HIGH SCORE!
EXPANDED

THE ILLUSTRATED HISTORY OF ELECTRONIC GAMES
3RD EDITION

RUSEL DEMARIA

CRC Press
Taylor & Francis Group
Boca Raton London New York

CRC Press is an imprint of the
Taylor & Francis Group, an informa business

CRC Press
Taylor & Francis Group
6000 Broken Sound Parkway NW, Suite 300
Boca Raton, FL 33487-2742

© 2019 by Rusel DeMaria
CRC Press is an imprint of Taylor & Francis Group, an Informa business

No claim to original U.S. Government works

Printed in Canada on acid-free paper

International Standard Book Number-13: 978-1-138-36720-3 (Hardback) 978-1-138-36719-7 (Paperback)

Visit the Taylor & Francis Web site at
http://www.taylorandfrancis.com

and the CRC Press Web site at
http://www.crcpress.com

Table of Contents

1   Before the Beginning

A short tour of the prehistory of electronic games—including an homage to early pinball games—and the key technological breakthroughs that made electronic gaming possible. Meet the earliest pioneers and experimenters who dreamed of using video screens for interactive entertainment.

17   The Seventies

Against the backdrop of a new era in social awareness and youth-oriented culture, the stage is set technologically for the birth of a new industry. Visionaries Ralph Baer and Nolan Bushnell lead the way, and Pong becomes a household word.

61   The Eighties

The electronic games industry is ready to rock and roll. While one hit follows another in the arcades, millions of homes across America are being invaded by Atari, Intellivision and ColecoVision gaming systems. The personal computer and the floppy disk make it possible for anyone to become a game developer.

255   The Nineties

The CD-ROM, 3D graphics, and high-speed internet access radically change the face of electronic gaming. New rivalries create rapidly escalating technologies, immersive realism, and a wide range of crossovers and tie-ins. Development budgets skyrocket, interactive games become very big business, and the companies themselves begin to merge and consolidate.

371   Across the Pond

A short history of electronic games in the U.K. Early fans of computer gaming in Britain fondly remember "Uncle Clive," the "Speccy," and the "Beeb." Learn the inside stories of off-the-wall classics like Ant Attack and Chuckie Egg, publishing magnate Robert Maxwell's connection to electronic games, and the origins of such breakout hits as Tomb Raider and Grand Theft Auto.

415   Across the Pacific

A short history of electronic games in Japan. One of the world's biggest video game companies, Nintendo began in 1889 as a playing card company. The early days of Nintendo, Bandai, Taito, Namco and other founders of the Japanese electronic games industry are traced in this section, which concludes with a timeline of important events in Japanese game development history.

High Score Acknowledgments

Thank you to Johnny L. Wilson for his contributions to the original High Score.

Special thanks must also go to those people who opened their homes to us and let us dig through their histories: Trip Hawkins, Doug Carlston, Richard Garriott, John Romero and Stevie Case, Al Alcorn, Rob Fullop, Ed Logg, Chris Crawford, Damon Slye, Jeff Tunnell, Jon Freeman, Anne Westfall, and Lyle Rains.

Finally, our gratitude to Ralph Baer, the Father of Video Games, for sharing his history with us and taking us way back to the beginning.

Take a deep breath now. Other wonderful people in the electronic games industry who provided us with valuable assistance include Michael Abrash, Phil Adam, Ernest Adams, Scott Adams, Wilfredo Aguilar, Mike Albaugh, Dave Albert, Ed Annunciata, Minoru Arakawa, Mike Arkin, Steve Arnold, Tony Barnes, Doug Barnett, Jeronimo Barrera, Hal Barwood, Bob Bates, Michael Becker, Ellen Beeman, Adam Belin, Scott Berfield, Mary Bihr, Joel Billings, Bob Bishop, Marc Blank, Don Bluth, Sue Bohle, Stewart Bonn, Bruno Bonnell, Hugh Bowen, David Bradley, Jeff Braun, Michael Bremer, Steve Barstow, Eric Bromley, Bill Budge, Roger Buoy, Nolan Bushnell, Paul Butler (Artech), Tom Byron, Billy Joe Cain, Doug Carlston, John Carmack, Louis Castle, Dr. Cat, Mark Cerny, Doug Church, Bob Clardy, Kevin Cloud, Pat Cook, Kraig Count, David Crane, Chris Crawford, Michael Crick, John Cutter, Don Daglow, Warren Davis (Q*Bert), Joe Decuir, Graeme Divine, Eddie Dombrower, Jerome Domurat, John Dondzila, Mike Dornberg, Diane Drosnes, Clint Dyer, Noah Falstein, Brian Fargo, Jamie Fenton, Andy Finkel, Gregory Fischbach, Kelly Flock, Nancy Fong, David Fox, Dean Fox, John Freeman, Brad Fregger, Ed Fries, Tom Frisina, John Garcia, Ron Gilbert, Ken Goldstein, Tony Goodman, Bing Gordon, Jim Gordon, Dan Gorlin, Paul Grace, Kirk Green, Andrew Greenberg, Arnold Greenberg, Clyde Grossman, Bill Grubb, James Hague, Holly Hartz, Gano Haine, Mike Halley, Cynthia Hamilton, John Hardy, Neil Harris, Will Harvey, Andy Heike, Bill (Becky) Heineman, Guido Henkel, Richard Hicks, Rich Hilleman, Bill Hindorff, Larry Holand, Dave Holle, Todd Hollenshead, Andy Hoyos, Dan Illowsky, Brent Iverson, Bob Jacobs, Dov Jacobson, Jane Jensen, Jerry Jewell, Greg Johnson, Mike Kalinske, Larry Kaplan, Arnie Katz, Bert Kerzsey, Ed Kilham, Gary Kitchen, Michael Kosaka, Stuart Kosoy, Chuck Kroegel, Ann Kronen, Bill Kunkel, Craig Lafferty, Rob Landeros, Lorne Lanning, Peter Leahy, Dave Lebling, Harvey Lee, Dick Lehrberg, Ned Lerner, LeveLord, David Levine, Howard Lincoln, Bob Lindstrom, Peter Lipson, Starr Long, Gilman Louie, Al Lowe, David Lubar, Peter Main, John Manley, Susan Manley, Christy Marx, David Maynard, Kevin McGrath, Sherry McKeena, Jordan Mechner, Dave Menconi, Sid Meier, Steve Meretszky, Susan Lee Merrow, RJ Mical, Al Miller, Jim Miller, Rand Miller, Scott Miller, Shigeru Miyamoto, Peter Molyneux, Brian Moriarty, Richard Muldoon, David Mullich, Bob Nall, Dave Needle, PS. Neeley, Paul Neurath, Al Nilsen, Alexey Pajitnov, Alan Pavlish, Mark Pelczarski, Teri Perl, Dave Perry, Wallace Poulter, Philip Price, Kent Quirk, John Ray, Sherry Graner Ray, Wolfe Reichart, Paul Reiche III, Mark Rein, Bert Reiner, Steve Richie, David Riordan, Lane Roathe, Chris Roberts, Warren Robinett, Keith Robinson, Henk Rogers, Bill Roper, Dave Rosen, Ed Rotberg, Howie Rubin, Jason Rubin, Peter S. Langston, Jim Sachs, Louis Saekow, John Salwitz, George Alistair Sanger (The Fat Man), Keith Schaefer, Dan Scherlis, Roger Schiffman, Bert Schroeder, Joe Scirica, Jim Seifert, Mike Sellers, Jim Simmons, Norm Sirotek, Robert Sirotek, Tim Skelly, Tom Sloper, Chuck Summerville, Damon Slye, John Smedley, Doug Smith, Jay Smith, Warren Spector, "Wild" Bill Stealey, Kevin Sullivan, Gregg Tavares, Chris Taylor, Doug TenNapel, Dave Theurer, Chris Thompson, Ray Tobey, Matt Toschlog, David Todd, Mark Tsai, Jeff Tunnell, Mark Turmell, Ronald Unrath, Jon Van Caneghem, Dan Van Elderen, Mark Voorsanger, Darlene Waddington, Gordon Walton, David Warhol, Silas Warner, Howard Scott Warshaw, CJ Welch, David Wessman, Anne Westfall, Bob Whitehead, Jay Wilbur, John Williams, Ken Williams, Roberta Williams, Ken Wirt, Jerry Wolosenko, Robert Woodhead, Steve Wozniak, Will Wright, Al Yarusso (www.atariage.com), and Joe Ybarra.

And then there are all the amazing people who provided support and/or material for the book: Chase (Sega), Fatskicky (www.fatbabies.com), Opi, Matthew Henzel, (VideoGameObsession.com, Sarinee Achavnuntakul (theunderdogs.org), Allen Adler (3DO), Eddie Adlum (RePlay Magazine), Haru Akenaga, Gale Alies (Infogrames), Matt Atwood (Capcom), Kevin Bachus (Microsoft), Rick Banks (Artech), Mike Beirne (Fujitsu), Dean Bender (Bender & Associates), Benjamin Bent (New World Computing), David Bergeaud, David Berk (Moby Games), Paul Berker, Jeff Blattner, Laura Bond (Williams), Jay Boor (Atari Games/Midway), Chris Brandkemp (Cyan), Mike Braun (Tandy), Reilly Brennan, James Bright (quarterarcade.com), Nance Brisco (Smithsonian Museum), Jeffery Brown (Electronic Arts), Ken Brown (Computer Gaming World), Lisa Bucek, Karen Busch (Sony Online), Nancy Bushkin (Infogrames), Nancy Bushnell, Paul Butler (Artech), Tracy Butler (Simutronics), Tony Byus (Taito), Michelle Caddell (assistant to Richard Garriott), Cathy Campos (Lionhead Studios), Chris Carro, Vickie Carson (National Park Service), Annette Carter (Acclaim), Jeff Castaneda (Rockstar Games), David Chen (Konami), Willy Chiu (IBM), John Chowenec (Cinemaware), Sarita Churchill (Dynamix), Rhonda Collette (Infogrames), Kevin Compton (AT&T), Philip Crews (Thumbs Plus), Florence De Martino, Brian Dear (PLATO), Chris Deering (Infogrames), Chris Dern, Christopher DiSalvio (assistant to Doug Carlston), Marcelyn Ditter (Midway), Garrett Dockery, Evelyn Dubocq (The Learning Company), Tim Eckel (arcade@home), Max Ehrman, Rob Ellis II (NearDeathstudios.com, Meridian 59), Margo Engel (Interplay), Eugene Evans (Infinite Ventures), John eXidy (arcade-classics.com), Amy Farris (Westwood), Sandie Fitzgerald (Electronic Arts), Nancy Fong (Electronic Arts), Chris Forman (www.yois.biz), David Foster, Beth Freeman (Sierra), Lars Fuhrken-Batista (the new Cinemaware, www.cinemawarc.com), Mary Fujihara (Atari), Sue Garfield (Electronic Arts, Joe Garity (Origin History Museum), Mike Gedeon (videogame connection.com), Christalle Gesler (Infogrames), Deboray Geyer (Midway), Kelley Gilmore (Firaxis Games), Michael Greene (Interplay), Heather Greer (Interplay), Jos Grupping (http://simflight/com/history/fhs/index.com), Lisa Gutridge (Electronic Arts), Lars Hannig (Atari-jaguar64.de), Tom Harlin (Nintendo), Dan Harnett, Kate Hedstrom (300), Laura Heeb (Enix), Kathy Helgason (Interplay), Dana Henry (Microsoft), Richard Hernandez (Apple), Steve Hildrew (gamesdomain. com), Conway Ho (Hana Ho Games – Hotrod: The Ultimate Joystick), Sheldon Hochheiser (AT&T), Kenn Hoekstra, Chris Hoffman (Working Designs), Mike Hogan, (Turbine), Robin Holland (Totally Games), Darren Horwitz (Sony PlayStation), Carla Hosein (Oriental Institute, University of Chicago), Keita Lida (Atari Gaming Headquarters, www.atarihq.com), Amos Ip (Koei), Russ Jensen, Kathy Johnson (Oddworld) Dan Jonin, Brian K. Youngblood, Perrin Kaplan (Ninten-do), Cindy Keirstead (Bandai), Mika Kelly (Infogrames), Sean Kelly (Classic Games Expo), Brian Kemp (Microsoft), Steven Kent (author, The First Quarter, aka The Ultimate History of Video Games), Zachary Knolls, Jane Koropsak (Brookhaven), Chris Kramer (Konami), Bill Kunkel, Bill Lamphear (Epyx), Maryanne Lataif (Activision), Frank Laugh, Jeff Lee, Jim Leonard (Moby Games), Sari Levy (for Sen. Joe Lieberman), Alan Lewis (Acclaim), Bill Linn (Linn PR), Lindsay Lowe, Alan Lundell, Kathryn Lynch (Infogrames), Anthony M. Pietrak (www.quarterarcade.com), Jenny Majalca (Sega), Jan Marsel (Activision), Peter Matisse (Infogrames), Michael Mcart (Ensemble Studios) Scott McDaniel (Sony Online), Sun McNamee, Edmond Meinfelder, Alexis Mervin (LucasArts), Mike Meyers (300) Kathy Miller (Sierra), Kyoko Mitchell (Blue Planet Software), Melinda Mongeluzzo (Capcom), Rik Morgan, Becca Morn, Trudy Muller (EA), Mashahiro Nakagawa (Sega Japan), James Namestka, Aaron Nanto (pcenginefx.com), Rae Nell Hicks (300), George Ngo, Michelle Nino (Activision), Janet O'Brien (Seattle Mariners), Masaaki Ohzuno (Taito), Chris Olmstead (Nintendo), Charlotte Ostar (Infogrames), Jeff Oswalt (Cyan), Alysa Padia (Infogrames), Charlotte Panther (Sony PlayStation), Del Penny, Steve Pereira, Tom Peters (Electronic Arts), Greg Peterson, Heather Philips (Interplay), Francoise Pietroforte (Infogrames), Bill Pitts (Stanford), Jonathan Poon (Cinemaware), Teresa Potts (Origin), Matt Pritchard (Ensemble Studios), Occan Quigley (Maxis), Brian Raffel (Raven), Keiko Randolf, Mary Resnick (Canon USA), Hugo Reyes (Namco), Tom Richardson (Infogrames), Linda Ripperger (assistant to Gilman Louie), Aaron Roberts (Digital Anvil), Robert Robertson (Apple Computer), Edward Rogers (Blue Planet Software), G.S. Sachdev, Gail Salamanca (Infogrames), Nicola Salmoria (M.A.M.E.), Mike Sandwick (Atari Football), Joe Santulli (Digital Press), Tom Sarris (LucasArts), Sandy Schneider, Mychelle Seebach, (Eidos), Carrie Seib, Jenny Shaheen (Oddworld), Robin Sherrer (assistant to Keith Schaefer), Gil Shif (Blizzard), Marjorie Simon (Electronic Arts), Mark Smotroff, Key Snodgress (RePlay Magazine), Stephanie Sonnleitner, Dawn Stanford (IBM), Andrew Stein, Marty Stratton (id Software), Tom Stratton (Nintendo), Topher Straus (assistant to Chris Roberts), Nathan Strum (M.A.M.E. images), Debbie Sue Wolfscale (Origin), Barbara Sweeney (AT&T), Jessica Switzer (Switzer Communications), David Swofford (Origin/ Destination Games), Pete Takaichi (Atari), Eileen Tanner (Nintendo), Mike Teal (Shiny), Michael Thomasson (www.goodDealGames.com), Adam Trionfo (As-trocade), Ummagumma (www.emuunlim.com/doteaters), Ronda Valenzuela (Electronic Arts), Mike Valgalder (Jaguar), Ornar Vega, Cassie Vogel, Pam Wagner, Leighton Webb (AOL), Eric Wein (Microsoft), Laura Wheeler (Westwood), Gio Wiederhold (Stanford), David Winter (pong-story.com), Sean Wolff (Ensemble Studios), Jeane Wong (Electronic Arts), David Woolley (PLATO), Chris Wopat, Hideo Yotsuya (SQEA, Inc.), Jesse Young (Midway), and Bo Zimmerman (Com-modore). Extra special thanks to Viola Brumbaugh for being there throughout this project in all its phases and expansions.

Special thanks must go to Scott Rogers for originally championing the book and for being a cool gamer, to Roger Stewart for his support of the project and for bringing me into it.

We have to thank the creators of the internet and the World Wide Web, which provided just about every obscure bit of information we needed. Special thanks go to Moby Games (www.mobygames.com), to the Killer List of Video Games (KLoV at www.klov.com) and to AtariAge (www.atariage.com).

And finally, more special thanks go to Canon USA for help; with photographic equipment, and to Thumbs Plus, which at the time was the best graphics organizer, and invaluable to this project.

Appendix A – The UK

Keith Ainsworth, Nigel Alderton, Alison Beasley, Ian Bell, Lee Blackwell, Olivier Boisseau (old-computers.com), David Braben, Cathy Campos, John Cook, Geoff Crammond, Jjarn Torkel Dahl, Terrie Dorrell, Phillippe Dubois, Marcus Dyson, Rich Eddy, Eugene Evans, Bruce Everiss, Exotica (http://exot-ica.fix.no), Mike Fairurst (UKretro.co.uk), Amy Farris, Steev Goodwin, James Hague, Richard Hanson, Dave Jones, Colin Macdonald, Ian Marshall, Alex McLintoch, Peter Molyneux, Melinda Mongelluzzo, Jeremy Parish, David Perry, Lee Rosini, Tammy Schachter, Dan Scott, Michelle Seebach, Jools Smyth, Steve Starvis, Jay Walters, Stefan Walters, Sandy White, Steve Wilcox, Roger Womack, Albert Yarusso.

Appendix B - Japan

Duncan Flett, Yuskhio Furusawa, Tara Hino, Dan Hower, Chris Kohler, Dominc Mallinson, Any Mastriona (Sony), Marsha Metz (Constantin Film Develop-ment), Keisuke Nitanda, Gerald Rogers, Henk Rogers, Junjiro Sintaku, Kevin Sullivan, Bill Swartz, Teiji Yutaka, www.nvg.ntnu.no, www.nvg.org.

For the Expanded edition:

Richard A. Bartle, Ed Fletcher, Stuart Moulder, Bill Pytlovny, Roy Trubshaw, Christopher Weaver, Ihor Wolosenko, Kevin Bachus, Ed Fries, the folks at Bungie, Alex Seropian, Nat Brown, Alex St. John, J Allard, and many more of the 89 people I interviewed for the Microsoft parts of the story.

Taylor and Francis

Special thanks to Sean Connolly and Jessica Vega

If we left anyone out, our sincere apologies.

Kickstarter Backers

I want to extend an extra special thank you to those of you who backed my Kickstarter campaign for High Score 3. Those of you who have followed my updates and posts are by now aware that I have had to cancel the project. There were too many obstacles in the way, not the least my health, but also the many changes in the industry and the difficulty of gaining the support needed to pull off yet another magnum opus. Hopefully, you will appreciate this expansion of the original books and accept my deep gratitude for your support.

Special Thanks to Digital Double (Kamal) and Jason West for their very extra generous pledges, and to David Perry, Chris Taylor, Lorne Lanning, Steve Meretzky, John Romero, Brenda Romero, Trip Hawkins, Bill Budge, Greg Johnson, Louis Castle, Eugene Evans, Jeff Tunnell, Gordon Walton, Carter Lipscomb, Tommy Tallarico, Ed Fries, Rebecca Heinemann, Will Wright, Sid Meier, Peter Molyneux for their generosity in donating their time.

Joshua Little, inXile Entertainment, Kenneth Bowen, Tom Bennett, James Sylvanus, Eric Freeman, Michael Labbo, Nils Goette, Elizabeth Shoemaker, Liam Burke, Gareth Jenkins, Rebecca Ingle, Nathan Forget, Sean Gubelman, FRMHungers, Jennifer Sward, James Hurst, Patrick Scott Patterson, Frank Rodriguez, Neil Roberts, Benoit Moiny, Andrew Gilmartin, David McEwen, Rod Reddekopp, Raffaello Rosselli Baslini, Borje Karlsson, FredericRP, Mark Hulme-Jones, Sam Wright, Andrew Bredencamp, David, Sam Jeffreys, Matthew Mather, Alexander Dietrich, Sharita Nelson, Mike Jerry, Jamie Sherlock, Ryan Cann, Edwin Falter, Stephen J Broida, Thomas Treplow, Kaylin Antè Norman, Chris Morris, Andrew Marquis, Brenda Romero, Michael Grimes, Douglas Whatley, Karen Clark, Daniel New, Grandy Peace, Harmik Khoronia, Peter Lyle-Dugas, Destin Bales, Steven Crump, Andy Nuttall, Corvus Elrod, Naomi Clark, Noah Falstein, Chris Edwards, Eddy L O Jansson, Fridtjof Lexberg, Joel "LowPolyCount Gonzales, Aaron (EgoAnt) Clifford, Colin Ybarra, Michael McHale, Samantha Kalman, John Phillip Fontecha, Miguel Sicart, Matt Hirschfelt, Falk Sonnabend, John Passfield, Francois Messier, Brannon Zahand, Axel Kothe, Jean-Claude Padilla, Jeremy Snead, Ken Allen, Kelly Konkol, Jordan Maynard, Stephen Kitt, Martin Rudat, Zack Johnson, Patrick Tullman, Vek, Kun-Wei Lin, Jung-Sheng Lin, Phil Bordelon, Ssaga, Brian Seward, Christopher Lard, Simon Wistow, Jennell Allyn, Cassandra Stapleton, Nabil Maynard, Byron Storey, Lynn Hernandez, Juan Orendain, Damien Bernard, Rajen Savjani, Michael Keith, Zaqster, Eric Nikolaisen, Kimberly Unger, Todd Blake, Ryan Mitchell, Erin Hoffman, Sigurbern Finnsson, Brian Haury, Jun Hyun Park, bchan84, Alexander Brideson, Ben Speakmon, Jorge Capote, Andrew Keil, Angelo L. Cruz, Geoff Richardson, Rayna Anderson & Chris Ractliffe, Joe Santulli, Cliff Garrett, MannyC, Nick Pham, MetalWing, Collin Ayers, Andy Molloy, Justin roiland, Matthew Kellar, Sabastien Boissonneault, Neal Lewis, Dick Lehrberg, Jonathan Desrosiers, Erik Odeldahl, Jens Bergensten, Bryan Cash, Michael Stum, M. Ian Graham, Aya Nakazato, Randy Cornetta, Bruno Campagnolo de Paula, Raymond Holmes, Steve Gargolinski, Justin Waldron, Rich D. Romanski, Joe Streeky, Jurie Horneman, Jeffrey Hilbert, Joshua Diaz, John Brewer, Tim Lindvall, Nida Zada, Josh Martel, Mattias Tuoremaa, Johan Schmetzer, Tony Huynh, gfactor, Csongor Baranyai, Michael Crandall, Will

Hinds, Mark DeLoura, Mike Villasuso, Brad Mohr, Will Jennings, Carl Chiniara, Craig Makk, Sela Davis, Arnd Beenen, William G Dourte IV, Giacomino Veltri, Chaz Wilke, Nick Terranova, Andre Kishimoto, Matthew Q. Brown, David Catlin, Brian Gilbert, Bryan J Polk, John Hanold, Kyle Overby, Brian Peek, Andre Berg Bragason, Melv Ng, Hunter, Scott Berfield, Karl Reinsch, J. Eddy, Ed Fries, David Fox, Thomas Hahn, Sam Pacheco, Spencer Oklobdzija, Benoit Tremblay, Adam Olivero, Andre Nylander, Andre Bergei, Tim Borrelli, Singapore-MIT GAMBIT Game Lab, Jefferson Ietto Novo, Bret Victor, Royce Sellers, Tony Van, Tom Hall, Christopher Muzatko, Rebecca Heineman, Jon Lambert, Christoph 'Sicarius' Hofmann, Joshua Beale, Sascha Fichtner, Steven Colby, Angela Kugler, Tom W. Minton, Chris Charla, Troy Tuttle, Eric Ronning, André Hagspiel, Gideon Boomer, William Marks, Mike Dorval, Kevin James Zimmerman, Christian Klein, Randy Padawer, Glenn White, Justin Krenz, Scott Borror, Michael Quandt, Conor and Rory Yule, Matty S., Michael Zytkow, Charles Feduke, Elling Hauge, Brice Coquereau, Beau Gunderson, Joseph Russo, Michael Kwan, Justin Legrande, Joel Goodsell, Joseph Cardenas, John Richards, Kyle Lowry, Luke Boonstra, Tom Larrow, Denis Marion, Kevin Savetz, Marc Meadows, Andrew Kane, Kevin Burns, Malcolm Tredinnick, Michael Haydel, Robert Lim, Duncan Harris, David Bedford, Kate Edwards, Simon Dampier, Jonathan Gillespie, Ivan Nikitin, Stephen Jacobs, Vitas Varnas, David Johnson, Robert Hagenstrom, Jason A. Zelek, Andrew Kwon, Chris P, Tone Houshmand, Steven Beach, Lloyd Cualoping, Abdullatif Alomar, Peter Bjorklund, Chris Tremmel, Jim Randall, Harlech Quinn, Katheryn "RaQin/Whaitera" Phillips, Craig Harris, Chad Keck, Chris ORegan, Scott Tkachuk, Phil Norton, Greg Izzi, Heejae Chang, Andrew 'Ewzzy' Rayburn, Maarten de Koning, J. Piatscheck, Jose Pablo Monge, Matt Lee, Patrick Wade, Bevan Sly, Barnabas Cleave, David McGreavy, Bryanna Lindsey, Harry Fields, Mark Tsai, Rick Rambo, Kevin Pickell, Don Rual & Tequila Works, Maria Harrington, Ryan Seney, Stuart Baker, Patrik Tennberg, John Tomic, John Albano, Zach Robinson, Luca Galli, Jay Moore, Jonathan Scheltema, Christopher Yim, Adrienne Grant, Jonas Lee, Jason Scott, Sheri Graner Ray, Kuowen Lo, Michael Bert, Tony Royko, Clinton Thornton, David Grinton, Larry Zieminski, David Campbell, Robert Drescher, Graeme Devine, Steven Sanders, David Bennett, Trond Nilsen, Derek Reeve, Luigi Venezia, James Riggall, Thomas Børnes, Ron Pieket, Mika Flinkman, Allan Nienhuis, Eugene Zheng, Vinay Giri, James C. Smith, Zizhuang Yang, Robert Beattie, Roland Ruth, Angel Montero Jr., Casey O'Donnell, Paul Bakaus, Piotr Gliźniewicz, Daniel Salas, Arenegeth, Michael Rubin, John Idlor, Peter Armstrong, Mikael Olofsson, Anders Flink, Carter Lipscomb, Ken Nagasako, Benjamin Herzog, Alan Hinchcliffe, Simon Ruehrschneck, Scott Hartsman, Jay Miller, Greg Meyer, Bruno Fonseca, Lukas Mathis, Jesse Schell, David A Mayo II, Kyle K Boyd, Riesz Williams, Jean-Luc Heusdain, Mike Prasad, Sean O'Reilly, Skip Clarke, Christof Sigel, Gavin Locke, Leslie Law, Ariel Benzakein, Neil Harris, Pete Morrish, Steven Meretzky, Benedikt Esser, Vic DeLeon, Terry Redfield, Raighne Hogan, John Cunningham, Gil Megidish, George Alexiades , Steven Dengler, Joline Desrosiers, Michelle Hinn, Seumas Froemke, David Whelan, Tyler Davis, Dan Hulton, Mike Acton, Terri Perkins, Bryan Phan, Yana Malysheva, Pether Chumioque, Giordano Bruno Contestabile, Steven Zakulec, Jason Kapalka, Jerome Braune, Dave MacPhail, Chris Van Graas, Jill Sullivan, Jay Wilbur, Gordon Walton, David Ehrman, kur4ido, Samu Lassila, Josh Samuels, James Latimer, Chris Darbro, Ashok Meena, Suzie Q Sailaway, Courtnee Papastathis, Michelle Man, Lin Jen-Shin, Christian Heublein, Roger Stewart, Ben Bertoli, Eric, Frankie J Appelgate

High Score! Expanded
Introduction

High Score! Expanded is, as its name suggests, a version of the original *High Score!* and *High Score! 2nd Edition* that has been further expanded with new content relevant to the period covered, which is roughly from the earliest glimpses of electronic games through about 2002 or 2003. The original books went out of print years ago when the original publisher Osborne/McGraw-Hill determined that it was not consistent with their general catalog of books.

I did a Kickstarter campaign to help fund the creation of a third edition of High Score, but found quickly that the industry and my contacts within it had changed. I decided to work on some other projects first, and then tackle *High Score 3* after (hopefully) reestablishing myself in the industry so I could get more cooperation. The first challenge I chose was to resurrect High Score in some form. After some confusion with a publisher, I realized that I would have to do the job on my own.

One problem was that the original layout files for High Score had been lost, and so I had to recreate the entire book from scratch, working from the graphics I had saved and raw, unedited stories I had written back in 2002. It was a daunting project, but it was also liberating because I could in some cases improve on what had been done originally and also add new content. It's the new content that I hope fans of the original book will find especially worthwhile. So in many ways, this is an entirely new book, reborn from the ashes of the originals.

Obviously, I must acknowledge the work of my original partner in High Score, Johnny Wilson. Johnny was involved with me in the early planning of the first edition, and contributed several specific pieces for that book. But the vast majority of the writing, design, and all other aspects of the project fell upon me, and it is for that reason, by agreement, that I am listed as sole author of this new edition, which represented a great challenge that I took upon myself to complete. With the help of my editor, Jillian Werner, I hope I have created a worthy successor to the previous books.

—Rusel DeMaria

Rusel DeMaria

Rusel DeMaria is the author or coauthor of more than sixty books, most of them in the gaming field, including *Myst: The Official Strategy Guide*, which sold more than 1.2 million copies, as well as one of the most comprehensive histories of the industry, *High Score! The Illustrated History of Electronic Games* (now updated in this book), a 2-volume set of Microsoft's history in games – *Game of X v.1* and *Game of X v.2*, and a book about the positive potential of games, *Reset: Changing the Way We Look at Video Games*. He founded and served as creative director for the most successful strategy guide publishing imprint in the industry and is a former senior editor and columnist for several national and international video game magazines. In addition, DeMaria has worked as a game designer and consultant, a tree climbing instructor, a tai chi instructor, and a city councilor.

Before the Beginning

In this section, we very briefly turn back the clock to revisit some of the key events in the history of technology, without which there could have been no electronic games. In setting the stage, we pay homage to pinball games, which in many ways paved the way for the electronic game revolution. We also look at the earliest known pioneers: the experimenters who first conceived and created entertainment on video screens and who, in some cases, helped inspire the generation of game designers that followed.

A PDP-1 terminal (scanned from Creative Computing Magazine).

Prologue:
Games People Played

Humankind has gamed throughout its history. Whether we look at the dice and primitive board games from King Tut's tomb or the graffiti representing game boards used by waiting patricians in the Roman Forum, people have left artifacts indicating play as part of their legacy. Is it any wonder that as our technology has changed, so has our capacity for play?

Remarkably, it is now possible to play the hottest games of the year 2000... 2000 B.C., that is. All it takes is a search of the Internet.

You can download shareware versions of games from ancient history. Games like the Moorish Quirkat, Mayan Bul, Chinese Shap Luk Kon Tseung Kwon and other games from ancient cultures ranging from those of the ancient Egyptians to the Vikings. Each game comes with a lot of background and a guided tutorial, since you probably have never seen these games before in your local toy store.

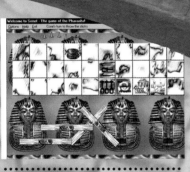

Ancient Egyptian Senet board and Windows version of Senet.

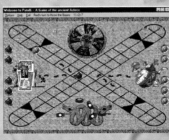

Background: An ancient Egyption Mehen board–The Forbidden Game of the Snake–and a screenshot of the Windows Version.

Top Left: Patoli
Bottom Left: Ur

Top Right: Bul
Bottom Right: Quirkat

Landmarks of Electronic Game Prehistory

Intellivision from Mattel

1889

The Marufuku Company is established in Japan by Fusajiro Yamauchi to make Hanafuda playing cards, and by 1907 they expand to Western playing cards. In 1951, the company becomes the Nintendo Playing Card Company. Nintendo translates as "leave luck to heaven."
—see pages 242, 412

1891

In the Netherlands, Gerard Philips begins to manufacture incandescent lamps and other electrical products. Philips eventually becomes a worldwide conglomerate that owns electronics companies, music labels, and much more, including Magnavox, the company that produces the first home video game, the Odyssey. Philips also develops the audiocassette and shares the honors with Sony for the development of the CD. Later, they also create the CDI system.
—see page 18

Sony's PlayStation

1918

The Matsushita Electric Housewares Manufacturing Works is established by Konosuke Matsushita. Matsushita is the parent company of Panasonic, who manufactured the first 3DO consoles and also had its own game development company in the 1990s.
—see page 266

1932

The original Connecticut Leather Company building

Russian immigrant Maurice Greenberg starts the Connecticut Leather Company and creates leather products for shoes. Under the guidance of Leonard and Arnold Greenberg, Maurice's sons, the company expands into plastic swimming pools, home toys, and eventually games and game systems under the name Coleco.
—see page 36

1945

Naming their picture frame business, Harold Matson and Elliot Handler combine their names and end up with Mattel. Using scraps left over from making the frames, Elliot begins making dollhouse furniture. Mattel ultimately creates a game division, manufactures the first hand-held games, and, later, the Intellivision console. Still later, they find success with their line of games based on the Barbie franchise.
—see page 74

1947

The Tokyo Telecommunications Engineering Company is founded by Akio Morita and Masaru Ibuka. They rise to prominence when they license transistor technology from Bell Labs and create the world's first pocket transistor radio. For worldwide marketing, they change their name to Sony, taken from the Latin word *sonus*, which means "sound." Ultimately, Sony becomes a giant in the world of electronics and introduces their PlayStation to the U.S. in 1995, establishing themselves as one of the most important game companies in the world.
—see page 295

1954

Service Games, created by Korean War vet David Rosen, is formed to export coin-operated amusement games to Japan. Later, deciding to create his own games in Japan, he purchases an old jukebox and slot-machine company. The name of the company becomes Sega, for SErvice GAmes. Sega produces many coin-operated arcade games and eventually becomes Nintendo's chief competitor in the home console business during the late 1980s and early 1990s.
—see page 244

Sega's founder, Dave Rosen, in 1966

3

Homage to Pinball

A full treatment of pinball games is far beyond the scope of this book. Indeed, whole books have been written about the history, the art and the culture of pinball games. We include this brief retrospective, however, because for many of us pinball was the precursor to our affinity for and love of video and computer games.

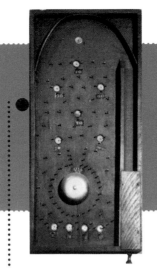

1871 REDGRAVE PARLOR BAGATELLE
The first game to use a spring-loaded plunger.

1876 REDGRAVE ORIGINAL PARLOR BAGATTELLE
Montague Redgrave's 1876 model.

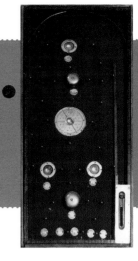

1898 REDGRAVE "TWO BELL" PARLOR BAGATTELLE
Note the slot in the spring-loaded plunger housing.

1933 THE PRESIDENT
Released in February 1933, it is nearly identical to the Mills Official Pin Table, which was released in July 1932.

1933 PACIFIC AMUSEMENT CO. CONTACT
First game to use electricity instead of only gravity. First game to have an electrical ringing bell. First game to be designed by Harry Williams, who later founded Williams Pinball.

1936 BALLY BUMPER
The first game with scoring electric bumpers.

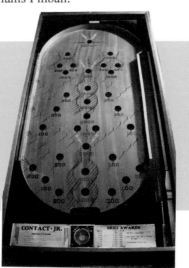

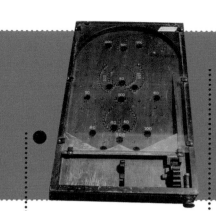

1931 AUTOMATIC INDUS-TRIES BABY WHIFFLE

Generally regarded as the first production "pin game."

1931 GOTTLIEB BAFFLE BALL

Gottlieb's first pin game. The game that launched the entire pinball industry.

1932 BALLY BALLYHOO

The game that started Bally Corporation.

1932 MILLS OFFICIAL

The first game to be advertised as "pinball." The name has been used ever since.

1947 GOTTLIEB HUMPTY DUMPTY

The first pinball game to use flippers, forever altering the direction of pinball games.

STAR SERIES

Early mechanical baseball game from Williams.

U.S .MARSHALL

U.S. Marshall was produced by Mike Munves Company in the 1950s. It is very similar to the ABT Challenger gun game series that had been produced since the 1930s. The game shot small ball bearings at targets.

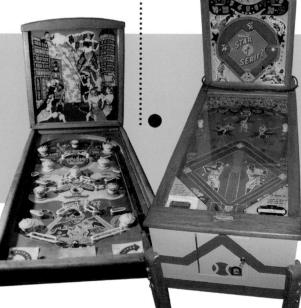

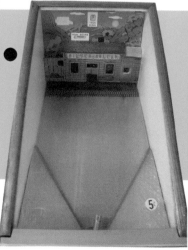

Early Technology
Advancement to the Information Age

While the concept of a computing device may not be as ancient as that of playing games, it has an interesting history. One of the earliest devices, dating back to at least 300 B.C., was the counting board (later the abacus), which was a storage device used to help keep track of numbers. Not true calculating devices, these are still the earliest known aids to mathematical calculation.

1890 article in *Scientific American* showing Hollerith's machine.

Much, much later, but still as early as 1645, Blaise Pascal invented a mechanical adding machine, for which he received a patent from King Louis XIV. This could hardly be called a computer, but it was a calculating device and a very early step on the road to the computers of today.

Herman Hollerith's census tabulating machine in 1890.

Charles Babbage and Augusta Ada Byron

Back in the early days of the Industrial Revolution, the idea of a computer that could think intrigued a few intellectuals, but frightened most people who even bothered to consider the idea. One man who was particularly obsessed with the concept of computing machines was Charles Babbage, a British inventor, astronomer, and mathematician. As early as 1833, Babbage was working on the problem. Babbage conceived of two mechanical computing devices: the "Analytical Engine" and the "Difference Engine," both of which were designed to automate mathematical calculations. Babbage was never able to build either one, but his colleague and patron, Augusta Ada Byron, wrote and published several papers describing Babbage's work. Byron, the future Lady Lovelace, was the daughter of Lord Byron, and arguably the first computer programmer. Even though the Analytical Engine was never built, Byron wrote instruction sets for the solving of mathematical problems.

Charles Babbage

Augusta Ada Byron

Only Logical

In order for computers to evolve, many key concepts had to emerge. The idea that logic could be represented by machinery was one such concept. An expert on George Boole's work of the mid-1800s, American logician Charles Sanders Peirce was able to see that simple true/false calculations of Boolean algebra could be emulated by electrical circuitry, which could be switched between "on" or "off" states. By 1880, Peirce had devised a "switching circuit" that could be used to switch states and therefore emulate Boolean conditions of true/false, on/off. Up to this point, any attempts to make a computing device had relied entirely on mechanical components. Using electrical switches made possible smaller, faster, and somewhat quieter machines.

Humble Beginnings

Hermann Hollerith's 1890 census tabulating machine may not seem important to you, but if you play games on a Windows machine, consider that this humble invention was a more or less direct ancestor of the original IBM PC. Hollerith's company became the International Business Machines Corporation, known more simply as IBM. In the 1930s, IBM funded the development of an electromechanical computer known as the Mark I. By the time it was completed in 1944, however, it was already obsolete. Already, the speed of innovation was outstripping the speed of development.

General Purposes

Like Hollerith's census tabulation device, early computing machines were designed to accomplish a specific task. However, in the 1930s, British mathematician Alan Turing envisioned a machine whose entire function would be described by the instructions it was given. Instead of a machine dedicated to one purpose only, Turing's machine would be useful for multiple purposes, although it's initial function was to break Nazi codes during World War II. Turing's concepts bore fruit in the hands of another mathematician, John Von Neumann, who created the concept of the stored computer program.

Herman Hollerith, 1888

Tubin'

While the Mark I was under construction, John Atanasoff and Clifford Berry were conceiving the first electronic computer that used vacuum tubes in place of the mechanical relays used in previous devices. Their ABC, or Atanasoff-Berry Computer, "was the world's first electronic digital computer. It was built by John Vincent Atanasoff and Clifford Berry at Iowa State University during 1937-42. It incorporated several major innovations in computing including the use of binary arithmetic, regenerative memory, parallel processing, and separation of memory and computing functions."*

For many years, the patents and glory went to John Mauchley and J. Presper Eckert, the designers of the ENIAC, which was considered to be the first all-electronic computer. It wasn't until 1973 that a court ruled in favor of Atanasoff as creator of the first electronic computer.

ENIAC was impressive, however, if only for sheer size. Consisting of 30 separate units, it weighed in at more than 30 tons and contained 19,000 vacuum tubes, 1,500 relays, and hundreds of thousands of other pieces. Its electrical consumption was a whopping 200 kilowatts, and it required a forced-air cooling system.

Despite its monstrous size, ENIAC was a modern, pre-solid state computer, whose model for computer design is the basis for modern computers.

Source: http://www.cs.iastate.edu/jva/jva-archive.shtml

IBM's original logo c.1924.

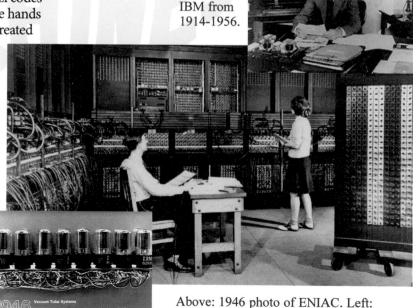

Thomas J. Watson Sr., CEO of IBM from 1914-1956.

Above: 1946 photo of ENIAC. Left: Vacuum tubes from the ENIAC era.

1947: A Tiny Breakthrough

Based on experiments in quantum physics, researchers became intrigued by the predicted behavior of certain crystals when electricity was run through them. These crystals behaved neither as conductors nor insulators, and came to be known as *semiconductors*. William Shockley headed one team of researchers that included Walter Brattain and John Bardeen. The trio of Shockley, Bardeen, and Brattain ultimately discovered how to run and modulate electricity through a semiconductor and created the first transistor.

The transistor was perhaps the single most important development in the history of electronics. Now electronic devices that once required a forklift to move could be held in the palm of your hand. They were more reliable and produced less heat. The electronics revolution truly began with the development of the transistor. In 1955, Shockley founded Shockley Semiconductor in Palo Alto, California, which ultimately set the stage for other semiconductor companies to move into the area. Because of its flourishing semiconductor industry, the area ultimately came to be called Silicon Valley.

1950s: Transistors at Work

Believe it or not, the monstrosity above is a transistorized calculator.

1958 Transistors and Printed Circuit Systems. New, small, solid state transistors, accompanied with printed circuit techniques, permit greater speed and better reliability. Ferrite core technology replaces vacuum tubes for stored programs. Now two ten-digit numbers can be multiplied 100,000 times per second.

Early transistor circuit boards–precursors to the integrated circuit.

Shockley and his team at work.

The first transistor.

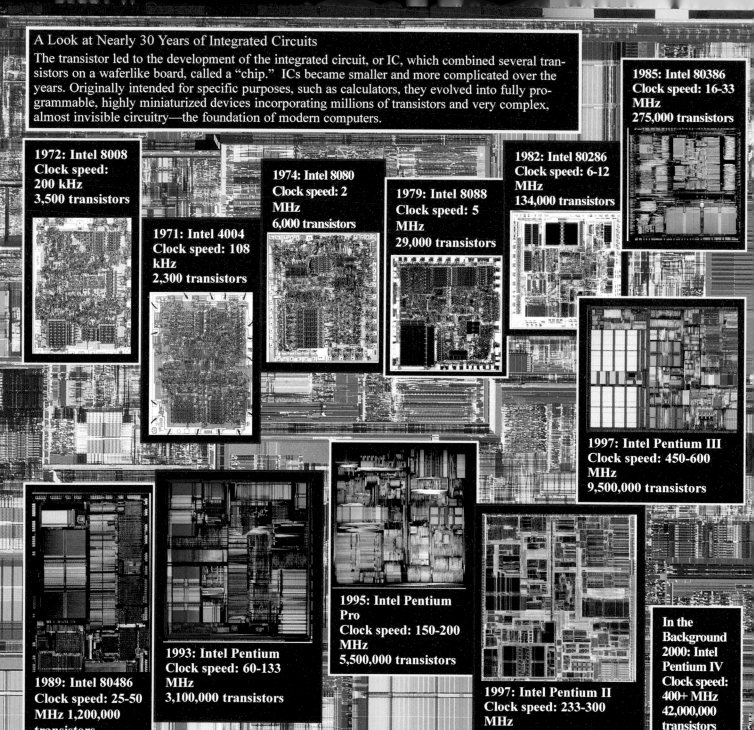

A Look at Nearly 30 Years of Integrated Circuits

The transistor led to the development of the integrated circuit, or IC, which combined several transistors on a waferlike board, called a "chip." ICs became smaller and more complicated over the years. Originally intended for specific purposes, such as calculators, they evolved into fully programmable, highly miniaturized devices incorporating millions of transistors and very complex, almost invisible circuitry—the foundation of modern computers.

1985: Intel 80386
Clock speed: 16-33
MHz
275,000 transistors

1972: Intel 8008
Clock speed:
200 kHz
3,500 transistors

1974: Intel 8080
Clock speed: 2
MHz
6,000 transistors

1979: Intel 8088
Clock speed: 5
MHz
29,000 transistors

1982: Intel 80286
Clock speed: 6-12
MHz
134,000 transistors

1971: Intel 4004
Clock speed: 108
kHz
2,300 transistors

1997: Intel Pentium III
Clock speed: 450-600
MHz
9,500,000 transistors

1995: Intel Pentium
Pro
Clock speed: 150-200
MHz
5,500,000 transistors

In the
Background
2000: Intel
Pentium IV
Clock speed:
400+ MHz
42,000,000
transistors

1989: Intel 80486
Clock speed: 25-50
MHz 1,200,000
transistors

1993: Intel Pentium
Clock speed: 60-133
MHz
3,100,000 transistors

1997: Intel Pentium II
Clock speed: 233-300
MHz
7,500,000 transistors

Tennis for Two:
The First Electronic Game?

Willy Higginbotham was a renowned physicist working at Brookhaven National Laboratories in the 1950s. As a designer of electronic circuits for the Manhattan Project during World War II, Higginbotham came to Brookhaven in 1947, when it opened. In 1958, as head of instrumentation design, he decided to put some pop in the annual visitor day by creating a little interactive game using an oscilloscope, an analog computer and some simple push buttons. The result was a simple tennis game, more than a decade before the advent of Pong. Willy Higginbotham´s ¨Tennis for Two¨ is the earliest known electronic game.

Tennis for Two was a big hit, and lines formed to get a chance to play it. However, Higginbotham had no interest in marketing the idea. For one thing, he said if he had patented the idea, it would have been assigned to the U.S. government and he would have made maybe ten dollars on it. In any case, Tennis for Two remained operational for two years and was finally dismantled in favor of an exhibit that showed cosmic rays.

The whole thing would probably have been forgotten except that teenager David Ahl saw it on a field trip to Brookhaven. Ahl later founded *Creative Computing Magazine*, the pioneer magazine of the electronic age.

This was the setup at Brookhaven, including Tennis For Two.

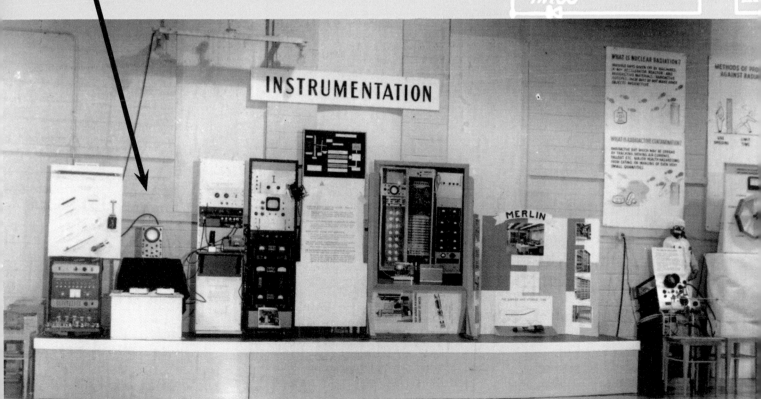

HOW TO PLAY

by Willy Higginbotham
"The display showed a two-dimensional side view of a tennis court. A horizontal line, below center, represented the floor of the court. A shorter vertical line in the center represented the net. Before the start of play the ball was shown at a fixed position above one or the other end of the court. Each player had a small box, which he held in one hand. On the box were a knob to aim at the ball (up, down, or level) and a push button. To start play, the person with the ball at his or her end of the court would select an angle and push the button, whereupon the ball would proceed over the net or hit the net and bounce back. If it went over the net, the other payer would select an angle and attempt to return the ball. He could hit the ball as soon as it passed the net or after it bounced, or wait and see if it landed beyond the end of the court. There was some wind resistance, as some energy was lost in each bounce. The racquet was not shown and the strike velocity was pre-set. We had controls for velocity but judged that a player would have trouble operating an additional control."

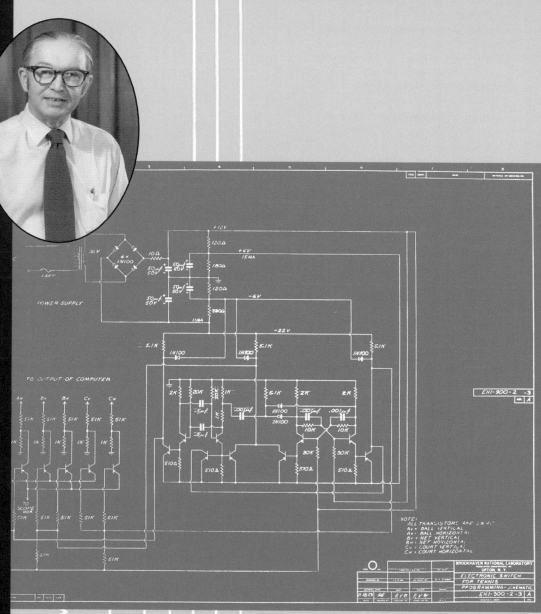

Willy Higginbotham and his schematic diagram for Tennis for Two.
Left: Higginbotham's own description of how Tennis for Two was played.

Spacewar!

In the summer of 1961, Steve "Slug" Russell* and some friends were trying to figure out how to best demonstrate the new PDP-1 computer that was being installed at MIT. In a time when most computers received input and delivered output in the form of punch cards or paper tape, the PDP-1 was remarkable in that it had a monitor display. Games played on paper tape were not nearly so interesting or immediate. The monitor changed everything.

In a 1981 article in *Creative Computing Magazine*, J. M. Graetz, one of those involved in brainstorming the idea for Spacewar!, reported that they came up with the following three precepts:

- **It should demonstrate as many of the computer's resources as possible, and tax those resources to the limit.**
- **Within a consistent framework, it should be interesting, which means every run should be different.**
- **It should involve the onlooker in a pleasurable and active way— in short, it should be a game.**

Inspired by E. E. "Doc" Smith's *The Lensman* and *Skylark* novels, Spacewar! was the first real computer game (other than perhaps a few small games of tic-tac-toe and the like), and a model of great game design that's still fun to play today.

The game was programmed into the PDP-1 in 1962, and for several years after, was disseminated to college campuses across the country, ultimately spawning a number of rather significant ripples in the fabric

A PDP-1 terminal

"Slug" was Russell's nickname because, according to co-worker Graetz, "he was never one to 'do something' when there was an alternative."

of space/time, or, more importantly, in the history of electronic games. Among those whose first influence could be traced back to Spacewar! are Nolan Bushnell, founder of Atari; and Joel Billings, founder of SSI.

In Spacewar!, two B-movie-style rocket ships (called the "Wedge" and the "Needle," because one was shaped like a fat cigar and the other looked like a long slender tube) battled in computer-generated space. Players would flick toggle switches to make the ships change direction, and the ships would respond much like the zero-G Asteroids ships that would animate coin-op and Atari 2600 screens almost two decades later. Each ship could fire up to 31 torpedoes that would, in turn, appear as little dots traveling in the direction of the other ship. If the dot actually managed to intersect the shape of the other ship, it "exploded" and the ship disappeared. There were no particle effects and no stereo sound effects to mark the explosion. The other ship simply disappeared and was replaced by a mad scramble of dots to represent the debris of the destroyed ship.

Even in 1962, the programmers/designers were discovering the trade-offs between realism and playability. Peter Samson decided that the random-dot star map that Russell had originally programmed was insufficient. He used a celestial atlas to program the star map as the actual galaxy down to fifth magnitude stars, calling it (with typical

Below: Screen from the original Spacewar!. The Wedge and the Needle start diagonally opposite each other. If you look closely, you may be able to identify some constellations among the stars.

nacker humor) "Expensive Planetari-um." Another student added a gravity option. Another added a hyperspace escape option, complete with a nifty stress signature to show where the ship had left the system. The problem with hyperspace was you never knew where you'd end up, and if you reappeared too close to the Sun and couldn't escape its gravity, well, you were toast. Later, "Slug" himself messed with the reliability of the torpedoes, but this was not well received by players, who liked their torpedoes to be accurate and reliable. Russell's refinements had leaped beyond his audience's ability to appreciate them.

Spacewar! remains one of the truly great milestones in electronic game history. It directly influenced several of the great pioneers who came later. It was created before there was an industry, on a computer whose $120,000 price tag made it an unlikely commercial product. And yet, it remains a true gem of a game, as much fun to play today as it was then.

Galaxy War, a version of Spacewar! appeared on the Stanford University campus in the early '70s and may have been the first coin-operated electronic game, as it may have been on display and used for business before Computer Space and Pong.

" In 1967, while hanging around at the Stanford University Student Union, I happened upon a strange machine that was the closest I had come to science fiction in real life. It was a game, but not a pinball game, which is what I thought a game that used electricity had to be. But this, though obvious-ly electrical in nature, consisted of nothing more than a TV-like screen and some buttons. By that time, the original toggle levers had been replaced by buttons. At any rate, it was Spacewar! It had several improvements by that time, including sun/no sun, negative or positive gravity (or "none" with no sun).

My friend Steven and I played it pretty much undisturbed at the beginning of the summer break. By the end of that summer, there were crowds six deep around the machine, and a satellite monitor had been mounted high on the wall so people could watch the games in progress. In hindsight, I wish I had understood what Nolan Bushnell knew when he saw the same game at the University of Utah. This was a phenomenon, and the beginning of a new era. What I saw was the coolest game I'd ever seen, but too many people between me and the controls. Popularity came with a price. "

—Rusel DeMaria

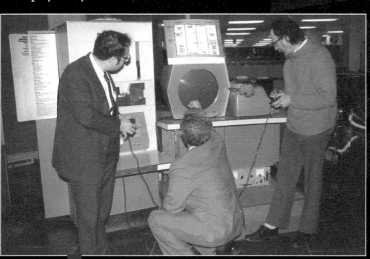

Steve "Slug" Russell and friends playing the original Spacewar! game.

Reputed to be the original PDP-1 of Spacewar! fame, now residing at the Computer History Museum at Moffett Field in Mountain View, California.

Top of page: Ralph Baer's original light gun.

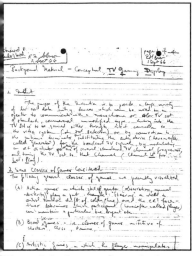

The original notes from the bus station where Baer's first concept of video games was formally documented.

Games on the TV?

Today it seems obvious that television sets were designed for of playing games. Right? Well, in the early days of TV, it wasn't obvious—except to one engineer, Ralph Baer. Baer was a consummate inventor, and, convinced that games and TVs were made for each other, he became the "Father of Video Games."

After World War II, in which he served in Army Intelligence, Baer obtained a degree in television engineering. His goal was to build television receivers. By 1951, he was working at Loral, then a small military contractor. He was given the job of building the "best TV set in the world." At that early date, Baer was already thinking about building TV sets with games built in.

"Somewhere along the line I suggested that we might include some novel features, like adding some form of TV game! That got the predictable negative reaction, and that was the end of that!"

It wasn't until 15 years later that Baer gave serious thought to the matter, but in 1966, he was still just about the only one doing so. Working at the time for another military contractor, Sanders & Associates, he scribbled some notes in a bus station in New York, and on Sept. 1, 1966, he wrote a four-page paper outlining his ideas for a TV game system. Within five days, he had completed a schematic of his proposed system.

The first task was to make something appear on the screen. One of Baer's early decisions was to send the signal through the antenna input (the only one available) and to use channels 3 and 4, which are the channels still used years later for video game consoles attached to the TV.

Baer got Bob Tremblay involved, and Tremblay built a vacuum tube device that could place two movable spots on the screen.

Fox and Hounds

"With that simple arrangement, we played a 'Chase Game' in which we pretended that one spot represented a fox and the other spot represented a 'hunter' or a 'hound,'" said Baer. "The object of the game was to have the 'hound' chase the 'fox' until he 'caught' him by touching the 'fox' spot with the 'hound' spot. It was primitive, all right, but it was a video game, it *was* fun, and we were encouraged to forge ahead."

The "Fox and Hounds" game hardware.

Shooter

Until this point, the entire effort was unofficial and had nothing at all to do with the work he was supposed to be doing. But Baer figured that he now had something to show, so he invited Herbert Campman, the company's corporate director of research and development, to see what he and Tremblay had created. The response was positive, and Baer received his first funding for the project—$2,000 plus $500 for materials.

Bill Harrison joined the team in January 1967. Baer's next innovation involved a toy gun, and Harrison designed some circuitry that allowed it to shoot the dots on the screen. "Now we could 'shoot' at that spot, and when we 'hit' it, the spot disappeared from the screen. Having the other player move the spot rapidly and randomly around the screen gave us a moving target. Gun games were born!"

The gun was a hit with Campman, too, and the team got more money and time to develop. New ideas and directions continued to flow, including some initial work with creating games to be played over cable TV. New people joined the project, including Bill Rusch, who had the idea to turn the video spot into a ball. "We batted around ideas of how we could implement games such as Ping-Pong, hockey, football, and other sports games. I am not sure that we recognized that we had crossed a watershed, "says Baer, "but that's what it amounted to."

Brown Box

By November 11, 1967, the team had produced a working two-player Ping-Pong game. What followed was a system for programmable games, culminating in what Baer calls the "Brown Box."

Ralph Baer and the Odyssey box, 1972.

What remained was to find a way to market the device. After showing it to all the major TV makers, a negotiation started with RCA. However, the RCA deal fell apart. But Bill Enders, a "Brown Box" supporter, left RCA and joined Magnavox. At Magnavox, Enders championed Baer's game product, and ultimately the deal was struck.

The first home video game system, the Magnavox Odyssey, was launched in 1972. The Odyssey's legacy was far-reaching. Although it was a marginal commercial success, partially hampered by Magnavox's marketing strategies, it may have been the inspiration for Nolan Bushnell's introduction of Pong. (See story on *page 19*.)

Ralph Baer didn't stop with the Odyssey. He helped develop Coleco's Telstar gaming system and invented Simon, Maniac, and a lot of other games and devices. He holds many patents.

(Ralph Baer died in late 2014. His spirit and innovations live on.)

Ralph Baer's 1971 patent for "Television Gaming and Training Apparatus."

The Brown Box system that ultimately became the Odyssey.

Ralph Baer and a few of his inventions.

Sometimes a Great Notion

The first part of Nolan Bushnell's story takes place in the 1960s. You might call it serendipity. You might call it visionary. Whatever you call it, the day Nolan Bushnell first encountered Spacewar! was most fortuitous. It was on the campus of the University of Utah. It was the mid-60s. It was especially fortuitous because Bushnell not only recognized a good game when he saw it, but he knew what it could become.

"You need to see it in the context of me as an engineering student first, but also as the manager of games at the local amusement park, my part-time job. In some ways I was smitten by Spacewar! not just because it was fun to play, but I also saw commercial opportunity; I knew how much good games earned. But it was something I put at the back of my mind. It was running on an IBM 7900 or something like that. A big IBM machine. Certainly too expensive to be feasible economically. The serendipity for me is that I knew the economics and the technology.

"Now fast-forward to me coming to California in 1969 to work at Ampex. I was an amateur-ranked Go player, and one of the guys I played Go with worked up at the AI lab at Stanford. He told me about the Spacewar! game they had and I told him, 'I played that in college. I'd like to see how it works.' So he took me up there one evening and we played a lot of Spacewar! That rekindled my enthusiasm for the game and my belief in its commercial potential."

Bushnell's first project was Computer Space, a single-player version of Spacewar! that he created in his spare time using various parts scrounged from Ampex and other sources. For his workshop, he converted his daughter's room, and two-year-old Britta slept in the living room.

"My original plan was quite different from how it turned out. I originally planned to do it based on a Data General 1600—to have a minicomputer running multiple games. My technical addition, as I originally saw it, was going to be a very cheap monitor. Then what kept happening, the computer kept running out of cycle time—it was so blindingly slow. I thought the cost of the machine would outstrip its ability to earn. I almost gave it up. I cut down to four games, but that put the economics on the edge. I kept having to make the monitors smarter, taking over tasks. Then I had my real epiphany. 'Hell,' I thought, 'I'm not going to use the Data General. I'll do it all in hardware.' So I went from using a $4,000 computer to maybe $100 worth of components."

Ultimately, he completed the design of Computer Space, creating the whole thing in hardware. But he still had to find a way to market it. How that came about was another bit of serendipity.

"I had a dentist appointment and my dentist had another patient who worked at Nutting & Associates. I was chatting with the dentist through a mouthful of cotton about what I was working on. He said you should talk to this guy. And that's how I first heard about Nutting. They were a company who had done one product and were in trouble. They were not particularly successful at that time; they were looking for anything, so they jumped at it. Maybe a stronger company would not have taken the risk."

Computer Space released in 1971. It is widely considered an unsuccessful debut, but it did make money, and, more importantly, it gave Bushnell some idea of the demographics of video arcade games at a time when there was no such thing.

"Computer Space did very well on college campuses and in places where the education level was higher. However, there weren't any arcades as such back then. You had to put machines in bowling alleys and beer bars. That was the market. If you couldn't do well in Joe's Bar and Grill, you had no chance. Computer Space did horribly in the typical American beer bar."

The lesson learned from all this? Keep it simple.

A two-person version of Computer Space

THE 70s

Don't Look Back

The stage was set for the introduction of a new art form, and a new industry. The technological foundation was built. The earliest pioneers had seen farther than any others and had made their tentative steps along the path. The world was in flux, as new politics, new music, and new social consciousness began to spread throughout the United States and Europe. The '60s were over. A generation of young people dreamed new dreams and broke down the status quo. It was into that world that first Ralph Baer and then Nolan Bushnell made their humble offerings, and changed the world in ways no one could have foreseen. Once Pong became a household word, it was too late to turn back. The era of electronic games had begun…

ATARI

GOALS

FAIRNESS

Fairness is the best single word which means play the game by the rules. We play hard, play to win, but we will play by the rules of local, state, federal and international law, as well as the standards of ethical business practice and fair labor relations.

An unethical corporation has no right to existence in any social framework. Besides, winning by cheating is, at best, a hollow victory.

PEOPLE

A corporation is simply people banding together in an organized fashion to produce products or accomplishments which would not be possible otherwise. When the goals of Atari and the goals of its people are in harmony, Atari is strong and its people are happy and satisfied. Therefore, Atari will:

a. Provide maximum remuneration and benefits to its people based on their contribution to its profits and goals.

b. Provide a work atmosphere in which a person can maintain his dignity and identity.

c. Maintain a social atmosphere where we can be friends and comrades apart from the organizational hierarchy.

d. Encourage and promote personal growth through education and training such as that we may all reach our individual potentialities.

e. Judge all people on the basis of their skills and contribution and not tolerate discrimination on the basis of race, color, creed, national origin, sex, appearance or personal life. At Atari, discrimination of the whites against blacks or blacks against whites; of the short hairs against the long hairs or the long hairs against the short hairs; the trained against the untrained; the experienced against the unexperienced, will not be tolerated.

f. Bring together people who enjoy what they do and are willing to strive to build a strong and innovative corporation in which we can all take pride and satisfaction and know that our part is well done. Our corporation will only be as strong as the sum of its parts.

PROFITS

Eventually, without profits, a corporation cannot exist. Therefore, all other goals except the first must be subservient to profits.

Profits should be large enough to fund our growth, share with our employees, and strengthen our corporate base.

Our profits should also be reflective of our contribution to those that our products serve. The best and most lasting business relationships are those in which all persons involved make profits in proportion to their income. By fairly pricing our products, we can keep ourselves, as well as our customers, financially healthy, and contribute to the overall growth of the industry.

PRODUCTS

We define our product as innovative leisure. We will build the best products possible, and serve our markets in such a way that through time the Atari name is synonymous with: quality, imagination, research, after-sale service, and social responsibility.

GROWTH

Our goal of growth will be aimed at expanding our current market through innovative products, as well as increasing market share through better solutions to our customers' problems. We will also grow by cautious entrance into allied fields, fields in which we can use our current successes to give us a competitive edge. Our growth will be dramatic, fueled by excellence in all areas, whether it be in research, finance, manufacturing, marketing or management.

CITIZENSHIP

We will remember that this society and its institutions have provided this climate for business activity. We believe that corporate citizenship is important to keep our institutions strong. We will be politically active for causes we feel are just. Our colleges and universities will enjoy our financial and personal support, and charitable causes will be supported.

Nolan K. Bushnell

2

Nolan Bushnell's manifesto of Atari's early corporate identity. It reminds us of the idealistic beginnings of this industry and of how much it has changed.

1972: The Magnavox Odyssey

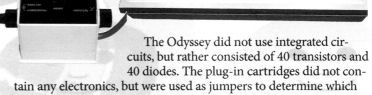

It was the first home video game system ever sold—anywhere! It was the first step toward what would ultimately become a multibillion dollar industry. It all started with Ralph Baer and his "brown box."

Ralph Baer took his "brown box" prototype to various TV manufacturers, convinced as always that video gaming was commercially viable. The first company to show interest was RCA, but after a long negotiation, the deal fell through. Baer told us, "Fortunately for us, one of the members of the RCA team—a guy by the name of Bill Enders—left RCA and became a vice president of marketing at Magnavox in their New York offices. And he had been very impressed with the demo."

Because of Bill Enders, Baer was invited to demonstrate the game to a group of Magnavox executives at the company's headquarters in Fort Wayne, Indiana. "We demonstrated to a whole room full of guys who didn't seem to react very favorably," said Baer. "But the boss who was there, Vice President of Marketing Jerry Martin, said, 'We go with it.' And that was it; that was the beginning."

It took many months to turn the Brown Box setup into a mass-market machine, but in May 1972, the Odyssey Home Entertainment System was distributed to Magnavox dealers all over the country.

The original Odyssey was an extremely simple machine capable of generating two square spots to represent the two players (the paddles), a ball, and a center line. There were no sound effects and no on-screen scoring. Using transparent colored overlays and six plug-in cartridges, the system could play 12 different games; however, many of the games required additional boards and other physical items such as dice or cards.

Color overlays used in the Odyssey games Simon Says, States, Roulette, and others.

The Odyssey did not use integrated circuits, but rather consisted of 40 transistors and 40 diodes. The plug-in cartridges did not contain any electronics, but were used as jumpers to determine which of the electronics systems would be used for a set of games.

Other games and peripherals were available for the Odyssey, including a light gun that would react to any light source, which meant it could be aimed at a lightbulb and react in the same way as when it hit a "target" on the game screen. However, since the system did not keep score, there was hardly any point in cheating.

Despite its relative simplicity by today's standards, the Odyssey might have done much better if it hadn't been for the perception, inadvertently and sometimes intentionally given by Magnavox salespeople, that the system would work only on Magnavox TVs. In its two-year lifetime, the Odyssey only sold around 100,000 units, though some sources report as many as 200,000. Only 20,000 light guns were sold.

The Odyssey was the culmination of Ralph Baer's experimentation that had begun way back in the 1960s, and it clearly marks him as the first creator of the home video game and a visionary inventor.

Let the Games Begin

There are myths and legends, pioneers and prophets. There are geniuses and visionaries. In some ways, Nolan Bushnell has been all of them. While Ralph Baer may be known legitimately as the "Father of the Video Game," Nolan Bushnell can lay claim to the title "Father of the Industry."

Birth of Atari

Unable to come to an agreement with Nutting & Associates for the next project following Computer Space, Nolan Bushnell decided to form his own company with partner Ted Dabney. The company's original name was Syzygy, a term they picked from the dictionary that means "either of two opposite points in the orbit of a planet or satellite, especially the moon, where it is in opposition or conjunction with the sun." Simply put, it is an alignment of heavenly bodies. The name appealed to them as techies. However, a candle company had that name, and in June 1972, Bushnell picked the name Atari from his Go playing background. "Atari" is what you say when you have surrounded your opponent's stones and are about to take them. This also had special meaning for Bushnell and says something about his business philosophy.

After his lessons with Computer Space, Bushnell was sure he wanted to create a sports game this time. Something simple. Apparently, he had obtained a contract to create a driving game for Bally, but he opted to begin even more simply. At this time, he was also managing a pinball route, to help fund the fledgling company.

He hired Al Alcorn, an engineer he'd worked with at Ampex, to do the engineering for the next game. But before attempting the driving game, he told Alcorn to do a much simpler ball and paddle game. It was supposed to be a throwaway project, just to get Alcorn's feet wet. But Bushnell didn't say that. He told Alcorn that he had a contract for the game with General Electric—a complete fabrication.

Registration of the Atari trademark in 1975 refers to the first use of Atari in June 1972. Note also that the design is described as "consisting of a stylized representation of Mount Fujiyama."

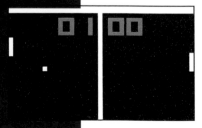

THE ROOTS OF PONG

Where there's innovation, there's often synchronicity. And so it was that, when Nutting heard about a home video game system being demonstrated at the traveling Magnavox Profit Caravan in May 1972, they sent Nolan Bushnell to check it out. Bushnell signed the guest book and saw the Odyssey.

Was this where the idea for Pong came from? Ralph Baer is convinced of it. Bushnell himself is not definitive.

"We already knew we were going to make a sports game. Simple is what we knew we had to do."

He did add, "Certainly I've never disputed that Ralph Baer created some of the first analog games. What we did was make them digital."

In any case, the decision to create a simple ball and paddle game may well have changed history. And, although Bushnell settled a lawsuit with Magnavox out of court and paid royalties for years after that, Pong was a monster hit, and the Age of Atari officially began late in 1972 when Pong was first introduced.

Alcorn laughs about it today. "It's about the art of management. By definition, anything that is revolutionary or truly earth shattering is going to seem wrong at first. There are several ways to get people do to something. You can demand people to do it. Building enthusiasm works. At Apple it was called the 'Reality Distortion Field,' a term sometimes used to describe founder Steve Jobs' uncanny ability to convince people of just about anything. A white lie—not a big lie—Nolan was simply trying to get me to do the right thing for the wrong reasons. I could have resented it, but I think it was amusing, his way of doing it. I was stubborn and ornery enough that if he had told me truth, I might not have worked so hard at it."

In fact, Alcorn completed the first hand-wired version of Pong in a week and a half. He then added some of the refinements that typified the great game, such as the "English" on the paddle and the ball's increase in speed as you played.

The Andy Capps Pong prototype, front and back. Note the hand-wired circuit board and the Hitachi TV set.

Originally, the paddles were just placeholders for a human figure holding the paddle, but the prototype proved to be fun to play. As Bushnell puts it, "Why gild the lily?"

Reality Distortion Fields

According to Alcorn, Bushnell actually did have a contract with Bally/Midway to produce a pinball game and a video game (possibly a driving game) and was receiving regular payments from Bally. When Pong was completed, he realized that he was on to something and did his best to convince Bally that they

Early photo of Atari folks with their baby, Pong. Depicted from left to right are Ted Dabney, Nolan Bushnell, Fred Marincheck, and Al Alcorn.

THE CASE OF THE CRAMMED CASHBOX

When the first Pong prototype was done, they did a test installation in a bar called Andy Capps in Sunnyvale. Late at night they received a frantic call that the game was broken. "We were worried about the games being reliable enough," says Alcorn. "They had to be robust enough to operate in a bar environment, which was relatively hostile. Silicon chips would burn out in those days, so we were concerned when we got the service call. We thought, 'Uh oh...' But the culprit was in fact the coin box, which was jammed up. That was very easy to fix. I can't say we really knew that this meant anything, but we did feel lots of relief. We really didn't know what we had at the time. We were just making it up as we went along."

didn't want the new game. First he told the Bally division that Midway wasn't interested. Then he told Midway that Bally didn't want it. In the end, he got them to pass on Pong. Having kept Pong for Atari, he decided to have Atari manufacture its own products. Alcorn remembers, "We originally intended to produce a game for the royalties, not make it ourselves. We had an argument about it at Andy Capps. Ted and I thought the whole idea of manufacturing was bullshit. Nolan had to convince us to be in the manufacturing business. In the end that turned out to be the best strategy."

Bushnell discovered that creating the cabinets came with its own headaches. He says, "We wanted to go into higher profile places, which meant we had to tone down some of our ideas. I found that you couldn't please everyone, though.

"The real problem we had in those days was that we had no money. Ven-

The original Pong sell sheet. The back includes lines like "a new product, a new concept, a new company." All in a "low-key cabinet suitable for sophisticated locations."

The 1972 commercial version of Pong.

ture capital was in its infancy at that time. In fact, we raised no VC until the company was highly successful. We always wanted to raise money. In those days we'd describe what we were doing and people would say, 'What? You want to put a computer inside a box and people put quarters in it. That sounds outlandish.'"

The end result, however, was staggering. As Al Alcorn puts it, "Pong was a runaway smash hit in the coin-op amusement business. Prior to Pong, what was the big smash hit? There were pinballs, claws, driving games. Nothing like this. Pong was the biggest success anyone had seen."

A closer look at the original wiring of the first Pong prototype.

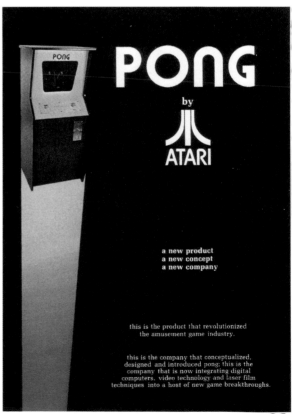

"The Jackals"

Joe Keenan and
Nolan Bushnell

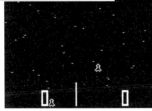

In Space Race, two side-by-side rocket ships would race toward the top of the screen while avoiding asteroids that flew horizontally across the screen. Midway's Asteroid was essentially the same game.

However they may have felt about being outmaneuvered by Bushnell, Midway quickly came out with their own Pong clone called Winner. But they weren't alone. Alcorn states, "Of all our first-run sales of Pong, I think a lot of them went to our future competitors."

In fact, by May 1973, Williams had introduced their version of Paddle Ball. By the end of the year, Chicago Coin had launched TV Hockey, Sega of Japan had introduced Hockey TV, Taito placed Pro Hockey in Japan, and even sports and amusement giant Brunswick dipped its toe in the water with Astro Hockey. Midway even built a follow-up machine to Winner called Leader, which allowed two or four players to play an elimination match of a Pong-style game. Leader's distinctive feature was the structure in the center of the screen (called the "center maze" in Midway's sales literature) that created interesting rebounds and ricochets.

Upon seeing the vast number of knockoffs of Pong, Bushnell and Alcorn realized that their own strength was in innovation. Alcorn says, "There were probably 10,000 Pong games made, Atari made maybe 3,000. Our defense was... 'OK. Let's make another video game. Something we can do that they can't do.' It wasn't easy. The company was building rapidly. It was much easier doing the first Pong with no distractions. Basically, though, it was a defensive decision to do more games. Even so, it took some time to come out with our next game... Space Race..."

Atari's second game was Space Race, which came out in July 1973. Midway released its own version of Space Race, called Asteroid (not to be confused with Atari's later megahit game, Asteroids). Nolan Bushnell referred to the people who produced copycat products as "the jackals" and was determined to beat them through innovation and originality.

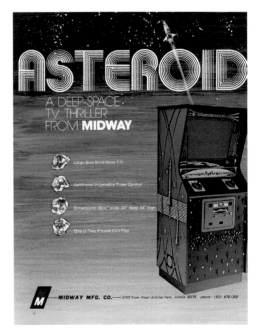

The original Space Race prototype box.

Kee Games

Sometimes getting around a barrier requires a little extra "innovation."

Atari quickly ran afoul of an established coin-op business practice wherein many regional distributors required exclusivity. "The problem was that our sales were limited by the nature of the distribution channel," says Alcorn. "One manufacturer could get only about one third of the market. Nolan's solution was to create another company that was perceived as a competitor. That company could grab another third of the market that we were losing to knockoffs."

Nolan convinced his next-door neighbor, Joe Keenan, to head the new company. When it started up, Kee Games "stole" two of Atari's top people, Gil Williams from manufacturing and Steve Bristow, Alcorn's top engineer. Publicly, the two companies were competitors, and there was considerable animosity between Bushnell and the upstart company, but secretly, they were one and the same. "Nolan and I even sat on the board of Kee Games," says Alcorn.

The two interrelated companies often used the same basic games

in different cabinets, with minor modifications. For example, Spike by Kee is the same as Atari's Rebound (but with a special "spike" button), and Quadrapong by Atari is Elimination by Kee.

Combined, Atari/Kee released four titles in 1973 and an amazing 18 new titles (6 of which were variants on Pong) in 1974, including the next big hit game, Tank, which ironically came from Kee Games. Tank was the first arcade game to use ROM (Read-Only Memory) to remember the graphics, and it had an on-screen maze through which one or two players could maneuver. It was also so popular that dealers didn't care whether they had an exclusive on the machines or not. Meanwhile, Atari was running into management and cash-flow problems. Joe Keenan had turned out to be a highly effective leader for Kee Games, and so it was decided to merge the two companies and make Joe the president of both.

With the merger, Kee Games went from this...

KEE GAMES

KEE GAMES
a wholly owned subsidiary of Atari, Inc
...to this.

new FROM KEE GAMES

SPIKE

THE "SPIKE" MAN COMETH...

FROM KEE!

• FANTASTIC TWO-PLAYER GAME

• FOUR PADDLE GAME WITH HORIZONTAL & VERTICAL MOVEMENT

• SHORTER PLAYING TIME

KEE GAMES

"We started a football game called Xs and Os, but then we thought a game with tanks would be better and made Tank instead."
–Steve Bristow

Somebody's Gotta Be First

Midway debuted TV Basketball in 1974, complete with stubby, blocky players and two easily recognizable baskets. They also developed a video baseball game called Ball Park that cloned Ramtek's Baseball, released in October. In 1973, Atari also launched the first maze chase game with Gotcha and, in 1974, first video driving game with Gran Trak 10. The former didn't prove nearly as successful as Sega's later (1976) Blockade, and the overhead perspective of the latter didn't make it anywhere near the moneymaker of 1982's Pole Position. However, these were the first games of their kinds in genres that would later prove incredibly popular.

Even though Atari had started it all with Pong, there were other companies with bigger guns. One of them, Midway, licensed Taito's Gun Fight, a clever little quarter gobbler where two blocky yellow cowboys squared off with a cactus between them. Gun Fight was the first Japanese import, a harbinger of things to come.

More from Midway and Atari

Midway's cabinets became ubiquitous. Midway led in driving games in 1975 with Racer (a black-and-white driving game), Wheels (overhead perspective racing for one), and later, Wheels II (overhead perspective racing for one or two players). Atari's best counterpunch was to release a big, expensive console for one to eight players, called Indy 800.

Midway also made arcade operators happy in 1976. Sea Wolf, the classic submarine shooter with periscope and side-scrolling target ships, became an arcade standard. Midnight Racer, a 3D driving game with Hi/Low shifter, was a major hit. The company even launched The Amazing Maze, a puzzle game reported to have more than one million patterns. Sega had a major hit, as well, with Blockade. Blockade was a simple enough game where you tried to avoid getting boxed in while you tried to hedge in your opponent and force him or her to crash.

But Atari hadn't given up on the coin-op business. Two major games hit the cabinets for Atari in 1976. Night Driver depicted a car hood in color so you could drive on a totally black screen with white blocks representing the sides of the road. The action was similar to 1982's Pole Position, but the black screen allowed for a fast frame rate with the technology of an earlier generation. Of course, Atari's biggest hit in 1976 was Breakout.

There is some discrepancy as to whose idea Breakout was. Both Steve Jobs and Nolan Bushnell have claimed credit. Whatever the truth may be, Bushnell did hire Jobs to create the circuitry for Breakout. "Breakout was a funny situation," says Bushnell. "At that time, we had bonus programs, and engineers could bid on the projects they wanted. When we were considering Breakout, ball and paddle

Sea Wolf was another of Midway's early successes.

Gran Trak 10 used an overhead perspective. Screen image is from the original flyer.

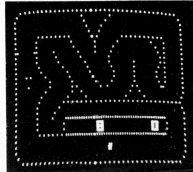

See more Atari posters on the following pages.

they could remove from the basic 75-chip design. In a 72-hour stint, Woz was able to remove more than 50 chips from the circuitry, and those who saw it considered it to be a true example of Wozniak's artistry. However, the final design was so tight, nobody could reproduce it. In the end, the circuits were redesigned with 100 chips.

Of course, Steve Jobs and Steve Wozniak went on to found Apple Computer (*see page 46*), but they do have a place in the Atari legend.

games were considered to be dead, and nobody would work on it. So that's why I gave it to Jobs and Woz, because nobody in the company wanted anything to do with it."

Jobs took the job and got Steve Wozniak to create the circuitry. The deal was that they would receive a nice bonus for every chip

Midway's Amazing Maze had you racing through the twists and turns of a complex maze trying to beat the computer to the finish.

In October 1976, Atari released Night Driver, a racing game that gave an illusion of speed with very simple graphics.

Taito's Gun Fight featured two cowboys and their six-guns and a variety of obstacles between them. The bullets, oddly, would bounce off the edges, making bank shots a pretty good strategy.

GAME DESIGN 101

Nolan's Theorem: All the best games are easy to learn and difficult to master. They should reward the first quarter and the hundredth.

Mike Albaugh's corollary (as told by Joe Decuir): The best games can be played with one hand, so you can have your beer or your girlfriend in the other.

Albaugh's response: "He may be referring to the time I beat him at Tank while holding a beer. Not easy, given the two-joystick controls. On the other hand, we had both had several beers at the time. Some folks believe they play better 'a little loose.' I know that it's true for me, some of the time. On the other hand, I lost five bucks by believing Ed Rot-

berg could beat his 'clean and sober' best at Space Invaders in an 'altered state.' Also, we deliberately sloped the control panels on games to prevent people setting drinks on them. We also put screened holes directly under the trackballs on Football, so if anybody poured a drink into it, it would just come out on his feet."

More Atari Posters

1975

1974

1974

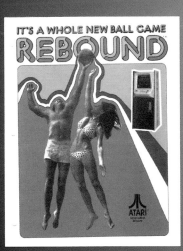

1974

1975

1975

1975

1976

1976

1976

1976

1977

1977

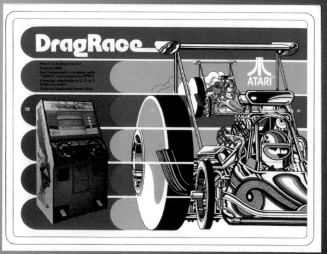

1977

1978

1978

1978

1978

1979

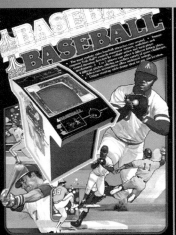

1979

1979

1980

1980

1982

1982

1982

1983

1983

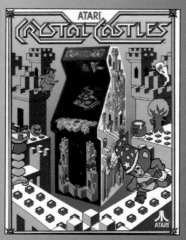

1983

1984

Al Alcorn with the original hand-wired Pong prototype sent to Sears. Below: The return address label from Tom Quinn back to Alcorn. According to Alcorn, the box had never been opened since the '70s before these pictures were taken.

Homing In

The first wafer containing multiple Pong chips.

Also in the mid-'70s, Atari began another project that would ultimately have as big an impact in the home as Pong had brought upon the arcade scene. In 1974, Alcorn had Harold Lee, a chip expert, working on a way to create a custom chip that couldn't be copied. Lee wasn't sure that was the best solution, given the rapid changes in technology, but he did say, "We can put all of Pong on a chip and hook it up to a TV set." Lee created the chip circuits, which Alcorn's wife would take each night to create wire-wrapped prototypes. Once the bugs were removed, Alcorn would return the corrected design. Ultimately, they had a chip design that they were pretty sure would work. They had created a feasible home system, but had no idea how they would market it.

Alcorn remembers, "We basically cold-called Sears & Roebuck in Chicago and stumbled across Tom Quinn, the buyer for sporting goods who was also the buyer for the Odyssey. He was at our doorstep within a few days. I think he perceived the potential better than we did."

But Quinn wanted exclusivity, and Bushnell wanted to explore his options, so they didn't

immediately make a deal. "We took the home unit to Toy Fair in New York. Lots of buyers looked at it, but we sold exactly zero." Everywhere, it was the same. Nobody was interested, except for Sears.

Sears Tele-Games

The first version of home Pong was still a wire-wrapped prototype. This was sent to Sears in a custom wooden box. When it came time to demonstrate it, however, it didn't work at first due to interference from a broadcast tower on the top of the building. Alcorn did get it running, and ultimately Sears placed a Christmas order for 150,000 Pong machines, which were called the Sears Tele-Games system. "They paid the bills, did all the advertising," says Alcorn. "It was the best thing that ever happened to us."

Still, in order to meet such a large order, Atari needed more money. Enter Don Valentine, the most influential venture capitalist of the time. Valentine was able to engineer a $10 million credit line, though part of his price was a seat on Atari's board, a position he took seriously.

Pong for the home sold for about $100, and was a phenomenal seller for Sears during the 1975 Christmas season. In focus group tests against the three-year-old Odyssey, Alcorn remembers, "What struck me was that, in the half hour the group was given to play each game, they spent most of their time putting the Odyssey together and making it work. With Pong, they hook it up and it's going

Pong-on-a-chip: the very first chip of the very first all-digital game.

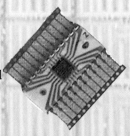

'beep, beep, beep' and people are having fun. Ironically, when they were asked what they would expect to pay, they rated the Odyssey higher because it had so many pieces. In retrospect, I think we underdesigned Pong. It was too simple."

Early Competition

After Atari's success in 1975, everyone wanted to get into the act by the holiday season of 1976. A staggering number of companies tried to introduce Tele-Games knockoffs in 1976, including Magnavox with their Odyssey 200 console.None could match Atari's success, until a former leather company who also made above ground swimming pools and a few toys entered the scene. Coleco introduced its Telstar system during that 1976 season, with some last-minute help from Ralph Baer who fixed a radio frequency radiation leak, and quickly, if briefly, rose to the top of the home TV game business.

Controversy Erupts

Also in 1976, video games made the headlines and began a trend of criticism that has lasted until this day when Exidy released their controversial Death Race arcade game. Based more or less on the movie *Death Race 2000*, players

Above: Prototype of the original home Pong unit mounted on a wooden box. Below: The final unit.

Nolan Bushnell posing with the original Sears Tele-Games unit.

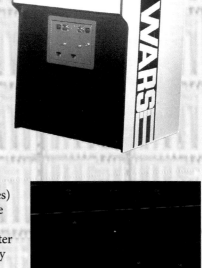

would compete at driving their cars over zombie pedestrians for points. The game started the violence controversy over video games and disturbed many in the game field. Atari, under Bushnell, had maintained a policy against killing recognizably human figures. Only 500 Death Race cabinets were ever made.

Cinematronics

In 1977, the next wave of innovation centered around vector graphics games. Cinematronics brought Larry Rosenthal's MIT master's thesis project to prominence by licensing and releasing the game. It was Space Wars, a new variant on Steve Russell's Spacewar! Using Rosenthal's "Vectorbeam" technology, on-screen images were created from detailed X,Y coordinates and produced crisper images than the blocky television-style graphics used in other games.

Space Wars had many of the variations that had earlier been added to Spacewar!, such as gravity/no gravity/negative gravity, sun/no sun, and hyperspace (which would instantly send your ship to a random location that might or might not be safe). It also added incremental damage so you could slowly cripple your opponent. In the original game, one hit was all it took.

The first Vectorbeam game after Space Wars was Warrior in 1978. This was a one-on-one sword-fighting game with players controlling their hacking, bashing warriors from an overhead perspective. The warrior figures, of course, were line-based figures displayed as

animated outlines on the screen. Tim Skelly, who was later to work on Armor Attack and Star Castle for the company, as well as Reactor for Gottlieb, not only worked on Warrior, but also helped design Rip Off in 1979. In Rip Off, players commanded futuristic tanks (little more than simple geometric shapes) on a playing field where triangles (representing fuel cells) filled the center of the screen and enemy tanks (in pairs and, at higher levels, in threes) would simultaneously try to remove the fuel cells and destroy the player's tanks. There was also a two-player mode where both players tried to fend off the enemy tanks in an early example of cooperative play.

In an interview, Skelly relates an amusing story that the starfield for Star Castle was actually the outline of a woman taken from a nudie magazine. Not many people recognized it for what it was, however.

In 1986, Pete Kauffman, chairman of Exidy, created an even gorier game called Chiller that many arcades refused to carry.

The Next Generation at Home

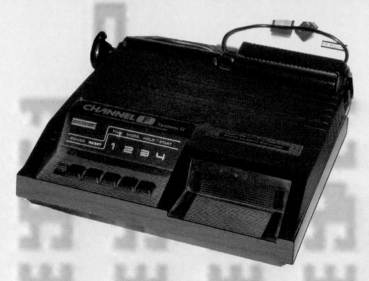

Fairchild's Channel F was one of the first multi-cartridge home consoles, but it achieved little success and was ultimately overshadowed by the VCS from Atari. Below: Several screen images from Channel F games.

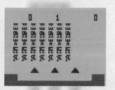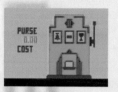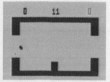

By 1976, the collective creativity of arcade game designers had produced a wide variety of games, but only Pong and its cousins had yet come to the home. It was time for a change. Interestingly enough, the first steps toward a more versatile home game system did not come from Atari.

The Fairchild VES

The Fairchild Video Entertainment System (VES) launched in 1976 with a built-in Hockey/Tennis game and eventually supported 21 cartridges before Fairchild pulled the plug and sold the rights to Zircon. Zircon added five more cartridges before allowing the system to fade. The system sold for $169.95, and the cartridges were $19.95 each. The first cartridge for the VES was a 4-in-1 "Videocart" and contained Tic-Tac-Toe, Shooting Gallery, Doodle, and Quadra-Doodle. This first cartridge was supplemented by Desert Fox, Video Blackjack, Spitfire, Space War, Master Mind, Labyrinth, and Backgammon/Acey Deucey during its first season. Ultimately renamed Channel F, the Fairchild system never sold well, and was soon to be overshadowed by Atari's next major advance, the Video Computer System, also known as the Atari VCS (later the Atari 2600—see page 41).

Studio II

Also in 1976, RCA launched its Studio II under the magic $150 price point for game machines and offered a variety of cartridges, also for $19.95 each (same as the Fairchild VES). The black-and-white graphics weren't very much better than the Atari/Sears machines, but there were four different series of cartridges available to freshen the game experience: TV Arcade, TV Casino, TV Mystic, and TV Schoolhouse. Studio II didn't make a ripple.

RCA's Studio II "Home TV Programmer" featured built-in keypad controls instead of paddles. It merits at least a footnote in the history of consoles for being one of the first cartridge-based units. Note that Studio II games included versions of Space War and Tennis.

A Brief History of Early Handheld Games

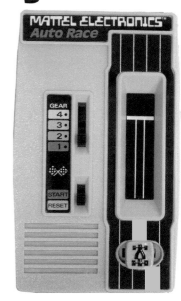

Handheld games first appeared in the 1970s. To a whole generation raised before Game Boy and other modern handheld game systems, a handheld game meant you got one—and only one—game. It was small and either sat in your hand or on a table in front of you, and it used a variety of different display types: anything from ordinary lights to Liquid Crystal Display (LCD) to Vacuum Flourescent Display (VFD).

The earliest instance of a handheld game that we've been able to discover was a game by Waco made back in 1972 called Electro Tic-Tac-Toe. This simple light-based tic-tac-toe game allowed players to slide plastic red or green tiles over the light to show they owned that square. After that Waco game, the first true electronic handheld games appeared around 1976 from Mattel.

Mattel

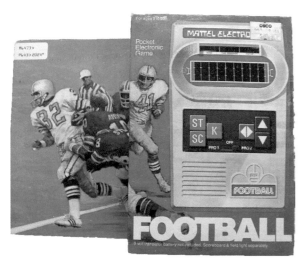

Mattel was the first company to release a truly all-electronic handheld electronic game (no mechanical moving parts, all solid-state electronics). The first of these games, such as Missile Attack, Auto Race, and Football, featured simple LED playfields with sound effects, and were immediate hits. Football, especially, sold in amazing quantities.

Michael Katz was director of marketing at Mattel at the time. "I first had the idea to make a game the size of a handheld calculator. I developed it with Richard Chang, who was the preliminary designer." Katz also says that the first game they released was Auto Race. "We wanted to test the market before we released Football, which we expected to do well."

According to Katz, these simple games turned into a "$400 million category." Mattel went on to release about 15 games of similar design/play for several different sports. They then moved into even smaller, LCD-based games and couple of more complex, two-player games. Their biggest competitor was Coleco (*see page 36*) with their similar line of sports games (although Coleco moved into the head-to-head two-player games much faster than Mattel).

Entex

Entex started out with simple LED-based sports games, most of which featured head-to-head play. These were a little more playable than Coleco's head-to-head games, although they were also significantly larger. Entex followed the head-to-head games with their Arcade series, which featured some very popular arcade games (and rather good handheld versions of them). They also made two cartridge-based games, Select-a-Game and Adventure Vision, that are very collectible today, but didn't due too well when they were released.

Bandai

Bandai began making handheld games in the mid-'70s with some very weak sports-themed games, and followed those with some arcade-themed games to compete with Entex. Bandai also released several promotional games for various companies, including Coca-Cola. Including foreign countries (especially Japan), Bandai released more handheld games than any other company in the '70s and '80s, and they are still producing them today in Japan, including games for home console systems and Game Boy.

Milton Bradley

Milton Bradley is best known in the handheld arena for Microvision, the first cartridge-based handheld game system. Very primitive by today's standards, it only had a 16x16 pixel LCD screen. It was very successful for a few years, but ironically, only 11 games were released for it (and a 12th one overseas). One problem was that MB refused to license games for the system—the only exception being Star Trek Phaser Strike (which

was later changed to just Phaser Strike after MB decided not to renew the license). Space Invaders was going to be released for this system, but when MB decided against licensing, the game was modified and released as Alien Raiders. MB also released

the far more successful and enduring game Simon in 1978.

Tomy

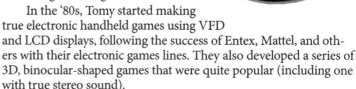

Tomy was one of the earliest handheld game companies. Their games in the early to mid-'70s were mostly mechanical (and wind-up) in nature, with very simple electronics (motors/gears or lights).

In the '80s, Tomy started making true electronic handheld games using VFD and LCD displays, following the success of Entex, Mattel, and others with their electronic games lines. They also developed a series of 3D, binocular-shaped games that were quite popular (including one with true stereo sound).

Other Companies of Note

Several other companies contributed to the development of handheld games:

Bambino: Sports games, competed with Mattel, Coleco

Nelsonic: Made Pac-Man, Frogger, Q*Bert watches

Nintendo: Early entry into handhelds with the Game & Watch series, very popular with collectors.

Parker Brothers: Merlin series, Q*Bert, Split Second, Bank Shot

Radio Shack (Tandy): Didn't develop their own games, but released a lot of handheld games licensed from companies like Bandai, Tiger, and Tomy.

Tiger: Made several rare tabletop games. Among the rarest is their tabletop version of Star Castle. Tiger still makes many LCD handheld games.

Note: This section was written with the help of Rik Morgan. To see a staggering collection of handheld games, visit Rik's online Handheld Museum at www.handheldmuseum.com.

Coleco

Founded by Russian immigrant Maurice Greenberg, The Connecticut Leather Company began operation in 1932, in the midst of the Great Depression. Over the years, Maurice and his son Leonard manufactured a great variety of items, gradually migrating into plastics and toys. They were enormously successful with many of their toys, especially their plastic wading pools.

In 1962, they sold off the leather goods portion of the company, became Coleco Industries, Inc., and went public at $5 a share. In 1966, Maurice's other son Arnold left his legal partnership to become Coleco's chief legal counsel and later its president. It was the combination of Maurice's hard work and optimism, Leonard's manufacturing and engineering talent, and Arnold's financial and marketing skills that took Coleco to the pinnacle of success. In 1971, the company was listed on the New York Stock Exchange.

Coleco was run by the Greenbergs—father and sons. Jim Gordon, who was director of creative services at Coleco, says, "Coleco was a New York Stock Exchange, Fortune 500 company, that was run like a Jewish delicatessen. Whoever screamed last or loudest always got what they wanted. I loved every minute of it."

Coleco's entry into the electronic game field came in 1976 when they introduced Telstar, a home Pong-type game. Arnold Greenberg relates that the company was heavily weighted toward spring and summer items. "Factory utilization was not as well

Where it started: The original Connecticut Leather Company building from the 1930s.
Below: Leonard Greenberg

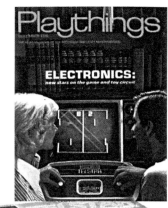

PLAY TENNIS HOCKEY WITH TELSTAR
TELSTAR
FOR VIDEO SPORTS GAMES ON ANY TV
COLECO

balanced as it should be, which whetted our appetites for the game business."

Eric Bromley, who came from Midway and became Coleco's chief electronics designer, remembers the breakthrough that led to Telstar. "Originally, Coleco was looking for an analog device, saving nickels and pennies to get it under $100. With the GI (General Instruments) single-chip solution, you put this chip on a board, made an RF generator out of an LC (or later RC) oscillator, some gates to convert RGB signal to black and white. The chipset was maybe $8-10 at the time. Add some pieces of 'glue' as we called it, and your cost was around $12 to $20. At that point, Coleco could sell a game for $69.95. The formula—the magic price point—was cost times three."

Telstar was a huge success and Coleco attempted to follow up by releasing eight new game systems in 1977, but a combination of events, including a 60-day dock strike, prevented them from meeting Christmas demand. They were forced to liquidate below cost. "There was a kind of steady electronic

May 25, 1971, first day of trading on NYSE: From left: Melvin Gershman, Arnold Greenberg, NYSE official, Maurice Greenberg, Leonard Greenberg.

Among the products that were late to market in 1978 was the Telstar Arcade, which, had it been shipped on time, would have been one of the first cartridge-based game machines.

Telstar Arcade cartridges were distinctively triangular and each carried a chip that contained the entire game. According to Eric Bromley, they were not originally going to be silver. "The oscillators were generating too much heat, so we used this aluminum coating as an RF shield."

Combat was a two-player tank game, another of Coleco's entries into the console market after the original Telstar.

trail—you would go from the basic Pong game into more sophisticated console-based dedicated video games. And by 1978, the world was changing and programmability was key and handheld was key."

The Fickle Hand of Fate

Forced to liquidate inventory after demand had subsided, Coleco suffered its worst losses in 30 years. They were in financial trouble, but their recovery was equally rapid. Mattel had released the first of their handheld games, and Coleco immediately saw an opportunity.

It wasn't unusual for Arnold Greenberg to walk straight from the lab, having witnessed an engineering breakthrough, and schedule a product demo for the very next day, causing the product's designers to have to scramble to put something presentable together. Eric Bromley tells a story where disaster turned into a bonanza. "One time, with almost no warning, we found ourselves demonstrating the prototype of our handheld football game, Electronic Quarterback, which was an upscale version of

Mattel's football game. Ours had passing, for one thing. The company's initial plan was to sell exclusively to Sears and move about 200,000 pieces. The salespeople had no faith in any product and if they could sell anything, they were happy. Well, we sent over a shoebox with the electronics and a hand-built game unit that had 92 tiny hand-wired LEDs in it—some kid with tweezers and a soldering iron had spent maybe four weeks on it. But at the demo, one of the Sears guys accidentally tripped over the umbilical cord that extended between the prototype and the actual electronics in the shoebox; he sent the handheld prototype flying. I got it back in a bag, smashed into a hundred pieces—this $6,000 prototype. It was the best thing that could have happened to us. Sears didn't buy it, and we sold three million of them."

Coleco entered the handheld market in a big way. One of their winning strategies was to air competitive TV commercials which featured two actors dressed up as Mattel's and Coleco's football games. This competitive ad predated the famous Intellivision/Atari 2600 competitive ad by a few years and was the first of its kind in the toy industry.

Coleco's handheld line included a variety of toys. Some of their most successful products, including their popular Head-to-Head line, are visible on the following pages.

Coleco's comparative TV commercial was the first of its kind in electronic game history.

Mattel was first to market with their handheld football game (which, as well as handheld baseball, was re-released years later). Coleco soon entered the handheld game business and produced a variety of products over the years.

In the '80s, Coleco and other handheld makers came out with mini arcade games based on popular arcade titles.

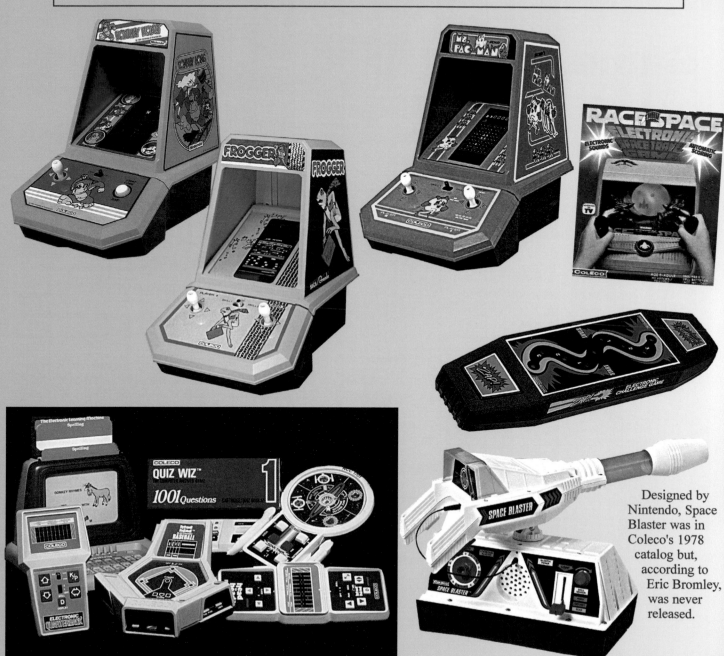

Designed by Nintendo, Space Blaster was in Coleco's 1978 catalog but, according to Eric Bromley, was never released.

Game Brain

Atari's first response to the new cart-based systems was to develop a very simple multi-game console called the Game Brain. In actuality, Game Brain had almost nothing inside it. The cartridges were each self-contained versions of games Atari had previously released as standalone systems, such as Super Pong, Ultra Pong, Stunt Cycle, Video Pinball, and Video Music.

Game Brain was never released—in part due to the far superior system Atari was in the process of completing—and is considered a very rare collectible, as only a small number were created as prototypes.

The original prototype of the VCS—code-named "Stella" after Joe Decuir's bicycle—the system that would ultimately become the first great home console game machine.

Stella

Even before Fairchild came out with their Channel F system, Nolan Bushnell and his team had begun development on an advanced new system that incorporated interchangeable cartridges. Al Alcorn says, "At that time, game development was very expensive and required a custom chip every time. A microprocessor-based cartridge system was much better. The challenge was to design a system or base unit that was flexible enough to play a lot of kinds of games."

Ultimately, they turned to their Grass Valley facility—Atari's think tank—to design the system. Steve Mayer found a chip that could handle the graphics and supply the speed and versatility to power the system they had in mind. It was the 6502 chip from MOS Technology, designed by Chuck Peddle, founder of MOS. The 6502 was powerful for its time, outperforming and selling for less than competitive chips such as the Intel 8080 and the Motorola 6800 chip. Ironically, the chip that Atari eventually chose for their game system, the 6507, was a slightly limited version of the 6502 used in the first generation of personal computers.

Once the chip was secured, the team was assembled and included Jay Miner, who was borrowed from Synertech (who designed custom chips for Atari); Ron Milner, who specialized on the sound module; Larry Wagner, a mathematician and game programmer; and Joe Decuir, a talented engineer.

The Atari VCS

The VCS entered the market with nine games: Combat (variations on Tank, packed with the system), Air-Sea Battle, Basic Math, Blackjack, Indy 500, Star Ship, Street Racer, Surround, and Video Olympics. It also introduced several improvements over previous home console products. Its games were far more colorful, and its controls, which contained the usual knobs for controlling tennis-style games, also introduced something new to the home game systems: the joystick. Other innovations included game selector switches and difficulty settings.

The VCS did have some limitations, however. It was originally designed to handle simple games like Pong and Tank, as the screenshots on the next page clearly show. Nobody quite anticipated the incredible variety of games this system would eventually support. Its true versatility and potential did not really appear at first.

The VCS failed to live up to expectations its first Christmas season, much to the chagrin of Warner, who had invested around $100 million by that time. There were various reasons for its lackluster performance, among them distribution problems and, possibly, competition from new handheld games, which were popular that season. Despite a slow start, the VCS was destined for greatness. Read on...

Stella, the bicycle... still owned and operated by Joe Decuir.

In those days, it was very expensive to create a new game, so when we designed Stella, our intention was to save money. We were able to move significant functions out of hardware and into software. In doing so, the unintended consequence was to create a far more open system, to put the functionality in the hands of creative people who went way beyond what we, as the original designers, had expected. It comes down to a very important engineering principle. I remember, years later, hearing Bill Joy, who became chief technologist at Sun Microsystems, mention this principle— that not all the smart people in the industry work for you. We followed this principle by accident, and Stella's success was directly related to it.
– Joe Decuir

Background: Hand-drawn schematic drawing of the VCS, courtesy of Joe Decuir.

The Competitive Advantage of the VCS

"The VCS was much cheaper to build than any other system," according to Al Alcorn. "All the other systems were designed by semiconductor companies, and there was no incentive to reduce the use of silicon. The VCS had no frame buffer; all the other systems did. In those days memory was very expensive.

"The VCS was the most successful system because of the variety of games it could play, which was largely due to its elegant architecture. The competitors' architecture was too constraining and limited the range of games they could produce. The minimal architecture of Stella wound up being more flexible than even its designers imagined."

Explaining the Frame Buffer

"Actually, it's quite simple. The obvious approach and the one used everywhere today is to have a large area of memory that represents each pixel on the display. That area is scanned out by special circuitry at high speed to drive a display. The computer can write to any part of the display and change the image. If the computer doesn't do anything, the display remains static. So if you had a display of 640x480 pixels of only 8 bits per pixel (256 colors), that would require 640x480 bytes or 307,200 bytes! Prohibitive in those days.

"So other game systems used larger pixels and 4 bits per pixel, but it was still the majority of the cost of the system. Stella relied on a very fast microprocessor and a custom chip (Stella) that generated two lines of video on the fly. If the computer stopped (like if you pulled out the cartridge when it was running), the display turned to garbage. We had only 128 bytes of memory versus thousands of bytes in the competition. It was a bitch to program because the software had to do the job in a limited number of cycles or it missed the end of a scan line."

We actually put audio hardware in instead of trying to make the microprocessor do all the sounds. Being able to go beyond beeps and buzzes with a programmable sound module meant that you could use random noise for things like gunshots, regular sounds for motors and that kind of thing, and, well… beeps and buzzes, too.
-Ron Milner

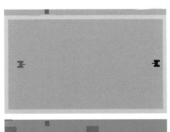
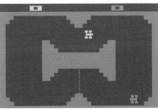
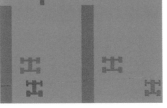

The first crop of games for the VCS were very simple and crude. Top: Screens for Combat and Indy 500. Bottom: Screens for Street Racer and Video Olympics.

Stella originally accommodated 4K cartridges, but our first games were on 2K carts because those were the cheapest ROMs at the time. We saved about $1 in cost by using a 28-pin 6502 derivative (the 6507) and a 24-pin cartridge connector. If we had used a full 40-pin 6502 and a 30-pin connector, we could have easily supported the full 64K address space in the cartridge, and RAM, and even an expansion box. As it turned out, many companies performed a lot of tricks with the VCS to fake a read-write strobe in the cartridges, so they could extend the address space by bank selection. At the time, we never anticipated the system's longevity or the need for so much memory. We opted to keep the costs as low as possible.
-Joe Decuir

WARREN ROBINETT AND THE EASTER EGG

It is standard procedure to place undocumented features and objects in games today. They are called Easter Eggs. But there had to be a first time, and it happened like this: Warren Robinett, a young programmer at Atari, would later go on to help found The Learning Company and to create the classic teaching game, Rocky's Boots, but he made his mark on game history first in 1979-1980.

"When I first went to Atari, I thought I'd died and gone to heaven. I was being paid to design games. But then, after about a year and a half, it started to dawn on me that Atari was making hundreds of millions of dollars and keeping us all anonymous. They didn't even give you a pizza if you designed a good game. There was no incentive at all. Nothing. That's when I has the idea of hiding my name in the game."

Warren created a very secret room in his VCS game Adventure that could only be accessed by selecting a single gray dot on a gray wall. If someone was clever (or lucky) enough to find the room, he found Warren's name written inside—completely against Atari policy. "I could have been

fired if anyone had discovered it, so I kept the secret of a year. It's damned hard to keep a secret for a year—especially a juicy secret like that—but I reasoned that if I couldn't keep the secret, then how could I expect my friends to do so? The game code would have been very easy for Atari to change if they had known about the secret room. But after 300,000 Adventure cartridges had been made and shipped around the world, it was too late.

"Being best known for inventing Easter Eggs in games is a bit irritating. I'd rather be known for inventing the action-adventure game. But, when it comes down to it, I'm happy anyone remembers my games from 20 years ago. At the time, I certainly wasn't looking 20 years ahead."

Although Robinett's Easter Egg was the first of its kind in a video game, hidden features were often incorporated into pinball games, according to former Midway and Coleco designer Eric Bromley. "At Midway, they had me create flaws, so if a kid banged on the box in a certain way, they would get a bonus score. Kids would look for these 'flaws,' but it would cost lots of quarters. We had a bunch of other tricks, too."

Box covers from the first Atari VCS games.

Big Changes at Atari

Meanwhile, back at Atari: Bushnell, ever the competitor, realized that he would need to release the VCS in quantity and overwhelm his competition. In order to manufacture enough units, Bushnell began to look for another infusion of cash. The market was unfavorable for making a public offering, so the Atari board of directors decided it was time to sell the company. Bushnell approached Universal and Disney, but neither company was interested. However, Warner Communications was interested, and they sent Manny Gerard, a VP and Wall Street entertainment analyst, to go check out Atari. Despite Atari's unorthodoxy, Gerard recommended that Warner buy the company. Put simply, the deal was consummated four months later for $28 million. It was the end of an era, though at first it seemed to be business as usual, but with more cash.

What happened next has been well documented in other books, including Steven Kent's *The First Quarter*. In short, the VCS did poorly its first Christmas, the video game business weakened significantly, and Bushnell's philoso-

phy clashed mightily with that of the East Coast Warner conglomerate. By the end of 1978, Gerard had invoked legal clauses in the sale contract and removed Bushnell from Atari.

Warner installed Ray Kassar, a former vice president of Burlington, a textile company, as the new CEO, and despite the fact that the true "Golden Age" of Atari was just around the corner, many people believe that the clash between Kassar's buttoned-down, autocratic style and Atari's freewheeling, pot-smoking, "Work smarter, not harder" attitudes ultimately caused the company to come apart at the seams. To many Atari employees, Kassar came to be known, not so affectionately, as the "sock king."

There were other tensions at Atari, which centered once again around Kassar, his plans for the company, and his treatment of his creative team members.

Computers or Games?

With the amazing success of Apple Computer, it became clear that the age of home computers had arrived, and Atari intended to be a part of that revolution. The first Atari home computers, the Atari 400 and Atari 800, debuted in late 1979. Altough Atari never really achieved anything like Apple's success, the attention paid to the computer side did affect the game side of the company.

In the background: Detail from the cover of one of Atari's newsletters.

One person who was directly affected was Al Alcorn, who was working at the time with a se- on a special project called the Cosmos—a system that used holographic technologies obtained when the developer of those technologies went bankrupt. the end, Kassar refused to release Cosmos, prompting Alcorn quit. With Bushnell already gone, the original team that had started the company was no longer there.

The Big Clash

Perhaps even more significant was the dissatisfaction of the chief designer/engi- at the company. Kassar had routinely refused to allow their names to be publi- with the games, and even changed some names when speaking about them to press. Moreover, he refused to pay royalties, so, while some games were making company many millions, the designers were given nothing to acknowledge their contributions. Take the case of Rob Fulop, whose Missile Command cart the VCS sold 2.5 million copies. His Christmas bonus was "the same as any secretary got—a certificate for a free Norbest turkey."

"He was classical management," says Atari game designer Howard Scott Warshaw of Kassar. "He was used to blue-collar and white-collar workers. You handled blue-collar workers, who were at the bottom of the org chart. You dealt with the white-collar workers. To him, software engineers, who were at the bottom of the org chart, were to be handled, but he didn't take into account that we were highly intelligent, creative people who didn't take well to being handled. He simply had no frame of reference for who we were."

Chris Crawford, pioneer game designer who worked for several years at Atari, also remembers Kassar's clash with the engineers. "He never could integrate smoothly with the engineers. There was always a war going on, which was stupid, wasteful, and destroyed morale." This situation ultimately led to the defection of some of Atari's brightest designers and the founding of competitive companies like Activision and Imagic.

Despite its problems, Atari was destined to make still more history during the Kassar years. The VCS did sell well the next Christmas, but it had still not reached its peak. Meanwhile, the unconventional designers at Atari were about to unleash some of the greatest games in video game history on the public. The Golden Age of Atari was just around the corner.

Meanwhile, Bushnell purchased back from Atari his pet project—the Pizza Time Theater franchise—for about $500,000, and proceeded to open the highly successful Chuck E. Cheese's chain of restaurants, where families could eat pizza and play games.

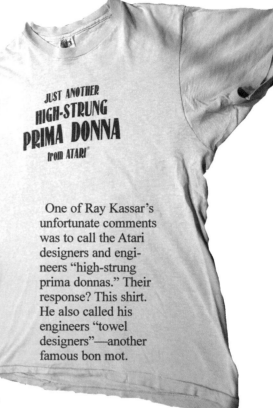

One of Ray Kassar's unfortunate comments was to call the Atari designers and engineers "high-strung prima donnas." Their response? This shirt. He also called his engineers "towel designers"—another famous bon mot.

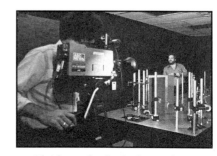

Al Alcorn in the holography lab, working on Cosmos.

Apple: A Modern Fairy Tale

Steve Wozniak, known popularly as simply "Woz," was already building electronic devices in the second grade. His obsession with building his own computer started almost as early. His first working computer was built in 1971 with his friend Bill Fernandez. They called it the "Cream Soda Computer" after the beverage of choice imbibed while designing it.

It was also Fernandez who introduced Woz to a skinny, quiet kid a few years younger, but full of self-confidence. At the age of 12, Steve Jobs had gotten parts for a home project by calling Bill Hewlett, the founder of Hewlett-Packard, on the phone. He had actually worked at HP during the summer of his 13th year.

Steve Jobs and Steve Wozniak working on the Apple II.

The combination of Woz and Jobs was incredibly fortuitous. Their diverse talents combined to create a true revolution. Both pranksters, they were notorious for their practical jokes, which often involved electronic devices created solely to freak people out. However, their first real enterprise was building "blue boxes" used to bypass long-distance charges on telephones. Inspired by an article in *Esquire* about the famous John Draper, aka "Captain Crunch," they built and sold "a ton" of them, according to Wozniak (who was known as Berkeley Blue to the phone phreakers).

The Apple Computer

While working at HP in 1976, Wozniak designed and built a computer based on the MOS Technology 6502 chip. The 6502 was a good chip, but most hobbyists of the time considered it harder to use as the "brains" of a computer than the Intel chips. However, its $20 price made it the chip of choice for Woz. It's unclear how this new computer got its name or why, but it's likely to have been Jobs' idea. After demonstrating the Apple I at the famous Homebrew Computer Club, where Woz freely passed out photocopies of his design to anyone interested, Jobs suggested starting a company. Woz, happy at HP, demurred; but Jobs' powers of persuasion were legendary, and ultimately they began Apple Computer on April Fool's Day, 1976.

Perhaps the rest would be a different history if it had not been for Jobs' confidence, ambition, and vision. After fulfilling an order for 50 Apple I computers to the Byte Shop, he went directly to Nolan Bushnell for advice on where to go next. Bushnell connected Jobs with legendary Silicon Valley venture capitalist Don Valentine who, in turn, connected him with Mike Markkula, who had retired a millionaire from Intel a year before and was enjoying his free time. Markkula ultimately invested a considerable sum in Apple and brought in Michael Scott from Intel to run the business. Meanwhile, Wozniak was working on his "dream" computer, the Apple II, which debuted at the first West Coast Computer Faire in April 1977.

The addition of Regis McKenna as Apple's PR representative was the last significant piece of the puzzle. McKenna's marketing savvy combined well with Woz's genius,

The original Apple computer—the Apple I.

Jobs' charisma, and Markkula's business and marketing sense. To make a long story short, the Apple II was a superior machine, capable of displaying color graphics on a TV set or monitor. The next year, Woz created the circuitry for Apple's first floppy disk drive, which was a critical addition to the machine, whose original cassette interface was slow, frustrating, and unreliable at best.

Then, one more critical element appeared—VisiCalc, the first spreadsheet program. With the addition of the floppy drive and the revolutionary new spreadsheet program available only on the Apple II, Apple's sales exploded, and the company came to dominate the world of personal computers—for a time, at least.

The original Apple II with cassette storage drive.

Above: Steve Jobs at the Apple booth at the West Coast Computer Faire.

Below: Steve Jobs in his garage workshop.

47

Apple's Early Games for the Apple II

Games always figured into the Apple story. In fact, as early as 2nd grade, Woz had created simple electronic games. Many of the engineers and programmers who helped create Apple had created games among their first efforts. And, of course, Jobs and Wozniak had both been affiliated with Atari at various times, including their famous "4-day wonder" version of Breakout (*see page 24* for Nolan Bushnell's version of the story).

Woz's super-efficient implementation of Pong earned him a job offer from Atari, which he turned down. His version of Breakout was a design wonder. "I hope that you run into the Atari folks who saw how few chips I used for Breakout," he told me. "But they couldn't understand my design. I probably couldn't either now." (As it turned out, not only did the Atari engineers not completely understand Wozniak's design, but they ended up having to redesign it for production—but that's another story.)

Wozniak's first implementation of the BASIC computer language was called Game BASIC. "I made trade-offs in it just for games," he said.

Ever the prankster, Woz related one amusing story to me. "Apple did ship a Brick Out tape at one time. I think it still had my 'Easter Egg' in it, where you could put the game into an auto-play mode and the paddles would jiggle as though you couldn't control them, but they would never miss. I tricked some people, notably Captain Crunch, with this."

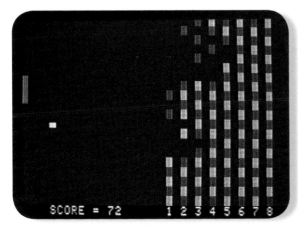

An early Apple II Breakout game.

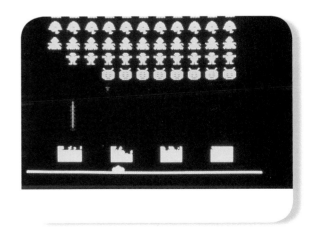

Apple's version of Space Invaders.

Apple put out several games early in their history, including a version of the popular game, Adventure, and a Hangman spelling game.

ALL IMAGES COURTESY OF APPLE
COMPUTER, INC. AND STEVE WOZNIAK.

49

The 1978 Invasion from Space... via Japan

Space Invaders was like nothing else. It captured the imagination of a whole generation, and may have been singly responsible for the rebirth of the flagging video game industry.

Taito was one of the first Japanese companies to enter the video game business, and they had quite early forged a distribution alliance with Midway, Atari's chief competitor in the U.S. The first Japanese game to be imported to the United States was Gun Fight, but the one that changed everything appeared in 1978, once again distributed by Midway. Space Invaders was in black and white only and used overlays to fake the colors at the top and bottom of the screen. It was the brainchild of Toshihiro Nishikado, a programmer at Taito, and there are many stories about its inception—most of them probably false. Whatever the truth, the implacable advance of the on-screen aliens and the *Jaws*-like

The original Space Invaders sell sheet.

THE SPACE INVADERS CRISIS

The citizens of Mesquite, Texas, became so furious at the misspent hours and dollars that they invoked a seldom-enforced city ordinance in order to drive Aladdin's Castle, a successful coin-op chain owned by Bally's (and later, Namco), from the local mall. The police chief cited a vague reference to Bally's alleged "connections to criminal elements," and the city created an artificial age limit of 17 years or older for patrons of the family-oriented arcade franchise. In lower courts, the city argued that they were trying to accomplish two purposes: (1) reduce truancy and (2) restrict minors from being exposed to people "who would promote gambling, sale of narcotics and other unlawful activities." The case

was argued before the U.S. Supreme Court in November 1981 (years after the initial legal action) and decided in 1982 (City of Mesquite v. Aladdin's Castle, Inc., 455 U.S. 283). The U.S. Supreme Court, like the appeals court before it, ruled that the 17-year-old age requirement violated both the U.S. and Texas constitutions because it violated guarantees of equal protection under the law.

By the time of the final decision in the Aladdin's Castle case, a golden age of coin-op games had flooded the Bally's chain of storefronts, other arcades, restaurants, theater lobbies, and anywhere else arcade games could be placed.

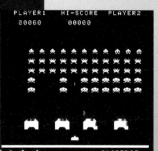

sound effects created a whole new kind of challenge and tension. It was a game of concentration, courage, and hair-trigger reflexes.

Space Invaders was a game you couldn't win. In the end, the aliens would destroy your bases and your laser turret. It was only a matter of time. But Space Invaders did introduce something almost as good as winning—the high score—although the practice of saving players' initials was not implemented, so you couldn't prove that the high score was yours!

Space Invaders made history in other ways, as well. It caused a shortage of 100 yen coins in Japan, and it inspired a legal crisis in Mesquite, Texas (see sidebar). The Space Invaders phenom was not quite finished, however, and it played a significant role as the decade of the '80s began.

Xs and Os

Neck and neck with Space Invaders—at least during the football season—was Atari Football, possibly the first sports simulation (as opposed to sports arcade) game, and certainly the first video football game to feature play selection. It featured four offensive plays and four defensive counter versions of the sweep, bomb, down & out, and keeper.

The game was based on another game called "Xs and Os" that had been conceived by Steve Bristow years earlier and abandoned in favor of Tank, and it retained its predecessor's use of letters to represent offensive (O) and defensive (X) players, giving it the look of an animated coach's playbook. The playfield also scrolled, displaying about 30 yards at a time, and stats appeared vertically along the sides of the playfield.

Atari Football was also possibly the first arcade game to feature a trackball. And it used the spherical control for all it was worth. A good game of Atari Football was a rigorous affair, with two-handed spinning of the controller, lots of body English, and plen

of blisters on the hands. The faster you spun the trackball, the faster your character (X or O) moved on the screen.

Atari Football scored big in the fall of 1978, keeping pace with the megahit Space Invaders—at least until the end of football season, when its sales dropped dramatically. The invading aliens hardly paused to notice.

In 1979, Atari came out with a two- or four-player version of the game that allowed for team play. In a four-player game on offense, one player was the quarterback while the other was the receiver. On defense, both players were tackles. The four-player version was even more fun than the original.

- The world's first video attraction to simulate the actual play action of American fooball.
- Two players
- New Trak Ball™ allows instant movement and control of key players in any direction.
- Offense can select 1 of 4 different run or pass plays.
- Defense can select 1 of 4 different plays.
- New add-a-coin feature adds contunuous time-play.
- Versatile new cabinet is height-adjustable to 40" for standing play. 31" for cocktail table play.
- Built-in self-test system.

ATARI
A Warner Communications Company

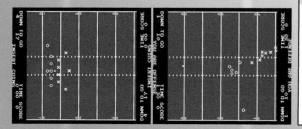

Bally Professional Arcade

Bally's Midway arcade division had been a strong competitor to Atari throughout the '70s, and Bally decided to enter the home console race under their own corporate name.

> *We thought we were changing the world, and I thought this was a way that we could empower people to be creative and imaginative. I saw that this was a revolution. For a few months I held the record for the world's cheapest computer.*
> —JAMIE FENTON, *BALLY PROFESSIONAL ARCADE DESIGNER*

Bally began in 1932 as Lion Manufacturing Co., and in 1936 they moved to Chicago and adopted a new name—Bally Manufacturing Corporation. In 1969, Bally became the first publicly traded gaming company on the New York Stock Exchange.

Their home system was first advertised in the JS&A mail-order catalog with a two-page ad for the Bally Home Library Computer in September 1977. The ad modestly claimed (in part) "The new Bally Home Library Computer provides more entertainment and services than man has ever dreamed possible from a consumer product."

Still known primarily for slot machines and pinball games, Bally had not entered the video game market before... until they introduced the Bally Professional Arcade system in 1978 through computer dealers (and some TV dealers). It was a pretty good machine for its time. Based around the Zilog Z-80 chip, it came with a number of interesting features. For instance, it came with two pistol-grip controllers with triggers and a rotating knob on the top. In addition to the controllers, it featured a keypad for data entry, and a version of BASIC for elementary programming.

Included on the system's ROM were Gun Fight (a color version of the Taito game originally distributed by Midway), Checkmate (a Blockade-style game), Calculator, and Scribbling (a sort of free-form doodle pad).

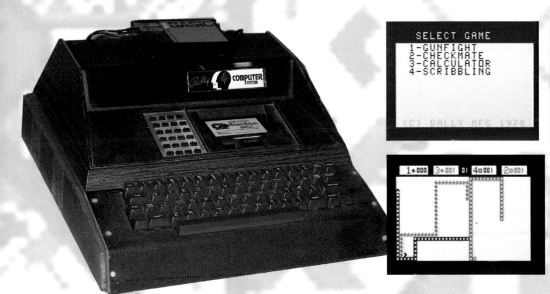

Very rare full Bally Computer System, complete with the keyboard that finally appeared years after the product's debut, plus some original game screens for Bally Gun Fight and Checkmate.

In the background: Scribbling.

Astrocade

The Bally Computer System featured a high price tag—$100 more than the Atari VCS—and it didn't sell well. Early shipments were plagued by defects and had to be returned. Released in February 1978, it was off the market within a couple of years. However, it was not dead and gone. It reappeared after Bally sold the rights to a new group of enthusiasts who formed a company called Astrovision. They marketed the new system first as the Bally Computer System, then, later as the Astrocade, which also became the company's new name. Although the Bally system was never a top contender, it did have a moment of fame, appearing briefly in the movie *National Lampoon's Vacation.*

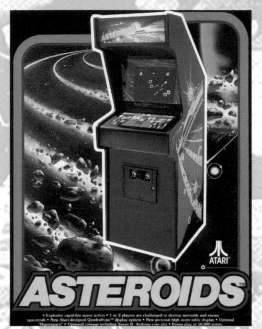

I remember that I bought it pretty much when it first came out. I eagerly awaited an announced keyboard that would have made the game system into a full computer, at least according to the local TV dealer where I purchased it. However, the keyboard never came out, and though I painstakingly entered some programs using the complex color-coded keypad overlay that came with the BASIC implementation, I abandoned my Bally system soon after Bally took it off the market. I had moved on to Intellivision by then, anyway, and ultimately got my dream computer when the Apple II came out. But I do remember playing many marathon sessions of Breakout on my Bally. (RDM)

1979: Atari Strikes Back

With the immense success of Space Invaders, Atari was losing ground in the coin-op arena. However, their response came in November 1979, and it was also quite out of this world.

Earlier that year, Atari had experimented with vector graphics games, releasing Howard Delman's Lunar Lander, which was a graphical version of an old mainframe rocket landing game. While destined to become a classic in its own right, Lunar Lander was quickly supplanted in the arcades by Ed Logg's first of several masterpieces, Asteroids. In fact, demand for Asteroids was so, well... astronomical... that several hundred Asteroids games were shipped in Lunar Lander cabinets just to fulfill the orders.

Ed Logg has provided us with some insight into the creative process that led to one of the all-time great arcade games. Not surprisingly, it started with Spacewar! (*see page 12*). "I had played Spacewar! In 1971 or 1972 at the Stanford University Artificial Intelligence Lab and later at the University Forum coffee shop. By the way, the Spacewar! game in the Forum was two PDP machines linked together and was coin operated. So, in a sense, this was the first coin-operated video game that I am aware of. Of course, Pong was the first 'commercially' produced video game. Spacewar! provided the controls and the shape of the ships in Asteroids."

The original idea came from Atari's head of engineering, Lyle Rains. "He based his idea on another game at Atari, which had a large asteroid, which the player could not destroy. But players tried anyway.

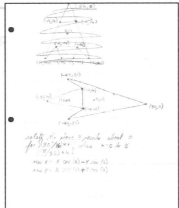

These original concept documents were taken directly from Ed Logg's original notebooks. They show how he created the vector formula for the Asteroids ship and also how he designed the fonts used in the game.

his aim became more accurate. The first three saucers were always the large saucer. Thereafter, the probability of a large saucer was reduced with each new saucer. The frequency of shots from the saucers was reduced with each new saucer, too."

The usual way a designer knew he had a hit on his hands was when the other designers all wanted to play the game he was working on. As-

teroids was no exception. "When the other engineers asked when I was leaving (so they could play), it became clear that I had an interesting game. Later in the project, when I added the high score table, I would come in and see that many games had been played the previous night. However, I must say I would never have predicted the sales of Asteroids would exceed anything the company had ever done before."

When we asked Ed for an interesting story about Asteroids, he said, "I have always been asked if I had thought of the lurking strategy, where people get high scores by just

From that idea, I suggested that larger asteroids break up into smaller pieces to provide some strategy other than shooting everything." Logg also suggested adding a flying saucer, "otherwise the player could stall when there were just a few asteroids on screen. The big saucer was a random shooting saucer that introduced the player to the idea that a saucer would come out when things appeared to be getting easy. The small saucer was more accurate because it aimed at the player with some amount of random error. As the score increased,

shooting the small saucer. The answer is, I tried this strategy, but could not pull it off. I must also point out that at one time the small saucer would fire a shot just as he entered the screen. Often, the saucer would not be visible and if you happened to be near, you would get hit before you had any idea where the saucer was. So I added a small delay before the saucer would take his first shot. This change was all that was needed to make the lurking strategy work."

Galaxian

Playing Space Invaders got to be a hypnotic exercise, and if you spent enough time shooting the moronic aliens, you could get pretty good at it. So then came Namco's Galaxian (also distributed by Midway), and it looked a lot like Space Invaders, but in color. Well, color is cool, and Galaxian was the first true color arcade game. However, what we remember is starting to fire at yet another, albeit prettier, rank of alien invaders, and having the evil suckers start to fly out of formation at me! And they were shooting the whole time! Yes, Galaxian's aliens were a whole lot smarter and more aggressive than those earlier invaders, and hooked a lot of quarters from many a would-be protector of Earth. Oddly, we never really destroyed them all, as evidenced by the repeated appearance of the red, yellow, and blue flagship, which made cameo appearances in later games such as Pac-Man, Galaga, and Gorf.

Way Back When. . .

Turning back the clock, we want to focus on the parallel evolution of computer games, which, like video and arcade games, can trace their roots back to mainframe computers. At the same time that Steve Russell was bringing Spacewar! to the PDP-1, Alan Kotok was finishing his B.S. project on the IBM 7090—a chess program that evaluated 1,100 positions per minute. By 1966, Richard D. Greenblatt's version, known as MacHack-6, became the first computerized chess program to enter an actual tournament. In the Massachusetts Amateur Chess Championship, the program scored one draw and lost four times (USCF rating of 1243). In 1967, the program became the first computerized chess program to beat a human player (USCF rating of 1510) by defeating Hubert Dreyfus. In four amateur tournaments, the program went 3-12-3 (3 wins, 12 losses, and 3 draws).

Another early experiment was John Horton Conway's Life (1970), a cellular automata program that allowed you to set rules and watch what happened to your computer-based "lifeforms."

Also, though there may have been some earlier Star Trek programs on college mainframes before 1971, Don Daglow, who ultimately founded Stormfront Studios, created one on the Pomona College mainframe during that year. Both Trek and Life went on to find renewed life in the personal computer world when Cygnus Software (later to become Interstel) released a slick version (for that era) of Trek called Star Fleet I, and Software Toolworks released Life as part of a Golden Oldies package.

1971 was also the year that Peter S. Langston, one of the original Lucasfilm Games team members, conceived of Empire while playing a board game with friends at Reed College. Inspired by the tabletop experience, he started coding the computer program in 1971. By the mid-1970s, the game had proliferated to mainframes all over the country and was widely played on both college mainframes and on the famous Rand Corporation's (RAND) computer.

In 1972, an assembly language programmer named William Crowther was developing software for the routers that enabled ARPAnet (the Advanced Research Projects Agency of the U.S. Department of Defense—later DARPAnet). This was the communications network commissioned in 1969 that was eventually to become the Internet. At that time, Crowther began work on a fantasy-based computer game based on his experiences as a spelunker. The game came to be known as Colossal Cave Adventure, or, more simply, as Adventure.

Because of Crowther's involvement with the proto-Internet, this simple program ended up on the computers of colleges and defense contractors all around the world, influencing a whole generation of adventure game designers. Later expanded by Donald Woods at Stanford, Adventure's influence extended to the East Coast (Infocom's Zork in 1979), the West Coast (Roberta Williams' Mystery House in 1980), the industrial Northeast (John Laird's Haunt in 1979), and to the tourist havens of the Southeast (Scott Adams' Adventureland in 1978). Internationally, it reached the UK in the form of Acheton, by Cambridge University's Jon Thackray, David Seal, and Jonathan Partington in 1978; Brand X (aka Philosopher's Quest), by Peter Killworth and Jonathan Mestel in 1979; and Roy Trubshaw and Richard Bartle's Essex MUD in 1979. In Finland, Olli Paavola created Lord in 1981; Brad Templeton and Kieran Carroll's Martian Adventure was completed in Canada in 1979; and Phillip Mitchell and Stuart Richie's The Hobbit went on sale in Australia by 1983.

Crowther's game, intentionally simplified to appeal to his daughters, featured the original two-word parser (GET KNIFE) that inspired the Infocom crew to create ZIL (Zork Implementation Language), which could understand complete sentences (*see page 118*). Another fan, Stuart Richie

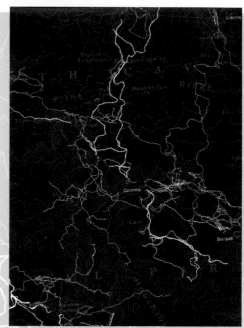

Will Crowther's Colossal Cave Adventure was in part based on the aptly named Mammoth Cave in Kentucky. Above and in the background is an actual map of the Mammoth Cave.

I loved the excitement and camaraderie that animated those movements—something that's completely missing today. Getting rich dominates today. Back then, nobody anticipated that there would be money in it. We knew we were changing the world, but it was not big in money terms. It was big in revolutionary terms.

—Chris Crawford, Game Design Pioneer

Chris Crawford's Gossip

Star Raiders

WUMPUS ROOM

Testimony to the status of Wumpus as a seminal game may be found in early versions of Zork where an adventurer entering the Bat Room without garlic would read the following description:

> Fweep!
> Fweep!
> Fweep!
> A deranged giant vampire bat (a reject from WUMPUS!) swoops down from his belfry and lifts you away...

of Australia's Melbourne House, put his linguistic training to work in designing a parser for The Hobbit. Richie called his parser Inglish. Roberta Williams loved playing Adventure on a remote terminal, but wondered why no one had put pictures with the text (*see page 138*). Yet, everyone considered Adventure to be the seminal text adventure.

As the '70s progressed, more and more game programs appeared on college and corporate mainframes. In 1973, Gregory Yob was visiting the People's Computer Company. He tried out a few games and realized that many of them were simply 10x10 grids where you played "Hide and Go Seek" with the computer. Finding this unsatisfying, Yob created a maze based on a dodecahedron. The dodecahedron is essentially the modern 12-sided die used in tabletop games, and Yob used the lines representing the edges or facets of this geometrical shape to represent the tunnels between the caves. Yob's game, Hunt the Wumpus, required players to explore the dodecahedron and attempt to slay the Wumpus, a malodorous beast who hid in caves surrounded by pits and superbats, and had suckers on his feet to keep him from falling into those pit traps. He would remain "asleep" until unwary or unwise adventurers would awaken him by firing an arrow and missing him. Once awakened, the Wumpus moved from cave to cave in a random pattern. If he ended up in the same room as the adventurer, he ate the adventurer. Hence, the odor associated with the Wumpus was designed to be an "olfactory" clue to the proximity of said monster. After all, the adventurer needed some hint that the monster was close before he or she ended up in the same room and the game was over.

The Home Computer Revolution

During the early 1970s, as video games evolved and the industry around them grew rapidly, on a distinctly parallel track a revolution was in the making, and the revolutionaries were geeky hobbyists with an enthusiasm for electronics and programming languages. The computer was miniaturizing and, for the first time, becoming available to regular people.

The first computers were complex machines used only by a select few. "Prior to 1975, computers were associated with technicians in lab coats—the 'high priests' of the big machines—who would retire to air-conditioned environments with a problem to solve and emerge sometime later with a printout."*

The Tandy/Radio Shack TRS-80

Then came the kits like the Altair and IMSAI and the clubs like the Homebrew Computer Club. Hobbyists drove a business that nobody expected, and few of them ever considered money as a part of the equation.

The hobbyist market was about to give way to something much bigger, however. In April 1977, both the Apple II and the Commodore PET were unveiled at the West Coast Computer Faire. Tandy's nationwide Radio Shack franchise introduced the TRS-80 in September of that year. All three home computers began selling in quantities right out of the starting gate, and others, including Atari, quickly jumped in with personal computers. The era of the personal computer had arrived.

Commodore PET

Chris Crawford talks about his first reaction to the Commodore PET: "It was simply incredible how much they could put together and sell for only $600. In parts, separately, it would have been $1,000 or $1,500. My original reaction was suspicion." In part, Crawford's skepticism might have been well-founded due to Commodore founder Jack Tramiel's reputation for heavy-handed business practices. "Business is war," he was quoted as saying. "I don't believe in compromising. I believe in winning." Regardless, the PET did sell for an incredible $599, and it consisted of a complete computer system, not a kit.

*Paul Freiberger and Michael Swaine, *Fire in the Valley*, McGraw-Hill, 2000

The Commodore PET

Neither the PET (which stood for Personal Electronic Transactor) nor the TRS-80 could display color graphics, but they sold for less than the Apple II. There were definitely different camps at the time, each one swearing by its favorite system, but in the end, the Apple II, with its open architecture and color graphics, outlasted the others by many years, with its chief competition coming from the Commodore 64, a system that significantly emulated the Apple II.

Atari Computers

At Atari, first Nolan Bushnell, then Ray Kassar saw correctly that microcomputers represented a great opportunity, and the company shifted some of its focus toward making personal computers to compete directly with Apple. Unfortunately, this shift in focus may have resulted in taking away from Atari's strength and its bread-and-butter business–games.

Like the Apple and Commodore computers, Atari used the MOS 6502 chip to power its computers, with the addition of the custom graphics CTIA (Color Television Interface Adapter) chip. However, Atari's designers were hampered by some FCC regulations limiting RF output. Apple had bypassed these regulations by not including an RF adapter with the system, which exempted them. (Apple RF adapters were sold as a third-party item.) Atari engineers rankled at the FCC restrictions, but had no choice but to design around them. Joe Decuir comments, "The disk drives were big and bulky, because they had to be managed by onboard microcomputer systems, and then they were slowed down by the 19,200 bps transfer rate. This was a crawl compared to the direct bus access that

IT LOOKS LIKE FUN TO ME

Chris Crawford, one of the game industry's distinguished pioneers, worked at Atari from September 1979 until March 1984 and experienced this rift first-hand. "The engineering department viewed the computers as the VCS on steroids. But Marketing saw the games and computers in two different markets. They were extremely suspicious of engineers doing games on the 800." On his first project for the computer division, Chris relates a story that in part exemplifies the rift. "My first product for the computer was called Energy Czar. I called it an 'energy environmental simulator.' Before I could take it past the preliminary design phase, I had to go through a marketing review. So I presented what I had in a big meeting, telling them how it would work, calling it an 'energy education simulation' because I had been warned not to call it a game. The lead marketing guy—a very sharp individual—stood up after my presentation and fixed me with a cold stare and asked, 'Is this a game?' 'No,' I answered. 'It's an educational simulation, not a game.' He said, 'I don't know. It looks like fun to me.'"

Apple had, but we were prevented from using the bus because of the FCC regulations."

The custom chips inside Atari's 400 and 800 computers were designed with games in mind. Again, according to Joe Decuir, "The Apple II was the obvious target to the engineering team, but we also conceived of the 800 as the next-generation gaming machine. In my opinion, it had no peer as a game console until the NES came out five years later in Japan." To cover both bets, Atari packaged the 800 with a real keyboard and some internal expansion capability, as the personal computer that could also play games, and the Atari 400 as the game machine that was also a computer. Later, Atari repackaged the chipset as a pure game machine, the 5200, which, unfortunately, wouldn't run 400/800 cartridges.

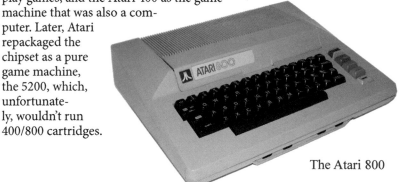

The Atari 800

Automated Simulations

Automated Simulations (later Epyx), one of the earliest computer game companies, emerged from a group of Dungeons & Dragons players, originally co-hosted by Jim Connelley and Jeff Johnson. In 1977, Jon Freeman was invited into the group by Susan Lee-Merrow, who went on to work for Electronic Arts at its beginning and later became a major marketing executive for Brøderbund and Lucas Learning. Freeman had written several articles for GAMES Magazine as well as a book, A Player's Guide to Table Games. He was working at the time on an updated version of The Playboy Winner's Guide to Board Games.

When Connelley purchased a Commodore PET to help with the bookkeeping side of his D&D campaign, he realized that if he could write and ship a game before the end of the tax year, he'd be able to write off the computer. So, he talked Freeman into adjusting the rules and creating data structures and scenarios (ship profiles, battle situations, maps, victory conditions, background stories, etc.) for a science fiction war game while Connelley did the programming. The game that launched Automated Simulations was called Starfleet Orion and took less than four months from conception (August 1978) to sales launch (December 1978). The company was named Automated Simulations sometime around Thanksgiving of the same year, primarily so that there would be a corporate entity for customers to pay.

The game was successful, in spite of the fact that it required

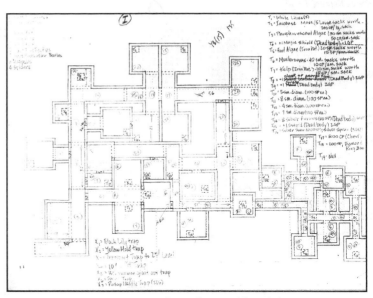

One of several hand-drawn maps used to create Temple of Apshai.

two players and had no computer opponent for solitaire play. "It was very simple, graphically," says Freeman. "Basically just dots on a screen. An explosion was an asterisk." Connelley and Freeman added a single-player mode in 1979 when they released Invasion Orion.

The highlight of the company's early history was their Dunjonquest series of role-playing games, featuring three Temple of Apshai games and, later, Sword of Fargoal. To distinguish the role-playing titles from the strict science fiction games, they chose the sub-brand name Epyx, but it wasn't until 1982 that Epyx became the company's official name. (More on that later.)

They followed the Temple of Apshai with Rescue at Rigel, a science fiction game based on the same role-playing engine, and followed that with Crush, Crumble and Chomp!, in which the player got to be a movie-style monster on the rampage. This was years before Rampage revised the same theme. Crush, Crumble and Chomp! came with a set of data cards describing each monster in detail.

RESCUE AT RIGEL

YOU'VE GOT 60 MINUTES — IN REAL TIME — TO FREE TEN PRISONERS FROM A MAZE-LIKE ALIEN MOONBASE!

EPYX

Crush, Crumble and Chomp!
The Movie Monster Game

EPYX

WREAK HAVOC! SPREAD MAYHEM AND DESTRUCTION AS YOUR FAVORITE MONSTER!

fall worked on some conversions of existing games, and the two worked together on Tuesday Morning Quarterback, which appeared first on the TRS-80 and later on the Apple II. They decided to strike out on their own in November 1981, and produced two games. One, called Pack Rat on the Atari 800, was never published. The other, Tax Dodge, was published by Steve Dompier's Island Graphics. Then one day their fortunes changed when they received a call from the head of a newly forming company. The "newly forming company" was Electronic Arts, and the call was from Trip Hawkins. Meanwhile, Jim Connelley officially changed the name of the company to Epyx and continued to run it until 1983 (*see page 158*).

Freeman remembers several other games created from 1979 through 1981, including The Datestones of Ryn, Morloc's Tower, Hellfire Warrior (the first real sequel to Temple of Apshai), Star Warrior ("Our first 'outdoor' quest"), Tuesday Morning Quarterback, Dragon's Eye, Upper Reaches of Apshai, The Keys of Acheron (level design by Paul Reiche), and Sorcerer of Siva.

Under a third label, Mind Toys, Automated Simulations created another pair of games—Jabbertalky and Ricochet—in 1981.

Meanwhile, Jon Freeman's life changed significantly when he met Anne Westfall, who was in a neighboring booth at the West Coast Computer Faire in March 1980. Their meeting began what was to become a lifelong partnership. West-

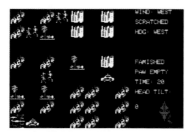

Crush, Crumble and Chomp! screen and data sheets.

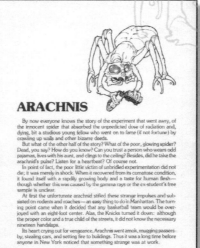

ARACHNIS

By now everyone knows the story of the experiment that went awry, of the innocent spider that absorbed the unpredicted dose of radiation and, dying, bit a studious young fellow who went on to fame (if not fortune) by crawling up walls and other bizarre deeds.

But what of the other half of the story? What of the poor, glowing spider? Dead, you say? How do you know? Can you trust a person who wears odd pajamas, lives with his aunt, and clings to the ceiling? Besides, did he take the arachnid's pulse? Listen for a heartbeat? Of course not.

In point of fact, the poor little victim of unbridled experimentation did not die; it was merely in shock. When it recovered from its comatose condition, it found itself with a rapidly growing body and a taste for human flesh—though whether this was caused by the gamma rays or the ex-student's free sample is unclear.

At first the unfortunate arachnid stifled these strange impulses and subsisted on rodents and roaches—an easy thing to do in Manhattan. The turning point came when it decided that any basketball team would be overjoyed with an eight-foot center. Alas, the Knicks turned it down: although the proper color and a true child of the streets, it did not know the necessary nineteen handslaps.

Its heart crying out for vengeance, Arachnis went amok, mugging passersby, stealing cars, and setting fire to buildings. Thus it was a long time before anyone in New York noticed that something strange was at work.

* * *

As Arachnis (as with Mantra), you lack the strength to be an effective Crumbler; to destroy buildings, you must do it with fire. Try to set your blazes so that the wind will cause the fires to spread to other buildings. Use your webs to slow pursuit into the area and to trap civilians emerging from the threatened buildings.

Don't let your hunger get out of control. You are fast enough to catch plenty of food, but a little paralysis won't hurt, either.

You can escape attack or go beneath fires by burrowing, but you will be vulnerable during your initial turn of digging.

Crush, Crumble and Chomp!
ARACHNIS

COMMAND		MEANING
R	Right	Turn right (90°)
L	Left	Turn left (90°)
H	Head	Turn head left/right 30° (aims Z & B)
N	Nothing	Do nothing (skip to end of turn)
M	Move	Move 1 square forward
J	Jump	Jump 2 squares forward (onto/over buildings)
D	Descend (Dig)	Descend and move subsurface (up to 5 spaces)
	N	North
	E	East
	S	South
	W	West
	U	Up to surface
G	Grab	Grab the human unit in the square in front of you
E	Eat	Eat the unit in your jaw (paw)
C	Crumble	Demolish the building/bridge in (the square in) front of you
W	Web	Weave an obstructing web in your square (bridge, road, or park only)
P	Paralyze	Cause nearby units to lose a turn
Z	Zap	Attack (with ray beam) flying units from the ground
B	Breathe Fire	Set fire to unit and/or building your head is facing
Q	Quit	Stop the game (temporarily or permanently)
#	Number (of points)	Check your current score

NOTES:
Arachnis has a weak Crumble (C) command, because its body lacks heft.

Copyright © 1981, Automated Simulations, Inc. P.O. Box 4247, Mountain View, CA 94040

Going Where No One Had Gone Before. . .

Early Activision execs

As 1979 drew to a close, the game industry was poised to explode in all directions. Arcade games were just hitting their peak, and some of the greatest classics of all time were just around the corner. And the Atari VCS, with six million units already in homes around the U.S., was about to soar.

But the VCS would soon have company in the console market. Mattel, the powerful toy company, saw opportunity knocking, and they test-marketed their Intellivision game console in 1979. The first real home console war was brewing.

There were only a few companies marketing computer games at the time—Brøderbund, California Pacific, Automated Simulations, and SSI, for starters. Game designers like Dan Bunten, Richard Garriott, Doug Carlston, Bill Budge, Jon Freeman, Dave Lebling, and Marc Blank were already at work on projects that were to set the stage for the first real generation of computer games. Many other young designers were discovering the wonders of the new personal computers and writing their first programs. For instance, it would be many years before John Romero would come to prominence with games like Doom and Quake, but he was delving into the secrets of Apple assembly language and graphics creation, writing programs in his head, and generally absorbing all he could.

Also at the end of the '70s, four Atari developers left and formed the first independent third-party game company to manufacture cartridges for the VCS, setting the stage for the future of the business. This company, Activision, was incorporated just as the first decade of video games came to an end, in late 1979.

The Last Straw

Activision came into being, at least in part as a result of Atari's policies regarding authorship credit and royalties for VCS game designers. The problem came to a head with Ray Kassar in 1979, but problems with royalties and bonuses actually started at Atari earlier in its history. According to Activision co-founder David Crane, during the VCS' first year there was a plan devised between engineering head Bob Brown and then president Joe Keenan that allocated 50 cents per console sold and a dime per cartridge to the engineering group, to be distributed as bonuses. However, that money never appeared, and management denied that the plan had ever existed. The engineers more or less laughed it off at the time.

Next, there was a written bonus plan, which was based on something called "Departmental Budgeted Operating Income" or DBOI. Some of the engineers referred to it as "Don't Bet On It." Somewhere in the tangle of legalese, this bonus also disappeared, though some of the top designers were taken behind closed doors, given 25% raises, and told not to tell anyone.

But the final straw dropped when marketing distributed a memo in 1979 that listed the percent of sales of each VCS cartridge sold the previous year and, referring to the top items on the list, it said something like, "These games are selling really well. Do more like this."

Meanwhile, Jim Levy was looking to form a computer software publishing firm. "I could see that the PC and video games were going to become as ubiquitous as hi-fi stereo/equipment sometime by the end of the '80s," says Levy. "I was sure that publishing games and other software for them would be potentially as large as the recorded music industry was at the time. I had been shopping a business plan for such an idea to the venture capital community." Fate brought the four Atari designers together with Levy, and the first third-party game company was formed, changing the business of games forever.

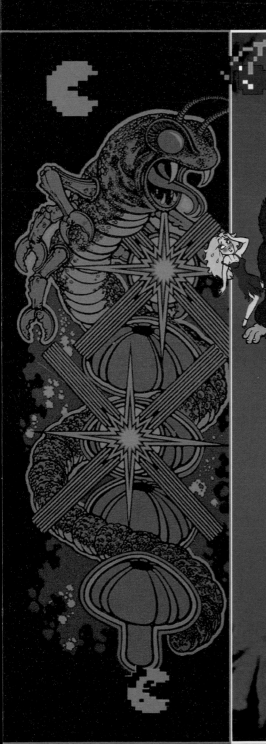

THE 80s

At the beginning of the 1980s, electronic gaming was entering its second decade as an industry, and it was ready to rock and roll. As always, arcade games set the stage, and one blockbuster game after another appeared on the scene. But now playing in people's homes was a rapidly growing list of titles—some original and some arcade conversions. Sales of the Atari VCS suddenly blossomed when they released a licensed version of Space Invaders. Renamed the Atari 2600, the venerable system suddenly leaped to the top of everybody's shopping list.

Mattel's Intellivision launched in 1980 as well, and its superior graphics soon caught the public's eye. It was followed a couple of years later by ColecoVision.

Another revolution was happening, and it centered around the home computer. For the first time, anyone with the patience and vision to do some programming and crude artwork could create and market a game. Whereas creating games for arcades or home consoles required considerable equipment and technical knowledge, and actually putting them on the market required even more equipment plus specialized silicon chips only available from certain companies, putting out a game for personal computers required only the computer itself and a disk drive with a blank floppy disk. (Even before disk drives, people put out games on cassette tapes, but those were tedious and unreliable. In order for computer games to succeed, it's a reasonable assumption that the disk drive was a requirement.)

And so the stage was set for a roller coaster decade of expansion, crashes, rebirths, technological advancement, and games galore!

1980: The Arcades

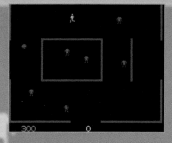

Cinematronic's philosophy of games:
'Make it loud, make it fast and make it shoot a lot.'
–Tim Skelly, **Cinematronics designer (Star Castle, Rip-Off, Armor Attack, etc., plus Reactor for Gottlieb and Sonic the Hedgehog 2 for Sega.)**

1978 had Space Invaders, and 1979 had Asteroids and Galaxian. But 1980 had to be the king of arcade years to date, boasting a bumper crop in the range of 100 new games released in the United States and Japan.* 1980 is distinguished, not just for quantity, but by the sheer magnitude of its introductions. Even though not all the new releases were big hits, many were great games setting new standards, and several 1980 games are all-time hall of famers—in particular, Missile Command, Defender, and Pac-Man.

As if anyone had any doubts, space was a big theme in the arcades, as it had always been. But in 1980 there were nearly 20 titles that began with the word "space" and another dozen or so that started with "moon" or "star."* Several others had space themes, even if their titles didn't necessarily reflect it. Out of the 100+ arcade releases of 1980, we've picked a few to look at.

sion—dumb yellow ones—were pushovers, since they couldn't shoot back. But later, you would have to handle the red robots, who did shoot back. Still, with some clever maneuvering, you could outshoot or outwit your enemies, all except for Evil Otto, a bouncing, fast-moving, and indestructible Happy Face, who would chase you inexorably to the death. The only hope was to make it to another room, and damn if your character didn't suddenly seem awfully slow, even if his animation looked like it was running. Berzerk was one of the early games from Stern Electronics, a company that released a couple of dozen other games from 1980 through 1984, including the Konami game Pooyan, in which players took on the role of a mother pig. Berzerk is notable for being one of the first games to include synthesized voice. It boasted 31 synthesized words, including "Chicken, fight like a robot" and the attract mode comment, "Coin detected in pocket."

Star Castle

Cinematronics had created several games after Space Wars, and in 1980 they came out with Star Castle, a game with stars, to be sure, but no recognizable castles. The stars, however, are part of the story. Looking for a different sort of star pattern, the designers used the outline of a centerfold from a girlie magazine.

Star Castle "centerfold" star field.

Berzerk

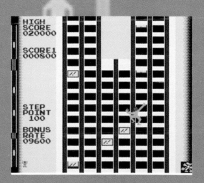

Evil Otto

Berzerk was, in some ways, the prototype of later games like Robotron: 2084, Gauntlet, Total Carnage, and Smash TV. When you began the game—to the disturbing sounds of "Intruder Alert! Intruder Alert!"—you found yourself in a room full of slow-moving robots that seemed to have it in for you. Although initially conceived in black and white, the first robots you encountered in the released color ver-

Crazy Climber

Crazy Climber was created by Nichibutsu and distributed by Taito. It was an odd little game with an equally odd hero. This guy just had to make it to the top of a 200-story building, despite having to dodge a lot of falling debris, nasty people who liked to close windows on his fingers, and an even nastier bird that pelted him with droppings.

Crazy Climber himself talked to you, which was relatively rare in games at the time. His repertoire of comments was limited, but the one we remember hearing most was "Oh, noooo...," his last words as he plummeted down to one of his three possible deaths.

Perhaps the most innovative aspect of Crazy Climber was the control system, which used dual joysticks to control the movement of his arms and legs in

*Source: Killer List of Video Games (KLOV) www.klov.com

sequence—the only way to maneuver him. This control system is reminiscent of working a marionette and was definitely a departure from any previous control methods.

Battlezone

Atari had scored a hit with Tank in 1974, and Battlezone, which is credited mainly to Ed Rotberg, repeated the theme but with a decidedly different point of view. In fact, Battlezone may have been the first true first-person game—a distant ancestor to Doom and Quake. Although games like Night Driver and Tim Skelly's Tail Gunner had featured first-person viewpoints, neither allowed free movement, which Battlezone introduced to the arcades.

"The idea for the game came out of a brainstorming session," says Rotberg. "We knew we had the technology to do that sort of game with advancements in processors and in our vector generator."

Using vector graphics, the game put you in the role of a tank gunner rolling across a somewhat surreal landscape dotted with out-of-place geometry—cubes and cones and such—distant mountains, and enemy tanks. The enemy wasn't shy about firing their howitzers at you, and you had to stick and move, using the dual joystick controls, to stay alive. The radar sounds and on-screen instructions for locating enemy tanks ("Enemy to right") soon immersed you in this life-and-death duel. Failure was graphically represented by the sight of an incoming shell and the severe cracking of your windshield. For the first time, you felt the hit as if it was your own. And, no, you could not drive to that distant volcano.

Battlezone boasted another distinction. It may have been the first commercial game commissioned into the U.S. military. Well, not quite commissioned, but the U.S. Army did ask Atari to create a training version of the game based on the Bradley Infantry Fighting Vehicle (IFV). Ed Rotberg worked a grueling three-month schedule to complete the project. The military version of Battlezone contained a host of features not found in the commercial version, including a variety of ordnance; realistic trajectories; both friendly and unfriendly vehicles; two additional magnification levels; and a controller system with thumb, finger, and palm switches, none of which appeared in the commercial version.

Rotberg had his reservations. "I was personally concerned that Atari was getting involved with the military, and I was very much against it. The deal I made with them is that I would be completely exempt from doing any other military product."

Rally-X

Although not the biggest game of 1980, Rally-X was at one time expected to be just that. At the 1980 Amusement Machine Operators of America (AMOA) show, four major releases were being shown: Defender, Battlezone, Pac-Man, and Rally-X. Ironically, the one that was picked to be the big winner was Rally-X.

In fairness, Rally-X looked pretty good for its time. It was a top-down racing game with colorful graphic and cartoonlike action. It departed from other games of the time in that it featured saturated color on the screen instead of color figures over a black background. Given how new color was to arcade games, it must have seemed pretty amazing. However, its main claim to fame in the history of games was the introduction of the first bonus round.

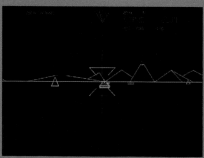

Missile Command

Missile Command was another adrenaline pumper that put you in the basically hopeless position of defending your cities against incoming nuclear blasts. A morbid theme, to be sure, and a game you really couldn't win, unless you emulated the Olympic torch bearers and kept a defensive vigil at the controls in perpetuity.

It wasn't a question of winning, only of scoring and lasting as long as you could. Many an hour was spent fending off the bombs that appeared eerily in the sky above your bases. Round after round you spun the Trak-Ball and carefully rationed the antinuke missiles from your three bases, often aiming for the intersection of several incoming missiles for maximum efficiency. It was high tragedy when you lost a city, worse if you lost a base that still had missiles.

Dave Theurer, the designer of Missile Command, describes the original concept: "Gene Lipkin told Steve Calfee that we should do a game where the country was being invaded by missiles. They showed me a picture of a radar screen and said take it from there. I hated radar screens because of the vanishing info, so I got rid of it. I used the Trak-Ball in my previous Soccer game, and decided it was the best

controller for the task. In those days the trackballs were pretty big. We even had one that was the size of a bowling ball just for yucks."

Only about five of the rare prototypes depicted here were ever made. According to Theurer, "The extra panel was originally designed to be part of the gameplay. We put it there to indicate the status of the various bases—how many missiles you had and the condition of your cities. We soon learned that when the players looked at the panel they lost track of what was happening on the screen. It was like if you had to drive your car and had to look on the floor of the backseat every five seconds. There were other reasons, such as the problem of lightbulbs burning out, and we figured the arcade operators wouldn't want to go through the trouble of replacing them, meaning they would be meaningless anyway. Finally, eliminating the panel did save money, which was always a consideration."

Atari assembly lines manufacturing Missile Command units.

Naming Missile Command

Missile Command went through a couple of name changes. Can you guess which of these were among the original titles for this classic?

GROUND ZERO
CITY COMMAND
NUCLEAR STRIKE
WORLD WAR THREE
ARMAGEDDON

Missile Command answers: Ground Zero and Armageddon

Defender

When it debuted at the 1980 AMOA show, Defender was universally considered too hard to be successful in the arcades. While the show attendees were betting on the ultra-simple Rally-X, Defender flew in under their radar to become one of the all-time great arcade classics.

They were right about one thing at AMOA. Defender was hardcore. Basically, the first time you played and tried to make sense of the two joysticks and five buttons, you generally died in a matter of seconds. Defender wasn't for the meek.

To succeed at Defender, you needed a Zenlike concentration and ultimate coolness under pressure, the unique ability to see what was happening all around you while monitoring the radar-like topside scanner, and at the same time, and a complete oneness with the controls so you could react to any situation without getting killed. You not only had to shoot the alien Landers, Baiters, Bombers, Pods, and truly evil Swarmers, but you also had to save the human abductees before they were turned into Mutants who would then add to your misery. No rest. Lotsa quarters. Once you achieved the zone, however, Defender could make you forget about everything else in life for as long as you could make that quarter last.

Stargate, aka Defender II, was even more insane than the original, and added yet another button control, which was used for the cloaking device.

Pac-Man

In the brief history of video games before 1980, inspiration had come from many sources—predominantly sports and science fiction. But once upon a time, when Toru Iwatani, a programmer for the Japanese amusement company Namco, stared at a pizza with one slice missing, it might have been the first and only time a game concept was inspired by an Italian entrée.

At any rate, Iwatani took his pizza and, with a bit of role reversal, turned it into a hungry character who just had to eat dots on a screen. This was the birth of Pac-Man.

But Iwatani's vision was unique for many reasons. He purposely set out to create a nonviolent game and a game that would appeal to female players. In both respects, he was more successful than anyone could have anticipated.

But wait… there's more. In fact, until this time there had never been a real character in a game. Typically, the game environment was filled with nameless cars and spaceships

The original Puckman cabinet. (Courtesy of *RePlay Magazine*.)

and featureless human stick figures. Though incredibly simple, Pac-Man was the first digital superstar of the video game era, the first character to capture the attention and imagination of the world. And he wasn't alone. His cute though implacable enemies each had names, though they were changed from the original Japanese names. In fact, there was a switch on the Pac-Man cabinet that allowed different names for the ghosts, each of which also had a nickname. In all, there were 23 names for Pac-Man's enemies, 16 for the Japanese version and seven more for the American (see sidebar). Moreover, each ghost had a distinct personality

Pac-Man was so popular that it spawned the first real licensing craze with toys, lunch-boxes, Pac-Man cereal, popular songs, and even a Saturday morning cartoon show. Pac-Man even appeared on the cover of Time.

Pac-Man was the first electronic game superstar and the first game character to join the ranks of pop icons like Mickey Mouse and Bugs Bunny. This, more than any other fact, sets Pac-Man apart. The adorable, dot-craving, essentially nonviolent maze crawler set the stage for later characters such as Mario, Sonic the Hedgehog, and Lara Croft.

An unusual white Pac-Man cabinet.

Originally titled Puck-Man, Namco and Midway wisely changed the name, fearing that vandals might alter the lettering with unfortunate and embarrassing results.

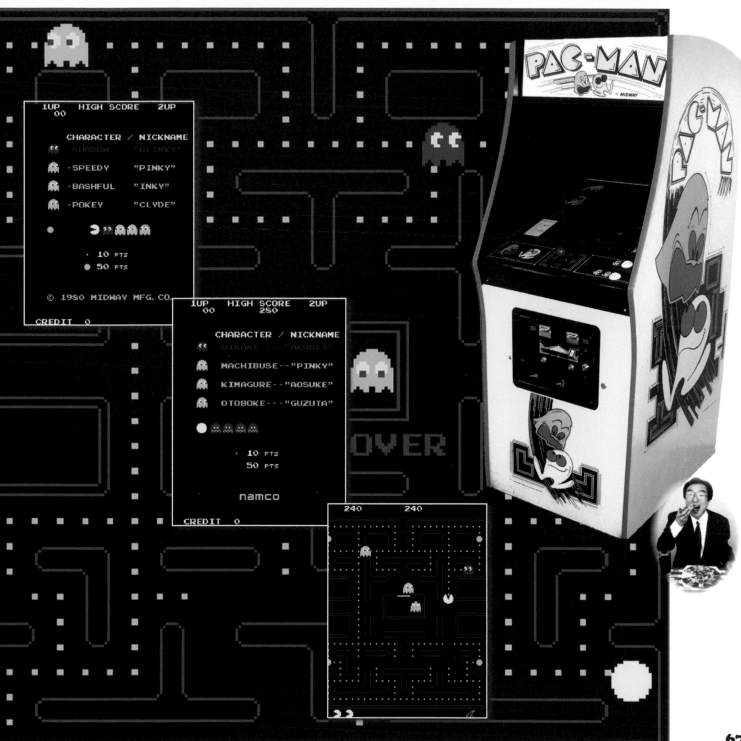

Despite its slow start, the Atari VCS had already sold around 6 million units by the end of 1979. In 1980, Warner struck a deal with Taito to release the hit game Space Invaders as a VCS cartridge. This was possibly the smartest move they ever made. Ray Kassar showed his marketing acumen by correctly predicting that people would go out and purchase the VCS just to get the Space Invaders game. And that's exactly what happened.

Releasing Space Invaders on the VCS caused Atari's sales to skyrocket and began the Golden Age of Atari.

Even as Atari was poised to enter its Golden Age, it was also losing some of its best talent because of the friction between the designers and management. First it was Miller, Crane, Whitehead, and Kaplan joining Jim Levy to start Activision, which became the first third-party publisher in game history. Then it was Bill Grubb starting Imagic—yet another competitor—and taking four important Atari folks with him. Despite the fact that Atari was starting to enjoy the greatest game sales ever seen, and became the fastest growing company in American history (until the dotcoms, anyway), the seeds of its doom were already being planted.

Activision started in late 1979 with $750,000 in venture capital and loans, unveiling their first games—Dragster, Boxing, Fishing Derby, and Checkers—at the Summer Consumer Electronics Show in Chicago. By early 1981 they had added Skiing and Bridge. It was only the beginning. Activision was to achieve instant success, and like Atari, it created a culture of its own as well as its own legacy of memorable titles.

Four of Activision's five founders were, of course, its first designers, and they reaped the rewards of success in a way they never had at Atari. According to Jim Levy, "We were famous for our parties at the trade shows. It was a wild time, and we made the most of it."

Activision quickly grew and began to expand, making games for Intellivision and, ultimately, home computers.

SPACE INVADERS*
VIDEO COMPUTER SYSTEM™
GAME PROGRAM™
112 VIDEO GAMES   MOVING SHIELDS • ZIGZAGGING LASER BOMBS • FAST LASER BOMBS • INVISIBLE INVADERS

ATARI
A Warner Communications Company

CX 2632

* SPACE INVADERS is the trademark of Taito America Corp. 1980

Activision employees getting ready for an early Consumer Electronics Show.

"When we made the decision to leave Atari, we still didn't know where we were going. We saw that we had essentially three choices: one was to leave Atari and work as consultants. Atari was paying consultants three to four times what we made. Why not quit, consult back, and double our salaries? Or we could create a development house—one of the first third-party development houses. Our third choice was to form a company to market and distribute games, but this option contained a steep ramp in risk versus reward. There were a lot of issues to deal with."
-David Crane, Activision Cofounder

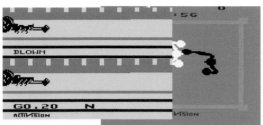

Screenshots from
two of Activision's first games–Dragster a
Boxing.

Activision
patches,
like this
one for
Kaboom!,
often were
humorous
and became
very popular
collectibles. Fans
would send in pictures
of themselves with their high
scores to obtain the patches.

River Raid's Carol
Shaw from an
early Activision
newsletter.

River Raid was orig-
inally going to be a
space game, but
ended up on a river.

Early Hits

Activision's instant success was further f
a string of popular titles such as Larry K
Kaboom!, which was reminiscent of Ata
lanche, Steve Cartwright's stunt flyer Ba
ing, Bob Whitehead's Defender-like Cho
Command, and Carol Shaw's River Raid

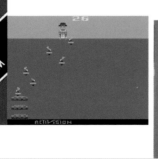

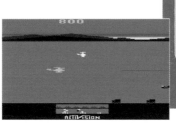

The early games from
Activision were fun and
addicting. Often, they were
based on arcade games, as in
the case of Kaboom! and
Chopper Command. Steve
Cartwright's Barnstorming
was an original game.

The Best of the Best

Activision's designers were the best Atari 2600 programmers around, and they pushed the system to its limit, often pulling off technical, as well as design, coups. For instance, David Crane's Freeway, a Frogger-like game, was the first VCS game that animated 24 sprites simultaneously.

In 1982, Crane created the best-known VCS game of all time. Pitfall! was a revelation, a tour de force for the VCS, and it helped usher in a whole new genre of games.

Pitfall! was the first game to feature a running, jumping hero in a side-scrolling environment. Put another way, it was the first platform game, of which there have been about a zillion since. Think Lode Runner, Super Mario, all the way up to the present day.

"Pitfall! was our 18th game," says Crane, "and the single most amazing fact about it is that it took me 10 minutes to design."

Crane continues, "Doing a game is really a very complicated activity. There are thousands of ideas in your mind at one time, so the entire thing is self-consistent. Keeping track of all the details... and then the 20-hour days. After completing a game we had a downtime, which we used to misname as 'post cartridge depression.' We would stare at the screen, play other guys' games, take time off. I was at that point, 'What am I going to do next?' I always wanted to do a game with a little running man, so I took a blank piece of paper and drew a man. 'Where is he?' Put in path. Put in jungle. 'Why is he running?' Put in treasure and obstacles.

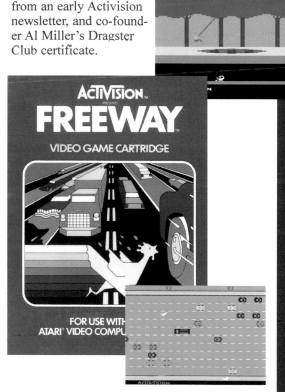

Designer Larry Miller, from an early Activision newsletter, and co-founder Al Miller's Dragster Club certificate.

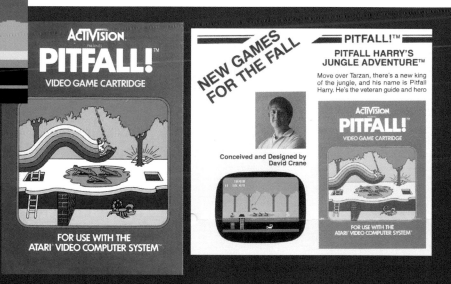

That was the design. Execution took about 1,000 hours at the keyboard."

Crane drew from various influences. One of the cooler features in Pitfall! was inspired by a Heckle and Jeckle cartoon in which they had to swing on vines over man-eating (or, in their case, crow-eating) alligators. In addition, the game's unique and clever above- and below-ground paths made brilliant use of limited space and increased the gameplay options. Pitfall Harry, the game's hero, had a greater repertoire of moves than any VCS hero to date, and he never even fired a gun or cracked a whip!

By 1982, when this picture was taken, Activision had grown considerably from its humble beginnings.

"These new Activision game cartridges for the Atari® Video Computer System™ are terrific!"

Activision was famous for their parties in the early 1980s.

Activision's wholesome first catalog featured their four released titles, plus the upcoming Skiing and Bridge.

HOW MANY ACTIVISION VIDEO GAMES   CAN YOU FIND IN THIS PICTURE?

ACTIVISION.
WE PUT YOU IN THE GAME.

Activision released several clever ads, such as the one below.

We had a pretty well-defined scheduled of proposed product releases for the first 18 months in the plan, but the exact titles were not discussed until after the designers left Atari and the money was committed to the venture. In late September, the guys told me what they planned as first releases: Boxing (Whitehead), Dragster (Crane), Checkers (Miller), and Bridge (Kaplan). David Crane and Al Miller left Atari in August and began working on designing a development system platform for Activision which was in process when the company was funded. They worked out of the second bedroom of Dave's apartment in Sunnyvale, a few blocks from our first real office. Whitehead did not leave Atari until Activision was funded. Larry Kaplan left Atari in August but held back from finally joining Activision until December.
–Jim Levy

Video Game Fans

Activision's promotion of their designers worked so well that fan letters began to pour in. Here are two happy customer service representatives surrounded by pictures of Activision fans.

Lots of fans sent in pictures of themselves, but none so fascinating as this one of a priest with an Activision patch sewn onto his robes.

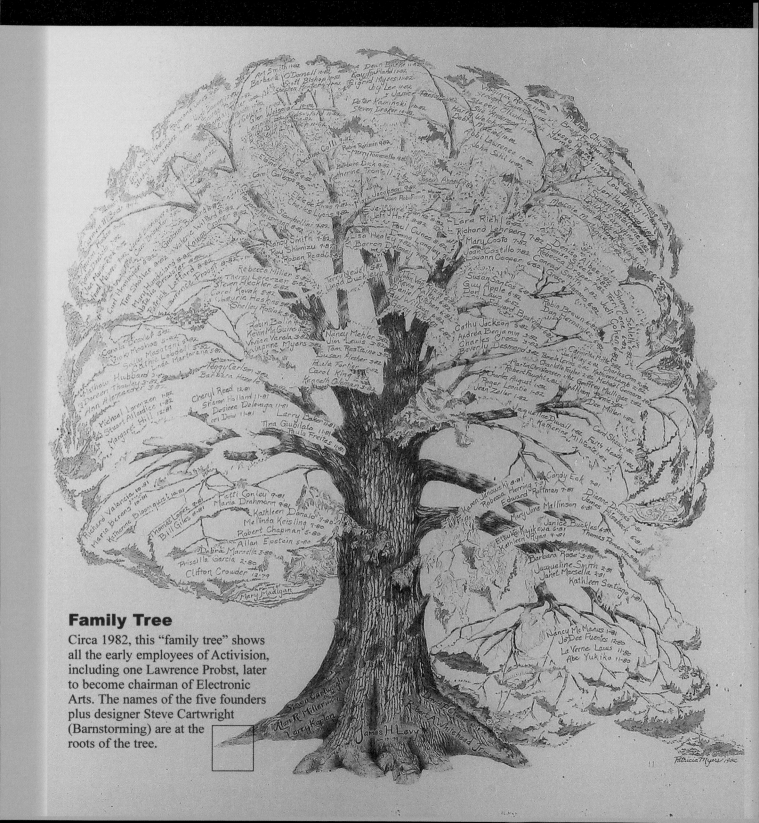

Family Tree

Circa 1982, this "family tree" shows all the early employees of Activision, including one Lawrence Probst, later to become chairman of Electronic Arts. The names of the five founders plus designer Steve Cartwright (Barnstorming) are at the roots of the tree.

Intellivision

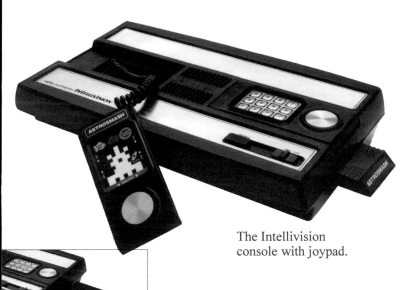

The Intellivision console with joypad.

The Intellivoice module that came with three synthesized game voices.

In the late '70s Mattel was the biggest toy company in the world. They had scored big time with their first electronic foray—handheld games—and they were ready for more. In late 1979, they test-marketed their first video game system. In 1980, Intellivision (short for "Intelligent Television") hit the streets.

At first, Mattel was cautious. They hired contractors for low pay to produce the first games. When they did start making games in-house, they hired kids out of college. According to Intellivision designer Keith Robinson, who now runs Intellivision Productions, Inc., "The company's marketing was oriented toward education and family products. Intellivision was seen as the heart of a computer system that would do family planning, stock analysis, teach you guitar… that sort of thing."

In 1981, Intellivision changed its focus and began the second unofficial age of Intellivision by releasing

hard-hitting print and TV ads that directly compared their graphics to those of Atari's 2600. Intellivision clearly came out on top in those ads and quickly grabbed a 20 percent market share, outperforming the rest of Mattel.

Mattel's aggressive ads were seen as the first shot in a console war—the first of its kind—and the media was quick to respond. Although today we consider it commonplace to have competing video game systems on the market at all times, back then it was almost unheard of. Although Coleco had once run head-to-head ads against Mattel comparing handheld games, (see page 37), this was the first such video game ad. For the first time in the brand-new video game business, consumers had a choice. Robinson puts it this way: "Before, the question was, 'Should I buy a video game system for my kid?' After, it became, 'Which video game system should I get my kid?'" Like Activision's challenge to Atari the previous year, this was a rite of passage for the young industry.

At around this time, amid visions of a long and profitable future, Mattel opened Mattel Electronics, a whole new division of the company that had pioneered handheld games and brought us Barbie.

The team of programmers and designers who made Intellivision's in-house games were called the "Blue Sky Rangers." They were kept strictly under wraps; Mattel was afraid of their being stolen by the competition.

In addition to expanding the Blue Sky Rangers' ranks from 20 to more than 100 developers during the heyday of Intelli-

Mattel released the Intellivision console with other names in certain retail outlets. It was known as the "Tele-Games Super Video Arcade" in Sears stores, the "Tandyvision One" at Radio Shack, and (as in the photo), the "Sylvania Intellivision" in GTE phone stores.

vision, Mattel also attempted to expand the system into something approximating the computer that had been part of the original vision. The first add-on module for the system was Intellivoice, a module that synthesized speech. Games like B-17 Bomber used the voice module effectively.

Mattel also promised a keyboard to complete its computer aspirations, but somehow the promised keyboard didn't make it to market at the time. Much later, when they did release a keyboard, it was a shadow of the promised peripheral, and was, in essence, too little, too late.

TWO PICTURES ARE WORTH A THOUSAND WORDS.

Atari vs. Intellivision?
Nothing I could say would be more persuasive
than what your own two eyes will tell you.
So compare for yourself. Game for game, feature
for feature, I think you'll find Intellivison
is clearly superior.
— George Plimpton —

MATTEL ELECTRONICS®
INTELLIVISION®
Intelligent Television

For the dealer nearest you
Call 1 (800) 323-1715
In Illinois 1 (800) 942-8881
*Trademark of and licensed by
Major League Baseball
Promotion Corp.
©Mattel, Inc. 1982.
All Rights Reserved.

ATARI®
HOME RUN™ BASEBALL

INTELLIVISION®
MAJOR LEAGUE BASEBALL™

Mattel's initial focus was to position Intellivision as the family computer system, but their winning strategy was to play hardball. Although we may never again see a more unlikely spokesperson for video games than George Plimpton, it was comforting to believe that the literati also played games. You can just imagine families all over the United States saying, "If it is good enough for George..."

Mattel eventually attempted to produce the long-awaited computer from scratch, but the resulting Aquarius was even less impressive and even

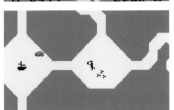

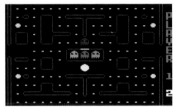

later than the ill-fated keyboard. Programmers considered it punishment to be assigned to create games for Aquarius, and designer Bob Del Principe's slogan for the system, which was released in 1983, was "Aquarius: System for the '70s."

At any rate, timing is everything. Perhaps Aquarius would have succeeded in the 70s, but in 1983, it was just in time–along with Coleco's equally ill-fated Adam computer–to see the end of an era.

Screens of Major League Baseball, Advanced Dungeons & Dragons, Donkey Kong, and Atari Pac-Man.

For, even in the midst of unparalleled success, Mattel and Intellivision's ride at the top was to be short-lived.

As always, there were many contributing factors. For one, their own advertising, which stressed superior graphics, backfired on them when ColecoVision was released in 1982 with still better graphics. And second, the fateful year 1984 loomed ahead, and Intellivision's crash, along with the whole industry, was enough to cause Mattel to close down Mattel Electronics. Intellivision was dead. Or was it?

The senior VP of marketing for Mattel Electronics, Terrence E. Valeski, bought the rights to the system and, using many of the Blue Sky Rangers, continued releasing games through his INTV corporation. Intellivision went on to be come the only classic video game console from the early 1980s to compete against the Nintendo and Sega consoles until nearly the end of the decade. INTV Corp. finally stopped production of the Intellivision system in 1991, more than 10 years after its introduction.

And still Intellivision lives on. Blue Sky Rangers Keith Robinson and Stephen Roney bought the rights from Valeski in 1997 and formed Intellivision Productions, which has brought the classic games to new platforms, including Mac, PlayStation, and cell phones.

Minkoff's Measures team was named for a hiring test given to prospective programmers. Back row: Mike Minkoff, Steve Ettinger, Bill Fisher, Keith Robinson, Joe Ferreira, Ron Surratt. Front row: Julie Hoshizaki, Steve Tatsumi, Dale Lynn, Eric Del Sesto, Tom Lohff, Stephen Roney, Tony Ettaro. Both photographs taken by Blue Sky Ranger Lee Barnes.

Don Daglow's Intellivision softball team, the Decles (a made-up word to describe the 10-bit programming for Intellivision). Back row: Gary Johnson, David Warhol, Robert Reeder, Eddie Dombrower, and Don Daglow. Kneeling: Tom Priestley. Front row: Judy Mason, Minh Chau Tran, Daniel Bass, Robert Newstadt, Mark Buchignani, and Mark Urbaniec (lying down).

Some Intellivision Titles

Armor Battle

Astrosmash

Beauty and the Beast

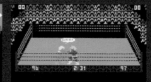
Body Slam! Super Pro Wrestling

Boxing

Championship Tennis

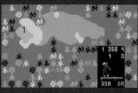
Chip Shot: Super Pro Golf

Commando

Deep Pockets *(unreleased)*

Dracula

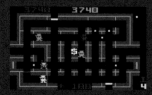
The Empire Strikes Back

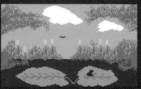
Frog Box

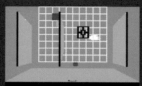
Grid Shock *(unreleased)*

Horse Racing

Hover Force

Lock 'n' Chase

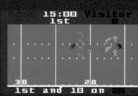
NFL Football

Microsurgeon

Motocross

Night Stalker

Space Armada

Happy Holidays *(unreleased)*

Sub Hunt

Swords & Serpents

Maze-A-Tron

Imagic

After 16 years at Black & Decker and another two and a half at Atari, Bill Grubb resigned as Atari's vice president of marketing and sales in January 1981, intending to start a small marketing firm and get out of the world of big business. One of his clients was Activision, and seeing their success, he began to think there was room for another third-party company in the world of video games. It turned out that Dennis Koble, who had been a designer at Atari for five years, was thinking the same thing. Soon there were nine people, including Rob Fulop, Bob Smith, and Mark Bradley from Atari, plus Bob Goldberger and Brian Dougherty from Mattel, whom Grubb had met while consulting.

Formed in 1982, Imagic was considered by some to be one of the best developers for the Atari 2600, relying less on arcade game remakes and more on original

remembers, "The company was founded with venture money, and the plan was to go public and make a big score. We were expecting a four- to five-year turnaround, but the rocket took off, and we rode the rocket. We went from zero to 350 people and sales of about $77 million in the first year."

The ride was a short one, however. Koble describes the atmosphere at the end, and some reasons for the discontinuation of the company: "We used to have a staff meeting every morn-

Cosmic Ark/17,500 (Gold Thumb 30,000) Rob Fulop, 25/Designer of Demon Attack and Cosmic Ark. You'll have to beat Rob at his own game.

Rob Fulop's picture from Imagic's fanzine, *NumbThumb.*

I left Atari because they basically gave me no additional compensation except the free poultry for Missile Command. At that point in my life at 23, 10,000 bucks could have bought me a car. I got 2 percent and my name on my games at Imagic. It made my career.
—ROB FULOP, FORMER ATARI AND IMAGIC GAME DESIGNER

When I started at Atari, there were only 35 people. By the time I left, it was huge. At Imagic, I could get back down into the trenches... I remember a retreat at Pajaro Dunes and saying to Bob Smith, 'Bob, this is as good as it gets.' And it was true.
—DENNIS KOBLE, FORMER ATARI AND IMAGIC GAME DESIGNER

titles. They ultimately made games for Intellivision and ColecoVision, as well as for Commodore and Atari home computers.

In addition to their various innovative game designs, such as linking two games (Atlantis and Cosmic Ark) as part of the same story, Imagic came out with some of the most colorful cover artwork of the time, some of which is reproduced here.

Imagic shot out of the gate, achieving instant success. Dennis Koble

ing at 8:00 a.m. The industry was starting to fall apart, and every morning it was bad news. Like the operations guy would say that we have more than 100,000 ROMs coming in next week, and we've already paid for them, but we didn't have orders for the games. The company was like a juggernaut, and you couldn't stop it on a dime. There were many financial commitments that couldn't be pulled back. Lots of people on staff. And meanwhile, the consumers had stopped buying."

Along with great games, Imagic created lots of great artwork for their box covers. Here's a small sample, along with some screenshots from Atlantis, Cosmic Ark, and Demon Attack.

The Atari VCS wasn't very forgiving, and trying to learn the technology and invent a new game was like trying to build a house from toothpicks.
-ROB FULOP

I don't know. It's fun to be known and all the rest of it—the whole ego thing. But I guess I'd just as soon be rich and anonymous as rich and famous.
-Dennis Koble

Mark my words: There's going to be more money spent on video game advertising this winter than there will be on beer.
-BILL GRUBB, REFERRING TO IMAGIC'S PLANS TO ADVERTISE ON TV EARLY IN 1983

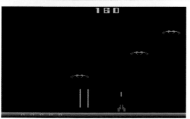

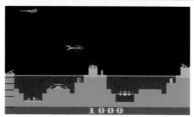

1981 at the Arcades

One of the wonderful features of game playing is that when something is fun, it's fun. And what's fun can be made even more fun. This principle has been followed again and again in the history of electronic games, beginning with Pong and continuing to the present day.

One of the best examples of an idea that evolved into something better and better was the Space Invaders concept. Before Space Invaders, there had never been a game where you had a ship at the bottom of a screen and had to shoot down hordes of alien craft. But after Space Invaders, this became a game genre in itself, and games based on this premise kept getting better. Space Invaders led to Galaxian. After Galaxian came Galaga, and Galaga was like Galaxian on steroids

Galaga

It's a good thing Galaga didn't come out first, or Earth would have been destroyed before we could pump up our wrists and fingers to fight them off.

Success in Galaga required the usual nerves of steel, but even more, a tireless button-pressing finger. Fortunately, if you could survive a while, you could gain a bonus ship. Yes, you had double the firepower, though you also had double the exposure to enemy fire and low-flying kamikaze alien ships. You also had to watch out for the tractor beam aliens who could steal one of your fighters if you were careless or unlucky enough to fall into their trap. With a well-placed shot, you could free it, but a careless or unlucky shot would kill your own man, causing you to increase your aggression level several times over. And Galaga had other surprises and unpleasant challenges. The game was full of tricks.

After a few waves of aliens, you were rewarded with a turkey shoot of a bonus round called the Challenging Stage. A bunch of ships flew out in predictable formation, but to get the whopping 10,000-point bonus, you had to hit 40 out of 40 of the suckers!

Gorf

Carrying the tradition of Space Invaders yet further, Gorf added its own inimitable presence. With an impressive vocabulary of phrases, Gorf hardly ever shut up, and it rarely had anything nice to say. One of Gorf's main innovations was the multi-mission arcade game. "I was a big fan of film history and D. W. Griffith," says designer Jamie Fenton. "I thought video games should have more than one theme."

In fact, Gorf consisted of five distinct missions, each a unique game. First there was the distinctly Space Invaders-like Astro Battles. Piece of cake. Next you had Laser Attack, in which you fought off more aliens, but had to watch out for the laser-firing support ships that could severely limit your mobility, and fry you instantaneously. Next came Galaxians. Yes, "We are Galaxians" again. From Galaxians you fought off a bunch of ships squirting out of a space warp, and finally, as in Star Wars, you attempted to fire into the alien Flag Ship's reactor port to blow it up. The Flag Ship flew above you behind a shield and protected itself by dropping fireballs and chunks of its neutronium hull when you hit it.

Gorf was also the first to suggest a bit of role-playing by means of its multi-stage story line and also by its use of military-inspired ranks (six in all—ranging from Space Cadet to Space Avenger) to reward players' accomplishments.

USS Gorf?

Gorf almost wasn't Gorf at all. "The game was originally going to be a tie-in with the first Star Trek movie. We were already talking with Paramount about it," says Gorf designer Jamie Fenton. "But the plot of the movie was dreadful for a video game. So we pitched an independent game." Maybe that's why the alien Flag Ship looks a little like the USS Enterprise.

Frogger

Probably everybody who ever played Frogger (and every writer who wrote about it) asked the question, "Why did froggy cross the road?" Why indeed? My answer is, "It was fun." Not for the frog, of course, but for the rest of us.

Frogger is one of those perennial classics that has been much imitated over the years and has managed to find a home in the consciousness of everyone who played it.

The object was to get the frog across a bustling highway, then jump from log to log and turtle to treacherous turtle across a stretch of river to one of the awaiting slots on the opposite bank, where there were sometimes tasty flies as bonus treats. Sometimes you could offer a chivalrous ride to a Ms. Froggy, which also resulted in a bonus score. The pace of everything increased as you progressed through the game. The fact that I once spent innumerable quarters in pursuit of this goal is somewhat astounding, but there you have it.

Ultimately easy to begin, Frogger was surprisingly tricky to master, especially at higher levels—true to Nolan Bushnell's law of video game design (*page 25 sidebar*)—and its appeal was widespread and enduring, making it one of the true classics of arcade history.

Qix

In the early days of arcade game design, just about anything might turn out to be fun, and Taito's Qix was a pretty good example of how diverse games could be in the days before 3D graphics. This geometry lesson of a game required you to grab screen real estate by moving a small cursor across the blackness of Qix-infested space. The Qix was

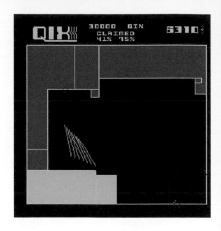

some malevolent (from your viewpoint, anyway) creature that would destroy your helpless cursor (it was called a marker, but today it would be your cursor) if it even touched the line you were drawing across the blackness. Other enemies, Sparx, chased you mindlessly, but relentlessly, and occasionally the line you were drawing would develop a fuse, which would burn down until you were toast.

If you could land the cursor safely on one of the screen's edges, however, or on the edge of already-captured space, you defined a new rectangular claim and reduced the Qix's domain while simultaneously gaining points, which were greater if you used the "slow" button. Each round had a goal—the amount of screen you had to capture to win.

For fans of the famous Etch A Sketch, there was some familiarity, as your cursor could only move in 90-degree angles and could only traverse space along the edges of its known universe, except when venturing out into the danger-filled blackness where the Qix moved randomly around. Qix players developed the extra benefit of being able to tell when 75 percent of a rectangle was filled in—a useful skill somewhere.

Ms. Pac-Man

Sequels often fall flat, but Ms. Pac-Man came on sassy and delivered the goods. With numerous subtle but effective improve-

ments to the original game, Ms. Pac-Man was even better than the original. And for the first time in video game history, women had a protagonist, and they spent quarters in unprecedented numbers. If there was ever a love affair between women and video games, it had to be with Ms. Pac-Man.

Ms. Pac-Man came into being not in some Japanese pizza parlor, but on the MIT campus in Boston and was the result of work done on enhancement boards for existing arcade machines.

The original intent was to create add-on boards that improved on gameplay for existing arcade games, thereby extending their viable life span in the arcade. However, following a lawsuit by Atari and subsequent out-of-court settlement, the designers approached Midway with an add-on board for Pac-Man, still thinking to market the board. Midway, instead, suggested putting out a whole new game.

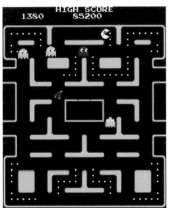

The original add-on had a Pac-Man-like character with legs, but that was not an acceptable option. Eventually, however, the concept of a female Pac-Man came up. She was first Miss Pac-Man, then Mrs. Pac-Man, and ultimately she became the ultra-liberated Ms. Pac-Man, the protagonist of the best-selling arcade game in U.S. history.

Ms. Pac-Man was an improvement over the original game, while still remaining true to its predecessor. The game was faster and included four mazes instead of one. Moreover, it did not allow for the kind of pattern memorization that many players had developed with Pac-Man. You had to play with skill, not patterns.

The four ghosts were back, but one was now named Sue (apparently after the sister of one of the designers), and the fruits got mobile, instead of waiting passively to be gobbled for bonus points.

Men and women, girls and boys, all played Ms. Pac-Man, and the world had a new heroine.

Centipede

I know Ed Logg didn't live in the house I once occupied in Hawaii where foot-long centipedes occasionally dropped from the ceiling to scare the bejeezus out of us, but ironically, he was designing one of my favorite arcade games at about the same time I was dodging the genuine article. Thus, I have a very personal relationship with Centipede. Centipede was a brilliant game in all respects. I loved the smoothness of motion using the Trak-Ball, and the rapid-fire attack, which could whittle away a mushroom faster than you could say "millipede." The title character itself seemed to have many lives and, once hit, the centipede's segments would strike out on their own, taking new paths through the forest of mushrooms. Dodging the ever-annoying spider while attempting to get the maximum points by blasting it at point-blank range added to the intensity, and of course there were cameo appearances by some of our other favorite insects: poisonous scorpions and fast-falling fleas that left a trail of new fungus behind and announced their presence with a descending slide whistle sound. —RDM

"We initially had the centipede running in a field of mushrooms that could not be destroyed. The spider was created from the start, just like the small saucer in Asteroids. It was designed to keep the player moving. At our first review, Dan Van Elderen asked why we could not shoot the mushrooms. From that suggestion the game really changed. The centipede segments would leave mushrooms when killed, the spider would remove them, and the flea created columns of mushrooms, which I thought would be the ideal strategy to trap the centipede. The earwig would cause the centipede to drop to the bottom to create a sense of panic.

Many years after Centipede was released, I happened to be walking by Industrial Design and noticed that the players were only playing the second player on a cocktail version of Centipede. A cocktail cabinet has the second player facing the first so the software must reverse the field of play. I asked them why there were doing this, and they said the second player gets better scores. I checked my game code and indeed there was a bug. Instead of the spider reducing his range as the player's score increases, the second player's spider was increasing his range, making it easier for the player."
—**Ed Logg**

Two Centipede posters... The one on the left is the one Atari released. The original poster (from Ed Logg's personal collection) featured a somewhat blurry naked green woman coming out of a colorful mushroom patch. Judged too risque, it was abandoned, and this may be the only one remaining.

Centipede board game from Milton Badley

[On Millipede] There were several ideas we wanted to add to Centipede to make the game more interesting. For example, having multiple spiders made the game really frantic. I also wanted to add some variations, like waves of mosquitoes and other bugs that come after certain levels. After one level, the field of mushrooms changed based on the Game of Life* (a mushroom would grow if there were two or three neighboring mushrooms). This was created to break up any pattern the players might have created that I had not foreseen.
–*Ed Logg*

*See page 55 [Ed Conway's Game of Life]

Tempest

The first game featuring Atari's color vector graphics, Tempest was a bright and colorful game that could baffle the unwary. Instead of the linear movement of Space Invaders games, you got to spin your odd crablike ship around one of 96 geometric shapes. Clockwise or counterclockwise, you spun, shooting at the advancing menace of flip-flopping red thingies and avoiding, at all costs, *avoiding* the spikes.

Tempest was an unreal game that required you to rethink your approach and stretch new video game muscles. It was all too easy to find yourself overwhelmed and not know, literally, which way to turn. And the game was tons of fun to play. You may not have had a clue what it was about or why you were bent on destroying these odd bits of alien geometry, but you just knew it had to be in a good cause.

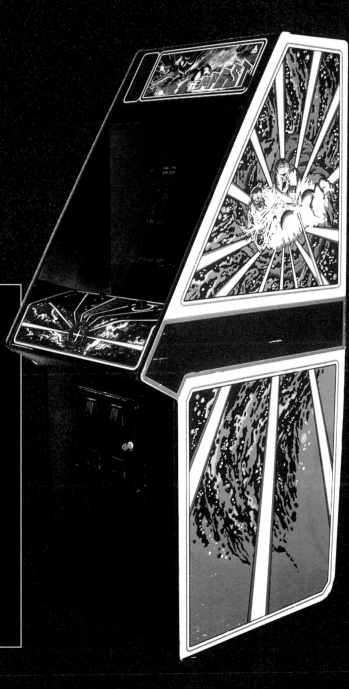

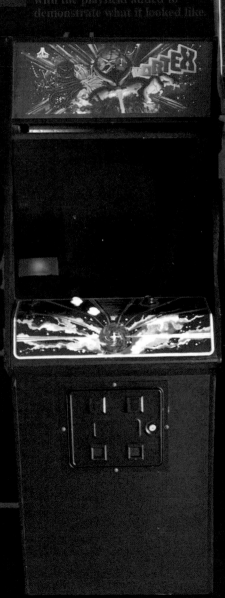

66 *We had a book of ideas that we kept, and one idea I had wanted to do was a first-person Space Invaders. I loved Space Invaders, and I thought it would be great in first person. Atari had a new color vector display under development, and they said I could use it. But when I completed my first version of the game, it was OK, but nothing special. At the first design review, Gene Lipkin said it sucked, and that was my feeling, too, but I still thought with some changes I could make it work. I mentioned a nightmare I had with monsters coming out of a hole in the ground and said, 'I can take this first-person Space Invaders and make it into a tube, and the monsters will come out like a hole in the ground,' and they said, 'Try it.' So I made a bunch of different shapes and made the necessary changes, and at that point people started coming into the lab and playing it a lot and making it hard for me to get my work done, which was the traditional way we knew we were onto something. When we field-tested it, it did really well. A large part of the game's popularity was that the controller was fun, and you could sit there and spin when you were waiting for something to happen. It had a nice feel to it.*
-**Dave Theurer, Tempest Designer** 99

Like Missile Command, Tempest went through some name changes. Its first moniker was Alien, which was the name of a famous Ridley Scott movie. Next came Vortex, which might have made some sense in the context, but, as designer Dave Theurer states, "I kept having a bad feeling. It reminded me of a feminine hygiene product." Put to a committee vote, the name that stuck was also Dave's favorite alternate—Tempest.

Donkey Kong

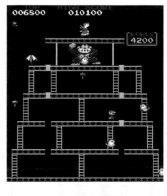

The story of Donkey Kong has been told often. And for good reason. It was in Donkey Kong that we first met one of video game history's most enduring characters, even if he was only a carpenter known as Jumpman at the time. It was legendary designer Shigeru Miyamoto's first video game (*see page 238* for an interview). It was the beginning of an era and a portent of the future.

Nintendo had not done well in the United States, though their Radar Scope game had only slightly trailed Pac-Man in Japan. But, of 3,000 Radar Scopes shipped to the United States, 2,000 remained unsold. When Miyamoto was given his first game assignment, the plan was to use the remaining 2,000 cabinets for the new game. A far-too conservative plan, as it turned out.

Miyamoto created a storyline about a gorilla who runs away from his master, a carpenter, and steals the carpenter's girlfriend. The carpenter must chase the gorilla through a series of industrial settings to rescue the girl. The name Donkey Kong was Miyamoto's best dictionary-aided attempt at creating an English title meaning "stubborn gorilla."

Other than a lawsuit by Universal Pictures over the similarity of Donkey Kong to King Kong (which Nintendo won), the game climbed the charts a lot faster than that carpenter was able to climb those girders. It was a tremendous hit. It introduced what we like to call the "save the princess" theme that would later be repeated in Miyamoto's Mario and Zelda series, as well as other games such as Prince of Persia.

Donkey Kong's protagonist—no, not the ape, but the man—was originally called Jumpman. But later, he was renamed after head of Nintendo U.S. Minoru Arakawa's landlord. He became Mario, and later changed professions to become a plumber. But that was all to come.

The game itself was clever and required patience, good timing, and whatever it takes for a puny human to go up against a giant ape. The cartoonlike musical background was similar to the music of later Nintendo games.

1982 at the Arcades

Arguably, 1980 and 1981 were the most significant years in arcade game history. However, creativity and technology continued to advance, and 1982 brought us several additional all-time favs.

Food Themes

Two games brought food to the forefront of the arcades: Atari's Food Fight and Midway's BurgerTime. Food Fight was an all-out brawl, with watermelons, pies, and other delectables flying as you tried to pick off some decidedly unfriendly chefs. BurgerTime was far more constructive in its vocational training. The ultimate goal here was to walk across various hamburger parts to cause them to fall onto platters, ultimately constructing tasty burgers. Would-be short order chefs would be advised not to tromp on the burger parts during assembly, but the technique worked for our hero, Peter Pepper, whose only defense against his various enemies—Misters Hot Dog, Pickle, and Egg—was to hustle his portly butt up and down ladders or to spray pepper in their faces to freeze them temporarily.

Dig Dug

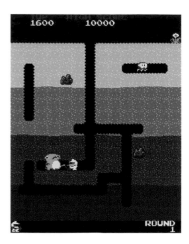

The title starts out like some grammar lesson on the verb "to dig," but the game itself is a classic. Dig Dug himself was a little guy who liked to tunnel underground and do some vermin eradication by means of his handy-dandy pump weapon. The pump would literally blow Dig Dug's enemies up like balloons until they popped. Of course, for extra cleverness points, you could lure a few pursuing Pookas and Fygars under a rock, which you conveniently cause to fall at just the right time. The real trick was that your enemies had a way of moving around without tunnels, which often meant curtains for the unwary Dig Dug.

In a way, in contrast to the early arcade maze games, Dig Dug was like a make-your-own maze game. Its clever play style, cute graphics, and nifty challenges elevated it to an all-time favorite. Many games imitated it, and even Maxis' SimAnt, which came out years later, brought back Dig Duggian memories.

Created by Namco, Dig Dug was the first coin-op import licensed by Atari.

Mr. Do!

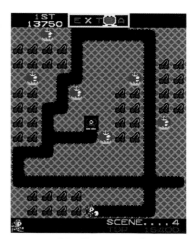

At about the same time as Dig Dug, Universal released the first of several Mr. Do! games. Mr. Do! was a clown who carried around a magic ball and ate cherries. Not that it has to make sense or anything, but Mr. Do! was similar to Dig Dug, and pretty much as fun to play. However, it lacked that certain something to take it to Dig Dug's heights... er, depths?

Mr. Do screenshot

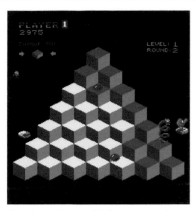

Get the ultimate high score and become the Supreme Noser!

YOU DID IT!

YOU HAVE USURPED ALL
OTHERS TO BECOME THE
SUPREME NOSER!

KINDLY ENTER YOUR INITIALS
FOR ALL TO SEE

A B C D E F

G H I J K L

M N O P Q R

S T U V W X

Y Z   .   RUB END

TIME 27

Before it was Q*bert,
it was @!#?@!

Q*bert

Although Dig Dug and Mr. Do! were definite runners-up for 1982's "cute award," that year's unquestioned winner had to be that ultra-endearing alien hop-meister, Q*bert. This nonviolent critter just had a need to hop around, changing the colors of the platform tiles on a playfield that gave the illusion of being 3D—no doubt part of its appeal. And instead of hopping in a straight line, Q*bert took the angles and hopped diagonally, just to keep the spatially challenged on their toes.

Q*bert was plenty of fun to play with its strange cast of characters, including Coily the snake (dumb as a limp rope*); Slick and Sam, who liked to undo Q's hard work; and Ugg and Wrong-way, whose trick was to turn our hero's world upside down. Q*bert talked a little during the game, but his words were really gibberish pieced together by messing around with the speech synthesis.

Originally, Q*bert was meant to shoot from his rather ample proboscis, and the first proposed title of the game was "Snots and Boogers," which, for obvious reasons, was scrapped. The second title, "@!#?@!," was actually printed on some test cabinets that went out, but ultimately the good folks at Gottlieb realized that a pronounceable name was something of a plus. In a brainstorming session, they came up with the idea of combining cube and Hubert, making Cubert, then Q-bert, and, finally, Q*bert—the winner!

Pole Position

When you hear the name Pole Position, think of every racing game that has come since because Pole Position defined the genre. It was the first driving game to capture the feeling of the track, and the skill involved required all

your attention. Shifting gears, anticipating the next turn, dodging aggressive drivers, and making that first qualifying lap were all a part of the experience. Pole Position was the first great driving game, and the first that truly satisfied our need for speed at the arcades.

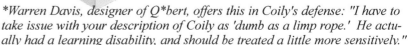

*Warren Davis, designer of Q*bert, offers this in Coily's defense: "I have to take issue with your description of Coily as 'dumb as a limp rope.' He actually had a learning disability, and should be treated a little more sensitively."*

Joust

Joust always struck me as one of the weirdest games I'd ever seen, and one of the most novel. Gravity definitely played a major role in the game; you were mounted on an ostrich (a flightless bird, as I recall) with a lance in hand, and would fall to the nearest platform (or into the molten lava below) if you stopped flapping, which entailed constantly hitting

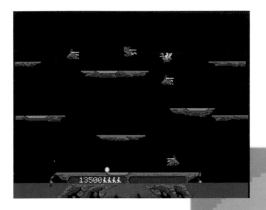

the "flap" button. This odd means of transportation, combined with the fascinating physics built into the game, made it completely absorbing. The game's stilted use of Ye Olde English (as in "Thy Game Is Over") clashed with common sense about as much as flightless birds... flying.

Oddly, unlike real jousting, altitude was very helpful, which in some ways made it similar to dog-fighting in very unwieldy, underpowered aircraft. You couldn't vanquish your foes from below, but only from above, so you would sometimes flap-flap-flap into a superior position, then drop on your unsuspecting victim.

Joust boasted its share of enemies, including several types of buzzard-mounted jousters, the dreaded pterodactyl, and the mysterious hand that would reach out from the lava and grab your bird. But by far the best opponent was generally standing (or sitting) right next to you. In two-player mode, you could choose to play cooperatively, which had its merits, but there was no challenge so satisfying as going up against your friend. A co-operative game could suddenly turn into a full-on surreal joust to the death between friends.

Tron

It might have been a box office flop, but Disney's Tron was just this side of orgasmic for geeky gamers like me. It was our secret fantasy brought to the big screen. And so discovering Midway's Tron in the arcades was the closest thing to being in the movie that any of us could ever hope for. I'll admit that lust for the total immersion of the Tron experience has since been replaced by holodeck fantasies from Star Trek, but in those days, Tron was it.

The cabinet had that je ne sais quoi, that glow of neon that was just cool, and the joystick that was completely satisfying in your hand. The game itself was plenty hard, which meant lots of quarters spent in order to experience all of its scenes, the best of which was based on the famous light cycle sequence in the movie. Cool scene, cool gameplay.

Tron was the first game based on a movie license, and promised a wonderful synergy between Hollywood and games. However, later attempts to link movies and games soon disillusioned us and proved that Tron was the exception, rather than the rule.

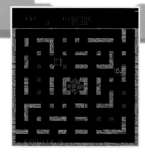

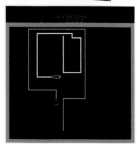

Donkey Kong Jr.

Clearly, Shigeru Miyamoto wasn't monkeying around when he decided to do a sequel to Donkey Kong. In Donkey Kong Jr., he flip-flopped roles on us, and we were perfectly happy about it. Instead of playing the irate carpenter, this time you got to play the ultra-cute scion of the original ape as he attempted to rescue papa from that very same carpenter, now named Mario. Mario would one day soon change professions and become our favorite plumber-hero, but not now. In this game, he was the heavy, and it was Junior who had to save the day.

Donkey Kong Jr. wasn't just the first official appearance of Mario, it was also a great game, much improved from the original. It is another indication of Miyamoto's budding genius that the sequel to his first hit game showed so much improvement. Its four levels were loaded with challenges, rewards, and imaginative touches galore. Junior's personality shines throughout, and Miyamoto's comic touches and melodramatic music set the stage beautifully.

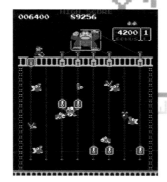

Robotron: 2084

After Defender, Eugene Jarvis did the even more intense Stargate, then took a little time off. When he came back to Williams, what he gave us was Robotron: 2084, which I like to think of as Berzerk gone berserk. Jarvis obviously

didn't subscribe to Isaac Asimov's laws of robotics; the mechanical monstrosities of Robotron were out to destroy all humanity. Your mission was to save the last human family—Mommy, Daddy, and little Mikey—who seemed to have a tendency to wander aimlessly among hordes of robotic assassins of various shapes and sizes. The most insulting enemies were the Brain Robotrons, who could turn Mommy, Daddy, or Mikey into zombielike killing machines called Progs. Some of Robotron's metal menagerie, like the Hulks, were blocky and indestructible, but most would succumb to a well-placed shot.

The real charm of Robotron, in addition to its high adrenaline production, was its use of two 8-direction joysticks, one for running (which you did a lot) and one for shooting. That meant you could shoot in just about any direction while you were on the move, which did give you an increased tactical advantage if you could keep a cool head. But there were way too many dangers to relax for a moment, except perhaps briefly after you had cleared one of the incessant waves. In Robotron, you knew that death was just around the corner, and every minute you survived was a victory. If you had met Eugene Jarvis back then, you would have shaken his hand and then bummed a quarter off him so you could play again.

Zaxxon

If people occasionally had trouble with the pseudo-3D perspective of Q*bert, they really freaked out when they first encountered Zaxxon. This little gem of a game initially caused bafflement among the ranks of players for whom the two-dimensional game had become second nature.

Somehow most of us made the necessary perceptual leap and, keeping half an eye on the altimeter conveniently positioned on the left side of the screen, courageously maneuvered and blasted our way over and under the obstacles of the fortress, past the oncoming delta-winged spacecraft in the space level, and finally into the confrontation with Zaxxon himself.

The most fun was had blasting away the various fuel tanks, antennae, and other oddments that littered the fortress—all good for extra points, of course—but therein lay the danger. If you got too greedy while flying low and strafing Zaxxon's infrastructure, you often found yourself screaming, "Pull up! Pull up!" and hauling back on the controls, only to watch your nifty little craft plunge nose first into a brick wall or electric barrier.

Ultimately, we came to call Zaxxon's POV an "isometric perspective," and it has been used effectively for years in other games, such as Diablo. But once upon a time, it was brand spanking new.

Time Pilot

While neither the history nor the avionics of Time Pilot would stand the test of close scrutiny, the game itself was a blast. The backstory had something to do with traveling in time through five stages from 1910 (the very genesis of manned flight) through the year 2001, which at the time was the far, far future. The bottom line was that you got to shoot a lot of stuff all over the place while doing loop-the-loops with your aircraft in two-dimensional space and laying down a carpet of rather large, slow bullets. Granted, the enemies you faced in each successive time period got tougher, but the premise remained the same: shoot everything. Well, except for the occasional parachutist, whom you could collect for a nifty bonus score.

One of the greatest feelings in Time Pilot was the ability to go forward and backward. Sure, that sounds like no big deal, but it did give you a great sense of freedom in a time when many games were essentially "rail" games that kept you going in one direction all the time.

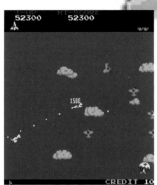

You had to shoot down a lot of enemies to advance to the next level, which was fun, but it sometimes became an endurance test to see how long you could avoid making some bonehead move and zigging instead of zagging, which often landed you smack on another plane or an incoming bullet or missile. In any case, Time Pilot deserves to be remembered, not for its science, but certainly for its great gameplay.

Moon Patrol

Cruisin' on an afternoon in your moon buggy would have been relaxing, if it hadn't been for all those nasty flying saucers, giant potholes, boulders, and other menacing obstacles that kept appearing. Good thing your particular vehicle came equipped with dual-firing guns (up and forward) as well as a handy jump control. Although Moon Patrol might not qualify as one of the all-time great games, it did distinguish itself by being the first game to feature parallax scrolling, in which the background moved at a different rate than the foreground, which provided a slightly more realistic distance effect. Moon Patrol was also the only imported game licensed by Williams (from Irem in Japan). Finally, Moon Patrol was one of the early titles to allow you to continue a game by inserting a quarter before a timer ran out

1983 at the Arcades

The hits kept on coming all through 1982, and 1983 began the same way. Several pivotal games were released in 1983, not the least of which were Dragon's Lair, the first laserdisc game; and Mario Bros., which first introduced the world to Mario and Luigi. Although the arcade business was about to take a tumble, companies such as Artari, Midway, Cinematronics, and Nintendo continued to produce great games.

Ultimately the persistent player was treated to a reunion scene with the sexy Daphne, and a road map of the game imprinted in his or her head. It is interesting to note that Gottlieb's M.A.C.H. 3, which came out within two weeks of Dragon's Lair, did better business. But Dragon's Lair is remembered as a landmark product, synonymous with the introduction of the laserdisc game.

Dragon's Lair

Dirk the Daring was kept pretty busy finding his way to the great dragon Singe, who had, for reasons only dragons know, kidnapped the fair Daphne. Even at 50 cents a pop, Cinematronics' Dragon's Lair—the first laserdisc game to be released (if not the first to be developed)—caused an instant sensation. With art and animation from Don Bluth Films, who also did the Secret of NIMH, the game was stunning, funny, and more graphically rich than anything previously seen in the arcades. It was like stepping into a Saturday morning cartoon.

Dragon's Lair's weakness, however, was gameplay. The game consisted of a series of branching decision points. Learning which decision was right or wrong could cost quite a few quarters and require you to see your hero, Dirk, turn into a crumbling skeleton before your eyes countless times.

3D Dragon's Lair figures on these pages are from the much later 2002 Dragon's Lair 3D title, almost 10 years after the game's initial release.

Mario Bros.

You met him first as the aggrieved victim of a giant malevolent ape in Donkey Kong. He was a carpenter then.

Next, with a new name (Mario) and still a carpenter, he morphed into a nasty man who had captured the giant ape, forcing poor Junior to risk life and limb to rescue his daddy in Donkey Kong Jr. Finally, he must have gone through some self-help seminars and vocational training, because now he was just about the most endearing character since Mickey Mouse, and he was a plumber, to boot.

Joined in two-player action by his sidekick Luigi, Mario had a knack for clearing the sewer of unwanted turtles called Shellcreepers, aggro Sidesteppers, irritating Fighterflies, and the treacherous Slipice that could make Mario and Luigi stick frozen to the ground.

Gameplay was pretty simple. Get under a creature and jump to flip it over, then kick it off the screen. You got points for kicking it, and you could also collect a bonus coin when it rolled out. The crablike Sidesteppers required two bumps from below and got pretty worked up after the first one, picking up speed and looking kinda angry.

The game was at its best as a two-player arena. You could play cooperatively, but more often than not, one person would flip something over and the other player would go grab the points. Not fair, you say? But that was Mario Bros. And you could get revenge with a well-timed bump on your buddy, sending him into an oncoming enemy. So there!

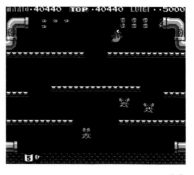

Star Wars

The Force was with Atari when Ed Rotberg began his last game, Warp Speed, before leaving the company. Don't remember Warp Speed? Maybe that's because it never came out. But under a new team and with a powerhouse license from George Lucas, it did become a most awesome and adrenaline-pumping game of Star Wars. According to Rotberg, "The guys who completed it did a great job. About the only piece that I contributed was the controller." At any rate, it makes a good trivia question.

Star Wars was a marvel of design. The cabinet art and control layout were superb, and the gameplay was intense. Of course, you played Luke Skywalker at the controls of an X-wing fighter, and you frequently heard voices—the voice of Darth Vader, "I'm on the leader," or Obi-Wan Kenobi, "Use the Force, Luke!" Meanwhile, R2-D2 would be talking to you in the background, but you probably didn't understand what the little droid was saying. Or did you?

True to the movie plot, you had to engage in some nasty dogfighting with a horde of TIE fighters in the first stage, then blast away at the gun towers on the surface of the Death Star. Finally, if you made it this far, you got to fly the dramatic trench run, avoiding all dangers and remembering the Force until you tossed your torpedoes into the miniscule exhaust vent that was the Death Star's Achilles' heel. If you were good enough, you'd be inducted into Princess Leia's Rebel Honor Guard—the high scorers' honors.

Of course, the other two movies from the original trilogy also came to the arcades, but it was the original Star Wars that most of us will remember

Atari's Don Osborne shows George Lucas how to use the Force in this cockpit version of Star Wars.

best. And Star Wars in the arcades was a harbinger of great games to come. Later products for the home computer, such as X-Wing and TIE Fighter, involved us even more deeply in the movie plot, but nothing could compare to the experience of playing at the arcade, especially in the cockpit version of the game. Inside the dark confines of the cockpit, you came to believe, as long as your quarters lasted anyway, that you really did live a long time ago, in a galaxy far away.

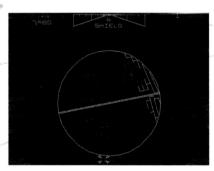

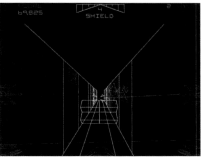

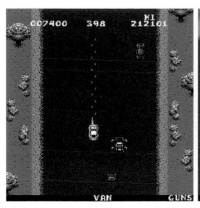

VAN   GUNS   GUNS

Spy Hunter

Pole Position might be the first driving game we really hauled ass in, but we were limited to a racetrack and a couple of gears. By 1983, we were ready for something a little more deadly. Enter Bally/Midway's Spy Hunter, which introduced to the arcades a car fit for 007, enemies to shoot and destroy, and cool Peter Gunn music. There was even a weapons van that you drove into at high speed, reminiscent of the popular TV show *Knight Rider*.

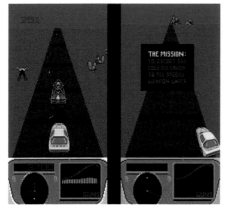

THE MISSION:

Spy Hunter 2 came out with a two-person view and a new isometric perspective, neither of which was a hit with arcade fans.

You had a deadly assortment of weapons, ranging from smoke screens to missiles, with which to cream whatever got in your way. Or, you could play bumper cars and simply knock those nasty bad guys off the road, where they'd crash and burn satisfyingly. Of course, they often tried to return the favor.

Spy Hunter let you play through on a timer with unlimited cars. You could crash as many times as you liked, and your trusty replacement truck would dish out another car. Of course, crashing wasn't recommended, but it happened as your car often skittered out of control in the heat of the battle. In the later stages, you traded in your Bond car for an equally fast and deadly speedboat on a river (switching from asphalt to water), but the idea remained the same.

I, Robot

I, Robot was not one of the greatest arcade games of all time, but it did have the distinction of having a cool name (insired by Isaac Asimov's seminal book), and of being the first game to use full 3D polygon graphics. It was the first of many, to be sure. It was a strange game, but fun to play. And its sense of humor was evident right from the beginning, when our heroic robot is told he can't jump. That's right. The rule from on high is, "No jumping!" And so began the saga of the robot who must jump. And, when you weren't jumping, you could just make cool pictures in "Doodle City" for a few minutes.

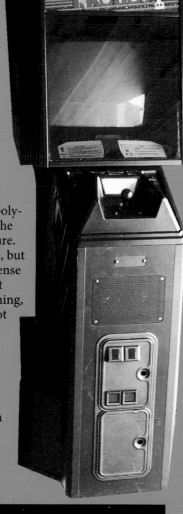

CREDITS   0   3 COINS 1 PLAY

1984 at the Arcades

By 1984, the arcade business had hit bottom, and the number of top games dwindled considerably. However, two fighting games—Karate Champ and Punch-Out!!— and one classic marble game did appear that year.

Punch-Out!!

Nintendo's Punch-Out!! simply reeked of personality, and it was a lot of fun, as well. Taking on the likes of Glass Joe, Bald Bull, or Mr. Sandman with your wire-framed, goofy-faced challenger, you couldn't help but smile—until you tasted the canvas, anyway. The game included a play-by-play announcer, which although it sounded as if it had a fishbowl over its head, nevertheless made you feel like you were at Madison Square Garden.

When the K.O. bar lit up, it was time to deliver the final blow, the *coup de grâce*, the big whomper. To deck the dude!

Punch-Out!! was a great boxing game, and the first of its kind. You had to mix it up, and each successive challenger required better technique. You had to vary your punches, use defense, and finish the guy off when the K.O. lit up.

In true Nintendo style, the characters were very cartoonlike, and some of them could even stick and move pretty well.

Marble Madness

Whereas "Roll Out the Barrels" would have been a good theme song for Donkey Kong, TV's *Rawhide* theme ("Rolling, rolling, rolling...") would have fit Atari's Marble Madness at least as well. As a marble, what else could you do? But, while the spherical protagonist of this game was a geometric shape without superpowers, it rolled through a truly surreal 3D world. Even in arcade games where, let's face it, reality is not the benchmark, Marble Madness set new standards for imagination and was much imitated in subsequent years.

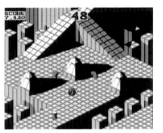

Mark Cerny was a champion arcade gamer and, while working on a physics degree at UC Berkeley in the '70s, managed to be the first documented player to roll over the scoreboard on Defender. He subsequently got a job as a teenage wonder programmer at Atari, where he was asked, "Why do you want to spend the best years of your life before you burn out at Atari?" His answer? "I didn't think I'd burn out." Ironically, Cerny's resume was sent to Atari's human resources department, and, thinking that it was a job application, they sent him a rejection letter. "It said, 'We'll keep you on file,'" remembers Cerny. "Lucky I didn't go through normal channels to get my job."

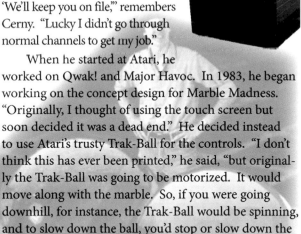

When he started at Atari, he worked on Qwak! and Major Havoc. In 1983, he began working on the concept design for Marble Madness. "Originally, I thought of using the touch screen but soon decided it was a dead end." He decided instead to use Atari's trusty Trak-Ball for the controls. "I don't think this has ever been printed," he said, "but originally the Trak-Ball was going to be motorized. It would move along with the marble. So, if you were going downhill, for instance, the Trak-Ball would be spinning, and to slow down the ball, you'd stop or slow down the spin. But it was too hard to implement."

Cerny went on to work on many games and was part of the teams that did Crash Bandicoot and Spyro the Dragon. After serving as president of Universal Interactive in the mid-'90s, he left and ultimately created his own company, Cerny Games. He's still making games, and assures us that he hasn't burned out yet. In fact, most recently, he was the lead architect for both PlayStation 4 and PlayStation Vita.

Vectrex

It was the first vector graphics console system for the home. Vectrex was first shown by General Consumer Electronics (GCE) at the Consumer Electronics Show (CES) in Chicago during the summer of 1982. It hit the market in time for Christmas with a price tag of $199. The system included an Asteroids-like game called Minestorm. Milton Bradley purchased GCE in 1983, but despite critical praise, sales were disappointing and by 1984 Vectrex was discontinued.

The Vectrex box, with its nine-inch screen, looked like a black version of Apple's Macintosh, which appeared some years later. Despite the fact that it was the perfect system on which to play home versions of games like Asteroids, Battlezone, and Tempest, to name a few, Vectrex's timing was bad. It came out at a time when the video game industry was on the verge of collapse. Only 30 games were produced for the system.

Vectrex was also monochromatic, which might have been perceived as a limitation. To display color in games, Vectrex used colored plastic overlays, harkening back to the first Odyssey system. (A color version with a clever layered color phosphor system was developed, but never marketed. One prototype still exists.)

Whatever the reasons, not that many Vectrex machines were sold, and yet it remains one of the most fascinating and innovative products that never got to live up to its potential.

> "Jay had made a speech-sampling device. One day he had us all shout, 'Back to work!' in unison. He put it in the box and whenever he thought someone was shirking, he'd pull it out and play 'Back to work!' from it. That was how I got the inspiration to put the voice in Spike."
> —TOM SLOPER, GAME SYSTEM DESIGNER

Jay Smith* on Vectrex

One day John Ross picked up a one-inch CRT that had been used in some military instrumentation. It was maybe six inches long and I think it had just a numerical display. But that started us thinking about making a handheld game from a TV tube. This led to a small game that was optioned to Kenner Toys. It was called a Mini-Arcade and used a five-inch CRT. We proposed using a vector scan instead of raster, and our first prototypes used oscilloscopes. But Kenner was pretty much a pure toy company, so they ended up turning it back to us.

Ed Krakauer, who had been at Mattel and later started General Consumer Electronics, saw our prototype around September 1981. He got very excited, but said it needed a larger screen and had to be done by the next CES in June.

We put on an incredible crash effort to do it. We gave it a nine-inch screen and turned it vertical so it would look different from a TV. It was designed using the Motorola 6809 processor, and the entire ROM was 8K—4K for the built-in game, Minestorm, and 4K for the operating system.

*Jay Smith was the head of Western Technology and is known by fans as the father of the Vectrex.

In the Background: Pole Position on Vectrex.

ColecoVision

Coleco was a serious player through the '70s, but they hit their zenith—and their nadir—in the '80s. It started with a fateful trip to the bathroom.

The high point of the arc came with the release of the graphically superior ColecoVision console system. ColecoVision was a far superior game system at the time, and Coleco marketed it aggressively. From its debut in August 1982 until its demise in 1984, hundreds of thousands of consoles and close to 10 million cartridges were sold for the system. In all, 170 games were made for ColecoVision, but the one that made all the difference was Shigeru Miyamoto's classic, Donkey Kong.

How Coleco scooped the home market with Donkey Kong is a story in itself. It started with Eric Bromley, Coleco's head of game design and development, who was visiting Japanese companies looking for content for the upcoming system. "While at Nintendo, I had to use the bathroom, which was on a different floor, and I walked past a machine that intrigued me. I asked if they would show it to me. It was Donkey Kong, and I knew immediately that we had to have it. They said they wanted, I think, one or two dollars per cart, which was a great deal back then, but they also wanted about $200,000 wired to them within 24 hours.

"I waited until it was about 7 a.m. in the States, then called Arnold Greenberg, Coleco's president. I said, 'Arnold, are you sitting down? I got the greatest game I've ever seen. The deal is reasonable. They only want a buck or two per unit. However, they want two hundred thousand in advance.' I took the phone off my ear and waited for the screaming to die down. Finally he asked, 'What's it called?' And I said, 'It's called Donkey Kong.' He asked, 'Why do they call it that?' I told him, 'Because they think it's funny.' First thing he wanted to do was change the name. Anyway, he said yes, and I went out to a restaurant with Yamauchi-san and his daughter and we wrote the contract on a cloth napkin. I kept the napkin."

But that wasn't the end of the story. Later, Nintendo actually made a better deal with Atari, and in a hotel room during a Consumer Electronics Show, Bromley was told to get it back at all costs. He got Minoru Arakawa, founder and president of Nintendo of America, out of bed and spent two hours "arguing, begging, pleading and cajoling." In the end, Arakawa agreed to return the deal to Coleco, saying, according to Bromley, that he'd "never seen any American stay up all night pleading for something like this, and if you put that much into the product we can't lose."

ColecoVision expansion modules included a fancy joystick, a driving module (which included a plug-in pedal), a trackball, and the Atari 2600 converter.

Besides having superior graphics, ColecoVision also boasted the ability to play all Atari 2600 cartridges using a special adapter called "Expansion Module #1," the first cross-platform adapter. Of course, this spurred a lawsuit by Atari, but Coleco prevailed. With the adapter, ColecoVision could legitimately claim to run more software titles than any other system.

Coleco followed their Atari adapter with a standalone Atari 2600 clone called the Gemini, again the first time a manufacturer had cloned a competitor's game system.

Screens, top to bottom, left to right: Coleco's Super Action Baseball featured windowed graphics and an isometric perspective. It was the best baseball game of its time. Zaxxon, Buck Rogers, Pit Stop, Rocky Super Action Boxing, Cosmic Avenger, Space Fury, Galaxian, and Jumpman from Epix.

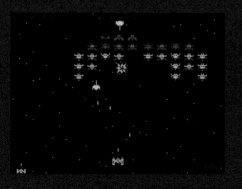

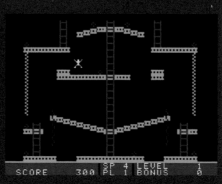

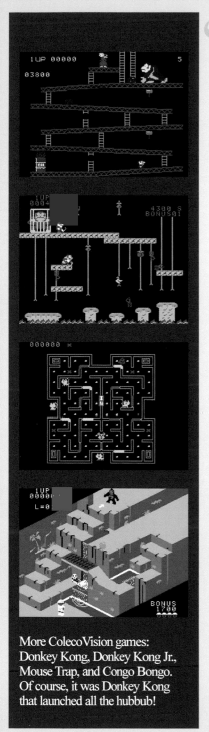

More ColecoVision games: Donkey Kong, Donkey Kong Jr., Mouse Trap, and Congo Bongo. Of course, it was Donkey Kong that launched all the hubbub!

"I went to Japan with Leonard Greenberg and we visited Yamauchi, the president of Nintendo. At the time, we were doing some joint product development with them. They were interested in buying ColecoVision from us for ten percent above our cost, but Leonard wanted to sell it to them for ten percent below our regular selling price. The negotiations broke down and Yamauchi said, 'We'll develop our own game system, then.' I heard Leonard laughing, thinking these guys wouldn't come up with anything that could compete.
-Bert Reiner, Coleco's head of engineering and production

Coleco's other bestseller was the Cabbage Patch doll. They even had a Cabbage Patch Kids game.

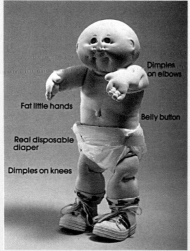

Dimples on elbows

Fat little hands

Belly button

Real disposable diaper

Dimples on knees

Adam

Perhaps no system demonstrated the adage, "Timing is everything" better than Adam.

Adam was an incredible idea—an inexpensive computer system, complete with monitor and printer, for little more than the price of a video game system. The Adam plan, according to designer Eric Bromley, was to create the ultimate user-friendly computer system. It was a bold and exciting idea. Unfortunately, Adam had many reliability problems, and a great

many of them had to be returned. And talk about bad timing, it hit the market just before the first wave of the video game phenomenon went boom and died.

"Adam was capable of having no instruction manual. We just needed a place for the warranty and how to plug it in," says Bromley. "If there were three possible ways to do something, they would all work. You could do things in any order. The theory about Adam computer was that the operating system and the three major applications were the same. You plug in one chip and up came the word processor. Plug in another chip and it would be a spreadsheet/database, or a graphics program. The operating system was underneath, so we just bank selected the part of the operating system we wanted. There was no loading, just the application with a simple menu system for operating it."

The big marketing coup of Adam was the release of an exclusive version of Donkey Kong Jr., and consequently there was a lot of

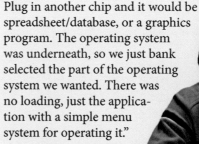

excitement around the Coleco booth at that Winter CES in Las Vegas. People were lined up four deep around the displays, and there were dramatic presentations of Adam.

However, Adam's ability to play Donkey Kong and Donkey Kong Jr. caused a bit of havoc. Nintendo had licensed the video game rights to Coleco, but had licensed the computer rights to Atari. Given that Adam was able to play ColecoVision cartridges, but was at the same time a computer, a great brouhaha erupted. Nintendo's Arakawa sums it up with classic understatement: "It was a big mess. How do you define the line between computer and video games? We had a difficult time trying to statisfy both of them."

Also avalable for Adam were several computer and arcade titles, such as Dragon's Lair (pictured).

In the end, Coleco won the right to sell both versions of Donkey Kong. They were also parties in a lawsuit brought by Universal Studios, owners of King Kong. Nintendo and Coleco won the legal battle, but even the great Kong couldn't save Adam.

MESSAGE TO GEORGE KISS FROM ATARI

Found hidden in the code of the Coleco version of Centipede:
"IF YOU ARE READING THIS, AND YOU WORK AT COLECO, THEN PLEASE TELL GEORGE KISS I SAID HELLO. THANKS. SINCERELY, LARRY CLAGUE"

The video game crash and the disaster of Adam nearly killed Coleco. The company was saved by its Cabbage Patch Kids dolls, which were hitting their peak at the time. However, only a few years later, Coleco finally succumbed and went out of business. Adam was their last foray into the world of electronic devices.

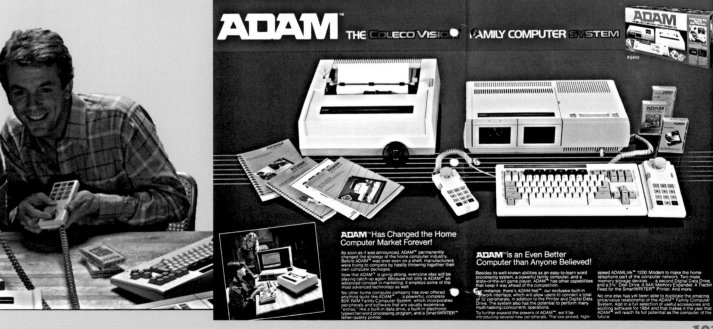

Meanwhile, Back at Atari

In the early 1980s, Atari was sitting on top of the world. VCS sales took off, and, at its peak, around 26 million systems had made it into people's homes—an unprecedented number. Likewise, cartridge sales were in the millions for top titles. The arcade division was pumping out hits in a booming market. Money was pouring in. It was Atari's "Golden Age."

Atari Stories

The Atari 2600 required its own breed of programmers. It was difficult to program for, and it took a particular kind of person to pull the best performance out of the games. Many Atari 2600 game developers were highly independent and eccentric, and there are a lot of stories about the freewheeling atmosphere at Atari in those days. Nolan Bushnell called it a "passionate, almost religious quest. And the more religious fervor, the better and more interesting the games turned out to be."

Once Upon Atari

In the golden days of Atari, money flowed so freely that they jokingly made their own credit card.

Howard Scott Warshaw not only designed games during the so-called Golden Age of Atari, but he has also created a one-of-a-kind video documentary series entitled,

Before he left Atari, Nolan Bushnell held a huge party at his mansion in Woodside, CA, which had previously belonged to Abigail Folger of the Folgers Coffee family.

Once Upon Atari. The video series features interviews with several of the principal engineers at Atari during the early '80s.

Among the most interesting stories is one that involves George Kiss, then director of software (whose morning question upon arriving at work was, "Is there anyone in jail?") and Larry Kaplan, who had helped found Activision and then returned to Atari as a vice president. Kaplan offered Kiss a specific salary bonus, "Or," he said, "You can have your score in Defender." According to the story, Kiss racked up a great Defender score.

Ray Kassar with then Mayor Dianne Feinstein at a cable car fundraiser in San Francisco. Kassar took the opportunity to show off Atari's Model 800 computer..

BANKATARICARD

VIVA

GOOD THRU

408 745 250 0 013080

Crown Prince Henri of Luxembourg poses with the Millipede game he took back home with him after touring Atari in 1983.

After the formation of Activision, the concept of designer royalties was back on the table, though it was still not the standard arrangement. One colorful character, Tod Frye, whose exploits involved something his colleagues called "walking the walls," and who believed that "lack of direction promoted initiative," went to Ray Kassar with a proposal... or maybe it was a proverbial "gun to the head." At any rate, he demanded a royalty for the game he was working on or he would quit and join Activision. The game was Pac-Man, and if Frye had stopped work on it at that time, they would have missed the Christmas season and lost a fortune. Kassar had no choice but to say yes. Frye received a dime for each 2600 Pac-Man cartridge sold. Atari sold ten million. Frye pocketed a million bucks.

In *Once Upon Atari*, Frye states, "In some ways it was irresponsible of Atari. I mean, it was a life-threatening thing to put that much money in the hands of such monomaniac, egomaniac, neurotic freaks who were under so much stress to produce. The only reason you did well at Atari is for some reason you wanted to be stressed."

Probably the biggest irony is that Frye's Pac-Man port was a very poor imitation of the arcade version and, despite its stellar sales, tarnished Atari's reputation at a time when the competition was heating up.

E.T. Phone Home

Back in the day, when Howard Scott Warshaw was creating games for the Atari VCS, he was given the opportunity to create one very big game. The catch was that he had to create it in only six weeks. Although some people might have refused so parsimonious a deadline, Warshaw saw it as a challenge. The game was E.T.

Atari had paid something like $20 million to Steven Spielberg for the rights to the game, and they expected it to be huge. However, despite the fact that Warshaw was actually able to get a game up and running in five weeks, the game had a snowball's chance in hell of meeting consumer expectations—not in 5 weeks or even 25 weeks. However you look at it, E.T. was a very well-publicized failure, not something Atari needed that 1982 Christmas season. Following the problems with Atari's 2600 version of Pac-Man, E.T.'s failure has been held responsible for further eroding consumer confidence in Atari products and in video games in general. Athough at the time few people at Atari were anticipating it, they stood on the brink of a massive meltdown.

George Oppenheimer was the creative force most responsible for Atari's ads and brochures.

Publicity shot showing Don Osborne (national sales manager), Lyle Rains (chief of engineering), and Mary Fujihara (VP of marketing).

During the early 1980s, Atari was divided into two camps—the arcade division and the VCS developers.

 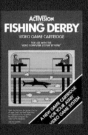      

With the release of Space Invaders on the VCS, sales rose astronomically. Suddenly Atari was selling millions of cartridges.

Out of hundreds of VCS games, we've put 30 on these pages. Can you match the boxes with the screen images on the next page?

Answers on page 107

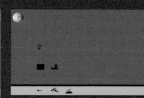

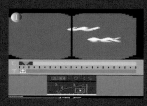

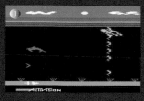

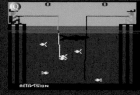

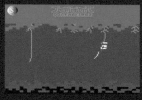

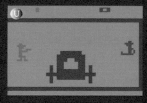

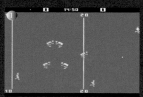

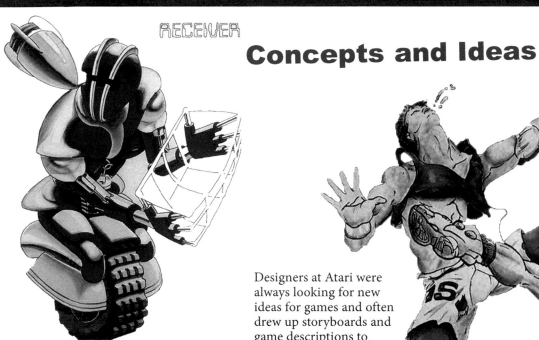

Concepts and Ideas

Designers at Atari were always looking for new ideas for games and often drew up storyboards and game descriptions to illustrate those concepts. On these two pages are several games that were drawn up, but never released, including Cyberball, Hoop Fighter, The Great Pogo Race, Lumberjack, Haunted Mansion and Pack Rat... a rare glimpse into the conceptual work of Atari's designers.

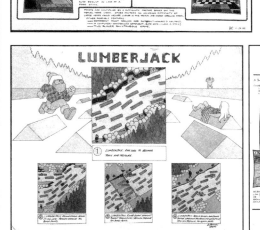

THE GREAT POGO RACE

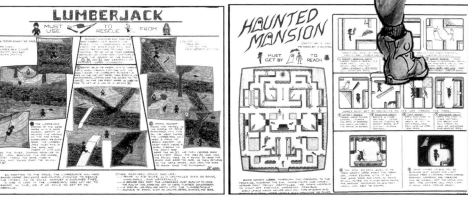

LUMBERJACK

LUMBERJACK

HAUNTED MANSION

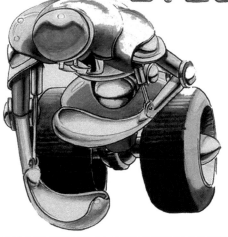

The Boom and the Bust

The home console business was changing. After only a few boom years, the astronomical growth of the industry finally caught up with it. The video game crashed, and crashed hard, in 1983-1984. There are many causes for the meltdown of the video game industry. After Activision successfully defended against Atari's lawsuits, the way was open to third-party publishers. Jim Levy, Activision's president, remembers, "Imagic started in 1981, and I remember that by the Consumer Electronics Show in the spring of '82 there were as many as 50 software companies."

The Crash

If you look at the history of video game technology going back to Pong, there's a rough cycle of six to eight years between the introduction of a new technology and the time that it peaks. What happens in a technology-driven market when it peaks depends on what happens at the beginning of the next cycle. Pong games gave way to the VCS and the cartridge-based home systems. In later years, at the end of the Nintendo Entertainment System's cycle—the cycle of 8-bit consoles—there were once again massive losses. Other cycles were not as disastrous, as long as a new platform was ready to carry the sales at the time of transition, such as when the Super NES reached its peak and the Nintendo 64 and Sony PlayStation were introduced. Each cycle of six to eight years, a new technology is introduced to a new generation of gamers, primarily those players between 9 and 16 years old.

Answers to VCS/2600 Quiz

A. Tennis	J. Dolphin	U. Outlaw
B. Star Wars:	K. Double Dragon	V. Breakout
The Arcade Game	L. Mario Bros.	W. Journey Escape
C. Megamania	M. Wizard of Wor	X. Basketball
D. Dig Dug	N. Night Driver	Y. Asteroids
E. Spider Fighter	O. Kung-Fu Master	Z. Boxing
F. Stampede	P. Lock 'n' Chase	1. RealSports Football
G. Swordquest:	Q. Fishing Derby	2. Defender
Earthworld	R. Battlezone	3. Video Pinball
H. Miner 2049er	S. Jungle Hunt	4. Revenge of the
I. Space Shuttle	T. Oink!	Beefsteak Tomatoes

Back in the early '80s, third-party software companies began to sell game software, each looking for a share of the market. By spring of 1982 there were at least 50 companies creating games for the Atari 2600, and each was looking for maybe five percent of the total market. According to Jim Levy, "Our projections at Activision, which we believe were pretty accurate, estimated that the total 1982 cartridge market would be about 60 million units. Activision had between 12-15% of the market. We planned to sell maybe seven or eight million cartridges and manufactured accordingly."

But Atari was caught up in their success and didn't take into account the new competitors when forecasting how many cartridges they would sell. They planned to sell 60 million cartridges—which would be 100% of the market! And each of the new software makers planned to sell 1-2 million cartridges themselves. If you do the math, there were simply too many games coming out—as much as 200% of market demand and many of these were rush jobs of dubious quality and appeal. This situation would create a huge problem by the end of the year.

By the end of 1982 there were huge backlogs of software sitting in warehouses. A whole bunch of what Levy calls "the Johnny-come-latelies" were getting no sell-through and were running out of cash. They were not getting paid because their product was not selling through at retail, but they still they had to pay their suppliers. Many of these newer companies began dumping products at cut-rate prices.

Even though some products, like Activision's Pitfall! and River Raid, continued to sell extremely well, there was widespread concern during 1983. Early in that year, Mattel announced that they were getting out of the electronic games business, closing the doors of Mattel Electronics. Activision sold off some of their older inventory at reduced prices. By the second quarter of 1983, Atari began to dump products, both financially and literally. It is now well known that Atari took millions of cartridges out into the desert in New Mexico and buried them, although it was not common knowledge at the time. Panic began to set in. Once again, according to Jim Levy, "By the middle of 1983, it was run for the exits and hope you could get there before the building collapsed.

"I kept wondering when Atari was going to dump all that inventory—they had huge inventories—and the answer they gave me was that they wouldn't dump… that it had value," says Levy. "But they did start dumping at really low prices, and once they started to dump, it was over. Atari collapsed and it took the whole industry with it."

Aftermath

By 1984, the business of video games was in shambles. Jim Levy remembers it well: "We had 400 people at our peak in mid-1983 and 95 at the bottom 18 months later. We went from $50 million revenue per quarter to maybe six or seven. And we were lucky. We were coming into PC software, although it was a small market then, and we had strong international sales. We also had plenty of cash. If we had been exclusively Atari 2600 in the U.S., we would have gone out of business."

Even though the crash has generally been associated only with the video game market, it had significant effects on the computer game market. Trip Hawkins, whose Electronic Arts was new and still small at the time, also remembers it well.

"It was terrible for everyone. Almost all of the retailers that had been carrying games were either driven out of business or dropped the category as

Atari went down. So, it took two years to rebuild a new retail network. Also, consumers saw so much bad press about Atari that they got the idea that video games were 'out' and cut back on game purchases. It was a tremendously difficult platform transition and wiped out many companies.

"Computer game companies like EA were struggling in a very small, difficult market, and it was not until Commodore sold a lot of C64 disk drives and Tandy sold a lot of PC-compatibles that the market got strong enough to keep EA and others going. After that, the NES took off."

It took years for the industry to recover. The young computer game industry continued to grow as more and more computers found their way into people's homes. But the single biggest reason for the recovery of the video game market has to be laid at the plunger of our favorite plumber —Mario—and the coming of the Nintendo Entertainment System to America.

Despite their ultimate success, even Nintendo felt the effects of the crash. According to Howard Lincoln, former chairman of Nintendo of America, "It was a really incredible collapse, and the impact of it lasted for years. Even after the NES was successful we kept hearing about the Atari collapse— all the way into the 1990s. For years, during the dog days of summer when sales typically drop, we'd have retailers saying it must be the start of another collapse."

Even after the NES was successful, we kept hearing about the Atari collapse—all the way into the 1990s.
–Howard Lincoln

FACTORS IN THE VIDEO GAME CRASH OF 1983-1984 (ANALYSIS BY JIM LEVY AND RUSEL DeMARIA)

Transition Cycles: 1983-84 would have been natural transition years for the business, according to the cycles we've observed since. And there wasn't anything really sitting there to take up the slack. The home computer couldn't do it. And Nintendo's next generation system wasn't out yet. Coleco-Vision was not quite enough of an advance, and, in any case, Coleco wasn't a company that could drive the transition.

Atari's Hubris: Atari believed that no matter what anyone else did, they could sell 60 million cartridges in 1982. And much of their 1982 creative output was very weak. One executive was heard to boast, "I can put horseshit in a cartridge and sell a million of them." In fact, Atari produced more Pac-Man cartridges than there were systems. When asked why, one Atari manager said that they thought people would want to have a second copy at their ski house. Yes, someone said that.

Oversupply: You had 50 software companies when there should have been five, every one producing a couple of million carts—60 million by Atari. Activision produced probably 6-7 million and sold 80-85 percent. What you ended up with was over 200 percent of demand being produced, and half of it was still in warehouses or on shelves at the end of the year. In 1983-84, everything went into the toilet. Games were selling for $5. "The only thing that saved Activision was that we had plenty of cash," says Levy, "and even so, it took three years before we were able to break even again."

Perceived Competition from Home Computers: Some people in the business wondered if home computers would supplant home video systems. Arnold Greenberg, former president of Coleco, says, "We joined the parade of those who got caught up with the coming of the home computers; even as we developed it the drumbeats could be heard." Fear of competition by home computers was definitely in some people's minds.

Lack of Faith: "I remember being on the show floor at CES during 1983 and 1984 and hearing many of the retailers, and even some of the press, referring to video games as a fad and comparing it to the hula hoop, one of the famous fads of the '50s that more or less defined the transitory nature of fad-based businesses. In those people's minds, video games were a short-lived phenomenon, something that would die and never be seen again. No wonder they were ready to bail and get out." (RDM)

After the Crash, Arcades Live On

The video and arcade game industry took some time to rebound, but Atari did release two all-time classics—Paperboy in 1984 and Gauntlet in 1985.

Paperboy

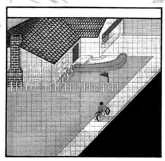

Original Paperboy design sketches showing different (mostly unfortunate) outcomes.

Paperboy was conceived by Dave Ralston, who also did the hit arcade game 720°. According to Paperboy programmer John Salwitz, "Dave was working on one of Gravitar designer Rich Adams' games. We called it Akkaahhr (which stood for 'also known as Rich Adams'). Dave had been talking about a game involving a paperboy on a bicycle for some time—it had won the 'best game' at a brainstorming session, though most of the best brainstorming games never got built. But Dave had been a paperboy as a kid, so that was part of his inspiration. At the brainstorming session, he showed a transparency of a street much like the final game images, then flipped it over to show riding on the other side."

One of the few other games that directly influenced Paperboy was Sega's Zaxxon, with its 3/4 isometric view. Otherwise, Paperboy was something unique and different. In fact, it was even more different at the beginning. Salwitz remembers, "Originally, it was downright wacky. It always had the riding dynamics and the paper throwing, but for a while it was kind of bizarre. We had pianos running down the streets, huge nails, and ducks in business suits."

After some "horrific focus groups," the project was nearly killed. But Don Traeger, who came in as a new marketing lead on the project, helped save it by bringing it back to something more accessible. Again, Salwitz remembers, "Instead of pianos, there were cars. Some things that are incredibly obvious now were not so obvious then. That refocusing and refiltering was as much an invention as anything. What we learned was that any time you diverge from what is accessible or mainstream, unless you are incredibly lucky or gifted—or both—you cut out a big portion of your market."

Gauntlet

As we did with Asteroids and Centipede, we asked designer Ed Logg to share some of his insights into his classic game, Gauntlet. He relates some of the inspirations that led to the game's concepts as well as some of the challenges inherent in creating a four-player game with hordes of enemies on technologically primitive equipment.

"My son was heavy into Dungeons and Dragons (D&D), which was very popular at the time. The original proposal for Gauntlet was made with characters and pieces straight out of D&D. Other inspirations included a game called Dandy, which gave me the idea of having multiple players play at the same time as well as the concept of items, which would increase the player's health.

"Gauntlet had some interesting challenges because the game could not have been done the way I wanted on the hardware that existed. So the engineer, Pat McCarthy, added additional features on top of existing hardware. In addition, I planned to have as many as 1,000 characters running around at any one time. So with the slow processors we were using I had to come up with a technique to solve the collision problem. Once we had the hardware and software algorithm, the rest of the game came together very well. Of course, with a game like this we needed many levels to challenge the players. So while I was on vacation, many other programmers and engineers came up with many of the level designs you see in the game today.

"Balancing the game also presented challenges, especially when more than two players were involved simulta-

Screenshot from Gauntlet

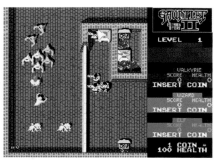

Screenshot from Gauntlet 2

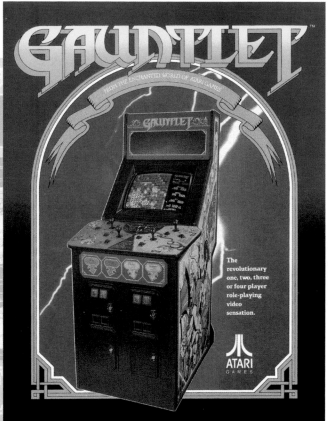

The revolutionary one, two, three or four player role-playing video sensation.

neously. We went through several variations before settling on the final algorithm. However, I recently looked over the initial proposal, and I must say the game turned out more or less just as it was initially envisioned.

"The first time we field-tested this game at a small arcade, the entire industry knew about it within a few days. Since field tests were supposed to be secret, this was extremely unusual. In fact, the operator had installed a sign above the game limiting the number of coins a player could play at any one time because so many players had come in to play it."

Logg also relates a story about a secret technique: "Through Namco, we sold many Gauntlet units in Japan. However, reports came in that players were playing forever just like they had done with Asteroids and Centipede. I could not believe this until I received a video tape showing their technique. Indeed it was possible with two of the four characters. I will leave as an exercise to the readers to figure out which two." Hmmm….

Playing with Keyboards—The Computer Cometh

"VIC Commandos": This photo was taken by team member, Neil Harris, who describes the people: "Frank Ditizio (a friend of mine who worked at a Commodore-owned Mr. Calculator store in 1979) — not a commando; Michael Tomczyk, VIC-20 product manager; Kim Tomczyk (standing, Mike's wife at the time); Bill Hindorff with his hand on his chin; Bernard Falkoff looking at the camera; and with the beard on the right, Andy Finkel."

Even as the arcade and home video game businesses were passing through their Golden Ages and into their Dark Ages, home computers were becoming ever more common in people's homes and at the workplace. Products like VisiCalc on the Apple II and, later, Lotus 1-2-3 on the IBM PC helped legitimate personal computers and increase sales. And that meant more customers for computer games. During the period from 1979-80, a staggering number of companies began creating computer games. The list is basically the story of the '80s—Origin, Sirius, SSI, Muse, The Learning Company, Sir-Tech, Edu-Ware, plus Brøderbund and Epyx, which had begun slightly before 1979. And, with the growing popularity of micro computers, more companies were entering the home compuer market.

Commodore

Commodore was founded by Auschwitz survivor Jack Tramiel in 1954, originally to repair typewriters. But Tramiel was willing to gamble on new technologies, and over the years he developed adding machines, office furniture, and, in the early '70s, transistorized calculators.

Sales of transistor calculators was highly competitive, and Commodore came close to going out of business. Tramiel saved the company by borrowing three million dollars from Irving Gould, a Canadian financier. He

Between TV series, William Shatner served as the spokesperson for Commodore's VIC-20.

also purchased MOS Technologies in order to control the cost and of the chips he needed. Looking toward the future, Tramiel shifted the gears of his company and began making home computers. He believed in "Computers for the masses, not the classes." In 1977, Commodore released its first home computer, the Commodore PET, which was designed by Chuck Peddle.

VIC-20

In the early 1980s, Commodore hit upon the ultimate product line—true, low cost, user-friendly machines. Introduced at the Consumer Electronics Show in 1980, the VIC-20 was originally called the MicroPET, but the name was changed before it was released in 1981.

With only 5K of system RAM, the VIC-20 was a highly underpowered color machine that was little more than a keyboard with a hookup to a TV. The story behind its miniscule RAM apparently goes back to Jack Tramiel's edict that the designers use 1K chips in the design because Commodore had a surplus. Despite, or perhaps because of, its simplicity, the VIC-20 sold phenomenally well. But this was just the teaser.

Commodore 64

In1982 the Commodore 64 was introduced, and it was a much-improved version of the VIC-20, with 64K RAM and a custom sound chip. The C64 went head-to-head against the Apple II as people's favorite game-playing machine, and most computer game makers began to support both systems almost routinely. Commodore sold 22 million C64s in 1983, and over its lifespan, the C64 sold more systems than any other single computer in history.

Amiga Stories

Once upon a time, two Florida doctors with a few million dollars to spare thought about opening a department store franchise, but somehow ended up funding a computer company. They hired Jay Miner from Atari and Dave Morse from Tonka Toys, and the team set about secretly creating the next killer game machine. The company's public name was Hi-Toro ("high bull"), according to co-designer RJ Mical.

As a cover, they began marketing peripheral game products like the Joyboard. They even hired the skier Suzy Chaffee (known for a series of ChapStick commercials) to demo the board. The team's activity of choice on the Joyboard, however, was to use it in a Zen Meditation game of their own devising, in which they attempted to remain perfectly motionless. But secretly, they were working on the ultimate game machine. According to Mical, "It was always a game system from the beginning. It only changed by definition because someone wrote on a piece of paper that it was a personal computer. When I met with the hardware guys and saw the diagram on the whiteboard that was clearly labeled 'computer,' and it had ports for disk drives and keyboards and the like, but I said, 'Game system?' and they chuckled and said, 'Game system!'"

Dave Morse

According to co-designer David Needle, David Morse deserves tremendous credit. "Without a doubt, there would be no Amiga if it were not for his strong and solid support and leadership at the corporate, product, engineering, and personal levels."

By the time the system had been developed, the company was deep in the hole. They offered the machine to many companies, but the only one that made an offer was Atari. However, Jack Tramiel was aware of their financial situation, and offered them a very low per share price, which kept going down the longer they dickered. The company was saved by a phone call from Commodore, Tramiel's former company, who ended up buying Hi-Toro for $4.25 per share—more than four times Tramiel's best offer.

They changed the name of the company to Amiga, "because it was friendly and welcoming, and it came before Apple and Atari in the alphabet," says Mical, whose title was director of intuition. (The name of the interface was "Intuition.")

The Amiga was an awesome computer system, but it ended up being overshadowed in the marketplace by the IBM PC and its clones and by the Apple Macintosh. But to its designers, it was a holy mission. "We all had a really deep passion for what we were doing," says Mical. "What we were doing was for the greater good of man. We believed that computers would become omnipresent. We wanted to create a computer that was as powerful as the big guy's computer, but at a low cost so everybody could afford it."

Not many game publishers specialized in games for the Amiga. Electronic Arts' Trip Hawkins supported it strongly at the beginning, but soon realized that the system's sales were not going to meet his expectations. One notable exception, however, was Cinemaware (*page. 224*), a company whose games often demonstrated the early superiority of the Amiga.

Amiga team photo.

This was the first Amiga prototype ever shown publicly–at the 1984 Consumer Electronics Show. According to co-designer RJ Mical, "The three stacks, two standing and one lying on its side, are the original prototypes of the three Amiga workhorse chips, with all the logic of the chip implemented using high speed CMOS. Each one connects via a monster cable into the motherboard which was nicknamed Lorraine after the wife of the boss, Dave Morse.

"People at CES didn't believe the Amiga could be that powerful, so during the show they kept looking under the skirt of the table to 'see where the real computer was.' Surprise! It was the Amiga, man!"

Jay Miner and co-designer, Mitchy the dog.

Accolade

Bob Whitehead's HardBall! featured smooth action and some interesting innovations, like determining pitch location. The HardBall series was very succesful and several versions were released.

In late 1984, two of the Atari refugees who had co-founded Activision decided that they had experienced enough of the cartridge world. They didn't like the fact that Activision seemed so rooted in the console world, even after the 1983 crash. So, Alan Miller and Bob Whitehead once again formed their own company to create games on home computers and, as they had at Activision, decided not to serve as corporate executives. And, once again, the company was given a name that began with an "A." This time, however, Miller deliberately scrutinized the dictionary to find a satisfactory name that would come before Activision in the phone book.

Miller and Whitehead settled on the name Accolade because the idea of applause suited their artistic sensibilities. "Interestingly," says Miller, "Acclaim was also on our short list of names and was later chosen by two other ex-Activision employees—Greg Fischbach and Jimmy Scoroposki—for their game company." Both Miller and Whitehead expressed their great appreciation of Jim Levy as the head of Activision, but they wanted to go their own way. "We always thought the world of his talent," says Whitehead. "But he was, in a way, trapped in the video game business. We wanted to go in a different direction."

Tom Frisina

Looking for someone to run the company and leave them free to be creative, they first turned to some Activision veterans, Tom Lopez and Allan Epstein. But Lopez decided to move on to Microsoft, and Epstein became a venture capitalist. Ironically, Epstein was later to step in as president and CEO at a crucial point in Accolade's history, but the inaugural president was Tom Frisina, a veteran of both home electronics and one of Nolan Bushnell's Catalyst companies. (Bushnell formed Catalyst Technologies in 1981 to serve as an incubator for new technology companies.)

Tom Frisina had left the home stereo industry to manage Androbot, Bushnell's robotics company, which attempted to build home personal robots. Frisina and Bushnell didn't see eye to eye, however, and so he was glad to take the reins at Accolade when the job was offered. Meanwhile, Miller and Whitehead targeted the Commodore 64 as their primary platform and started work on their pet projects. "The margins were completely different," says Whitehead. "You could produce a computer game on a floppy disk for probably a tenth of what it cost to produce a cartridge. Of course, you still had to create quality software to succeed."

From the Old West to Outer Space

Miller adds, "Our initial creative goal at Accolade was to expand the scope of what video games had been up to that time and appeal to a much wider audience. Bob and I had been doing games for eight years at that point and had in fact been developing them since the very beginning of programmable games. We were interested in emulating other, more popular forms of entertainment such as movies and television. In Law of the West, I chose to develop a game similar to the movie High Noon and tried to explore on screen interpersonal communication. Bob chose to emulate televised baseball and was brilliantly successful with HardBall!. Mike Lorenzen (who also came from Atari and Activision) emulated the television show Star Trek with Psi-5 Trading Company. We were also targeting an older audience than we had at Activision because we wanted to appeal to a larger audience. I would be remiss if I did not mention that Mimi

Alan Miller's Law of the West seemed like something right out of television's classic *Gunsmoke* when it first appeared.

Doggett created all of the art for these three games, and Ed Bogas composed the music."

Whitehead remembers the start-up mentality at the beginning: "What you need in a successful game is a balance between freshness and familiarity," says Whitehead. "In HardBall!, we achieved both. The over-the-shoulder view behind the pitcher was familiar to TV audiences. And we added some innovations for the time, such as being able to control the pitch using the joystick, being a coach, and having names for our player lineups." Amusingly, the player names were taken from Accolade's staff, their families, and employees of their advertising agency.

Accolade had a number of other significant products. Rex Bradford's original golf game, Mean 18, became the Jack Nicklaus Golf series. "It was a perfect fit," says Whitehead. "Jack Nicklaus prides himself on his course designs, and Mean 18 had a course designer. It was relatively easy to get the license."

Artech and Distinctive

One of Accolade's philosophies was to bring in outside talent to supplement their in-house designers. "At Accolade we tried to have about half of the original titles done by employee developers and half done by external development groups," says Miller. "It was our policy to have all ports done by external groups because the internal group's efforts were focused on original creations."

Two Canadian development teams made considerable contributions to Accolade's product line—Artech and Distinctive Software. Artech produced The Dam Busters, Ace of Aces, and Fight Night. Distinctive, after a couple of years doing ports for Accolade, ultimately developed Test Drive—the first in a highly successful series that helped set the standards for future driving games. They later went on to become a top design house for Electronic Arts' sports games.

New Directions

Eventually Frisina left and went on to form Three-Sixty Pacific, but Accolade continued to produce a variety of interesting titles. By the turn of the decade, they had created a graphic adventure engine with a reverse parser to compete with Lucasfilm's Secret of Monkey Island series and, more specifically, Sierra's Leisure Suit Larry series. Infocom veteran Mike Berlyn unveiled a wild adventure called Altered Destiny, and Activision veteran Steve Cartwright went head-to-head with Leisure Suit Larry, sending Les Manley on a Search for The King and getting him Lost in L.A. Another great series of games from Accolade was Star Control, by Paul Reiche and Fred Ford, which mixed space exploration with fun space battles and lots of weird aliens.

Although Ace of Aces had the same name as the booklet game from Nova Graphics, it featured a lot more action and had missions like the later flight simulators.

In the days before high-resolution, 3D, and animated cut scenes, the stage was set with still images.

Star Control

After Paul Reiche III finished working with Jon Freeman and Anne Westfall on Archon and Archon II (*see page 180*), he teamed up for a while with old friends Evan and Nicky Robinson at a company called R3 (pronounced "R-cubed"), though he also had his own company called Supreme Brain Software. R3 pitched a game called Teratosaurus (which means "mutant dinosaur"). The game eventually became EA's Mail Order Monsters. R3 also did World Tour Golf, but then Reiche went off to work as art and technical director for SoftAd.

"One day I found myself in Detroit wearing a suit and about to go visit Ford and General Motors, and I realized that the pods had gotten me." Reiche returned to what he loved—designing games. For his next project he wanted something that, in his words, "combined thoughtful aspects of gameplay and twitchy ones, scratching the same itch as Archon." Inspired by the original Spacewar! (*see page 12*), he decided to add some simple strategy to the space combat aspect of the game.

Working with his new partner, Fred Ford, he started with two ships and then began creating characters, eventually figuring that they'd be able to create 12 alien races and still have the game done in time. In the process, he created one of the all-time villainous races in the history of computer games—the Ur-Quan. "I'd seen an article in National Geographic about predatory caterpillars in Hawaii. There was a picture of one hanging and grabbing a moth from above. I was fascinated by the concept of a creature that clung from the ceiling and hung down over you." However, Reiche, who thinks about a lot of things other than computer games, knew he wanted a villain with more than just mindless

THE FIRST **12** MEGABIT GAME!

STAR CONTROL ™

↩ FOR USE WITH THE   SEGA' GENESIS' SYSTEM

destruction as a motive. "Why would they travel all that way, spend all that time and energy, just to blow you away? They'd have to have some economic or religious reason, or something." So, he created a race of slavers.

Another inspiration for the strategy portion of the game was Orson Scott Card's classic space strategy novel, Ender's Game. "I imagined what it was like fighting the Buggers remotely."

Star Control was released in 1990 and eventually appeared on several platforms, including Amiga, Amstrad CPC, Commodore 64, Sega Mega Drive/Genesis, MS-DOS, ZX Spectrum, and Macintosh.

Star Control was primarily a simple exploration and combat game. But its sequel, Star Control 2, is still called by many avid fans the best computer game ever written. "We wanted to do more than just whip out more ships and rule variants, so we thought, 'Let's try a

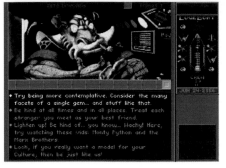

science fiction adventure role-playing game.' In the first Star Control, there was no timeline, so we had to rationalize the circumstances that caused these aliens to come all the way across the galaxy to enslave people. What was the ecological niche that caused the Ur-Quan to be solitary and violent? At the time, I was also curious about troubled childhoods and how they affect people's lives, so I thought maybe the behavior of the races could be defined by their past experience as well. Maybe they were slaves in the past. But who enslaved them, and why?"

That the graphics in Star Control 2 are rich and full of character is no accident. Reiche hired a number of excellent artists, including George Barr (who had done art for Archon II), Erol Otus, and Iain McCaig, to help create the characters and ships. With spot animations, they brought the 2D paintings to life. Reiche comments that later games, which used 3D-rendered characters, "didn't have the same charm as the hand-painted ones."

Fans of Lucasfilm Games' Monkey Island, Reiche and Ford created a complicated conversation system. Says Reiche, "The way Monkey Island handled conversations worked really well for humor. You had multiple choices in what you could say, and the contrast between your choices allowed you to lie or be crazy. In one sense, multiple choices blows the drama, but the contrasts are great for humor, and it also lets the player control how long they want to spend in the conversation tree.

"Originally, we thought to model the space science really accurately, and I did a lot of study of stars and planets, but we found that level of detail became boring, and anyway we mostly ended up generating ice balls or Venus-like worlds. We decided that some level of abstraction was necessary to keep people from losing themselves and getting lost in the details."

Star Control 2 came together as a beautifully crafted game with a great mix of action, exploration, humor, and a rich cast of alien characters and races such as the Chenjesu and Mmrnhrmm (who fused to become the Chmmr), the Zoq-Fot-Pik, the Syreen, the ever-cowardly Spathi, and many others.

Although there was a Star Control 3, it was not done by the original team and was not considered nearly up to the standard of its predecessor.

Star Control 2 was released in 1992 on DOS, 3DO, and Mac.

I know it probably sounds weird, but when I design a game like this, I make drawings of the characters and stare at them. I hold little conversations with them. 'What do you guys do?' And they tell me,
–Paul Reiche III

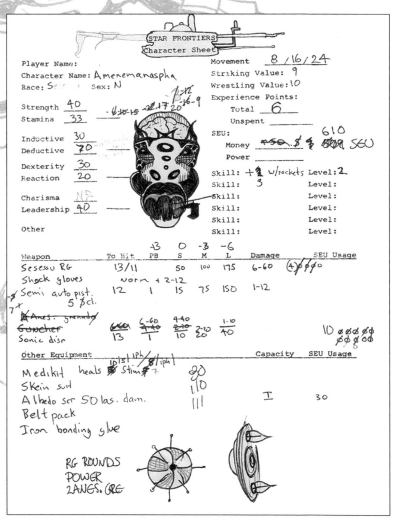

One of Paul Reiche's original stat sheets, used in developing Star Control.

Infocom

Infocom founders Marc Blank, Joel Berez, Albert Vezza, J.C.R. Licklider (Lick), Christopher Reeve.

If you ever thought that the name Infocom doesn't sound like a game company, your observation was more astute than you might have guessed. Although you probably read earlier in the book how MIT's Dave Lebling and Marc Blank were inspired by Adventure and began work on a game known as both Dungeon (its official name) and Zork (a reference used by the creators for any unfinished project), Infocom originally intended to exploit the popularity of Zork and move the profits into the much more lucrative world of business software.

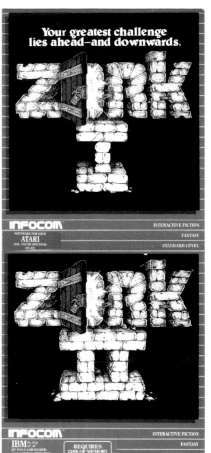

Al Vezza, one of the power brokers at the MIT computer lab, proudly demonstrated Dungeon at many conferences and realized that the game had commercial potential. On June 22, 1979, Vezza joined with Blank, Lebling, Joel Berez, and a few other students to capitalize Infocom. Their goal was to parlay game publishing into a software empire like the then-powerful Lotus Development Corporation. Indeed, the "Lotus obsession" was a major cause of Infocom's downfall.

Speaking Zorkian

Although the mainframe version of Zork (also known as Zork: The Great Underground Empire) had been fully functional since 1977, the TRS-80 and Apple II versions weren't released until late 1980. Unlike other adventure games of the time, Zork and its sequels, Zork II and Zork III, featured a language called ZIL (Zork Implementation Language). Marc Blank created ZIL using a language developed at MIT's Dynamic Modeling Group called MDL ("Muddle"), which in turn was based on LISP (which stands for "list processing"). ZIL, which was designed specifically for creating games, went beyond checking VERB and OBJECT against the game's database. Instead, ZIL interacted with the player to sort out clarifications and assumptions. If a player typed **open the door** in a room with more than one door, ZIL would return a question, "Which door do you mean?" As a result, ZIL was by far the strongest parser in gaming until reverse parsers, using word lists, came along to assist gamers further.

Razzle-Dazzle

Infocom's marketing department insisted that the finest graphics processor was the human mind and that they were serving computer gamers best by allowing players to imagine the action. Moreover, their text-based games did not require graphic conversions, so they could easily be ported to every machine imaginable, from mainframe through CPM-driven units to Apple, Atari, Commodore, IBM, Texas Instruments, and a half-dozen foreign operating systems.

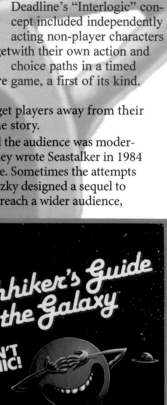

To compensate for the lack of razzle-dazzle on screen, Infocom soon developed a tradition for creative packaging. 1981's Deadline (Marc Blank), a classic murder mystery, came packaged with documentation designed to imitate a lab report, coroner's report, statements taken by police, and other forms of evidence. 1982's Starcross (Dave Lebling) was a science fiction game packaged in its own flying saucer. 1983's Suspended (Mike Berlyn) used the plastic mask of a cryogenic sleeper to make the product jump off the shelf and featured a map of the cryogenic complex and six vinyl markers to represent the robots. 1983's Planetfall (Steve Meretzky) featured color postcards from interplanetary tourist traps, a Stellar Patrol ID card, a recruitment brochure for the SP, and a personal diary. 1984's Cutthroats (Mike Berlyn and Jerry Wolper) came with a book that had a map of four shipwrecks, a price list/tide table in support of the player's treasure hunt, and a magazine parody called True Tales of Adventure.

Mind Food

Yet, the defining quality of Infocom was the excellence of their games. The stories within the games were so fascinating and the environments created by the "Infocommies" were so rich that other products were designed as well. Novels were published under the Infocom mark. Science fiction author George Alec Effinger novelized the original Zork, and fantasy author Robin Bailey did the same for Enchanter (Blank and Lebling's 1983 tale of an encounter with a wizard named Krill). Also, since Infocom games were noted for having tough puzzles, a force rose up to meet the need for clues. MIT graduate Mike Dornbrook built Z.U.G., the Zork Users Group. He developed a line of books called InvisiClues that enabled you to get help with one puzzle without having to glance at solutions to other puzzles. Later, Dornbrook became an official part of the Infocom marketing brain trust, but not until the profits from Z.U.G. had

built a beautiful home for him in which he still resides.

Despite its predilection for difficulty, Infocom wasn't trapped in a situation where its authors had to keep making the games harder and harder (and more esoteric) in order to satisfy the core audience. The designers tried several ways to shake up the mix. Zork III appeared in 1982 and reversed the course of the previous two games. Instead of gaining points for solving the hard puzzles, Zork III gave points to players for doing easy, obvious things like climbing down a cliff to get a treasure chest. Yet, you didn't get any points for solving hard puzzles like opening the treasure chest. There were only seven points to be earned in the entire game. The idea was to get players away from their obsession with points and back to the story.

Sometimes the attempt to expand the audience was moderately successful, such as when Stu Galley wrote Seastalker in 1984 to be Infocom's first "junior" adventure. Sometimes the attempts backfired. In 1984, for instance, Meretzky designed a sequel to Enchanter, using the title Sorcerer. To reach a wider audience, Sorcerer was advertised on the back cover of Boys' Life magazine. Controversy arose when one postal worker unilaterally (and illegally) decided that he would not deliver the magazines because they were advertising a satanic product. Could this event have subtly inspired Brian Moriarty's postman protagonist who tries to save his village in 1985's Wishbringer?

Deadline's "Interlogic" concept included independently acting non-player characters with their own action and choice paths in a timed game, a first of its kind.

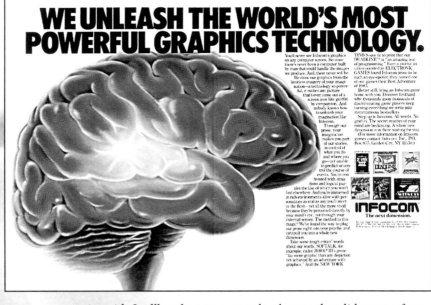
Infocom's early games may not have had graphics, but their ads were both graphical and funny.

Sometimes the attempt to widen the audience was phenomenally successful. 1984's *Hitchhiker's Guide to the Galaxy* paired Infocom's master of mirth, Steve Meretzky, with his novelist equivalent, the brilliant Douglas Adams. The game was proportionately as successful as its namesake, and a new audience discovered Marvin, the manic-depressive robot, and company while the old audience struggled with the Babel fish puzzle and pondered peril sensitive sunglasses.

When Brian Moriarty proposed his Infocom masterpiece, Trinity—a complex, ethically and emotionally challenging game built around the Manhattan Project—he was encouraged to go in a different direction. As a result, he published 1985's Wishbringer, an introductory-level game that sold remarkably well and was conceived around the idea of putting a glow-in-the-dark rock in the box as a marketing gimmick like the old maps, books, and postcards. At the same time, Dave Lebling was finishing the Enchanter

Douglas Adams and Steve Meretzky (pictured above) adapted Adams' classic *Hitchhiker's Guide to the Galaxy* to the computer.

series with Spellbreaker, an expert-level game that did not perform up to expectations.

Infocom had one other 1985 project that did not perform up to expectations. Entitled Cornerstone, it was a product without a plot. It was a database application firmly positioned between the programming-heavy dBase series by Ashton-Tate and the limited, but easy, VisiFile. It was more versatile than the latter, but didn't require the expertise of the former. Vezza, Berez, Blank, and Cornerstone author Brian "Spike" Berkowitz thought Cornerstone would be the foundation of the company's future. Indeed, Blank bet Berkowitz a dinner in Paris that Infocom stock would not sell for less than $20 per share by 1987. Instead, Infocom had become so weak by the end of 1985 that they became a takeover candidate.

The New Infocom

In February 1986, Activision purchased Infocom for approximately $7.5 million—considerably less than the $20 per share envisioned by Blank. At first, all parties tried to play well together. Activision CEO James Levy dressed up as a bride for a mock wedding ceremony at Infocom headquarters, and the company's official newsletter, *The Status Line* (formerly the *New Zork Times*), reported that "We'll still be the Infocom you know and love." The acquisition seemed cordial even when the company's humorous underground newsletter, *InfoDope*, made fun of Levy. Articles joked about Levy trying to get Infocom to widen their range of titles and create simulations. (*InfoDope* suggested titles like Tugboat Simulator and Empire State

Elevator Operator.) Infocom published more titles in 1986 under Activision than they had been able to market in 1985 and still more in 1987. Indeed, Activision hired the famed acting troupe Second City to perform at their party where they unveiled 1987 hits at that summer's Consumer Electronics Show. It seemed a well-made match.

Yet, the acquisition was no longer cordial when Levy stepped down and Bruce Davis took the reigns at Activision. Two years after the purchase Bruce Davis decided that, in retrospect, Activision had overpaid for Infocom, and initiated a lawsuit against the Infocom shareholders in an attempt to get some of the money back. The Infocom shareholders were shocked and incensed by this, and fought a prolonged litigation as a matter of principle. Davis, who was a lawyer, invoked a clause in the sale contract, "making vague claims, and, over time, increasing the amount he was requesting," according to Mike Dornbrook. Years later, even after Activision entered bankruptcy, the suit was settled for about two percent of the legal expenses that had been incurred, just to make it go away.

Davis also forced Infocom to publish Infocomics in 1988, an intriguing idea from Tom Snyder Productions that tried to capitalize on the crossover between comic readers and computer game players with $12 products that would come out on a serial basis. Unfortunately, the experiment overlooked how much comic readers enjoy art and decided to bypass established writers, artists, and intellectual properties in order to exploit the Infocom IP. Infocomics bombed, and as morale began to deteriorate, underground humorists began to publish such things as a memo to join the "Bruce Youth" movement and "turn in" their fellow employees whenever they heard a discouraging word against their corporate "fuehrer."

In addition to the Infocomics failure, Davis pushed and pushed for more graphics in Infocom releases. Activision's commitment to Apple caused them to publish Quarterstaff, a Macintosh-only game featuring lots of interface innovations, but sales were so low that it was never ported to another machine. Marc Blank wrote Journey, an illustrated adventure that allowed point-and-click navigation throughout. Dave Lebling attempted to create a Shogun that would do for Clavell's novel what Meretzky had done for Douglas Adams'

Improv group Second City performed for Activision at the 1987 Consumer Electronics Show.

masterpiece. Bob Bates attempted the same with the Arthurian legend in his game, Arthur. Yet, the marketplace perceived the graphics as either too little, too late, or as too incidental to the games, while Activision observed how quickly the graphics drove up the development budgets and reduced profit margins.

All of the corporate controversy and Hollywood-style accounting overshadowed the marvelous quality found in Meretzky's Zork Zero, 1988's graphical prequel to the series that had started it all, and BattleTech: The Crescent Hawk's Inception, Westwood Associates' role-playing game based on FASA's BattleTech universe. Those games were successful until corporate overhead butchered their financials. As a result, Activision sent Joe Ybarra to Massachusetts to reduce the overhead by an impossible amount or else pull the plug. By then, the "Great Underground Empire" was slated to be six feet underground. Other titles were marketed as Infocom titles, but the creative unit no longer existed.

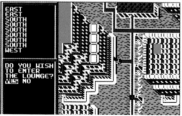

Screens from some of Infocom's later graphic adventures (top to bottom): Arthur, Circuit's Edge, BattleTech: The Crescent Hawk's Inception

Richard Garriott & Origin Systems

"Three important events happened in 1974," says Richard Garriott. "First, my sister-in-law gave me a copy of *Lord of the Rings*. Second, I discovered Dungeons & Dragons, and third, I became acquainted with my first computer. In combination, these three events began a love affair with the computer that has continued to this day." Garriott's passion for computer games soon surfaced. He even convinced his high school to let him use the one and only teletype machine to link to a remote computer so he could start writing his games, and to establish a special course "with no teacher, no other students, and no curriculum" whereby he could experiment. During high school, he wrote 28 small games, which he entitled D&D1 through D&D28. The game that ultimately became Akalabeth was D&D28B and was never intended for release. However, while working a summer job as a salesman at the local ComputerLand, he was encouraged to sell it. "I made a substantial investment of personal assets in Ziploc bags and Xerox copies and hung a few copies on the walls of the store. One of them found its way to California Pacific, and they offered to publish the game. They sold 30,000 units, and my royalty was $5 per unit. Something that had taken four to six weeks to create had earned me $150,000. 'Not bad,' I thought, and I started work on Ultima, which essentially used Akalabeth as a subroutine."

Richard Garriott with Akalabeth. In the inset, he's holding the paper tape, and to the left, the full reel #1 of the Akalabeth tape.

As a teenager, Garriott and friends (Jeff Hillhouse and Chuck "Chuckles" Bueche) built a ride they called the 'Nauseator.' "It was a ride that spun on two axes. When you were in it, you didn't feel dizzy, but 15 to 20 minutes later, everyone who rode it felt sick. So we called it the 'Nauseator'." Interestingly, Jeff Hillhouse was Origin's first employee and worked there until the company closed its doors in 2004.

Many Faces of Akalabeth

Garriott's first game was Akalabeth. On this page are several covers and pack-in sheets for the original game. Below, in a picture taken in 2001, Garriott is playing Akalabeth on an old Apple II.

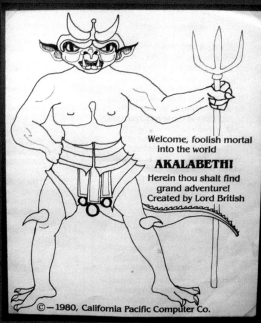

The Ultima Series

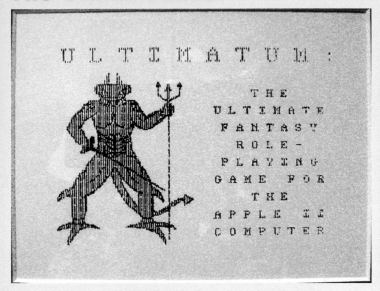

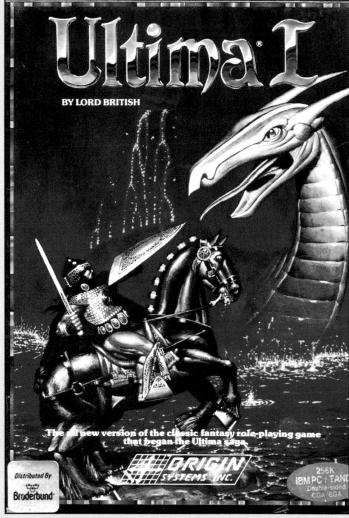

Each of the Ultima games included a cloth map and some-times other interesting items, such as coins and metal ankhs. Here are the cloth maps for the first two Ultimas.

"The first Ultima was originally titled Ultimatum but soon became Ultima I. I still remember how much fun it was to play—my first RPG." (RDM)

Screenshots from
Ultima I and
Ultima II (left).

(Far right) Ultima IV

Garriott's alter ego was Lord British, a character he played both in real life and in the Ultima series. His original game credits read "Lord British" as well.

Below: Raising the sign on Origin's first big office building in Austin, Texas.

Below Right: Garriott's role-playing roots continued in the new building with medieval duels on the front lawn.

Garriott put himself and his friends in the Ultima games. In addition to being Lord British, he was also Shamino, one of the recurring characters shown above in Ultima VI.

One of many wonderful paintings created by Denis Loubet for Origin's games. This is a photograph of the original art for Ultima VI.

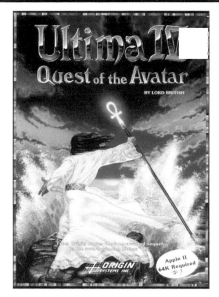

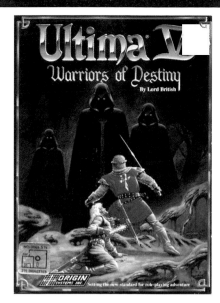

When California Pacific went out of business, Garriott found that many companies wanted to publish Ultima II, but only Sierra would package it the way he wanted, with a colorful box and cloth map. Ultima II was also the first assembly language program he had ever written. Up to this point, all his games had been written in BASIC.

Ultima III was Garriott's second assembly language program. It was during the programming of this game that Garriott made the decision to rewrite each new Ultima completely from the ground up, a practice he continued for each of the Ultima releases.

In Ultima IV, Garriott took a big risk. He included ethical puzzles and a concept of accountability in the game. "I was very worried that it would flop," he says, "but when

it came out, it became the first Ultima to make it to number one on the charts. Ultima IV is special, also, because if you think of the first three as 'Richard learns to program,' Ultima IV was where I learned to tell a story."

Ultimas V and VI continued the saga begun in Ultima IV, with some considerable story development and plot twists. It marked

Screenshots from Ultimas II, III, and IV.

FALSE IMPRESSIONS

In Ultimas V and VI, Garriott created a fearsome race of creatures called the Gargoyles. Throughout these games, you fought and killed them when you could, feeling good that you were ridding the land of a terrible enemy. But, by the end of Ultima VI, you discovered that the Gargoyles were really very civilized and that you had been systematically, if unknowingly, destroying their world. To me, this is one of the most brilliant moments in computer game history, where I was given the opportunity to come face to face with my own ability to create prejudice and how ignorance can create false impressions. (RDM)

considered story consistency. "The first Ultimas were really inconsistent and had a lot of disconnected elements. Starting with IV, I began to create a consistent world and storyline."

Ultima VII was a major rewrite of the code and game style. The graphics were far more three-dimensional, and there were a lot of addition-

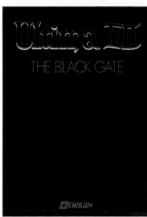

Ultima Underworld screens.

A Time of Transition

Following their sale to Electronic Arts, Origin continued work on the Ultima series with Ultima VIII. However, as Richard Garriott remembers it, there was considerable pressure to get it out, and it was released "before its time." Garriott recalls, "The high concept of the game was good, with a new balance of action-oriented puzzles and storyline, but it was the most unfinished of our projects."

Ultima IX was the final Ultima in the series. Because of the early indications of success of Ultima Online, its development was a difficult process, ultimately leading to Garriott leaving Origin. However, the game was completed and marked the end of the story begun back in the early 1980s.

In its early days, Origin was briefly located in New Hampshire. When they moved back to Texas, some of the employees remained behind and formed a new company, originally called Blue Sky Productions (not to be confused with the Blue Sky Rangers of Intellivision days). Led by Paul Neurath and Doug Church, they created state-of-the-art games, ultimately changing their name to Looking Glass. In 1992, they created a first-person 3D dungeon crawl that was set in the Ultima world and became Ultima Underworld. This groundbreaking product helped set the stage for the upcoming era of first-person games.

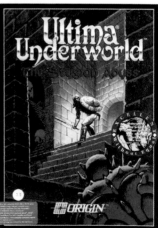

al activities available to the player, even baking bread. Garriott's comments: "I consider Ultima VII to be the most finished of the Ultimas. I liked the concept of the Black Gate that could allow the Guardian to step in. I love the pattern of the game and the pattern of play. One of the best stories. My own critique is that it was probably too large." Looking at Ultima Online, which was first conceived around the time of Ultima VII, you can see the basic elements of the online game to come.

Screenshots from Ultimas V, VI, and VII

Ultima VIII: Pagan was the second-to-last Ultima. Ultima IX: Assention was released, but experienced considerable changes. It's official release was in November 1999.

127

Brøderbund

Doug, Cathy, and Gary Carlston, founders of Brøderbund.

Even before Roberta Williams (*see page 138*) published Mystery House, The Wizard and the Princess, and Mission: Asteroid, Doug Carlston, who was a bored attorney at the time, had designed a space-opera style game called Galactic Saga on his TRS-80 computer. Carlston had taught at an integrated school in South Africa, and was once ousted from the country during the apartheid era for his sympathies. He used many African names for locations and people in Galactic Saga and subsequent games in the series. The name he chose for his company came, oddly, from an unsavory group of merchants called the Broederbond, an Afrikaans word meaning "association of brothers."

Carlston and his siblings, Gary and Kathy, started their business in Eugene, Orgeon, but eventually moved to the San Francisco area. They brought us such memorable games as Lode Runner, Prince of Persia, Carmen Sandiego, and, most popular of all—Myst (*see page 270*).

Starting in the late '70s, Doug Carlston's first games were episodes of the Galactic Saga written in BASIC for the TRS-80.

Pictured on this page are some of the manuals from games sold in plastic bags by Brøderbund Software, and on the following pages are many more images from their game legacy. Although Brøderbund later became influential in productivity software and distribution, they started out in games and distributed many influential titles, such as SimCity and other early Maxis titles, the MYST series, and even the Ultima series after Richard Garriott broke with Electronic Arts over a dispute over whether Ultima code was used in EA's 1987 game, Deathlord.

In their day, few people knew the origin of the company's name, and it was commonly believed that the name was Swedish, an impression reinforced by the use of the null sign instead of an "o" in Brøderbund. Whatever people believed about the name, Brøderbund was one of the first successful computer game companies.

Brøderbund released tons of products during the '80s, many of them classics destined to become models for the next generation of game designers.

In 1982, Brøderbund began selling games from the Japanese company Star Craft, with early game designers Tony Suzuki and Jun Wada, who were among the first Japanese game designers to achieve celebrity in the U.S.

1982

Choplifter was a huge game—the first game to beat VisiCalc on the Softalk charts, possibly the first game to go from computer game to coin-op, and one of the first games that involved rescuing hostages (after Defender). It came about a year after the Iran hostage crisis. The game's designer, Dan Gorlin, remembers, "I was in a computer store and watched as three mothers came in to get that game 'where you rescue the hostages.'" He continues: "A lot of professionals in the game business now tell me that Choplifter was a big influence on them. It kinda freaks me out, like inventing dynamite or something."

1983

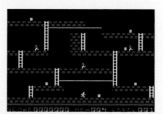

Lode Runner was similar to many other arcade games of the time, but it had a dizzying number of levels with a lot of clever puzzles. Brøderbund was one of the first companies to consider thier customers as designers, and Lode Runner one of the first arcade games to feature its own editor mode, which players could use to create their own levels—a true classic.

1984

The Ancient Art of War was a groundbreaking war game that featured troop formations and strategy, with various bits of advice from Sun Tzu. You picked your general and then operated on a grand strategic map. Once a battle was set up and you had decided how to deploy your troops, you could watch the action in an animated battle.

Next pages: A 1982 Brøderbund games catalog.

Let us introduce you to the next dimension of arcade adventure and excitement . . .

Brøderbund games stretch your vision and imagination to the limit. Computer gamesters everywhere are discovering our incomparable Atari, Apple, VIC-20, and IBM PC programs, and they're not going back to anything less. So next time you're looking for new worlds to conquer, look to Brøderbund.

Brand New from Broderbund !

A.E.™
by Jun Wada and Makoto Horai

The A.E. are coming! Beware! Squadrons of menacing sting rays are streaking down from the sky to attack you. Wave upon wave elude the firepower of your remotely-fired, trigger-action missiles. You're doomed to be pestered forever unless you drive these waves of A.E. ("rays") out of the solar system, deep into the outer wastelands of space. APPLE II/II+, 13 or 16 sector (48K Disk). Joystick or paddle controlled. Also available for ATARI 400/800 (48K Disk). Joystick controlled.

SERPENTINE™
by David Snider

Giant serpents set forth to slay their slithery cousins. To add to the fun, the snakes lay eggs and fight ferociously to protect their young! A fast arcade style game with many levels of play. APPLE II/II+, 13 or 16 sector (48K Disk). Keyboard or joystick controlled. Also available for ATARI 400/800, joystick controlled (8K Cartridge/16K Cassette/24K Disk).

THE ARCADE MACHINE™
by Chris Jochumson and Doug Carlston

Create your own arcade games! It's easy! No programming knowledge needed. Comes with a selection of full color monsters (or you design your own), dramatic explosions and sound effects, automatic high scoring features, and more. Requires APPLE II+ or an APPLE II with Applesoft in ROM or RAM and a 16 sector controller (48K Disk).

Pleasures and p

CHOPLIFTER!™
by Dan Gorlin

With realistic throttle action you maneuver a daredevil rescue chopper. You fight off enemy jet fighters and air mines above, and tank fire and air-to-ground missles below, to rescue hostages held behind the lines and bring them out alive! APPLE II/II+, 13 or 16 sector (48K Disk). Requires joystick with two buttons. Also available for ATARI 400/800, joystick controlled (16K Cartridge/48K Disk).

APPLE PANIC™
by Ben Serki (ATARI and IBM versions by Olaf Lubeck)

The apples will get you if you don't watch out! Forced to flee from pursuing apples in a multi-level mansion, you set traps for your pursuers along the way. A fast arcade style game with great graphics and animation. APPLE II/II+, 13 or 16 sector (48K Disk). Keyboard controlled. Also available for the ATARI 400/800, joystick controlled (16K Cassette/24K Disk), and for the IBM PC with graphics adapter card. Keyboard controlled (64K Disk).

STAR BLAZER™
by Tony Suzuki

Test your ability to attack and evade supersonic tanks, heat seeking missiles, explosive balloons, enemy jets and fuel guzzling bluebirds in your maneuverable fighter, as you battle to clear away the Flatlanders' radar, ICBM installations, and headquarters. Joystick or keyboard controlled. APPLE II/II+, 13 or 16 sector (48K Disk).

DAVID'S MIDNIGHT MAGIC™
by David Snider

Hi-res pinball at its best. Dual flipper controls, upper and lower playing levels, tilt mechanism, rollovers, multiple ball play, electromagnetic deflectors and many special effects. APPLE II/II+, 13 or 16 sector (48K Disk). Requires paddles or joystick. Also available for ATARI 400/800, paddle controlled (48K Disk).

TRACK ATTACK™
by Chris Jochumson

Steal gold from a moving train by intercepting it in your fast car! Jump the train and run across the top to take control of the engine. You'll need great timing and good peripheral vision. APPLE II/II+, 13 or 16 sector (48K Disk). Keyboard or joystick controlled. Also available for ATARI 400/800, joystick controlled (32K Disk).

DUELING DIGITS™
by Brian Couch

It's a dark age. The art and science of math is all but lost. You battle the forces of ignorance (or dangerous human opponents) to capture glowing "sacred" numbers and fit them into the "Expression." For one or two players. APPLE II/II+, 13 or 16 sector (48K Disk). Paddle controlled. Joystick will work for one player.

...erils found nowhere else in the galaxy!

STELLAR SHUTTLE™
by Matt Rutter

On a dangerous rescue mission to the planet Ttam, you must maneuver your shuttle craft through streaking asteroids to reach narrow landing wells and load refugees for the trip back to the mother ship. But beware of the dragons! They have a taste for Ttamians and will try to thwart your rescue attempt. An arcade style game. Available for ATARI 400/800 only, joystick controlled (16K Cassette/32K Disk).

SEAFOX™
by Ed Hobbs

In a lone submarine you take on a convoy of enemy ships and its escort, while dodging exploding depth charges, mines and torpedoes. You will need superior maneuvering ability, courage and a welcome aquatic ally to survive! APPLE II/II+, 13 or 16 sector (48K Disk). Keyboard, or joystick controlled. Also available for ATARI 400/800, joystick controlled (48K Disk).

LABYRINTH™
by Scott Schram (ATARI version by Corey Kosak)

Descend into the labyrinthian depths of Prince Julian's long abandoned diamond mines in search of treasure. You'll encounter terrifying creatures guarding dark corridors with walls that move constantly to expose entryways and seal off exits. APPLE II/II+, 13 or 16 sector (48K Disk). Keyboard controlled. Also available for ATARI 400/800, keyboard controlled (16K Cassette/24K Disk).

GENETIC DRIFT™
by Scott Schram

Quick! Save the world from domination by sharks, cockroaches and other more adaptable sorts. Control genetic drift by zapping unstable life forms that threaten you, and mutate them into friendly life forms that assure our mutual safe passage into the next age. APPLE II/II+, 13 or 16 sector (48K Disk). Keyboard controlled. Also available for ATARI 400/800, joystick controlled (16K Cassette/32K Disk).

Famous
Beginnings
at Brøderbund

1987

MacroMind's Maze Wars+ was distributed by Brøderbund and came out long before the company released Director (not to mention Dreamweaver or Flash) and changed their name to Macromedia.

1984

Raid on Bunge-ling Bay might not have been considered one of the great classics from Brøderbund,

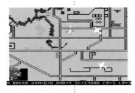

except for one thing: It was the first published game by a young designer named Will Wright. Wright created a tile editor to design the towns to bomb in Raid on Bungeling Bay. Even after he finished the game, he kept playing with the tile editor. He said it was part of his inspiration for SimCity.

1985

Jordan Mechner filmed his brother running and jumping, then rotoscoped the images into his first game, Karate-ka. Using kicks and punches, you had to run through a bunch of screens of baddies to rescue the princess. The ending was great. If you ran right up to the princess, she kicked you in the head, and it was game over. You had to start all over again. If you politely walked up to her, though, you won! Karateka was the initial model upon which Mechner later made the classic game Prince of Persia (1989), also from Brøder-bund (*see page 308*).

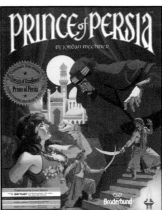

Quintessential Edutainment

Even though a few companies, such as The Learning Company, had previously combined entertainment and learning on computers, Brøderbund became known for such games and really popularized the so-called "edutainment" genre.

1992

The Living Books series, which featured animated and interactive children's books, was another wonderful addition to Brøderbund's legacy of edutainment titles.

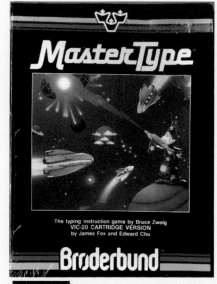

1983

One of the ultimate typing games, MasterType helped many budding typists have fun while learning, a theme that would continue throughout Brøderbund's history.

1985

The game that truly defined the term "edutainment," the Carmen Sandiego series remains one of the most popular educational games ever. Besides Where in the World, there were versions of the game for the U.S.A., America's Past, Space, Europe, Time, and a special edition for Japan. The game also inspired a Saturday morning cartoon series that ran for nearly five years.

Brøderbund Games of the Early 1980s

On this and the next few pages we've reproduced many of the game box covers done by Brøderbund in the '80s. These images were provided courtesy of company founder Doug Carlston, who graciously let us rummage through 31 huge boxes of games!

Games of 1981

Games of 1982

> *I vividly remember The Arcade Machine. I created a lot of little arcade games, and even placed second one month and fourth another in the contest Brøderbund held, which meant my games were published on the back of the next month's release. (RDM)*

Brøderbund Games of the mid-1980s

APPLE DISK
Spare Change
Works on The Apple IIc
Arcade Action and Antics by Dan and Mike Zeller

SHARK TRAP
An arcade-style game for the VIC-20
by Clifford Ramshaw
Brøderbund Software

Battle Map Poster Included!
OPERATION WHIRLWIND
A World War II Strategy Game For ATARI Home Computers
by Roger Damon
Disk Version
Brøderbund

STEALTH
BY TRACY LAGRONE AND RICHARD E. SANSOM
COMMODORE 64
Disk · 1 Player
Joystick
STEALTH
Brøderbund

SPELUNKER
ATARI COMPUTERS
Disk · 48K · 1 Player
Brøderbund

WINGS OF FURY
REVIEW COPY
Not For Resale
Brøderbund

BREAKERS
AN ELECTRONIC NOVEL
ESSEX
A SYNAPSE & BRØDERBUND PRODUCTION

The Castles of DOCTOR CREEP
COMMODORE 64
Disk · 1 or 2 Players
Brøderbund

135

**Brøderbund
Games of
1988/89**

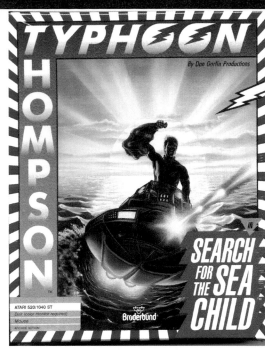

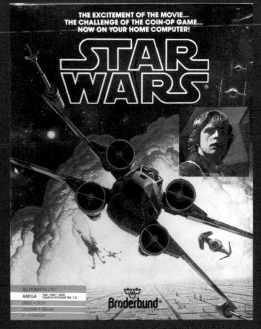

Lucasfilm was just
becoming a game
publisher, but they
hadn't yet started
on their own series
of Star Wars titles.

Other Broderbund products

In addition to the games depicted on these pages, Brøderbund also created the Living Books series, Print Shop, the Bank Street series, and many more products of all kinds, ranging from games to education to home productivity. They also distributed games for many other companies, including Origin, New World, Maxis, Synapse, and Cyan. They introduced such popular games as Prince of Persia, SimCity, and Myst.

We've included Diablo, which was only available in Japan, because of its very familiar title. No relation to Blizzard's megahit game of the 1990s.

Gary Carlston with Mark Canter, one of the founders of MacroMind, which later became Macromedia.

One of my favorite titles for a game. (RDM)

Sierra: Computer Game Pioneers

Colossal Cave changed my life. I owe a lot to Will Crowther.
—ROBERTA WILLIAMS

Ken and Roberta Williams

Although Brøderbund's name engendered language and nationality confusion, the name was there to stay. Another competitor in the "Battle of the Plastic Bags" taking place in '80s-era computer stores

began its life as On-Line Systems, but its most glorious history is as Sierra.

Sierra is one of the longest-lasting computer game companies still in existence today and has for many years been one of the biggest. In their first 20 years of operation, they published more than 150 products—most of them games—but they also published word compilers, word processors, and many other home productivity and educational products. Sierra employed hundreds of talented designers, artists, programmers, and other creative people and helped pioneer many of the most significant developments in the history of computer games. They were first with a graphic adventure game, first with a color-filled graphic adventure, first to use sound cards and video cards, first to put out a CD-ROM game (Mixed-Up

Mother Goose in 1988), and first to create a significant online enterprise (The Sierra Network in the early '90s). They also produced several of the longest-running series in gaming history, beginning with King's Quest.

The Adventure Begins

All of this history began from very humble origins. In 1979, Ken Williams started a small company called On-Line Systems. He was working for various clients, doing mostly financial, communications, and database work. When the Apple II computer came out, Ken saw the need for a Fortran compiler and began work on one.

Meanwhile, his wife Roberta was at home with a new baby and time on her hands. Ken had been bringing his TRS-80 computer home and had a link to the mainframe at one of the companies he was working with. Roberta discovered a game on that mainframe. It was called Colossal Cave—the original Adventure game. Working with a Teletype connection, which would print out the descriptions of the game's scenes, Roberta quickly became engrossed in this new form of entertainment.

After completing Colossal Cave, Roberta began looking for more games like it. Other than some games from Scott Adams' Adventure International, she found little. Suddenly inspired, she thought perhaps she could create a game of her own. "That's where I sat down at my famous kitchen table with tons of paper and started mapping and putting down ideas," says Roberta. "I wanted something with a good story, but it also had to be a game. Stories tend to be linear—beginning, middle, climax—and I needed to expand into, 'What if they want to do this? Or that?' My main inspirations were Agatha Christie's *Ten Little Indians* and the board game Clue. I used the idea of Clue to pull me out of linear thinking."

In about a month, the game was entirely designed, but Roberta was not an accomplished programmer, despite having

MYSTERY HOUSE
HI-RES ADVENTURE # 1
THE BEST IN HI-RES ADVENTURE
by
Ken & Roberta Williams

MYSTERY HOUSE
by
Ken & Roberta Williams

36575 MUDGE RANCH ROAD
COARSEGOLD, CA 93614
209-683-6858

some background with computer science. She needed Ken for the technical side, but he wasn't showing any interest. "Ken noticed what I was doing, but I think he thought, 'Isn't that cute?'" So one day Roberta hired a babysitter and invited Ken out to a nice romantic dinner. "Well, he should have been suspicious—and maybe he was. Maybe he wasn't as dumb as I thought. Anyway, we went to a steak place in Simi Valley and had a nice dinner and some wine. We talked about his Fortran compiler and the Apple computer. Then I said I wanted to tell him what I was doing, and I saw his eyes glaze over. Finally, he looked at his watch and said, 'I'll give you five minutes.' I still remember the moment when he started actually listening. I could see it in his eyes. I'll never forget it. It changed our lives."

The next day, Ken called his partner in the Fortran project and said he was dropping it. He was going to work with his wife on a game.

Mystery House

During their dinner conversation, Ken and Roberta had decided that the game should have pictures, and from that point the development happened very quickly. By May of 1980, On-Line Systems released Hi-Res Adventure #1: Mystery House, packed in Ziploc bags and often hand-delivered to computer stores… and they were still working on the kitchen table. They ultimately sold 80,000 copies at $24.95 each.

"Mystery House was the first computer game with real graphics in it," says Roberta. "About two months later, Richard Garriott came out with Akalabeth, which I would say had even nicer graphics, but Mystery House was the first. Before that it was all Pong-like lines and Xs and Os."

On-Line Systems gradually expanded, releasing at least three more games in 1980—Skeetshoot, the little-known Hi-Res Football, and The Wizard and the Princess/Adventure in Serenia—followed by seven more products in 1981. "When we started Sierra we had no idea how big the computer industry was going to become," remembers Roberta. "We thought computers and software would always be a small industry, of interest only to hackers and hobbyists like ourselves. Well, we were wrong. Our little software business quickly outgrew the space available on our kitchen table, and the operations had to be moved to the den and spare bedroom."

The Wizard and the Princess was a breakthrough game. Ken created the game to draw the lines on screen and then wrote a routine to fill in the colors. There's no way he could have fit all those graphics on a disk, but by using draw commands and the fill routine, he could put a ton of full-color graphics in the game. A lot of people afterward used similar techniques. Of course, if he had used page flipping, he could have made the graphics fill invisibly to the player, and we would have been wondering how he got all those images on the disk!

**—JOHN ROMERO
CO-FOUNDER, ID SOFTWARE**

KITCHEN MIRACLE

"Every time I visit the Sierra offices, I think of a little line my mom used to say when she brought dinner to the table. 'Here comes another miracle from the kitchen.' It was her favorite joke. Sierra On-Line is our miracle from the kitchen, and with every new product comes a new miracle."

—ROBERTA WILLIAMS, EARLY '80s

Three covers for The Wizard and the Princess—the second game in what became the Hi-Res Adventure series—one showing IBM's version, which was called Adventure in Serenia.

Porting the Arcades

Sierra didn't only make adventure games. They also made quite a few early action games, many of which were ports of arcade games. In 1981, On-Line Systems released Missile Defense (Missile Command), Crossfire (Exidy's Targ), Jawbreaker (Pac-Man), and Frogger—the only one they licensed, and the weakest of the lot.

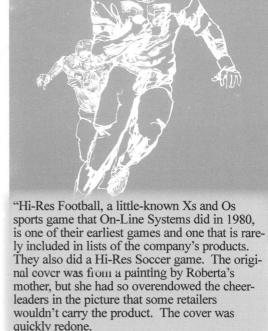

HI-RES FOOTBALL
© 1980 ON-LINE SYSTEMS
48 K Apple II or II Plus
$39.95

"Hi-Res Football, a little-known Xs and Os sports game that On-Line Systems did in 1980, is one of their earliest games and one that is rarely included in lists of the company's products. They also did a Hi-Res Soccer game. The original cover was from a painting by Roberta's mother, but she had so overendowed the cheerleaders in the picture that some retailers wouldn't carry the product. The cover was quickly redone.

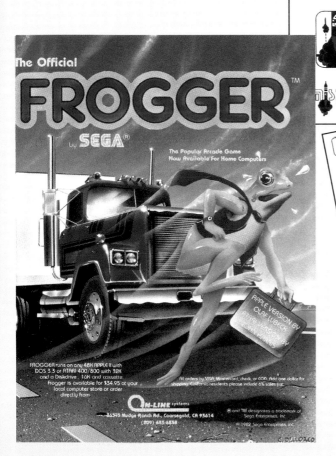

NO MORE CARTS FOR SIERRA

It is not well known, but Sierra also did, briefly, create some games for the Atari 2600, including Texas Chainsaw Massacre and Winnie the Pooh. However, caught in the video game crash of the mid-'80s, they ended up with a lot of excess inventory, which plunged them into financial troubles. This experience stayed with Ken Williams.

In 1984, he went to Japan and brought back Nintendo's Famicom system. Al Lowe says, "I vividly remember playing Mario, and we all thought it was so much fun." But when it came to producing titles for the NES when it came to the States, Ken said no. "Definitely, getting burned with excess inventory was a major reason why we never went into carts."

MISSION: ASTEROID
HI-RES ADVENTURE #0

$19.95
Disk
48K REQ

MISSION: ASTEROID is an introduction to the HI-RES ADVENTURE family of games. This adventure is slightly easier and a little shorter than our other HI-RES ADVENTURE games. MISSION: ASTEROID is designed to acquaint beginning Adventure players to the wonderful world of Hi-Res Adventure.

In this adventure you find that an Asteroid is about to hit the Earth and destroy it. It is your mission, as an Astronaut, to rocket to the Asteroid and blow it up before it reaches Earth. You must fight through the Red Tape at Mission Control, then enter the Rocket Ship and learn how to fly it. I hope you have a flight plan or you will never find your way through space to the Asteroid. Be careful with the explosives, as they can be very dangerous if not handled correctly. This game should provide weeks of Adventure.

OVER A HUNDRED HI-RES PICTURES. (Looks great on b/w and color televisions).

FULL 21-COLOR! HI-RES GRAPHICS. (Each room a work of art).

YOUR GAME MAY BE SAVED FOR LATER CONTINUANCE.

RUNS ON BOTH 48K APPLE-II AND APPLE-II PLUS.

THIS EXCITING GRAPHIC GAME WILL CHALLENGE YOUR IMAGINATION AND TEST YOUR CREATIVITY EVERY STEP OF THE WAY!

APPLE II/APPLE II PLUS
SOFTWARE.

ON-LINE SYSTEMS

Mission:Asteroid was actually created after The Wizard and the Princess, but was easier and smaller, so it was later renamed as Hi-Res Adventure #0.

1982's Time Zone was one of the most ambitious adventure games ever made. It shipped on an astounding six double-sided diskettes. It consisted of 1,500 screens and 39 interlocking scenarios. In many ways, it was a tour de force, but it was also more adventure than most could handle, and the original asking price of $99 was too steep for most people's wallets.

Apple Cider Spider was published under the SierraVision brand, which Sierra used for many of its early games.

After Time Zone came The Dark Crystal, which Roberta did with Jim Henson's group. "It was the first game I had done where it wasn't my own story," she says. "I gave the script to them, and this one guy covered it with marks. It came back more like his game than mine. I told the programmer to do it my way. The guy didn't speak to me again for several years, and, needless to say, we never did another product with them. My next project was Mickey's Space Adventure with Disney—the most boring project I ever did—but Ken really wanted the relationship with them. He said, 'Do what they say. Be a good girl. Be nice.'"

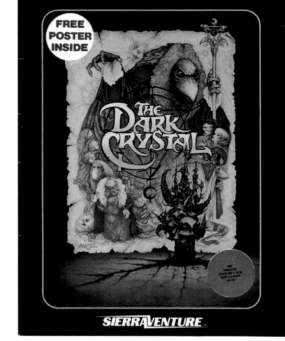

King's Quest

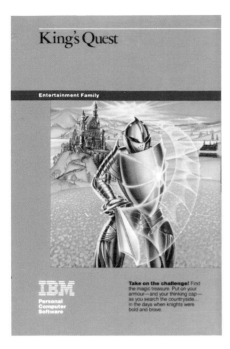

Sierra had developed a relationship with IBM early on when the computer giant published Adventure in Serenia. So when IBM was developing the PCjr (code-named Peanut), which was supposed to be a low-cost consumer machine, they approached Sierra to see whether they wanted to create a game for the new machine.

"They gave us prototypes and explained the capabilities of the machine. It could do a lot more than the Apple II at the time, with 128K of memory and more colors. They said, 'We want something like The Wizard and the Princess, but we want it to push the machine's capabilities,'" remembers Roberta. "I had always wanted to do animation in my games and have more colors. Up to then, the adventure games had been first-person perspective. I had the idea to do something

different, so I said, 'I want to create a world with a little guy running around and you control him.' But if you had a little guy running around, you had to give a sense of dimensionality in the picture. He has to go behind things like trees and rocks and stuff."

The concept of the third-person adventure game completely changed the way the genre was created, and Sierra had to design a whole new engine to produce Roberta's idea.

The change wasn't only technical, however. "In the old games," remembers Roberta, "they were stories that you experienced from your own eyes. Like in Time Zone—you're just walking through the trees outside your home, and suddenly there's a time machine. It's never been there before; it's just suddenly there. What is this? You don't even know what it is. This funny-looking machine... You look closer, then climb inside, look at the controls, and before you know it, you're off on an adventure. But it's just you.

"But with the little guy running round, it's not you, it's him or it's her. Suddenly that character has to be defined, and I actually think the story becomes more defined. Before, it was a little more loosey-goosey. There weren't a lot of really well-defined characters, and I think the worlds were a little more loosely organized, partly due to my own inexperience as a writer. But once you start thinking in third person instead of first or second, you have to think, 'Who is this person and how is he going to interact with other characters?' When it was you, it was your personality. Now it was someone else with his or her own personality."

About the time Roberta was beginning King's Quest, she was also completing The Black Cauldron.

Original drawings and map for King's Quest VII on this page and the next.

ROSELLA AS A TROLL

Roberta and Ken Williams and (below) their custom King's Quest license plate.

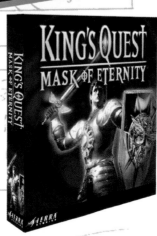

In the background: Level plan for King's Quest VII.

More Quests

With the success of King's Quest, Sierra launched several more Quest games, drawing upon a variety of designers, each of whom had a unique and individual approach to the newly formed third-person adventure game genre. Like King's Quest, each of the new games initiated a series of games, as they were all very successful. The first such game was Police Quest, designed by ex-cop Jim Walls. This was a serious crime adventure using the King's Quest engine.

Where King's Quest was a lighthearted fantasy adventure and Police Quest was an attempt at serious police drama, the next series had tongue firmly in cheek. When Scott Murphy and Mark Crowe (Two Guys from Andromeda) came up with an idea for an adventure game set in space, Ken Williams gave them the go-ahead. Williams had a great respect for the creative process and would let his team run with their ideas. "I wanted my designers to be the king of their product, and nobody was going to mess with their creativity. And if it didn't sell, they didn't get invited back."

Space Quest, starring a rather dimwitted janitor named Roger Wilco, sold very well, and Murphy and Crowe were definitely invited back to produce several sequels. Roger Wilco's adventures were loaded with odd puzzles, humorous situations, and quirky dialogue. Along with Leisure Suit Larry and Lucas' Maniac Mansion (which also released in 1987—*see page 208*), Space Quest helped usher in a new era of humor-based adventure games.

Screenshot from Space Quest

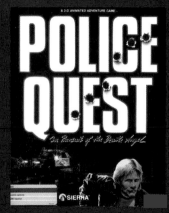

Leisure Suit Larry

At exactly the same time that Roger Wilco was being prepared to pratfall into the game market, veteran game designer Al Lowe was preparing to introduce another, at least equally lame character, basing the new game on Sierra's sole text-only game, Chuck Benson's Softporn Adventure. "I took the design for Softporn, kept the locations and puzzles pretty much, and then started on the text. Chuck was a great programmer but wrote dialogue like an engineer," says Lowe. "So we took Softporn, which has no central character…and created a dorky character. By this time, of course, we were doing all this new 3D technology, and so I commented that the original game was so old it should be wearing a leisure suit. I guess that's how Larry's outfit came into being. It was coincidental that Scott was doing something similar with Roger Wilco. However, Larry was even dorkier than Roger—he was simple and dim-witted. He operated further down on Maslow's hierarchy of needs."

Larry was a huge success, and there were two sequels, at which point Lowe considered the story to be done. "I wrapped it up and tied a big bow on it," he says. "I was tired of it. By the way I ended it, I thought I had made it pretty final. I had Larry fall out of his world and land in Sierra. It was my homage to Blazing Saddles. So Larry meets Ken Williams and gets a job. He starts typing, and he's programming the first scene for the first Leisure Suit Larry." However, the series had become so popular that people were asking for more. As a joke, Lowe did another game but called it Leisure Suit Larry V, and in it he referred to events from the fourth game that never really existed.

After finishing the Larry series, Lowe did a game called Freddy Pharkas: Frontier Pharmacist, a spoof on westerns inspired by the Zucker brothers' films, such as Airplane! The original version was very successful, so they did a second version with speech instead of printed text.

HOT TUBBING TO FAME

On-Line Systems' 1981 Softporn Adventure was actually a text-only adventure, but it is noteworthy for two reasons. First, it was the progenitor of the popular Leisure Suit Larry series that debuted in 1987. And second, co-founder Roberta Williams (far right) posed in the buff for the cover and print ads in magazines such as Softalk. The cover photo was reprinted in a 1981 article in Time magazine, but no mention was made of the presence of the company's co-founder in the tub. The back cover of the game says, in part, "WOMEN! EROTICA! DERELICTS! BOOZE! and MUCH MORE!!!" and "The subject matter is such that adult males should find this game quite interesting. Others may too—but be forewarned!!!!" The game carried a self-imposed R rating.

Gabriel Knight

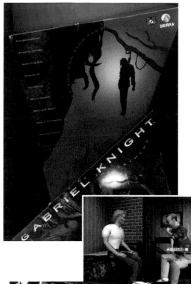

Originally hired as part of a group of in-house writers, Jane Jensen helped Jim Walls with Police Quest 3 and then wrote and designed with Roberta Williams on King's Quest VI. Following that, she was offered the opportunity to create her own series. "I guess at the time I wrote the proposal," says Jensen, "I was influenced by some of the adult graphic novels like Sandman and Hell Raiser. Also, I had already done some work on a mystery series concept that dealt with paranormal mysteries and featured a parapsychologist. All that got boiled down to Gabriel Knight."

The first Gabriel Knight game, Sins of the Fathers, featured an excellent voiceover cast, including Tim Curry, Michael Dorn, and Mark Hamill. Its dark, adult themes met with considerable critical success. Says Jensen, "It was very gothic and a little bit more violent and a little bit more sensual."

The sequel, The Beast Within, which was done with real actors in full-motion video, also, also received critical acclaim. But keeping the same depth of detail while shooting real actors was a challenge. "We shot a 600-page script," says Jensen. "It was very difficult, but we accomplished a lot, given our time and budget."

With the third in the series, Blood of the Sacred, Blood of the Damned, they moved from real actors to 3D characters. Jensen comments, "It's really difficult to get 3D actors to look good and to emote."

The Gabriel Knight series has an unusually large female fan base, according to Jensen. "It has a sort of mystery/romance feel to it. Especially with GK2, it had a very Anne Rice homoerotic quality." Of course, the heart and soul of the Gabriel Knight series was its stories, and Jensen proved it by publishing them as mystery novels at a later date.

Screens from Phantasmagoria. Above: The blue screen set. Right-hand corner: Scenes from the game.

Phantasmagoria

With the growing popularity of the CD-ROM, Roberta Williams became inspired to try something new. "I always liked horror or thrillers and suspenseful stories and movies. I thought it would be fun to see if it could be done in a computer game, but I was convinced that you couldn't really scare people like you could in movies. 'Hey, open that door!' I figured we needed to use real actors. I wanted it to be really scary. Most of the games that tried to be scary didn't seem scary to me."

Using blue screens and setting up each camera shot exactly to the 3D models of the house and rooms they had created, they began to shoot the actors to blend into the scenery. However, like 7th Guest, they ran into difficulties with a sort of halo effect around the actors, and had to spend a lot of time in postproduction, cleaning up the images by hand. "I got a nasty reputation around Sierra for being so picky," says Roberta. "I kept sending the pictures back because I could still see the blue at the edges."

Original Phantasmagoria storyboards.

The game shipped on a whopping seven CDs, garnering attention for sheer size, and it generated a good deal of controversy. It contained a lovemaking scene, va rape scene, drug abuse, and several violent death scenes (which could be turned on or off). It was definitely for adults, and Sierra suggested an age limit of 15. "Originally it had nudity in it, too," says Ken Williams, "but in the end we chickened out and removed it."

Despite some uneven press, the game sold well. Its puzzles were kept intentionally easy to allow new gamers to enjoy it, and it was very strongly marketed. Given its content, Phantasmagoria managed to stir up considerable controversy and was not only banned by various retailers but also by the Australian government.

The End of an Era

Sierra had grown to be a huge company with hundreds of employees and ultimately acquired smaller companies such as Dynamix. In 1996, Ken and Roberta Williams sold the company to Cendant Corporation, a multifaceted company whith many interests and subsidiaries. The couple then retired after 18 years of running Sierra. It was the end of an era. Sierra continued to make games, many of them exceptional, but the companiy's personality changed. It was no longer a mega–"mom and pop" concern. Among the many fine games from Sierra in the '90s was a first-person shooter—not one of the genres for which Sierra had been known previously.

Half-Life: Counter Strike

After Doom, the first-person shooter became the de facto standard for game publishers. One after an-

other, games imitated id's masterpiece. Some, such as Interplay's Descent, gave new dimension to the game by adding a mind-twisting flying element. Others, such as Apogee's Duke Nukem, added humor and attitude. And id's own Quake was an amazing 3D world and another technological breakthrough. But few in the genre, if any, really told a story.

Valve and Sierra changed that. Half-Life, while still in the mold of a first-person shooter, added drama, story, and character interaction to a great action game. Perhaps because of that (or even in spite of it), Half-Life was received both in the market and critically as one of the best games of 1998, spawning a number of sequels. Following in the tradition first established by id with its Doom WAD editor, which allowed anyone to create levels for Doom, Valve also included an editor with Half-Life, which meant that lots of additional scenarios ("mods") were created and shared by users on the Internet. Some of these Half-Life mods were good enough to be included included in the excellent 2000 release, Half-Life: Counter Strike.

Sierra put out a staggering number of games in more than two decades of production, and we've included a few of them here. Also of note was the Quest for Glory series. Under the Dynamix label, Sierra put out even more great games, such as The Incredible Machine and the Tribes series (see Dynamix, next).

In the background, a level design map for Phantasmagoria.

Dynamix

Damon Slye began programming on an 8K Commodore PET during high school—versions of existing games like Mastermind and Star Trek. Against his parents' better judgment, he went out and bought an Apple II. "They thought I should save the money for college. They had no idea what I was doing in my room all that time." What he was doing was programming his first original game—Stellar 7. At the time, Jeff Tunnell was running a computer store and Slye began working for him. "Damon was working on a font-making program, and I was doing some games in the back room," recalls Tunnell. "One day I needed a routine written, and Damon did it for me in assembly language. I realized then that I was never going to be that good a programmer, and I began thinking about being a producer and designer and doing the business aspects."

EA photo from Arcticfox with Kevin Ryan, Jeff Tunnell, Damon Slye, and Richard Hicks.

They formed Dynamix in 1984 and soon published Slye's first game, Stellar 7, through SEC and Chris Cole's Sword of Kadash through Penguin, a company that sold games and graphics tools for Apple II and C64.

Sales of Stellar 7 were somewhat disappointing, despite the fact that a lot of people seemed to have the game. Slye says, "I think we sold around 8,000 units. Hit games were selling on the order of 80,000 units back then. I was mystified, especially since everyone I met had played it and loved it. Apparently it had been heavily pirated." The game had many fans, however, including author Tom Clancy, who once called Slye to tell him how had played it every day when it came out.

Fateful Decisions

With the disappointing sales of their first games, the young company was just scraping by, but they received some encouragement when Joe Ybarra from Electronic Arts called out the blue to suggest making a deal with them. However, nothing happened for several months. "Finally we were about to give up, so we gave him one last call. We let him know it was now or never—we needed a contract or we'd have to close up. He sounded surprised. 'Why didn't you say so earlier?' So he finally invited us to come to EA to pitch a game idea. We all piled in a van and made the long drive to San Mateo." They pitched a game to EA. "After the pitch, all the EA guys around the table one by one gave us the green light," says Slye. "It seemed like a done deal. After they all left the room, Joe nixed the idea! It was quite a letdown." But Ybarra had another idea—a tank game for the still unreleased Amiga. "Joe told us the Amiga was on the order of 10-20 times more powerful than a Commodore 64. And EA was supporting it heavily. So of course we jumped at the chance to develop on it."

While they were developing the tank game, they worked on prototype systems that, according to Slye, "looked like something out of a mad scientist's experiment… It was a steel black box with wires coming out everywhere, and the keyboard had a wooden case. After many all-nighters, and lots of pizza, the result of our efforts was Arcticfox. The game was really an evolution of Stellar 7. Instead of having seven little basic arcade levels, Arcticfox was one epic quest with many simulation and strategy elements. Instead of monochrome wireframe graphics, it had

Early Stellar 7 covers, all designed by Damon Slye.

32 colors and solid-fill. Arcticfox was a cool game, and it was the first original title that EA shipped on the Amiga.

"Unfortunately, the Amiga didn't sell as well as we'd all hoped. I remember an email Trip Hawkins sent out to all the Amiga developers that was titled 'If You Know 6502 Assembly Language, Start Coding!' It was quite a shock after Trip had been singing its praises for so long. But Trip was a smart guy, and his quick about-face was the right decision."

Tunnell remembers a near tragedy that happened during the development of Arcticfox, when their hard drive went down. "It just about took down the whole company. Because of that, we realized we needed to expand." Tunnell found other opportunities for the company, including doing some non-game related projects for Activision.

While Tunnell worked on Skyfox II for EA, Slye went to work on his next original game, Abrams Battle Tank. "Both Spectrum HoloByte and MicroProse had very realistic tank simulations in the works. In our game, the player was put in a command of a lone tank and would take off across the countryside, taking on everything that came his way, including not only other tanks and infantry, but helicopters as well! Ours was not very realistic. Tank warfare does not really lend itself to a solo experience: it's about platoons of tanks mixed in with infantry and air support, but our approach was a reflection of our prior games."

While Slye was working on Abrams Battle Tank, Tunnell became interested in adventure themes and movie-like techniques with a game called Project Firestart.

After Abrams Battle Tank was released in 1988, Dynamix expanded their relationship with Activision and spent the year doing ports and conversions for them. "Damon was working on his next hardcore simulation, A-10 Tank Killer, and I was running the company and managing the other projects." The company actually released an astounding eight products in 1989, including multiple ports for Activision (among them the original MechWarrior game and Ghostbusters II) and their first two as an affiliate publisher for Activision—A-10 Tank Killer and David Wolf: Secret Agent.

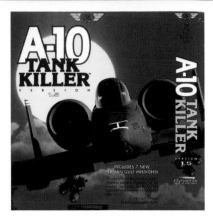

I like to find a subject that offers interesting choices to the player. You don't try to simulate the facts, but to create the same kinds of tensions that would occur in the real world. The important thing is the psychology. I was beginning to develop this understanding in A-10 Tank Killer, and continued it through my other products.
–Damon Slye

DAMON SLYE: WHY THE TANK KILLER?

"A-10 Tank Killer was a big advance—especially for me in understanding how to make a really good simulation. I'd always wanted to do a flight sim for the PC, but I wanted something different from the standard jet sim, which had been done many times. We had learned that basic marketing teaches that when you develop a new product, you can either build something a little better than the competition, or make something different; and that it's almost always smarter to make something different. Find an untapped niche. When I was searching for a cool combat airplane to simulate, I came across the A-10. It was the antithesis of the F-16 and the other modern jets: instead of a sleek, beautiful, swept-wing, supersonic, high-tech dogfighting machine, the A-10 was a green, ugly, straight-winged, slow airplane designed to fight down low,

alongside the grunts on the battlefield. What it lacked in grace and beauty, it made up for in personality and fire power. This was an untapped niche.

"In addition, it seemed to me that since the A-10 was designed to work closely in conjunction with friendly forces on the ground, and against enemy ground units, all of these additional elements would create more compelling gameplay, and more choices for the player, as well as the possibility of introducing some storytelling (through radio messages and requests from friendly ground forces). A-10 Tank Killer was the first game Dynamix published as a label, and it was also the first simulation that supported the new 256-color VGA graphics. It sold very well. Later when the Gulf War came along, the A-10 was featured in many CNN pieces, and the sales of the game really took off."

"Hey, We Should Just Buy You Guys."

"We had to raise about about $1.5 million to become a publisher and fund our own development," remembers Tunnell. "At that time, I brought in Tony Reyneke to help with the business end."

They also sold some 3D technology to Sierra to raise additional capital. Tunnell says, "'Ken [Williams, of Sierra] liked us, and so he said, 'Hey, we should just buy you guys.' Tony and I were tired of the constant financial battles, so we said yes."

"It was a difficult decision for us since we were so emotionally invested in Dynamix," says Slye, "but it was the right decision. Ken, who understood entrepreneurial motivation, did a great job with the transition. He allowed us to maintain our identity and most of our autonomy, provided sufficient incentives to us, and gave us the support we needed to grow into a successful label for Sierra."

The company grew rapidly then, expanding from around 30 people to more than 100. In 1991, they released four titles, including The Adventures of Willy Beamish, Heart of China (in which renowned Oregon-based martial arts instructor Sifu David Leung played a principal role), Nova 9, and Red Baron.

Red Baron was a great game. Set in the biplanes of WWI, it captured the feeling of the relatively slow-moving dog fighting of the era and was a delight to flight simulator fans. Slye comments that "jousting in biplanes at slow speeds, up-close

Some of Damon Slye's research photographs of a real Fokker, from the making of Red Baron.

and personal with the opponent, creates a pretty exciting, compelling experience. It remains one of my personal favorites of the games I've worked on."

Around this time, Tunnell, like Bilbo with the Ring, "was feeling stretched and thin." He broke away to form his own development company, Jeff Tunnell Productions (JTP), but continued to produce products for Dynamix. "We did a remake of Lode Runner, before retro became big, 3-D Ultra Pinball, and Trophy Bass. I remember when I suggested Trophy Bass, everybody laughed at us, and Ken Williams looking me in the eye and saying, 'This had better work.'" It did work. In fact, Trophy Bass was one of Dynamix's most successful games along with 3-D Ultra Pinball. "Few people realize that the simulation games for which we are so well known actually were not our biggest money makers. When I returned as the head of Dynamix in 1995, I developed the idea of making the simpler games like 3-D Ultra to pay for the others."

After Red Baron, Slye began work on Aces of the Pacific, which covered the air war in WWII in the Pacific Theater. "We (or I) were a little too ambitious and optimistic on our goals for this product. Consequently, it was the most grueling development experience the rest of my team members and I ever went through. There was a lot of overtime, and far too many all-nighters. We made the classic mistake of adding people to the project when it was behind schedule, in the hopes of speeding things up. This added to the chaos and probably made it even later that it would have been. Eventually we did finish it (though it had lots of bugs and we had to do a patch), and fortunately it was a big hit. I think we built the right game, but I think my mistake was not realizing how long it would take to build. Had we known, we could have planned a more orderly development."

Slye's last product at Dynamix was Aces Over Europe, which featured WWII air combat in Europe. "We added more combat AI, support for better graphic resolution, new planes, campaigns, and maps. Having learned from our mistakes, we released a clean product with very few bugs, and we managed to work only a modest amount of overtime. This was necessary since many of the team members had been pushing hard for several years. After that I left Dynamix to go back to the University of Oregon for my Bachelor of Science in Math."

In the same year that Aces Over Europe was released, Dynamix released a little game that made a big impression.

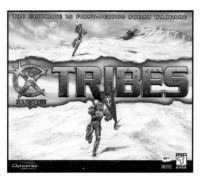

"The idea came from a comment that Damon made, maybe ten years earlier," recalls Tunnel. "It was at a time when products like Music Construction Set were popular. Damon said, 'It would work if we could put together little machines.' I thought, 'Man, that's cool,' and ran off and did a little design. I held onto that design for ten years, but when I started JTP, I thought it was time to do it."

Incredible Fun

Working with Kevin Ryan, Tunnell created the ultimate Rube Goldberg computer game, in which the player had to solve puzzles or create free-form gadgets by putting together an odd assortment of items, such as cannons, light bulbs, bowling balls, cats, pulleys, scissors, and various gears and widgets.

"Incredible Machine was put together by me, one programmer, and one artist on a total budget of about $35,000," says Tunnell. "We did a second product as an add-on and put it in a cool package. We sold about 250,000 units for a total budget of around $75,000 at that point." The Incredible Machine quickly became one of Dynamix's most memorable products.

Dynamix continued to produce quite a few games, but one of the most notable series evolved from the fact that Dynamix had done the first MechWarrior game. When MechWarrior-style games began to be very popular, Dynamix decided to create one of their own and came out with Metaltech: Earthsiege in 1994. Tunnell, who was still at JTP at the time, describes it as a "giant fighting robot game." After

> *I think one of the secrets to a great simulation is the idea that what you want to model—what's really important—is not the specific facts and data associated with the vehicles, but rather the experience and choices that exist in the mind of player. It's all about psychology. So, the designer's focus should not be on the vehicles, but on the experience created within the player's brain. Due to shortcomings in computing power, it's not possible to model reality; therefore, sometimes you have to change the 'facts' to get closer to the truth. I began to understand this in A-10 Tank Killer, and utilized this principle more fully in Red Baron, Aces of the Pacific, and Aces Over Europe.*
> —Damon Slye

several more products in the Earthsiege world, Dynamix took the backstory of Earthsiege and created a much bigger universe for Starseige in 1998. However, Starseige was costly to produce and fell short of the company's expectations. "I think people had grown tired of giant fighting robot games," comments Tunnell.

However, also in 1998, Dynamix came out with Starsiege: Tribes, a first-person shooter designed to be played online by teams of 16 players. Tribes was the first such online cooperative team game, and also featured the ability to play indoors and outside on a large landscape, with the players flying around using personal jet packs. Thousands of Tribes teams were developed and the product was a significant success for Dynamix.

In 2001, Sierra officially closed down the Dynamix offices in Eugene, Oregon, sadly closing a chapter in this history.

Sirius Software

Gebelli was a brilliant programmer whom John Romero describes as "a god." Most of the Apple II programmers of the day imitated Gebelli, to the point of using some of his code. He was a magician with the Apple II computer.

Jerry Jewell relates an interesting story about being approached by Steve Wozniak, the creator of the Apple II. "Wozniak came up to me at the third West Coast Computer Faire, and he wanted to thank me and Nasir. He said, 'I had an airplane accident not long ago and had amnesia. While I was convalescing, they brought me my Apple and your games. I think your games helped me recover my memory.' For years after that, he would invite us to parties and get us VIP tickets to things like the US Festival."

Competing for attention on those racks and shelves (earlier described in the computer stores of the late '70s and early '80s) were the Apple II masterpieces of Nasir Gebelli, designed and crafted for Sirius Software. Like so many early computer game companies, Sirius began in the late '70s, when Jerry Jewell met Nasir Gebelli while working at the local ComputerLand in Sacramento, California. Gebelli had made a little slideshow on the Apple II which the pair turned into the first graphics editing product for the Apple—E-Z Draw. Gebelli then began producing games—first Duck Hunt/Both Barrels and then the Galaxian-like Space Eggs, which he programmed in 30 hours straight. Gebelli next produced Gorgon, a game so much like Defender that Sirius later settled with Williams to avoid a copyright suit.

The early days of Sirius were like those of so many pioneering companies, with work going on in apartments and at night or on weekends. But the sales of Space Eggs and Gorgon really skyrocketed, and then Apple Computer placed a $1.5 million order for their products for redistribution. "We had a $3.5 million first year," says Jewell. "Not bad. Of course, the inventory that Apple bought sat in warehouses and was never distributed."

Iron-on tattoo that came with Space Eggs.

> *"Everybody knew each other. I mean Sierra, Brøderbund. Like if we were going to come out with a racecar game, we'd tell them, and they wouldn't do a racecar game right then. We didn't share programmers or anything, but we did cooperate in that way to avoid diluting the market."*
> –Jerry Jewell

Nasir Gebelli later went on to form his own software company and placed ads like this.

Synapse Software

In 1979, Ihor Wolosenko left a very successful career in high-end commercial photography and cinematography in Boston: "I really got sick of working with art directors." He moved to Berkeley, California and began a personal exploration of the human body and mind. He also encountered video games, notably Galaxian. While conducting hypnosis workshops, he began thinking about the underlying challenges and opportunities offered by video games. "With my studies of neuro-linguistic programming and Tibetan teachings, I was thinking about what's lost in translation without understanding the entire emotional context of a language… How do you translate that into some parallel, but not exactly the same, experience?"

In order to manage his business, he had purchased an Atari 800 computer ("because the Apple II couldn't play Star Raiders, and I wanted this computer to play Star Raiders"), but soon realized that there was only one database program for the computer. Through a friend he had met at an Atari user group, he was introduced to Ken Grant, a database expert. He and Grant spent a year refining a database that Grant had previously hacked together. Their first attempts, released as early as May of '81, were too buggy, and it wasn't until October that they were able to ship the stable product, FileManager 800, under the Synapse Software label. Wolosenko decided to ship in a box instead of the more common baggie. His approach was to use a plain box with a plastic top. By changing the cover sheet on the box, he could ship any software he wanted without having to do a lot of new development.

Wolosenko reasoned that he couldn't go to market with only one product, and Atari user group member Rob Re had the answer—a game he had created called Dodge Racer. Wolosenko made a deal with Re, offering a royalty (somewhere between 10% and 20%) with no money up front. Then another user group member named Mike Potter came forth with a Defender-like game called Protector. Potter had previously published the game with Crystalware, but a dispute over royalties got him fired. Wolosenko published Protector after working with Potter to make some improvements and published it under the Synapse label. Potter went on to produce four more games for Synapse—Protector II, Chicken, Nautilus, and Shadow World (the latter two of which featured split-screen gameplay).

Wolosenko was working with Potter on Chicken and had hired another developer to work on another of his game concepts called Slime, but the other guy turned out to be flaky. "He wasn't getting anywhere and he became impossible to work with. Finally he started having psychic experiences with his disk drive-such as fire coming out of it." By this time, Steve Hales, a high school buddy of Potter's who had been writing $5 Atari 2600 cassette games for a start-up company called Starpath, had joined the team. (Starpath later merged with Epyx in 1983.)

Hales was given the task of completing Slime, but he scrapped the previous work, which wasn't comprehensible, and just started from scratch. Hales accepted the royalty-only deal that had become standard at Synapse, although he later commented, "I look back at that now and I'm just amazed that I just sort of said 'OK'. You know,

I mean I think it's because I was 20 years old." A few months after shipping Slime, however, he realized why he'd signed the contract. "I just remember getting a big check after, you know, couple of months, and that kind of opened my eyes… oh yeah, there is a way to make this work."

Hales' next project was Fort Apocalypse, which had some similarity to the highly popular game Choplifter. "Dan Gorlin and I pretty much came up with the idea just about the same time," says Hales. "I actually met with him years later and had a chat about that. We compared timelines and notes and, you know, we were probably mostly inspired by the failed helicopter rescue in Iran in 1979. For whatever reason that gelled in our brains and we're like, Ok, let's do this. Think about it: Helicopters flying over deserts, flat ground, picking up people and coming back."

Hales differentiates the two games, stating that Gorlin used more physics with more of a "real" feeling to the controls, whereas Hales focused on scrolling through a large open underground world in a helicopter, rescuing people. "A lot of interesting similarities, but very different approach."

Meanwhile, Synapse was growing quickly, and soon they had to move out

of Wolosenko's Berkeley apartment to accommodate 100 people, some of whom were employees, but many of whom were artists working for royalties and using the space and equipment supplied by Synapse. In fact, they moved several times, from a six-bedroom apartment to a 6,500 square foot space and then to a 22,000 square foot office complex. When asked about the size of the new digs soon after the move, Wolosenko quipped, "Well, I like to play basketball in my office."

However, running a company with 100 people to manage wasn't quite the same as having just three or four people around, and Wolosenko became restless. He was spending most of his time helping design and develop the games, like New York City and Picnic Paranoia, and wasn't so interested in solving the day-to-day business problems.

Still, Synapse continued to grow, developing games for the popular Commodore 64 and IBM PC. Hales developed an ambitious game called Dimension X, which tried to synthesize elements of two highly popular games, Star Raiders and the early Star Trek game. Hales attempted to create a more action-oriented game using a 3D graphics effect that he had learned from another high school friend, Stephen Landrum (who later became one of the key engineers for the Atari Lynx). Later describing Dimension X as "a lesson in creative failure," his attempts to develop around this graphical technique led to delays, while Synapse was hyping the game in print. After six months of hype and delays, the game failed to live up to expectations, "and everyone was let down."

Another star developer at Synapse was Cathryn Mataga (then "William"), who created the hit games Shamus and Shamus: Case II, based on the Berzerk style of games but with artistic differences.

155

After their successes, Hales and Mataga teamed up to tackle a new challenge. They believed that there was a market for text-based games, drawing inspiration from Infocom and Scott Adams. Their concept, however, was to bring in real writers (beginning with Robert Pinsky, who wasn't famous yet) and provide them with specialized tools which they named BTZ (Better Than Zork). Hales describes BTZ as a "virtual machine… a natural language parser with very sophisticated macros." They also first coined the term "electronic novel." Here's how Pinsky describes his first phone call with Ihor Wolosenko:

He said, "Are you familiar with computer text adventures?"
I said, "No."
He asked whether I owned a computer.
I said, "No."
Had I ever heard of Zork?
"No."
Would I be interested in writing the text for an interactive computer work?
I said, "Yes, I might be."

According to Pinsky, they had asked him to provide several ideas for these games, which he did. The one he called the "silliest" involved sending the player "on a journey through four minds: an assassinated rock star with a messiah complex, clearly modeled on John Lennon; a bloody dictator inspired by Hitler and Stalin and the rest of the twentieth century's sad litany; a brilliant scientist reminiscent of Marie Curie; and a poet, a nod to the game's creator himself." Much to Pinsky's surprise, this treatment was the one that Wolosenko and company opted for. That idea became Mindwheel, which was a huge hit for Synapse despite the fact that it required two floppy disk drives to run. Synapse had plans for five or six electronic novels, but only three more were released—Essex, Breakers, and Brimstone.

Hales credits Wolosenko for his insight, stating, "Every product Synapse produced had Ihor's touch. I believe that because of Ihor, our quality was better, the designs were more unique, and I was pushed beyond what I thought was possible."

Previous quotes from www.filfre.net/2014/03/mindwhell-or-the-poet-and-the-hackers/ Also recommended for further reading is Nick Montfort's book on interactive fiction, Twisty Little Passages.

Tramieled

In order to diversify, Wolosenko returned to the original Synapse roots and developed several productivity applications for the Atari 800, including an up-to-date database manager/spreadsheet, a word processor, plus stock charting, and statistical analysis programs. He did a deal with Atari, which would sell them under the Synapse brand. "It was just in that time when Jack Tramiel bought Atari and things were going south," adds Wolosenko.

Synapse had to invest a lot of money—over $1.5 million—in producing the software, which would be loaded onto expensive ROM carts, but when they went to a meeting at Atari with Sam Tramiel (Jack's son and the new president), they received some surprising news. According to Hales, "They weren't paying us. He took the contract and ripped it up in front of me. He said, 'This isn't worth the paper that it's printed on.' And he said, 'You can sue me if you want to. You know, I have everybody suing me. If you get 10 cents on the dollar, you know, you're gonna be really lucky. So get the fuck outta here.'"

Strapped for cash, Wolosenko sold Synapse to Brøderbund with the intention of continuing to produce software, but before a year was out, Synapse was gone.

The lawsuit with Atari dragged on with "depositions up the wazoo" and an attorney representing Atari, "a really obnoxious attorney who perfectly mirrored the Tramiels and

SHAMUS: CASE II

their world view. It was a zoo." In the end, however, Atari settled the case for $2.5 million—a million dollars more than they owed. Wolosenko split the money among the other Synapse employees and moved to Hawaii. Later, he started Virtual Arts and worked with Maxis and Will Wright for a while.

Epyx

Epyx games, including the obscure 1982 title New World.

Epyx evolved from Automated Simulations (*see page 58*), and went through several incarnations during the 1980s and into the early 1990s. After Jon Freeman and Anne Westfall left, Jim Connelley continued the company. He released Randy Glover's 1983 hit, Jumpman, which, ironically, was based on the main character from Donkey Kong. By that time, Donkey Kong's Jumpman had become Mario, and apparently Nintendo wasn't concerned about the similarity game, nor of of Jumpman to their similarity to the sequel Jumpman Jr.'s Donkey Kong Jr.

Meanwhile, tensions erupted at Epyx, and Connelley and a bunch of programmers left the company. Michael Katz then took over as head of the Epyx.

Katz instituted immediate changes. "Epyx was known for strategy games," he says, "and the board members wanted to see the company be more mainstream, which meant action. We created a new category, action/strategy, and changed our company logo to show The Thinker with a joystick. The first product in that category was Pitstop, a pure auto race game in which you had to decide based on gas usage and tire wear when to go into the pits. If you waited too long, you'd either run out of gas or tires would blow. You also controlled the pit crew. Pitstop became the demonstration model and lead product of the new positioning of Epyx."

Katz also mentions that Epyx was the first software company to make activity products from toy licenses, such as Mattel's Barbie and Hot Wheels and Hasbro's G.I. Joe.

Epyx was also the first company to categorize their game types and to put a recognizable logo on their products so that consumers could tell what kind of game they were buying. For instance, a mortarboard represented an educational product, while a joystick represented an action game.

Also in 1983, Epyx merged with Starpath (formerly Arcadia), headed by Bob Brown, who had been one of the chief architects of the Atari VCS. Again, according to Katz, "They had shelved a multi-event sports product. We saw it, and with the 1984 Olympics coming to Los Angeles, we told them to finish it and make it an Olympic product. That was Summer Games."

Summer Games was an excellent title that featured several Olympic events and allowed up to eight players to compete. In some cases, two players could compete at the same time. Each event had its own control system and generally involved some frantic keyboarding or joystick manipulations.

Summer Games was the beginning of a highly successful franchise for Epyx, which often defines the company historically. They produced a sequel to Summer Games as well as Winter Games, World Games, and the very popular California Games, in which you competed in skateboarding, footbag, surfing, roller skating, a Frisbee-like game, and BMX racing. 1990's California Games II added hang gliding, jet skiing, skateboarding, bodyboarding, and snowboarding to the series. Perhaps the weirdest game, though not officially part of the "Games" series, was Purple Saturn Day, which involved a sort of intergalactic Olympics with pseudo-futuristic events like time/space piloting.

Epyx produced quite a few other games, including Impossible Mission, an excellent action platform game; their Street Sports line of games; Sub Battle Simulator; and Dragonriders of Pern (based on the Anne McCaffrey novels). Epyx also was the original publisher for the first games from George Lucas' Games Group (*see page 206*).

On the following two pages, we've included a variety of Epyx's titles over the years.

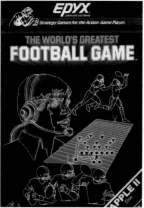

The World's Greatest Football Game was developed by Gilman Louie's Nexa Corporation, later to merge with Spectrum HoloByte (*see page 200*).

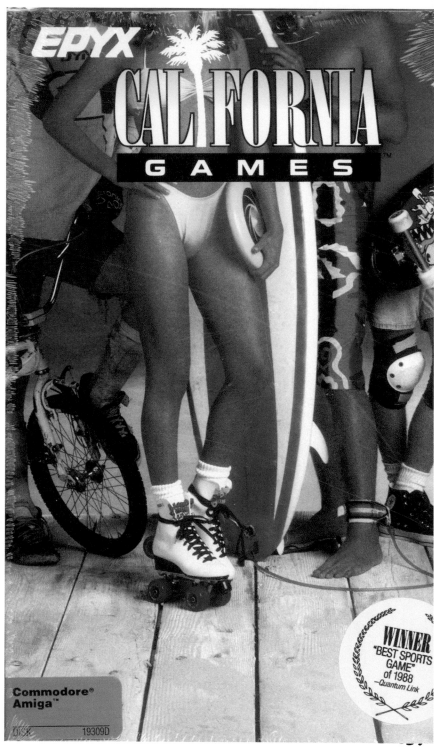

Above: Israeli version of Project Neptune (1989), developed by Info-grames, published in the U.S. by Epyx.

The Computer Game Developers Conference

Chris Crawford had been a game evangelist at Atari. It wasn't surprising when he gathered some of his developer friends at his home in March 1986 for the first Computer Game Developers Conference (although it was dubbed a "symposium" originally). "We sat around in a circle," remembers Crawford, "and everybody just talked about game design issues. I had a clipboard with questions to ask, just in case, but I never needed it. We talked about game design in the morning and business issues in the afternoon."

Original board of directors. Back row: Nicky Robinson, John Powers, Dave Walker, Brenda Laurel; Front row: Tim Brengle, Stephen Friedman, Chris Crawford.

After the first small gathering, Crawford realized how valuable the experience had been. "We learned an enormous amount from each other." So he planned a second conference for September of the same year. This one was more organized, and it took place in a hotel in Milpitas, California. This time 120 people showed up. "I won't say that everybody came," says Crawford, "but a sizeable proportion of the design community showed up. Everybody was wandering around thinking, 'Golly gee, look at all those people facing the same problems as me. I used to be all alone, and now I'm not.'"

Crawford deliberately chose small spaces to ensure that the conference would feel crowded, which would force people to mingle. This mingling was to become a significant aspect of later Computer Game Developers Conferences, until the show went mainstream.

Originally, CGDC gave out awards to publishers. At the time, says Crawford, the publishers were concerned that these conferences were going to become a game designers' union. "They had every right to be concerned—when the developers put their heads together they realized that many were getting screwed. " However, the real purpose of the conferences was to mingle and share information.

Crawford was against having design awards, but ultimately he was outvoted. In the early days, there would be a banquet to accompany the awards ceremony, and most of the developers came in costumes. A guest speaker would deliver some message to the gathered crowd of developers. "The most memorable speaker was novelist Bruce Sterling, who told us we, as game designers, were writing in sand," recalls Crawford. "He gave quite a rousing speech."

The Game Developers Conference expanded. In a politically charged atmosphere, Crawford left the leadership role, and the conference was ultimately sold to publishing company Miller Freeman. The conference now hosts thousands of attendees; however, many who attended it in the early years look back nostalgically to a time when it was just "us," the core developers. Many industries have major shows where manufacturers and publishers display their work. The game industry has always attended shows such as the West Coast Computer Faire, the Consumer Electronics Show, and more recently the games-only Electronic Entertainment Expo (E3), but the Game Developers Conference was unique. It was about the creation of games. It established a community of developers and fostered mutual respect and lifelong friendships.

The original meeting in Chris Crawford's living room. Back:Chris, Brenda Laurel, Cliff Johnson, Brian Moriarty, Dave Walker; Front: Dan Daglow, Tim Brengel, Amanda Goodenough, and unidentified person.

A couple of game designer costumes for the annual costume banquet. Above left: Softalk magazine editor Margot Comstock and Rusel DeMaria at the banquet.

The first Computer Game Developers Symposium. Front row: Gilman Louie, unknown, Jeff Johannigman, Ivan Manley, unknown, unknown, Chris Crawford; Back rows: Stephen Friedman, Sean Barger, unknown, Kellyn Beck, Cliff Johnson, unknown, unknown, Brian Moriarty, Carole Manley, Tim Brengel, Gordon Walton, unknown, Thurston Searfoss, Mike Jones.

The Wizardry of Sir-Tech

(Note: The story of the Wizardry series is very difficult to tell perfectly and completely. Unfortunately, there is considerable contention and disagreement among the principal players in the story, and we have chosen not to take sides. Here, then, are the highly-condensed basics.)

GALACTIC ATTACK

A real-time space war simulation written in USCD PASCAL for your APPLE II or III

Sir-tech SOFTWARE, INC.
6 MAIN STREET, OGDENSBURG, N.Y. 13669
(315) 393-6633

RUNS ON ANY APPLE
(DOS 3.3 or PASCAL, 48K and 1 disk required)

Mortal Enemies

Other than Electronic Arts, most of the early computer game companies were started and run by the game developers themselves. Another exception was Sir-Tech Software, which began more like modern companies, with a combination of creative and business people. In some ways, it all started at Cornell University when Robert Woodhead had a nasty surprise. "I was thrown out of college for a year for low grades. I guess I had been spending too much time programming and playing games on the PLATO network."

Andrew Greenberg was the system administrator for that same PLATO system Woodhead had been spending too much time on. "Part of my job was to kick people off of the games, and Robert had made it his mission in life to play games on PLATO. So we were automatically each other's enemies."

During his imposed year off, Woodhead wrote Galactic Attack, a single-player version of one of the PLATO games, and began work on a dungeon-style game he was going to call "Paladin." A few weeks after beginning Paladin, he heard about another student who had written a dungeon game. It was Andrew Greenberg, who remembers, "He was stunned to hear that I'd written a game because I was, by definition, a professional spoilsport."

Woodhead remembers, "Andrew had two things going for him. He had already written a game in BASIC, and he had a really good name for it—Wizardry." The two met and agreed to collaborate, dividing responsibilities during a weekend meeting. However, their partnership was anything but smooth. Greenberg recounts their working style: "We were like night and day. We spent all our time quibbling and criticizing each other. Our friends said if you locked us in a room together, there'd be a lot of screaming and yelling, and later, when you opened the door, there'd be blood dripping from the walls, and in the center of the room there would be a diskette." Today, the two are great friends, but their mutual respect only became clear later, when they each read positive statements about the other in the media.

During that same period, Woodhead had been programming some database and accounting programs for Fred Sirotek, an entrepreneur who owned several businesses. After showing some products at a computer show, Woodhead and Norm Sirotek, Fred's youngest son, decided to form Sirotech Software in 1981. Their first product was Info-Tree, a database created by Woodhead. The company was ultimately renamed Sir-Tech, according to Robert Sirotek, "because Norm and I kept getting phone calls in the middle of the night and early morning from end users."

Wizardry inspired and entertained a whole generation of game players, including Robin Williams, Harry Anderson, and the Crown Prince of Bahrain, who actually called Sir-Tech on the phone.

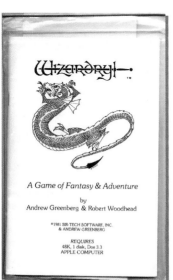

Wizardry

Months later, at the first Boston Applefest in 1981, Woodhead brought with him possibly the first public beta version of a computer game. The beta version was called Dungeons of Despair, and it consisted of a few specially designed levels of Wizardry. He sold them at full price, promising the completed game later and asking for feedback. "We had a clue that we were onto something when we counted the money that night in the hotel room and there were several thousand dollars on the bed.

"The Dungeons of Despair scenario was us exercising everything we could do to make sure the game was solid," says Woodhead. "We wanted people who bought it to test it for us. Proving Grounds of the Mad Overlord was later play-tested for two to three months by fanatical players running 24 hours a day. They found very subtle bugs and really did tweak and tune the difficulty of the game considerably."

One of Wizardry's ultimate strengths was the extent to which it was tested and played before it was finally released. Both Woodhead and Greenberg admit that they

owe a great deal to the many testers who spent hours on the game. They also drew inspiration from Dungeons & Dragons and from the PLATO games. "We added a concept of story and plotline to what we'd seen on PLATO, where it was 'hack-hack-kill-kill-occasionally something interesting happens-run away…'" adds Woodhead. Proving Grounds of the Mad Overlord, the first Wizardry game, was a great success. More importantly, through a combination of mesmerizing gameplay and effective marketing, it became one of the most influential products in the early history of computer games. Rob and Norm Sirotek, who ran the company, concentrated on marketing the games and building the infrastructure of the business while the design duo of Woodhead

The first Wizardry, which featured a faux-3D maze, a host of imaginative enemies, and lots of diabolical tricks and traps, was also one of the first computer products to come out in a box.

163

and Greenberg came right back with a sequel, Knight of Diamonds—essentially a scenario disk for the same game with new dungeons and some tougher puzzles. (Clever players with advanced characters figured out how to teleport to the bottom and work their way back, thereby avoiding some of the challenges.)

Sometime around the creation of the third Wizardry, Legacy of Llylgamyn, Greenberg moved to Boston to begin work on Star Saga, an amazing text-based science fiction adventure. Woodhead then created The Return of Werdna (Wizardry IV), the toughest of the initial Wizardry epics, with Roe Adams. The concept was great—this time you play the evil Werdna out for revenge—but in the end, Wizardry IV proved possibly too difficult. In addition, it was completed late, coming out in December 1987, and by then the Wizardry series was losing ground.

The Next Phase

Enter David Bradley, whose first published game was Battle of the Parthian Kings from Avalon Hill. Afterward, he began working on a role-playing game, but Avalon Hill didn't want to compete with Sir-Tech and suggested he offer his game to them.

Bradley went to Sir-Tech and struck a deal to create Wizardry V: Heart of the Maelstrom. However, Wizardry IV wasn't yet complete, and Sir-Tech opted to wait and deliver the games in order. According to Bradley, it was two years before Wizardry V finally came out in November 1988, although it was completed much earlier. Wizardry V also included story elements and an introduction by Andrew Greenberg and his wife, Sheila.

According to Robert Sirotek, Bradley's work on Heart of the Maelstrom may have saved the company.

"Wizardry IV was by far our worst commercial failure. Wizardry V saved the Wizardry product line. We very likely would not have continued the Wizardry products if it were not for the success of Wizardry V."

Along with Woodhead, Bradley credits Richard Garriott's Ultima series with being one of his main inspirations. "I considered that Heart of the Maelstrom was a greatly expanded role-playing game. Ultima was the other series putting content back into the games, and, as Garriott went with a third-person view of the characters, I elected to stay with the traditional Wizardry first-person viewpoint."

Bradley knows Wizardry as few others could, given that he rewrote the whole system from the ground up in Wizardry VI: Bane of the Cosmic Forge. He expresses great respect for the work of Woodhead and Greenberg, and worked hard to preserve what he calls, "the spirit that makes Wizardry Wizardry." Among the changes Bradley implemented was the use of full-color graphics for the first time in the Wizardry series, which up until that point had stayed with the original line-drawn mazes.

Wizardry VII: Crusaders of the Dark Savant was a complex game that pitted the player against several computer-controlled enemies, all seeking the same 13 map pieces that could lead to a great artifact. In this game, players were transported from the world of the previous Wizardry titles into a new scenario, which included some surprises

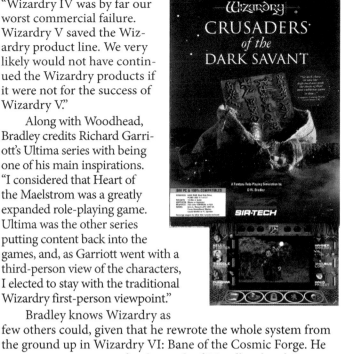

Deep Space was one of Sir-Tech's few non-Wizardry titles, most notable because it was created by Paul Neurath and Edward Lerner, who later went on to form Looking Glass Studios and produce many great games, including Ultima Underworld.

such as aliens and space travel. Bradley comments, "I regard this game as my true masterpiece. It was very non-predictable and nonlinear. Everybody who played it had a different experience."

Brenda Brathwaite (Romero) joined Sir-Tech in the early '80s after learning of the company in a casual conversation with a friend at a basketball game. Over the years, she watched and learned from previous designers and credits Bradley as her primary design mentor. In 2001, Sir-Tech finally released Wizardry 8, possibly the final installment of this great series, and one of the best. Designed by Brathwaite, it won multiple awards from the games press.

Below: Another one of Sir-Tech's early products was a great maze game called Star Maze. You flew a sort of Asteroids-style ship through a complex series of mazes, shooting and avoiding surreal enemies like the crawling caterpillar and often bouncing off the walls. It was great fun.

"These cards are from a Japanese card game based on the Legacy of Llylgamyn, called Tiltowait. Wizardry fans will remember that Tiltowait was one of the most powerful spells in the game. I was pleased to learn that their Fighter character is called Mifune because, back when I played the game obsessively, my Samurai was also named Mifune, after the great Japanese actor Toshiro Mifune." (RDM)

Wizardry was huge internationally. Here are a French version of Wizardry, a Japanese board game, and a detail from a Japanese anime laserdisc. Also below are Sir-Tech's founders in Japan with executives from Banpresto Co. Ltd., a division of Bandai, while they were opening up connections with the Japanese console makers. Wizardry was among the first computer games ported to the Famicom and Nintendo Entertainment System.

Opportunity Knocks: The Story of SSI

Joel Billings in 1980.

In the summer of 1979, Joel Billings was on vacation and preparing to start business school in the fall. A champion player of paper and board war games, Billings considered creating war games on computers, thinking there might be potential sales in the emerging microcomputer market. Having just studied marketing surveys in school, he decided to start by putting out a questionnaire in a couple of local hobby/game shops. Being in Silicon Valley at the time, he found that about 20 percent of the war gamers who filled out his survey had access to computers. On the questionnaire he had written,

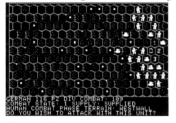
The 116th Panzer Division (next to the #3 attacker) is ready to join in the attack on the unfortunate U.S. 106th Infantry Division in 1981's Tigers in the Snow, a hex-based version of Battle of the Bulge.

"If you're a programmer and interested in programming war games, call me "

Two important events occurred then. First, he received a call from John Lyons, an experienced programmer and a war gamer. Lyons' comment was, "Now I know what opportunity looks like when it knocks."

The second important event was meeting Trip Hawkins, then at Apple, who convinced Billings that the Apple II was the way to go. "I credit Trip with evangelizing the Apple II to me, whereas I only knew about the TRS-80, which would have been the wrong computer."

Billings met with investors, which is how he first heard about Trip, but ultimately started Strategic Simulations, Inc. using family money instead of outside investment. SSI's first game was Computer Bismarck. Billings says, "We started with an easy situation. John called it a Fox and

Hounds game. We realized that artificial intelligence would be a real challenge, but in this one all you had to worry about was, 'I'm the Bismarck and all I want to do is run away.' Our early AI was more like an expert system. Using our expert war game experience, we asked ourselves what should it do in each situation and had it pick path 1 or path 2, and so forth." Despite its simplicity, the artificial opponent for the solitaire game—Otto von Computer, as the programmers called him—was so respected that he stayed around for 1981's Torpedo Fire.

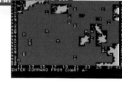
After several simulated days, the British admiral (human player) has yet to catch sight of the legendary Bismarck as its artificial admiral (Otto von Computer) attempts to break out into the North Atlantic.

Business in High Gear

By 1982, SSI had published 17 games, with eight of them using the familiar hex grids of war games. Most importantly, the fledgling SSI had already recruited several designers and programmers for a raft of new games. Charlie Merrow (later to design Fighter Command) would design Computer Air Combat (the game that inspired Russell Sipe to start Computer Gaming World magazine) and Computer Baseball. Dan Bunten (*see page 182*) was recruited to design Computer Quarterback and Cartels & Cutthroats. Roger Keating (later of SSG fame with Reach for the Stars and Warlords) would program Southern Command with its version of the Arab-Israeli War of 1973; Gary Grigsby (later of Kampfgruppe, War in Russia, Pacific War, and Battle of Britain fame) to design several games; and the trio of David Landry, Chuck Kroegel, and Dave Walker were recruited to program Tigers in the Snow and Battle of Shiloh.

In addition to these games, SSI published two hybrid board game/computer game efforts: Napoleon's Campaigns 1813 & 1815 and Road to Gettysburg. Both games came with board game maps, but all movement and combat was resolved on the computer. The games were not entirely popular because they portrayed "fog of war" and "limited intelligence" all too well. It was difficult to tell what was going on, even with the map. Later, a version of Napoleon's Campaigns allowed you to resolve battles with 15mm miniatures and type in the results so that the computer could referee strategic movement and set up smaller battles for you.

Although Gary Grigsby would unveil the first two "monster games" on the computer during 1982 (Guadalcanal Campaign) and 1983 (Bomb Alley), and AI genius Roger Keating was putting the finishing touches on RDF 1985 (his hypothetical war between the U.S. and Soviets in the Persian Gulf), SSI wasn't betting all of its marbles on historical combat. Contemporary with Grigsby's games were Paul Murray's The Warp Factor (ship-to-ship combat in outer space) and Tom Reamy's Galactic Gladiators (man-to-man tactical combat with a scenario editor).

Also in 1983, SSI unveiled a boxing strategy game called Ringside Seat. The boxing game played well and featured statistics on all the famous athletes in the days before player associations and major sports federations demanded a royalty for such use. There was only one problem. The freelance designer who sold the game to SSI used the statistics from an Avalon Hill board game called Title Bout to create his database. Indeed, entire game mechanics were stolen from the board game. Naturally, Avalon Hill took legal action against SSI—also including Computer Bismark in the case. It was ultimately settled out of court. Ironically, Avalon Hill had published a computer version of Title Bout, but it was only available on one computer platform, and it didn't sell very well. However, James V. Trunzo, the game's designer, later used his database and mechanics to create other computer boxing games, such as APBA Pro Boxing.

Joel Billings was flabbergasted at the Ringside Seat designer, because he had specifically asked if any games had been used as source material. Now, he had to settle out of court with Avalon Hill yet again.

SSI put out three other titles in 1983 that offered nonmilitary challenges. Epidemic! required players to stop a space spore–spawned epidemic. Geopolitique 1990 required diplomatic as well as military acuity, and Fortress was an abstract war game (somewhere between Othello and Go) that "learned" how you played and built strategies against you.

In 1984, the company broke into the fantasy adventure field with Questron. Once again, they became embroiled in a legal situation when it turned out that the designers of Questron had basically redone Ultima. "We were showing Questron at a trade show in January, two weeks before it was to come out," says Billings, "and some Origin guys came out and said it was a rip-off of Ultima." Some tough negotiations later, SSI worked out an agreement. "At that stage, there was no way we were not going to release it," Billings recalls. Questron was not only popular with SSI's customer base, but was successful

John Lyons

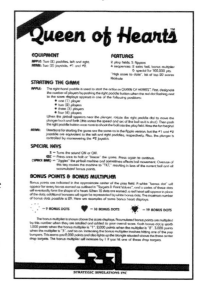

SSI did mostly war games, but they did put out a few other titles. Here's the instruction manual to an obscure pinball game called Queen of Hearts.

enough to attract the attention of the new powerhouse on the block, Electronic Arts. EA hired the brothers who designed Questron to build Legacy of the Ancients for their 1987 season. This time, SSI was the company taking legal action, and the brothers were required to fulfill their Questron contract and design Questron II for SSI. Of course, real gamers knew that Questron II was pretty much Questron III. The same brothers went on to create The Legend of Blacksilver for Epyx, which could be considered Questron IV.

With Napoleon's Campaigns 1813 & 1815 and Road to Gettysburg, the maps were so large that you needed reference points on the screen and a printed map on the side in order to keep up with the action.

Maze Rats: An entire gang of robots (G,A,R,M,S.) has ganged up on the Armour team (Q, L) after traversing the maze from right to left.

Ringside Seat: Using the Stick & Move strategy, Ali was able to hold off Sonny Liston for a unanimous decision in three rounds.

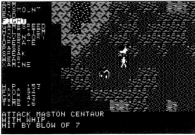

Any resemblance between Questron's graphics and those of the Ultima series was purely intentional.

50 Mission Crush was not a very action-packed game, and, although this WWII bomber simulator lacked any kind of flight simulator mechanics or visuals, it actually simulated the frightening sense of impending doom that the bomber crew might have felt while dodging flak and enemy fighters. A lot of missions failed, and as a player, there was nothing you could do about it.

As always, SSI continued to intersperse war games of the highest possible quality into the mix. The military games included Gary Grigsby's War in Russia and a couple of new takes on the genre—a tactical battle game called Field of Fire and a flight simulator of sorts called 50 Mission Crush. Yet, the publisher was unafraid to experiment with games like Rails West! (railroad building in the western frontier of the U.S.) and Colonial Conquest (multiplayer strategy in the expansionist era).

For war gamers, however, the high-water marks for SSI war games came in the mid-'80s. Kampfgruppe, the award-winning game of armored combat on WWII's eastern front, was hailed by every reviewer and made Grigsby into a cult hero among military buffs. It was also the era of Gettysburg: The Turning Point by Chuck Kroegel and David Landrey. The game marked the beginning of an American Civil War series where, unlike previous games with their fixed historical orders of battle, you could be surprised in the same way that a real general could be surprised. The Civil War series was a staple for the company until everything was overwhelmed by the Advanced Dungeons & Dragons phenomenon.

Yet many people forget that SSI's venture into the world of AD&D actually followed a successful line of fantasy releases, such as Wizard's Crown, Gemstone Warrior, and Phantasie. In fact, the original idea for the AD&D series was to use the Wizard's Crown engine and force-feed the licensed game's role-playing mechanics into it. Fortunately, that didn't happen, and the Gold Box engine evolved out of this initiative. (See the following "Dungeons & Dragons" section for more information.)

War gamers felt slightly miffed when SSI became so successful with its role-playing license, but the truth was that

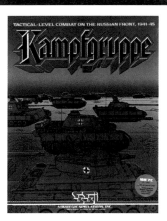

during the height of AD&D success, SSI was publishing more military titles per year than ever before. Plus, some of Gary Grigsby's most intricate designs appeared in this era.

The Confederate commander avoids conventional wisdom and charges the Union cavalry on the first turn of Gettysburg: The Turning Point.

Games like the Panzer Strike series, Second Front (War in Russia on a grand scale), and eventually, Pacific War, offered challenges never experienced before. The granddaddy of all strategic-level war games, Pacific War was so intricate that experienced war gamers used a two-page checklist to make sure they took advantage of every move.

Dungeons & Dragons

In 1987, TSR Incorporated informed interested bidders that it was ready to license Dungeons & Dragons to a computer game company. D&D had inspired many games already, such as Dungeon Master, Wizardry, and Ultima, but none of them were licensed, and TSR got nothing from them. They had looked into making computer

Advanced Dungeons & Dragons
COMPUTER PRODUCT

POOL OF RADIANCE

C-64/128

APPLE

AMIGA

A FORGOTTEN REALMS
Fantasy Role-Playing Epic, Vol. 1

SSI

STRATEGIC SIMULATIONS, INC.

games themselves (such as a combat flight simulator with wire-framed graphics based on their Dawn Patrol game) and discovered that it was not as easy as it looked and not a practical direction for them.

At least ten companies contended for the potentially rich license. One of them was SSI, and Joel Billings remembers: "If you think of it, they were really doing war games. So we thought, who would be better for it than us? Most of our guys were both war gamers and RPG players, so we took this very seriously and outlined a whole series of different products, not just one. In the final decision, we were up against EA and Origin, but they were just proposing one title, sort of like the movie license model. I think our broader vision won us the contract."

The deal was consummated at CES, and SSI started work on several titles: Pool of Radiance, an adventure that took place in TSR's Forgotten Realms campaign setting and the first of the Gold Box series; Heroes of the Lance, an action game that was developed in Europe by U.S. Gold and did best on the Nintendo Entertainment System; and Dungeon Master's Assistant, for use with D&D campaigns.

Similar in appearance to Interplay's The Bard's Tale, Pool of Radiance offered much more detail and number crunching. More importantly, it offered authentic D&D statistics, character classes, alignment, mechanics, and nomenclature. Among other innovations, the game placed the characters in a mock-3D terrain and used three levels of sprite graphics to suggest the differences between short-, medium-, and long-range encounters.

The next Gold Box game was Curse of the Azure Bonds, where SSI ran into a play balance dilemma. By allowing players to bring experienced characters from Pool of Radiance, they had to make the game playable for beginners and for people with built-up characters. Their solution was to have most of the player's

weapons and equipment stolen at the beginning of the game. They took a lot of criticism for this decision and had to come up with new solutions for play balancing in the future.

The D&D license was a huge boost for SSI. War games had always had a limited audience. Fantasy had more players, and D&D was as big as you could get in the fantasy genre. At that time, SSI entered into a complex distribution deal with Electronic Arts, which had the best distribution in the business, giving up 20 percent of the company for a $2 million cash infusion. However, by the time SSI paid substantial royalties to TSR and the distribution share to Electronic Arts, their overall profitability suffered. Billings had this to say: "The deal with EA was both good and bad for SSI. It ended up being one of the key factors in SSI's ultimate demise. But if I had it to do over again, I'd probably do the same thing. I'm not much for second-guessing."

SSI did continue to produce war games, but it was clear that the fantasy genre was their best source of revenue, and much of their resources were devoted to those games going into the 1990s.

By 1990, SSI realized it was time to look for a new approach, and so they teamed up with Westwood and used their 3D flight engine to create the landmark product, Eye of the Beholder, where you flew dragons instead of airplanes.

Publicity photo of Trip Hawkins and Joel Billings announcing the partnership between EA and SSI.

Panzer General, Steel Panthers, and Other Generals

One of the most successful and innovative war games of the 1990s was inspired largely by Daisenryaku, a Japanese war game for the Sega Genesis that was never released in the U.S. This game managed to captivate the interest of many of the designers at SSI. The title it inspired was Panzer General, a campaign game which placed the player in the role of a German general fighting a series of battles played across beautiful landscapes. Panzer General's success spawned a number of other products, and the graphics continued to improve with almost every new version.

In the initial Panzer General, you could only play the role of a German commander. Later releases allowed you to take any side of both the historical and fantasy conflicts portrayed.

The units in People's General looked so crisp that they made the battlefields and buildings look unrealistic.

Although Allied General, the first sequel, was a disappointment (having been created by an outside developer), later products included Fantasy General, which introduced fantasy elements to the series (such as mage or warrior campaigns); Panzer General II, with options to play German, U.S., British, or Russian sides; and People's General, which was set in the post–Cold War era. Finally, they released Rites of War, a well-designed Warhammer variant based on the Panzer General II engine, and Panzer General 3D Assault, but these last two suffered from coming out after the company had been purchased by a series of new owners and never got much marketing. By the time the company released People's General, a postmodern Communist campaign using the same basic engine, the units looked so real that they upstaged the landscapes on the battlefields, causing them to look phony by comparison.

Panzer General II not only offered multiplayer play and better graphics than its predecessor, it also featured campaigns from four different sides: U.S., British, German, and Soviet.

All the General series games featured smooth-as-silk mouse interfaces. The games flowed well, and the sound effects and voice acting were terrific. The games were not without controversy, however. The details of explosions and bodies flying caused some stir, and there was criticism of the game's perspective being exclusively from the Nazi side.

The truth is that SSI's Joel Billings knew all too well the alliterative marketing axiom that nothing makes money in war games except for "Nukes, Nazis, and NATO (and sometimes, Napoleon)." In addition, Billings knew that in games that revolved around tanks and planes, the Germans had the best equipment through much of the war. So, it is no surprise that the first entry in what came to be known as the General series was based on German air and armor.

Steel Panthers

In 1995, about 18 months in marketing time after Panzer General's phenomenal success, another series did extremely well for SSI. Again, the subject matter was tied to World War II. SSI's longtime genius, Gary Grigsby, returned to the scene of many of his finest moments. The designer of Kampfgruppe, Overrun, Panzer Strike, Typhoon of Steel, Guadalcanal Campaign, Bomb Alley, War in Russia, Second Front, and the great classic, Pacific War, created what many believe to be the ultimate armor simulation in Steel Panthers.

The original Steel Panthers offered tactical combat with meticulously modeled tanks and terrain that looked almost three-dimensional. Scenarios could be played in a couple of hours, and a scenario editor allowed players to build their own combat scenarios. The complexity of play was represented by the program's translucent calculations for armor penetration, movement effects upon aim, and terrain effects. The simplicity was enhanced by having each unit's movement range highlighted on the map, as well as a host of additional options for moving entire tank divisions at once (in formation!).

Where Panzer General had great explosions and special effects to reflect the results of battles, Steel Panthers allowed you to lay down smoke to avoid battles or use indirect fire to attack the enemy. Instead of merely seeing the final results of combat, war gamers were treated to watching shells bounce harmlessly off approaching Tiger tanks and infantry ambushes pop up in the detailed wooded terrain. Steel Panthers also offered a robust morale model that often had outnumbered and outgunned units retreating whether you ordered them to do so or not.

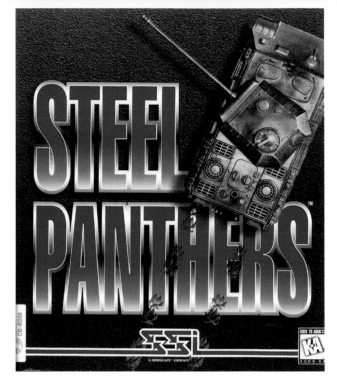

DAISENRYAKU

I remember seeing a parade of people coming in and out of Chuck Kroegel's office when I was visiting in late 1993. They were playing Daisenryaku, a Sega Genesis game from Japan. I remember their comments about the fluid way that you could order units about with the Sega controller, as well as the emotional stake you would gain by shepherding units from one battle to the next. The next time I visited SSI, the Daisenryaku addicts had managed to incubate that something special into something even more special—Panzer General. (JW)

More Panthers and Still More Scenarios

User-generated scenarios started to proliferate and to be swapped over the still-new World Wide Web. Then came Steel Panthers II in 1996. Where Grigsby's modern armor sequel to Kampfgruppe in the mid-'80s, Mech Brigade, had been superior in design but inferior in sales, the modern armor sequel to Steel Panthers was a major success. Perhaps the successful implementation of armor in Desert Storm affected sales. Perhaps it was the ability to use a familiar system in launching guided missiles and building tactics around reactive armor, or the ability to play campaigns where you could upgrade units after, and purchase support units before, the battle. Players who thought Desert Storm was too one-sided could play earlier Arab-Israeli conflicts or simulate Korean and Vietnamese conflict actions. Better yet, they could continue to build their own scenarios… and they did.

In 1997, Steel Panthers III released. It used the same basic engine as the prior two efforts, but it was significantly more complex. Steel Panthers III offered 40 scenarios and six campaigns. The scale was enlarged to 200 yards per hexagon, compared to the 50-yard hexes of the previous games. Most importantly, players could no longer simply charge forward in a modern parody of the Light Brigade. A new command control point system meant that players had to make reasonable decisions that reflected solid combined arms doctrine. Although Steel Panthers III covered everything from WWII to the modern day, it was more of a complete modern warfare game than its predecessors. Combined arms were much more important, and aficionados are continuing to build their own scenarios and distribute them on the web to this day.

Trip Hawkins & Electronic Arts

It seems that some people are destined to do great things. Trip Hawkins is one of them. Most people know that Trip Hawkins started Electronic Arts and helped create a revolution in the business of computer games. Few, however, know his roots.

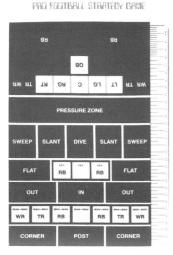

"I got my professional feet wet by starting a little business to market a tabletop football game I'd devised in 1972," says Hawkins. "In the days before computers, I played not just board games, but the kind of board games that simulated interesting things, like NFL football. Accu-Stat was an excellent game and used dice and charts to allow realistic uses of strategy and player characteristics and stats. It was the precursor to John Madden Football.

"Of course, I was 19 years old and had no idea what I was doing, so the business failed. But it was perhaps the most important experience of my work life because I discovered my love for creating games could combine with a passion for entrepreneurship, and that failure could be used to just add fuel to the furnace. For years, my best friends would say that the only reason I started EA was so that someday I could make another football game.

"In 1980, I had only been out of school for two years, and yet I knew that I was already part of something very special and powerful and that I would have a very interesting career. At Apple I learned a lot about thinking big from Mike Markkula and Steve Jobs, and I learned how you could be a small company in a huge industry and still think and be the leader. This was reflected in the 1980 National Computer Conference trade show, where tiny Apple was a darling of the show and showed a lot of class by taking all the show attendees to Disneyland for free.

Electronic Arts: The Plan

Not EA, but an interesting poster found on the wall in Trip's home.

The original plan for Electronic Arts involved three principles that turned out to be prescient. "After failing with Accu-Stat, I was determined to start another business and to do so successfully," recounts Hawkins. "So I

Trip Hawkins with John Couch in 1981, examining a memory subsystem circuit board for the Apple Lisa. "Since I helped Apple get a great story," says Hawkins, "Steve Jobs was pleased and had this photo framed and gave it to me as a gift."

was more deliberate and patient about timing and wisdom. I knew what I wanted to do and collected ideas and thoughts over a period of years. But I also felt that a really 'big idea' was required to make a business work.

"The big idea for EA was the concept of the software artist—treating the creative talent like artists. But there were two other ideas at the founding, represented in this plan, that proved in the long run to be equally critical. One was organized, efficient, cross-platform development using our own proprietary tools and technology. The other was direct distribution to retail stores. This original plan document is a bit amazing in how well it predicts the future, although our financial model for EA was ludicrously optimistic, as is the case for many start-ups. What made EA a winning company was the combination of strategic vision with the raw ability to adapt from mistakes and adjust and stick with it."

October 8, 1982: Page from the original business plan for Electronic Arts, then called SoftArt.

In famous venture capitalist Don Valentine's office in 1982, presenting the plan. Dave Evans was one of the new company's first producers. Trip came up with the idea of a game producer by combining aspects of film, recording, and business software development project management into the job. The role of "producer" has remained a standard part of game development ever since.

SUMMARY

THE OPPORTUNITY

The retail value of home computer software will grow from $100 million in 1982 to $2.9 billion in 1987. During this time the home computer will emerge as a significant new communications medium for play, discovery, fantasy, and experience for 22 million upper income, well-educated families worldwide. SoftArt hopes to become one of the leading software suppliers to this market.

THE BUSINESS

A system for producing and marketing a broad line of advanced consumer computer software developed by independent designers.

THE STRATEGY

Starting in 1983 with 18 products, primarily "better games", SoftArt will develop a broad software product line for the home. It will be critical to develop three assets: Talent, The Marketing Delivery System, and Technical Leadership.

TALENT will be developed via a group of "Producers" who will synthesize the functions of movie producers, record industry A & R people, and technical product managers. Their goal will be to get the best possible home computer software products out of independent designers working under contract.

THE MARKETING DELIVERY SYSTEM will include direct sales to retailers, bold and visionary print advertising, and innovative and distinctive product packaging and point of sale merchandising. The goal is to achieve broad distribution with a broad, branded product line that sells itself.

TECHNICAL LEADERSHIP will include the development of advanced software tools, anticipating hardware technology advances, and providing assistance and creative stimulation to designers. The goal is to efficiently produce better products that get the most out of the consumer's computer.

KEY FIRST YEAR EVENTS:
10-82	First designers sign
11-82	Company debuts at AppleFest
12-82	Major financing complete
1-83	Show first products at CES
4-83	First products ship
9-83	Company turns profitable

FINANCIAL GOALS:
	'83 Sales	'84 Sales	'87 Sales	Long-Term PAT
	$4.2M	$20M	$192M	12%

FUNDING REQUIREMENTS: $2,000,000 additional investment ($206,000 already invested)

Presenting the EA business plan, with Rich Melmon, the first employee Hawkins hired as the initial sales and marketing executive. Hawkins is leaning on his "trusty" Apple II, which was also used by Bruce Zweig to program initial versions of his best-selling MasterType game.

173

Leave the Room,
Lose Your Vote

Hawkins' first proposed name for the new company was Amazin' Software, which was universally disliked by the first 11 employees, including Bing Gordon, who recounts the naming meeting: "We were going to go with SoftArt, but it was taken, so we had a meeting at Pajaro Dunes to determine a name. Trip said we had to have a name before the night was over, and anyone who went to sleep lost their vote. That was typical of Trip. Trip could always wear people out. He could go and go. If you leave the room, you lose your vote. The other part is, if you're in the room, you get a vote. Anyway, I liked Electronic Artists because it reminded me of Mary Pickford and the original United Artists 'anti-studios' in Hollywood. However, Steve Hayes pointed out that we weren't the artists... that we worked with them. We didn't develop our own in-house project until five years later, with Skate or Die. Tim Mott suggested Electronic Arts. It was after midnight by then, and that's the name we adopted."

David Maynard at one of the early cross-platform artist stations, circa 1984.

"EA's first real office, where we had a lease and our own furniture, was in San Mateo on Campus Drive with a nice view," according to Trip Hawkins. "Here, in one of the two conference rooms with windows, Steve Hayes and I are obviously enjoying the view while contemplating something important. This would have been in 1983. Steve and David Maynard were the first two technical staff hired by EA, both joining in 1982 prior to our first venture funding."

Bing Gordon holding the football (below) at one of EA's Pajaro Dunes retreats, probably circa 1984.

EA's first retailer proudly displaying his Electronic Arts releases.

Early Days at EA

May 1983 at the first EA warehouse in South San Francisco. "All 21 employees at that time went to the warehouse to pack and ship the first orders in company history," says Hawkins. "I was taking a break and probably looking around for something else to do. I would later personally hand off the first order to a customer who drove over to pick it up."

I founded EA in 1982, and we shipped our first games in May of 1983. By September, we were already way behind on our plan and feeling like we might go bust. These key objectives were posted around the company walls and given to everyone during that stressful launch period, and much discussion took place about them on an ongoing basis. These objectives became a rallying cry for survival and a kiln for the EA culture.

–Trip Hawkins, founder, Electronic Arts

KEY OBJECTIVES
TO BE MET BY 10/1/83

1. 800 GALLERIES PROPERLY INSTALLED

2. 8 COMMODORE PRODUCTS "IN THE BAG"

3. 1,000 COMMODORE OUTLETS SIGNED UP

4. ALL SET FOR COMMODORE AND IBM OPERATIONS

5. "BETA" SOFTWARE FOR 2 HOME MANAGEMENT TITLES

6. EVERYONE READY FOR SEASONAL VOLUME

7. SUCCESSFULLY HOLD OVERHEAD SPENDING AND HEADCOUNT

8. EVERYONE'S SANITY INTACT!

90% done

impossible! we're all insane already!

Among the early employees depicted packing software are Susan Lee-Merrow (above left), who went on to become a long-time executive at Brøderbund and Lucas Learning, and Nancy Fong (right), now senior director of global brand partnerships

175

We See Farther

Right: This handmade mockup of EA's "We See Farther" poster was used at the West Coast Computer Faire in 1982. It became part of what was then known as "The Manifesto."

"This poster, made in 1982, captured in one image the concepts and vision of Electronic Arts," Trip Hawkins tells us. "'We See Farther' became our rallying cry and a touchstone in hard times that made us keep going. It was conceived of by Andy Berlin and Rich Silverstein, who EA worked with as freelancers and who made EA their first client when they formed their own agency. GBS became a major force in advertising and did the famous 'SEGA!' campaign years later."

"Can a Computer Make You Cry?" was the first EA poster/ad generally distributed. It appeared in several magazines in 1982, including Scientific American. For the first time, the actual developers of games were featured. Included in the picture are Mike Abbott and Mark Alexander (far left front and back rows), who created Hard Hat Mack, EA's first platform hit; Dan Bunten (back row, second from left), who created M.U.L.E. for EA; Jon Freeman and Anne Westfall (third and fourth from left, back row), creators of Archon and co-creators of Murder on the Zinderneuf; Bill Budge (far right, back row), creator of Pinball Construction Set; John Field (second from left in front), who created Axis Assassin and The Last Gladiator; David Maynard (front right), who created Worms?

Top left: An early EA group shot, including a very young Paul Reiche III, who helped design both Archon and Murder on the Zinderneuf. Top Right: Year by year, the company continued to grow, as evidenced by this later photo. Among the recognizable faces in the crowd is Chris Crawford, who worked at EA at one point in his long career.

WE SEE FARTHER

The next important promotional poster was the famous "We See Farther" poster and ad. Using the same photo as the "Cry" ad, this poster further illustrated EA's philosophy of featuring the artists while publicly stating the company's manifesto.

Bill Budge

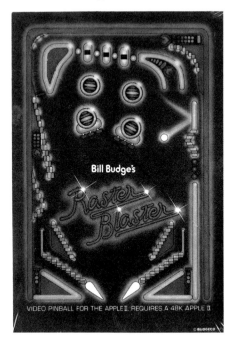

VIDEO PINBALL FOR THE APPLE II; REQUIRES A 48K APPLE II

Rare BudgeCo poster for Pinball Construction Set.

For me, the ultimate video game has always been playing with computers to create the ultimate video game.
–Bill Budge

Games with built-in scenario design software have become a staple today's game market. Thanks to independent programmer, EA came one of the first companies to market a game that let you "roll your own" games.

Bill Budge began programming in high school. He worked Apple Computer for a short time, where he first met Trip Hawkins, programming for the Apple II and somewhat for the Lisa project. At Apple, he created Raster Blaster, a pinball simulation that featured realistic physics, raster graphics, and a do-it-yourself game product (though it did require some programming), which was sold by California Pacific. In 1981, he started BudgeCo to market Raster Blaster.

While at Apple, he spent time around the early Macintosh developers, and it was the Mac's graphical interface that inspired a couple of his products. One was a Mac-like toolbox and product called MousePaint for the Apple II, and the other was the Pinball Construction Set, which he first released through BudgeCo. Pinball Construction Set was one of the first game products that set the player's creativity loose, and after Trip Hawkins approached Budge with a good offer, it became one of the flagship products for Electronic Arts' debut.

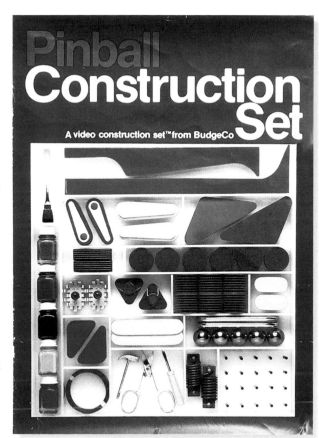

Pinball
Construction
Set

A video construction set™ from BudgeCo

Screenshot of the Apple II version of Pinball Construction Set.

Bill Budge at work in the '80s.

> *Electronic Arts sent me on an 'Artists Tour' to promote their games, like a book author or a rock star. I showed up at one department store in Boston wearing blue jeans, a t-shirt, and sneakers. The manager was expecting me to work behind the counter selling games, so I had to buy a whole new outfit in the men's department. That was when I realized that game programmers weren't rock stars.*
> **–Bill Budge**

Bill Budge wants to write a program so human that turning it off would be an act of murder.

ARE YOU SURE YOU WANT TO CALL THIS GUY AN ARTIST?

Budge's notoriety grew quickly, and EA even made him a "poster child."

Video game creator Bill Budge with latest invention, do-it-yourself pinball

Young video game maker's life rife with paradoxes

In an ambassadorial trip to Japan in 1981, Budge and Brøderbund's Gary Carlston met with Japanese programmers, including Tony Suzuki (Alien Rain and Galaxian) and Jun Wada (A.E.). Budge also ran into a very young Bill Gates.

Jon Freeman
& Anne Westfall

In the good old days before paint programs, character graphics on computers were often drawn on graph paper first. When the filled and empty spaces of the drawing were then converted—by hand—into ones and zeros, the resulting binary numbers, which could then be typed into the computer, literally reflected the pattern of the graphics. Depicted here are several characters for Archon.

Jon Freeman and Anne Westfall were among the original software "artists" who helped to launch Electronic Arts. However, they were already veterans of the young industry, having created several games for Automated Simulations and on their own.

"One day we got a call from Trip Hawkins—the day that EA was incorporated," Freeman recalls. "It truly came out of the blue. He contacted us based on a classified ad that we'd placed, basically as a favor to a magazine, in its new classified section. It was a pretty big surprise because our copy of the magazine was missing the classified page. We didn't know it was there. When Trip called and said he'd seen that ad, we were pretty skeptical. We thought it was some sort of weird scam.

"We agreed to meet Trip, however, and were impressed that he was the first person we had ever encountered who offered an advance against royalties," Freeman continues. "Although the cash involved was incredibly meager by current standards, it was far more than anyone else had ever offered. At that point, advances were not commonplace. His notion that the developers make games and the company handles the publishing sounded very good. We had left Automated because we wanted to concentrate on developing games, not on running companies and dealing with politics. Of course, we had no idea if EA was going to succeed, or what it would become.

"Ultimately, our talks settled on our two strongest ideas—Archon and Murder on the Zinderneuf—and we said, 'Pick one,' and Trip said, 'Why don't we do both?' It was exciting and somewhat scary at the same time.

"I had met Paul Reiche at a trade show, and, with two games to do in six months, we asked him to join us along with our friend, Robert Leyland. Robert did the programming on Zinderneuf, and Anne programmed Archon. Paul and I worked on design for both products."

Archon was simply an amazing game—in my opinion, the quintessential computer board game. It had great rules and strategies, like chess, with the addition of arcade-style battles that made it a true computer game. The shifting balance of light and dark was brilliant. One of my all-time favorites. (RDM)

Archon featured
both board play on
an ever-changing
board and real-time
battles in a separate
arcade battlefield.

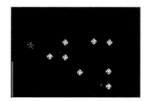

Murder on the Zinderneuf was
a murder mystery set on a diri-
gible. You were given a choice
of detectives you could play;
each of them had various
styles of questioning suspects.

George Barr is a noted science fiction and fantasy
artist who worked on sev-
eral game projects with
both Jon Freeman and
Paul Reiche. Here is an
original drawing depicting
one of two possible victory screens in Archon Ultra.

The detective (you)
on the Zinderneuf
had to question sus-
pects and locate
clues to solve the
murder mystery.

Dani Bunten Berry

She started life as Dan Bunten and was one of the young visionaries of the genesis of computer gaming. The first and most ardent proponent of social and online gaming, Dani Bunten Berry died in 1998, leaving a legacy of games, articles, personal courage, great friends, and an esteemed position in the history of electronic games. When she made the transition from SSI to EA, Bunten created game history—with a game that was just "too weird" to sell.

1981: Cartels & Cutthroats was Bunten's second Apple II title for SSI. This economic simulation game was designed for up to six simultaneous players. Trip Hawkins tried to obtain the rights to it from SSI, and when they refused, Bunten offered to produce another game for the newly forming Electronic Arts.

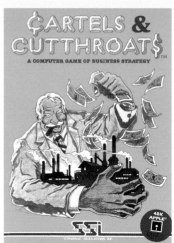

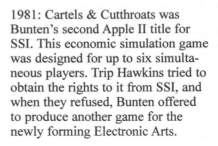

1978: Wheeler Dealers, a multiplayer stock market simulation game for the Apple II, came in a cardboard box, not a Ziploc bag, and sold for an astounding $35. It included special buttons used to play the game. A truly innovative product of which only 50 were sold.

1980: Bunten created Computer Quarterback for SSI. Originally a two-person game only, a single-player mode was added at the last minute at SSI's insistence.

1982: Cytron Masters was Bunten's last game for SSI. It featured strategy and real-time action and pushed the Apple II hardware to its limit.

1983: Based loosely on ideas from Robert Heinlein's Time Enough for Love, M.U.L.E. was, and is, one of the great classic games of all time. This was the first game credited to Bunten's company, Ozark Softscape. Brian Moriarty, a longtime friend and colleague of Bunten's, described it as an "unprecedented example of computer-moderated parlor gaming. By combining the resource management of Cartels & Cutthroats, the auctioneering of Wheeler Dealers, and the futuristic setting of Cytron Masters, M.U.L.E. sustained an exquisite play balance of teamwork and rivalry, bitter cooperation, and delicious treachery." Though it initially sold only 30,000 copies, it has inspired many game developers as well as ongoing websites devoted to it.

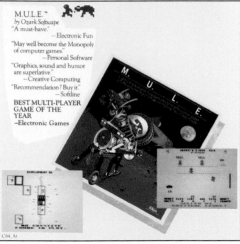

Many people (including one "Hawk Trippins") prized their M.U.L.E. Skinner certificates and still have them today.

Login was a major Japanese game magazine, and they named our game, M.U.L.E., the best game of 1983. Of all the myriad awards I have received over the years, this is one of my favorites because our notoriety had spread to Japan and also because M.U.L.E. richly deserved it. M.U.L.E. won more awards than any game in EA history, and yet it did not sell well because it was too weird.
—Trip Hawkins

1984: The Seven Cities of Gold was Bunten's first real commercial hit, selling 150,000 copies and winning several awards. Following his own traditions, he created a game that featured real-time action, strategy, and exploration with a historical context and even some educational value. The one irony was that it was his first single-player-only title.

1986: Heart of Africa was the last game Ozark produced for a single player. With Robot Rascals they went in opposite direction and required the participation of four players. Featuring a deck of real playing cards, this game was a turn-based action and strategy game. Billed as a "family game," it was mostly ignored by the buying public.

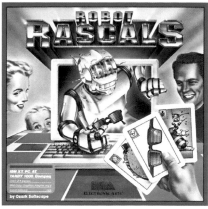

1985: The next game Ozark wanted to produce was based on an Avalon Hill board game, but the execs at EA applied some leverage and convinced them to produce a sequel to The Seven Cities of Gold. Heart of Africa was not, however, nearly as successful as its predecessor. Ironically, some years later, Sid Meier did tackle that Avalon Hill game. It was called Civilization.

JOEL BILLINGS ON THE EARLY DAYS

"In hindsight, Dan Bunten was critical to SSI's development. He was the first non-employee to submit to and publish a game with SSI, and his game was the first non-war game published by SSI. Up until then I assumed we would create all our games in-house. In early 1980, just after Computer Bismarck was published, Dan contacted me and submitted his beta version of Computer Quarterback. We published it in September 1980, and it was the office favorite for at least a year. We organized a league that included employees at SSI and others working at other companies involved in the production and printing of the game. It was clearly the most fun two-player game we made in the early years, and arguably in the history of SSI.

Dan was very low-key, funny, and easy and enjoyable to work with. After publishing three games with SSI, Dan let me know that he and Trip Hawkins had spoken about the possibility of his doing his next game with EA. (This was when EA was just forming.) He was very interested in having his games make it big by going with EA, but at the same time expressed worry that EA might not survive. No one knew whether the market could support the money EA was going to put behind its products.

Trip offered to give SSI stock in EA to buy out our option on Dan's future work. In what turned out to be a financial mistake, I didn't jump at the chance to get EA stock. Trip ended up offering Dan a contract we

couldn't match, and Dan decided to take a chance with EA. M.U.L.E. was the result. Despite the awkwardness of Dan's move from SSI to EA, you couldn't help but root for this tall (at least that's how I remember him), smiling guy who wanted to make games people could enjoy together. In that way he was unique among all the computer game designers I've met.

I probably hadn't seen Dan for ten years when I bumped into him at an E3 in L.A. in 1995 or 1996. Although his sex had changed, she was the same tall, happy, smiling person I had known ten years before. I will always remember her fondly as a great game designer and uniquely warm personality in the computer gaming business."

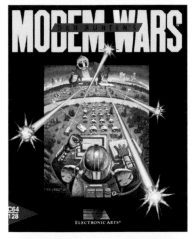

1990: Command H.Q. was released by MicroProse and, like Modem Wars, featured modem-based war gaming.

1992: Global Conquest featured four-player online war gaming and, according to Brian Moriarty, its absorbing mix of real-time action and resource development was the design proto-type for an entire generation of combat simulations, including Dune II, Warcraft, and Command and Conquer.

1988: Constantly innovating and pushing the envelope, Bunten's last game for EA was Modem Wars, the first game from a major publisher to feature modem-to-modem play. Many of the synchronization and latency challenges faced later by online game developers were first solved in this game.

Dan Bunten with Brian Moriarty, Chris Crawford, Steve Peterson, Eric Goldberg, and Robert Gehorsam at an early Computer Game Developers Conference.

EA Sports

It is little known, because he didn't publicize it much at the time, but the earliest games in what has become the immensely popular EA Sports line were principally designed by Trip Hawkins, EA's founder. He personally recruited celebrity figures such as Larry Bird, Dr. J, Earl Weaver, and John Madden, and he worked directly with them to formulate some of the greatest and most influential sports games of computer game history. Hawkins spent extensive amounts of time with his experts. For instance, he tells us, "The first design session I had with Madden took place over a three-day period on a train winding its way across the USA."

Making History with Basketball's Superstars

1983's One on One was the first true licensed sports computer game, and as such, it marks the beginning of an era. Moreover, it was a great game to play. Despite its very crude graphics, the game was painstakingly crafted to simulate one-on-one basketball play between two of the living legends of the game, Julius Erving and Larry Bird. Erving met with Trip Hawkins and Eric Hammond and shared his insights into the game with them, helping bring more realism to the player's experience.

The following quotes in this section from Julius Erving came from a design session with Hawkins and Hammond.

BY ERIC HAMMOND, LARRY BIRD & JULIUS ERVING

AMIGA 500, 1000, 2000
256K; 1 or 2 players; Kickstart 1.2
Extra Features with 512K
1 or 2 joysticks recommended
ONE-ON-ONE   1083

Things will break for you if you have patience. That's very high on the list.
–Julius Erving

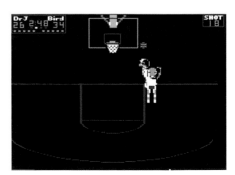

Publicity photo of Michael Jordan checking out the Commodore 64 version of Jordan vs. Bird: One on One.

Jordan vs. Bird: One on One

It was natural to follow a great one-on-one game with an even greater one. With Michael Jordan's rise to prominence in the NBA, Electronic Arts made the logical choice for a sequel to their first One on One product and paired Jordan and Bird in this 1988 release. This game, like its predecessor, was great fun to play, whether you liked to stand back and pop three-pointers with Bird or drive to the hoop and perform 360 jams with Jordan. The players' images improved noticeably as well and were based on actual images of players in action.

> *The capability to make a shot is, I think, directly attributed to having the right to miss it. If I can go to the foul line, and I have the right to miss the shot, I will make it more often than if I didn't have the right to miss it. If you have made five or six baskets in a row, you have the right to miss it anywhere on the court. So you are going to go out there and you are going to take that shot.*
>
> —Julius Erving

ONE ON ONE WITH GODZILLLA

Asked who would win the most in ten games between him and Larry Bird, Erving replied, "I could play ten games against Godzilla and I'd feel that I'd win most of them."

Earl Weaver Baseball

EARL WEAVER Baseball™

By Eddie Dombrower, Teri Mason, Earl Weaver

APL

ELECTRONIC ARTS®

Baseball has often been described as something of a ballet, where athletes stretch, pirouette, and jump with amazing and graceful agility. So, it should be no wonder that one of the finest computer baseball games ever made had its inception in ballet. A young programmer named Eddie Dombrower was fascinated by ballet and created the world's first computerized dance notation program. With Earl Weaver Baseball, Dombrower was able to combine the programming of intricate body movements with his love of baseball. He had already created World Series Baseball for Mattel's short-lived Intellivision console system. Now, he was ready to program a game where the ball reacted according to a physics model and the on-screen athletes moved like they should.

The grand slam came when Earl Weaver, the Hall of Fame manager for the Baltimore Orioles, agreed to consult on the game. With Weaver's help, Dombrower was able to get it all right: movement, physics, and strategy. The lineups followed Weaver's philosophy, the default positioning of fielders was based on Weaver's handling of similar game situations, and there was even an interactive database where players could "Ask Earl" what he would do in a given game situation (based on Weaver's book, Weaver on Strategy).

The physics model for Earl Weaver Baseball was state of the art, and although later games would improve on the model, EWB was the first of its kind. In fact, Don Daglow, the producer of EWB, would eventually direct his own Stormfront Studios to produce Tony La Russa Baseball II with temperature and humidity factors, height of grass, and slant of the basepaths for every major stadium. Yet, Earl Weaver Baseball was the first game to truly cross-reference the statistical matrix of random

John Madden Football

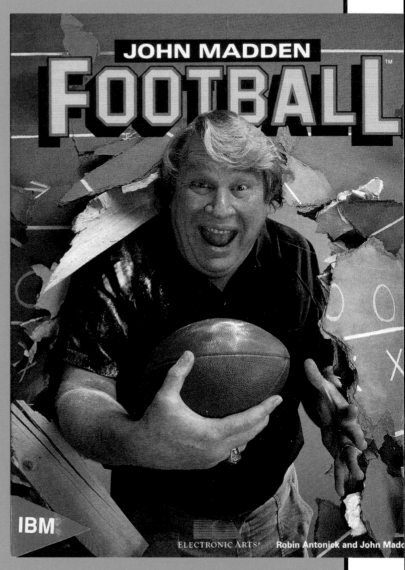

EA's first football game was called Touchdown Football and it came out in the early '80s. However, the game that was to burst onto the scene, set the new standard, and become the best-selling series in EA's history was ignited by the irrepressible John Madden. It isn't well known that Trip Hawkins actually worked directly with John Madden to develop the game. The result was a true classic and a great series, as well as the first to bring playbooks and realistic detail to electronic football games.

Of course, the game was delayed by almost a year because EA showed the original game to Madden, and the celebrity didn't get it. Since the game was going to debut on the Apple II, Robin Antonick had abstracted the number of players on the field so that each team had fewer than 11 players on each side. According to Hawkins, Madden exclaimed, "This isn't football!" Robin went back to work and accomplished the seemingly impossible—getting 22 players on the field.

numbers and existing statistics with formulas that considered wind, outfield wall distance and height, fielder's speed, runner's speed, and ball velocity. Unlike the pure statistics-based sports games and the pure reflex-based arcade games that were published prior to EWB, players suddenly had to consider the configuration of the stadium and the simulated weather when they were planning line-ups and strategy.

Original Madden play diagram framed and hanging on Trip's wall.

More Electronic Arts Games

After its dramatic debut in 1983, Electronic Arts quickly became one of the most important computer game companies in the world. With only six products in May 1983, they exploded a year later with 42 products.

EA Games of the '80s

Chuck Yeager's Advanced Flight Trainer

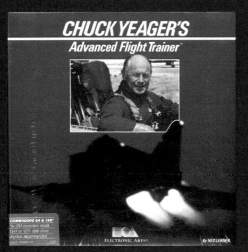

Two things made the 1987 product Chuck Yeager's Advanced Flight Trainer notable. First, it really was what it said it was: a flight trainer. For those of us who were one jet shy of liftoff, AFT was aerial boot camp but much more fun. The second distinguishing characteristic was Chuck Yeager himself, although the product was well underway before EA struck a deal with General Yeager. The wry humor of Yeager's comments when you nose-dived into the turf—such as, "That's no way to treat a plane"—somehow made all the difference. As they had with many of their sports titles, EA arranged for their designer, Edward (Ned) Lerner, to meet with Yeager to glean some of his particular wisdom. "It was something of a culture clash," remembers Lerner. "The design team were all of 25, and he was over 60 at the time. I remember him touching the joystick somewhat disdainfully and saying, 'I do the real thing.' But he was a good sport about it."

Unlike complex flight simulators such as Falcon, F-15 Strike Eagle, and Battlehawks 1942, AFT and its sequels were approachable and fun, and for some of us led to greater success in all future cyber flight endeavors.

Budokan: The Martial Spirit

Budokan was a wonderful martial arts game that came out in 1989. Michael Kosaka, an artist working at Electronic Arts, designed the game to be a "serious" martial arts game. Kosaka was studying the Japanese martial art Aikido at the time and wanted to do something that captured the spirit of real martial arts training. "I remember that the concept was sold accompanied by one of my really crude hand-drawings of two guys in Kendo uniforms hitting each other in a dojo. No full-color storyboards and dialogue scripts, no elaborate pre-production with models and overhead slides. It was seat-of-the-pants, get-outta-the-way development back then."

Using martial arts books for reference, Kosaka and several other artists worked with EA's proprietary animation tools to draw each frame of the animation by hand. The result was well worth it, because Budokan had exceptionally smooth animation for its time. Attempts to videotape EA employees falling on wrestling mats "ended up being more for staff comic relief than actual animation reference," adds Kosaka.

The name Budokan was taken from a yearly martial arts festival in Japan, but Kosaka later found out that it is actually just the name of a big auditorium. "It would be like calling a game 'San Francisco Cow Palace.' But to us, it sounded cool and exotic, and we also remembered the rock album *Cheap Trick at Budokan*."

Starflight

Starflight was EA's first role-playing game on the IBM PC, although it started out on the Atari 800 and then the Commodore 64. The decision to make the game on the IBM PC was, at the time, a radical thought. According to designer Greg Johnson, "People were saying that the PC was not a machine anyone wanted to play games on." In 1986, after three years of effort, the game was released. "When we were building Starflight, we were just about as naive as they come," says Johnson. "Electronic Arts was still very new and had only about 30 employees. For all of us on the team, it was our first game; most of us were straight out of college. We really didn't have a clue about how to build a game like that."

What Johnson calls "a game like that" was an ambitious and complex effort, especially for its time. Starflight allowed the exploration of a vast galaxy that was never the same twice because each planet was generated as fractal graphics on the fly. In some ways, it was like Star Control, which came out years later.* There were ships, random planets to explore, aliens to encounter, and the opportunity to build up wealth by mining and colonizing the planets. It was also a lot of fun to play.

Starflight was the first PC game to go platinum (sell more than 250,000 units). It helped prove that the PC could be a gamer's machine, but despite its success, there were many challenges. According to Johnson, "The game was almost canceled any number of times. I think most of our success was due to the amazing focus of our lead programmer, Tim Lee. Several of us had a hard time surviving through those three years, and there were countless disappointments. It was all driven by the idealistic dream of walking into a store and seeing your game on the shelf, all the time only half-believing that was really possible. In retrospect, it was one of those life-defining experiences you're grateful for but would never want to have to live through again."

Greg Johnson went on to help design Starflight 2 and made some contributions to Star Control (**page 116**). After working with so many aliens, it's not too surprising that he eventually created two of the wackiest aliens ever—ToeJam and Earl (**page 261**).

Sentinel Worlds I: Future Magic

Karl Buiter had published a detailed space exploration game on the Apple II called EOS, or Earth Orbit Stations. It required tons of disk-switching and had an interface that seemed complicated enough to require NASA training. The good news was that he learned enough from the experience to put together a tremendous effort called Sentinel Worlds I: Future Magic.

Like Starflight before it, Sentient Worlds I: Future Magic required you to build and train a crew before you could launch. Unlike Starflight, you weren't likely to lose the chance to get the ultimate win from botching one encounter (unless, of course, you died). Gamers who preferred puzzles and resource management gravitated toward Starflight, while players who wanted immersive RPG elements may have preferred Sentinel Worlds.

Indianapolis 500: The Simulation

Indianapolis 500: The Simulation, from Papyrus, was just what it claimed. It modeled racecar performance and featured working rearview mirrors, variable race lengths, and a lot of additional detail. Prior to 1989, most racing games were about as realistic as the Autopia at Disneyland. Design teams might get the top speeds and exterior design right, but little attention was paid to physics, the effects of damage and wind, oversteering, gear ratios, and fuel limits, among a thousand other details. In fact, you drove on such a rail in earlier games that you didn't even see your car spin out, much less turn around the wrong way. Indianapolis 500 was the first racing game that allowed you to spin the car completely around and travel the wrong way on the track. Hardly good racing, but it did add some excitement. Indianapolis 500 established the baseline for what other racing games would become.

Johnson and partner Mark Voorsanger regularly shared ideas with Paul Reiche and his group. "Paul Reiche was really the mastermind behind the communications system in Starflight," says Johnson. "And I made some contributions to Star Control. We often helped each other out."

Nestwood

Louis Castle

Brett Sperry

1985 saw the humble beginnings of a company that would ultimately change the face of computer gaming. Their first project, a C64 port of the Temple of Apshai series, netted them all of $16,000—just enough to cover expenses.

Louis Castle, who co-founded Westwood with Brett Sperry, relates how they very nearly created the first real-time action RPG. "We literally rewrote the entire product, graphics and programming.... We made it real-time, a top-down, real-time dungeon crawl—like a very primitive version of Diablo or Gauntlet. But that's not what Epyx was expecting, and they said, 'No you can't do that. It needs to be turn-based.'"

Even though the Apshai port was released as a turn-based game, the lure of real-time action remained. The young company continued to port games and worked on several titles for Epyx, including World Games and Super Cycle, ultimately getting the chance to create games of their own design.

Westwood's first original game was Mars Saga for Electronic Arts. "We lacked the experience to finish a totally original product. Mars Saga turned out okay, but it could have been great. It had great fundamentals but lacked a strong story element and presentation. It needed more characters and events to pin it together."

Their first big product was Eye of the Beholder, which was published by SSI. "We wanted to do a D&D game," says Castle,

"but SSI was pretty tight with the license, so we did a couple of other games for them—Questron, which was not D&D, and Hillsfar, which was sort of a D&D puzzle game." Next came Eye of the Beholder in 1990, which was inspired by FTL's Dungeon Master from the previous year. Eye of the Beholder was a real-time dungeon crawl set in the D&D system, and it was a big hit.

Westwood was sold to Virgin in 1992, which gave them an infusion of cash. Virgin then released Westwood's first true adventure game, Fables & Fiends: The Legend of Kyrandia - Book One.

At the time, Westwood was working on another real-time game based around medieval knights and sorcery. Concerned about the game's potential appeal, they began to consider changing it to something more contemporary. "Think tanks and money as a resource, oil wells, and other stuff like that," Castle recalls. "We were fascinated by Rescue Raiders (Choplifter with units) and Military Madness. And Brett was a huge *Dune* fan. When Virgin said they had the *Dune* license, it all fell into place. Brett realized that spice was the perfect common resource for both sides to fight over."

The original name for the game was Dune, but Virgin had a *Dune* adventure game project under way. Known as Dune II, the resulting game became the model for the real-time strategy (RTS) genre. "We knew it had to be a multilayered game with building and protecting buildings and units, not a game of wanton destruction." In many ways, Dune II was the culmination of the work that had begun with that original Apshai port. Real-time games soon exploded, with Blizzard's Warcraft and Westwood's Command & Conquer series playing leading roles. Westwood even returned to the well over six years later with Dune 2000 and Emperor: Battle for Dune. Ironically, it all started with a swords and sorcery game that took a few unexpected turns and became a science fiction classic.

In late 1990, SSI teamed with Westwood again for their first true 3D product in their AD&D line. They had a fresh face in Dragon-Strike, but not a commercial success. DragonStrike was a 3D flight simu-

lator in which players would fly astride fighting dragons in a mission-based campaign setting. It was designed for both the PC and the Amiga, though much of the low-level copper and blitter code had to be rewritten in order to get a decent frame rate on the Amiga. To show how much technology has changed, the entire 3D code library for DS fit in 10 kilobytes of memory, and the routines could generate around 1.5 megabytes of map data. The

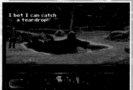

data had to be compressed and generated with each frame because the program had to reuse the memory and didn't have enough buffer to keep even the visual part of the map in the buffer.

Westwood has gone through many identities. They were originally known for porting existing products, but have been variously known for sports, RPGs, adventures, and real-time strategy games. This is only a small look at their origins and early landmark products. As a part of Electronic Arts, they continued to make great games throughout the '90s and beyond.

DUNE·II
The Building of A Dynasty

Westwood STUDIOS
Distributed exclusively by VIRGIN GAMES

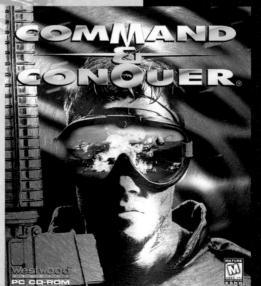

Companies that skyrocket up are on a path to explode. Lots of young companies make one hit, and if you let that get to your head, it can really destroy you. You can be a victim of success as easily as a victim of failure.

—LOUIS CASTLE

MicroProse

Another of the most influential computer game companies of the 1980s, MicroProse began after a challenge playing a coin-op arcade game. The scene was a coin-op arcade at the old MGM Grand Hotel (now Bally's) in Las Vegas. Both J. W. "Wild Bill" Stealey and Sid Meier were working for a Baltimore-based defense contractor and were attending a meeting for the company at that hotel. They met over an Atari coin-op game called Red Baron (not the Dynamix/Sierra game for the PC), where "Wild Bill" was challenging all comers.

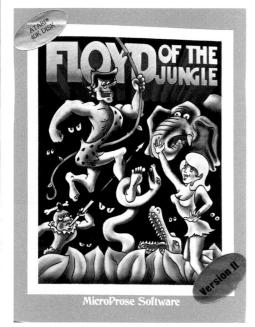

Red Baron used wireframed graphics to depict World War I aircraft. Most of the units had a console cabinet with a seat that allowed you to sit in a cockpit and shoot down enemy planes with your unlimited supply of ammunition. Sid Meier watched Stealey racking up victories and finally decided to take the challenge. When Meier blitzed past all of the experienced pilot's high scores, Stealey couldn't believe it. He asked Meier about his flight experience and was chagrined to discover that he was merely a computer systems analyst and had beaten the high scores by analyzing the simple moves used by the artificial pilots in the game and predicting those moves in advance.

Since Stealey had already done some bragging, Meier countered with a bold assertion of his own. Meier claimed that he could design a better game in one week on his home computer

than the Red Baron game that was raking in quarters in front of them. Stealey didn't want to be outdone, so he assured Meier, "If you can write the games, I'll sell 'em."

It took longer than a week. In a tradition that goes back to the earliest days of programming, Meier's schedule slipped, and it took a whole two months to finish the game. As promised, Stealey took Hellcat Ace on the road and immediately sold 50 copies on his first sales call. As a result, it seemed like money in the bank to form a company. According to Stealey, "MicroProse started on a bet between us. We decided to sell just enough software to pay off our cars. Then, in the first year, with me carrying all of MicroProse in a satchel, we did $200,000 on the back of Hellcat Ace."

The original idea was to call the new company "Smugger's Software," based on the acronym S.M.U.G., which stood for Sid Meier's User Group. Fortunately, they opted for a more assonant double pun. MicroProse was supposed to stand for the micro-professionals who designed and programmed the games. It also represented the idea that their code was prose in the sense of being an art form, like literature. Even so, the small company started out as a homespun operation, with products distributed in plastic bags with dot matrix–printed manuals.

The company's first products were Hellcat Ace, Chopper Rescue, and Floyd of the Jungle. Stealey says, "Floyd of the Jungle was my favorite. It was the first game to allow you to hook up four joysticks on the Atari 800. And Chopper Rescue let you play with two players—one pilot and one gunner."

Sid Meier relates that he had many influences through the years. Games such as Space Invaders, and even Pong, convinced him that the electronic medium could generate intensity. He also mentions the work of Dani Bunten Berry (née Dan Bunten)—especially The Seven Cities of Gold. "I was blown away by how epic it was. It probably led to Sid Meier's Civilization. Up until that time, I was writing airplane, submarine…smaller games in scope. I saw how you could spread out across the map and didn't have to be constrained by the size of the screen. I did Pirates! right after seeing Seven Cities. Later, Dani told me that in Pirates! we had done all the stuff she had

MicroProse Software

wanted to do with Seven Cities, which turned her loose to concentrate on multiplayer games. She was evangelical about multiplayer."

Sid Meier is legitimately considered one of the greatest game designers in history, and he had a rather unique approach to game design. Instead of plotting everything out in detailed design documents and flowcharts, Meier would spend late nights coding working prototypes of the game long before the alpha stage and bring in new builds almost daily for his co-workers to play, test, and critique. Later, as he added researchers, musicians, artists, and co-designers to his teams, they would shake down the semidaily builds and make suggestions which, in turn, Meier would turn into improved code. At times, Meier would have perfectly working code and would rip it all out with his typical refrain, "We had it in there, but it wasn't fun, so we took it out." There are very few designers who can code as rapidly as Sid Meier, nor any that also have his instinct for fun.

Commentary from Sid Meier

Sid Meier has graciously provided us with commentary on each of his games over the years, starting with Hellcat Ace. He tells a story not only of his own accomplishments, but of many aspects of the evolution of game design during the '80s and into the '90s.

Hellcat Ace

"My first attempt at a combat flight simulator, based on a trick I had worked out that rotated the horizon quickly and moved it up and down. We could only push so many pixels back then, so I used this trick to make it look like you were flying. Today, we laugh at it."

Chopper Rescue

"This was a side-scrolling arcade game like Choplifter, but Choplifter had a better swooping effect. It was a game where I was discovering player missile graphics on the Atari—a million things flying around shooting at you,

hostages waving on the ground—a full-bore arcade game…dropping bombs and shooting everything…. It was not realistic in any sense."

Solo Flight

"This was the first game that really broke out nationally. It came when I was learning to show a 3D world. It came out around the same time as subLOGIC's (later Microsoft) Flight Simulator, but ours was easier to fly and not quite as detailed. I think we were the first to show a shadow on the ground so you could gauge your altitude. It helped set the tone for us—the combination of realism and fun. My personal aphorism is, 'When fun and realism clash, fun wins.'"

NATO Commander

"It was not even fun to play. It was just bad."

F-15 Strike Eagle

"F-15 started with our experiments in wireframe rotations. When that became an airplane, it said 'dog fight.' We found ways to show that onscreen with fairly complex ideas for the time—radar, bomb sites…ideas direct from the real Air Force. Bill put a lot of his knowledge into it. I think we were the first to have chaff and flares. Also, a bit of a MicroProse trademark, we included a 100-page manual, so you felt like you got some insight about how things were done in the real world. It was something that seemed realistic and was fun to play."

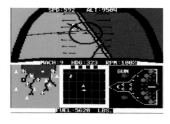

Sid Meier's F-15 Strike Eagle raised the ante on flight simulation by adding realistic features and a huge manual. Here is a Spanish version of the game, which was distributed in many languages.

Conflict in Vietnam/Crusade in Europe/Decision in the Desert

Decision in the Desert was a real-time combat game before they were popular.

"These were aberrations—hex-based war games that were part of my growing up but didn't make the best translations to computers. But these games turned us loose to find a new language for computer games that was not tied to board games. Overall, the fun of the industry is figuring out how to use a new medium, finding a new model."

Silent Service

"One of my better games. There was a game called Gato (*see page 201*) somewhat before us, and I remember playing it and saying, 'Hey, this could be a good game.' But in my mind it had copped out in some ways and didn't have the mixture of fun and realism that I thought would be fun. So, we basically stole the idea and made a cool WWII submarine game set in the Pacific. The innovation I remember was the map you could zoom into and keep zooming down even to individual islands. We used a sort of fractal idea that included the whole Pacific. It was a gigantic playground to play with submarines. This was the first time I had done a significant amount of research on a topic.

"For a long time it was just subs with torpedoes, but Stealey said we needed something more exciting. 'Can't you get on the surface and shoot it out with guns?' He said it so many times that we finally said okay and put in a deck gun. From that moment on, he was a game designer, and he would just have to say 'deck gun' to mean that we needed excitement and cheap thrills. It was a running joke. (In fact, 'Wild Bill' relates that he was demonstrating Silent Service to a potentially big client who was skeptical of a submarine game. 'There were three ships and I got one of them, and then the other two were chasing me. I got blown to the surface, got one with a torpedo, and shot the last with the deck gun, and they all cheered and ordered 25,000 units. Thank god for the deck gun.')"

Pirates!

"Pirates! was a reaction to the RPGs, where it was kill this monster, get five exp, kill that monster. I didn't enjoy them. And adventure games, which I called

Pirates! is one of the finest games ever made and probably the best example of mixing strategy, role playing, and action in one game. Anyone who hasn't played Pirates! should. (RDM)

'pick up the stick games'.. you know. You're in a room with a glass, a stick, a brush. You pick up the stick. They promised excitement, storytelling, and plot that I didn't think they delivered. I said to myself, 'I'm going to try to write an adventure role-playing game that is the way I want it, with the focus on excitement, romance, story... and takes you from one high point to the next and doesn't bog you down in killing the same monster again and again.' Pirates! was a neat topic, and I took a movie fun/excitement approach to it as opposed to a realistic approach. We had no shame in putting a lot of 'Arrghh mateys' in there. It seemed like a nice combination of sword fighting, exploring the big map, meeting with a governor and wooing his daughter, land battles... well, we won't talk about the land battles. But one mistake we didn't make was to make the action parts too involving, like we did later in Covert Action. You don't want the player to get too involved in the action and lose the thread of the story."

Red Storm Rising

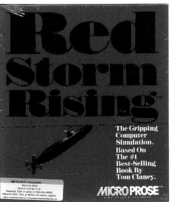

"We all read the book and thought it was cool, but what I recall about that was meeting Tom Clancy. Before we could do the game we had to have an audience with Tom Clancy. Bill had what I call his 'virtual flight suit' on and was totally in Air Force mode. He wanted to convince Tom that we were legit and knew what we were doing. And we did have a good meeting with Clancy. And we were lucky. They gave us plenty of leeway. I worked a lot with Larry Bond (who later did Harpoon), and he was a very heavy-duty simulation kind of guy. We tried to be pretty hardcore with that game. It was a pretty good game, but not one of my favorites—maybe more complex than fun. In the end, I found that I didn't like doing licensed games."

Gunship

"That was a fun game and became a test bed for everything I knew about flight games. The one unique thing was learning how a helicopter worked, how different it was from an airplane. It was also the first game where I didn't write all the code. We started to have teams of programmers once we got into 3D. We had a very smart guy, Andy Hollis, who did the 3D programming on Gunship."

Note: Hollis went on to garner fame as the lead designer on EA's Jane's series of simulations.

F-19 Stealth Fighter

"F-19 was probably our biggest out-the-door success. It was also the first game we wrote for the IBM PC. We had a cool mapping system that I sort of borrowed from Pirates!—a big map, where if you swooped down toward the ground there were buildings and roads and the idea of a big world. Of course, we did it by cheating. And also there was the idea of an airplane that half the time would try to avoid fighting. It added a suspense element that was a little bit new. We were riding a wave of militarism and modern high-tech; the Cold War was still on. There were rumors about the stealth bomber in the news. It was the right product at the right time. And we had the technology, too…the different views like the missile cam, the bomb cam. We claim to have invented a lot of those camera views, as well as the full-time camera in the corner of the cockpit that showed you the plane you were locked onto. This solved the problem of having planes in the distance be dots on the screen, and you couldn't tell what they were doing. With all the views, we almost felt like movie directors. F-19 was the last flight simulator that I wrote. I felt that it was everything I knew about how to write a flight simulator, and I never felt the need to write another one after that. That didn't mean that Bill didn't keep asking me to write them, though."

Covert Action

"We have a problem we call the 'Covert Action problem,' which is when action sequences take over the game. It was an international spy game with clues to unravel in different cities, and as you played, the game would break into various action sequences—break into building, car chase, decode message—and each game was cool on its own, but almost too cool in that it took you too far away from the plot. It pointed out clearly how lucky we had been with Pirates! to have balanced the plot and action segments so well. This was a case where the whole was less than the sum of its parts."

Railroad Tycoon

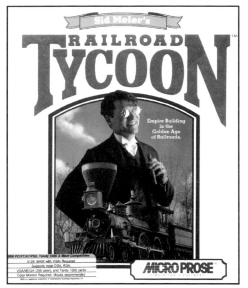

"This was the first game that started the whole 'Sid's god game' thing, but it started off simply as a model railroading game about laying down track and watching trains with switches and signals. I showed it to Bruce Shelley, and he was into railroads and history and had done a board game called 1830 about trains, so I developed the rest of the game to make Bruce happy. I put in all sorts of stuff that I knew he would like, and he really contributed a lot to the game. We tried to make it fun and touch on all the cool parts like building track, seeing the economics, the tycoons of the day, covering the sweep of history."

Civilization

"My first intention with Civilization was to make a real-time game that would emulate SimCity on a global scale, but it didn't work. I put it aside and wrote Covert Action. When I came back to it, a light went on in my head, and I realized that it would be a turn-based game. From that point on, Civilization was one of the smoothest developments of all the games I've made. It's amazing how few things we had to undo in the game. Even the tech tree. I just threw together a bunch of technologies, expecting to have to go to the history books afterward, but that ended up, with one or two exceptions, to be the tree we used in the game.

"Civilization had many influences. SimCity in its turning the world away from destruction toward construction, the idea

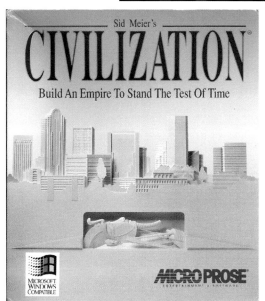

that it's just as much fun to build something as to destroy it. Empire, which had that 'uncover-the-map' quality. Railroad Tycoon with the idea of economics and building and all it had.

"One defining quality of Civilization is the concept of simple systems interacting to create complexity. On their own, the finances, military, and so forth are all easy to understand, but combined, they create a complex experience. And also there's the concept that you are the king. You get to make all the decisions that influence the course of history. Civilization is reputed to have this 'one more turn' quality. You're always planning ten moves ahead, and you just gotta play one more turn. You've ordered a lot of chariots, you're researching gunpowder—you're always in the middle of things and projecting ahead. There's seldom a good stopping point. There were lots of cool touches. In a solid game system, you can do so much cool stuff. You could take one of your populace and turn them into something like a tax collector or an entertainer. Our entertainers looked like Elvis. One of our little jokes."

CPU Bach

"How do you top Civilization? I admit I ducked the issue and let other people do Civ II. So I went off and did CPU Bach, which was as far away as you could get from what I had done before—on purpose. If I tried to top myself every time, I'd go crazy. I started it on the PC, but somehow Trip Hawkins convinced me that there would be a 3DO machine in every living room, right next to the stereo. And it did have a lot going for it, even if it didn't turn out exactly that way. At any rate, CPU Bach was a fun product, and I'm proud to have an aberration like that in my life."

Magic: The Gathering

"The most complex, bizarre, strange development process I've ever been through. The irony is that halfway through the project, we had a great game, but during the second half we made it worse and worse. We had to make a lot of changes to fit the licensor's requirements and had to take a lot of the cool stuff out."

Gettysburg!

"Gettysburg! was a game I'd been wanting to write for at least 20 years. When I was eight years old, I was sent off to Switzerland where my father's family lives, and the bribe to get me to go peacefully was an American Heritage book on the Civil War. It was the most amazing book, with full-page battle maps, paintings that looked like the battle was actually happening. I always wanted to capture that in a computer game, but it took advancements in technology to allow a thousand figures to march across the screen, shooting and marching and all. It's a niche product, but I think it's the best Civil War game out there, and I'm happy with how it turned out."

Civilization III

"Where Civ II added more units, more technology, more stuff, Civ III takes the approach of widening the game, like having culture, diplomacy, trade resources, things that were overshadowed perhaps by the military aspects of the original game. It's true to the spirit of the original with new gameplay elements that interact in the same way. Much of what we put into Civ III came from our players. We've gotten a lot of feedback, and many people have asked for ways to win besides capturing the world. And we've added some interface elements from real-time strategy games, putting as much on the main screen as possible."

More from MicroProse

In addition to Sid Meier's brilliant designs, MicroProse was the home of a host of other talented designers. Arnold Hendrick, formerly of board game publisher SPI, and Lawrence Schick, formerly of Coleco's electronic game division, collaborated on a Japanese version of Pirates! Mixing tactical battles, role-playing elements, and action sequences, Sword of the Samurai was a great game that never received the acclaim of its predecessor. While Schick went on to craft Task Force 1942, a detailed WWII naval simulation, and later headed up

AOL's game division, Hendrick parlayed his military history background into the original M1 Tank Platoon. Then, Hendrick created the most detailed role-playing game imaginable. Darklands was one part detailed historical setting (Germany during the 15th century AD) and another part open-ended fantasy. Unfortunately, Darklands arrived over budget, past due, and with hundreds of thousands of lines of discrete code instead of the promised software engine that could craft 15th-century Italy and 15th-century Britain as its heirs apparent. It also arrived with so many bugs that it ran through seven patches before it was playable on the average machine.

MicroProse also scored with a group out of Texas. Steve Barcia's SimTex group gave the company a megahit in Master of Orion and duplicated the feat with Master of Magic. The former was often called "Civilization in Space" by hardcore gamers, and the latter used elements from Civilization and the new trading card game phenomenon, Magic: The Gathering, to craft a game that was truly unique. In 1994, MicroProse also collaborated with Mythos Games to produce X-COM, which set new standards in turn-based strategy gaming. X-COM was followed by several sequels.

The MicroProse trademark has gone through several acquisitions, from Spectrum HoloByte to Hasbro to Infogrames, and most recently to Cybergun, although the company, as such, no longer exists. Sid Meier founded Firaxis Games in 1996 and continues to produce great games.

Spectrum HoloByte: Converging Paths

Around 1979–80, Gilman Louie was developing TRS-80 games for a company called Voyager—the first being a Star Trek type of product. He later began working with the Apple II and Atari 800 systems and formed a development firm called Nexa, working for companies such as Activision and Epyx.

"My big break came when I was at our six-by-six booth at the West Coast Computer Faire in 1983 and a young executive from Microsoft/ASCII approached me, saying he didn't know there were any Japanese-American game companies. I'm not Japanese, but I didn't say anything. At the time, I was consulting and doing various jobs out of my

The original Falcon, distributed on a cartridge for the Japanese MSX system.

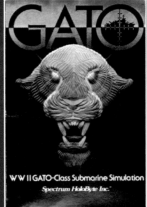

1984: Starship Simulator, another MSX cart, "My third Star Trek game."
—GILMAN LOUIE

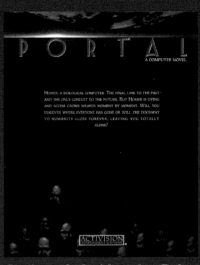

Louie worked with author Rob Swigart to produce Portal, arguably the first computer novel, not to be confused with the later hit indie game of the same name.

1980: "Battle Trek for TRS-80, the first game I designed and sold."
—GILMAN LOUIE

The Real Dogfight Simulator.

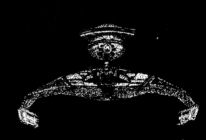

The F-16 Fighter Simulation
Spectrum HoloByte

ADVANCED TECHNOLOGY
The F-16 Fighter Simulation
Spectrum HoloByte

ELECTRONIC BATTLEFIELD SERIES
FALCON
3.0
DOS 5.0
required
Spectrum HoloByte
INCLUDES 2-PLAYER MODEM VERSION

FALCON
4.0

Joining Forces

Meanwhile, in 1983 Phil Adam and Jeff Sauter started a company called Spectrum HoloByte ("Spectrum meaning color. Holo meaning 3D, as in hologram. Byte being a digital representation.") and produced a WWII submarine simulation called Gato. "We had trouble getting it on the shelves," says Adam, "so I sent out 3,000 games at no charge to various stores, then called all 3,000 the following week. The first time we got a purchase order for 48 pieces, we popped open the champagne." By the fall of 1984, Gato became the number one game on many charts. Adam adds, "Not many people know that Gato was originally designed for the PCjr. Not many companies were founded around the PCjr and survived."

Spectrum followed by creating Orbiter, a space shuttle simulation. It came out two weeks before the Challenger disaster.

About that time, Paul Saffo, for the Institute for the Future, showed Louie's Falcon game to technology writer and pundit Stewart Alsop. Alsop knew about Gato and brought the two companies together, suspecting a good match. Meanwhile, despite the fact that Adam and Sauter were already in negotiations with Activision to sell their company, Gilman Louie managed to convince them to work out a business plan to form a publishing company and do Falcon for the Macintosh and the Amiga. Somehow, Activision got a copy of the business plan and, according to Louie, "offered me a $250,000 development deal to make it go away. I knew we had something then, and I ran out of that meeting to talk to Phil while Jeff was in another meeting with Activision.

Above: 1988 CES booth. Phil Adam is on the right. Also, 1989's booth.

Below: Gilman Louie getting the chance to check out an F-16.

mom's house with all my fraternity brothers from San Francisco State."

Shortly thereafter, he received a surprise visit from eight Japanese businessmen who had called from the San Francisco airport. While his mother was serving tea and asking embarrassing questions, somehow he was offered funding to do a flight simulator for the MSX—a Z80-based computer in Japan. He could choose the F-15 or the F-16. He'd be working with 16K of RAM and a 16K cartridge.

"I was embarrassed and could only imagine what these guys, whose cards had ASCII on one side and Microsoft on the other, were thinking. Then Mr. Hamada said in thick English, 'We started in a house half this size.' I said yes to everything." The product he created was called F-16 Fighting Falcon.

"It was complex and allowed head-to-head fighting on two computers using the joystick port and some nifty communication software we wrote. I figured it was pretty niche-y and that we'd sell maybe 10,000 of them, but we sold 100,000, and Sega licensed it for their Master System in 1984." The game debuted in the U.S. in 1985.

Gilman Louie was featured in a national magazine ad for the Amiga with a screenshot from Vette!

But Phil

Spectrum's Tank is based on the U.S. military's networked training simulation, SIMNET.

was getting ready to go to England to meet with Mirrorsoft, so I went with him. We showed our business plan to the British and ended up doing a deal with Robert Maxwell and forming Sphere, Inc. as the holding company, with Spectrum HoloByte as the publisher."

The deal gave Maxwell 80 percent of the company. Louie and Adam each took 10 percent. Sauter took Spectrum's hardware division, which was not part of the Maxwell deal. Four years later, Adam left to join Interplay, but not before participating in several big developments in the company's history.

Ironically, one of the first projects the new company had set its sights on was to create a game based on Tom Clancy's Red Storm Rising, but the deal with Maxwell got held up, according to Adam "because Gilman had a computer system he wanted to be a company asset, and Maxwell's people didn't want to pay for it." *The Red Storm Rising* contract went to MicroProse instead (*see page 197*).

Despite hitting some turbulence along the way, Falcon was a huge critical and commercial success upon release, ultimately

coming out on the IBM PC in 1987. Known for its realism and technical accuracy, Falcon went on to be the quintessential modern jet simulator—the standard by which other modern combat simulations were to be judged for years afterward.

Tetris

While Falcon was flying high, another game more or less airdropped into their laps. It came to Spectrum by way of Hungary and they paid $11,000 for the rights to it. It was the antithesis of a detailed simulation like Falcon. It contained a mere seven blocky shapes, no Gouraud shading, no complex rules of engagement, and no huge manual. The game was called Tetris. However, the Tetris story is convoluted and often confusing. See the next chapter for more.

Bankruptcies and Near Misses

Falcon was so realistic that Spectrum HoloByte was approached to create a low-cost military trainer through General Dynamics. They were given access to many design specifications and other information, but then it turned out that they couldn't do it after all, since they weren't military contractors and didn't work in Ada. "So we took all the design specs and the information we learned working with General Dynamics and the pilots, and we made Falcon 3.0" says Louie.

However, as Falcon 3.0 was approaching its launch date, Robert Maxwell died in a mysterious boating incident, and it later turned out that the Maxwell empire was bankrupt. Moreover, the bankruptcy trustees were convinced that millions of dollars of missing pension funds were somehow hidden at Spectrum HoloByte. As part of the liquidation of the Maxwell businesses, the bankruptcy officers were going to sell Spectrum if Louie couldn't raise enough money to buy it back. "I told Bill Stealey at Micro-Prose about my situation, and he immediately loaned me $300,000, saying, 'We can figure out what to do about it later.' He literally wired me the money the next day."

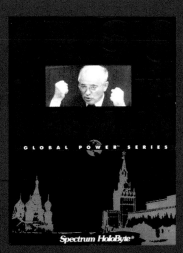

1991: Crisis in the Kremlin, a bold product that places you in the role of Mikhail Gorbachev, ironically predicted the coup attempt on his leadership of the Soviet Union.

1989: Fun driving through the streets of San Francisco, with a full, accurate, and drivable map of the streets of the City by the Bay. Also, the first 3D driving game for the PC.

The money from Stealey bailed out the company temporarily, but it wasn't a long-term solution. So Louie went to venture capitalist Vinod Khosla, who was working with Trip Hawkins at the time on the funding of the 3DO. With Khosla's investment, the company was able to continue, and even secured an investment from Paramount and, along with it, the license to do Star Trek games.

While all this was taking place, however, Spectrum was forced to release an already-delayed and badly bug-ridden Falcon 3.0 before it was really ready. It was months before a series of patches finally produced a stable version. The product sold well despite its problems, and when it was finally patched together, it flourished.

With new investment, the company took on new life. With Tetris, Falcon, and the Star Trek license obtained from Paramount, they grew quickly from a $7 million company to a $26 million company. It was at the height of this success that Bill Stealey came back to Louie with a problem of his own. His board was going to take the company from him if he didn't raise something like $12 million in ten days. With Khosla from Kleiner Perkins and Spectrum HoloByte's CEO Pat Feely, Louie launched a campaign to purchase MicroProse and allow Stealey to keep his shares. Ultimately, they were successful, and the two companies essentially merged.

Louie remembers that the merger worked out well for the first year, but then it became clear that the two companies had very different cultures and expectations. The company's

Having fun with chess, this insert was included in National Lampoon's 1993 spoof of the Chessmaster series, Chess Maniac 5 Billion and 1.

stock went up, but then started to fall as the two cultures clashed. After trying to sell unsuccessfully several times, they sold the combined company to Hasbro and ultimately were purchased by Infogrames. Gilman Louie left after that and started working for the CIA.

Pajitnov with Spectrum
HoloByte's Phil Adam
and Gilman Louie.

ТЕТРИС
(TETRIS)

Now Compatible With
IBM
PS/1

IBM PC or Tandy 1000
• 256K RAM
• Hercules, CGA, EGA, or
  Tandy 1000 16-color
• 5¼" & 3½" disks enclosed
• Joystick optional
RAM-resident version included

The Soviet Challenge
Spectrum HoloByte

Tetris

Alexey Pajitnov

Pajitnov with Henk Rogers
and colleague Vladimir
Pokhilko.

The original Japanese Game
Boy version of Tetris.

Alexey Pajitnov graduated from
the Moscow Institute of Aviation with a degree in applied
mathematics in 1979. From the
university, he went to work at the
Academy of Sciences, the main
research institute in the Soviet
Union. His job involved work
on artificial intelligence, speech
recognition, and what he calls
"really serious, well-established
boring work." He adds, "I liked it,
though, and spent 60 hours a
week programming this stuff."

But Pajitnov had other interests. "Basically, for all my life I
was interested in kinds of mathematical puzzles or diversions, or
some deep intelligent jokes," he
says. "When I got access to computers, that passion immediately
found a place, and once I had a
more or less reasonable operating
system, I started putting together
games and puzzles."

Pajitnov's first inspiration for
Tetris was a game called Pentominos. "It was available at toy stores
in Russia. It contained shapes that would fit into a box. You would
take out all the shapes, and then you spent a good hour putting them
back." Pajitnov became quite good at Pentominos and even read a
book written about it.

"One day, I decided to put together a game based on this
puzzle, and I decided to put it on the computer. When I wrote
the procedure to rotate the shapes, it worked very quickly when
you pressed a key, and it was so amazing to see it moving on the
screen that I wanted to see a game in real time. That's how the
idea of Tetris was born."

There were other steps to take, however. First, since the original five-square shapes of Pentominos created too great a variety
for Pajitnov's intentions, he reduced it to four squares per shape,
making a total combination of seven possible shapes.

From this point, naming the game was easy. "Pentominos
was named from the Greek for the number five. I figured I
would take the Greek word for the number four, tetra, and that
became Tetris. But I soon realized that if you just placed the
shapes into the box, the game would soon be over. I needed a
way to get rid of the shapes so the game could continue. And I
noticed that when an entire line was full, it was kind of dead—
you can't do anything with it—so I decided to take it away and
leave space for more pieces."

The scoring system was another aspect that made the game
unique. "You get a score in advance with each piece as it appears,
and you spend part of the advance score while you think about

where to put the piece. There are no bonus points for combinations, no points for clearing lines. There's simply a certain potential of points for each piece. And, of course, as the game progresses, the amount of the advance increases, but the pieces fall faster and you have to think faster."

The pieces appear randomly, and Pajitnov points out that "it was truly random. There was no bias to one shape over another." But Pajitnov did consider other refinements, such as a garbage area and making the square shapes invisible, "since you didn't have to rotate them, anyway." But in the end, he kept it simple. "I realized that I had better not touch anything because I could spoil it by adding complications."

The original game was developed in 1984 on an Electronica 60 computer with a monochrome monitor. When it was ported to the IBM PC in 1985, with a whole 16 colors, the pieces were each given an individual color. "I do remember that the T piece was yellow," adds Pajitnov.

A game of Tetris running on a Russian system much like the one used to program the game.

A RIGHT TWISTY TALE

The story of how Tetris found its way to the world is very complex and involves a lot of legal folderol and international maneuvering. Here is a very brief summary of events as remembered by Henk Rogers (one of the people responsible for bringing Tetris to the West and currently co-owner of The Tetris Company, which handles all worldwide Tetris-related products) and Phil Adam, who was at Spectrum HoloByte when Tetris was introduced.

- 1984: Alexey Pajitnov invents Tetris.
- Tetris somehow finds its way onto computers in Iron Curtain companies.
- Robert Stein, who has a company of developers working in Hungary, discovers Tetris and licenses rights to Mirrorsoft in England. He subsequently goes to Russia and acquires some of the game rights he has already licensed to Mirrorsoft, but not all of them.
- Mirrorsoft licenses computer rights to Spectrum HoloByte, which then licenses console rights to Atari spin-off Tengen.
- Spectrum HoloByte packages the game for personal computers in the U.S., stressing the Russian angle, even hiring Ronald Reagan and Mikhail Gorbachev look-alikes.
- In 1987, Henk Rogers, a computer game publisher in Japan, discovers Tetris at the Spectrum HoloByte booth at the Computer Electronics Show (CES). From them, he licenses personal computer rights for Japan.
- Rogers seeks console rights, first from Spectrum HoloByte, then from Tengen, and publishes Tetris on Nintendo's Famicom system in Japan. Robert Stein agrees to represent Rogers in seeking Tetris rights for handheld systems, such as Game Boy.
- Months pass, and Stein does not deliver handheld rights. Rogers learns that someone has approached Nintendo to do a Game Boy Tetris. Rogers asks Nintendo president Minoru Arakawa to give him a little time and heads off to Moscow.
- Meanwhile, Spectrum HoloByte has

approached Nintendo about Game Boy rights as well. Kevin Maxwell, son of Mirrorsoft owner Robert Maxwell, goes to Moscow to negotiate Game Boy rights for Spectrum HoloByte.

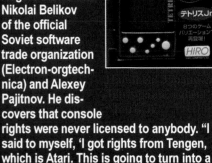

- In February 1989, Rogers meets with Nikolai Belikov of the official Soviet software trade organization (Electron-orgtechnica) and Alexey Pajitnov. He discovers that console rights were never licensed to anybody. "I said to myself, 'I got rights from Tengen, which is Atari. This is going to turn into a major lawsuit.'"
- The Russians send a fax to England, giving Kevin Maxwell 48 hours to respond. Ironically, Maxwell is in Moscow and doesn't receive the fax. The Russians then agree to license the rights to Rogers.
- Rogers returns to Nintendo and explains the situation. They promise to back him up against Atari, whom they are about to sue over Tengen's unauthorized distribution of NES cartridges. They grant Rogers continued publishing rights in Japan in exchange for assistance in getting the console rights worldwide.
- In March 1989, Rogers, Arakawa, and Nintendo Vice President Howard Lincoln all fly to Moscow to complete negotiations for console and handheld rights.
- In 1996, all rights to Tetris are placed in The Tetris Company; Blue Planet Software becomes the exclusive agent, and all Tetris players play happily ever after.
- Tetris for Game Boy sells well over 30 million units since its release on all platforms in 1989. More than 70 million units had been sold worldwide, as of 2002, when this summary was written.

The Games Group: Early History of Games at Lucasfilm

It was originally called the Games Group, and, like Industrial Light & Magic and Pixar, it spun out of the vast creative empire of George Lucas. And like those other companies, it has been a consistent leader in its field. Now known as LucasArts, the original Games Group was a small cadre of talented people looking for ways to make better games.

They started with a million-dollar investment from Atari, who wanted Lucasfilm to develop games for them. Ed Catmull, who was running an advanced technology group at Lucasfilm (the Computer Division), then hired Peter Langston, who had done a bunch of games in the '70s, including one of the earliest versions of Empire (*see page 237*) and an intriguing program called the Internet Oracle. (More information about this amusing program available at *http://livinginternet.com/l/la_known_oracle.htm.*)

Rotofoil for the cover of Ballblazer.

Original Games Group Members: David Levine, Charlie Kellner, Peter Langston, David Fox, Loren Carpenter, and Gary Winnick

Langston then hired David Fox, who had written a book about computer animation and had a dream of working for Lucasfilm; programmers David Levine, Charlie Kellner (one of the first Apple employees), and Chip Morning-

star; and artist Gary Winnick. Also present at the inception was David Riordan, who was a consultant at the time and had completed a research project on cable television opportunities for Lucasfilm.

"Everybody contributed game ideas," says Langston, "and the two from David Fox and David Levine were our favorites." The two ideas Langston mentioned were Levine's Ballblazer and Fox's Rescue on Fractalus!, though the original names were Ballblaster and Rescue Mission (or, alternatively, Behind Jaggi Lines).

There are a lot of stories surrounding these first games. They were somehow pirated before release and put out on the Internet. The various vehicles depicted on the game covers were actual models made by ILM technicians just for the covers. David Fox is the guy in the helmet on Rescue on Fractalus!, which was originally inspired by Loren Carpenter's early work with fractals.

"I asked Loren, 'Do you think it's possible to do fractals on Atari computers?'" remembers Fox. "He said, 'Well, maybe.' After a few days he took an Atari 800 home, learned 6502 assembly code, and came back with the first pass of a fractal landscape. Meanwhile, I had started designing Rescue on Fractalus!"

Saucer for Rescue on Fractalus!

(Catmull, Carpenter, and Alvy Ray Smith went on to form Pixar with substantial early investment from Steve Jobs.)

David Levine created accurate physics algorithms for Ballblazer, and there was even a tricky maneuver called the "Back Wall Charlie" named after Charlie Kellner. The music on Ballblazer was interactive and was modified by the player's controller movements. A musician himself, Langston got both Pat Metheny and Lyle Mays (among others) to contribute riffs for Ballblazer. Longtime Newsweek technology editor, Michael Rogers, wrote the original Ballblazer manual (although it's possible that Riordan and his partner, Garry Hare, also wrote a manual—history is unclear on this matter).

At the time they were ready to release these early games, Atari had changed hands and was now owned by Jack Tramiel. Unwilling to accept Tramiel's terms, the Games Group looked elsewhere, ultimately making a deal with Epyx. According to former Epyx president Michael Katz, "Their games were pretty esoteric, though great graphically. Hell, we couldn't even pronounce some of their early titles. But we wanted a relationship with Lucasfilm." Epyx wanted disk games, not cartridges, so that further delayed the release of the products, which finally came out in 1985.

The next two games, also published by Epyx, were Kellner's The Eidolon and Koronis Rift by Sinistar designer Noah Falstein, who had joined the team from

Before 3D computer modeling, the Games Group had ILM actually create scale models of the type they had made for the Star Wars movies, including a detailed saucer and landing craft for Rescue on Fractalus!, and a rotofoil for Ballblazer.

Williams. "In some ways, Koronis Rift was a forerunner to first-person shooter games," says Falstein. "You traveled around a 3D sort of landscape with weak weapons and shield, and you'd find burnt-out tanks and integrate their capabilities."

The Games Group, which by that time was known as Lucasfilm Games, developed several titles for other publishers. David Fox worked on Labyrinth (published by Activision) and comments, "It was in some ways a better game than a film." Falstein, inspired by Sid Meier's Hellcats and F-15 Strike Eagle, began to research military themes, ultimately featuring the hydrofoil in PHM Pegasus for Electronic Arts and inspiring David Levine to write an anti-war poem called "Blood on the Water" in protest. Levine's protest did cause the group to consider their treatment of war games, and according to Falstein, "Starting with Battlehawks 1942, we made it a policy to show both sides of the war."

During these years, several changes of personnel occurred.

Before becoming a publisher, Lucasfilm Games produced two excellent war simulations for Electronic Arts. Producers on these titles were Rich Hilleman (still at EA) and Randy Breen, who went on to become VP of product development at LucasArts.

Steve Arnold came from Atari to help manage the division. Shortly thereafter, Levine left the company, as did Langston, who was lured away to "a job I couldn't refuse" at Bell Labs, and several notable programmers came on the scene. Graeme Devine (who later co-founded Trilobyte) did a conversion of Ballblazer and spent some time at the Skywalker Ranch (where Lucasfilm Games was located from 1985-1989). Larry Holland did an Apple II conversion of PHM Pegasus, and Ron Gilbert did a C64 conversion of Koronis Rift.

Falstein next worked with Larry Holland on Strike Fleet, an innovative naval warfare game that allowed the player to control fleets as an admiral or to captain individual ships. Strike Fleet, published by EA, was the last game the group developed for an outside publisher.

The Two-Fold Path

The next phase of Lucasfilm Games' development was led by two former programmers for a short-lived company called Human Engineered Software (or HESware), Ron Gilbert and Larry Holland.

SCUMM Is Born

Up to this point, Lucasfilm's games had been innovative and technically excellent, but their impact on the art of computer game design had only just begun. The new era began in 1987, when they released their first game as a publisher, Maniac Mansion. The idea for the game originated from discussions between Ron Gilbert and artist Gary Winnick. To make it easier to develop, Aric Wilmunder and Gilbert developed a scripting language they called Script Creation Utility for Maniac Mansion, which was later shortened to SCUMM, and it was the SCUMM system that was used to create all the subsequent adventure games the company produced for years afterward. (David Fox offers the following comment: "Knowing Ron, he came up with the name SCUMM first, and then figured out what to call it… just like another tool was called MMUCUS, Earwax, and another SPUTM—do you see a trend here?")

Gilbert, who had played text adventure games such as the original Adventure and Zork, wanted something different, so he developed a game with no typing. All possible verbs were listed on the screen, and the player simply clicked on the verb and then clicked on the object on the screen.

The script, written by Gilbert and David Fox, was notably irreverent and humorous, a trademark of later Lucasfilm adventure games. In part, this was a way to avoid the obvious absurdities involved in adventure games. Gilbert cites a theoretical example of a game where you are in Los Angeles and you need a pencil to solve a problem, but in the game, the pencil is in New York. "It's kind of silly to think that there are no pencils in L.A., but in many adventure games, that is how the world seems to be. Using humor lets you turn a weakness into an advantage. You can use crazy ideas to solve puzzles, and when the situation makes no sense, people don't grumble about it. If they are laughing, they are much less likely to groan and say, 'What was that all about?'"

Maniac Mansion was one of the landmark products in the history of LucasArts games. Its combination of wacky humor, innovative interface, and story development set the stage for many amazing games to come, such as The Secret of Monkey Island, Zak McKracken and the Alien Mindbenders, Zombies Ate My Neighbors, Grim Fandango, and Day of the Tentacle, to name only a few.

About the time that Gilbert was getting started on The Secret of Monkey Island, Noah Falstein was meeting with George Lucas and Steven Spielberg. He was charged with the task of creating a game based on the upcoming movie Indiana Jones and the Last Crusade. This was late 1988. The movie was due out in May 1989. There was no way to do a good game alone in that short a time, but possibly with a team and SCUMM…

Steve Arnold assigned his best team—Falstein, Fox, and Gilbert—to work together and produce the game. The team produced the game

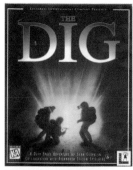

in record time, according to Falstein, but they had different opinions about the game's ending. Falstein favored a serious ending, and Gilbert favored humor. In the end, they opted to create different endings. According to Falstein, Gilbert created a random number generator that presented different combinations of ending scenes, so that players would get different combinations of serious and comic endings. "I went over Ron's code to be sure he didn't bias it," adds Falstein with a smile. (Fox adds that he remembers writing the ending code using Gilbert's random number generator.)

Steven Spielberg was a great fan of computer games and made frequent visits to the Ranch, where the games division was located. Noah Falstein relates a story about Spielberg playing Battle of Britain while the ILM crew waited to show him the first dinosaurs for *Jurassic Park*. So, when he wanted to do a game based on "The Dig," an original story he had penned for his *Amazing Stories* TV series, he turned to Lucasfilm. "Working with both George Lucas and Steven Spielberg was one of the high points of my career," says Falstein, who was tapped originally to lead the project. Unfortunately, Lucas' management changed teams more than once on the project, which ultimately took six years to complete from initial meetings to shipping the game. In the end, although it had

beautiful artwork, The Dig was one of the very few disappointing games put out by the Lucasfilm crew and remains notable primarily because of Spielberg's involvement.

In 1990, Lucasfilm Games released one of its most evocative games—Brian Moriarty's Loom. This unusual game featured an intriguing storyline, innovative gameplay, and beautiful graphics. Unlike most of the early SCUMM games, Loom was a more serious game with a deeper and more thought-provoking fantasy involving a mythical world of magic. Loom had no inventory, and all the puzzles were solved with the use of musical sequences, which the player learned while exploring the world. Loom was closer to a modern fairy tale, with timeless imagery and a hero's quest that evokes ancient myth.

Also in 1990, Rob Gilbert completed one of the funniest games of all time, The Secret of Monkey Island. Monkey Island was a pirate adventure full of wisecracks and jokes, and it featured several dialogue puzzles. "My favorite dialogue," says Gilbert, "was between Guybrush (Monkey's protagonist) and Stan the used ship salesman. Stan is trying to convince Guybrush that he needs all these extra options. It's the classic used car salesman encounter. You have to leave and come back a couple of times. We wanted it to be slightly frustrating and a little irritating, but not too much so. We were treading that thin line where the player would be amused at the parody, the satire, with a tinge of frustration, but not so much as to be angry with the game."

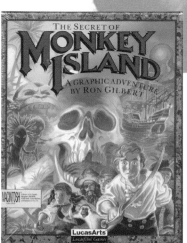

more than once on the project, which ultimately took six years to complete from initial meetings to shipping the game. In the end, although it had

Gilbert also shared the secret behind the strange name of Monkey's protagonist. For a long time, the character who wanted to be a pirate had no name. The artists had created a "brush" in Deluxe Paint for the character and, in the absence of a name, labeled the file GUY.BRUSH. They started calling the character "Guy-brush," and the name stuck. The last name came from the fact that Gilbert's wife was reading P. G. Wodehouse's Heavy Weather, where the rather bizarre family has the surname Threepwood. She shared the amusing name with Gilbert, and a "star" was born.

After The Secret of Monkey Island, there was no stopping them. Adventure games became one of the mainstays of Lucasfilm Games, which ultimately changed its name to LucasArts in the early '90s. There followed an impressive list of titles, including LeChuck's Revenge (Monkey Island 2), Indiana Jones and the Fate of Atlantis, Day of the Tentacle, Sam & Max Hit the Road, Zombies Ate My Neighbors, Full Throttle, The Curse of Monkey Island, Outlaws, Escape from Monkey Island, and the hilarious Grim Fandango.

LucasArts also entered the console market with several successful games, starting in 1991 with Star Wars for the NES and following the next year with The Empire Strikes Back and Defenders of Dynatron City. Also in 1992, they released Super Star Wars for the Super NES, following with several additional SNES titles over the next two years. In 1997, they even released Ballblazer Champions for the Sony PlayStation.

Taking Flight

After Strike Fleet in 1986, Larry Holland and Noah Falstein were thinking about the next step. "We got quite ambitious and grandiose and wanted to create entire theaters of operation," says Holland. Stuck doing a hi-res Apple II version of Zak McKracken, Holland was anxious to go back to military combat. In his readings, he became fascinated with the Battle of Midway in WWII. "I wanted to base the game on what really happened, on moments in history. Reading about tales of Midway really crystallized it—it still gives me chills. It was the most important five or ten minutes in the last 50 years. In minutes, three Japanese carriers were sunk; it was the moment the war changed. I wanted to capture that kind of impact and show how a small number of people can change everything... the moment when things were in the balance."

The game he and Falstein produced was Battlehawks 1942, which was released in 1988 and was the first of three great World War II air combat games. Holland was just getting warmed up, and by the next year he had produced Their Finest Hour: The Battle of Britain, in which he continued to improve technically while expanding the realism and human connection of his games. Depicting both sides of the air war, and with missions based in history, Their Finest Hour let players engage in one of the most dramatic conflicts of the war. "There were great heroes on both sides of the conflict," says Holland, "and our task was to let players experience even the German pilots without lionizing or demonizing them." Holland also came up with an innovative replay mechanism that allowed players to reenter a battle during the replay at any time.

In 1991, Holland completed his final WWII product, Secret Weapons of the Luftwaffe (SWOTL), a huge project that incorporated not only individual flight missions, but a vast overall campaign mode, great graphics, and huge fleets of B-17s. But there were lessons for Holland in doing the game, which was many months late. "I fell into the common trap of the overly ambitious and threw the kitchen sink into this game. I learned that even incremental elements can make a game far more complex. There are stories about the security guard coming by at 3 a.m. and finding me asleep on the couch. I think I lived at Lucasfilm for about a year. But what I loved about that game was the message—what war means to technological innovation, and strange turns it can take."

Ironically, Lucasfilm had licensed *Star Wars* game rights to Brøderbund, and it wasn't until 1992 that the rights reverted to the company that made the films. At that time, following SWOTL, Holland was ready to move on. Brian Moriarty made a comment to him that if Larry didn't do an X-Wing game, he would. "When Brian said that, I thought 'I have to do it now!'" And so Holland took all his experience with WWII games and applied it to the first Star Wars game, X-Wing.

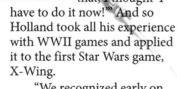

"We recognized early on that, although we wanted to tell both sides, as we had in the previous flight games, we also wanted to tell the David and Goliath story. We didn't want to do the movie over again, though, but put in the familiar elements in a similar story."

X-Wing* succeeded phenomenally and gave rise to a series of great games, each of which expanded the genre and became more graphically rich, with ever deeper stories and mission threads. Star Wars: TIE Fighter took the Empire's side. But playing the evil Empire created its challenges. "In most great works, the villain or evil side has a lot of intrigue, and we wanted to design with that in mind. We gave the Empire shades of gray and gave the player a chance to achieve some nobility."

In Star Wars: X-Wing vs. TIE Fighter, which came out in 1997, Holland and his team off-handedly agreed to incorporate Internet play. "We got into it and said, 'Oh, my god...' We discovered how difficult it was to put in real-time action on the Internet. I remember testing into the pre-dawn hours, and we'd think we had finally fixed a problem. Then, later in the day the 'fixed' version would not be any better than before. This happened several times until we finally understood that the problem was bottlenecks in the Internet itself." Ironically, most players only played the deathmatch mode. "We put in a lot of cooperative missions, story, and cool military engagements, but people mostly played the deathmatches. In the end, I felt that only about five percent of the game was actually played."

Finally, with Star Wars: X-Wing Alliance, Holland was able to expand the game genre even further. "X-Wing Alliance was an opportunity to bring together a lot of what we had learned over the past five years. The design allowed us to do things we had wanted to do, like fly the Millennium Falcon and be a gunner, do the Battle of Endor in grand scope. It was a nice wrap-up of the series." Of course, LucasArts produced many more Star Wars games for both the first series of movies and for Episode I.

I had the great privilege of being hired to write limited edition novellas for both X-Wing and TIE Fighter, and was able to carry forward the stories of my characters, Keyan Farlander and Maarek Stele, in the subsequent strategy guides. I hope someday to continue their stories in a series of novels. (RDM)

"When I was a kid, I was always designing games, but in those days computers were something the size of a blue whale and run by men in white lab coats," says Hal Barwood, veteran designer at LucasArts. "So I followed my other passion and went to film school." One of Barwood's film school buddies was George Lucas, which turns out to be significant.

To make a long story short, Barwood did teach himself to program and even made a couple of games. One unreleased game of his from the early '80s was an epic action adventure on the Apple II he called Space Snatchers. "I fully intend to take that game one day and release it on the Internet," he says. Meanwhile, we've got a screenshot.

Barwood's Hollywood credits range from "extensive, but uncredited" writing on *Close Encounters of the Third Kind* (but if you pay close attention to the pilots who come out of the mothership at the end of the movie, one will identify himself as Barwood) to producing *Dragonslayer*, which also happened to be the first non-Lucas film that Lucas' great special effects house, Industrial Light & Magic, worked on.

In time, Barwood returned to his passion for games. His first game at Lucas was Indiana Jones and the Fate of Atlantis. He continued to work as a writer, designer, and production manager at LucasArts for more than two decades, but is currently working on independent projects. Among his LucasArts projects were the SNES title Big Sky Trooper, published by JVC ("too long in development—a great game, but an 8-bit title in a 32-bit world"); Indiana Jones and

His Desktop Adventures ("the concept of developing modular games using similar elements, the way the chessboard squares and pieces are always the same, but no two games are alike"); Indiana Jones and the Infernal Machine ("some of the best level design I've ever seen, an absolutely wonderful game trapped in a defective 3D engine"); and Rebel Assault II: The Hidden Empire ("returning to my roots, I helped with the video and directed the shoot").

Barwood credits his movie experience very little in his game design work. However, he admits that it has influenced him in various ways. "In movies, narrative runs everything. It's the same with adventure games. People still come to me saying that movies are linear and games are nonlinear, and therefore can't tell a story. But of course they can, although there are subtleties and pitfalls you have to look out for."

Barwood then referred to an interesting bit of dialogue from the movie *The War of the Worlds*.

Dr. Clayton Forrester (Gene Barry), a physicist, is in an army bunker watching the Martian invaders. General Mann (Les Tremayne) joins him:

General Mann: "From the data, from that picture the Air Force took tonight, what we've got out there is the original pilot ship. On the basis of its observations, the others were guided down. Pattern-wise, one lands, then two, making groups of three, joined magnetically. Is that possible?"

Dr. Forrester: "If they do it, it is."

Point made...

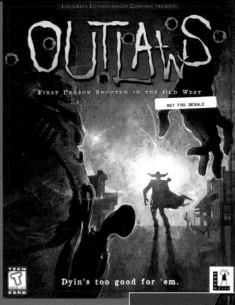

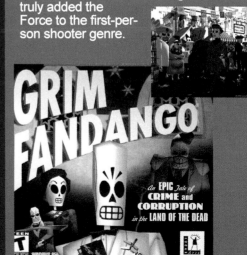

LucasArts has produced so many great games that it's hard to decide which ones to include here. We wish we could feature them all. Certainly, two great games were Outlaws (a first-person shooter set in the Old West) and Grim Fandango (set in a strange, modern world of the dead, and one of the most twisted and hysterical of the modern adventure games). Also, there were the Star Wars: Dark Forces games, which truly added the Force to the first-person shooter genre.

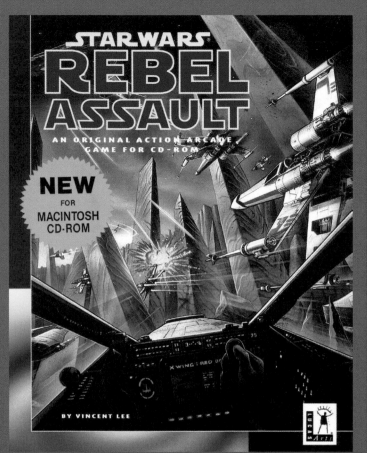

Star Wars: Rebel Assault featured some great graphics and intense flying and shooting. In many ways, it was the modern equivalent of Rescue on Fractalus!

In more modern times, LucasArts has produced many games based on *Star Wars: Episode I* and the world that predates the original *Star Wars*. Star Wars: Episode I: The Phantom Menace was an action/adventure game and one of the first of the new era of games from LucasArts.

Chris Roberts: Wing Commander

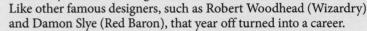

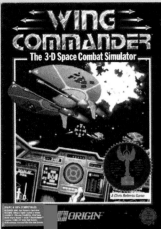

There was a time when Origin Systems was known almost exclusively for the Ultima series of role-playing games. However, that was before Chris Roberts joined the company. Roberts grew up in England, and his exposure to games started in the arcades. "When I was a young kid I was an artist, and I guess I was fascinated by storytelling and movies. At the same time, I went to arcades and played games like Space Wars, Galaxian, and Galaga.... I was fascinated by the ability of computers to animate images onscreen. So I taught myself to program on a Sinclair ZX81 with 1K of memory and tried to merge my two passions—storytelling and games."

He created his first games as a teenager on the BBC Micro computer. His first published game was called Wizadore and was published by Imagine (a subsidiary of Ocean Software) in 1984. It spent eight weeks as number one on the English charts. His next game, a soccer game called Match Day,

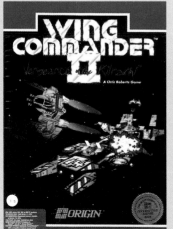

*See the UK section of this book for more of Roberts' early work.

spent 12 weeks at number one. He followed that with Stryker's Run.* "It was a sideways-scrolling game set on a futuristic war-torn planet. You had to get a message across no-man's-land to your HQ. You could get into aircraft and fly them."

At that point, before going to university, Roberts decided to take a year off to write games. Like other famous designers, such as Robert Woodhead (Wizardry) and Damon Slye (Red Baron), that year off turned into a career.

In 1987, he began designing Times of Lore for the Commodore 64, creating his own development system on an IBM PC and using a cross-assembler and his own download software to port it to a Commodore 64. About that time, his father moved to Austin, Texas, and Roberts decided he liked the weather and all the movie theaters, so he moved, too.

While visiting a local D&D gaming spot, he noticed some cool graphics on the walls depicting various characters. He asked the artist if he'd like to work on his game with him. Two weeks later, that same artist, Denis Loubet (*see page 125*), went to work at Origin Systems. Soon after, Roberts worked out a deal to have Origin publish Times of Lore.

Roberts' next game was a post-apocalyptic role-playing game called Bad Blood, also for Origin, but he was already thinking about a space epic he wanted to create. "I had grown up with Star Wars and Battlestar Galactica, and I read tons of science fiction. I remembered the game Elite, which I thought was pretty cool," says Roberts. "I was originally going to call my space game Squadron and create a fleet combat game from a top-down perspective. I started buying books and doing research. About that time, I had a chance to see Sid Meier's F-19 Stealth Fighter. It wasn't out yet, but it was running at ten frames per second on a 386 25 MHz machine—at the time a $10,000 system. It was beautiful, but I thought, 'Who would buy this game?' You needed the best machine for it to perform with any reasonable frame rate. Of course, it went on to become one of the biggest hits that year. I was also inspired by Larry Holland's Battlehawks 1942, and I liked his technique of using bitmaps to represent 3D images." In fact, there was some talk of locating the game in the Star Wars universe, but at

Lucasfilm, the idea of doing their own Star Wars games was gaining strength.

In creating his own outer space fantasy world, Roberts was inspired by the themes of the Pacific Theater in WWII. "The Pacific Ocean is analogous to the vastness of space, with islands and atolls being the equivalent of planets." Roberts then created the two warring sides—the Kilrathi and the Confederation, modeled roughly on the Japanese and the Americans in WWII.

In Times of Lore, Roberts had done a remarkable job of condensing code, "squeezing as much code and data as I could into the Commodore's meager memory. The whole game fit in 64K—a necessity for the European market, which was still tape-driven, but irrelevant in the U.S., where everyone had floppy drives," he says. "But did anyone notice?" he asks. The answer would appear to be no. "After the success of F-19 Stealth Fighter, I decided that people just wanted to have the best, coolest game possible, period, and it was irrelevant whether it ran really well on their particular machine. So for Wing Commander, I went 'balls to the wall' and really pushed the technology." No more squeezing. Roberts also tapped his fascination with movies to create more story and atmosphere. "All the elements of character, details in the ship, and action sort of came together and created something that was more than just a game. It was like a departure into another world."

Roberts knew he was on the right track when, still in development, most of Origin was playing the game. Later, after the game's release, Roberts was further vindicated by players' responses to the game. "I'd go on CompuServe and see that they were talking about the world and the characters, not just what their high score was."

Of course, the original Wing Commander and its sequels were created by ever-larger teams of people, including some of Origin's most creative talents, such as Loubet, Warren Spector, Steve Beeman, Ellen Guon—later Ellen Beeman, and many others. Each succeeding game became ever more movie-like, with animated cut scenes, lots of characters, and lots of environmental details. They were more than simple flight combat games. They were true adventures with a taste of role-playing that captured players' imaginations. Roberts created four Wing Commander games, each more ambitious than the last.

Chris Roberts with Mark Hamill and Malcolm McDowell at Planet Hollywood, dedicating WC IV costumes.

Also in 1991, a spin-off of the Wing Commander series, Privateer,

debuted to a warm reception, with an expansion pack, Privateer: Righteous Fire, and a sequel, Privateer 2: The Darkening, to follow.

By 1993, Roberts was involved in creating the ambitious and groundbreaking game Strike Commander, which featured amazing 3D technology and required game fans to purchase state-of-the-art hardware even to run it. The technology for Strike Commander was ready in 1991, though the game didn't release until 1993. But even in 1993, it was at the top of the technology curve, pre-CD-ROM.

Wing Commander III was even more ambitious, evolving the Strike Commander technology and incorporating full live-action sequences with actors set against digital sets. Roberts went for an all-star cast, including Mark Hamill, John Rhys-Davies, Tim Curry, and Malcolm McDowell in the filming. It was a very expensive project and benefited from the 1994 sale of Origin to Electronic Arts, who provided much-needed financial resources.

Coming out in December 1994, WC III did so well for EA that they wanted another game from Roberts by the next Christmas. Wing Commander IV released in February 1996, again with a big cast of actors. "We didn't have time to retool the technology, so we spent our time and money on the story and content, shooting film and creating the missions."

After finishing Wing Commander IV, Roberts decided to strike out on his own, forming the company Digital Anvil and ultimately going on to make movies. Origin continued to create Wing Commander products, including Wing Commander: Prophecy (known as WC V), Wing Commander: Armada, and Wing Commander: Academy.

Interplay

"I was a big *Lord of the Rings* fan, comic books, movies…I read a lot of fiction. Everything pointed me toward games," says Interplay's founder, Brian Fargo. In the mid-'70s, Fargo got a Magnavox Odyssey, followed by an Atari VCS. Fascinated by how these games were being made, at 16 years old he started calling publishers and asking them questions. "They were no help at all," he recalls. "One guy said something to the effect that 'if you don't know now, you'll never know.' Then, around 1979 or so, I got an Apple II computer, and that's when a light went on above my head. It had 48K of memory, and there was a 16K add-on. I thought, 'What a waste. What would you do with all that memory?'"

The Demon's Forge
By Brian Fargo

Above: A young Brian Fargo.

Right: Brian Fargo and Bill Heineman demonstrating Dragon Wars to Johnny Wilson.

Fargo's first game on the Apple was an adventure game called The Demon's Forge, which he published under the label Saber Software. He would call computer stores and ask if they had it and then refer them to the ad in Softalk, which he had spent half his business budget on. Later, he'd get a call from those same stores ordering his game. (This is pretty much the same trick Bill Stealey used in the early days of MicroProse.)

Then some Stanford graduates approached Fargo to form a company called Boone Corporation. After about a year, Fargo decided to go off on his own again. Dick Lehrberg, formerly executive vice president of Interplay, relates, "At one of the Boone board meetings, all the other

The earliest press photograph of Brian Fargo at Boone Corporation in 1983. From left to right: Mike Boone, Bill (now Rebecca) "Burger" Heineman, Brad Davis, Troy Worrell, Brian Fargo, and Dave Shore.

executives broke into a fistfight. That's when Brian left to form Interplay Productions." That was October 1983. The company began with conversions and other odd software projects. "When you start a company, there's what you want to do and what you have to do," says Fargo. And so they did various jobs, such as conversions of products for a division of K-Tel Records and even some military work for Loral. Finally, Interplay landed a three-product contract with Activision.

"They had an incredibly sophisticated 3D engine for a golf game, some graphic adventures, and also a fantasy role-playing game with three-frame animations in this giant window—which you look at now and say, 'Oh my god, it's so small,'" remembers Lehrberg, who was at Activision then. "But I thought it would be right up our alley. However, when I mentioned it to Jim Levy, he said role-playing games were 'nicheware for nerds' and passed on the RPG." Eventually, Interplay did strike a deal with Activision. For $100,000, they agreed to create Mind Shadow (based loosely on Robert Ludlum's The Bourne Identity), The Tracer Sanction, and Borrowed Time (with Arnie Katz) for three different machines—essentially a nine-product deal. Later, a golf game developed by some, in Fargo's words, "Stephen Hawking-smart" Stanford graduates was added to the mix and became the first 3D Gold game sold under Activision's Gamestar line.

The role-playing game Activision passed up was written by Brian Fargo's high school buddy, Michael Cranford, although Fargo did contribute some scenario design. Electronic Arts' Joe Ybarra liked the game and signed up Interplay to do it. It was called Tales of the Unknown Volume 1: The Bard's Tale, but it ultimately became known simply as The Bard's Tale.

The Bard's Tale was a great success, selling around 300,000 copies. Interplay followed with a pair of sequels and Wasteland (pg. 238), a more modern RPG using the Bard's Tale engine. However, Fargo was aware that, as developers, they were missing out on the real money. "We had solid products, but we weren't really making that much money. Individual designers like Eric Hammond, who did the One on One series, did really well."

After some, in Fargo's words, "big hairy negotiations," Interplay became an affiliate label of Activision, which meant that they took more of the risk but would make more of the profit. Meanwhile, in a turnabout, Electronic Arts passed on Interplay's next product, thinking it was a terrible idea, and Activision this time published what was to be Interplay's next big hit—Battle Chess, a game at least partially inspired by the great chess scene in Star Wars.

William Gibson's Neuromancer was the inspiration for Interplay's game of the same name, notable in part because they worked with Timothy Leary in developing the story and used the rock group Devo for the music.

By this time, Interplay had broken off from EA and was distributing through Activision, but by 1990, Fargo once again decided it was time to make a change and turn Interplay into a full publisher. Unfortunately, Activision was in trouble at that time, and there was a lot of unsold inventory. Fargo hired veteran Phil Adam to head up his marketing and sales. "I had wanted to create a marketing and sales company to work with Origin, Interplay, and Dynamix," Adam remembers, "but Brian said, 'Why not just do that for Interplay?' So I joined in late 1990, but with Activision having problems, I told Brian we might have to go six months without revenue while we cleaned up the mess."

Fortunately for Interplay, their next product was Castles, a wonderful game of medieval building and warfare. "We sold 50,000 Castles in one day," says Adam. Fargo adds, "The idea came to me when I was watching a BBC miniseries on castles, and they said that castles weren't really

homes, but were military machines. But I never quite got it to where I wanted it to be. I had a real-time strategy game in mind. When I see Ensemble's Age of Empires, I think, 'That's what I wanted. They just nailed it.'"

Shortly after releasing Castles, Interplay hit it big with Star Trek: 25th Anniversary, which was the first really successful *Star Trek* game. In fact, Fargo remembers, "When we got the rights to *Trek*, people thought it would be a slam-dunk seller, but retailers were pretty much down on the concept due to the poor versions that came before it." Later, Interplay released a CD-ROM version of the game with actual voiceovers from the cast and crew of the original *Enterprise*. It was at the recording sessions for this product that William Shatner saw the complex interactive script and commented that it was more like three movies.

Interplay also created some cartridge games for the NES, including Swords and Serpents for Acclaim, Rad Gravity for Activision, and a game called Rock N' Roll Racing by Allen Adham, one of the founders of Blizzard, who also did The Lost Vikings and Blackthorne for Interplay.

Interplay created some great games in the '90s, including Descent, which took the first-person shooter concept popularized by Doom and gave it new dimensions. They also began working with some outside studios—BioWare and Shiny Entertainment. Bio-Ware's first product, Shattered Steel, didn't do very well, but Interplay stayed with them and was rewarded by the critically acclaimed Baldur's Gate series of role-playing games. Meanwhile, they purchased Dave Perry's Shiny Entertainment (*see page 288*) to have a strong cartridge development house, only to find Perry more interested in doing primarily computer games such

> *I remember showing Battle Chess at a trade show, and Ken Williams from Sierra comes up to look at it. He says, 'I think when I watch the combat, there should be different outcomes.' But I said, 'That wouldn't be chess, and anyway, it would double our graphics load.' He said, 'You'll just have to try harder, I guess.'*
> **–Brian Fargo**

as MDK, Messiah, and Sacrifice. (Fargo relates that in their final negotiation phase, they played a game of pool to settle a particular issue involving who paid taxes. Fargo claims to have won approximately $20,000 by sinking the eight ball. "My previous biggest gamble was five dollars," he adds.)

Next page: Baldur's Gate was just the beginning for BioWare, which became a publisher in its own right and has developed some of the great games of the '90s and beyond, including the Mass Effect and Dragon Age series, as well as Star Wars: Knights of the Old Republic (*see pg 300*).

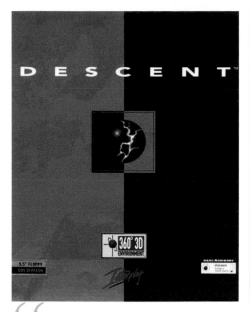

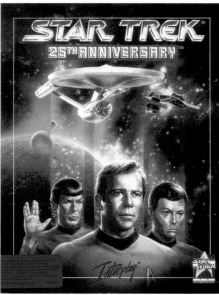

The last years of Interplay were quite stressful and I was able to spend much less time in development than I wanted. We were caught between the changes in the PC business and the explosive development costs of a console business for which we had no big hit. Despite having a wonderful slate of PC games, we were not adequately financed for the 21st century. I knew I needed to come up with a solution and I found a buyer for the company in 2002, but there were far too many shareholder issues to allow the transaction to happen and my biggest shareholder wished to do things their way. With no control and a different vision of the company than Titus, I flipped them the keys and wished them luck. It was sad to walk away from the company I created, but it was time to get back to my roots and start a new company.
–**Brian Fargo**

Interplay closed its doors in 2004-2007 following a run of acquisitions, success and failures, and multiple trials and tribulations. However, before this blackout they did acquire David Perry's Shiny Entertainment, which resulted in multiple hit games; they produced the post-apocalyptic RPG Wasteland for Electronic Arts; and later developed Fallout, a post-apocalyptic RPG with similarities to Wasteland, which set off an epic series continued by Bethesda today.

New World Computing

In 1983, Jon Van Caneghem began work on a game inspired by Ultima, Wizardry, and his D&D experience. In 1986 he completed the game, started New World Computing, and released Might and Magic Book One: The Secret of the Inner Sanctum. "It was such an awesome feeling to complete Might and Magic," Van Caneghem tells us. "This was my first creation, and it combined the best of other games I liked with the kinds of features I wanted." Might and Magic was the first RPG to feature really well-drawn indoor and outdoor locations and to allow full exploration of both.

"In 1988, with Might and Magic II, we tried to push the envelope on the Apple II, doing things with color and resolution that nobody had done to that point," says Van Caneghem. "Our efforts were somewhat eclipsed by the introduction of VGA graphics on the PC, though.

"Might and Magic III came out in 1991, and it marked several exciting milestones. It was the first time I had other programmers to help me. It was our first PC title. We also pioneered an item concatenation system,

Above: Mark Caldwell and Jon Van Caneghem, co-founders of New World Computing.

First Impressions

In 1986, I was asked by my editor at *A+ Magazine* if I wanted to review a new program called Might and Magic Book One: The Secret of the Inner Sanctum. I remember chuckling over the name, which pretty much summed up the role-playing genre nicely. I also remember calling up the guy who created the game to ask him some questions about it, wondering who the heck he was and where he came from. I wondered at the time how such a great game had come seemingly out of nowhere. Might and Magic was an eye-opening RPG; the packaging was bold and original; yet, I had never heard of New World Computing or Jon Van Caneghem before. I consider Might and Magic one of those gems you discover every once in a while and I had no hesitation in giving it a great review. (RDM)

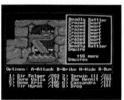

where, for instance, a sword might be the 'flaming sword of mayhem' or something. Some say it was our best Might and Magic, and certainly it won many awards and was translated into a staggering number of languages."

Might and Magic IV and V (1992 and 1993) were pure genius. No one has quite duplicated this design in the history of computer games. If you owned M&M IV and M&M V and had them installed on the same hard drive, M&M V would open up a bridge, a dimension door, between the two games and the locations represented therein. Since the universe represented in IV was the flipside of the universe represented in V, this meant that you could go from one type of gaming experience to another. But that's not all. If the two games were connected, there was not only a dimension door between the games, but there was an addition that amounted to approximately one third of the game—an extra quest, a new endgame, and additional dungeons that opened up if you had both games on your hard drive.

Might and Magic VI came out in 1998 and represented New World's first 3D graphics RPG. The team faced many unexpected challenges. "Working in 3D for the first time, we had to guess about the size of the game, the map size. It was very new and, in retrospect, several times we were inches away from guessing way wrong."

Might and Magic VII was based on the M&M VI engine and therefore didn't require a lot of technical development. The design team concentrated on story and gameplay, with the result that VII was four times the size of VI. Might and Magic VIII is one of Van Caneghem's least favorites. It was based on the same engine again, which by this time was quite obsolete, and it was released in what he considers an "unfinished" state—ironically, suffering the same fate as Ultima VIII.

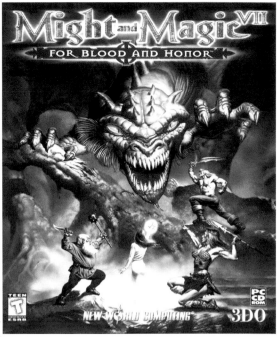

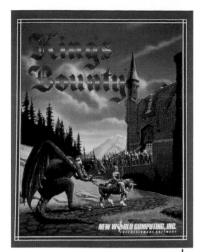

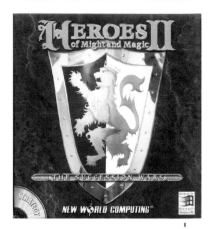

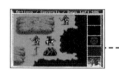

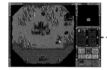

King's Bounty

"I love role-playing and I love strategy, and I wanted a game in which I could control armies of creatures," says Van Caneghem about King's Bounty. This small, turn-based RPG adventure game came out in 1990 and was a very pleasant surprise. It was, by comparison with to the Might and Magic games, quite small, and games were short in duration. And that was part of its appeal.

Years later, New World revised the King's Bounty games with the Heroes of Might and Magic series. "My wife, Debbie, loved King's Bounty and so she pressured me to do more. So I finally gave in and made Heroes," relates Van Caneghem. "A good thing I listened."

Since this book was originally published, New World Computing, which had become a division of 3DO, has gone out of business. However, for King's Bounty fans, there's a great new version published by Atari, called King's Bounty: The Legend.

Jon Van Caneghem later became one of the founders of Trion Worlds and then moved over to Electronic Arts to head their Los Angeles studio.

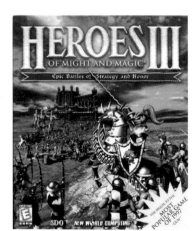

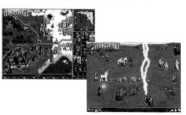

223

Cinemaware: Made for CD

When Activision bought Gamestar, I quit and was looking for a new job. Bob Jacobs offered me an opportunity, but I was skeptical. I took my wife with me to the interview for a reality check. Bob took us back to a lab where he had an Amiga. It was the first time I'd seen one. He showed me the title page of Defender with its cool glinting metal effect and letters etched into the wall. I had never seen anything like it before. My wife leaned over and whispered, 'Take the job.'
—**John Cutter,**
    Cinemaware's first employee and producer of many of their titles

Master Designer Software Presents
A CINEMAWARE™ Production DEFENDER OF THE CROWN
Directed by KELLYN BEECK Computography and Art Direction by JAMES SACHS
Editing by Sculptured Software Inc. Special Effects by BRYAN BRANDENBURG
Original Score Composed by JIM CUOMO Unit publicist: MARC HALBERSTADT
Executive Producers: ROBERT & PHYLLIS JACOB
© 1986 Master Designer Software Inc. all rights reserved.

One of the most intriguing companies to come and go (and recently come back again) in computer game history, Cinemaware had a profound effect on a lot of us. Many of the alumni of this company are well-known developers who have continued long careers, including RJ Mical, John Cutter, Pat Cook, David Riordan, David Todd, and Doug Barnett.

Started in 1986 by Bob and Phyllis Jacobs, Cinemaware's initial mission was to produce games for the CD-ROM. Ironically, the CD didn't really catch on until after Cinemaware had closed its doors. But for glitz and glamour, nobody did it better. The box covers alone were worth the price, and the games were often offbeat, funny, and great to play.

Most of the games were originally created on the Commodore Amiga, much to the regret of those of us who were primarily using Apples and PCs.

Cinemaware's first release in 1986 was Kellyn Beck's Defender of the Crown, a game set in England during the heyday of knights and fair maidens. It even included jousting, as well as castle raids and assaults. It started out as Robin Hood, but Kellyn wanted to create his own storyboard. It also had a nude scene, even if it was depicted in silhouette.

"When I'm talking to people about interface, the first example I give is S.D.I. The other example I give is Rocket Ranger," says Cinemare producer John Cutter. "We had a fistfighting sequence against the Nazis in Rocket Ranger. When we first put the sequence together, it was missing something. For sound effects, we were using white noise, which was a common programmer's shortcut. But the Amiga could do real digitized sound effects, so we contact-

ed Bill Williams, who had done everything for S.D.I. He actually went out and got a John

Sinbad and the Throne of the Falcon was another of Cinemaware's experiments in interactive cinema. "It was the first game I had seen where there was an active zoom feature triggered by the mouse. As the cursor moved across the map, you would click with the mouse to open up a window

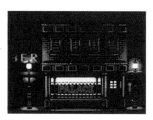

magnifying sections of the map. It had the effect of looking like you were peering at the map through a magnifying glass." (JLW)

In The King of Chicago, you played a character named Pinky Callahan, and the object was to rise to power in the Mob in post-Capone Chicago. "I remember the original Macintosh version of King of Chicago. It was downright weird. It featured clay-molded characters in a wicked, backstabbing gangster adventure. This was definitely a 'do unto others before they do it to you' sort of game, and I loved it!" (RDM)

John Cutter likes to use S.D.I. as an example of the power of graphics in games: "We had already completed a version of S.D.I., but after seeing the graphics Jim Sachs did in Defender of the Crown, we real-

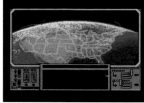

ized we wanted better art. We hired professional artists and redid all the graphics. A month later, we got a new version back from Sculptured Software, who was programming the game. We were convinced that they had made all kinds of changes to the gameplay, but it turned out that they had not. It was just the improved graphics and some sound additions that made the game much, much better."

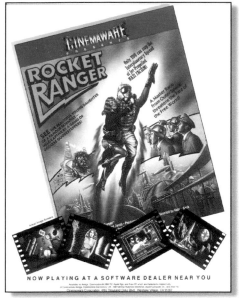

"I remember one day, maybe six months after Stooges came out," says Cutter, "and we had some European reviewers visiting. It was a big dog and pony show, and I heard them outside my door saying how much they loved our games. I'm beaming. But then they came to the Three Stooges game, the one I was most responsible for in design, and said, 'We hated it.'

Stooges did not do well in Europe, though it did well in the States. My favorite part was the intro, where it began with the Defender of the Crown title screen—just long enough—then the Stooges would come out. We even had a digitized line from one of their films saying, 'We're in the wrong game, idiot.'"

Wayne movie and recorded a fistfight and used that sound as a punching sound. All of a sudden the fight became so much fun, in part, I suppose, because it really subconsciously sounded like a John Wayne movie. It's an example of how our emotions are affected, even when we don't know why or where it's coming from."

The TV Sports line of games that Cinemaware released attempted to create the same sort of atmosphere as sports on television, except, of course, that you got to control play of the game. But they had announcers, cheerleaders, and even funny commercials. The games themselves were pretty fun to play, too.

John Cutter says, "My favorite of the TV Sports games was TV Sports Football. Our passing interface was great. It required you to lead the receiver to complete the pass. One of my personal high points was when I beat Pat Cook in the finals

of our tournament. Pat was a great game player, and to this day he swears I had the programmer tweak the game." Says Cook, "He's still telling that story? Of course he fixed it."

Designed by Doug Barnett, who also did all the graphics and sounds for the game, and programmed by David Todd, Lords of the Rising Sun was possibly the most ambitious of Cinemaware's games. Barnett says, "I really got into it, reading books and buying swords—I couldn't eat sushi for a year after finishing the game." And David Todd adds, "Doug's original design had everything in it. A book an inch and a half thick. We had to trim it some."

Lords of the Rising Sun featured a stylized map of Japan set in the year 1180, during a famous period called the Gempei War. It featured two brothers, one more skilled in military matters and the other a superior politician. During the game, you had a first-person point of view

(POV) in the ninja attack sequences, clever real-time battle formations, castle sieges, and various cut scenes. Barnett remembers, "This period of history had a lot of gameplay jumping out of it and saying, 'Do me!' And in the end, one brother turns on the other, so you had to gauge when you were close to victory. That's when you'd lose half your forces."

During the development of the game, they flew Barnett to Dallas so he and Todd could work together more closely. "Every morning, the Dallas Cowboys cheerleaders would practice across the street. It was a good way to start the day," says Barnett. "David was married. He probably didn't even notice," he adds.

David Riordan began in the music business, went to making films, and ultimately helped start Lucasfilm's game division at the request of George Lucas. Still, by the time he came to Cinemaware, he hadn't yet designed a game.

CINEMAWARE PRESENTS

BUY ONE GET ONE FREE
SEE DETAILS INSIDE

IT CAME FROM THE DESERT

SEE DECENT AMERICANS TERRORIZED!

HEAR TEENAGE GIRLS SQUEAL!

PRESENTED IN THRILL-O-VISION!

MAKE THEM ANTS CRY UNCLE!

IBM PC, Tandy and 100% Compatibles
VGA, EGA, Tandy 16-color
640K Ram required
Supports Ad lib, Soundblaster and

Early Cinemaware pamplet including Pat Cook, David Riordan, John Cutter in the front, and Bob Jacobs in the back row.

"Bob Jacobs used to come over and lay down a little seagull management. He'd flap in, poop all over everything, and leave. But he had such a passion for what he wanted. I'm still grateful for the crystal gems of wisdom he shared with me. Cinemaware had, per capita, one of the most creative and talented groups I ever worked with.
—PAT COOK, CINEMAWARE DESIGNER AND PRODUCER

It Came from the Desert was his debut as a designer. "I first came to Cinemaware at a time when I was considering quitting games and going back to films," says Riordan. "Then I saw my first Amiga, and the game on it was Defender of the Crown. I wrote Bob Jacobs a fan letter. Before I knew it, I was working for him. So then the time came to create a game for Cinemaware. I was thinking what kind of game I'd do. Something cinematic. I'm a big fan of the movie Them. So I asked Bob, 'What about a bug movie?' And he answered, 'Why not?'

"My original design was way too big. David Todd said to me, 'This is at least ten disks. Hell, maybe it's 100.' So I asked myself, 'How do you do it all, keep it to a reasonable size and have it be fun without huge holes? How you plot what we called a 'real-time environment'?' I wanted the feeling that the ants were coming and things were happening where you were not. We thought we were heading to a time when we could really make movies, and that's how we approached it."

> *What I liked most about Wings was the diary, which would continue with the story even if your pilot got killed. There was nothing to stop you from finishing the game, and lots of people commented that this was one of the first games they had been able to complete. We tried to give a good feeling for what it was like to be a pilot in World War I. When Bob first approached me to do the design, I wasn't very interested. But after an hour in the library reading about aviation in WWI, I was hooked. It was amazing, these young kids—often 18 or 19 years old—flying around and shooting at each other at a time when airplanes were so new.*
> —John Cutter, Cinemaware producer

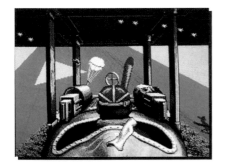

> *This was the first time I'd ever been put in a game. My first and last names were part of the random pool of pilot names, and once I even played as Jules DeMaria. (RDM)*

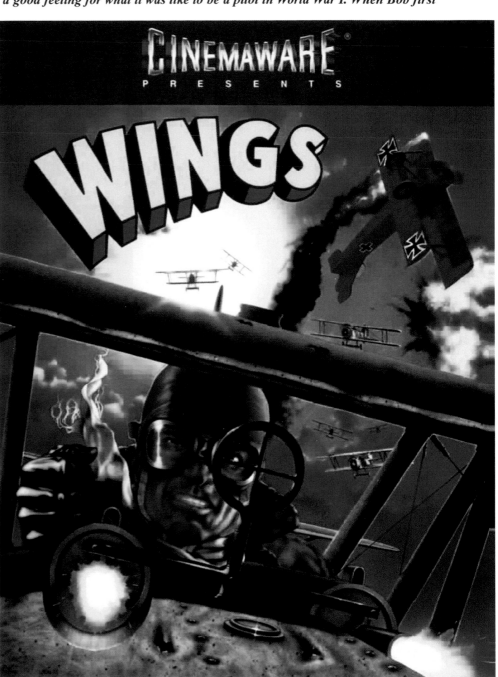

Bethesda Softworks

Christopher Weaver

In the late '70s, after finishing graduate school with degrees in physics and Japanese, Chris Weaver spent several years working at companies like ABC and the National Cable Television Association. He also completed a stint as chief engineer for the House Committee on Communications, which led to the formation of his first company, Videomagic Laboratories. Videomagic was focused on real-time video simulations based on work they had previously done under a DARPA grant at MIT. When Videomagic shut down in 1984 Weaver started Media Technology, which did engineering and media consulting for Fortune 500, network, and government organizations. There he met Ed Fletcher, who one day suggested that they explore video games, an idea that Weaver supported because he believed that personal computers would continue to proliferate. Fletcher's passion was for football, and so he set out to create a computer football game.

For Weaver, the idea of games wasn't that big a stretch. "Much of my undergraduate and graduate career focused on computers, networks, user interaction, simulation, spatial data management, and synthetic environments."

Ed Fletcher had earned an electrical engineering degree from the University of Florida. He got his first taste of games on a roommate's Heathkit H8 with 4K of RAM, playing a game called Starcraft (not the Blizzard RTS) and dabbling in gameplay programming. As he remembers it, he moved to Rockville, Maryland about a year after graduation to join Videomagic Laboratories as a digital engineer, where Chris Weaver was vice president. Videomagic was working on laserdisc technology to create video games that were even higher-end than Dragon's Lair. Then, after two years of toiling to make laserdisc games, the arcade market crashed. "I had spent the whole time building the CPU for the arcade game,"

Fletcher says. "During that time I kind of got the sense that when it comes to games, the software people are having more fun than the hardware people."

After Videomagic went bankrupt in 1984, Fletcher joined Weaver to start a new company. It turned out that the architecture of the machine they had been building was similar in architecture to the Amiga. "So we thought, what we'd do is develop some really good technology on interactive stuff with the laserdisc." At that time, interactive training videos were a growing business on laserdiscs, so they thought that was a good direction to go. They decided on the Amiga because it was compatible with the system they had already developed.

While they were waiting to find a contract, Fletcher decided to make a game as a way of learning the Amiga's graphics system and get a good feel for how the new machine worked. They got their first Amiga 500 in September of 1985, and Fletcher started working on a football simulator called Gridiron! Weaver remembers that Fletcher's first approach was to use lookup tables to determine outcomes—a standard practice at the time—but Weaver didn't think the result was impressive enough, and together they decided to implement real physics in the game. Although Fletcher had promised to complete the game in three months, it ended up taking six. Fletcher remembers that Weaver was able to secure enough financing to pay him a salary, and because they were actually based in Weaver's home in Bethesda, Maryland, they were able to keep their expenses low.

Weaver officially started Bethesda Softworks in 1985 with a personal investment of $100,000 "and a lot of sweat equity." With Weaver and Fletcher doing most of the work, there was plenty to do to complete the game and prepare to market it.

(According to Fletcher, the company name was inspired by BMW / Bavarian Motor Works, which he remembered visiting as a kid. Since Weaver's house where they were working was in Bethesda, Maryland, Bethesda Softworks seemed like a logical name. Weaver originally wanted to call it Bethesda Softwerke, but another company in Virginia had that name, so ultimately he changed the name. Weaver also recalls wanting at one time to incorporate "magic" in the company name because of the Arthur C. Clarke quote, "Any sufficiently advanced technology is indistinguishable from magic.")

Gridiron! was released for Amiga in spring 1986 and it sold about 5,000 copies. "Back then, that was a hit," says Fletcher. "We even got an award from Family Computing magazine, tying with Earl Weaver Baseball for the best sports simulation of the year." Gridiron! was also released on the Atari ST the same year, achieving still more success.

The success of Gridiron! changed the whole focus of the company, and they decided to ditch laserdisc training and focus on games. Although Gridiron! would never win awards for its graphics—the players were all represented by either black or white dots on a flat green "field"—what made the game remarkable was that each of those dots was based on the first realistic sports physics simulation, and the "players" would block, run, throw, and tackle accurately. Because of this, sports game Gridiron! was also called a simulation. Despite this early success, Weaver kept the company in what he called a "bunker mentality"—frugal and always prepared for the inevitable challenges—claiming later that this approach allowed them to survive when many bigger companies, such as Software Toolworks, Mediagenic, Epyx, and Commodore did not.

Gridiron! caught the attention of Trip Hawkins at Electronic Arts, most likely because of their realistic use of physics. The story most commonly told is that Bethesda contracted with EA to publish Gridiron! and also to develop a 16-bit version of John Madden Football. The companies had a falling out, however, and there are conflicting versions of what ultimately caused the rift. Whatever happened, EA did not sell many copies of Gridiron!, so neither company was happy with the arrangement. Meanwhile, Robin Antonick programmed Madden, and there was some dispute about whether he had used any of the Gridiron! physics code in the game. Trip Hawkins says categorically no. "There is no trace, either in code or concept, of any Bethesda work in any version of Madden in history. The first Madden code base was 6502 assembler by Robin Antonick, and it debuted in 1988 and was later ported to 8086 and was the only Madden code base released for home or personal computers." Weaver doesn't claim that Antonick use the code outright, but he asserts that the Madden code was highly influenced by Ed Fletcher's code, which is plausible. In any case,

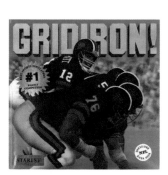

there was a lawsuit which was ultimately settled, and the two companies went in their separate directions. (Antonick later sued EA, claiming that they failed to pay him contractual royalties for later versions of Madden that still implemented his code. The courts originally found in favor of Antonick, but that ruling was since overturned and the case is still in appeals.)

Meanwhile, time had not stood still, and Bethesda was already working on another sports game. They chose hockey because, according to Fletcher, "The ones out there were just really crappy." He adds, "I knew nothing about hockey; I went to Florida for college, for Christ's sake." Initially, they approached Bobby Orr's agent, but "he wanted an exorbitant sum of money even though he'd been retired for a number of years." (Although Weaver remembers Orr himself being very generous with them on a personal level.) On a whim, they approached Wayne Gretzky's agent. Gretzky had recently been traded from the Oilers to the L.A. Kings and, according to Fletcher, Bethesda got a good licensing deal because Gretzky's people saw it as good PR.

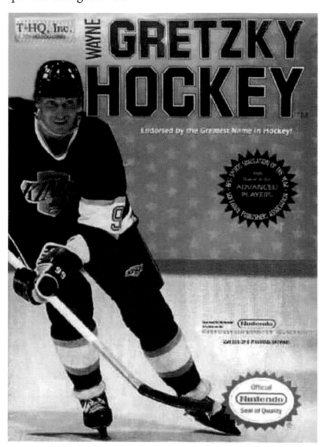

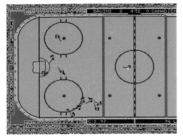

Wayne Gretzky Hockey on Amiga

With a lot of help from people in the hockey community—particularly from the local Washington Capitals team—Weaver and Fletcher were able to get a real education in how the sport worked, along with expert help in the game's development. They used the Gridiron! physics models again and produced the most realistic hockey game for its time.

Wayne Gretzky Hockey was Bethesda's first breakout game. Published initially on the Amiga in 1988, Wayne Gretzky Hockey won the Best Sports Simulation award from the Software Publishers Association that year, and was ported to the PC, Atari ST, Commodore 64, Macintosh, and ultimately to the NES (by THQ). The game spawned two sequels as well, putting Bethesda firmly on the map.

After the success of their first hockey game, according to Fletcher, "We got to the point where we could start hiring people and become a real company." They started working on the sequel, Wayne Gretzky Hockey 2, aiming to release the game in time for the Christmas season. Weaver's goal was to get the game into Radio Shacks in time for its fall distribution, which at that time would lead to a "boatload of sales." What occurred was a classic case of marketing versus development. From Fletcher's point of view, Weaver wanted to rush the game out the door, but from Weaver's perspective, the team needed to allot enough time to fully test the game so that it could be ready for production and released on time.

What happened is that they finalized the game according to Weaver's schedule and burned 75,000 CDs, only to discover a fatal "no ship" bug. All 75,000 CDs had to be destroyed. Fletcher believed that rushing development, even to achieve greater profits, would force them into making what he called "low quality" products, and that Weaver was more concerned with the money side than the quality side of the equation. Weaver, on the other hand, saw that the Christmas season accounted for at least 20% of a product's sales—sales that you would never get back later. For a small company in its early stages, he just didn't think they could afford to miss that window. It was a fundamental, but very common, difference of perspective between product developers and management/marketing.

After shipping Wayne Gretzky Hockey 2, the situation got worse from Fletcher's point of view. Weaver decided to take over 100% of the ownership of Bethesda Softworks, justifying the decision because he was the only one with an actual financial stake from the original investment he had made when founding the company. Legally, he was right, and Fletcher had always been treated as an employee. When Fletcher complained, Weaver offered him 5% of the profits as reported on their income taxes, but Fletcher didn't believe it would amount to much if it was based on the tax forms. With clever accounting, he figured the yearly profit would be "as close to zero as possible."

Although in retrospect Weaver can understand Fletcher's feelings, he does add that he paid his employees well—better than himself in the early day—contributing 15% to an IRA (without any employee contribution) and providing healthcare. At any rate, Fletcher had begun to lose faith in Bethesda and left to start a company of his own.

Part of Fletcher's frustration might have come from some managerial approaches Weaver had implemented based, in part, on two books by Steve McConnell—Rapid Development and Code Complete. Weaver is the first to admit that his schooling had been in science and not in business, so he was doing his best to run Bethesda successfully. There was considerable pressure to produce games on time and on budget with a small crew that did everything in-house, from conception and design to programming, box art and design, manuals, distribution and sales, and even disk duplication. Although doing everything in-house provided greater product control, potentially faster turnaround times, and lower costs, it also required strict discipline and long hours to hit financially critical shipping dates.

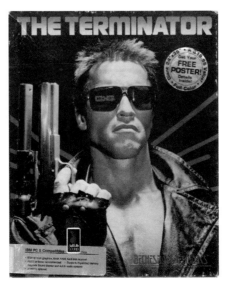

Bethesda continued to produce games, beginning with a third Gretzky hockey game followed by The Terminator—a progenitor of first-person shooters—in 1990 (with several sequels to follow). Weaver knew that, although licensed games had built-in audiences and marketing, original properties would be the best way to make money in the long run. So when Julian LeFay proposed an ambitious role-playing game, he said yes, even providing the name for the first one: Elder Scrolls: Arena. "I did provide a name," says Weaver, "but it was Julian who really had the idea and made it work." The first two Elder Scrolls games, Arena (1994) and Daggerfall (1996), introduced the background for the series and were followed by An Elder Scrolls Legend: Battlespire (1997) and The Elder Scrolls Adventures: Redguard (1998).

LeFay left the company after the release of Battlespire, later writing on a Daggerfall comment board that he had left out of frustration over the lack of adequate staff, the pressure from management to ship the projects on time instead of when they

were truly ready (sound familiar?), dropped features, and other similar complaints. In the case of Daggerfall, which he thought could have been far better, LeFay was the only programmer. On Battlespire, he had more control over the project, but said that it, too, suffered from inadequate resources and support.

Weaver had come to realize that to become a real powerhouse in the industry, you had to develop games asynchronously, and Bethesda Softworks wasn't set up for doing multiple games. So in 1999, Weaver teamed up with influential Washington lawyer and businessman Robert A. Altman (who was also married to Wonder Woman star Lynda Carter) to form ZeniMax Media. In addition to becoming Bethesda's parent company, Weaver and Altman intended for ZeniMax to enter into a cross-media arena producing not just games, but other mobile, web, and interactive TV content. Weaver used his Bethesda stock to help obtain funding for the new venture. Altman took on the role of CEO, while Weaver was made CTO.

In all, Bethesda and associated studios released about 36 games between 1986 and 2002. The crowning achievement of this era was The Elder Scrolls III: Morrowind (2002), a major hit that set the stage for some of the company's biggest future hit games.

The Elder Scrolls: Morrowind was a landmark game for Bethesda. It was an open world RPG on a huge scale, with nearly endless opportunities to explore. Morrowind and its successors—Oblivion and Skyrim—would help redefine the nature of single-player RPGs and propel ZeniMax/Bethesda to even greater levels of success and opportunity.

2002 was also the year that Weaver's contract with ZeniMax was due to expire. At the time, he was taking some time to teach at MIT, while tensions began to build up between him and Altman. There's a long story involving a complex and drawn-out lawsuit, but the shorter version is that Weaver's contract was not renewed. He left the company to go into teaching full time, which he now says is exactly what he loves most. At the time of this writing, Weaver is teaching Comparative Media Studies at MIT and working on projects to bring effective digital, game-based education to K-12 education.

However messy the case of ZeniMax v. Weaver was, it did not seem to blunt the company's progress or its mission to create great games. ZeniMax/Bethesda has continued to develop hits, becoming one of the powerhouse companies in the game industry.

Lynda Carter and Robert Altman

Morrowind cover and Daggerfall screen.

T..r..e-Sixty..a..cific

In mid-1987, Tom Frisina left Accolade—which he had been running for about two years—and decided to start a company of his own. Frisina had a vision of building a company around products that would appeal to a wider audience than the core computer gamer. At the beginning, however, he drew inspi-

ration from Tom Clancy's novels. MicroProse had released Red Storm Rising, and Frisina was thinking about how to go even further with a submarine game. He knew that Clancy had used Larry Bond's Harpoon board game to work out some of his naval scenarios, so Frisina went directly to Bond, a former NATO referee for naval exercises.

I'D RATHER DO IT MYSELF!
Tom Frisina told *Computer Gaming World*'s editorial staff that he planned to leave Accolade and start his own company, Three-Sixty Pacific. Ironically, when news of this was printed in the "Rumor Bag" column with Frisina's permission, Frisina called up all his investors and demanded to know where the leak came from. Later, reminded that he had given the story himself, he was astonished. "I was my own leak," he said, laughing.

Going for depth first and celebrity second, Three-Sixty not only published Bond's classic war game Harpoon, but also Dale Brown's Megafortress (a brilliant game version of Brown's best-selling thriller, Flight of the Old Dog), Jim Dunnigan's Victory at Sea (a campaign game set in the South Pacific theater of WWII using data compiled by Dunnigan, aka the dean of war game designers), and Patriot (a game based on the Gulf War using the research compiled by veteran war game designer Frank Chadwick).

Frisina was savvy enough not to tie his future onto military strategy games alone (though those became Three-Sixty's bread and butter). He had a vision of publishing software that would make even more of a difference. Working with former NASA

psychologist Taibi Kahler (author of The *Mastery of Management*), he published a software product called Bridges that tested for elements of six personality types using the prototyping developed by Kahler at NASA. Unfortunately, the buyers at the software chains simply wouldn't take seriously a psychological product developed by a "mere" game company.

Three-Sixty Pacific's biggest problem, however, was the fact that they sunk too much money into products that didn't fully satisfy their customer base in between the innovative titles. For instance, Artech (the Canadian group that had worked with Frisina since Accolade) talked Three-Sixty into publishing an abstract puzzle game called Theatre of War. It was to war games what sophisticated jazz was to popular music, and proved unsatisfying to the company's usual customer base. In

addition, buggy initial versions made Patriot and Victory at Sea unplayable at launch, and Three-Sixty started to become cash-flow negative. Barely finishing Harpoon II after a "shotgun wedding" with Intracorp, who also funded Capstone, Three-Sixty Pacific became one of those "coulda' been a contender" companies that faded into history.

More Favorite Games of the '80s

The Edu-Ware team in 1983.

In addition to major companies who had a huge impact on the computer game industry, many small companies produced amazing game classics. There were also some games from major publishers that we wanted to acknowledge on their own—games such as Wasteland, Alter Ego, Shanghai, and Little Computer People. In the following section, we'll look at some of our favorite games of the '80s, starting with one of the least graphical, and yet most mental of games—David Mullich's The Prisoner.

The Prisoner

David Mullich worked for Edu-Ware while still in college, later joining the company and becoming VP of product development. Sherwin Steffin and Steve Pederson started Edu-Ware in 1978 for the purpose of creating educational software, but, according to Mullich, "they got more publicity out of their entertainment software."

Edu-Ware published several games, including

Space, a port of the popular board game Traveller; as well as Terrorist; and Windfall, which was an economic simulation about the oil crisis. They also did Network, in which they cast the player in the role of a TV network programmer trying for the highest ratings.

By far their most noteworthy game, however, was The Prisoner, which was inspired both by the TV show of the same name and by an experiment Mullich had learned about in a psychology class (see "Rules of the Game" in the sidebar).

"I was so enthusiastic about the show and the whole idea of this community that was all geared toward trying to get information out of a spy by tricking him... playing mind games on him. I wanted to create a computer game that would play mind games on players, lead them down false alleys, change the rules on the fly, trick them into doing something they shouldn't do."

Castle Wolfenstein and RobotWar

At approximately the same time that The Avalon Hill Game Company was making its first venture into the world of computer games, another Baltimore company made its appearance.Muse Software appeared on the entertainment software horizon after they recruited a programmer named Silas Warner. Warner had worked for Commercial Credit Corporation, supervising their PLATO accounts and writing a sales call simulator as part of the company's training program. The simulator was programmed in two weeks after the company had undergone a role-playing experience as part of its training.

When Warner arrived at Muse Software, he designed two of the games that defined the early era of computing, Castle Wolfenstein and RobotWar. The former was an action-adventure game that inspired id Software's Wolfenstein 3D. The latter was a programmer's dream, where players would use a special pseudo-code to program robotic behavior. Then, much like the BattleBots of today, they would be placed in an arena and allowed to fight it out. The last robot standing was the winner. Although the game fostered numerous tournaments in regional user groups and a play-by-mail tournament for Computer Gaming World magazine (where competitors saved their source code to disk, which they mailed to the magazine for the editors to place their robots into tournament matches), it was more of a cult classic than a bestselling blockbuster. Tributes to RobotWar include Origin's OMEGA game and the shareware version of CROBOTS, available online.

Magazine ads for Castle Wolfenstein and RobotWar.

ROBOTWAR BATTLEFIELD (4 ROBOTS)
PRESS ESC. TO STOP.

Castle Wolfenstein and RobotWar screens.

Although best known for Castle Wolfenstein and RobotWar, Muse also published action games such as ABM (similar to Missile Command), Frazzle (similar to Asteroids but with a spatial twist), and Firebug (a reverse Pac-Man where the player is destroying the maze of a building instead of avoiding ghosts). Firebug was later changed to Firefly because the publisher didn't want to be accused of promoting arson. Perhaps the most interesting thing about Firebug was its delightful pun whenever one lost the game. The screen would go dark and then display, "You made an ash of yourself!" Talk about adding insult to injury!

Muse Software quit publishing in the mid-'80s, but Silas Warner went on to become the conversion guru for MicroProse Software. At MicroProse, he converted Sid Meier's Pirates! to the Apple IIGS, Red Storm Rising to the C64, Silent Service to the Atari ST, and Gunship to the Amiga.

The Perfect General

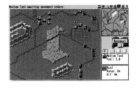

One of the finest tactical war games ever produced on the computer was the result of 12 years of play-testing. Bruce Williams Zaccagnino, who had built what the Smithsonian called the World's Largest Model Railroad, also had a passion for military miniatures. His local war game club had developed rules for playing with miniature tanks and soldiers on scale-model terrains.

Zaccagnino started Quantum Quality Productions (QQP) with the idea of bringing his war game experience to the home computer. He drafted Mark Baldwin and Bob Rakosky of Empire (and later, Empire Deluxe fame) to design the interface and artificial intelligence for two games—The Perfect General and The Lost Admiral—both of which were released in 1991.

The Perfect General offered an easy point-and-click interface for movement and targeting, as well as three levels of difficulty for the AI. Using the tabletop miniatures model, all QQP games allowed you to purchase units for points. The Perfect General was also one of the early point-to-point modem games, and for years it was one of the most-played games on the web. Perfect General II still has quite a following, with new scenarios available free.

> When we first got The Perfect General at Computer Gaming World, one of our editors, Alan Emrich, lost five out of the next seven workdays to the game. I, being a responsible editor, only lost two out of the next three. (JLW)

Empire: Wargame of the Century

Like many other computer games, the history of Empire begins in the analog world of tabletop gaming. Peter S. Langston and friends were playing an abstract war game at Reed College in the early '70s. Langston wondered about using a computer to run the game and simulate the "fog of war" effect, which would prevent players from seeing the whole battlefield—something very difficult to accomplish with tabletop games.

Langston's Empire, begun in 1971, was a text-only multiplayer game. The world was updated once per day (usually at midnight). However, attacks were handled instantaneously, which led to some interesting ploys by avid players.

After Langston, Walter Bright continued to advance and popularize the game, drawing inspiration from the British war room in the film *Battle of Britain* and from the board game Risk. Bright made refinements on the multiplayer game, and in the mid-'80s, he developed a single-player game for personal computers. Bright's version was turned down by many of the major game publishers, however, largely for its out-of-date graphics and interface.

Independently, Mark Baldwin did a version of Empire for Interstel, and his version looked terrific on both the Atari ST and the Commodore Amiga. He brought the game to current interface standards, offering point-and-click movement and pop-up menus. For the first time, players could escort transports with destroyers and group task forces efficiently. This Baldwin and Bright version of Empire: Wargame of the Century was to be converted to a half-dozen different computer platforms and was one of Interstel's best titles ever. It was also released with a play-by-mail feature so that players could trade disks via snail mail (and later, files via email).

After Interstel's collapse, Baldwin joined with a frequent collaborator named Bob Rakosky to create Empire Deluxe for New World Computing. This enhanced rewrite was a Windows-based program complete with a versatile construction set and three different levels of gameplay to make it more accessible (Basic, Standard, and Advanced). Empire Deluxe was successful enough that the team dipped into the well again and released Empire II, a tactical war game construction set using the expertise in AI design and interface development created for Empire Deluxe.

Peter Langston's favorite story about Empire is the one about the vice president of a large corporation who was so agitated by an attack on his country that he allegedly walked into the computer room and flipped the main circuit breaker to abort the attack. Then there's the Harvard student who refused to go to bed until everyone logged out of Empire. So the other players took turns staying up late in order to foil his dedicated plan for "national security."

Walter Bright tells a story about the sysops at Caltech who didn't want gamers tying up the PDP-10 with games, so they severely restricted the hours that students could play Empire. Bright simply switched the name of the game to "test" and played anytime he wanted for months before the sysops caught on.

Walter Bright's original version of Empire required a lot of command input and waiting while the computer thought, but it still featured addictive play.

Mark Baldwin's refinement of Bright's design in Empire: Wargame of the Century significantly improved the interface.

The Modern Version Of The Award Winning Classic

EMPIRE Deluxe

By Mark Baldwin and Bob Rakosky

Wasteland

Wasteland was created at Interplay and distributed by Electronic Arts, and although its interface bore a great resemblance to Interplay's The Bard's Tale, the game itself was quite different and had plenty of innovation. Many players still consider it to be among the greatest role-playing games ever written. Wasteland differed from other games by being based, not in some medieval fantasy world, but on the modern science fiction tabletop role-playing game called Mercenaries, Spies, & Private Eyes. The game demanded the use of modern weapons, and Wasteland was the first computer role-playing game (CRPG) to feature an encounter with an armored vehicle. This, in turn, required the use of armor-piercing shells and some additional programming to modify the damage calculations. Wasteland also offered a robust skill-based system that allowed characters to improve without engaging in combat.

Wasteland's excellent design team included bestselling novelist Michael A. Stackpole, the creator of Mercenaries, Spies, & Private Eyes. The game was set in a post-apocalyptic desert world. Stackpole designed some of the game maps himself, and farmed out maps to others, including Ken St. Andre (designer of Tunnels & Trolls) and fantasy artist Liz Danforth. Danforth is the wicked designer who created the "rabid dog dilemma." You needed to kill the rabid dog to get out of a cave on her map. If you killed the dog, a little boy followed you and complained, "You killed my dog, you dirty Rangers!" Some players ended up avoiding the town where Bobby was, just to evade the nuisance of his constant accusation. Others heartlessly killed Bobby to remove the annoyance factor. Vince DeNardo, Computer Gaming World's art director at the time, restarted the game and kept saving and resaving the game until he could escape from the cave without killing the dog. As a result of such encounters, Wasteland became similar to Ultima IV as one of the few CRPGs that forced you to ask questions before you shot anything.

Shanghai

If the basic solitaire game and FreeCell variation that are bundled with Microsoft Windows are the most-played games in the personal computer world, Shanghai must be a close second. It has been converted to dozens of operating systems, from PCs

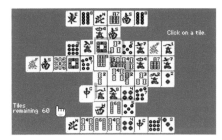

Shanghai screen

to consoles and handhelds, including an amazing number of versions in Japan that ran on what were formerly "dedicated" word processors.

It is a simple concept: take the beautiful tiles from a mahjong set and assemble them onscreen in the formation known for centuries as "The Turtle." Then, dismantle "The Turtle" by matching pairs until no tiles remain. The result is a simple and compelling solitaire game perfectly suited to the computer, where it takes mere seconds to set up, as opposed to the much more laborious task of setting up the real tiles.

Bill Swartz, longtime president of Activision Japan, remembers that no matter how many times Activision licensed the game in the Asia-Pacific region, no one would believe that the computer game was designed by a Westerner. Still less could anyone believe that every tile was painted and every line coded by a brilliant man who could not move from the neck down.

Brodie Lockard was a Stanford University gymnast who suffered a terrible accident. After the accident, his body was confined to a wheelchair, but his mind and spirit could not be confined. Lockard accepted a job at Stanford as his career, but he continued to program educational projects on his own time. Fascinated with "The Turtle" mahjong variation, he programmed it as an online game for one of the early communications services that antedated the World Wide Web. It quickly became the most-played game on the service, despite the fact that the meter was always running when people played. When the color Macintosh appeared, Lockard painted elaborate tiles, holding a special stylus in his mouth.

Activision producer Brad Fregger (who also produced the first computer solitaire game, Spectrum HoloByte's Solitaire Royale) saw the game on Christmas Eve of 1985. Borrowing a copy from Lockard, he took it home. Everybody who played it got instantly hooked. And, as they say, the rest is history.

Alter Ego

Electronic Arts often used "celebrity designers" for their games, picking their brains concerning their field of expertise. When EA published a psychological game (Mind Mirror), they consulted with Dr. Timothy Leary, the foremost advocate for mind expansion via mind-altering drugs in the U.S.

When Activision published its psychological game, the emphasis was on fun. Designed by Peter J. Favaro, the adolescent and child psychologist who wrote *Smart Parenting*, Alter Ego had different versions for male or female characters. The game functioned as a role-playing game that pulled back the veil on psychological development. Onscreen, the game looked like a graphic flowchart. Players would choose from various options on the decision tree represented by a family crest for family matters, a heart for emotional decisions, a fluoroscope for physical decisions, and faces for social decisions. Often, the situations were humorous (particularly when players did the wrong thing on purpose), and sometimes, they were sexual (particularly during the adolescent phase of the game). Usually, the situations presented a dilemma to which the player would respond by choosing a mood and an action. Then, just as in a role-playing game, players would see their characters improve in physical characteristics, mental discipline, social skills, and occupational potential. Other icons represented opportunities for relationships, jobs, scholarship, and recreation. Alter Ego was an interesting experiment in nonviolent games that related to real life. It didn't sell enough to suit Activision's goals, but it is certainly one of the more interesting and fun-to-play games of its era.

Little Computer People

Little Computer People was a relatively obscure game, but one that created a lasting impact on the people who played it. Perhaps the first example of a commercial "artificial life" product, a decade before Tamagotchi (*see page 343*), this game was seminal.

Here are some comments from designer David Crane: "If it is little known that I was the author of Activision's Little Computer People, then it is even less known that this product began life as something else.

"An independent, creative guy in L.A. by the name of Rich Gold had an idea to bring the Pet Rock concept to video games. He got some funding and developed a noninteractive product he called 'Pet Person,' containing much of the animation and sound effects of the ultimate LCP product. It was his intention that the product would be used like a fishbowl. You turn it on and just watch it all day without any interactivity. He was unable to get it published in that form, but we got a look at it, saw its potential, and bought his early work.

In Alter Ego, you could start at any of life's stages...

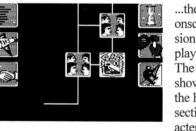

...then use the onscreen decision points to play the game. The screen shows part of the high school section. As characters matured, additional options such as High School, Relationships, Job, and Recreation were added to the choices at the side of the flowchart.

Screen from Little Computer People.

"The graphics and animations were superb, and I kept them pretty much intact—adding sounds, music, and additional capabilities. I then put almost a year into it, turning the character into an interactive, semi-intelligent, and responsive simulation. We came up with a way to customize every diskette so that each Computer Person would be unique in every way—appearance, personality, etc. Added to the technical effort was some great creative support from marketing. They developed the concept of invisible people living in your computer, the research publication, and all of the support materials that made the game something special. In spite of all that, the product was never a big success. That was unfortunate because we had all sorts of plans for follow-up products if it had been successful.

"Not that it was a failure; everybody's development costs got covered with a little profit. But we were all prepared to make an apartment building with dozens of Computer People, all interacting with one another and trading equipment and furnishings, etc. We had hopes to create disks full of new stuff and/or new houses that you could buy to customize your Computer Person's environment. But you don't do sequels unless the market demands it, and that demand never materialized. Oh well.

"Some users would write to us in a panic when a Commodore crash damaged their diskette. They would beg us to fix their 'Aaron' (or whatever the name). So I created an 'LCP hospital' computer so that our customer service people could make a fresh diskette that incorporated the 2048-bit personality parameter from the old one. We were able to 'save' hundreds of Little Computer People in our hospital.

"All in all, it was a fun project. I may yet do another product along those lines if the right deal comes along."

Millionaire

In 1982, after learning some hard lessons in the stock market, Jim Zuber founded Blue Chip Software and published Millionaire, a stock market simulation that tracked earnings, volume, and general and industry-specific trends. As in real life, stock performance tended to reflect overall market performance (bullish uptrends, bearish downturns, and mixed markets), industry group strength, corporate strength, and news.

Looking at the simulation provides a snapshot of the '70s and early '80s. Industry groups included Computer (Control Data, IBM, and NCR), Oil and Gas (Conoco, Exxon, and Mobil), Retail (Kmart, Sears, and Tandy), Automobile (General Motors, American Motors, and Bendix), and Heavy Industry (Dow Chemical, U.S. Steel, and Caterpillar tractor).

The game (and its sequels) presented general market trends, industry sector trends, and individual stock performance in chart form. Less sophisticated than charts used by technical investors, they taught you a lot, nonetheless. Also, in what became a tradition for Blue Chip Software games, players could leverage their investments into more risky portfolios as they earned money up to certain thresholds. You started with $10,000 and could improve your investment power with several techniques, such as margin buying, puts and calls, and selling short. Each technique required higher earning thresholds.

Zuber followed up Millionaire's positive reception with his most interesting game, Tycoon. Using the same system, virtual investors could play the commodities market. Tycoon was faster moving than the stock market game and offered enough historical data that players could invest as fundamentalists (following basic inferences on potential supply/demand for each commodity) or technicians (creating a strategy based on past performance charted against current trends).

Less successful were Blue Chip's games Baron, a real estate simulation, and Squire, an investment game that included such things as art and collectibles. They did come out with one more game with the quality and precision of Millionaire and Tycoon—American Dream, an IBM game in which you managed your own business.

Blue Chip was ultimately acquired by Britannica Software, but their only interesting release after that was a more detailed $99 version of Millionaire called American Investor, created for serious investors with assistance from the

Screen from Tycoon.

American Stock Exchange (AMEX). When Britannica Software became Compton's NewMedia (the company who claimed a patent on multimedia products in the early '90s), the company faded to the backlist and off the shelf.

Rocky's Boots

In 1979, when Warren Robinett left Atari, after creating the first video game Easter Egg in his VCS game, Adventure (*page 43*), he backpacked around Europe for a while and thought about what he'd do next. "I wanted to do another adventure game, and I wanted it to be one where you had to build machines to defeat monsters. I thought up two classes of machines—sensors and actuators. Sensors would put out signals that would go to the actuators. For instance, a monster sensor would activate a bomb."

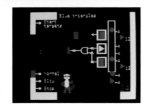

When he got back from his travels, he was introduced to three women who were proposing to do games. These women—Anne Piestrup (now McCormick), Leslie Grim, and Teri Perl—were all highly educated academics. Working with money from a grant from the National Science Foundation, they started The Learning Company. Their first product was called Logic Tools, which was the precursor to the group's first game, and one of the true classics of computer gaming, Rocky's Boots.

Rocky's Boots was a construction set, ultimately, that allowed you to wire together machines that would use logic

Warren Robinett testing Rocky's Boots at a Palo Alto, California, elementary school in 1982.

circuits (AND gates, OR gates, NOT gates, flip-flops) to trigger a big boot, which would sense and eliminate target items, such as red triangles or anything but green circles, as they passed by. The game was innovative and fascinating to play and was, in some ways, a precursor to later construction games, such as The Incredible Machine.

Of course, The Learning Company went on to become the most successful educational game company in the history of electronic games, distributing many classic educational game series, including Reader Rabbit and Oregon Trail. And it all started with the boot.

Flight Simulator

Bruce Artwick's 1975 thesis at the University of Illinois was entitled, "A Versatile Computer-Generated Dynamic Flight Display." From this thesis evolved one of the all-time classic products, Flight Simulator. Originally published by subLOGIC in 1979 for Apple II and TRS-80 computers, Flight Simulator came to the attention of Bill Gates and Microsoft, which Artwick thought of as a "nice small company." Microsoft obtained the license and released its first version of Flight Simulator in 1982. The rest is history.

Some believe that Bruce Artwick was influenced by a game called Airfight on the PLATO system. This may or may not be the case, but it is plausible.

Flight Simulator was known for its accuracy and realism, and subsequent versions became ever more accurate and detailed, with continued improvement in graphics. Scenery disks ultimately became available so you could fly over your favorite city or landscape. The combat aspect of Flight Simulator was always secondary to its realistic flight model, and pilots-in-training could even satisfy some of their requirements using the program. Flight Simulator was a perennial software leader for years, until Microsoft inexplicably disbanded the division in 2009, but there's news that a new Flight Simulator is in the works.

Home Systems of the Late '80s

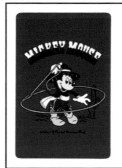

After almost two decades of growth, the video game industry faced a meltdown in the mid-'80s. The home computer game business was expanding, but the audience was too small to save the industry. Worse, the majority of the world just viewed computers as business utilities. Let's face it: Games were considered frivolous.

However, some bold players from Japan went against conventional wisdom. Because they were willing to take risks, the video game business bounced back—ultimately stronger than before. The point position in this new campaign was taken not by Atari, whose credibility by this time was at an all-time low, but by Nintendo, whose previous successes had all been in the coin-operated arena.

Nintendo

Today, Nintendo is a household name throughout the world, virtually synonymous with video games, but its march to dominance began over 100 years ago. In 1889, Fusajiro Yamauchi

Nintendo's early playing cards, Disney branded and traditional Hanafuda.

founded Nintendo as a playing card company. Over the next 50 years Nintendo grew to prominence. By 1959, they printed and sold cards with Disney characters on them, opening up the market for children's playing cards.

In the '60s, Nintendo branched out and began to manufacture games. Their new game division was led by the legendary Gunpei Yokoi, whose first game product was a mechanical hand called the Ultra Hand that sold more than a million units. Yokoi followed the hand with the Ultra Machine, an indoor baseball-pitching machine; a periscope toy called the Ultra Scope; and a very popular Love Tester that actually measured electric current flowing between two people. In 1970, Yokoi hired Masayuki Uemura, who was selling solar cells for Sharp Electronics at the time. The two teamed up to create Nintendo's Beam Gun, a game that used optics and electronics together. People shot the guns, and the targets would fall over. The Beam Gun marked Nintendo's entry into the world of electronic games.

During the '70s, Nintendo created a number of electronic toys, including a video recording (EVR) player in conjunction with Mitsubishi Electric. They also licensed the Magnavox Odyssey for sale in Japan and began to create coin-operated video games. Then, in 1980, Nintendo introduced Yokoi's next brainchild—the fantastically popular and much-imitated Game & Watch series. These small, highly addictive handheld games also featured a digital watch and alarm.

Flyer for Radar Scope, one of Nintendo's first coin-operated arcade games.

As the '70s drew to a close, Nintendo released their first coin-operated arcade game, Radar Scope, which was second in popularity only to Galaxian in Japan. However, Radar Scope didn't sell well in the U.S. Heading the U.S. operations, initially from New Jersey, was Minoru Arakawa, son-in-law to Nintendo's president, Hiroshi Yamauchi.

Arakawa remembers the early days: "We brought all the Radar Scope machines from Japan via Panama to New Jersey. By the time they reached us, the game's market opportunity was already half dead. We asked Japan to come up with the next great game, but all the R&D heads were busy and didn't want to do anything for us. So they appointed a young guy who had just joined Nintendo to develop a game for us." The game was Donkey Kong. The young employee was Shigeru Miyamoto.

But Donkey Kong wasn't an instant hit with the employees at Nintendo of America. "Donkey Kong was really different from the existing shoot-'em-up games," Arakawa recalls. "All the employees at NOA were disappointed and started looking for new jobs. They saw no future with us. So we put it in a local tavern, and the next day there was $30 in the cash box. The day after it was $35. That was really good back then. By the third day we thought, 'This is not a joke. It's a really good game!'"

At the time, Ron Judy, Nintendo's U.S. distributor, had just taken a bath trying unsuccessfully to distribute Radar Scope machines, but he took Arakawa to meet a lawyer friend named Howard Lincoln in spring 1981. Lincoln vividly recalls his first meeting with Judy and Arakawa. "Arakawa wanted help trademarking a game. I remember Ron's face when he said the name Donkey Kong. It's a name that's incomprehensible to English-speaking people. I had to get the spelling first. But then they released the game, and it took off like wildfire. I didn't see Ron again until September, when he came to me to incorporate because he was making so much money."

In 1983, Yamauchi decided it was time to incorporate the U.S. subsidiary Nintendo of America (NOA) with Arakawa at its head. Lincoln soon joined NOA, first as senior vice president, and the next year as chairman. (When we originallyzzzzzzzzzz interviewed him in 2001, he was the chairman of the Seattle Mariners.)

Nintendo Vs. arcade system

Donkey Kong figured heavily in the launch of both ColecoVision and the Adam computer, and it was during that time that Universal brought suit against Nintendo and Coleco over the similarity between Donkey Kong and their property, King Kong. Lincoln recalls, "It was very risky for NOA, which was still relatively small. And when somebody like Sid Sheinberg sends you a cease and desist, it gets your attention. The litigation was protracted, but in hindsight it turned out the right way." And, in the end, Nintendo was able to continue marketing Donkey Kong.

In the early '80s, Nintendo began work on a next-generation home game machine, introducing the Family Computer (or Famicom) in Japan in 1983, where it was very successful. However, the timing was bad for bringing it to the U.S. The video game industry was in the midst of its great collapse. Still, Nintendo knew they had a good thing going, and they negotiated with Atari to OEM the system. But Atari was falling apart. Nintendo's Arakawa remembers, "During the negotiations quite a few people at Atari were fired or laid off between meetings, and every meeting was attended by different people." Needless to say, the negotiations did not go well. "It was the best thing that happened to Nintendo," says Arakawa. "If Atari had taken the product, it's doubtful that Nintendo of America would exist today." Unable to introduce the Family Computer in the U.S., Nintendo created a series of coin-operated games for the arcades called the Vs. System, which was actually run by the Famicom hardware and featured many of the early Famicom games. "We found from our testing in certain locations that the systems made lots of cash, and we knew our quality was good. We were confident by 1985 that people would like our system, but the re-

Nintendo's Family Computer (Famicom)

Original Nintendo Entertainment System and Robotic Operating Buddy (R.O.B.) below.

tailers were a different story," says Arakawa.

To get past the once-burned-twice-shy retailers, Nintendo came up with the idea of bundling the Famicom, now renamed the Nintendo Entertainment System (NES), with a toy robot called R.O.B., or Robotic Operating Buddy. The system also included a light pistol (the Zapper) and the games Duck Hunt and Super Mario Bros.

It worked. The NES grew in popularity as consumers, once jaded by the early '80s machines, flocked to purchase the NES and play Super Mario Bros. and the other great games that began to appear on the new console. Arakawa once again: "The players were not tired of games. They were just tired of average games."

In 1986, Nintendo introduced what they called the Famicom Disk System in Japan. This system featured erasable disks that Famicom users could attach to their systems and then record games onto the disks. Originally scheduled for release exclusively on the Disk System were Super Mario Bros. 2, The Legend of Zelda, and Metroid. However, the Disk System was never released in the U.S., and these games (and others) were all eventually released on cartridges.

Sega

In 1952, two Americans, Dick Stewart and Ray Lemaire, went to Japan and started a company to place jukeboxes on U.S. military bases. The company was called Service Games, and they eventually expanded to 5,000 locations all over Japan. In 1953, Dave Rosen also came to Japan and formed an art and a general import business, which collectively he called Rosen Enterprises, Ltd.

By 1956 or so, the Japanese economy was starting to revive, and there was more disposable income and time for enter-

tainment. Rosen decided to import mechanical games from the States. "It was very difficult to obtain the import license," recalls Rosen. "At that time, such licenses were only granted for necessities, and they didn't classify this as a necessity."

Rosen's idea worked splendidly, however, and within a short time he had established arcades in virtually every town and city in Japan. "These arcades were not like the arcades in the U.S.," he says. "It wasn't just a matter of placing the machines in a location. There were backdrops, and the machines were built into the scenery." Among the most successful games were the rifle shooting games. The Japanese were not allowed to own guns, and they flocked to these games.

Sega co-founder Dave Rosen with some of Sega's early games.

Some of Sega's pre-video games, including Punching Bag (1962); Rifleman, the first mechanical game they made (1967); Periscope (1968); and their last mechanical game (other than pinball), Jet Rocket (1970).

Rosen remembers becoming more and more dissatisfied with the quality of games he was importing, many of which were older models. "By the mid-'60s," he says, "it became apparent that the Chicago game manufacturers, such as Bally, Midway, Williams, Chicago Coin, and Gottlieb, were not really manufacturing games that were novel and new, but were satisfying themselves with cosmetic changes on the same games. So in 1965, I merged Rosen Enterprises with Service Games, which had since shortened its name to Sega. The new company was Sega Enterprises, Ltd. One of our main purposes was to begin to develop and manufacture our own games for the arcade locations we had."

Sega began developing new games, as many as ten a year at one point, and by 1967 had begun exporting them to the States. "The first game we built was Rifleman. Our first big success was Periscope," says Rosen. In 1969, they were purchased by the multinational corporation Gulf & Western, and in 1974 they incorporated in the U.S. "From 1967 through 1979 we manufactured 140 different games, but soon afterward the Chicago companies began copying our games. In fact, our last game, and one of the finest mechanicals ever built, was Jet Rocket, and somehow a bunch of other companies had learned about it. Bally, Williams, and Chicago Coin each had a version of it when we brought it out."

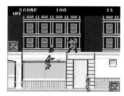

In 1979, Sega began to build arcade video games, and in 1980 they acquired Gremlin, a San Diego–based company with a large manufacturing plant. Ironically, according to Rosen, Sega was the first distributor for Nintendo's Beam Gun product in the U.S.

In addition to arcade systems, Sega began producing and licensing games for the home systems. At about this same time, Sega was made part of Gulf & Western's Paramount group, best known for their movie business. Rosen joined the board of Paramount, and movie moguls Michael Eisner and Barry Diller joined Sega's board.

Although he had seen it coming, Rosen could do nothing to prevent the effects of the video game collapse of the early '80s, and consequently Gulf & Western decided to sell off Sega. Rosen bought it, along with the head of the Japanese operation, Hayao Nakayama, and an investor, Isao Okawa. Nakayama became president, Okawa became chairman in Japan, while Rosen agreed to run the U.S. operation, but only for a few years.

The Master System

"Everybody was looking to produce a better product back in the Coleco days," says Rosen, "and we had developed a machine, but we were not really very aggressive in pushing it. We were more interested in attempting to sell software." Then, after the collapse, he adds, "The industry was fairly well written off. We had product in the pipeline, but we had put it on the shelf. We took it off the shelf when we started to see what was happening with Nintendo. But we were a year behind Nintendo, and that was a very difficult hurdle to overcome. Nintendo had a very deep foothold in the Japanese market and very strong alliances with third-party developers. We found ourselves in the position of having to scramble in the U.S., so we made a distribution deal with Tonka Toys."

In addition to being late, the Master System also suffered from having very little original software at the beginning. Nintendo had locked up most of the third-party Japanese developers with exclusive contracts. Sega drew from its well of popular arcade games, but remakes of arcade games couldn't compete with the original fare provided by Nintendo and its third-party developers. Sega did ultimately come out with more original games, "but by that time it was becoming obvious to us that we would be, at best, a poor second," admits Rosen. Among the best of the Master System's games was Phantasy Star, the first in Sega's excellent RPG series.

While the Master System struggled to gain a foothold in the U.S., Sega was already working on their next machine—a true 16-bit home game

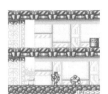

A Boy and His Blob and Bionic Commando for Game Boy.

console. "There was a difference of opinion in Japan over how to distribute the new machine. Some wanted to find a partner and do a joint venture, but I thought that would be difficult. The margins on the hardware were not great. The true profits were in the software. Still, we did approach several toy companies and others, including Atari, to distribute the new machine. But it all came to naught," says Rosen, "and we were left with the option of going out and doing it on our own."

Handheld Games

Handheld games had enjoyed considerable popularity in the late '70s and during the '80s, but the idea of a complete handheld game system really came into its own in the late '80s. Initially, there were four main contenders, each with its strengths and weaknesses. In the end, there was one clear winner.

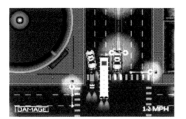

Midnight Club and Madden 2002 for Game Boy Advance.

any other console system in history. Of course, having Tetris bundled with the system in the U.S. was a brilliant stroke. It was the perfect game for the system.

Game Boy was the only major handheld game system that was monochrome, but Nintendo eventually rectified this situation—first in 1994, by introducing the Super Game Boy, which was an attachment to the Super NES that allowed Game Boy games to be played in color on a TV. Later, in 1998, they released Game Boy Color; then, in 2001, they released the long-anticipated Game Boy Advance, with superior color graphics and far more sophisticated gameplay.

Game Boy

In 1989, Gunpei Yokoi, who had designed Nintendo's popular Game & Watch hardware, produced a cartridge-based handheld device, which Nintendo called Game Boy. The system was compact and well built, but it only featured graphics in four shades of gray. Compared to other handheld systems of the time, it seemed quite crude and unimpressive. But Nintendo's genius for marketing and for controlling their markets once again shone, and in the end, none of the other handheld game systems survived long, while the Game Boy went on to sell more than 500 million units—more than

TurboExpress

NEC's TurboExpress was in some ways the premier handheld system. It was a full TurboGrafx-16 system and used the exact same HuCard games. Of course, it couldn't play the CD games, but its library of available games was much greater than any other system. Its color LCD screen gave a crisp, clean image. TurboExpress was even the first handheld game system to offer an optional TV tuner peripheral so you could watch your favorite shows between games. However, the system was costly ($249.99 versus $89.99 for Game Boy—even the TurboGrafx-16 system was only $199), and despite a large game library, its primary audience was players who already had the TurboGrafx-16, and therefore already had the games. Buying an even more expensive system to play the same games—even an ultra-cool handheld device—was probably not in most players' budgets.

Metal Gear Solid for Game Boy Color.

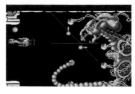

Left: Screens for R-Type and Ninja Spirit for TurboGrafx-16. Ninja Spirit was the first game to receive a perfect 10 from *Electronic Gaming Monthly* magazine.

Game Gear

The Game Gear was Sega's entry into the handheld market, but it did not fare well against the competition. It featured a color display and some good games, but it was a battery hog and was neither as crisp nor as advanced as the TurboExpress. And, although it did have a couple of exclusive Sonic the Hedgehog titles, it lacked the third-party support or marketing of its main competition, Nintendo's Game Boy.

TENGEN

Atari Games formed a new division called Tengen to create games primarily for the NES. Originally a legitimate Nintendo licensee, they didn't like the hefty cut of profits that Nintendo took. At the time, Nintendo kept strict control over all games produced for the NES, manufacturing the cartridges themselves and including a special microprocessor called the "lockout chip," which prevented any but those carts produced by Nintendo

from working in the machine. Tengen reverse-engineered the lockout chip and announced that they were going to produce games independently, bypassing Nintendo altogether. Nintendo altogether. Nintendo took them to court for copyright infringement. Tengen was able to stay in the NES business for a while, and one of the first Tengen titles was Tetris. However, it ended up that they had bought the rights from Mirrorsoft, who, in the end, did not own them. Then, in 1991, the courts upheld Nintendo's case against Tengen, and they were forced to stop producing games for NES entirely. Meanwhile, Nintendo had purchased the legitimate Tetris rights and released their own versions of the product. For more about Tetris, *see pages 204-205.*

THE ATARI LYNX

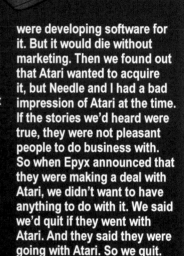

Originally called the Handy Game, the Lynx was an advanced system, but suffered from Atari's reputation and competition from Nintendo. Here's the story, as told by co-designer RJ Mical (see also *pages 113, 224 and 266*):

"There were three guys—Dave Morse, Dave Needle, and me. Dave Morse's son said one day, 'Dad, you should take that Amiga idea and do something small that you can hold in your hand.' So we went to a restaurant and did some drawings on napkins to see what it would look like. We stole the napkins. We decided we should start a company, but then we found Epyx, which was a cool company and decided to throw our lot in with them. We became part of Epyx and completed the design. But due to reasons out of our control, Epyx had spent too much money on other things and dipped into our project. They didn't have enough money to market it. The Lynx was done. It was in a phase where the hardware and tools were done and people were developing software for it. But it would die without marketing. Then we found out that Atari wanted to acquire it, but Needle and I had a bad impression of Atari at the time. If the stories we'd heard were true, they were not pleasant people to do business with. So when Epyx announced that they were making a deal with Atari, we didn't want to have anything to do with it. We said we'd quit if they went with Atari. And they said they were going with Atari. So we quit.

"The next time we were free to meet, we went to another restaurant and began drawing the 3DO system on napkins. We stole those napkins, too.

"The Lynx was a good color handheld system, and probably deserved to do better than it did, but, like all the other handhelds other than Game Boy, it had a short life."

Mario & Zelda

It's amazing to remember that it all started with Donkey Kong, but the career of Shigeru Miyamoto began with the rampaging ape, and his genius for game character development and design has continued to delight and entertain millions worldwide ever since. These pages celebrate two of Miyamoto's most significant series: Mario and Zelda.

The first home Mario games were on the Nintendo Entertainment System. They continued to evolve in complexity and depth over the succeeding versions.

Mario leaped into our homes again as the launch title for the Super NES.

The first 3D version of Super Mario, for the Nintendo 64, was a marvel of game design and perspective.

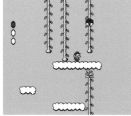

Screens from NES versions of Mario: Mario Bros., Super Mario Bros., Super Mario Bros. 2, and Super Mario Bros. 3.

Mario inspired many products, among the best being Super Mario Kart and Super Smash Bros.

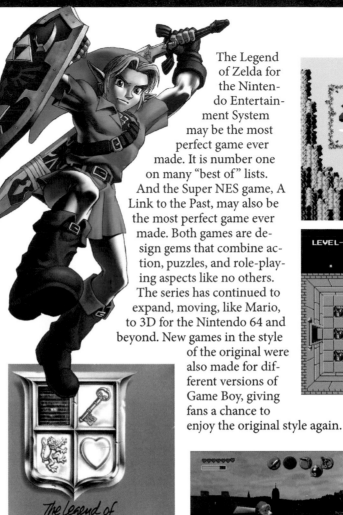

The Legend of Zelda for the Nintendo Entertainment System may be the most perfect game ever made. It is number one on many "best of" lists. And the Super NES game, A Link to the Past, may also be the most perfect game ever made. Both games are design gems that combine action, puzzles, and role-playing aspects like no others. The series has continued to expand, moving, like Mario, to 3D for the Nintendo 64 and beyond. New games in the style of the original were also made for different versions of Game Boy, giving fans a chance to enjoy the original style again.

Original Legend of Zelda screens.

Super Smash Bros.

Link takes a swing at 3D in Ocarina of Time on the N64

Miyamoto Speaks!

Shigeru Miyamoto is certainly one of the most influential and successful designers in the history of electronic games. His importance to the success of Nintendo cannot be overstated. Today, he is a super-producer, designing games and also overseeing Nintendo's many development groups. "He is a fantastic tutor for new producers," says Minoru Arakawa, founder and president of Nintendo of America. On these pages, Miyamoto-san comments on various aspects of his games and career.

Shigeru Miyamoto with SimCity designer Will Wright in 1988.

On the Origins of Mario

The Donkey Kong arcade game hit the market in 1981. Before that time, I had been designing posters to be affixed onto arcade game consoles or supporting others who were making video games. When the idea of this "new game to replace an old one" was proposed to teams of game designers in the form of an internal Nintendo company competition, I submitted several different ideas for Donkey Kong. As for the name, I just wanted to create an English name meaning "silly gorilla." As I consulted with my dictionary, there was the word "donkey" for "silly." Since apes were often called "kong" in Japan back then, I mixed them together.

On the Evolution of Mario's Identity

One of the new fun things I really wanted to realize on Donkey Kong was that players could move the character around and jump all over the screen for the very first time in the history of arcade games. However, due to the technical restrictions of those days, I could not depict the movement of hair when Mario jumps, so I had to put a cap on him. Likewise, to make the movement of arms more visible for the players, I had to put a shirt on him with overalls, etc. In other words, in order to evade the technical restraints, I came up with a very rational design for the original Mario character.

Nintendo internally decided to name and promote each character for Donkey Kong. Because I wanted Mario to appear in many of the later games with a variety of different roles, I just made a vague set of characteristics for him as "a middle-aged man with a strong sense of justice who is not handsome." When we made Mario Bros., because the setting was an underground world, Mario's image as a plumber was set, which is still alive now.

When we were making Super Mario Bros., I wanted players to control a Mario character who was bigger than ever. When we made the prototype of the big Mario, we did not feel he was big enough. So, we came up with the idea of showing the smaller Mario first, who could be made bigger later in the game ("super"); then players could see and feel that he was bigger.

When we were making Donkey Kong, we did not incorporate all the ideas I had initially conceived, so when we developed Donkey Kong Jr., we included some of the unused ideas from Donkey Kong. I originally wanted to make "Donkey Kong's revenge" as the main theme for this sequel, but Donkey Kong was too big a character for players to manipulate back then, so I made the story based upon Donkey Kong Jr. As for Donkey Kong 3, because the game was designed with another game called Green House for Game & Watch in mind, we decided not to use Mario.

On Easter Eggs and Secrets in the Early Mario Games

The first experiment we did for the game was to control big Mario. Because the development of Disk System was already underway at that time, we tried to pull out the best of NES's ability with Super Mario Bros., which might have become the very last NES game. I recall the basic game design was completed about three months after we started the experiment, when we were satisfied with the control of big Mario and when we had completed the designing of small Mario and of such items as mushrooms. It is true that we had incorporated some of the programming errors and unexpected reproductions during the course of development as the official "secrets." However, the majority of them were intentionally designed by us. To name some of the unintentional secrets, "serial coin appearance block" and Mario's "walking on the ceiling" had originally been programming errors that we later employed as the official secrets, while the "Zero World" was the error that we found only after the game hit the market.

On the Evolution of the Original Legend of Zelda

The first Legend of Zelda was created based upon the original concept of a "miniature garden that you can put inside your drawer," inside of which the player can freely explore. As you can see it in the recent Pikmin game, too, I make it a point of making games where the player becomes more creative by playing the game. The Legend of Zelda was the first game that has successfully incorporated such a concept. I tried to make a game where the next move the player is supposed to take is not already determined. Each player has to decide the route he or she thinks is best and take the best possible action, and, by doing so, players can encounter a variety of wonders.

Another big element is that players themselves can grow. In the game you see and feel that Link actually grows. At the same time, players can become better game players. I believe that this is the most definitive difference with RPG games that make use of parameters to show such a growth. In 2002, we will introduce you to the new Zelda game on Nintendo GameCube. This one is also going to be a unique, unprecedented game full of fresh surprises. Please look forward to it!

On the Trade-offs between 2D and 3D Game Design

I think a great advantage of 3D is that players can feel that they are inside the game. Also, we are able to create a greater number of character animations within a much shorter time. On the other hand, it is true that the number of difficult-to-play games has increased because, for example, we have to let players get accustomed to the way the camera works, and creators themselves have to understand the best possible way to use the camera.

Was Pikmin Set in His Personal Garden?

No, no! The fact of the matter is that one of the reasons why I hit upon the Pikmin idea was because I was intrigued by the movements of a group of ants and the ecology of plants when I was gardening. There's got to be some mix here. Come to think about it, however, it may be an interesting idea to place Pikmin dolls in my garden. I would have to put hundreds of them in order for people to see that such small figurines are actually there, since the real-size Pikmin is just about two centimeters high, though.

On Future Challenges in Game Design

I know people think Pikmin is a fairly unique game. On the other hand, I think it is not unique enough. Because my job is to surprise people all around the world, I must continue to create more unique and fresh entertainment all the time.

On the Games He Wants to Make in the Future

There are too many such ideas to identify one. There are just fractions of comprehensive ideas. Integrating them together may need new technologies to develop them.

On Other Games He Plays

When I am working, I hardly play video games, but I do not get inspiration by playing others' video games. When I am asked about my most favorite video game ever made by someone else, I make it a point of answering, "Pac-Man."

On His Greatest Moment as a Designer

Because I am always trying to realize the best possible unique entertainment in each day and age, I find the utmost joy whenever a new game is completed. Among the best moments is the time when I saw Nintendo employees enjoying themselves with the Donkey Kong arcade game that we had just completed. It was an especially delightful moment for me. Another time I recall is when I received the Hall of Fame Award at the E3 show a few years ago. When I received the applause of the audience, it was really something special for me.

Mega Man
(Capcom)

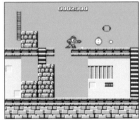
Operation Wolf
(Taito)

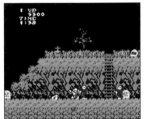
Ghosts 'n Goblins
(Capcom)

Kid Icarus
(Nintendo)

A Boy and His Blob
(Absolute)

Metal Gear
(Konami)

Snake's Revenge
(Konami)

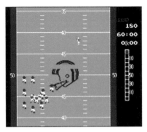
10-Yard Fight
(Irem)

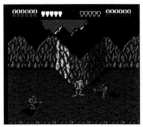
Battletoads *(Rare)*

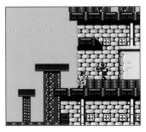
Bionic Commando
(Capcom)

Bases Loaded
(Jaleco)

Ballblazer *(Lucasfilm Games)*

Batman *(Sunsoft)*

Blades of Steel
(Konami)

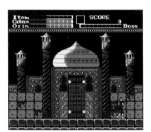
8 Eyes *(Taxan)*

Castlevania
(Konami)

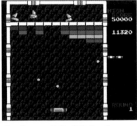
Arkanoid *(Taito)*

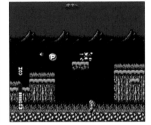
Blaster Master
(Sunsoft)

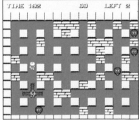
Bomberman
(Hudson Soft)

Crystalis *(SNK)*

Duck Hunt *(Nintendo)*

Attack of the Killer Tomatoes *(THQ)*

Double Dribble *(Konami)*

Little Nemo: The Dream Master *(Capcom)*

Mike Tyson's Punch-Out!! *(Nintendo)*

The Lone Ranger *(Konami)*

Dragon Warrior *(Enix)*

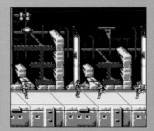
Super C *(Konami)*

Tetris *(Nintendo)*

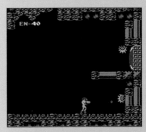
Metroid *(Nintendo)*

R.C. Pro-Am *(Rare/ Nintendo)*

Smash T.V. *(Acclaim)*

Street Fighter 2010 *(Capcom)*

Teenage Mutant Ninja Turtles *(Konami)*

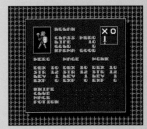
Super Black Onyx *(BPS)*

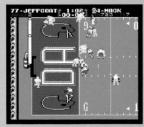
Tecmo Bowl *(Tecmo)*

Wild Gunman *(Nintendo)*

Wizards & Warriors *(Acclaim)*

Ys *(Falcom)*

The New Console Wars

By 1989, the NES was unquestionably dominant in the U.S., but in Japan a different story was unfolding. In 1987, electronics giant NEC introduced a next-generation machine. The PC Engine was touted as the first 16-bit system, although its CPU was actually an 8-bit chip. The system did feature an upgraded graphics processor, however, and ran games both on credit card-sized HuCards and on CD. Yes, the PC Engine was the first home system to feature the CD-ROM.

The PC Engine was immensely popular in Japan, and by 1989, there were hundreds of titles available for it. A little after PC Engine, Sega introduced its 16-bit Mega Drive system (which was based on its arcade technology), but they were unable to push the PC Engine out of its position.

The stage was set for the ultimate launch of both the PC Engine, which was renamed TurboGrafx-16, and the Mega Drive, which became the Sega Genesis, into the U.S. market. And although both systems were released late in 1989, they are very much a part of the story of the '90s, when console games came of age.

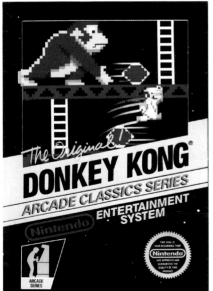

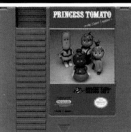

Hudson Soft's most popular NES game was Princess Tomato in the Salad Kingdom, which was created because one of the founders' daughter didn't like vegetables.

THE '90s

If the '70s were characterized by innovation and the '80s were about expansion, the '90s were a time of maturation. The CD-ROM, in particular, opened a virtual Pandora's box of good and evil. Like the CD, and in some even more significant ways, 3D technology radically changed the face of game design and development. Some designers decried it as the bane of good design, while others saw it as the path toward ultra-realism and games with movie-quality worlds.

Because of these changes, games grew both in size and technical quality, and new types of games became possible; but all this growth was not without its costs. Game budgets skyrocketed, and development cycles often expanded from months to years. It was no longer possible for a game developer to be a one-man show. To succeed, games required teams of specialists and generally huge marketing machines. By the late '90s, with thousands of games coming out, the retail shelf life of a game could be measured in weeks if it didn't do well out the gate.

Because of all these changes, telling the stories of the '90s is often very different from telling the stories of earlier decades. There were still a few wild and woolly events, like the rivalry between Nintendo and Sega and the emergence of companies like Blizzard, id Software, and Eidos. However, once electronic games moved from being seen as a fluke or a passing fad

and began to mature into a legitimate industry for which annual venues totalled in the billions of dollars, the personal stories of individual creators often began to give way to products that are developed in highly corporate environments.

This is not to say that passion and and creativity are missing from the corporate development environment—far from it—but it has become more difficult to track the stories in the same personal terms possible in the less structured environments of the '70s and '80s. By the end of the '90s, a few companies, such as Electronic Arts, Infogrames, and Ubisoft owned most of the computer game companies and their trademarks, even if many of those companies technically no longer existed.

Just as the movie industry grew from silent beginnings, passed through the Golden Age of the studio system, and emerged into today's wide-open market of technological and storytelling innovation, so the business of electronic games has gone through its own evolution, which still continues.

1990

Another Three-Way Race

The phenomenal success of the Nintendo Entertainment System in the U.S. paved the way for other companies to consider the lucrative American market; however, Nintendo's commanding market share made the prospect somewhat daunting. At Sega, after trying to find someone to partner the Mega Drive, the decision was made to bite the bullet and introduce their 16-bit console to the U.S. market. This was what the Sega of America team wanted all along.

After considering several new names for the machine, including Cyclone and "something with a fox logo," according to Al Nilsen—who became head of marketing for the new product—they decided to call it Genesis. "It had positive biblical connotations," says Nilsen, "a new beginning. Also, it had a *Star Trek* connotation from the Genesis Project movie."

The American team received their orders from Nakayama in Japan. "*Hyakumandai!!*" became their slogan. It meant "Sell a million units!" That was the goal to reach by the end of 1990. Of course, this was easier said than done. Not only did Nintendo have 90 percent of the market at the time, but NEC was also getting ready to introduce their PC Engine to the U.S. market. Nilsen remembers the pre-launch sales meeting, held in Monterey, California. "I remember one of the retailers telling us, 'You guys are really nice guys, and I like you, but NEC is going to blow you out of the water. Be prepared that on December 26th, I'm going to return it all to you.' What mattered to us, however, was that we had sell-in."

This is the first Keith Courage in Alpha Zones chip. Keith Courage was named after Keith Schaefer; this chip was given to him to commemorate the fact.

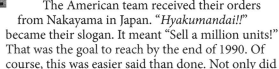

Sega launched Genesis a day early, beating NEC to the punch and shipping seven titles (two more than promised), including arcade hits Altered Beast and Golden Axe, as well as Tommy Lasorda Baseball and Arnold Palmer Tournament Golf. "After a week, we had 65 percent of the market, and by Christmas, we had over a 90 percent market share," remembers Nilsen. "We had done our research. We realized that the initial NES players had gotten older and entered their teens. Their systems ended up in closets. They discovered girls. So we positioned Genesis as the product you graduated to. Once you put away your toys, you got Sega. And we gave them arcade games and sports."

Meanwhile, Nintendo was not terribly concerned, having just completed their best year ever. "Being first to market is not of prime concern," says Peter Main, who was Nintendo's executive vice president of sales and marketing at the time of the Genesis launch. "In any product, it's the third through the fifth year when the software to hardware ratio goes through the roof. Our business plan said that our new software releases would carry the NES through 1991, and that we'd introduce the Super NES at that time."

TurboGrafx-16

The PC Engine, which in the States was called TurboGrafx-16, was originally designed by Hudson Soft, a Japanese game company started by two brothers. According to Ken Wirt, vice president and general manager of NEC's Home Division for TurboGrafx-16, the Kudo brothers grew up on the island of Hokkaido, "very poor, next to the railroad tracks."

They started a little electronics shop and got into CB radios. Their technician, Nakamoto, was programming some computer games and ported them to Nintendo's Famicom when it came out. "They made a ton of money," says Wirt. "And they were real characters. One of the brothers wore cowboy boots and drove around Japan in a Dodge Ram pickup. They also spent about a million dollars restoring the old steam engine that used to run by their house when they were children. There's a number on the Hudson logo, which is the number on the steam engine they restored."

Hudson Soft tried to get Nintendo interested in the machine they had developed, but were turned down; so

Two of developer Working Designs' (Arc the Lad) earliest games—Parasol Stars and Cadash.

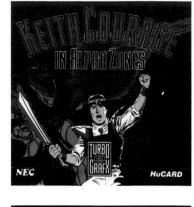

they tried elsewhere, ultimately striking a deal with consumer electronics giant NEC, who brought out the PC Engine in 1987.

In Japan, NEC's PC Engine was powerful and successful, and, having released earlier, was far more popular than Sega's Mega Drive. So, when NEC decided to bring the system to the U.S. and European markets, they were sure they would succeed. According to Keith Schaefer, executive vice president of NEC Technologies, "We had a better system, with a bigger, faster 16-bit graphics chip. Our marketing dollars were the same, we were in all the key distribution locations, and our price point was competitive."

However, in the all-important Christmas season of 1990, Sega emerged the clear winner. What happened? Again, according to Schaefer, "Sega Genesis came to market with what I consider to be inferior hardware, but a superior selection of software that was Americanized for the American consumer. TurboGrafx-16 came out with exactly the same software that was popular on the PC Engine in Japan. These games were not the right games for the American audience."

Part of the problem was that all the software came from Japanese developers through Hudson Soft, who had an exclusive deal with NEC to produce all the software for the system. The titles

were mostly unknown in the U.S., while Sega launched with a combination of familiar arcade titles and sports games. "We saw the problem coming," says Schaefer, "but there was nothing we could do about it." So, despite having a huge number of games already made for the system in Japan, they turned out to be the wrong games.

Another problem with the launch of the TurboGrafx-16 traces its roots to the Japanese sense of honor. "We initially had orders for a million units over the first 12 months," says Schaefer, "so NEC went ahead and ordered production of 600,000 from their Taiwanese manufacturers. But the orders dwindled, and we ended up only selling through 250,000 units. When we saw the orders shrinking, we wanted to cut back on manufacturing, but for NEC it was a matter of honor, and they would not go back on their order with the Taiwanese. It's a very laudable quality of Japanese companies—their sense of honor—though if we had been able to cancel the excess manufacturing, we might have continued the product for a second or even third year."

NEC attempted to make their caveman, Bonk, into a character like Mario or Sonic, but without much luck. J.J. & Jeff, on the other hand, mostly resembled Beavis & Butt-Head.

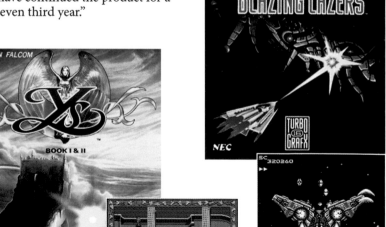

257

Neo-Geo

In 1990, Nintendo licensee SNK (creators of the games Ikari Warriors and Crystalis) came out with the ultimate gamer's system, the 24-bit Neo-Geo. Unfortunately, its ultimate price of $649 was beyond the reach of most gamers in 1990. On the other hand, Neo-Geo was so close to arcade quality, with a lineup heavy on action/fighting games, that it was actually used in many commercial arcades. There wasn't much in the way of deep game development, but it was the console to have if you were an ultra-extreme hardcore gamer. Neo-Geo remained a fringe product, however, and never achieved the level of sales of the major systems.

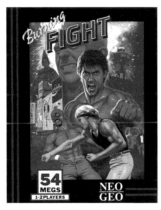

Screens from Super Baseball 2020, Double Dragon, Fatal Fury, and Art of Fighting.

1991

Hedgehog vs. Plumber

After its launch in the U.S., Genesis sales were good, but not great. Nintendo remained the leader, and they were preparing to launch their own 16-bit system, the Super NES. And Nintendo had something that Sega did not—Mario! So Sega enlisted their employees in Japan and held a competition to see who could come up with the best character. One of the women had been reading a book about animals and thought hedgehogs were cool. Hers was one of two winners. The other was a very young preschool-type anime done in pastels. Al Nilsen remembers going into a conference room with Shinobu Toyoda, one of Sega's longtime top executives, and seeing the two winning drawings. "Here, pick one," he was told.

"So, here was this image of Sonic the Hedgehog in a rock band with his blonde, human girlfriend, Madonna. There was no game design or story. Just this image, but it was the less objectionable of the two. So I said 'Do Sonic, but get rid of Madonna,' and we sent it back to Japan."

Six months later, Nilsen was in Japan, having long since forgotten about the hedgehog, when the R&D group showed a non-playable demo of the

first Sonic game. Nilsen was blown away. Two months later, they had the first playable level ready. "It was just incredible," says Nilsen.

The designers were justifiably proud and wanted to show the game at an upcoming Tokyo game show, but the marketing team said no. They knew that Nintendo was planning the U.S. launch of the Super NES at the June 1991 CES in Chicago. "We immediately decided not to tell anyone about this thing," says Nilsen. "This could be our secret weapon."

Tom Kalinske

To help run the company, Sega hired former Mattel President Tom Kalinske. "I was on vacation in Hawaii. I had left Mattel and helped bring Matchbox Toys out of bankruptcy, buying it for $21 million and selling it three years later to Tyco for $120 million. I was on vacation when Nakayama found me. He and Rosen ganged up on me and convinced me to fly to Tokyo to see the Genesis and the product that became the Game Gear. Some months later, I got excited enough about it to go in and take on Nintendo."

By the time Kalinske joined Sega, the Genesis had launched, but after a few weeks, he began to make some changes. He wanted to lower the price from $189 to $129, take out Altered Beast, which he said "looked like devil worship in the Midwest," and take on Nintendo in aggressive, competitive advertising. He also wanted to move some of the developers to the States. "My deal with Nakayama was that I made the decisions, so I went to Japan and announced my plan. At the end of a long discourse, all the Japanese executives began buzzing in Japanese, and I didn't have a clue what they were saying. At the end of about an hour of this, Nakayama said finally that nobody in the room agreed with me. They thought bundling Sonic would weaken profits. You didn't mention your competition, especially if you were

in a weaker position. They couldn't afford establishing a development group in the States. And on and on. Nakayama began to leave the room, and I thought this was the shortest career on record. Then, at the door, he turned and said, 'When I hired you, I told you I wouldn't interfere. So do what you set out to do, and we'll support you.'"

Sega played a chess game, publicly expressing concern about the launch of Super Mario, saying they hoped it didn't get bundled with the Super NES (SNES), but secretly hoping it did. In head-to-head tests, Sonic had done better than Mario. They knew what they had. Nilsen adds, "It was a competitive business, but they were both great games. I've never denied that I played Nintendo games. But at the time, you looked at Sonic and you said 'This is next generation.' Mario was maybe 50 percent toward the next generation at the time."

Nintendo's Arakawa comments further on the head games being played: "Tom Kalinske is a brilliant marketer, and the first thing he did was to pick up on a newspaper quote from Mr. Yamauchi in which he said, 'Sega is nothing.' Kalinske put it on every door in the Sega offices."

Sonic did make great waves at CES and stole some of Nintendo's thunder that year, but despite Sega's marketing spin, SNES did very well, and their launch title, Super Mario World, turned out to be a great game.

With TurboGrafx-16 still hanging in, it became a legitimate three-way race... for awhile. Ultimately, it came down to Sega and Nintendo.

Electronic Arts and Sega

Another boost to Genesis occurred when Trip Hawkins decided that Electronic Arts would reverse engineer the Genesis cartridges and start making their own Genesis games. This was a market departure for EA, which had stayed with computer software almost exclusively until then. "It happened right when I joined Sega," remembers Kalinske. "Trip had informed Sega that he intended to publish Genesis games without a license. The situation grew heated, and there were threats of lawsuits. We wanted to resolve it, and we needed publishers. At the time, Nintendo would threaten their third-party publishers with reprisals if they published Genesis games. I never revealed the deal, but in the end we granted EA a favorable arrangement relative to everyone else. That was fine. They got a good deal and we got a strong third-party publisher. You have to understand that no platform was ever really successful without third-party support."

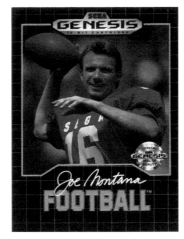

Original press kit photos for Joe Montana Football and Michael Jackson's Moonwalker.

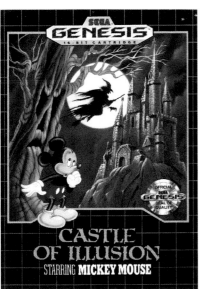

The successful introduction of the SNES as well as the resurgence of the Genesis with Sonic the Hedgehog and third-party support from Electronic Arts helped to galvanize the industry. They were playing hardball, but they also gave each other mutual respect. Nintendo's Arakawa comments, "It was good for competition. It was good for the industry, too."

Indeed, the specter of the Atari collapse was beginning to fade, and video games enjoyed another age of expansion.

In addition to their success with Sonic the Hedgehog, Sega created many successful games with celebrity endorsements from Joe Montana, Michael Jackson, Mickey Mouse, David Robinson, and others. In general, Sega's celebrity games were of high quality and fun to play.

YO! WHA'S UP? THE STORY OF TOEJAM & EARL

ToeJam & Earl was certainly one of the funniest and wackiest games ever released. And, in addition to its originality, it featured excellent game design. It was definitely a romp on the side of hipness. Co-designer Greg Johnson relates the background of one of our all-time favorite Sega Genesis games.

"This game was born out of a release from stress. Both Starflight I and II were huge, weighty projects that were very demanding. ToeJam was an opportunity to kick back and do something silly and just for the hell of it. I remember the genesis of the idea happened at about four in the morning when I stumbled out of bed and scribbled a bit of dialogue onto a scrap of paper. It went like...

'Yo. Greetings and various apropos felicitations. My name is ToeJam and this is my homeboy, Big Rappin' Earl. Say Wha's up, Earl.'

'Wha's up.'

'Earl and myself are highly funky aliens from the planet Funkotron.'

"Well, that's where it started, with the characters. I love the hipness of black street culture (I'm half black) and old school R&B music, and I also have always loved aliens (at least the ones I've met).

"Making ToeJam and Earl, more than anything else, was a way to have some fun. That's why it was such a great two-player game... so my business partner Mark Voorsanger and I could play all the time. The reason it was a random world was so we could keep playing it without getting tired of it.

"When I was in college I was totally addicted to Rogue—that was a truly great game. I would stay up till 3 and 4 a.m. watching the little C get chased around the screen by the little V on the mainframe computer, trying to get deeper than I'd been before in the dungeon. Structurally ToeJam and Earl is Rogue. It has all of the same elements, right down to the potions that do unidentified things."

261

Sega Genesis

Of the many popular Genesis (and some Sega CD) games, we've included a few more screens to inspire memories of games gone by.

Sonic the Hedgehog (*Sega*)

Sonic the Hedgehog 2 (*Sega*)

Sonic the Hedgehog 3 (*Sega*)

Sonic the Hedgehog 4 (unreleased beta) (*Sega*)

Alex Kidd in the Enchanted Castle (*Sega*)

Joe Montana II: Sports Talk Football (*Sega*)

Michael Jackson's Moonwalker (*Sega*)

Castle of Illusion Starring Mickey Mouse (*Sega*)

The Revenge of Shinobi (*Sega*)

Sonic & Knuckles (*Sega*)

Sonic 3D Blast (*Sega*)

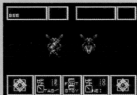

Phantasy Star II (*Sega*)

Virtua Fighter 2 (*Sega*)

Shining Force (*Sega*)

Mario Lemieux Hockey (*Sega*)

David Crane's Amazing Tennis (*Absolute*)

David Robinson's Supreme Court (*Sega*)

Flashback (*Delphine*/*U.S. Gold*)

Revolution X (*Midway*/*Acclaim*)

Decap Attack (*Sega*)

Ecco the Dolphin (*Sega*)

Dick Tracy (*Sega*)

Alisia Dragoon (*Game Arts*)

Ninja Gaiden (unreleased beta) (*Tecmo*)

NBA Jam (*Acclaim*)

Strider (*Capcom*)

Altered Beast (*Sega*)

Golden Axe (*Sega*)

Gunstar Heroes (*Sega*)

 **Herzog Zwei** (*Sega*)

 **Landstalker** (*Sega*)

 **Kid Chameleon** (*Sega*)

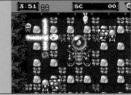 **Mega Bomberman** (*Hudson Soft*)

 **Mega Turrican** (*Data East*)

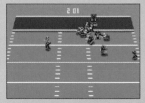 **Cyberball** (*Tengen*)

 **Nobunaga's Ambition** (*Koei*)

 **Pit Fighter** (*Tengen*)

 **Powerball** (*Namco*)

 **Primal Rage** (*Time Warner*)

 **Rings of Power** (*Electronic Arts*)

 **Cadash** (*Taito*)

 **Shining in the Darkness** (*Japanese version*) (*Sega*)

 **Super Smash T.V.** (*Acclaim*)

 **Sokoban** (*Thinking Rabbit*)

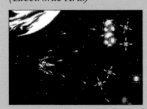 **Sol-Deace** (*Sega*)

 **Space Harrier II** (*Sega*)

 **Rastan Saga II** (*Taito*)

 **Steel Talons** (*Tengen*)

 **The Addams Family** (*Ocean/Acclaim*)

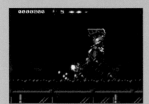 **The Terminator** (*Virgin*)

 **Tintin in Tibet** (*Infogrames*)

 **Ms. Pac-Man** (*Tengen*)

 **Lunar: The Silver Star** (*Working Designs*)

 **Lunar: Eternal Blue** (*Working Designs*)

 **Burning Force** (*Namco*)

 **James 'Buster' Douglas Knockout Boxing** (*Sega*)

 **Chuck Rock** (*Core Design*)

 **Batman** (*Sunsoft*)

 **Vectorman** (*Sega*) **263**

Super NES

There were hundreds of games made for the Super NES. Here are screens from some of the best-remembered titles.

Super Mario World *(Nintendo)*

Batman Forever *(Konami)*

Barkley: Shut Up and Jam! *(Accolade)*

Super Punch-Out!! *(Nintendo)*

Contra III *(Konami)*

Darius Twin *(Taito)*

ActRaiser *(Enix)*

Demon's Crest *(Capcom)*

Super Godzilla *(Toho)*

The Death and Return of Superman *(Sunsoft)*

Lufia & the Fortress of Doom *(Taito)*

Kirby's Dream Course *(Nintendo)*

Return of Double Dragon *(Tradewest)*

Dragon: The Bruce Lee Story *(Virgin)*

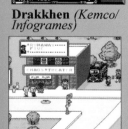

Drakkhen *(Kemco/ Infogrames)*

Mickey Mania *(Sony Electronics/Disney)*

The Addams Family *(Ocean)*

Illusion of Gaia *(Nintendo)*

California Games II *(Epyx)*

EarthBound *(Nintendo)*

Castlevania: Dracula X *(Konami)*

Extra Innings *(Sony Imagesoft)*

Dungeon Master *(JVC Musical)*

Pocky & Rocky 2 *(Natsume)*

F-Zero *(Nintendo)*

Final Fight 2 *(Capcom)*

Gradius III *(Konami)*

Micro Machines *(Taito)*

Dr. Mario *(Nintendo)*

NBA Live 95
(Electronic Arts)

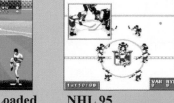

Madden NFL '97
(Electronic Arts)

Mario Excitebike
(Japanese) (Nintendo)

Super Castlevania IV *(Konami)*

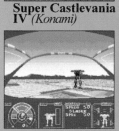

R-Type III: The Third Lightning *(Irem)*

Super Bases Loaded
(Jaleco)

NHL 95
(Electronic Arts)

Super Adventure Island *(Hudson Soft)*

MechWarrior
(Activision)

Super Virgin Girl (Japan Only) *(TGL)*

Ninja Gaiden Trilogy
(Tecmo)

Street Fighter II Turbo *(Capcom)*

Super Off Road
(Tradewest)

Super Turrican 2
(Ocean)

Ys IV *(Japan Only)*
(Falcom)

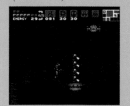

Super Star Wars
(LucasArts)

Space Ace *(Absolute Entertainment/Seika)*

Wizardry *(Japanese) (Sir-Tech/ASCII)*

Final Fantasy II
(Nintendo)

Sküljagger
(*American Softworks*)

Super Metroid *(Nintendo)*

Star Fox *(Nintendo)*

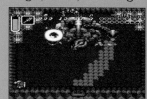

Sonic Blast Man *(Taito)*

Total Carnage *(Malibu)*

Mega Man X *(Capcom)*

Pilotwings *(Nintendo)*

ClayFighter *(Interplay)*

Zombies Ate My Neighbors *(Konami)*

The Legend of Zelda: A Link to the Past *(Nintendo)*

1992
3DO

ELECTRONIC ARTS®

FOR USE WITH

Twisted
The Game Show

By Studio 3DO

3DO

Electronic Arts founder Trip Hawkins, having guided EA into the video game world, now left the company to start a bold new venture. Once a critic of video games, and a hardcore computer game supporter, Hawkins had seen the light (so to speak) and was ready to go head-to-head against Nintendo and Sega, with support from (among others) Time Warner, Matsushita, and MCA.

The 3DO Company was originally incorporated in 1991 as SMSG, Inc. and in that same year entered into a development agreement with NTG Engineering, which included Amiga/Lynx designers RJ Mical and Dave Needle. "Trip had a vision, but needed a machine to do the vision," says Mical. "We had a machine, but nobody knew about us. We were in stealth mode. Ultimately, we were introduced to each other through a mutual friend, who couldn't talk to either of us due to conflicting nondisclosures."

NTG was a different sort of company from the beginning. Employees didn't work for the normal stock options, but for a percentage of profits based on what they contributed to each project. "It was almost a utopian socialist idea," says Mical, " and it might have worked, but the 3DO was too good. We were working on several projects, but within a year and a half, all we were doing was 3DO. Then Trip bought us and we were employees. Certainly 3DO was one of the most remarkable places I've ever worked because of the density of really smart people who worked there."

Hawkins' eloquent evangelism of 3DO swayed many in the industry, who came to believe that the 3DO machine would become a ubiquitous appliance like the telephone or the TV. Says co-designer RJ Mical, "In our wildest dreams, we imagined getting into home-of-the-future trials where the 3DO was built into the wall, not only to do entertainment, but to allow interactive video content to be received in the home as well."

Though it got plenty of press and had an impressive public offering even before they had a product, 3DO ultimately suffered from too high a price tag ($699.99 at launch) and some rushed titles, including the highly anticipated but disappointing Jurassic Park. Another of the launch titles, Crash 'N Burn was a fun battle racing game, but not a strong enough title to drive hardware sales. Although 3DO couldn't boast the number of third-party developers that Nintendo had, they did have a couple of notable ones. On one side was a company called Rocket Science, one of the most impressive collections of talent assembled to do games—and one of the biggest disappointments. Despite the presence of some amazing designers, programmers, and artists, the company took a wrong turn from the beginning, concentrating on "rail games" that were ultimately not that interesting.

On the other side of the coin was Crystal Dynamics, whose game The Horde was certainly one of the best games to come out for the 3DO. Crystal Dynamics has continued to create great games, while Rocket Science folded up and disappeared.

Electronic Arts published Twisted, a game show in a game, one of the more interesting 3DO titles. The wacky spoof of TV game shows featured full-motion video and some amusing games.

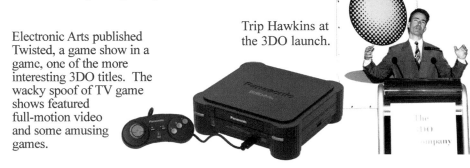

Trip Hawkins at the 3DO launch.

American Laser Games came out with a version of Mad Dog McCree for 3DO that featured more full-motion video.

Also on 3DO was Humongous Entertainment's excellent and highly entertaining (even for some of us adults) Putt-Putt series of games for children.

Other games came out in Japan, but were never released in the U.S.

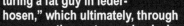

267

Trilobyte

Graeme Devine and Rob Landeros were both industry veterans by the time they joined forces in 1989. Devine had begun programming in the late '70s on TRS-80 computers and ultimately worked on porting games, including Ballblazer, for Atarisoft's British offices. In time, he ended up on Lucas' Skywalker Ranch, working with the Games Group there, but returned to England to form IC&D Software. IC&D stood for Ice Cream and Donuts, which Devine says, "was a fine name for a game company."

The company did some original games, such as an adventure game called Metropolis; and they did ports for a company called Arcadia, which became Virgin Mastertronic. "We were doing really well at making money," Devine recalls. Then Mastertronic asked if he'd be interested in coming to America again to help start their U.S. office. "I said I could do that for a while. Then, fourteen years later... I was still there. I was employee number seven."

That's where he met Rob Landeros, who had moved to Virgin/Mastertronic after a couple of years as Cinemaware's art director. "I didn't start with computers young. I had done some scrimshaw and, for a while, some political cartooning. When I saw the Amiga, I knew I had to have one. I was down in Redlands, California, and I happened to meet Jim Sachs, who giving a demonstration of the art he was doing for Cinemaware's Defender of the Crown. I was blown away and went home to try to emulate the quality of what he had done. Ultimately, we got to know each other and when Cinemaware

was looking for an art director, he said, 'Why don't you go for it?' So I did get the job, and it was trial by fire. I learned how to be an art director by the seat of my pants."

Ultimately, Landeros left to take a job at Virgin, where he met Devine. For a while, he was happy there, but Virgin wasn't focused primarily on AAA titles, and they began doing a lot of licensed products. While most of these products were forgettable, one exception was Spot, their first ever NES game, which used the 7Up Spot character. "We worked from Japanese documents to create the NES cartridge—four months of intense work, culminating in a mad overnight drive to make CES in Las Vegas with the first working carts, which Dan Chang and I had made by converting old Legend of Zelda cartridges." Spot was actually a very fun game, well put together, and it did well. However, both Landeros and Devine were getting itchy feet. Says Landeros, "They were moving in a different direction. They asked me, do I want to work on a McDonald's license, and I said, 'McNo.'"

Actually, the two had already begun brainstorming at a New York airport for a new game, right after attending a show dedicated to new CD-ROM multimedia technology. "We first thought about the board game Clue, because Virgin had that license," says Devine. "But we were also big

fans of Twin Peaks. We even thought about having a Twin Peaks product that just let you wander around the town, but that ultimately evolved into a game we called 'Guest.' When we got back, we showed our proposal to Martin Alper, who was the head of Virgin Mastertronic, and he took us out to lunch and fired us. He said, 'I can't produce this in-house, but I can give you a contract to do it as an independent developer. Just promise us a floppy disk version, because we probably

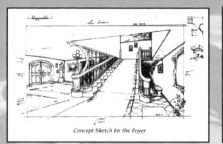
Concept Sketch for the Foyer

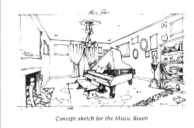
Concept sketch for the Music Room

Chess puzzle from The 7th Guest.

can't sell enough CDs, and don't move more than 50 miles away.'"

Grateful for the opportunity, Devine and Landeros formed Trilobyte Software, set up offices in Jacksonville, Oregon (more than 800 miles away), and produced the first huge megahit CD-ROM game, The 7th Guest. There was no floppy version. There was also no complaint from Virgin, in the end, because the product sold more than a million copies.

The development of The 7th Guest was an adventure in itself. Working for the first time with CD technology and rendering some of the first 3D animation sequences and complex morphing, they had many technical hurdles to overcome. First Devine backward-engineered a hi-res animation format called SLC and made an animation player, which he released as shareware. Autodesk's Gary Yost saw it and ended up providing the young company with several copies of Autodesk's 3D Studio software.

The rendered sequences in The 7th Guest were huge by current storage standards; the sequence going up the

stairway was more than 20 megabytes. They ended up having to get a huge $10,000 hard disk to store the material. Another problem they encountered turned into a feature in the game: They shot all the actors against blue screens, but apparently, they either used the wrong shade of blue or should have used a green screen. Whatever the problem, every image had a ghostly aura around it, and it was prohibitively expensive and time-consuming to remove all those pixels, so they turned the actors into ghosts and adapted the game to fit the graphics.

Ultimately, they added a lot of complex brain-teasing puzzles, without which the game would have been more of an interactive movie than a game. Landeros and scriptwriter Matthew Costello did a lot of puzzle research. One of the hardest puzzles, the infamous Microscope Puzzle, was actually a game of Spot set on the highest level. (Going back to the cluebook in the Library actually lowered the difficulty level of the puzzle each time, though it wasn't much help solving the puzzle, otherwise.)

After the amazing success of The 7th Guest, Trilobyte started working on a real-time strategy game called Cyber War. Devine describes it as "SimCity with a war going on." But they were also contractually obligated to do a sequel to The 7th Guest, and so they began work on The 11th Hour, which was a technical nightmare. The story of The 11th Hour was similar to that of The 7th Guest and easier to follow, but the game wasn't nearly as successful. By this time, CD-ROMs were less of a novelty, and another game called Myst had taken the world by storm.

In time, Trilobyte closed its doors, and Devine and Landeros went their separate ways. But they will always retain their place in the history of electronic games with The 7th Guest.

Henry Stauff, the mad villain of The 7th Guest.

Cyan: Tales from Two Brothers

This is the story of two brothers who made worlds. They began with the intention of creating an interactive children's book, but somehow, along the way, Rand and Robyn Miller made the one game that everyone had to have in the early '90s.

Their first product, The Manhole, was completed in 1987. The Miller brothers also started their company, which they originally named Prolog, in the same year, soon after changing the company name to Cyan. "We started with the idea of mapping the book medium to interactive, but the first page was so intriguing that we discovered we could go deeper instead of linear," says Rand Miller. "You click on the manhole and the cover slides open, a beanstalk grows out of the hole. There's a little door on the fire hydrant. At that point, our plans didn't matter. It was draw what's here, then draw a door. We didn't know what was behind it." he adds. "Honestly, when we created it, we had no plan. It came on five floppy disks and you had to have a hard disk to play it. If we had examined the market, we'd have been cancelled." However, when they showed the product at a HyperCard convention, the brothers sold all their copies and ultimately made a publishing deal with Activision. "They offered maybe $20,000. It was serious money for something we'd enjoyed doing for six months."

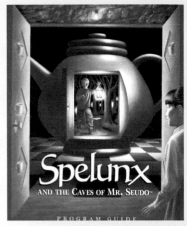

The Manhole was a delightful, surreal, and fully interactive journey in which everything you clicked on caused some event to occur. It wasn't truly a game, but an exploration of a world so malleable that a straw could become a tunnel and a tunnel could be the inside of a creature, and you might end up floating in a whirlpool in a glass of iced tea being drunk by a giant walrus. Or something like that. Originally created with rich black-and-white images on the Macintosh, The Manhole was a fascinating experience for young and old alike. (Ironically, it wasn't until 1992 that Brøderbund brought out the first of the Living Books series, which was very much what the Millers had originally conceived, though by then they were already working on Myst.)

The Miller brothers followed with Cosmic Osmo and

the Worlds Beyond the Mackerel. Also published by Activision, in 1990, Osmo was bigger and even more interactive than The Manhole, and it had a story and a main character. "It's amazing to us how much Myst evolved out of our earlier products. Osmo gave us the opportunity to have an unlimited universe. Osmo was also the first game where we began to put bits of story in it." Osmo was also the first game they did for CD-ROM, which opened their eyes to some expansive vistas to come.

Unfortunately, at the time Cosmic Osmo released, Activision was going bankrupt. Undaunted, the Millers created Spelunx and the Caves of Mr. Seudo, an educational game. "We wanted to motivate more than educate. Force-feeding information is never as effective as having someone want to suck you dry because they're so interested in what they're looking at," says Miller.

But it was their next product that made history. It was 1993 and the CD-ROM was becoming a de facto part of every new home computer. Two products really pushed the envelope and demonstrated the power and potential of the new storage medium—The 7th Guest and Myst.

It started with a call from Sunsoft, a Japanese company who had been trying to contact the Millers for a year to create a game for adults. "We had already created a concept called A Grey Summons. It was designed to be a fantastic world that adults would lose themselves in. Completely different from Myst in many ways, but the publishers we saw said no to it," says Miller. "So, when Sunsoft asked for a proposal, we sent them four pages—basically a map with a top-down view of some islands, with a one-page description of these brothers and these books and how you'd get to go to these islands and explore them and go to different ages." They estimated their budget at around $400,000. "We ended up spending double that, and paid for the extra on our own."

Screens from Cyan's massively multiplayer online game, Myst Online: Uru Live (Originally billed as Parable, but not released until years later.)

In a great piece of irony, Sunsoft only wanted the console rights, anticipating a CD-ROM add-on from Nintendo that ultimately never came out. The Millers kept the PC rights.

They took the PC rights and showed the early version of the game to several publishers. At Maxis, they showed it to Will Wright and Jeff Braun (see page 274). "Will seemed to love it, and Jeff said, 'I'm not sure I get it, but if Will likes it, I love it.'" They didn't publish with Maxis, however, but struck a publishing deal with Brøderbund, where the response was overwhelmingly positive.

Myst first released on the Macintosh in the fall of 1993, with the PC version following shortly after. And very soon, it became the product everybody had to have. Not a traditional game, its incredibly beautiful scenes set in a stark world simply compelled you to explore more. Nothing like it had been seen on home computers before.

"In Myst, you can't separate the graphics from the gameplay. It was the visuals that pulled people forward. It was the carrot that pulled people around the corner," adds Miller. "It sounds like marketing drivel, but if you're sitting in a room with the lights low and the sound turned up, we want you to think you're really in that place. The box said, 'A surrealistic adventure that will become your world.' That's what we wanted."

With the unprecedented success of Myst, the Millers had the money to get the best equipment and the luxury to take their time. In the sequel, Riven, they were able to complete the Myst story—at least to their satisfaction. "We didn't worry about making it a real-time game but took the Myst concept and went as far as we could with that world. Riven wrapped it up for us, and we weren't interested in doing more sequels. We'd told this story. We were interested in creating a larger, online world, something that goes back to what we've always done. However," admits Miller, "Myst fans did want more." In 2000, they released realMyst, a more dynamic version of the original game, and they licensed Ubisoft to create the third game, Myst III: Exile.

RIVEN
THE SEQUEL TO MYST

Maxis

Jeff Braun, referring to the original SimCity cover: "We got sued by Toho and had to pay them big bucks for infringing on *Godzilla*. We never used the word 'Godzilla,' honest, just a doll that wasn't Godzilla but was confused as Godzilla in a number of magazine reviews."

Meanwhile, Jeff Braun and Ed Kilham had gotten together to "form a game company for adults," as Braun described it, soon to be joined by A.J. Redmer.* Braun remembers how he met Will Wright: "I asked a friend in the game industry how to meet game programmers; he said, 'It's simple… beer and pizza.' So I threw a few game programmer pizza/ beer parties and Will showed up at one.

Will Wright's first game was Raid on Bungeling Bay, which was published by Brøderbund (*see page 128*) in 1984. After that, he began working on two more games. One Wright describes as a "weird strategy game" called Probot. The other game was called Micropolis. Probot was never released, but Micropolis was another story.

The concept for Micropolis came, in part, from the game editor Wright had written for Bungeling Bay and also from two books he read, *Urban Dynamics and System Dynamics*, by Jay Forrester. Drawing also from John Conway's work with cellular automata and his Game of Life, in 1985 Wright ultimately completed a game for the Commodore 64, but had no luck finding a publisher.

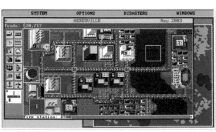

Once I saw Will's 'city builder' (pre-Micropolis) on the C64, I knew this was what Maxis should be doing."

Working out of Braun's apartment, the small company began to revise the original game. Along the way, they found out that there was a disk drive manufacturer called Micropolis, so they searched for a new name for the product. "I think it was our writer, Michael Bremer, who came up with the name," remembers Wright. "Bremer was also also the first to call the city's inhabitants 'sims.' He saved us much pointless work over the ensuing years coming up with titles for our games."

The original Micropolis game was rewritten for the Macintosh and Amiga. Then, going against convention, the small company released SimCity in February 1989, well after the traditional Christmas selling season. Brøderbund distributed it. Ironically, remembers Wright, "A lot of our later games also came out around that same time of year… SimCity 2000 and 3000, even The Sims." Whatever they did, it worked. Shortly after the release of the game, a reporter from Newsweek called and did a full-page article on the game and the fledgling company. "We made a lot of mistakes in developing the company," says Wright, "but SimCity was successful enough to pay for those mistakes, and then some." Classic understatement from Wright.

*Kilham later went on to create an intriguing battle game, RoboSport, for Maxis, then moved on to join Larry Holland's team on X-Wing and TIE Fighter. Eventually, he formed his own company, Ronin Entertainment, with Lucas veteran Kalani Streicher. Redmer also moved over to Lucasfilm and has continued to work with various companies in the industry.

If you haven't already figured it out, Will Wright is an avid reader and is always fascinated by new ideas. His next game, which he thought should be on a grander scale, was based on the work of James Lovelock, to whom he was introduced by Whole Earth's Stuart Brand. SimEarth was far less popular than SimCity, but Wright enjoyed the research into geology, climatology, evolution, ecology, and so forth. With SimCity, Maxis had begun a tradition of writing very detailed manuals and contracting out to experts to write scholarly sections. In SimEarth, says Wright, "the best thing, for me, was the manual, which contained the best 30 pages on Earth science ever written." One of the little-known facts about SimEarth was its ability to play music based on particular layers of the simulation. For instance, you could set up the music to correspond to the air temperature or the mixture of atmospheric gasses.

Instead of moving logically to SimGalaxy or some other even larger topic, Wright went small for his next game and wrote SimAnt with high school friend Justin McCormick. SimAnt was based largely on Wright's fascination with ants and on the work of E.O. Wilson, who wrote the Pulitzer Prize-winning book *The Ants*. "It was much more playful than SimEarth—a much more approachable game. I was hoping to show grown-ups how cool ants were, but we had our biggest following with younger kids."

It was at about this time that Wright began his fascination with a game that for years went by the name Project X and eventually became The Sims. But he had to put aside this game many times. He worked first with Fred Haslam to complete SimCity 2000. "We actually took the code I'd developed for Project X, and that became the code base for 2000. All the references in the code are like 'draw house' and 'draw yard' and so forth." SimCity 2000 added new perspectives and layers to the game. "We got to add in a lot of stuff we'd had to leave out of SimCity, and I personally went through hundreds of letters to see what players wanted."

SimCopter was an ambitious project. The idea was to let people actually go into a 3D model of the cities they had built in SimCity. Still with one part of his mind on Project X, Wright tackled the challenge of producing a 3D game in which the world would be created based on an unpredictable set of criteria—a player's own SimCity. "We had to look at the buildings, the crime

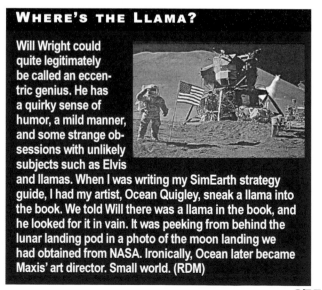

The early Maxis team: Left Right Photo, front row: Steve Hales, Photo, left to right: Jeff Braun, Jeff Braun, Will Wright; Back row: Ed Daniel Goldman, Will Wright, Kilham (Maxis' first employee), Brett Michael Bremer, unknown, Durett, A.J. Redmer, Brian Witt, Rob David Caggiano, Tim Johnson, Strobel.

WHERE'S THE LLAMA?

Will Wright could quite legitimately be called an eccentric genius. He has a quirky sense of humor, a mild manner, and some strange obsessions with unlikely subjects such as Elvis and llamas. When I was writing my SimEarth strategy guide, I had my artist, Ocean Quigley, sneak a llama into the book. We told Will there was a llama in the book, and he looked for it in vain. It was peeking from behind the lunar landing pod in a photo of the moon landing we had obtained from NASA. Ironically, Ocean later became Maxis' art director. Small world. (RDM)

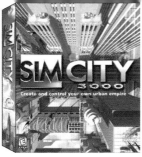
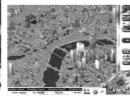

SimCity came out in many new versions, each with new features and more graphically detailed.

In SimCopter, Maxis attempted a living world based on unpredictable parameters—a players' own SimCity.

and population density at that spot, and many other factors. Really, it was probably too ambitious for the size of the development team we had. Recently I saw the concept done really well in Rockstar's Grand Theft Auto III. Many of the same elements were there, but done much better."

In 1995, Maxis went public, just before Netscape. At their peak they hit a market cap of over $500 million. Then, in 1997, they were sold to Electronic Arts.

Although Will Wright has always been the creative heart and soul of Maxis, many talented people worked there and contributed to Sim titles not created by Wright, such as SimLife, SimTower and SimFarm, even SimCity 3000. But ultimately, after nine years of working on it, and after overcoming all sorts of corporate roadblocks, Wright finally completed his pet project, Project X.

Project X—AKA, The Sims

Inspiration for The Sims began with another pair of books—a book on architecture called *A Pattern Language* by Chris Alexander and Understanding Comics by Scott McCloud. Wright first came across

A Pattern Language, which he describes as the Western equivalent of the Chinese art feng shui, back around the time he was writing SimCity. "My original concept was to do a game based around architecture the way SimCity was about cities. There were several home design packages on the market at the time, but none of these were fun to use." From *Understanding Comics*, Wright came across the concept of levels of abstraction. "The book shows a range of faces, from photographic to a simple smiley face. It becomes clear that the photographic image leaves little room for interpretation, whereas a more abstract image is easier for someone else to read in what they want to see— themselves, for instance, or a friend or neighbor. We used the concept of abstraction quite a bit in The Sims, especially in the visual language they speak."

Sim behavior was modeled, to some degree, on the ant behavior he had worked with in SimAnt. "Some of the elements of The Sims were in SimAnt… the guy with his house and the ants' responses to their environment. "How the Sims react to objects in their world is modeled roughly on ant behavior," says Wright. "What I call a 'proximity pheromone' model. What this means is that the people in The Sims will generally respond to objects that are close to them. So, if the urge for some entertainment is strong and they are near a TV, they might switch it on and watch. But if they are nearer to the fish tank, then that is where they

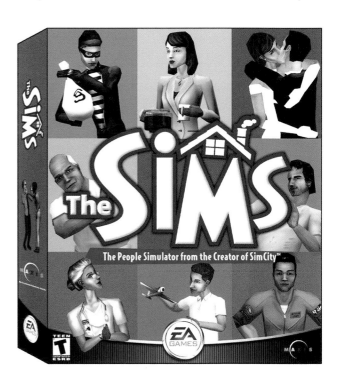

might go. This depends on specifics of the Sim's personality, of course. They seek out whatever will increase their happiness the most, which depends on all their needs and personality traits. Of course, if there is something very compelling, like a hot tub or someone they love around, they'll go all the way across the house."

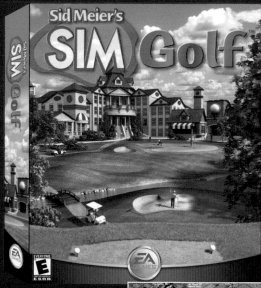

In 2002, the incomparable Sid Meier turned his attention to the links and produced SimGolf for Maxis/Electronic Arts. SimGolf allowed players to design their own golf courses and play on them.

Several Sims expansion packs have come out since the original debuted, including The Sims: Livin' Large, House Party, Hot Date, and Vacation. In fact, The Sims is available in some form on just about any gaming platform, including mobile, online multiplayer, and social games.

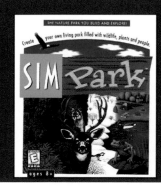

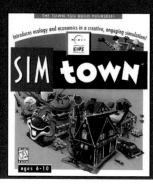

Maxis published many other games in addition to those designed by Will Wright, and many talented people have contributed to all their products. Still, Will Wright can be considered the soul and inspiration of Maxis.

God Gamer

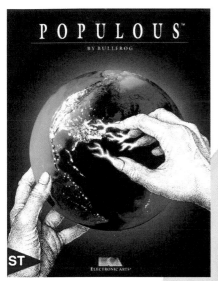

Often credited with being the inventor of the "god game" category, Peter Molyneux started producing software in the mid-'80s. His first company was Taurus, founded with his partner, Les Edgar. They intended to produce business database software, but the company wasn't going anywhere fast. Then one day they were invited to a meeting with Commodore. "They started saying how much they loved our product and how they really wanted to see it on the Amiga," says Molyneux. "I felt extremely flattered and then delighted when they offered to supply us with ten free machines. Slowly the realization dawned on me that they thought they were dealing with another company called Torus, who were doing something with networking, but times were hard so I kept quiet and in time took delivery of our free machines."

Molyneux quickly realized that the Amiga could be a great game machine, "so, as ardent gamers, we happily switched to developing games." They started out with a port of Druid II from the Atari ST and used the money to begin their own project.

They changed the name of the company to Bullfrog. "We were

Flood was an obscure Bullfrog game by Sean Cooper.

both Taureans," recalls Molyneux, "which is where the 'bull' comes from. We chose 'frog' because at the time we were both big fans of the game Frogger."

Bullfrog's debut product was called Populous, and in it the player got to be a god looking down on his or her world and doing various godlike things while worshipers act out their dramas on the surface. "The idea of being all-powerful is something that has always fascinated me since I was a kid," says Molyneux. "Much later I can remember going up in one of those scenic lifts and looking down at all the little people below going about their lives, and this also made me think about using little people to convey this feeling of power. Then Glenn Corpes, one of the original Bullfrog team, showed me a landscape engine that he had been working on, and I suddenly knew that this engine would give me the most perfect view for the game I had in mind."

Populous was a huge hit, and one of those rare games that spawns a genre of its own. It featured a great isometric view, humor, and intriguing gameplay. It was similar to SimCity, which came out around the same time, in that you affected a world full of simulated people, but didn't interact with them directly. It also had something in common with real-time strategy games in that your followers would build up villages and would wage war on the followers of rival gods.

Bullfrog followed Populous with a game of territory and resource management called PowerMonger. PowerMonger was not as popular as Populous, but it was also a very clever game that involved building armies as well as villages and technologies. It consisted of a large map divided into segments, and each segment represented a different scenario. The goal was to conquer the map segments to take over the world. Molyneux, ever his own worst critic, says PowerMonger "was a good world simulation, but it had an overly complex interface and no story." It was fun, though.

A "QUIRKY IDEA"

"Populous was my first ever game and, in some ways, after Black & White, it is still the game of which I am most proud. Never in my wildest dreams did I imagine it would sell over 4 million copies. I thought maybe a few people would appreciate this rather quirky idea we had come up with. Populous was essentially a simple game. It had no story or goal, so that ultimately the gameplay was extremely repetitive."
-Peter Molyneux

Bullfrog came out with a succession of clever games, including Syndicate, Theme Park, Magic Carpet, Dungeon Keeper, and several sequels to Populous. Each was unique and interesting in its own right, though not always commercially successful. In particular, Theme Park did very well in Europe and Japan, but poorly in the States. Molyneux comments that the graphics might have been "too childish" for the U.S. market and that "Theme Park could have been improved with more disasters and more kinds of challenges."

Dungeon Keeper was really enjoyable in many ways. The ultimate anti-hero, you played the demonic keeper of a dungeon, building up your troops of nasties to take on the invading heroes. Although the game was great fun to play, its interface was unnecessarily complex.

Black & White

Molyneux's most recent work, created for his new company, Lionhead Studios, was also his most ambitious work at the time this was written. The inspiration came in part from an episode of the *The Outer Limits* called "Sand Kings," in which a scientist discovers a new species who then worship him as a god. The other inspiration came from an electronic pet Molyneux obtained during the final weeks of the Dungeon Keeper project. "I managed to keep my Tamagotchi fed and watered despite being totally exhausted, but we were cooped up in a very small office, and its beeping was driving everyone else mad. Finally, Andy Robson, who is now head of testing at Lionhead, snapped and drowned it in a cup of coffee. I was stunned at how upset I felt at the 'death' of my helpless pet, but then it occurred to me that if I had become so attached to an egg-shaped piece of plastic, how much more attached might I and other people become to a unique computer creature."

Black & White not only allowed you to play god in a much more direct way with your worshipful populous, but it also introduced the concept of an artificially intelligent, unique, and often quirky creature who becomes your pet and ultimately develops its personality based on its experiences and your training methods.

Black & White also allowed players to create their own kind of world. They can be a dark, cruel god or a good and beneficent deity—or anything in between—and the world shapes itself in the image of its master.

Next Steps

Although the scope of this book technically ends in 2000, it would be remiss to leave out Molyneux's most compelling work to date: Fable. The Fable series of games continues Molyneux's quest for games in which the player's actions have an impact. We'll have more about Fable and Molyneux's future directions in the next book.

> *When I look back at my past work, I cannot honestly say I am proud of any of it.*
> —PETER MOLYNEUX

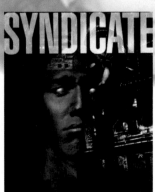

Blizzard

When Allen Adham got a couple of friends—Mike Morhaime and Frank Pearce—together to form a company called Silicon & Synapse in 1991, none of them had any idea what lay ahead for them, or for the rest of the game-playing world. To start the new company, Adham and Morhaime each put up $10,000. Their loftiest goal at the time was to make great games and have fun.

Adham had done some play-testing for Brian Fargo at Interplay and had been involved in Fargo's Demon's Forge project, so it was natural that the new company started out doing conversions of existing games to new platforms for Interplay. After a couple of years, Silicon & Synapse began creating original console games such as Rock N' Roll Racing and The Lost Vikings for Interplay. Adham comments on those early years: "We got to see how games were made. We were just sponges, absorbing information."

Above: Screen from Rock N' Roll Racing for Genesis.

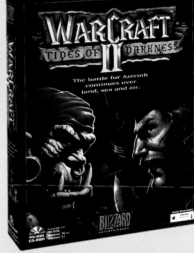

Although their games were moderately successful, the young company was still living on the edge. "We were living from paycheck to paycheck," says Morhaime. "One late check from a publisher would have put us in the red." Living in debt, both Morhaime and Adham often used their credit cards to make payroll.

In 1994, it all changed. Silicon & Synapse (which had by now become Chaos Studios) changed its name again to Blizzard Entertainment.

The original Silicon & Synapse logo.

Original Blizzard concept art for Warcraft.

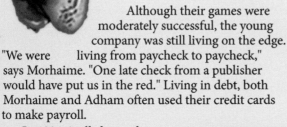

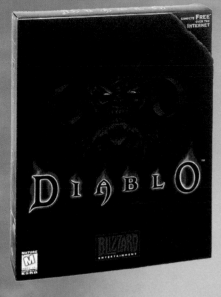

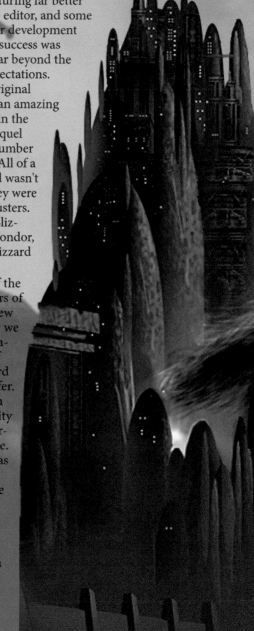

ruin the strategy of the turn-based action." However, co-designer Dave Brevik agreed to prototype the real-time implementation. Within three hours, he had a mockup. When he clicked on the monster, his character started swinging, the monster went down, and it was suddenly clear that real-time was the way to go.

Meanwhile, Warcraft II shipped in late 1995, featuring far better graphics, a map editor, and some added character development and humor. Its success was astronomical, far beyond the developers' expectations. Whereas the original game had sold an amazing 100,000 copies in the first year, the sequel exceeded that number ten times over. All of a sudden Blizzard wasn't making hits, they were making blockbusters. In early 1996, Blizzard acquired Condor, which became Blizzard North.

With the merger of the companies, the designers of Diablo experienced a new sense of freedom. "Now we could make the best Diablo we could, instead of basically building toward milestones," says Schaefer. At that time, they began to consider the possibility of playing over the Internet, and Blizzard's Battle.net was born. Diablo was finally released in late December 1996, too late to catch any Christmas sales. However, the holiday boost proved unnecessary. Diablo exploded off the shelves and was a runaway hit.

Blizzard was far

Adham and Morhaime sold the company to "edutainment" giant Davidson & Associates for several million dollars (*see page 217*), and completed Blackthorne for Interplay and The Death and Return of Superman for Sunsoft. They also introduced their first Blizzard product and their first big computer game hit, Warcraft: Orcs & Humans. Along with Westwood's Command & Conquer, Warcraft helped to usher in a new genre: real-time strategy (RTS).

Meanwhile, a small development group called Condor was looking for an opportunity, shopping a proposal for a game around CES, but getting no takers. Some employees at both Condor and Blizzard had worked on ports of Justice League Task Force for Sunsoft, and so they knew each other. When Condor co-founder David Brevik called his friend Allen Adham to ask for a copy of Warcraft, the conversation eventually got around to what Condor was doing. Brevik mentioned the proposal that had been universally turned down. The game was called Diablo.

Ultimately, Blizzard decided to contract with Condor to do the game, though it was somewhat different in its original conception. "Originally, we modeled our world and look after XCOM," says Max Schaefer. "Then, late in the spring, someone from Blizzard proposed that the game be real-time. We fought heavily against it. We said it would

Above: StarCraft screens.
Below Right: Brood War screen.

from finished making hit games. While the Diablo team got started on the sequel, another game was in development. Originally, StarCraft was meant to be like Warcraft but in space, but an early preview at the Electronic Entertainment Expo in 1996 convinced the team that it needed work. They redesigned the Warcraft II engine to allow the graphic effects they wanted for the game and revamped the design. By August 1997, they had entered the crunch mode of the project. Programmer/designer Bob Fitch remembers how the project consumed him. Going from 50 hours a week ultimately to 80 hours a week and basically living at Blizzard, he remembers, "People would bring me food. I was sleeping on the couch and despite all of that, I still wanted to play the game. I thought, if it is this bad—if I want to play the game when I am sleeping here, showering here, and people are bringing me my food—then this game is going to be great."

Fitch was right. The game shipped in March 1998 and within three months had already sold a million copies. The expansion pack, Brood War, was even better according to Fitch. "People call Brood War an expansion, but really, Brood War is the game that StarCraft should have been."

StarCraft's amazing speed off the shelves was later eclipsed by Blizzard's long-awaited Diablo II, which sold its first million copies in only 18 days. By Blizzard's tenth anniversary, Diablo II had sold more than 2.5 million copies worldwide, and Battle.net had nearly 9 million active accounts playing more than a million games a day. Diablo II was worth the wait, too. It was every bit as intense as the original Diablo, but with new char-

acter classes and a whole new story. There was plenty of hack and plenty of slash, and a plethora of cool stuff to find. And the Diablo II expansion pack, Lord of Destruction, added new characters still, and much more cool stuff.

In 2001, Sierra, Blizzard, and Universal Interactive all combined to become Vivendi Universal Interactive. World of Warcraft launched in 2004, 10 years after the debut of Warcraft. In July 2008, Activision merged with Vivendi Universal Interactive in a deal reportedly worth $18 billion to become Activision Blizzard, Inc. Blizzard by any name, however, has continued to create nothing but great games.

id Software

John Romero (top) and John Carmack (bottom) at their computers.

Screen from the first Kroz adventure (above) and Commander Keen (right).

They've rocked the world of computer games since 1991, but the story of id Software began much earlier. For John Romero, it began in 1979 when he learned to program on an HP 9000 mainframe at Sierra College in Rocklin, California. A year later, he discovered the Apple II, and he was off and coding. Romero, who is today a walking encyclopedia of Apple II game information, eventually taught himself assembly language programming—without a computer. "We had moved to England, and my Apple was on the boat for six months. I had to teach myself assembly language in my head. Amazingly, I wrote down the code for my first assembly game, and when I got my computer, I input it and it worked!"

After graduating from high school, Romero moved back to California. He wanted to work for a game company, and ultimately he landed a job as a programmer at Origin Systems' New Hampshire offices. He was also publishing games in magazines such as A+ and Nibble (where he received the prestigious December cover three years in a row). He left Origin to start Inside Out Software, a company dedicated to porting games to different systems. The company didn't do well, and he moved on to Softdisk, a monthly magazine-on-disk company located in Shreveport, Louisiana. There he caused the formation of a game division within the company. He also met Tom Hall, Jay Wilbur, and artist Kevin Cloud (all of whom became part of the original id Software) and worked with another experienced programmer, Lane Roathe.

One of the contractors who contributed to Softdisk was a kid who worked in a pizza parlor in Kansas. His name was John Carmack,

and he also started programming early on the Radio Shack TRS-80 and the Apple II. Impressed by Carmack's work, Romero invited him to join them at Softdisk. Carmack had twice refused to join Softdisk, but when Romero invited him he said yes and came to Shreveport. "It was pretty cool for me," says Carmack. "I got to meet really good programmers like John Romero and Lane Roathe. I had never known any other good programmers. I learned a lot in my first six months at Softdisk." Carmack's first project at Softdisk was Catacomb for the Apple II.

In short order, Carmack came up with a technique for creating smoothly-scrolling graphics on the PC, something that hadn't been done previously. As a prank, he and Tom Hall recreated the first level of Super Mario Bros. 3, pixel by pixel, replacing Mario with their own character, Dangerous Dave. They completed it at 5 a.m. after pulling an all-nighter, and showed it to Romero. Carmack called the game, "Dangerous Dave in Copyright Infringement." The results were just short of miraculous. "I was thunderstruck by Carmack's smooth-scrolling code," says Romero, "and made a big deal about it to the other guys, saying, 'This is it, guys. We're outta here.' Very seriously. Jay was laughing, but I looked at him seriously and said, 'Dude, I'm not joking.' Then he slowly closed the door so we could talk." When a full version (with Mario, not Dave) was presented to Nintendo, however, the console company said they weren't interested. Dangerous Dave went on to have more adventures, but not in Marioland.

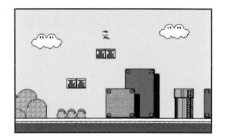

Dangerous Dave in Copyright Infringement.

A Real Get-Rich-Quick Scheme

As a high school student, Scott Miller was a big fan of games like Rogue, M.U.L.E., Archon, and Spelunker. He was also making games of his own. "Back in 1985," says Apogee's Miller,

ideas from the deep

6777 rasberry lane, *821
shreveport, la 71129
318-687-5941

he roath   john romero

Romero's early business card, before id.

"The management at Softdisk was very protective, and I knew I had to be stealthy in contacting Romero, so I began sending him letters praising his games," says Apogee founder Scott Miller. Romero remembers the letters well. "Scott was writing me all these letters, using different names. I thought they were fan mail, so I pinned them to the wall. Then I read an article about Apogee and Kroz and I noticed the address. I thought to myself, 'I know that address.' I looked, and sure enough, all the fan letters were from that address. I was pissed at first and wrote a scathing letter to him. But then I wrote a nice letter, and included the scathing one with it. He didn't care. He told me he wanted me to make a new version of Pyramids of Egypt for Apogee. I told him the stuff we were working on was way better and sent him our Super Mario 3 demo."

"I was making games and releasing them into shareware, but they weren't making any money. I spoke with other shareware authors, such as Nels Anderson, who did EGA Trek, and Mike Denio, who did Captain Comic, and they weren't making any money either. There were good games out in shareware, but they weren't making money."

In 1987, Miller came up with a stroke of genius. He split his latest game, Kroz*, into three parts and released only the first part for free. Players who wanted the rest would have to pay for it. Miller's scheme was immensely successful, and he started Apogee with the idea of finding other Shareware game authors and marketing their games according to this very lucrative plan. Among the authors he contacted were Anderson and Denio. At the top of his list was John Romero. (See the "Fan Letters" sidebar to learn how he made contact.)

Miller tried to convince Romero to create a game for him, but Romero was unconvinced. Miller tells it this way: "He had a pyramid game for Softdisk, and I said it would be perfect for shareware, but John thought it was bullshit. But when I told him how much money Kroz was making, he finally said, 'Are you willing to put your money where your mouth is?' I said I'd send him a $3,000 advance. I had $5,000 in my bank account."

Romero agreed and got his friends at Softdisk to work with him. Tom Hall came up with the idea for their first shareware game—Commander Keen—in about 15 minutes. (The full proposal is reproduced in the sidebar on the next page.)

Meanwhile, Romero had spotted Adrian Carmack (no relation to John) in what he calls the "five-buck-an-hour art farm" at Softdisk. According to Adrian, "I was told by my college art professor that an internship position was open at Softdisk. The job was to create artwork for monthly computer games. I worked in the computer art department, but Romero and Carmack wanted me to be in their group. Romero went to the owner with his complaint, and after a

meeting between the two groups I was switched over to the game department. Shortly after that John Carmack asked me if I wanted to work with them on a side project, which was Commander Keen." The team was complete.

Three months later, Commander Keen: Invasion of the Vorticons was ready

Wolfenstein 3D screenshot.

to ship, and a month after that they received their first royalty check for $10,500. Immediately they realized that staying at Softdisk, working on salary, was a dead end. Other than Jay Wilbur and Kevin Cloud, the whole group resigned but agreed to produce games for six more bimonthly Softdisk installments. They formed id Software on February 1, 1991.

id Software Goes 3D

John Carmack wasn't finished innovating. After creating his smooth-scrolling technology, he went to work creating a 3D game engine. The first games using that engine—Hovertank One and Catacombs 3-D—were published by Softdisk between April and November 1991—the first first-person 3D shooters ever made. Hovertank One used flat shading, while Catacombs 3-D had full texture mapping, but in EGA graphics mode. Both games are virtually unknown today. It was id's third 3D game that blew the lid off.

Scott Miller, anxious to get the team to work on a 3D game for shareware release, actually had his Apogee team create one of the games (ScubaVenture) to complete id's Softdisk contract. Miller remembers, "I guaranteed that they would make at least $100,000 on a 3D game."

In September of 1991, id moved its offices from Shreveport to Madison, Wisconsin, because Tom Hall had told them it was cool. According to Jay Wilbur, "No one realized that when Tom said 'cool,' he meant 'cold!'" Preferring warmer climates, the company moved again on April 1, 1992, this time to Dallas, Texas. They hired Jay Wilbur to run the business side, and they hired artist Kevin Cloud, both of

*Miller's other favorite game? Spell Kroz backward.

285

Two of the many shareware DOOM boxes.

whom had previously remained at Softdisk.

Shortly after completing their obligations to Softdisk, the id team also completed their second set of Commander Keen episodes for Apogee (in December 1991) and turned their attention to the 3D game Scott Miller wanted so badly. Their first idea was to do a game involving a bio-lab mutant, for which Tom Hall had coined the name, "It's Green and Pissed"; but in the end decided that was trite. (Jay Wilbur swears that the name somehow was also used during the early development of DOOM.) Then Romero suggested doing a game inspired by Silas Warner's classic Castle Wolfenstein (see page 236). The original design for Wolfenstein 3D included some strategy elements, where you could search corpses for items and drag the dead Nazis out of sight to escape detection, but they eventually dropped those elements and made the game a pure shooter.

Wolfenstein 3D was a smash hit, and true to his promise, Miller was able to deliver the id team the promised $100,000—the first month! The team followed up with a commercial release called Spear of Destiny.

id's brief stay in Wisconsin did have one significant result. They met and befriended another small game development group called Raven Software, and let them use a modified version of their Wolfenstein engine for ShadowCaster, a game Raven was doing for Electronic Arts. This was the basis for a lasting relationship between the two companies.

Breaking the Mold

After the release of Wolfenstein 3D, id realized they could go it alone, and decided to stop publishing through Apogee. (The breakup between id and Apogee is a story in itself. This is the short version.) "They had lots of money and had learned how to make money with shareware," says Miller. And, according to Jay Wilbur, "Basically, all we needed was someone to answer phones and lick stamps."

According to Wilbur, "Carmack was working on his next-generation game engine. One day he came out of his office and said, 'I have a perfect name for the game. DOOM.' We all thought it was perfect."

The conceptual inspiration, according to Romero, was to somehow combine elements of two movies—Aliens with Evil Dead—demons and monsters in space. But they had to rethink their philosophy of design because Carmack's DOOM engine was way more powerful than the previous one. "Now we had ceilings of any height, walls with angles, lighting, and floors. We had to break out of our Wolfenstein design mold and push the engine. I came up with a design motto that we don't want anything we do to look like you could have made it with our previous technology."

With superior level design; multiple artifacts, weapons, and monsters; superbly moody music; and fast 35 frames-per-second 3D set in a world full of danger; DOOM was the perfect game for its time. Where Wolfenstein 3D had been a huge success, DOOM was a revelation, a phenomenon, and practically an industry unto itself. It was the basis for much of what has come from the game industry in the years since. Ironically, according to Romero, "DOOM was released in December 1993, the day after Senator Lieberman did his big speech at the violence hearings." Talk about timing!

Once again, the first few levels of DOOM were offered as shareware, and anybody could sell that version. "There were as many as ten different boxes of the product. You walked up to the count-

A KEEN PROPOSAL

Billy Blaze, eight year-old genius, working diligently in his backyard clubhouse, has created an interstellar starship from old soup cans, rubber cement, and plastic tubing. While his folks are out on the town and the babysitter has fallen asleep, Billy sneaks into his backyard workshop, dons his brother's football helmet, and transforms into...

COMMANDER KEEN—defender of Earth!

In his ship, the Bean-with-Bacon Megarocket, Keen dispenses galactic justice with an iron hand!

From the Publisher of DOOM !

HERETIC

er and took your pick. They were all the same, except for the packaging," says Romero.

Another of the innovations that DOOM offered was peer-to-peer play over the modem or LAN. There was a cooperative mode in which up to four players could hunt the enemy together. This required id to rewire the game so that the monsters would randomly target a different player each frame. And then there was the deathmatch mode. DOOM introduced the deathmatch to multiplayer gaming and started something that can only be thought of as a new sporting event still popular today. (Romero claims credit for first using the term "deathmatch.")

The relationship with Raven Software then bore new fruit as id and Raven teamed up to create both Heretic and Hexen using the DOOM engine as well as DOOM II, an impressive expansion of the original product that released in October 1994. But there was more to come.

Quake

How do you top DOOM? Well, technologically, Carmack was up to his usual tricks, and he created an engine that was as much a step forward as DOOM had been from Wolfenstein. However, developing groundbreaking technology has its challenges, and Carmack created at least 12 versions of the engine before it was complete. Meanwhile, they brought in programmer Michael Abrash (who had written a book called Power Graphics Programming) from Microsoft. ("Bill Gates tried to talk him out of it, but it didn't work," says Romero.)

The original concept was to have the player go through the game with a big hammer. No DOOM-like weapons here. And, although the exploration would be in the now-familiar first-person view, the fighting would be in a perspective, "like Tekken 3," according to Romero. But, according to Kevin Cloud, despite some good elements in the early design, "about halfway through the development process, id decided to change directions and focus on further developing the fast action gameplay that made Wolfenstein and DOOM so popular."

"The design process of Quake wore us all out, and I was upset that we had to abandon our original concepts," says Romero. "At the end of the project, I was all alone uploading it to the 'net and mastering the CDs. In the past, we had all been together, celebrating, but everybody else was at home."

After Quake shipped, id and Romero parted ways, and Romero went on to form Ion Storm. Quake was a huge hit, as DOOM had been before it. And, like DOOM, but to an even greater degree, it inspired the evolution of the "mod" community—allowing players to create their own levels and modifications by releasing the source code. Although they were no longer alone in the market, with other

Both Carmack and Romero were famous for their matching Ferarri Testarossas.

JOHN CARMACK ON 3D

"If you look at our 3D games, they were basically like 2D overhead games, but with a fresh perspective. We took the same game design concepts, but it became much more exciting when, instead of a 16-pixel blob on the screen, we put you in it. We created a brand-new generation of games—the first-person shooter—but it's really an overhead action shooter game with a new perspective."

game engines such as Apogee's Build engine, Bethesda's XnGine, and the Unreal engine from Epic MegaGames competing, id continued to produce great games, such as Quake II and Quake III, each of which further improved on the speed and depth of the Quake engine, as well as substantially improving online deathmatch play. Versions of the Quake engine have been licensed to produce a staggering legacy of games including Half-Life and its sequels, Medal of Honor: Allied Assault, Star Trek Voyager: Elite Force, American McGee's Alice, Return to Castle Wolfenstein, 007: The World is Not Enough, Star Wars Jedi Knight II: Jedi Outcast, and many more.

Shiny Entertainment

After years of creating games in England and the States, Dave Perry started Shiny Entertainment in October 1993, right after getting his green card.

Perry had done several games for the UK company Virgin Interactive, including one based on a McDonald's license, called Global Gladiators. "I remember working my ass off—sleeping in the parking lot at Virgin," says Perry. "But the game won Game of the Year on the Genesis." He also developed Cool Spot, based on the 7Up license and using the Global Gladiators engine, as well as Disney's Aladdin, where he and his team developed sophisticated paper-to-digital animation techniques called Animotion.

Earthworm Jim

When he started Shiny, Perry took with him many of Virgin's best designers and artists, including longtime associates Nick Bruty, Mike Dietz, Ed Schofield, and Steve Crow. Later they were joined by Andy Astor,

Nick Jones, and Tom Tanaka. At about this time, yet another Virgin employee, animator and cartoonist Doug TenNapel, decided it was time to move on, and applied to Shiny for a job.

According to TenNapel, "Mike Dietz told me to come up with a character and maybe animate a walk cycle. 'We'll see if you're Shiny material,' he said. So I went home and put on a Fleetwood Mac album. By the time the album finished, I had designed Earthworm Jim, Peter Puppy, the Queen—every major character in the Earthworm Jim world."

With Perry's background in doing licensed games, and with investment from Playmates and Interactive Entertainment backing the company, the concept of Earthworm Jim was planned from the start as a multifaceted attack—toys, TV, comic books, and video games. The result was one of the oddest heroes of all time and several

Original early drawings of Jim and The Evil Queen Pulsating, Bloated, Festering, Sweaty, Pus-filled, Malformed, Slug-for-a-Butt.

Original cover art and screenshots for Earthworm Jim.

Storyboards for Earthworm Jim TV show.

truly great games.

TenNapel, who later went on to create The Neverhood for DreamWorks (*see page 310*), deserves a lot of the credit for the original concept, but he also spreads the credit around. "We worked round the clock—animated our asses off—but we all brought a lot of experience with us. Nick Bruty added a lot. He's probably the best game designer I've ever worked with. Mike Dietz is an old school animator, while I'm like wild lightning, and he had a lot of influence on the game. Combined, we had all done hundreds of games. We finished it in a year."

After EWJ

After the phenomenal success of Earthworm Jim and its sequel, Shiny continued to make great games, but they were faced with a changing industry. "After we did EWJ 2, 3D technology had become the standard," says Perry, "and it caused a division at Shiny. Many of our team didn't want to move from 2D traditional animation to 3D. And it was expensive. I was funding the company out of my own pockets—buying Silicon Graphics systems and motion capture… It was very expensive. 'What? Another suite of Alias? How much? It's just a piece of software.'" (According to TenNapel, it was not so much the switch to 3D but the fact that there were financial issues arising from the sale to Interplay (see below) that caused several team members to leave.)

Ultimately, Shiny did move into 3D. But in the middle of developing their next game (a 3D shooter called MDK), they accepted an offer to become part of Interplay. "We acquired Shiny because of their strength in the console market," says Inter-

Mithra

Model sheet for Psy-Crow.

play's Brian Fargo (*see page 219*). "Dave's a great visionary, and they had great technology. Ironically, their next projects were for high-end PC products, not the mass market console products we were anticipating."

Despite Fargo's comment, MDK sold more than 500,000 copies and was successful on both PC and PlayStation platforms. They followed with another wacky PlayStation game, Wild 9, and Messiah, a highly innovative PC title. There was considerable hubbub about some of the content of Messiah, which includes such features as the ability of the player's angel character to possess the bodies of other beings, including prostitutes.

After Messiah, Shiny created Sacrifice, an ambitious story-based game of strategy, action, and magic set in a 3D world. Shiny's games were consistently imaginative, groundbreaking, and critically acclaimed.

Enter the Matrix

Deeply into Sacrifice, Perry initially turned down the opportunity to create a game based on The Matrix, but he jumped on the chance after seeing the movie. "The directors offered to make the movie and game 'one project,' the point being that they would create new footage and story for the game that tied in perfectly with the movie. Like in the movie when Morpheus falls off the truck onto the hood of Niobe's car, in the game it was you getting the car there to save him. When Monica Bellucci kisses Neo in the movie, she kisses Jada Pinkett Smith in the the game. It was a big idea." Enter the Matrix and its sequel, Path of Neo, were successful, though challenging games to create. These were the last two games Perry would make with Shiny. As Atari was selling Shiny to Foundation 9, Perry made his exit. He moved into free-to-play MMOs and later built up, and then sold, streaming game service Gaikai to Sony.

Sacrifice was actually based on the old-style wizards games. However, its state-of-the-art engine really gave it a special look and made the experience a lot more immersive.

There is still life in the games where you play as a wizard, collect incredibly powerful spells, build an army, and then go and sacrifice the bodies of your enemies to your god.
—Dave Perry

Doug TenNapel at work.

1993

Jaguar

Top to bottom: Atari Karts, Alien vs. Predator, Battlemorph.

In the early '90s, Atari attempted to come back to the console business one more time. The company was simultaneously developing a 32-bit system called the Panther—which was scheduled to release in 1991 at the same time as the Super NES—and an even more advanced system called the Jaguar. Touted as the first 64-bit system (which was astounding when compared with the 16-bit Genesis), Jaguar was impressive on paper, and Atari was able to line up several third-party publishers. At launch in 1993, the system sold well, although at a price tag of $250—far higher than Atari had originally announced.

The Jaguar was a sleek and powerful machine, but its initial software did little to convince consumers that the machine could live up to its hype. The development system proved to be difficult to work with, and many third-party titles either released very late or were never completed. Ultimately, however, some fine games were released for the Jaguar, including Tempest 2000 and versions of DOOM, Wolfenstein 3D, and Alien vs. Predator; but the initial reaction held the system back. Most of these games were available on other systems, anyway. Jaguar really had no "killer app" and too small a list of titles to keep growing.

In a weak selling year in general, hobbled by a lack of good titles, and with Sega's Saturn on the horizon, Jaguar did poorly. With the release of PlayStation in late 1995, its fate was sealed. Despite its claims to be a superior 64-bit system, the new 32-bit consoles, Saturn and PlayStation, both produced superior products. Although Atari introduced a CD add-on and even had a more powerful Jaguar II in production, their support lasted only a matter of months. Jaguar was discontinued in 1996.

Star Alliance - Battle for Earth from JDC (courtesy of Lars Hannig).

1994

Peripheral Madness

At the time of Nintendo's SNES introduction, Sega was on the rise. The competition between Nintendo and Sega grew ever tighter as they shared the market and NEC ultimately faded. For the first time, there were two nearly evenly successful console systems. According to Nintendo's numbers, they ultimately sold 18.5 million SNES to 16.4 million of Sega's Genesis.

However, Sega may have leaned a little two hard on Sonic. Although many other great games did come out for the Genesis, including Phantasy Star II, Revenge of Shinobi, Virtua Fighter 2, and Shining Force (which in many ways was the forerunner to Square's Final Fantasy Tactics), Sonic was the only real franchise character Sega had. He was featured in comic books and cartoons and was definitely a big hit,

but Sega came out with more Sonic games than you could shake a stick at. Even the introduction of the popular character Tails in Sonic the Hedgehog 2 wasn't enough to carry the company.

But perhaps Sega's bigger problem came in their various attempts to expand the Genesis. They tried different peripheral devices, including the Sega CD unit, but none were immensely successful, and their 32X add-on for the Genesis—a hybrid CD enhancement with its own games—simply diluted their market and left a bad taste in the mouths of both consumers and retailers. If you had Sega CD and 32X attached to your Genesis, the sleekly designed console was transformed into an ungainly jumble of badly fitting parts. In the end, Nintendo's franchise games and its immense third-party support kept them strong, while Sega began to stumble amidst increasing competition from new console makers.

The Violence Controversy

In 1993, games like Mortal Kombat and Night Trap came to the attention of U.S. Senators Joseph Lieberman and Herb Kohl, who launched a campaign against video game violence and the "culture of carnage" rampant throughout the entertainment industry. There were valid arguments on both sides, but certainly the game industry wasn't about to succumb to outright censorship and the possible loss of revenues. Violence was a part of gaming, and the improving technology allowed increasing realism. Ultimately the game industry offered a compromise— the Entertainment Software Rating Board (ESRB), which created a rating system for video games. This rating system alerts parents to possibly offensive material but does not necessarily prevent young kids from gaining access to violent games or other games deemed unsuitable for young minds.

TIME TRAVELER

One of Sega's more interesting attempts was a system called Time Traveler, which was billed as "the world's first three-dimensional holographic video game." Created with technology called "the Micro-theater," which was developed by independent inventors Steve Zuloff and Barry Benjamin, Time Traveler was a nonlinear holographic game. The creator of Time Traveler was Rick Dyer, who had previously worked with Mattel, Coleco, and others, and was the designer of the first Laserdisc game, Dragon's Lair.

Time Traveler was a big production, with 40 actors and actresses and a team of 100 people. Initial responses in the arcade community were very positive, as well. People were impressed with the technology.

Sega's Dave Cantrelle with "Princess Kyla," Rick Dyer, and ADG's Jim Masterson at ACME, where the game previewed to the trade.

Street Fighter II

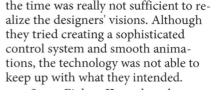

In 1991, when Capcom's Street Fighter II hit the arcades, it looked like the cavalry coming to the rescue in some B western. Instead of the sound of bugles, however, it announced itself with a resounding "Hadouken!"

Street Fighter II was far from the first fighting game. The history of fighting games goes back at least to the '80s, and there were several types of games that featured punches and kicks. Many early games involved the "beat 'em up" theme, such as Double Dragon and Final Fight. The Teenage Mutant Ninja Turtles games were popular fighters in both the arcades and on home systems. A few early games attempted to provide one-on-one excitement, such as Data East's 1984 Karate Champ and even Activision's Kung-Fu Master. In 1987, Capcom came out with Street Fighter, their first attempt to make a one-on-one fighting game. However, technology of

the time was really not sufficient to realize the designers' visions. Although they tried creating a sophisticated control system and smooth animations, the technology was not able to keep up with what they intended.

Street Fighter II, on the other hand, introduced the smoothest animation and the fastest, most complex controls ever seen. When it came out, the arcades suddenly breathed new life, and one-on-one fighters rapidly became the new killer app. Street Fighter II also provided a truly imaginative assortment of fighters, each with his or her own basic and secret moves, and strengths and weaknesses. It was cartoons come to life, and it was a game in which mastery mattered. Over the next few years, Capcom came out with several revisions of the game, though each represented primarily incremental improvements and no giant leaps ahead.

Imitators abounded. On both arcade and home systems, fighting games were everywhere following the release of Street Fighter II. It's safe to say that games inspired by Street Fighter II dominated the scene until DOOM and the first-person shooter took over around 1994.

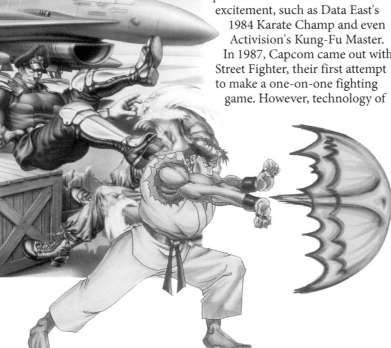

ORIGINAL STREET FIGHTER II ART COURTESY OF CAPCOM.

Mortal Kombat

One of the most significant games to enter the market in the wake of Street Fighter II was Midway's blockbuster 1992 release, Mortal Kombat.

In gameplay, it rivaled Street Fighter II, with secret moves, death moves, and something that even Street Fighter II did not have—real actors digitized into the game. Instead of cartoon characters, you were fighting with and against more or less realistic depictions of people.

The so-called realism of Mortal Kombat was part of its appeal, and part of its controversy. While fighting, blood spurted from every hit, and the finishing moves, once an opponent was sufficiently beaten down, were gory to the point of absurdity—like ripping the unfortunate loser's heart out of their chest or yanking their whole spinal column out.

Mortal Kombat was more than just a lot of gory graphics and an intense fighting game, however. It also had an ongoing story—one that grew increasingly complex for some fans as Midway continued the game series, released movies and other ancillary products, and furthered the story in a variety of ways. Most of all, Mortal Kombat is remembered for its innovation, intensity, and great effects. The series has continued, with new releases all the way until 2015, and shows no sign of disappearing.

293

1995

Saturn

In late 1994, Sega introduced the Saturn in Japan. The system was initially successful in Japan, though its U.S. launch was troubled. Sega's reputation had been tarnished by several poorly received add-ons for the Genesis (notably the short-lived 32X system), as well as some that were announced but never shipped (such as the modem called Tele-Genesis). Further, at least partly as a result of Sony's planned launch of PlayStation later in the year, Sega decided suddenly to move Saturn's U.S. debut up from September to May 1995. This meant that Saturn was initially released in limited quantities in limited markets, and, because of the early launch, it had far too few titles at launch—none of which had the marketing impact of Sonic. To make matters worse, some of the better titles from Japan—including games from Capcom and SNK—were not brought over to the U.S., further damaging Saturn's prospects.

Left to right, top to bottom Albert Odyssey, Dragon Force, Vampire Savior, and Dungeons & Dragons: Tower of Doom.

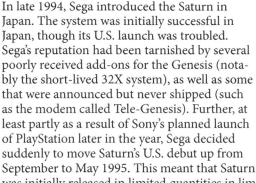

Releasing early did gain Sega some sales, but their success was short-lived. With a $399 sticker price, the system initially sold for $100 more than PlayStation. In addition, Sony virtually owned the consumer electronics market. With their deep pockets and marketing expertise, they were able to take the game market by storm, quickly eclipsing Saturn's sales.

One of Sega's early marketing points for Saturn was a 28.8 kbps modem add-on called NetLink, which would allow users to access the Web, check email, and play online games. By 1994, Sega had launched the Sega Channel in partnership with Time Warner and TCI. With NetLink, Saturn became the first fully internet-enabled game console, demonstrating Sega's visionary, though possibly premature, commitment to expanding the parameters of the franchise.

Top to bottom: Sega's Panzer Dragoon Saga, Shining Force III, and Game Arts' Grandia.

NetLink for the Sega Saturn.

Saturn's flagship title at launch was Nights into Dreams, by Sonic and Phantasy Star designer Yuji Naka. Nights was an intriguing game, with many Sonic-like aspects (although it did not feature Sonic). However, Nights was not popular enough to drive sales of the system. Other excellent games ultimately appeared on the Saturn, including Panzer Dragoon Saga, a huge action RPG that deserved a much bigger audience. Virtua Fighter 2 and Sega Rally Championship headed up a strong arcade conversion list. Between 1995 and 1998, Saturn only sold about a million units and then was discontinued as Sega prepared to launch its "next-gen" system, Dreamcast.

PlayStation

Big ideas have to start somewhere, and the story behind Sony's entry into the console market comes predominantly from the vision and drive of one man. Although it took some support from the top and a team of dedicated developers to produce Sony's first game console system, it was all set in motion when Ken Kutaragi, then working in Sony's sound labs, bought a Nintendo game system for his daughter.

Kutaragi didn't think the sound from the Famicom/NES was as good as it could be, and he thought he could improve it. After getting permission at Sony to engage in some outside contract work, he approached Nintendo and went to work designing a digital sound chip for them. After the sound chip, Kutaragi continued to work as an outside contractor for Nintendo, but not everybody at Sony was happy. Several Sony executives opposed the arrangement, but Sony's CEO Norio Ohga stepped in and supported Kutaragi's efforts and allowed him to continue.

In 1988, Sony and Nintendo began a joint venture, with Kutaragi working with Nintendo to develop a 16-bit "Super Disc" CD-ROM-based game system. According to some sources, the goal was to create a Super Famicom system capable of playing both cartridges and games on CD-ROM, which was meant to compete with similar systems coming from Sega and NEC. Images such as those shown in this section claim to be prototypes of a system called "Nintendo Play Station." One shows a standalone system based on the Super Famicom, originally called the Super Disc, and the other, an add-on meant to attach beneath the unit. In fact, Sony introduced the standalone machine at the Chicago Consumer Electronics Show in 1991, but immediately afterward, Nintendo announced that they were going to use Philips as their CD-ROM supplier, not Sony.

Part of the original agreement with Nintendo had allowed them to license their own games, and it soon became clear that Sony intended to leverage their extensive music and film properties. Many believe that Nintendo, who always controlled game licensing very tightly, foresaw a serious threat from Sony, causing them to break the agreement and switch their CD development partnership to Philips.

The breakup caused bad feelings on both sides. But Ken Kutaragi, who had designed the SNES sound chip and led the original development of the prototypes, wasn't about to let all that work go to waste. He approached Ohga again, advocating for Sony to continue the work that he had started with Nintendo and develop their own version of the Play Station. Again, Ohga agreed and lent his support to Kutaragi's vision, which led to the formation of the Sony Computer Entertainment division.

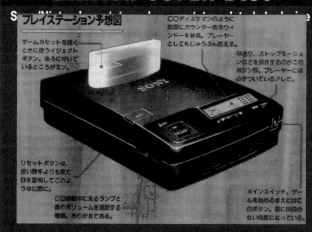

SONY/NINTENDO PLAY STATION SUPER DISC

from the upper left corner:

- **Playstation Forecast Figure**
- **Eject button used for pulling the cassette out. Cool to have it in this location.**
- **Like CD Disc Man, there is a display screen. This player can be used as a CD player.**
- **Buttons for fast forward, stop, etc. Other players have these kinds of functions.**
- **Main switch to start the game. The angle of the switch makes you not turn it off easily.**
- **The lamp glows while CD is playing. There is a button for volume. It's common to have these on players.**
- **Reset button is located here—emphasis on appearance more than function.**

Early Play Station prototype with unit on top of disc player.

295

Although the original plan was to continue development of the original Play Station concept, ultimately a new deal was struck with Nintendo in which Nintendo would control content licensing—a partnership that was short-lived. Sony reset its sights on the next generation of hardware. Kutaragi went back to the drawing board and created a new standalone 32-bit system from scratch. The result, the Sony PlayStation (or PSX), was released in Japan at the end of 1994, and came to America on September 9, 1995. PlayStation was designed for ease of game development, and Sony didn't restrict developers the way Nintendo had. Because of this, some developers, such as Squaresoft, defected from Nintendo to join the ranks of Sony's content creators. In the end, with games like Final Fantasy VII and Gran Turismo leading the way, Sony became the leader in the console field.

In early 2000, Sony redesigned the original PSX into a personal CD player-sized console called the PSone, while PlayStation 2 went on to dominate the game world after its release later that same

PlayStation™

PlayStation™

Prepare yourself for a blast of ultimate game system power. Sony's breakthrough 32-bit processor, CD-ROM architecture delivers real-time experience with ever-changing 3-D perspectives and stereo CD-quality sound. Custom multiple processors including a dedicated 32-bit RISC CPU pulse at the heart of the system. Result? Gameplay will never be the same.

Features

- Custom multiple processors for the most realistic 3-D graphics rendered in real-time and the most responsive gameplay ever.
- 360-degree movement provides ever changing 3-D perspectives to enhance realism.
- Full frame video at 30 frames per second for the highest quality images.
- 360,000 polygons per second giving a smoother, more realistic look to the graphics and movement of the games.
- 16.8 million simultaneous colors.
- 2MB of RAM, 1MB VRAM. Players can download an entire game into RAM memory.
- Custom ports for two controllers and two memory cards.
- Includes custom controller, AC power cord and stereo AV cable.

Marketing

Support within the PlayStation's unprecedented marketing campaign includes:
- National TV
- National Print
- Full PR and Editorial Coverage
- Retail Promotions and Merchandising
- Sony Home Page Web Site Coverage

Product Profile

Available: September 9, 1995
Part No: SCPH-1001/94000

One of the top games for the new PlayStation: Tomb Raider (Eidos)

year. The next generation introduced more significant challengers, and with rivalries from Microsoft's Xbox 360 and Nintendo's Wii, Sony found their PlayStation 3 in a three-way race for console superiority.

Nintendo PlayStation

With Nintendo supplying the guts, all it needed was Sony to supply CD-ROM storage technology and the happy alliance would be sealed. Except one company did not have faith in optical storage, leaving the other to take the concept on its own...

Left to right, top to bottom: DOOM (Williams), Spyro the Dragon (Sony), Gran Turismo (Sony), Tony Hawk's Pro Skater 3 (Activision), Twisted Metal 2 (Sony), Final Fantasy VII (Squaresoft).

297

 **Breath of Fire IV** *(Capcom)*

 **Bloody Roar** *(Hudson Soft)*

 **Suikoden II** *(Konami)*

 **Tekken** *(Namco)*

 **007 Racing** *(Electronic Arts)*

 **Crash Bandicoot** *(Naughty Dog)*

 **Azure Dreams** *(Konami)*

 **Ridge Racer** *(Namco)*

 **Dragon Quest IV** *(Japan only)* *(Enix)*

 **Dragon Warrior VII** *(Enix)*

 **Madden NFL 2002** *(Electronic Arts)*

 **NCAA Final Four 2002** *(Electronic Arts)*

 **Tiger Woods PGA Tour Golf** *(Electronic Arts)*

 **007: The World is Not Enough** *(Electronic Arts)*

 **The Legend of Dragoon** *(Sony)*

 **Soul of the Samurai** *(Konami)*

 **Metal Gear Solid** *(Konami)*

 **Nightmare Creatures II** *(Konami)*

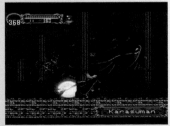 **Castlevania: Symphony of the Night** *(Konami)*

 **Tenchu 2** *(Activision)*

Darkstalkers: The Night Warriors (*Capcom*)

Marvel Super Heroes (*Capcom*)

Street Fighter Alpha 3 (*Capcom*)

Dance Dance Revolution (*Konami*)

Alundra (*Working Designs*)

Jumping Flash! 2 (*Sony*)

MLB 2001 (*Sony*)

Final Fantasy IX (*Squaresoft*)

Final Fantasy VII (*Squaresoft*)

Final Fantasy VIII (*Squaresoft*)

PaRappa the Rapper (*Sony Computer Entertainment*)

Spyro: Year of the Dragon (*Insomniac/Sony*)

Arc the Lad (*Working Designs*)

Lunar 2: Eternal Blue Complete (*Working Designs*)

WWF Smackdown! 2: Know Your Role (*THQ*)

Working Design's Arc the Lad collection.

299

BioWare

Many of the pioneers of the game industry found their passion for making games early. People like Nolan Bushnell, Richard Garriott, Roberta Williams, Will Wright, and others hadn't pursued a serious career before embarking on their creative path. Not so with Ray Muzyka and Greg Zeschuk, whose passion for games overwhelmed their desire to continue as medical doctors.

Having worked on some medical education software while at medical school, they had already shown the ability to complete, and sell, digital products. "When the opportunity came up to work with some really talented people," says Muzyka, "we seized it. We took our capital and basically started working more and more as BioWare and less and less as doctors, in transition from the medical side… it took a few years during the early '90s."

"To really tell the people part," adds Zeschuk, "there were a ton of talented people, but the interesting thing is that none of them were from video games. During the first three or four years, they were all people from school, other fields—community programmers, graphic designers, graphic artists, commercial ones—a lot of folks that had a passion for games but didn't have the outlet."

Still working as doctors, they formed BioWare in 1995 with another classmate, Augustine Yip; set up shop in Edmonton, Canada (definitely not a hub for game development at the time); put together a team of novice developers; and had

at it. Although they both continued their medical practices for many years after starting BioWare—in part to pay the salaries of BioWare employees—little by little they shifted from weekend work to full-time game developers, while Yip ultimately decided to return to medicine in 1997.

"We would go back and work as MDs on the weekend," says Muzyka, "and oftentimes we'd be putting in more money to supplement the funds and taking loans against our medical incomes, so it was almost like the medical work almost became the hobby that was funding the career, the video game career."

Their first game was Shattered Steel, a MechWarrior-like sci-fi action game that was published by Interplay. According to Zeschuk, Shattered Steel featured "deformable terrains with 3D robots running around—which was pretty state-of-the-art back in the early mid-'90s."

Although Shattered Steel got them in the door as a studio, their real passion was for RPGs. When asked about their influences, they took turns rattling off a litany of great RPGs, including the Ultima and Wizardry series, Wasteland, The Bard's Tale, the Gold Box D&D games, the Legend of Zelda series, Final Fantasy, Chrono Trigger, Chrono Cross, Shining Force… Their passion was clear, and even as they were producing Shattered Steel, the seeds of their first RPG project were taking shape.

"I remember we'd have all these lunches where we'd discuss game design ideas and we came up with the concept called 'Battleground Infinity,'" says Zeschuk. Muzyka continues, "Battleground Infinity was a really ambitious design in retrospect. It was almost an MMO, but we didn't know it at the time. It had these dimensions you'd go into; it was multiplayer; it was going to be cutting-edge graphics at the time, which, inevitably, in the '90s were not as impressive as they became later. Nevertheless, it would have been pretty cool." Their proposed budget in the low six figures wasn't realistic, but they did create a prototype of their idea and showed it to five publishers, four of whom made offers. Even though Interplay wasn't initially too interested because they had a good RPG line with the D&D license, the prototype impressed them and they signed a deal, but not for Battleground Infinity. At that point, BioWare dropped the Battleground Infinity idea. Instead, they developed the very successful RPG, Baldur's Gate, which used the D&D license. They did, however, retain the original project's name in their game engine—the Infinity Engine—which was later used in several other projects.

At the time Baldur's Gate was released, there was a feeling in the market that RPGs were no longer a viable genre, with the possible exception of popular Japanese games like Final Fantasy. "We remembered the great experiences we had growing up playing these rich RPGs," says Zeschuk. "Getting to explore and

BioWare's first game: Shattered Steel.

be a hero, the knight in shining armor, exploring through a post-apocalyptic wasteland, the diversity of options you could play, the types of characters… You could form the stories you got to live through where you're both the director and actor at the same time. It was really powerful to us. We thought, 'No, this is a genre that really deserves to be preserved and reborn and revitalized.' It never really occurred to us that we could fail at it, which is probably good in retrospect."

Baldur's Gate was a game changer. Its success came largely because of its high degree of attention to detail and quality writing. To the two doctors, quality, in everything from the workplace to the product, was always the keyword. Another contributor to the success of the game was likely their experience with pen-and-paper role-playing games and their focus on story. "We really wanted to create tactical combat, and give each story a very, very broad experience, very flexible with what you could do," says Zeschuk. "It turned out to be a monstrosity, in a positive way, especially for a team that had never done it before."

Baldur's Gate helped form the vision of BioWare as a company. "It was really about driving emotionally genuine engagement that felt credible, real," explains Muzyka. "The idea of narrative not being only story, but story being one of the ways that's manifested in dialogue, in characters, but also the narrative of the explorer, or the narrative of the combat, the narrative of the hero's journey, and other forms of narrative, too."

One of the early concepts at BioWare was to run multiple teams on separate products. Even as Baldur's Gate was taking shape, they had a team working on Shattered Steel 2, which became MDK 2, the sequel to Shiny Entertainment's MDK. However, the vision of a multiplayer RPG fueled their dreams at the time, so even as they were working on Baldur's Gate II: Shadows of Amn (plus an expansion pack, Throne of Bhaal) and MDK 2, they were also working on the next step towards an MMO. That step—or "half step" according to Zeschuk—was Neverwinter Nights, published in 2002.

Neverwinter Nights accomplished much of what Muzyka and Zeschuk had envisioned at the time, allowing players to enjoy the game as either a single-player or a multiplayer experience. The game even had a DM (Dungeon Master) mode in the tradition of live D&D games. This mode allowed one player to guide others in an online experience and included a fully functional game editor—the Aurora toolset—that allowed players to create their own versions (mods) of the game.

BioWare was highly successful at the time, selling millions of game units to a growing audience, but in many ways it was just getting started. What followed over the next decade were the original product, Jade Empire; a highly productive relationship with LucasArts and the Star Wars franchise (including the truly massive MMORPG, Star Wars: The Old Republic); and two new blockbuster franchises—Dragon Age and Mass Effect. More to come in *High Score 3*.

Art from Baldur's Gate.

Screenshots: Baldur's Gate above, Neverwinter Nights to left.

Eidos

Lara Croft has become the first electronic gaming sex symbol, with the possible exception of Ms. Pac-Man.

In 1990, Eidos was a brand-new company specializing in video compression technology. By 1996, they were right at the top of the game charts with Tomb Raider. Who would have guessed that by purchasing two relatively average companies—Domark in 1995 and U.S. Gold in 1996—they would suddenly transform into a gaming giant? Of course, they also got Core Design along with the U.S. Gold deal, which turned out to be a fortuitous twist of fate. It was Core Design that came up with Lara Croft and Tomb Raider, a game that first released in 1996 for Saturn, PC, and PlayStation.

Tomb Raider was a huge hit. It helped establish the PlayStation as the leading console system, and it made significant waves throughout the PC gaming community. Moreover, Tomb Raider somehow proved the ultimate value of 3D action worlds, incorporating exploration and acrobatics reminiscent of the classic Prince of Persia games with a dynamite new character, the female Indiana Jones of electronic games— Lara Croft.

Originally, the design emphasis was on creating the environment for the game, but during brainstorming sessions, it became clear that the game's lead character should be something different from the usual buffed, battering ram male protagonist. The role called for someone with physical skills combined with flexibility, and with flexibility, the designers reasoned, came an element of gracefulness. The more they considered it, the more they leaned toward a female protagonist. The first character was Lara Cruz, a buffed and Amazonian sort—still too close to the male stereotype. Cruz soon gave way to Croft, however, and Lara was born, complete with her own story—a well-educated young woman from a wealthy background, more the female James Bond than Rambo.

Soul Reaver 2
screenshots.

Concept artwork for Soul Reaver 2.

Angelina Jolie as Lara Croft.

Lara Croft has become an icon over the years. Once there was a question of whether male game audiences would be interested in playing a female lead character. That question has been answered definitively.

Eidos has made its fortune largely on the strength of the Tomb Raider series, but they have also done distribution deals with various companies, including Ion Storm, the compay John Romero founded after leaving id Software. They have also acquired or invested in several other successful development companies, including Crystal Dynamics (Gex, Soul Reaver series), Michael Crichton's Timeline Studios, Elixir Studios (Theme Park), Free Radical Design (GoldenEye), and others.

In 2001, Tomb Raider became one of the few electronic games to make it to the silver screen, with Angelina Jolie in the leading role. Although not an across-the-board critical success, financially the movie did extremely well, grossing over $300 million worldwide, and it spurred even more sales of games in the already popular series.

More recently, Eidos licensed the 2002 Winter Olympics, and they have released the controversial Hitman and Hitman 2 from Norwegian developers IO Interactive. They are also continuing to develop more games in Crystal Dynamics' Soul Reaver series and from Ion Storm with Deus Ex 2. Eidos was purchased by Square Enix in 2009.

Story of an Odd World

When Lorne Lanning saw his first example of computer graphics, he knew.

"I knew that was the future, and it was my future," he tells us. Perhaps that recognition was due in part to the influence of his father, who was in the navy and worked on nuclear submarines. "We were still drooling in Pampers," says Lanning, "when he'd come home with a transistor and tell us how this little thing used to take rooms full of vacuum tubes, and we'd say 'What?'"

When Lanning was in his teens, his father went to work for Coleco. Meanwhile, Lanning was sneaking into bars and drinking in order to play arcade games like Asteroids and Missile Command.

Slog and Slig, two of Abe's main meanies.

Many years later, as a painter and student at the School of Visual Arts, he was dissatisfied with photo-realistic paintings and illustrations. "They were like Polaroids—no sound, no movement. I wanted to create living fantasy worlds that looked believable." He packed his bags and moved from New York City to Los Angeles and enrolled at CalArts to study visual effects and traditional animation techniques.

In 1987, after completing his studies, he found that there was very little work for a computer graphics artist. He did, however, land a job at TRW, working on the Strategic Defense Initiative (SDI) program, sometimes referred to by the press as "Star Wars."

"Working on space visualization graphics allowed me to get a glimpse of what was

Oddworld co-founders Sherry McKenna and Lorne Lanning.

happening on the super high end of simulations as well as real-time databases the military was using to simulate F-14s, for instance. It was mind-blowing. I was aware of how the military blazed the trail for technology, so I could see that these big expensive simulations were going to become your average consumer video game experience in time. I saw virtual reality, the ancestors of today's multiplayer worlds—the military was doing that long ago with tanks, planes, ships, and submarines all in the same database."

Lanning went to work at Los Angeles–based effects house Rhythm & Hues (creators of the famous Coca-Cola Polar Bears, among many other projects). At first, he was placed in the role of art director, but he wanted to be a technical director. "Only computer programmers were in that role." Ultimately breaking the mold, Lanning spent a couple of years honing his CG chops in animation, choreography, texture mapping, and other techniques that he would eventually employ in making

games. He was learning while waiting for the right time.

That time came with the advent of the CD-ROM and 32-bit graphics. Lanning finally started on what he really wanted to do, to make storytelling—Storydwelling®—worlds. He approached Sherry McKenna, an award-winning film, commercial, and location-based special effects producer, and proposed forming a game company. Her response? "Why do I care?" McKenna was not into computer games, which she considered incapable of producing the results she was used to in film and location-based entertainment.

Lanning, however, is nothing if not impassioned. He presented a plan to McKenna that involved story, characters you care about, and graphics that were close to movie-quality. It was 1994, and Oddworld Inhabitants was born. Lanning and McKenna set up shop in San Luis Obispo, California, and began producing a string of hit games in Lanning's Oddworld brainchild.

Oddworld: Abe's Oddysee® was the company's first product, a highly imaginative story and game with, of all things, a character who didn't fight or wield a weapon. It's one thing to have a great technology and superior art and animation, which Abe did, but it's another to have brilliant and original game design. And Abe had that, too. The game played like a series of logic puzzles that could only be solved by precise movements and appropriate use of Abe's unusual abilities, which included sneaking in shadows and chanting to possess the minds of some enemies. Abe also could run, jump, and climb—much in the mold of Prince of Persia—and the game made great use of his abilities.

Oddworld: Abe's Exoddus® was a worthy sequel to the first game, and added a few new wrinkles. It was much bigger and in some ways trickier, although the main character was more or less the same and the basic gameplay remained.

Another feature, which began in the first game and has evolved

Production sketch and final game screen from Oddworld: Munch's Oddysee®.

in later products, was the concept of GameSpeak® and the ability of Oddworld's characters to communicate with each other and to work cooperatively. Many of the puzzles in Abe's Oddysee, and to an even greater extent in Oddworld's later games, required the player to find ways to communicate with other characters in the game, and to control them purely by the use of cleverly designed word commands.

Oddworld: Munch's Oddysee®, introduced a new character, Munch, and their first fully 3D world for the Xbox. Munch was a far more ambitious project than the original Abe's Oddysee, still retaining Lanning's vision of storytelling and the highest production values.

In the end, even a successful run of hit games didn't fully satisfy Lanning, who walked away from the video game industry in 2005, frustrated with the lack of publisher support for his critically acclaimed, but poorly selling final game, Oddworld: Stranger's Wrath®.

Returning to games, Oddworld's newest title is Oddworld: New 'n' Tasty, launched in 2014.)

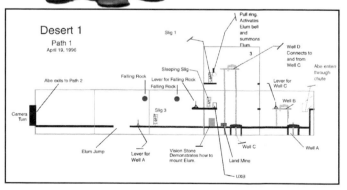

Level design from Oddworld: Abe's Oddysee®.

1996

Nintendo 64

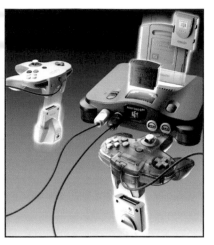

The Legend of Zelda: Ocarina of Time

Nintendo made a rare false move with their 1995 release of the 3D game system Virtual Boy. However, they revealed the Silicon Graphics-powered Ultra 64 console in Japan that same year, following with the 1996 release of the same system, now renamed Nintendo 64 (or N64 for short), worldwide and sold unprecedented quantities in their first months after release. Mario made the move from 2D to 3D in Super Mario 64, and in the process blew everyone away (including many computer game designers), paving the way for a succession of 3D games from Nintendo. At the top of the list was the first 3D Legend of Zelda title, Ocarina of Time. Nintendo also released several games from one of their premier developers, Rare, Ltd., including Killer Instinct Gold, Golden-Eye, Banjo-Kazooie, and Donkey Kong 64.

Nintendo continued to support a cartridge-only machine—no CD, no Internet—and did it very well. Meanwhile, Sony reduced the price of the PlayStation to $199, and Sega, already in trouble, was forced to follow suit. Over the next few years, both N64 and PlayStation continued to sell well, but PlayStation

Top to bottom: Mario Party, Paper Mario, Mario Tennis

The Legend of Zelda: Majora's Mask

proved the stronger system. "At the end of our 12th month, N64 had a bigger installed base than PlayStation," says Nintendo's Peter Main, "but in our second year, their third, they smoked right by us. At the time we launched the GameCube, we had sold about 18 million N64s to about 27 million PlayStations. It happened in the second or third year and had to do with who had the most compelling software story to tell. We didn't have a broad enough array."

The Nintendo 64 continued to be a very popular system for years, however, and was Nintendo's flagship console until the release of the GameCube in 2001. Many great games came out for N64, some of which we've memorialized on these pages.

Super Mario 64

EXPANSION PAK INCLUDED!

DONKEY KONG 64

PLAYERS CHOICE MILLION SELLER

REQUIRES N64 Expansion Pak™

Designed For N64 Rumble Pak™

1-4 Players Simultaneous

EVERYONE E

COLLECTOR'S EDITION YELLOW GAME PAK

DOLBY SURROUND

Yoshi's Story, Wave Race 64, Pilotwings 64, Banjo-Kazooie

THE NEW TETRIS

NINTENDO 64 Only For

4-Player Frenzy!

EVERYONE E

N64 GAMES BY RARE, LTD.

Rareware, as they're called, are games from one of Nintendo's finest developers. Based in the UK, Rare, Ltd. has produced consistently great games for Nintendo consoles, going all the way back to Battletoads for NES.

Donkey Kong 64

Right to left: Blast Corps, Jet Force Gemini, Diddy Kong Racing

GoldenEye 007, Conker's Bad Fur Day, Killer Instict Gold, Perfect Dark

STAR WARS ROGUE SQUADRON

PLAYERS CHOICE MILLION SELLER

TEEN T

More Games of the '90s

Out of hundreds of games that made an impact on our lives in the '90s, here are a few we just had to include.

Prince of Persia and
The Last Express

Jordan Mechner (*see also page 132*) published his first game, Karateka, while attending Yale University in 1984. Interested in filmmaking techniques, he experimented with rotoscoping, which takes actual film, then colors in the images in cartoon-like fashion. The result is very smooth and realistic animation. Mechner first experimented with rotoscoping in Karateka.

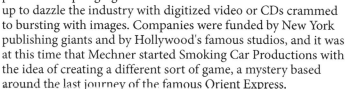

In 1989, Mechner completed his next game, which was to become a classic. Prince of Persia, like Karateka, was published by Brøderbund (*see page 128*), and again used rotoscoping techniques. Mechner used his younger brother as a model for the title character, who could run, leap, and climb with exceptionally smooth animation. Of course, the Prince needed all his skills to avoid the numerous, and quite devious, traps that Mechner built into his game. Prince of Persia and its sequel, The Shadow & The Flame, are among the most inspirational games of all time and

influenced game makers for years to come. Fans of the games wrote many letters praising them. One such letter came from Saudi Arabia, and among the comments, the writer said, "…you are truly the Prince of America… You frighten me a lot, You excite me a lot, You Enjoy me a lot." Amen.

Mechner's next major epoch began during the height of the multimedia craze. New companies were springing up to dazzle the industry with digitized video or CDs crammed to bursting with images. Companies were funded by New York publishing giants and by Hollywood's famous studios, and it was at this time that Mechner started Smoking Car Productions with the idea of creating a different sort of game, a mystery based around the last journey of the famous Orient Express.

In The Last Express (1997), Mechner returned to rotoscoping on a grand scale. He and his colleagues at Smoking Car did meticulous research, finding and accurately modeling surviving

Archival photograph of an Orient Express car. On the next page is the game screen.

Three of the developers, testing the rotoscoping process: Jordan Mechner, Nicole Tostevin (art director), and Robert Cook (technical director).

cars from the Orient Express, poring over transportation records discovered by a bit of sleuthing in Paris, and creating a story of international intrigue and murder in a historical setting.

The project turned out to be horrendously difficult—a labor of love and dedication for Mechner and his staff. Each scene was filmed with real actors over a blue screen backdrop, then each image was meticulously redrawn using special software to create the rotoscoping effect. The postproduction

An example of the rotoscoping technique used to put actors in the scene.

took far longer than anticipated, and the project went way over budget.

Regardless of budgets and technical challenges, The Last Express was a pure gem, a remarkable game that creates an exceptionally rich atmosphere all its own. The characters are strongly written, and the use of people speaking in their native languages further enhances the realism and compelling sense of detail in the game. A lush musical score from film and television composer Elia Cmiral (*Somebody is Waiting* and *Nash Bridges*) further enhanced the international flavor of the story, providing aural counterpoint to the colorful and accurate graphic presentation. In some ways, The Last Express is reminiscent of one of those murder mystery train excursions where you have to eavesdrop and observe everything in order to piece together the entire story.

Unfortunately, in an era when first-person shooters and fast-paced action was the rule of the day, The Last Express offered a pace too slow for many gamers, and the open-ended flow of play was too confusing for others. On top of that, The Last Express was over-budget and under-marketed. The result was a commercial failure that still offers an aesthetic and cerebral treat to anyone who plays the game to this day.

Along the bottom of the page is an entire sequence showing how the scenes were produced, from sketches to final rotoscoped images in the game.

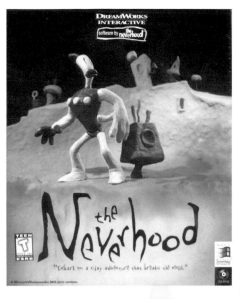

The Neverhood

After working on Earthworm Jim 2, Doug TenNapel joined with Ed Schofield, Steve Crow, and Mark Lorenzen and left Shiny Entertainment, looking for another opportunity. According to TenNapel, "Steven Spielberg was a huge Earthworm Jim fan. And Jeffrey Katzenberg had wanted it for Disney, but Shiny went with Universal. So, when they formed DreamWorks, they invited me to pitch a game." The game they pitched was called The Neverhood, a game done all in claymation and inspired by a series of paintings TenNapel had done in the late '80s called "A Beautiful Day in the Neverhood." The deal to produce this unusual game was struck at a meeting at Spielberg's house. According to TenNapel, "Steven is probably the only executive who would have the balls to make that kind of decision."

Nobody had ever tried a fully animated game using all claymation before (although the original King of Chicago for the Macintosh and a few others had used clay figures). The project was unusual and risky.

"We invented almost everything we did," remembers TenNapel. "We researched cameras and ended up working with $10,000 beta versions of Minolta digital cameras, which would melt down every once in a while. They'd send us another one. We literally built a miniature world coated in clay in a 60' by 60' warehouse. We set it off the ground and built a hub and rail camera system through it."

Since all of the animators on the project were traditional cel animators,

they did all the first drawings on paper and then applied the animation directly to the clay figures.

The game was completed in a year, though it took three months just to build the set. However, The Neverhood was

not a commercial success. Like many experimental and artistic games, it failed to reach a significant audience, although, according to TenNapel, "We got letters from old men and little children—people who had never touched a PC before—telling us how much fun they'd had wandering around in our world and thanking us for creating it."

And, although The Neverhood contained interesting puzzles and some very funny animation, even TenNapel admits that it was not exactly a game. "It's a fine artwork that ten people made and DreamWorks funded," he says. Game or not, The Neverhood, like Jordan Mechner's The Last Express, was a notable and creative attempt to do something different. One of a kind... until the sequel, Armikrog, came out in 2015.

The creation of The Neverhood involved a clay-covered set and cameras on rails. to the left are images of Doug TenNapel repositioning figures in the set.

100 Brand New Lemmings™ Adventures!

Lemmings

You've probably heard of lemmings—those little rodents that are reputed to flock en masse over cliffs and into raging rivers, committing mass suicide when societal urges push them to their population limit. It's a myth, but did you ever figure this as the premise of a game? Dave Jones of DMA Design did, and in the process, he produced one of the greatest puzzle games in computer game history.

Psygnosis' Lemmings might have gotten the "cute" award for games of the '90s, except that it was not only cute, but also devious, humorous, cruel, and brilliant. Those ultra-cute critters would just keep on going, heedless of all perils, and it was up to you to save their furry little butts, often by judiciously sacrificing one or two of the horde for the common good. In the end, if you saved the required number, you advanced to the next, probably even more devious, level.

Lemmings seemed to have endless permutations, and the characters, though tiny on the screen, became endearing figures in several sequels and on a staggering variety of ancillary products ranging from mouse pads to lunch pails. Moving a long way from Lemmings, DMA Design has more recently producd games such as Grand Theft Auto III and State of Emergency.

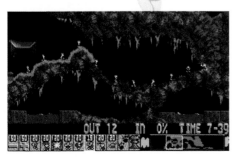

Lemmings mouse pad and screenshot.

System Shock

One of our favorite producer/designers is Warren Spector, who has worked variously at Steve Jackson Games, TSR, Origin Systems, Blue Sky Productions/Looking Glass Studios, and at Ion Storm. He worked often as a producer and designer, with multiple credits, including several Ultima and Ultima Underworld games and several Wing Commander games. He was the producer on the groundbreaking game, System Shock, which set the stage for 3D first-person adventure games. System Shock was developed by Looking Glass, the same great team who brought us the Ultima Underworld games, with Doug Church as the project lead.

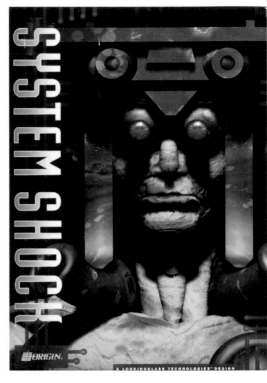

"I think Doug Church, Looking Glass studio head Paul Neurath, and I were so tired of fantasy games," says Spector. "We just wanted to move into a different genre entirely. The science fiction setting had a strong appeal. But mostly, I think,

IT's ALL IN THE DETAILS

Warren Spector comments on the special attention that went into the details in System Shock: "I just remember being blown away (and, I admit, terrified) at the team's audacity. They'd do stuff like take time out from actually finishing the game to implement little minigames you could download in cyberspace, or make a starfield outside the station window appear to move, or start security cameras rotating the day before we signed off. Drove the poor producer crazy, but it's stuff like that that takes a game from really good to great... That's what I keep telling myself, anyway."

it was an attempt to bring even more depth—of story, of simulation, of player experience—to gaming."

Spector speaks about the collaborative nature of the project: "Doug Church was clearly a guy with a vision, and I kibitzed mightily, but the design work was spread around as much as

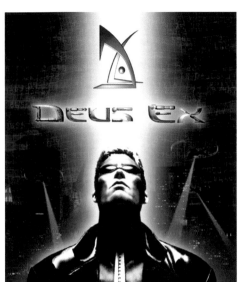

I've ever experienced. Programmers came up with system designs... writers came up with story elements... designers built levels... but there were some incredible team meetings where high-level conceptual stuff got hammered out, as well as a lot of details, in an atmosphere of total respect and commitment to quality. That was a cohesive team, I can tell you..."

Like many games, System Shock nearly didn't make it out the door. "On Shock, the biggest challenge from my perspective as out-of-house producer, was communicating what the game was all about to a management group that didn't always get what the team was trying to do," said Spector. "You don't want to know how many times the game came this close to getting killed (or how late in the project)."

Deus Ex

Later, Spector got the opportunity of a lifetime when John Romero offered him the chance to make "the game he's always wanted to make" for Romero's newly established company, Ion Storm. The game Spector made, Deus Ex, has been hailed by players and press as one of the most innovative action adventure games ever made. In a time when so many games were plotless firefests, Deus Ex offered deep stories, characters, real dilemmas, and alternative methods of play.

Again, Spector comments: "I was really feeling like I had to prove something to the execs, journalists, and fans who had pounded into me the idea that the kind of games I loved were doomed to be nichey and appealing only to the hardcore. I wanted so badly to prove them all wrong. I think we did okay on that score!

"Deus Ex was the next logical step, at least in my mind, along an evolutionary path that started with the Underworlds and then Shock and then Thief. I spent a year working with the Thief team and found myself a little frustrated at how narrowly focused that game was shaping up to be. That's not a bad thing, but I just kept arguing that we could allow players more freedom of action than Thief allowed. We could let them fight their way through problems as well as sneak... We could allow them to interact directly with NPCs as well as overhear them and avoid them... None of those ideas had any place in Thief, so I knew I had to find a way to make a game that allowed a broader range of player choices than any other game ever had.

"On Deus Ex, the biggest challenge, in terms of process, was dealing with a game that was, by design, unfocused. We didn't want it to be a shooter or an RPG or an adventure game or a strategy game. We wanted it to incorporate elements of all of those game types. And I (perhaps foolishly) assembled a team of people who, well, let's just say they didn't always agree on what made a good game, a bad game, and so on. Merging disparate opinions and differing design and implementation styles into a reasonably coherent end product was tough! In terms of design and implementation, the biggest challenge was probably making sure that a wide enough variety of play style choices was supported at the macro level and at the micro level. Every problem had to have multiple solutions. Every character development choice—every augmentation, every skill, every item—had to be useful in enough circumstances to be worthy of inclusion in the game. And the emergent gameplay possibilities were so broad that we couldn't always predict what circumstances players would find themselves in! Balancing DX was the toughest challenge I've experienced."

Age of Empires

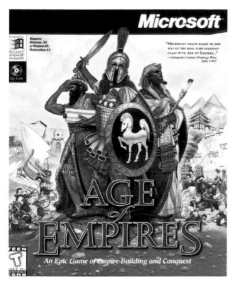

Age of Empires appeared on the scene in the midst of the real-time strategy game glut. Nearly 50 new real-time strategy game titles clogged the channel during that era, and most of them were "more of the same" mediocre efforts where the player who could click the fastest would win. Rick Goodman (who later went on to create the massive Empire Earth for Sierra) and his brother Tony had a broader vision. Noticing how most other real-time strategy games tended to be extremely repetitive and didn't offer a great deal of variety in terms of their style of play, they started working in 1995 on a game that would evolve with the players.

Since the brothers envisioned the game as something of a faster-paced Sid Meier's Civilization and they knew Sid was working on his own new game, they recruited Sid's co-designer from Civilization and Railroad Tycoon, Bruce Shelley. Shelley joined the team and immediately began adding the little touches to make each civilization in the game have different strengths, weaknesses, and styles.

At the same time, the artists involved with the project went to extraordinary lengths to develop a grittier and more realistic look, as opposed to the sterile, tiled effects seen in many of the real-time strategy games of that era. Ensemble Studios, as the brothers were to name their development house, probably had more pictures of dirt and grass as reference photos than a forensic laboratory. Their artists overlaid their work onto these reference images, and if the art didn't look right against the realistic terrain, they went back to the drawing board.

The result of all the attention to detail was that Age of Empires rose above the noise of its competition. Hitting in late 1997, it managed to rack up a number of Game of the Year awards, and the designers achieved the ultimate accolade from their peers: the knowledge that the playing of Age of Empires caused slippage on competitive products. More Age of Empires releases were to follow: Age of Empires II: The Age of Kings and Age of Empires II: The Conquerors. The AOE engine was also used in Star Wars: Galactic Battlegrounds from LucasArts.

Age of Wonders

To some, Age of Wonders was a throwback to the ancient days of turn-based gaming. It was an aberration in the age of real-time strategy games. A fantasy game with the best elements of a Sid Meier's Civilization-style game (a global map that you gradually uncover by discovery and the necessity of city-by-city or stronghold-by-stronghold conquest), Master of Magic (a research tree for magical spells revolving around an axis of five spheres of magical power), and Fantasy General (tactical turn-based combat where terrain makes a difference), Age of Wonders was a superb example of the "Just one more move, honey!" syndrome. Playing the campaign game could easily involve 60-80 hours of gameplay.

With two full campaigns, one for the good guys and one for the bad guys, players would usually end up playing all of the races in the game during the course of the campaigns. Each race had different weapons and units. Plus, if you kept them with one of your leaders, you could use the best units or weapons of a conquered race as part of your assault group. If you didn't keep the conquered troops with a strong leader, they were likely to desert. Another interesting feature of Age of Wonders was the idea of having a new population migrate into a conquered city.

Age of Empires composite map.

Several months before GPL was released, I was in Boston meeting with Kaemmer and the team. We hooked up the current version on the Papyrus LAN, and we were all racing in Lotus-Fords. The physics were in to handle most of the collisions and damage, but the team hadn't much time to simulate what happened when cars went airborne. Kaemmer was on my tail going into a corner of the Nürburgring circuit and I hit my rear wheel because I was getting loose as he passed me. Kaemmer's car flipped up into the air and went end over end, spinning and spinning through the air. It was so funny that Kaemmer called everyone in the studio in to see the replay. The next build I played didn't feature the outer space atmosphere of that build. (JLW)

1 Grand Prix. He chose that era because the sophisticated technology and aerodynamics of the current period hadn't come into play. Cars could still become airborne, and more than one engine and chassis were competitive.

In addition to the bells and whistles of the VCR replays, the joy of seeing lost logos from a bygone era, the seven great models (Lotus, Brabham, Eagle, BRM, and three fantasy V12s), and the sheer beauty of the graphics (perfectly modeled cars and lovingly recreated tracks), the entire driving experience of Grand Prix Legends was authentic. Kaemmer didn't just consider tire damage and how it affected the car. He figured in fuel consumption, individual tire pressure and damage, steering linearity and ratio, static ride height, as well as transmission and drive ratios. No matter what chassis you selected in GPL, you had all of these options and more to play with. Want to up the realism? GPL was the first simulation to truly simulate a clutch, using optional wheel and peddle controllers.

It was the glory days of realism in racing simulations. For many, it was so realistic and so difficult to drive that the sim didn't put up the kind of numbers in sales that Kaemmer and the Papyrus team had seen in multiple releases of IndyCar Racing and NASCAR Racing. For many of us, however, it was the high-water mark of racing simulations.

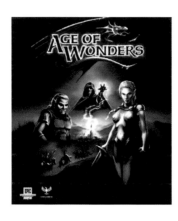

Migrations reduced the necessity of keeping large garrisons in the city to keep the conquered citizens in line.

Age of Wonders was one of those games that went through many hands and publishing relationships before it came to market, a symptom of the '90s. The developer was Triumph Studios, a group associated with Epic MegaGames (makers of Unreal). The publisher was Mars Publishing, who in turn had a distribution deal with Gathering of Developers. By the time the game was being distributed, Gathering of Developers had been acquired by Take-Two Interactive. So, in a very real sense, Age of Wonders was the quintessential end-of-the-decade game, a product that was touched by many hands and felt somewhat dated by the time it was released. Fortunately, it did spawn an Age of Wonders II in 2002.

Grand Prix Legends

There is simply no automobile racing simulation in the history of computer games that is as faithful to its subject as Grand Prix Legends. Not only was GPL a dream come true for Dave Kaemmer, the genius behind it, but it was the apex of reality-based automobile simulations. Although the game was released in the latter part of the decade, Kaemmer opted for the nostalgia of '60s-era Formula

Jane's Combat Simulations

Look over the annual awards in the latter half of the '90s and you'll notice that, most of the time, the winners in the Simulations category are titles in the Jane's Combat Simulations series. There is a very good reason for this. Electronic Arts already had dominance in the Sports category and had experienced great success with the Chuck Yeager series of games. In the early '90s, EA made a commitment to dominate in the Simulation category. In addition to Paul Grace, their in-house designer and producer who had been working in this category since the earliest Yeager releases, EA went after Andy Hollis, the veteran designer and program-

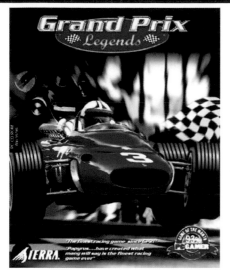

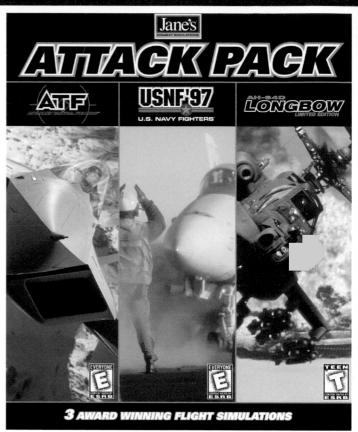

mer from the MicroProse stable. Not satisfied with celebrity designers, EA also went after celebrity specialists—the world's foremost research group for military information, Jane's Information Group, Ltd.

Andy Hollis had created his own simulation, Mig Alley Ace, contemporaneous with Sid Meier's Hellcat Ace in the formative years of MicroProse. In addition, Hollis had collaborated with Meier on a couple of versions of F-15 Strike Eagle and on F-19 Stealth Fighter. When Meier moved on to other interests, Hollis stuck with aviation. In 1993, he started work on an AH-64D Longbow simulation. In 1996, this became Jane's AH-64D Longbow, which, along with Jane's Advanced Tactical Fighters were the first in the award-winning series. The beauty of the simulation, in addition to the awesome graphic presentation, was that a beginner could get in and experience instant action without the frustration of having to learn every possible system, while experts could spend hours upon hours mastering tactics and systems.

As the series expanded into F-15, Longbow 2, Israeli Air Force, World War II Fighters, USAF, 688(I) Hunter/Killer, and F/A-18 Simulator, this hallmark of easy entry mixed with a challenging growth path continued. One title, Jane's Fleet Command, offered such a realistic view of the modern world situation that its screens adorned network newscasts during more than one Middle Eastern crisis. Of all the titles in the series, Fleet Command was the only one that was more of a strategy game than a simulator; it was Harpoon taken up a notch.

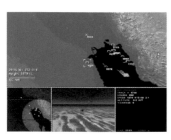

In Jane's Fleet Command, carrier-based Hornets are intercepted on their way to bomb a secret Iraqi chemical plant.

An F/A-18 pilot looks to his left to spot an approaching MiG-23 in Jane's F/A-18 Simulator.

Unreal®

In the early '90s, Epic MegaGames (now known as Epic Games, Inc.) was a small company known for their Jazz Jackrabbit platform series and Extreme Pinball. No one would have suspected that they

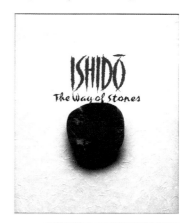

were only a few years away from creating a ground-breaking game technology.

The concept began with James Schmalz; he had an idea for something he thought of as a magic carpet game with robots. He showed the prototype to fellow designer Cliff Bleszinski and Epic founder Tim Sweeney. There wasn't much to it at first, but everyone agreed it had promise and a loosely coordinated development effort began.

Years went by, as a small group of developers literally spread all over the world, forming a virtual team of talented programmers, artists, and designers to work on it. For the last year of the project, they closeted themselves together in Waterloo, Ontario, where they began working insane hours. Unable to come up with a name that satisfied the whole team, they ultimately called the game—and the underlying technology—Unreal. And, in many ways, it was.

When it was released by GT Interactive in 1998, Unreal had the hottest technology around and some of the best level designs of any game to date. Its integrated engine and level editor (which was archi-

tected by Tim Sweeney and contributed to the great level design) were considered the best. The artificial intelligence, including Steve Polge's AI bots that let people practice deathmatches offline, further set the game apart. Unreal garnered a lot of attention from the press and quickly gained fans all over the world. Ultimately, several sequels, including Unreal II, Unreal Tournament, and Unreal Championship, continued to expand and improve the Unreal product line. For its power and flexibility, the Unreal engine has become one of the standard engines in games from many publishers all around the world.

Short Takes

Ishido

Next to Archon, Michael Feinberg's Ishido is one of the finest original adaptations of a board game concept to the computer. This game of stones featured an innovative rule set tailored perfectly to the computer,

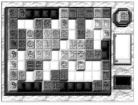

addictive play, and a variety of wonderful stone sets by Brodie Lockard, (of Shanghai fame).

Duke Nukem 3D

When id Software released DOOM, they not only started the first-person shooter phenomenon, but were also the acknowledged kings of the genre. However, Apogee's (AKA 3D Realms) Duke Nukem 3D added some elements, especially a really cool character and lots of humor. Duke Nukem's world full of strippers, nightclubs, and weird aliens offered plenty of opportunities for interactive fun, and clearly distinguished itself from the moody quality of id's games. Not just an imitator, Duke blasted his own path, and a damn good path it was. Not to mention the jiggle factor.

Battlecruiser 3000AD

Derek Smart had a vision for Battlecruiser 3000AD. He wanted its entire universe to become so real that it would become more interesting than real life. He had such a clear vision that he fought his way through relationships with multiple publishers and is still supporting and selling the latest versions of his game on the web. Players assume the role of commander of a starship. The feeling was that of a more realistic Battlestar Galactica, long before Homeworld gave us the same idea from a different perspective. Battlecruiser 3000AD put players on the bridge and let them interact with a huge crew, each programmed with AI to have their own skills and individual agendas based on their crew assignment. In an era when everyone was expecting Wing Commander redone, many were disappointed with Battlecruiser 3000AD, but today there are probably more people still playing Smart's game than Chris Roberts' magnum opus.

Where Duke had jiggle, Battlecruiser had a rather deplorable ad that got banned in some places. You can see for yourself why. It was created by publisher TakeTwo Interactive, and Smart had to threaten to sue to force them to remove all versions of it, including some that were very minimally censored.

Hollywood Mogul

When Carey DeVuono sold his first script over the transom, he thought his dream had come true. After a few months of script meetings and a period in which his script went into the never-never land of "turn around," he decided to transform his hard-earned lessons about Hollywood into a marvelous strategy game. Although the game is written in simple Visual Basic with crude graphics and no on-screen action beyond text over blocky buildings and theaters, this is a marvelous little game that can still be purchased on the web. Players become the head of a studio. They buy ready-made original scripts, rights to make scripts from literary blockbusters, or they order scripts to be written from their ideas. Would-be moguls get to set budgets, film locations, and select everyone from producer to supporting actress, not to mention test-screening the films and determining the size and scale of the opening weekends. In short, everything you could want in a movie-making strategy game is here except a toolkit to make your own movies.

Detroit

Impressions Software was a strategy game company that began with a business simulation where players could run their own software company. It was a crude effort that loaded from a cassette tape into a Spectrum or Amstrad, but it was successful enough to give David Lester (creator of Lords of the Realm I and II and Caesar I-III) his start in the PC games business. In spite of their best-selling historical games, Impressions never lost sight of the fact that it was a real-life business simulation that got the company going. Air Bucks let you set everything about the airline business, from route through planes flown to seat configuration and on to marketing and fare calculations. Detroit accomplished the same thing for automobile manufacturing. Players tried to balance marketing, manufacturing, research, and safety needs against the dreaded monster called profitability.

The '90s and Consolidation

Mergers and acquisitions are an inexorable fact of life in the business world. Entrepreneurial companies get gobbled up by big, diversified corporations after the original company outgrows the skills of the management team; small companies fall upon hard times during economic downturns and are purchased by companies with deep pockets to acquire their intellectual property, or a start-up company has to be sold in order for the venture capitalists to reap the harvest of the investments they seeded.

Whatever the reason, the '80s was a time of expansion, with companies springing up like homesteaders staking their claims. By by the end of the '90s, many of these pioneers were gone or were absorbed by much larger entities.

To be sure, big acquisitions had taken place before. For instance, in the '80s, Activision picked up Infocom and Gamestar for a song, and Sierra took over Dynamix and Coktel Vision. By 1996, Sierra itself was sold to Cendant Corporation, and during the next decade first became part of Vivendi Universal and finally, before closing its doors, was absorbed into Activision Blizzard through the merger of Activision and Vivendi.

Electronic Arts started its acquisitions in 1987 with Batteries Included, then in 1991 with the acquisition of Distinctive Software, which became EA Canada. The next year they acquired Origin Systems. EA ultimately became a juggernaut, acquiring approximately 38 companies by 2012, including Bullfrog Productions, Maxis, Westwood, DreamWorks (game division), Kesmai, Mythic Entertainment, BioWare, Playfish, Chillingo, and PopCap.

EA's acquisitions, while numerous and highly significant, have been, for the most part, fairly simple to follow. In contrast, there's the story of Mindscape, which acquired Strategic Simulations, Inc., then became The Software Toolworks, which was ultimately purchased, along with Brøderbund, by The Learning Company. The Learning Company was then sold to Mattel, but massive losses ultimately caused Mattel to bail out, and the whole bundle ultimately went to French publisher Ubisoft.

In another complex series of transactions, Spectrum HoloByte bought MicroProse, but was then purchased by Hasbro, who already owned Avalon Hill. But Hasbro was unable to achieve the kinds of profits they expected, and they ultimately sold their game companies, along with the classic Atari license, to another French publisher, Infogrames, which promptly changed their name to Atari.

Elsewhere, Sony acquired Psygnosis, and Sierra locked up deals to buy Blizzard Entertainment, Papyrus Design Group, and Impressions. 3DO acquired New World Computing, and Microsoft acquired Access Software (publisher of Links, the classic golf program that became Microsoft Golf). Then Microsoft turned to the online world and purchased VR-1 (Fighter Ace), before snapping up FASA (the paper game company that published BattleTech, Shadowrun, and Crimson Skies) as soon as it hit the market. By the end of the decade, Microsoft had also purchased Ensemble (Age of Empires), Bungie (Myth and later, Halo), part of Oddworld (Munch's Oddysee), and Chris "Wing Commander" Roberts' Digital Anvil.

On the East Coast, GT Interactive (from the people who brought us GoodTimes Video and GoodTimes Food) decided that computer games could be marketed as easily as food and home video. They started on a profitable note with distribution of id Software's products (prior to being usurped by Activision), but ultimately their quest for the mass market was their undoing as the public grew tired of cheap versions of legacy software and multiple retreads of Deer Hunter. At first, the company tried to fill in the gaps by signing a deal with Epic MegaGames for Unreal and purchasing Humongous Entertainment in order to get the Putt-Putt and Blue's Clues business. Humongous used the GT funds to fuel their Cavedog division and published the best-selling real-time strategy game, Total Annihilation, which was designed by Chris Taylor (who later started Gas Powered Games and designed the Dungeon Siege series). TA was an impressive hit for GT, but its sequel, Total Annihilation: Kingdoms, was less successful, and GT eventually pulled the plug and went under.

One more tale to tell: Take-Two Interactive. Founded by the son of a Manhattan real estate wheeler-dealer, Take-Two Interactive began with the acquisition of a small Pennsylvania developer/publisher called Paragon Software. Paragon had published a number of games in the '80s and had been an affiliate label for Electronic Arts before moving to MicroProse as their second-tier developer/publisher.

Take-Two purchased Paragon and went on to publish some of the worst games ever. Hell: A Cyberpunk Thriller featured a cast of well-known actors but no play value whatsoever. Yet, the company eventually pulled itself together and created some interesting products, including Star Crusader, Ripper, and Black Dahlia, before purchasing war game specialty shop TalonSoft, and the action specialists at GodGames and Rockstar (GTA III), and later, Sid Meier's Firaxis.

Sometimes, acquisitions and mergers worked out well for all involved and everyone thrived, even exceeding expectations. Other times, the relationships would sour, the expectations and management styles would clash, and companies with great records, such as Origin Systems and Ensemble, would be shut down. In other cases, whatever made the company unique would be drained out, and with layoffs and massive personnel changes, the original company vision would be lost.

With all this industry consolidation came a more businesslike approach to game development overall, but often at the cost of innovation. Companies with fresh perspectives and approaches had difficulty cracking the monolithic retail barrier established between huge corporate publishers and the retail chains, and it became tougher than

Consolidation king EA has absorbed a staggering number of companies.

ever for clever designers to get support for their projects. A new relationship in retail channels had arrived, in which MDF (Marketing Development Funds), end caps, shelving/stocking fees, and other costs became the established way of doing business. Shelf space diminished, and large retailers even got away with requiring game companies to reduce the size of their boxes to accommodate their shelf sizes. By the beginning of the new millennium, the face of game development and marketing had changed radically from its wild and woolly beginnings. Although it seemed doomed to remain that way, the new millennium had its share of surprises in store...

A Brief History of Early Online Gaming

Empire and Avatar on PLATO, much as they used to look.

You could say it started with Sputnik and the Space Race of the '50s and '60s. The launch of the Soviet satellite in 1957 spurred the U.S. to create ARPA (Advanced Research Projects Agency). One ARPA agency, the Information Processing Techniques Office (IPTO), eventually created something called an Interface Messenger Processor. The ancestor to the modern-day Internet, ARPANET began with four IMP nodes at UCLA, UC Santa Barbara, Stanford Research Institute, and the University of Utah.

PLATO

The first real online community emerged from a system first conceived in 1960 by Don Bitzer, a professor and electrical engineer at the University of Illinois. Bitzer was trying to answer a question posed by one of his professors, who wondered about using computers for education. What evolved ultimately was a system called PLATO, which several years later was turned into the acronym: "Programmed Logic for Automatic Teaching Operations" to satisfy journalists who wanted to know what it stood for.

The PLATO system, which eventually migrated to college campuses all over the country, was a true model of things to come. It included email, newsgroups, split-screen chat, and, of course, online games. PLATO had a profound impact on the future history not only of games but of the Internet and the World Wide Web, as most of the early structures of online communities were first developed on PLATO systems.

Game designers such as Silas Warner (RobotWar, Castle Wolfenstein), Robert Woodhead and Andrew Greenberg (Wizardry), and Peter Langston (a non-PLATO version of Empire, early Lucasfilm games) fondly remember the PLATO communities and the early inspirations they got from PLATO. The creative atmosphere of PLATO was wide open in all aspects. "We were craftsmen," says Silas Warner. Another notable inspiration includes the game Airfight, which may have been the progenitor of what eventually became Microsoft Flight Simulator. "One of the central games on PLATO," remembers Warner, "was a huge space war simulation called Empire." But, according to David Woolley, one of the designers of the PLATO system, "The most popular game was called Avatar, which logged even more hours than Empire." He continues, " I think the very first PLATO game was written by Rick Blomme in the 1960s. It was Spacewar!, a copy of the MIT game, and very simple graphically. As I recall, the spaceships were represented just by X and O characters that moved around the screen." Woolley wrote the second PLATO game, a horse racing game. "There would be three horses, represented by letters, which would race around an oval racetrack."

Originally run on funding from ARPA and the National Science Foundation, PLATO was ultimately sold to Control Data, but failed to remain prominent under their guidance.

If you want to learn more about this fascinating chapter in the history of online computing, check out Brian Dear's website for information about his book—more than 15 years in the making—on PLATO: *http://friendlyorangeglow.com/*

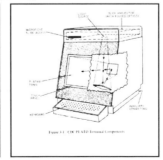

Images from the 1976 PLATO System Overview showing a typical PLATO workstation and touchscreen details.

MUD

"People like me and Roy Trubshaw weren't supposed to go to university back then because it was all middle class types or above," says Richard A. Bartle, co-creator of the Multi-User Dungeon, better known as MUD. Bartle and Trubshaw were "working class" blokes who, according to Bartle, were easily recognized as such because of how they talked. Bartle says, "I've got a northern accent, from the North of England, which is like the South of America. Everyone thinks you're a yokel. And Roy Trubshaw comes from the West Midlands. He sounds like he should be working in a factory. People in Parliament don't have our accents."

To all of our good fortune, England expanded their university system in the '60s, and some universities even taught subjects such as engineering and computer science, and, as Bartle observed, the middle class parents didn't want their children studying something like engineering. "An engineer is somebody you send up on a telegraph pole to fix the line and that kind of thing." So Trubshaw and Bartle were both able to enroll at the University of Essex, which taught both mathematics and computer science.

According to Bartle, the MUD has its roots in the class system of English society. "We raged against this class system, so we made one that didn't... made a world of our own." The idea was to create a world that ignored people's origins and only saw them for their strength of character and how they behaved.

Trubshaw, who was a year ahead of Bartle at university, initially wanted to find a way to send messages across the network on the DEC System 10 mainframe with only blocks of memory, measured in bytes. (For our modern readers, that's not kilobytes, megabytes or gigabytes. Just bytes of memory.) Trubshaw was able to overcome the technical hurdles by taking liberties with the system's memory hierarchy. Upon completing his message-sending program sometime late in 1978, it immediately became clear that text messages were not the only thing that could be sent. Bartle says, "He immediately set about creating the world because... why wouldn't you?"

Around that time, Trubshaw and Bartle teamed up. While Trubshaw worked out the physics of the world they wanted to create, Bartle—who had played games in the past, most notably Colossal Cave Adventure—set about building the world. After about a year of coding directly in assembly language, which required a trained engineer, Trubshaw decided to rewrite the whole system around a more accessible language which he called Multi-User Dungeon Definition Language, or MUDDL for short. "So you'd code it into MUDDL, and the compiler, which was called DBASE—short for database. You could only have six letters for file names so that was why it was just DBASE. And so DBASE read in your MUDDL stuff and then it dropped assembly language, which you then put through the assembler and that converted it into relocatable binary files, which were then loaded into memory by the game engine. It was quite complicated, but doing this was a way that we could get human-creatable worlds and convert it into quite compact binary form, which was then correctly accessible by the main MUD engine."

Trubshaw and Bartle wanted MUD to be shared, and MUDDL helped democratize the system. And with a connection to ARPANET through a nearby post office (which at the time was also a part of British Telecom's research division), they were able to share MUD through the growing network that would eventually become the Internet. People began playing MUDs in the U.S. and even in Japan. Before he graduated, Trubshaw passed code ownership to Bartle, who continued to work on promoting MUDs worldwide.

The original purpose of MUD was to create a world that didn't suck, and spreading that world was one of their primary missions. For that reason, they charged no money and encouraged people to create their own worlds. "We encouraged people to write their own games. Some of them played MUD, liked it, wrote their own. The only thing was that they had to say something to the effect that they weren't going to commercialize it. We didn't want other people profiting from our endeavors if we weren't going to profit from it. Some of those other games weren't so good, some of them were better."

As MUDs proliferated, some became very popular, such as AberMUD, which was developed by Alan Cox, Richard Acott, Jim Finnis, and Leon Thrane at the University of Wales, Aberystwyth. AberMUD, which was very game-oriented, made it to the U.S. and became popular there. However, some people, whom

THE D IN MUD

"The D in MUD was Dungeon, not because it was based on Dungeons & Dragons; it wasn't based on Dungeons & Dragons. Roy had never played Dungeons & Dragons. The D came because we wanted you to think about it as something that would explain to people what MUD was—a dungeon of sorts. And Roy also came across a Fortran version of Zork, called "Dungen" (which didn't have the O in it because only six characters were allowed). Zork was by far the best around, so we thought that these games would ultimately be called Zork. But it wasn't Zork. We didn't know it as Zork. We knew it as DUNGEN, so we thought these games were going to be called Dungeons. So MUD was like a multi-user dungeon. So that's why it was called Multi-User Dungeon, not because it had anything to do with Dungeons & Dragons."

–Richard Bartle

Bartle refers to as "socializers," decided to take the game out of MUD, the first example being called TinyMUD, which spawned various offshoots like MOO, MUSH, and MUCK. One very important version was called LamdaMOO, which Bartle refers to as "the Second Life of its day" because it allowed users to create their own objects for the game. Bartle asks, what do you do when you've got a world with no game? He answers that you create a game, or you make objects for that game, "and the final thing is you have sex." He adds that you also might complain about the resources, "because six months later the entire disk pack was of people's creations, and the whole thing collapsed."

Probably the two most influential MUDs—as far as future impact is concerned—were Scepter of Goth (1978) by Alan E. Klietz, which was one of the first commercial MUDs, and Diku-MUD, which was a much later version of MUD released in 1991, inspired by AberMUD.

Scepter of Goth became very popular in America and spawned other popular MUDs like Mordor and The Realm of Angmar. Former MUD creators went on to form companies of their own, such as Simutronics, co-founded by Tom and Susan Zelinski along with David Whatley and Rob Denton. Matt Firor and Don Campbell started Mythic Entertainment, first producing a MUD called Tempest. Tempest ultimately became Darkness Falls, which in turn was the codebase for their popular MMO Dark Age of Camelot. According to Bartle and others, Meridian 59, the first of the real MMOs, was also inspired by Scepter of Goth. However, its developer and lead designer, Mike Sellers,

says that this is, at best, only partially true. Although his assistant designer and a level designer had played Scepter of Goth, Sellers had not, and so he says that there was little, if any influence from that MUD. He says, "I had played a bunch of other MUDs though, and the general gameplay was definitely influenced by these—our initial goal was to make a 3D MUD (but with some advances, such as no resets), but honestly at this point it's difficult for me to pin down too many influences… games like Eye of the Beholder (single-player) and various MUDs (Aber, Diku, even Legend), plus tons and tons of pen-and-paper RPGs."

DikuMUD was a major influence on the earliest MMOs, and its effect has lasted through generations of games. The first such game was Ultima Online. Producer Starr Long states that DikuMUDs "were a huge influence. UO was MUD-based and EQ [EverQuest] was specifically DikuMUD-based," adding, "and everything since EQ has been derivative of the DikuMUD model."

Raph Koster, lead designer of Ultima Online, has written a very detailed article (among many of his great writings) that describes DikuMUD in detail, including its direct impact on games that came later. Players of MMORPGs may be amazed to find that just about everything we see in modern MMOs had already been designed into DikuMUD, and although he states correctly that among the early MMORPGs, Ultima Online played the least like DikuMUD, he fully acknowledges the influence Diku and other MUDs had on the game's design. Koster's full discussion can be found at *http://raphkoster.com/2009/01/09/what-is-a-diku/*

Richard Garriott, the creator of the Ultima brand, also acknowledges the influence of MUDs. "While I literally never played a MUD, I was always well aware of them. My team members had often played them, but while I longed for the multiplayer aspects, I could not abide by either the early lack of graphics nor the scale limiting dial-up service pricing. Every year that went by, we would research the work of others and wonder if we were yet at the year where we could make a truly grand, multiplayer Ultima. 'MUltima' was pitched internally and eventually to EA almost every year until the WWW began to grow, then we knew now was our time, and we basically FORCED Larry Probst to let us start UO!"

DikuMUD was unquestionably a major influence on the hit MMO EverQuest, whose influence continued on to inspire many of the MMOs that followed, including the granddaddy of them all, World of Warcraft. Bartle says, "EverQuest is a DikuMUD with a graphics engine bolted onto it. They just bolted a graphics engine onto DikiMUD. You won't find them saying, 'Nonono this came from our own imaginations fully formed,' like the child of Zeus or something. The gameplay is absolutely Diku-MUD." There was even a short-lived dust-up over whether the EverQuest team used the DikuMUD codebase, but that was quickly resolved. Here's EverQuest designer Brad McQuaid on the influence of DikuMUD:

"Before designing the core of EverQuest, Steve Clover and I played a lot of text MUDs, especially Toril/Sojourn MUD, which was a DikuMUD derivative. We learned a lot from playing these MUDs, especially the psychology behind them, what made them so compelling to play, etc. We've always been open about this, even giving thanks to Toril/Sojourn MUD in the original credits of the game. We also paid homage to DikuMUDs by putting in the same text when you /con a mob.

A promotional MUD map issued with MUD2.

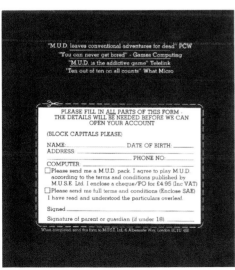

A commercial version of MUD with mail-in order form.

"Still, EverQuest was built from the ground up by the team. Even if we had wanted to (and we wouldn't have—it would have been unethical), it would have made no sense to use DikuMUD code. MMORPGs are fundamentally different than MUDs in many ways. Probably the most fundamental is that MUDs are room-based, whereas EQ and other MMOs take place in 3D graphical environments. This means you have to have completely different mob pathing and AI. Combat doesn't take place in one 'room,' but rather in a 3D environment, where both the player and the mob can roam freely. Also, since EQ was graphical it had a mouse and text-based UI. We also added quite a bit to EQ that wasn't present in the MUDs we had played, like the spell system, the crafting system, the faction system, and several other systems. That said, we were certainly influenced heavily by DikuMUDs and will be eternally grateful to those who took part in the evolution of MUDs from their very genesis to the MUDs we played."

MUD itself (and its successor, MUD2) is still around as the oldest, continuously running multiplayer game. You can still play it at *www.mud2.com.*

PlayNET

Howard Goldberg and Dave Panzl pioneered person-to-person communications that included games and graphics when they created PlayNET for the Commodore 64 in 1983. Bill Pytlovany, who later worked to adapt PlayNET's games to another platform—Q-Link—remembers the service better than most. "It was an incubator program for the RPI college up here… They had the idea of making it something that people would just be able to sign on with and not have to know all about security bits and stop bits and all that crap."

PlayNET offered many of the features that ultimately became standard in online services in addition to chat and graphics, such as email, bulletin boards, instant messaging, file sharing, and even online shopping. According to Pytlovany, Goldberg and Panzl were hoping to sell their service to Commodore, but it was another company, Control Video Corp (CVC), that outmaneuvered them.

Founded by William von Meister (who also founded the early service The Source), CVC marketed an online service for the Atari 2600 called GameLine. The business model for GameLine consisted of one-time charges for a special modem ($49.95) plus a setup fee ($15), and, because the service allowed Atari 2600 owners to download games (one at a time, with no way to save other than high scores), they charged $1 per game download. In 1983, the leadership of the company changed hands, with Steve Case joining as a marketing consultant and Jim Kimsey as a manufacturing consultant. By 1985, von Meister had left the company, which was renamed Quantum Computer Services with Kimsey as CEO and Marc Seriff as CTO. Case became VP of marketing, but was considered to be in line to become its CEO after Kimsey retired.

CVC's success could be attributed in part to Case's business acumen. Case was able to work out a deal with Commodore to include a disk containing CVC's product, Quantum Link (or Q-Link), with every modem they sold. Modems were not standard equipment at the time, which gave Q-Link a distinct advantage over PlayNET. "So PlayNET had nowhere to go, so they licensed their software to Quantum."

It was at that time that Pytlovany joined the Q-Link team at the renamed company, Quantum Computer Services. His job was to port PlayNET's games to Q-Link, but there were some problems that made games less viable than chat features. "PlayNET still had some issues, like it took two full minutes to load the software before you could connect your modem, and then two full minutes when you wanted to go from one section

to another section. So when we launched Q-Link at Quantum, games weren't the main feature." Even so, Q-Link did feature the former PlayNET games, including Backgammon, Chinese Checkers, Chess, Go, Reversi, and a Battleship-type game called Sea Strike, among others. None of the early games required massive graphics, animations, or major graphical changes during play. This allowed Q-Link to display both the game and the chat window on the same screen, so people could play and converse with each other without switching screens or modes.

Q-Link was highly successful in the small C64/C128 market, so Quantum looked for other areas of expansion. They worked with Apple to create AppleLink for Apple II and Macintosh computers and later launched PC-Link in conjunction with Tandy.

Quantum also hosted the beta test of the earliest experiment in large-scale commercial virtual communities—Habitat.

CHESS

Chess is a game famous for its complexity and challenge. We have not provided you with the rules for this game and have assumed that those of you who are interested in playing the Royal Game of Chess are aware of the basic rules of this game of skill and strategy.

PLAYERS	Two
PIECES	16 per player.
BOARD	8 rows of 8 alternating colored squares.
OBJECTIVE	To be the first player to capture (checkmate) your opponent's king.

PLAYNET INSTRUCTIONS

Setting Up

PlayNet sets up the board for you and keeps track of whose turn it is.

Moving

- Press **F3** to get into Move mode.
- Use the "move" keys (around the **S**) to position the cursor on the piece you want to move.
- Press **RETURN** to pick up the piece.
- Use the "move" keys to move the piece.
- Press **RETURN** to place the piece.
- To retake a move, select *RETAKE LAST MOVE* from the menu. Your opponent will be asked whether or not he objects. If your opponent objects to a replay, you may not retake your last move. If he does not object, your last move will be retracted and you are ready to replay. If your opponent made a move after the one you are retracting, his move also must be replayed.
- In order to castle, promote a pawn, or capture en passant while in Move mode, press **F7** to see menu, then select an item by pressing **F1**.

Ending

While in Talk mode, bring up the menu; then select *QUIT GAME* by pressing **F1**.

32

CHINESE CHECKERS

PLAYERS	Two to six
PIECES	Ten colored marbles per player.
BOARD	A six-point star, each point holding one player's marbles.
OBJECTIVE	To be the first player to move all your marbles to the opposite point.

PLAYNET INSTRUCTIONS

Setting Up

PlayNet sets up the board for the correct number of players, keeps track of whose turn it is and does not allow illegal moves.

Moving

- Press **F3** to get into Move mode.
- Use the "move" keys (around the **S**) to position the cursor on the marble you want to move.
- Press **RETURN** to pick up the marble.
- Use the "move" keys to move the marble.
- If your move involves multiple jumping, press the **SPACE BAR** after each jump.
- Press **RETURN** to place the marble and complete your turn.

Ending

While in Talk mode, bring up the menu; then select *QUIT GAME* by pressing **F1**.

GENERAL GAME RULES

- Move or jump in any direction, as long as you follow the lines on the board.
- Make as many legal jumps during a turn as possible.

33

Original PlayNET manual.

Habitat

Habitat was created in 1985 by Lucasfilm Games' Randy Farmer and Chip Morningstar. It is often referred to as a graphical MUD. It allowed players to create graphical avatars and to input commands via the joystick (Go, Get, Put, Do, and Talk), making it a little like a multiplayer point-and-click game environment. New objects were constantly being brought into the environment, and for years the first graphic cyburb continued to run in Japan via the Fujitsu network.

In 1993, Farmer described the service in somewhat technical terms:

"Habitat is 'a multi-participant online virtual environment', a cyberspace. Each participant ('player') uses a home computer [Commodore 64] as an intelligent, interactive client, communicating via modem and telephone, over a commercial packet-switching network to a centralized, mainframe host system. The client software provides the user interface, generating a real-time animated display of what is going on and translating input from the player into messages to the host. The host maintains the system's world model, enforcing the rules and keeping each player's client informed about the constantly changing state of the universe."

Source: *http://www.crockford.com/ec/citizenry.html*

Pytlovany remembers working on Habitat and the challenges it presented. "It was a great idea, an awesome, cool, ahead-of-its-time concept, but at the time the C64 just barely had enough memory, and some of the graphics capabilities we had trouble with to the point where to debug it people would rec___ sessions with a video tape machine at home and then bring in their video tape so we could see

Screen from Fujitsu's Habitat II. (Courtesy of Fujitsu Limited)

what the other person was seeing while we were seeing it, because it was an interactive world… your avatar was in the same room with another avatar. And that was one of the ways we had to debug it. And one of the things we finally determined was a problem was some Commodore 64s used a different video chip than other ones, and they didn't work, but the ones we had did work, so we narrowed it down to actually problems with certain chips that the C64 shipped with that wouldn't work, and some that did. So that was a screwy thing we had to deal with. That and the fact that we were creating a world that even on our servers didn't have the space to do what the vision that the guys at Lucasfilm really had, and so it was trimmed down into something called Club Caribe, which was, instead of a whole world, it was an island, so that way there was a limited amount of places you go and things that you could do. And that was something that was containable within the realm of what the computer could do at the time."

Habitat ran on Q-Link as Club Caribe for two years before being closed and its technology sold to Fujitsu in 1990. The legacy of Habitat is far-reaching. It was studied closely by both other game designers and academicians. The lessons it taught served as models for later attempts at online multiplayer gaming. For a seminal article on Habitat, check out this link, which is where we found the original screen image: *http://www.stanford.edu/class/history34q/readings/Virtual_Worlds/LucasfilmHabitat.html*

but a much reduced fee during the evening hours and weekends, plus each system also required a sign-up fee to join the service. Hourly pricing ranged from $5 in the non-peak hours to as high as $22.50 an hour.

All of the services offered an array of text-based games that had been bouncing around university and corporate systems for a while: Adventure, Blackjack, Football, Hangman, Lunar Lander, Maze, and Star Trek, among others. In addition, CompuServe and The Source offered Civil War, Hammurabi, and Hunt the Wumpus, while Delphi offered Empire and Geowar. CompuServe, however, proved to be the more aggressive game provider. In 1982, John Taylor and Kelton Flinn started programming for MUD and formed the company Kesmai. Their early programming efforts were published as Dungeons of Kesmai and Island of Kesmai. In addition, CompuServe purchased a multiplayer space combat simulator (using ASCII characters only) called DECWAR that Kesmai overhauled and relaunched as MegaWars, the first of what would become a popular trilogy. Since this program was one of CompuServe's big money generators for years, it's interesting to note that CompuServe purchased full rights to the program for $50.00, an amount that would

Along with the original MUDs, Habitat can legitimately be regarded as one of the chief influences on later, more commercially successful online role-playing games such as Ultima Online, EverQuest, and World of Warcraft.

Early Pay to Play

The early '80s marked a new era in online gaming when large companies realized they could charge money for ___ame computers during the slack times at night. Such early systems included The Source (Dow Jones), CompuServe (H&R Block), and Delphi (General Videotex). Users on these systems paid a premium during work hours

Original Habitat screen.

have been recouped as soon as the original maximum of ten players played even one off-peak hour at the game.

BBS

Gamers were willing to pony up fees that were exorbitant by today's standards, just for the experience of playing with other gamers all over the country. Of course, in a free market economy, other options soon appeared. The BBS, or Bulletin Board System, phenomenon was beginning to take shape. Individuals would run their own bulletin boards and invite others to play games by email, trade software (piracy was rampant), or swap hints and reviews about commercial games. Usually, a BBS only cost the user the price of a telephone call, but some had membership fees. The trick was to find one near you.

Many of these bulletin board systems offered play-by-email or play-by-bulletin board versions of tabletop role-playing games like Traveller and Dungeons & Dragons. Others offered games like those on CompuServe, Delphi, and The Source. Dragon's Lair (in California) offered Nukewar and Lunar Lander; Big-Top Games (Wisconsin) had Civil War and Blackjack; Signature Software (California) offered Star Trek, Blackjack, and Othello; A.R.C.A.D.E. (Michigan) provided Civil War, Island Jumper, and Horse Race for its users; ARK-NET (Arkansas) had Centipede and Rubik's Cube on its boards; and Lethbridge (Canada) had B-1 Bomber to go along with Wumpus. Many systems had text versions of adventure games to add to their selection. Nessy (in Illinois) published a version of Adventure in Time and Queen of Phobos; Drucom (Pennsylvania) had King Tut and Atlantis; and COMNET-80 (Ohio) offered Isle, Dog Star Adventure, and CIA.

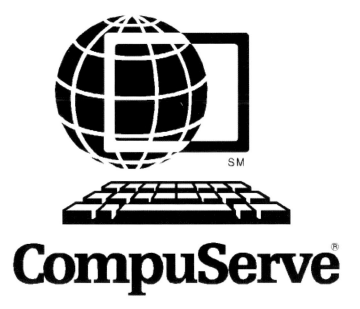

In addition, some BBS operators turned their hobbies into businesses. One entrepreneur was Harlow Stevens, Jr., who established The Mansion in Evanston, Illinois, to provide Medieval Conquest, 18 Wheeler, Cargo Master, GM Air Freight, Nuke Strike, Destination Midway, and Oil Baron. These multiplayer games stood alongside the standard play-by-email Diplomacy games that were appearing on virtually every system and the email role-playing games.

Of lasting significance was the experience of Mark Jacobs. He established a system in 1984 that was dedicated to playing one game—a text-based role-playing game called Aradath, which began with eight phone lines and charged gamers a flat rate of $40 per month to stay in the game before it evolved into the popular Dragon's Gate MUD, which would finally shut down in February 2007. Jacobs would eventually form AUSI and then Mythic Entertainment, creating almost a dozen online games over the years, including Online Diplomacy, Galaxy II, Godzilla Online, Independence Day Online, Silent Death Online, and his masterpiece, 2001's critically acclaimed Dark Age of Camelot, which still boasts an active community as of this writing.

1985: New Players

Bill Louden, the man who built the games business for CompuServe, found himself out of a job in 1985. He still loved games and was reputed to be addicted to CompuServe's Kesmai MUD, but he wanted more while CompuServe's management seemed willing to settle for the status quo. Louden began to look for another opportunity and found the excess bandwidth waiting for him at the General Electric Information Service (GEIS), the corporate backbone of GE's worldwide interests.

The GEnie (General Electric Network for Information Exchange) system launched in October 1985. GEnie quickly became the serious venue for gamers, primarily because it offered free support accounts to any software company and to a plethora of celebrity designers and authors. GEnie also added programs over the years, including MUDs like Simutronics' Gemstone (which still exists as Gemstone IV), Alan Lenton's Federation (which still exists as Federation II), and Mark Jacobs' Dragon's Gate; graphic simulation programs like

Kesmai's Air Warrior (eventually to become Air Warrior III), Kesmai's Multiplayer BattleTech, and Simutronics' CyberStrike (still available as CyberStrike 2); and multiplayer play-by-email games like Jim Dunnigan's Hundred Years War (www.hundredyearswar.com) and AUSI's Diplomacy, among others.

Meanwhile, in 1985—the same year that Island of Kesmai began its ten-year run—the seeds of massive change were sewn when, one month after the launch of GEnie, Quantum Computer Services launched Quantum Link. At first, Q-Link supported only Commodore 64/128 computers. It also had a pricing structure that could net slightly more than the existing services. It cost $9.95 per month and $5.00 per hour. Q-Link is notable for two things: Habitat, and its eventual identity as America Online (AOL), which has continued to provide online games ever since as part of its overall service.

Big Blue Blues

If you've noticed a pattern in online opportunities to this point, it would have to be that companies with large amounts of unused bandwidth on their mainframes decided to put their assets to work. In 1984, two giants of the commercial world formed a joint venture. IBM and Sears, Roebuck and Company created the Prodigy Network. Prodigy was originally designed with the mass market in mind and was based on the thinking— somewhat prematurely—that online advertising and online shopping were keys to the future. Like failed dot-coms on the Internet, Prodigy thought they could become the next television by providing mass market audiences with short bursts of information (*for some reason, every time I open a PowerPoint presentation, I think of Prodigy– RDM*) and using banner ads to drive commerce.

Unfortunately for Prodigy, once you assumed that your audience had a computer and a modem, you were no longer talking about a mass market.

Screens from Air Warrior.

329

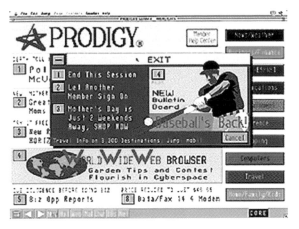

Worse yet, the rigid manner in which information had to be presented on Prodigy worked against doing games with graphic front ends and simultaneous users.

Despite its inherent problems and non-gaming direction, some interesting games appeared on the system. Rebel Space was a brilliant play-by-email space conquest game with minimal decorative graphics. It was designed by Beyond Software (later known as Stormfront Studios) and had two female system operators who kept the story interesting and matters lively. Business Simulator from Reality Technologies was designed by a Wall Street firm that understood serious business. It offered numerous decision points and spreadsheet presentations so you could compete against other virtual entrepreneurs as the CEO of your own fictitious company. MadMaze was largely the creation of Greg Costikyan of board game design fame (The Creature Who Ate Sheboygan, Paranoia). MadMaze tried to present the dungeon exploration experience in snapshots of action and puzzles. The Next President involved tens of thousands of players in choosing fictitious candidates for president and running detailed simulated campaigns.

Although it was a poll/survey-driven game, it was fascinating enough to run successfully during two different presidential elections. Baseball Manager was a classic fantasy

COSTIKYAN ON MADMAZE

In 1988, Robert Gehorsam was in charge of games for Prodigy, and contacted Eric Goldberg about doing a game for them. Eric had previously designed a maze navigation game for Trintex, the company that preceded Prodigy. Trintex had done a market test in Northern New Jersey; Eric's game had been one of the more popular products in that market test, so Robert found it fairly easy to sell upper management on the idea of a successor. Eric brought me into the project, both because he had other commitments, and because we had previously collaborated on many games.

One of the conditions imposed by management was that no new programming was to be used in implementing MadMaze. This was, of course, crazy, but it was a condition of the deal. We managed to figure out how to use two of Prodigy's existing software tools to create the game. One, called Q&A, was originally designed for the creation of online quizzes; we repurposed it to create the game's "places of power," locations in the maze where players had to supply the correct answer to some kind of puzzle or other. The other, called TTOPS, was originally designed to deploy news stories, but we used its navigational features to implement the maze itself.

Eric created the maze geography; I designed all the puzzles, and wrote all the text in the game. The graphics were executed by Prodigy staff artists, and were supplied in NAPLPS format. This now-defunct format basically drew monocolored shapes on the screen, but in the hands of a capable artist, were able to produce images that, while crude even by the standards of conventional PC games at the time (which of course are far cruder than today's) were at least... okay. When the game appeared on the service, it quickly became not only Prodigy's most successful game, but also one of the most intensively used applications on the service. Over the course of its lifetime, more than 2 million people played it. You'd think Prodigy would have been thrilled, but in fact, they thought this was a problem. You see, in their internal accounting, they assigned a high proportion of costs on the basis of modem usage, and lots of people were playing the game for long periods of time. So by their standards, supporting MadMaze was very costly. By their accounting system, the ideal application was one where people dialed up, spent a minute online, and went away— never mind the fact that we were providing a lot of value for Prodigy subscribers, presumably making it more likely that they would continue their subscriptions.

It has, of course, been useful in my subsequent career to be able to say "I designed the first online game to attract more than 1M players—in fact, 2M players," but in retrospect I can't say that I think MadMaze was that great a game. The miracle, really, was that it didn't suck, given the fact that it was cobbled together from existing tools, and with such primitive graphics.

sports league with a twist. If you set a lineup, there was a statistical engine that figured out how your game would evolve, even if a given manager didn't play a member of your roster on a given day. It was part simulation, part fantasy league.

The Jack Nicklaus Golf Tour was one of the boldest experiments by Prodigy. You could download a unique golf course and play one round offline. Then, you would upload a check file on your results and the service would post the "tour" results. Two great ideas never actually came to pass: A campaign game in the Star Wars universe where players would fight their TIE fighters offline and upload the results with a check file was stymied by Lucasfilm. Prodigy attempted to do the same thing with Secret Weapons of the Luftwaffe, but unfortunately, both games ended up grounded by dueling legal departments.

Peaks and Valleys

In the early '90s, two dedicated online game networks appeared, neither of them tied to the excess bandwidth of a major corporation. The Multi-Player Games Network (MPGN) was a tremendously graphical network built around a fantasy role-playing game called Drakkar (the first online game to allow players to create guilds and have guild clubhouses, hideouts, and so on) and the idea that board game players would like to play board games online. MPGN had some marvelous implementations of board games, many overseen by Marc Miller (designer of the Traveller role-playing game for Game Designers' Workshop): Operation Market Garden (a two-player

The map/menu of TSN, Sierra's very early online service.

WWII game), Empire Builder (one of the finest railroad strategy board games ever made), Imperium (space conquest), and Minion Hunter (brilliant implementation of a monster hunt game that used the racetrack board à la Monopoly and simple player statistics as in role-playing).

MPGN was something of a victim of its own success. Financed by a wealthy financial angel, the company never felt the pressure to make money until it was too late. Further,

Drakkar was so successful that it was difficult to pull regulars out of Drakkar long enough to fill a game of Junta (the multiplayer game of backstabbing and intrigue in a fictional banana republic) or any of the other strategy games. Great games were overlooked on MPGN.

The Sierra Network (TSN) was the brainchild of Sierra founder Ken Williams, who realized that the future of the interactive entertainment business would be online. Rather than purchase huge mainframes, Sierra built their network around a patchwork quilt of PCs. TSN was a real network, not a time-sharing service. It started with a graphical interface that allowed you to create a Habitat-style avatar, divided the games up into "lands" as though it were a theme park, and offered a mixture of common games (backgammon, card, and gambling), a children's area, premium games (a golf game for four players, but missing a chat feature), a popular area called Larryland (after Leisure Suit Larry), and Shadow of Yserbius. Yserbius was TSN's big game.

Shadow of Yserbius was overseen by Apple and early EA producer/designer Joe Ybarra; it was the first graphical online fantasy role-playing game to allow multiple players to join

Scenes from Shadow of Yserbius.

together in parties of four. The game was compelling, both because of its interesting quest-based design and because of the new experience of adventuring with other players in a graphical world. Although MUD players might have seen it as nothing new, its graphical environment introduced many new fans to online multiplayer gaming, and many TSN subscribers joined the service strictly to play Yserbius and never went anywhere else.

TSN ultimately became the ImagiNation Network (INN), was sold to AT&T, and closed up shop when AT&T decided not to continue with an ambitious cyberworld project under way at the time.

Changes and Experiments

In the mid-90s, the online world changed radically. The main online services, such as AOL, CompuServe, and Prodigy, were still the primary destinations for online gamers, but their dominance was about to end. First, the World Wide Web was born, and subsequently Netscape made it available to just about anyone with a modem and a mouse. Then id Software came out with DOOM and made it possible to play on direct modem and LAN connections. The clamor for web-based deathmatches was deafening, and it was only a matter of time before "deathmatch" became the home user's arcade game of choice. Meanwhile, Blizzard was inventing Battle.net and introducing players to online games. Soon, Quake would create an online obsession at home and in workplaces all over the world.

The Realm Online

Taking another direction, experiments in graphical role-playing games started to appear. Sierra's Oakhurst Studios began to beta test The Realm Online, which replaced INN as their online endeavor of the future. The Realm was somewhat stiff and graphically limited, and it didn't really set the world on fire nor did it represent the model of the future of online games. The funniest aspect of The Realm was that players could dress their avatars in different costumes, but if they removed all items of clothing, their characters would be walking around in their tighty whiteys.

Sierra gave up on The Realm when other, more open and sophisticated games began to appear, but the game has survived over the years, and you can still play it as of this writing by going to *www.realmserver.com*.

Meridian 59

Elsewhere, in their parents' garage, Andrew and Christopher Kirmse were assembling a virtual team of developers to create their online brainchild, Meridian 59. Andrew had attended MIT while Chris studied at Virginia Tech. Both of them had been summer interns at Microsoft in 1993 and had done some professional programming. But their real dream was to create a

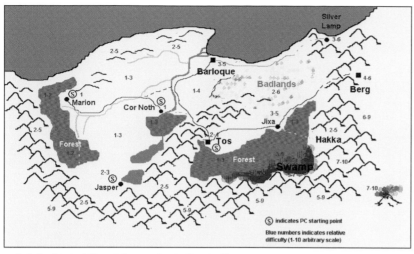

Original Meridian 59 map by Mike Sellers.

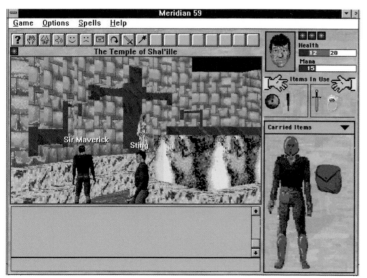

Screenshot from Meridian 59.

graphical RPG along the lines of Scepter of Goth, which they had played obsessively in high school. Like the MUD pioneers before them, they developed their own scripting language —Blakod—and began working on the technical aspects of their game. It took some years to complete, in part because they both returned to school and completed their studies. They had no experience with computer graphics, but found resources, and spent many hours playing DOOM II. Then they connected with Mike Sellers, who was completing his MBA at Berkeley, and with his help they obtained their first outside funding. Together they formed a company called Archetype Interactive.

Their project came to the notice of a programmer at 3DO and from there to Trip Hawkins. They agreed to an acquisition deal for $5 million in stock, and in September 1996, they launched the game.

Meridian 59 was crude and unpolished when it was first released, but it was also the first of its kind—a fully graphical massively multiplayer role-playing game—MMORPG. The early gameplay experience was best compared with the seminal book, Lord of the Flies. It was chaotic and wild, but it was, at the same time, an innovation and a glimpse of what was soon to become a massive part of the computer game industry.

Meridian 59 was a precursor to games that came later, such as Asheron's Call and EverQuest, and featured lots of hack 'n' slash role-playing combined with social interaction. In many ways, it was an early attempt at making graphical MUDs. But it was just a little ahead of its time. More than one developer has lamented the role of trailblazer: "You can recognize a pioneer by the arrows in his back." (-Beverly Rubik) Meridian 59's intense player vs. player gaming did not appeal to the mass market, and, in any case, the game suffered from the "arrows in the back" syndrome. Ultimately, 3DO closed down the servers in 2000. (However, the game has been revived by the Kirmse brothers and a devoted fan base. For more information, check out *www.meridian59.com/*.)

333

UO Charter Edition poster.

Ultima Online

Around the time that Meridian 59 was in its inception phase, Starr Long was working with Richard Garriott on Ultima IX. But around the end of 1994, his attention was pulled toward a new idea inspired by the emergence of the World Wide Web and experiences that he and other members of the team had with DikuMUD. "We looked at every online game we could find—INN, Air Warrior. We realized that we had to get in right now… this is the next thing," says Long. Garriott agreed, and told them to make a prototype. Two weeks later, they had a game called MUltima, which could support up to 50 players. There wasn't much action, only a sort of scavenger game based on Ultima V graphics. But the seed was there.

Origin's budget didn't have room for another project at the time, so they approached Larry Probst, who was the head of Electronic Arts, and Probst granted them $250,000 to begin work on the project. (*See page 324* for quotes from Long and Garriott.)

Ultima Online, as it was later renamed, was different from any others that had been seen. It was based around Richard Garriott's desire to create complete worlds and included a lot of noncombat skills. "It's all in the details," says Long. "A lot of our inspiration came from the infamous 'baking bread' in Ultima VII."

UO, as it came to be known by players, was a wide-open player vs. player world where the only safe places were within city limits. While later games created specific PvP areas for players to fight each other, UO was a dangerous place to explore, particularly for new characters, and when you died your belongings remained with your corpse.

Despite the dangers, UO quickly gained a following and for the first time proved the commercial MMO model. With

Screens from the original UO and Ultima Online: Third Dawn.

It could get pretty crowded sometimes in UO, and you couldn't move through other player characters.

was prevented from leaving by a few mischievous (or clueless) players who refused to clear the doorway. The speech bubbles in such situations were hilariously unreadable.

Despite its occasional quirkiness, UO was popular, fun to play, and constantly growing. Ultima Online was the first of

Richard Garriott & Starr Long

a $15 monthly subscription and 100,000 players, Garriott did the math. That was $1.5 million a month. And 100,000 players was just the beginning.

In addition to crafting skills, hunting, and fishing, UO also contained a local ecology that responded to the actions of players. For instance, if all the deer were killed for meat and leather, wolves would move closer to town and threaten players. Cutting down all the trees would have an effect on local weather. It was a clever idea, but not one that scaled well when you had thousands of players all trying to hunt deer and cut down trees.

UO also differed from later MMOs by using over-the-head speech bubbles common in single-player games for conversations instead of text lines with options for global, local, or private chat. When there were 20, 30, or 150 people in an area, the speech bubbles tended to overlap and make the whole thing unreadable. Plus, at the beginning, there was no way to communicate with someone who was not nearby. Another oddity was that players could block the passage of other players, which resulted in times when a whole room full of players

Ultima Online booth at E3.

several commercially successful massively multiplayer online games. Its deep skill system and detailed world based on the Ultima series created a dedicated group of players, and it's still going strong as of this writing.

Next up: EverQuest.

EverQuest

The world of Norath came into being because of the combined efforts of several key people, but sometimes it just takes one person with a vision and the determination to make it happen.

WarWizard screenshot.

John Smedley (known as "Smed" around the office) was that guy. Working at Sony's 989 Studios, he was involved in development that mostly focused on sports games for the PlayStation. However, Smedley, who had cut his RPG teeth on Dungeons & Dragons as a kid, discovered the joys—and the perils—of online RPGs in 1993 while playing CyberStrike on the GEnie network. He likes to tell the story about his new wife discovering his $600 bill for one month of GEnie. "That was the first time she knew that I was addicted to online games."

He took an idea for an online RPG to Russell Shanks, who was CTO at the time. Shanks remembers saying, "John, you work for a PlayStation company. How the heck are you going to make a PC online game?" Smedley was not discouraged, however, even when the studio's director of development showed no interest in the concept.

In March 1995, Kelly Flock took the reins of Sony subsidiary Imagesoft and became Smedley's boss. At Smedley's second meeting with Flock he pitched what was at the time called "Online Adventure Game" and got an immediate yes. Flock,

who had worked previously at LucasArts and Activision, had seen eary online games like Kesmai's Air Warrior and and Island of Kesmai. By August, Smedley had a pitch ready, a warm-up project called Tanarus to be developed with Simutronics. At this point, Flock presented the idea to Terry Tokunaka, the head of Sony Computer Entertainment, who told him that they would support PC games, but that they should "focus on the online side of things." Tokunaka added, "Don't go lose a lot of money," but he supported the project.

By February 1996, Smedley was back in Flock's office pitching his Online Adventure Game concept. Again, he got the go-ahead. He started looking for new talent and got a lead on a couple of developers who had made their own shareware RPG called WarWizard. And that's how he found Brad McQuaid and Steve Clover.

"Steve Clover and I were working at a wholesale plant nursery where I was the MIS director and Steve, a programmer," remembers McQuaid. "We did game programming in the evenings. We'd finished a shareware game called WarWizard and also WarWizard 2, which was just a demo. I'd recently put the WarWizard 2 demo out on the Net to see if we could find a publisher."

Smedley called on a Saturday in February 1996. They were blown away. "We immediately saw that a 3D online RPG would combine our experience developing a single-player RPG and the online MUDs we loved. We gave our notice at the nursery and started work at Sony in early March 1996.

"Being paid to do what we loved was incredible," says McQuaid. "We began work on a design document detailing the game's mechanics and interface. We had a white board, and I remember Steve and I were drawing the game's world and naming the major cities. We had Antonica, Odus,

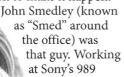

Faydwer, Kunark, and Velious—even though the latter two ended up being the first expansions."

Over time, the team grew, with Bill Trost taking over as lead designer while McQuaid became the producer and Clover continued as a programmer. They brought in friends and fellow gamers Kevin Burns and Tony Garcia as artists, and the project continued to gather steam. But it still didn't have an official name.

The name came when McQuaid and Clover were driving in the car and just blurting out whatever came to mind. After a few ideas that didn't catch on, Clover said, "Everquest," and they both knew—it was EverQuest!

The EverQuest team all believed they were making history, but were viewed as misfits by other Sony divisions. "We were in a console game development company and making this game," says Smedley. "Throughout the lifecycle of the development, Brad hired a lot of his friends." Brad's friends were not experienced game developers. They came from jobs as diverse as pizza delivery and TV sales, but they had one thing in common: a lot of experience playing role-playing games. Continues Smedley, "These were not a band of people who had made games before. They were a band that played games together before, and there's a very, very big difference."

What followed were years full of challenges and growth, and the evermaturing project that was to become the first monster hit MMORPG. EverQuest went into open beta in July 1998, and the response was overwhelming—so much so that their greatest challenge was keeping the servers from crashing as thousands of players poured into the newly birthed world.

The EverQuest team realized quickly that they would need to keep feeding the beast, or at least keep providing new and engaging content for their dedicated players. They embarked on an ambitious cycle of expansions, starting with The Ruins of Kunark in April of 2000, followed in December by The Scars of Velious, The Shadows of Luclin a year later, and The Planes of Power in October 2002. In all, there were 15 expansions for EverQuest, up until 2008. EverQuest II came out in November of 2004 and also continues to expand as of this writing.

EverQuest set a standard that was to last for many years, and it left a legacy that can still be found in many, if not most, of the MMOs that came after.

Sexy women were always a part of EverQuest's appeal, and there were even EQ pin-up girls.

Asheron's Call

By the time Ultima Online was released, there were other groups around the country working on massive multiplayer games, each with unique ideas. The EverQuest team was one of those groups. Another, starting as Second Nature and ultimately changing their name to Turbine Entertainment, consisted of a very small team led by industry veteran Dan Scherlis and first-time lead designer Toby Ragaini. In 1995, Second Nature began work on a very ambitious and innovative massively multiplayer game called Asheron's Call.

Among the key features in Asheron's Call was a method of sharing experience and encouraging group cooperative play. Previous games, such as Ultima Online and Meridian 59, had been notorious for the predominance of player killing, which many game players found too adversarial, and which oftentimes created frustration for new players. Asheron's Call attempted to change the focus from player killing to monster killing and group social dynamics.

Asheron's Call differed from other MMOs of the time in several ways. For one, it did not identify enemies using color coding, which EverQuest introduced, and which has become the standard for almost all MMOs since. Asheron's Call was in some ways more difficult and challenging to play than other MMOs of the time, and although it never gained the kind of massive following that EverQuest did, it was considered by its fans as the best of all the early MMOs.

After nearly two years in development, Turbine partnered with Microsoft, who released the game successfully as a premium service on the Microsoft Internet Gaming Zone in 1999, about nine months after the release of EverQuest. Ironically, the original release of Asheron's Call had been set for a year earlier, which would have put it ahead of EverQuest, but technical problems and the polish required by Microsoft caused the launch to be delayed.

Dark Age of Camelot

The Olthoi were among the deadliest of the early enemies in Asheron's Call.

AC enemies had a lot of stats, including various strengths and weaknesses (not shown here), and players would have to develop perception skills to "read" the enemy. Either that, or attack and die a lot.

Enraged Female Tusker		
Tusker	character level	120
Strength		435
Endurance		480
Coordination		330
Quickness		280
Focus		140
Self		200
Health		750/750 (100 %)
Stamina		977/980
Mana		200/200

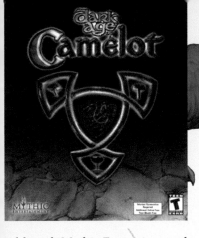

Although Mythic Entertainment began development of their massively multiplayer game Dark Age of Camelot late in 1999—much later than Origin, Sony, or Turbine—they were able to complete the game in 18 months and release it in October 2001.

Although they had set out to create what they called a "graphical MUD," what they ended up releasing to the public was another top-notch MMORPG based loosely in Arthurian legend, Norse mythology, and Celtic folklore. In large part, Mythic's fast turnaround can be attributed to two factors: years of experience creating online text-based RPGs, and the ability to see what the other MMO leaders had already accomplished.

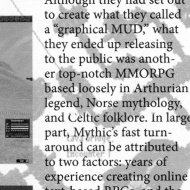

Set in three "realms"—an Arthurian Albion, the Norse-inspired Midgard, and the Celtic-based Hibernia—DAoC initially distinguished itself by its innovative way of approaching the player versus player experience. Each player character would belong to one of the three realms, and within that realm's borders they were safe from attack by other players. However, in areas

that existed outside of any realm, players could freely engage in combat against players from other realms and fight to gain control over various castles. Controlling castles conferred tangible benefits to all members of the winning realm, which added spice to the PvP play.

While some games create special worlds that are PvP- or PvE-only or a hybrid of the two, DAoC's solution to encounters offered the best of both worlds. Those who liked PvP could engage in full-on battles against enemy realms, while players who much preferred PvE play could have a full MMO experience without having to engage other players, all on the same server.

Several expansions followed the original release over the next six years, including Shrouded Isles, Foundations, Trials of Atlantis (which featured many large group quests), New Frontiers, Catacombs, Darkness Rising, Labyrinth of the Minotaur, and "New" New Frontiers.

I had the privilege of writing and designing many of the manuals, as well as a beginner's guide, for Dark Age of Camelot. It was a great opportunity to work with a fantastic team.—RDM

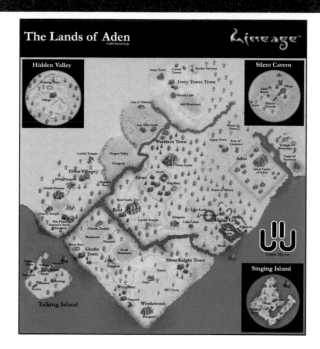

The Lands of Aden

Hidden Valley

Silent Cavern

Singing Island

Talking Island

Lineage

Chronologically appearing before EverQuest, Lineage, an MMO which was based on a popular comic book series of the same name, was launched by South Korean publisher NCsoft, with a subscriber base primarily in Korea. However, it was brought

to the U.S. in 1998, about six months before EverQuest.

Lineage didn't achieve the kind of popularity in the U.S. that it did in Korea, where it had at one time as many as three million subscribers—a staggering number at the time. Despite its comparative obscurity in the U.S. mar-

ket, NCsoft continued to expand into the U.S., first acquiring Richard Garriott's somewhat ill-fated Destination Games. But in 2003, they released the greatly improved Lineage II, which was far more successful in the U.S. than its predecessor, and in 2004 they published Cryptic Studios' popular superhero MMO, City of Heroes.

As of this writing, NCsoft has expanded all over the world, with several studios in the U.S., and continues to publish great MMOs, including Aion and the Guild Wars games from ArenaNet.

And Then...

EverQuest remained the king of MMOs for many years, with expansions every six months at first, then once a year after that. In addition to Dark Age of Camelot, 2001 saw the launches of RuneScape, Ultima Online: Third Dawn, and Anarchy Online.

Screen from Star Wars Galaxies.

Notable in 2002 was Squaresoft's first MMO released in North America, Final Fantasy XI. Asheron's Call 2, which didn't immediately satisfy the old guard players of AC, and The Sims Online also launched that year. Turbine began a beta to revive Asheron's Call 2 in 2012.

By 2003, the MMO gold rush was truly on. EverQuest still dominated, but a variety of new MMOs launched. Not all of them ultimately stood the test of time, but it was notable that the first Star Wars MMO—Star Wars Galaxies—launched that year; as did EVE Online, a game that innovated a dynamic in-game economy and a huge sci-fi world of exploration and combat; and Toontown Online, an MMO for kids from Disney.

2004 was a banner year for MMOs in many ways. There were more expansions from EverQuest, Dark Age of Camelot, Final Fantasy XI, Anarchy Online, Star Wars Galaxies, Meridian 59, Ultima Online, and EVE Online. City of Heroes also launched, while Anarchy Online was one of the first mainstream MMOs to switch to the free-to-play model, which ultimately became more and more common. But one release overshadowed all others. Almost instantly following its launch in November 2004, World of Warcraft became not just another MMO, it was the MMO!

More on World of Warcraft in come in *High Score 3*.

1999

Dreamcast

In 1999, Sega introduced certainly their finest machine of all—the Dreamcast. Although Sega of America had been working on a different machine (code-named Black Belt), Dreamcast was designed by Sega of Japan (originally code-named Dural, later Katana). This excellent 128-bit machine was far superior technically to the PlayStation and N64. It could render 3D graphics at amazing speeds, and it boasted a built-in 56K modem, optional keyboard and mouse, and quite a few innovative features. To support the online capabilities of the system, Sega launched SegaNet, an online gaming network.

At first, Sega's strategy seemed to work, and they quickly sold a million units, almost entirely just after its launch. However, despite Dreamcast's technical superiority and the excellence of its games, it was still up against the established market share of PlayStation and N64.

Moreover, Sega's reputation was working against them. Many potential Dreamcast owners had written Sega off by this time, having endured several failures. Sega had slipped from the second spot to the unhealthy third spot. Even their Sonic Adventure, a direct an-   swer to Nintendo's Super Mario 64, wasn't a strong enough ti-tle, though it had many fasci-nating features, including the use of the Tamagotchi-like memory card to incubate eggs for little pet creatures. Despite some good action seg-ments, Sonic Adventure seemed not to catch on with players in nearly the way that Super Mario 64 had done. Even their strong arcade conversions, innovation, and dedicat-ed support of online gaming, with games like NFL 2K and Phantasy Star Online (not to mention third-party games like Quake III Arena), couldn't unseat PlayStation. History will tell if this was Sega's last console system, but for the moment, it would seem so.

Sonic Adventure (Sega)

Sonic Adventure 2 (Sega)

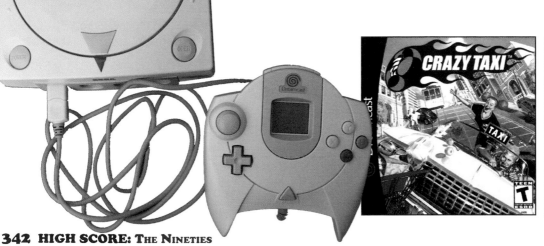

More Dreamcast Titles

Virtua Tennis (*Sega*)

Skies of Arcadia (*Sega*)

AirForce Delta (*Konami*)

Capcom vs. SNK (*Capcom*)

Shenmue (*Sega*)

SoulCalibur (*Namco*)

Mr. Driller (*Namco*)

Phantasy Star Online (*Sega*)

ChuChu Rocket! (*Sega*)

Jet Grind Radio (*Sega*)

Also in 1999...

Power Stone (*Capcom*)

Gunbird 2 (*Capcom*)

Grandia II (*Ubisoft*)

Resident Evil 2 (*Capcom*)

Sony released specifications for its upcoming PlayStation 2 product, while Nintendo kept mostly mum about a system code-named Dolphin and Microsoft, the 800-pound gorilla of the office software market, announced its intention to enter the home console market with something initially code-named Midway. For gamers, the 21st century promised a whole new round of technological improvements and gaming mayhem. And what we knew then was just the tip of the iceberg.

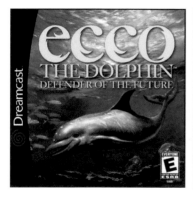

TAMAGOTCHI

Invented in 1996 by Japanese housewife Aki Maita (who was seeking a pet that was easy to care for), the Tamagotchi virtual pet was originally distributed in Japan by Bandai. This little egg-shaped electronic device quickly became an obsession, and when released throughout the rest of the world, it launched a new era of electronic toys, as well as many imitators (including Tiger Electronics' Giga Pets).

The concept behind Tamagotchi was that within the egg-shaped container there resided a cute little alien creature that required your care. It required food, cleaning, play, and sleep. If neglected, it would die. Amazingly, millions of Tamagotchis were sold, and people took them quite seriously. It wasn't uncommon for people to bring them to work to be sure to take good care of them. Ironically, at about the time that Tamagotchi hit, Sega and Bandai were discussing a merger, but that fell through, possibly because Bandai no longer needed Sega—not when they had their cyber pet Tamagotchis.

343

2000

PlayStation 2

The sequel to Sony's PlayStation was well worth the wait. This powerful system set the standard for console makers to match, and its ability to play DVDs added to its mass market appeal. On these pages are screens from just a few of the many phenomenal PlayStation 2 games.

Gran Turismo 3: A-Spec *(Sony)*

Jak and Daxter *(Sony/Naughty Dog)*

Spy Hunter *(Midway)*

Tekken Tag Tournament *(Namco)*

Maximo: Ghosts to Glory (*Capcom***)**

Silent Hill 2 *(Konami)*

NBA Street *(EA Sports)* **ICO** *(Sony)* **Metal Gear Solid 2** *(Konami)*

Street Fighter EX3 (*Capcom***)**

Jak & Daxter

Original PlayStation 2 console with the optional blue horizontal stand.

Quake III Revolution *(EA)*

James Bond 007: Agent Under Fire *(EA)*

Wizardry: Tale of the Forsaken Land *(Atlus)*

Knockout Kings 2002 *(EA Sports)*

Dead to Rights *(Namco)*

Midnight Club: Street Racing *(Rockstar)*

Pac-Man World 2 *(Namco)*

Unreal Tournament *(Epic Games)*

Ready to Rumble: Round 2's Lulu Valentine

Dynasty Warriors 4 *(Koei)*

Super Bust-A-Move *(Taito/Acclaim)*

Mortal Kombat: Armageddon *(Acclaim)*

Dead or Alive 2: Hardcore *(Tecmo)*

State of Emergency *(Rockstar)*

Gauntlet: Dark Legacy *(Midway)*

Ridge Racer V *(Namco)*

Grand Theft Auto III *(Rockstar)*

Star Wars: Starfighter *(LucasArts)*

Madden NFL 2002 *(EA Sports)*

NCAA March Madness 2002 *(EA Sports)*

345

2001

Pikmin: Miyamoto's signature game for the GameCube.

Game Boy   Advance and GameCube

As far back as 1996, Nintendo had plans for a new generation color handheld device code-named "Atlantis." However, development of the system was on-again, off-again. Several generations of Game Boy did come out, including Game Boy Pocket, Game Boy Light (a backlit Game Boy available in Japan), and Game Boy Color, which, ten years after the product's original introduction, finally brought color to the system. However, it wasn't until 2001 that Atlantis, now called Game Boy Advance, was released.

GameCube

First announced in 1999 and code-named "Dolphin," Nintendo finally released GameCube in time for Christmas 2001, almost simultaneous with the release of Xbox. Despite many rumors and products that were never released, GameCube was the first disk-based system from Nintendo, but it did not use the customary CD-ROM discs, or even the soon-to-be popular DVD format. Nintendo's discs were small optical minidiscs. The system's quality and power are demonstrated by the screenshots from early GameCube releases shown on these pages.

Game Boy Advance Games

Super Mario Advance
(Nintendo)

**Frogger's Adventures:
Temple of the Frog** *(Konami)*

**Mario Kart: Super
Circuit** *(Nintendo)*

Breath of Fire
(Capcom)

GameCube Games

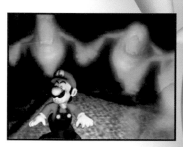

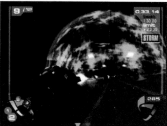

Luigi's Mansion *(Nintendo)*

Super Smash Bros. Melee
(Nintendo)

XG3 Extreme G-Racing
(Acclaim)

Crazy Taxi *(Acclaim)*

Wave Race: Blue Storm *(Nintendo)*

Wave Race Logo

Promotional image
for Luigi's Mansion

WarioWare: Twisted! (*Nintendo*)

The Legend of Zelda: The Minish Cap (*Nintendo*)

Mother 3 (Japan Only) (*Nintendo*)

Madden NFL 2002 (*EA Sports*)

Metroid Fusion (*Nintendo*)

More Game Boy Advance Games

Pokémon: LeafGreen Version (*Nintendo*)

Castlevania: Aria of Sorrow (*Konami*)

Advance Wars (*Nintendo*)

Fire Emblem: The Sacred Stones (*Nintendo*)

Golden Sun (*Nintendo*)

Final Fantasy Tactics Advance (*Square Enix*)

Kirby & the Amazing Mirror (*Nintendo*)

Mega Man Zero (*Capcom*)

Mario & Luigi: Superstar Saga (*Nintendo*)

<table>
<tr>
<td>

More GameCube Games

</td>
<td>

The Legend of Zelda: The Wind Waker (*Nintendo*)

</td>
<td>

Super Mario Sunshine (*Nintendo*)

</td>
</tr>
</table>

Tales of Symphonia (*Nintendo*)

Metal Gear Solid: The Twin Snakes (*Konami*)

Animal Crossing (*Nintendo*)

Metroid Prime (*Nintendo*)

Super Monkey Ball (*Sega*)

Viewtiful Joe (*Capcom*)

Xbox

Microsoft's entry into the world of video games was years in the making, and it took the combined efforts of a number of misfits, bullies, tricksters, renegades, geniuses, and visionaries, combined with a bit of slight of hand and political theater, to help usher in the Xbox era. Storybooks often have one beginning and one ending, but in real life there may be multiple beginnings, and endings are not always fully determined while the story is being told. And so it is with the story of Xbox.

Starting the EBU

In 1991, Tony Garcia left LucasArts where he was director of development and joined Microsoft, initially to work on the Windows Sound System, a sound card that Microsoft hoped to promote primarily for business applications. But being a "game guy," Garcia began thinking about game applications and wondering why Microsoft didn't have a game division. With the support of manager Bruce Jacobsen, he started a small games group with five people in 1992. At the time, Microsoft had a few games like Solitaire, Minesweeper, and Flight Simulator, but nothing else. Garcia ran what was called the Entertainment Business Unit (EBU), which grew to around 150 employees and contractors combined over the years that he was at its head. He also oversaw the acquisition of BAO (Flight Simulator developers) and made the deal to publish Microsoft's first hit game, Ensemble's Age of Empires, shortly before leaving, at which point Ed Fries took over in 1996.

Blood Wake
(Stormfront Studios/Microsoft)

Fuzion Frenzy
(Blitz Games/Microsoft)

Azurik: Rise of Perathia
(Adrenium Games/Microsoft)

Project Gotham Racing
(Bizarre Creations/Microsoft)

Halo: Combat Evolved
(Bungie/Microsoft)

NBA Inside Drive 2002
(High Voltage/Microsoft)

Madden NFL 2002
(EA Sports)

NFL Fever 2002
(Microsoft)

Amped: Freestyle Snowboarding
(Indie Built/Microsoft)

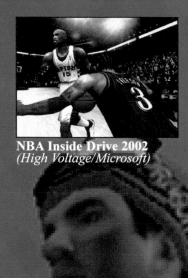

Dead or Alive 3
(Tecmo)

Mad Dash Racing
(Crystal Dynamics/Eidos)

BONELESS • MUTE BACKFLIP
4750 x2

Tony Hawk's Pro Skater 2x
(Activision)

THE GAME OF X

This chapter is a considerably condensed version of
the Xbox story, based on research for an upcoming
book: *Game of X* by Rusel DeMaria. *Game of X* is based
on more than 70 interviews with people involved in
the events and strategic thinking that led the world's
biggest enterprise company to enter the video game
console business.

Garcia's efforts were successful to a point, but they were hampered by timing, such as the switch from DOS to Windows, which caused considerable disruption among PC game developers; technical issues, such as the fact that Windows was initially a terrible platform for games; and finally, perhaps an overly cautious and deliberate approach. In any case, most of the company was either unaware of the games division or, at best, indifferent to it. When Fries took over the division, after a distinguished career in the Office divisions, he was told that doing so was career suicide.

To move games forward at Microsoft required the particular skills and vision that Fries brought to the job, but it also required some vision at the technical level, and a motivation bigger than simply to make games because it might be a good business someday, assuming that Windows ever became a suitable game platform

Fun, Games, and Competition

The proper motivation and group to move things forward at Microsoft made their appearance first in a white paper written by Alex St. John, Eric Engstrom, and Craig Eisler called "Taking Fun Seriously." At the time, St. John was a gamer, but his two partners were not. And their white paper was not primarily meant to convince people of the fun they might have making games; it wasn't meant to glorify game development. It was, in fact, a strategic document in Microsoft's battle against archrival Apple Computer. St. John, Engstrom, and Eisler were all members of Microsoft's Developer Relations Group—a division with the primary (and public) mission of providing support for Microsoft's developer community, which they took very seriously, and a secondary (and secret) mission of disrupting and even destroying competing platforms from major competitors, which they took equally seriously.

As St. John explains it, Apple owned computer video with QuickTime, and none of

Taking Fun Seriously

or "How to own PC games in two years, and take a bite out of the home game console market"

by: Alex St. John, Eric Engstrom, & Craig Eisler

Date: 11/18/1994

What's important about games?

The term "Multimedia" among DOS game developers today is a euphemism for "Poor game technology" or put another way "the best game technology GUI OS's can support" It's lets graphic, less interactive, and generally less dynamic than the kinds of interaction found in most modern DOS, and console video games. We recognize that multimedia technology will be extremely crucial to the success of Windows in the home, yet our "multimedia" technology to date does little to substantially distinguish itself from the functionality provided by our nearest competitors in this area, Apple, and IBM. We place an enormous emphasis on video technology, but is this because video is really the most important component of multimedia, and demanded consumer feature, or simply that it's the easiest problem to solve on a platform like Windows, and the only efficient form of distribution for mass market entertainment until the computer came along? The fact that the arcade business was bigger than the movie box office last year would tend indicate that interactivity is at the heart of today's consumer entertainment requirements.

To date most of the successful Windows based "games" have been little more than a series of beautifully rendered still frames, some animation, hot buttons, and maybe a video transition between scenes. Games that make serious money are consistently real-time dedicated applications. Ironically, Microsoft sells the number one PC based video game. Flight Simulator... a DOS application, and the folks who develop it for us steadfastly insist that it cannot be done as well under Windows. Further Sega+Nintendo titles pocket 87% of the revenue in the 4.5 billion dollar home entertainment market, while Windows is less than 1%... so consumer is writing Sega titles too.

Say why don't we fix that, eat DOS once and for all, grab a real chunk of that cash, and get a multimedia technology jump on IBM, SGI, and Apple a year wide, with a relatively minimal investment in solving some of the problems? Enter the Manhattan Game SDK, and a strategy for making Windows the premier game OS.

Executive Summary

Objectives
- Use Manhattan game SDK to enable Systems, ACT, and Consumer
- Kill DOS as game OS in two years
- Grow PC game revenue against console game machines

Market Observations
- Game market is huge
- Console market is in decline and must re-invent itself next year
- PC game market is severely suppressed because of difficulties with game installation, piracy and little hardware innovation under DOS for games.

Prepared by Alex St. John,
Eric Engstrom & Craig Eisler   *Microsoft Confidential*

Microsoft's video applications had come close to dislodging QuickTime's dominance. His idea was to dominate where Apple was weak, because Apple, and most importantly Steve Jobs, was not interested in video games.

At the time, Microsoft and Bill Gates weren't overly enthusiastic about video games on Windows, either, and given the platform's technical limitations, neither were game developers. Having determined their anti-Apple strategy, St. John and company refused to let technical details get in the way. By looking under the hood they discovered a way to make games work really well under Windows 95, essentially bypassing the extra services and bloat that Windows required, but games did not. However, to implement their vision they needed to work in stealth mode and perform some major feats of mirection and political ninjutsu to fend off other internal groups with competing interests.

The result of their efforts was DirectX. While Engstrom was designing and Eisler was coding, St. John, who was a brilliant provocateur and disrupter of the status quo, was using his considerable intelligence and talents to cause all kinds of trouble… trouble designed to distract people from what his partners were doing. He fended off the rival Windows NT division and numerous rival visions of how PC graphics should be handled. In addition to his natural abilities, he implemented the principles of the Chinese classic, The Art of War, taught to him as part of his DRG training by a shadowy figure at Microsoft who remained virtually invisible for years.

In the end, DirectX prevailed over its rivals and opened the door for high-quality games on the PC. This was a step in the right direction, and under Fries' management and the DRG's evangelism, Microsoft's game division slowly gained some traction in the industry. However, this was just the first salvo. The real goal at Microsoft was always to dominate the living room—to see PCs as ubiquitous appliances, all running Microsoft platforms and applications. But PCs were usually found in offices. It was the game consoles that were common in living rooms.

> *"Without those three guys, Windows gaming would have stalled for years, and my guess is that the Xbox would never have happened."*
>
> —Zack Simpson, former lead software engineer for Origin Systems

Some of Alex St. John's Microsoft relics, including his infamous "DirectAxe." Yes, there's a story...

Xbox Begins

Otto Berkes

Ted Hase

There are dozens of stories about the Developer Relations Group, and especially about Alex St. John and his over-the-top antics and events (many of which will be covered in depth in my upcoming book, Game of X), but the next step toward Xbox actually occurred soon after St. John left Microsoft.

It may have started toward the end of 1998 with some very casual hallway conversations between Otto Berkes, who was in charge of DirectX and OpenGL development, and Ted Hase, a DRG games evangelist. They were pondering the future of DirectX as a platform. "The conversations naturally led to looking at the console market," remembers Berkes, "looking at it through the lens of business, technology, and the developer ecosystem. You know, at that time, Sony was in its ascendancy. PlayStation was the hot new thing."

Over time, the discussion became more intriguing, and so they invited two guys with game backgrounds to join them informally: Kevin Bachus and Seamus Blackley. Although Berkes and Hase were initially considering a console-like version of a Windows PC, Bachus and Blackley were instantly envisioning a full-on Microsoft console like the PlayStation. Of course, everybody knew that was impossible, but people can dream, right?

The meetings continued, however, in Building 4, which Berkes said he preferred because the food was better there. It wasn't long before they decided to recruit one more co-conspirator—Nat Brown, a very bright guy stuck in an exceedingly dull job, and a guy who knew how to get things done. Brown was also a nose-to-the-grindstone researcher. Together, they began to form a plan, and Brown did background research on various possible approaches such as logo programs in which Microsoft would set standards for what would be officially recognized (logoed) third-party, DirectX-enabled Windows game PCs. He also delved into Sony's PlayStation finances and business model and sought weaknesses that could be exploited and used to convince Bill Gates to support their ideas.

By this time, the five co-conspirators had become serious, and even though they came from different divisions and had no official group or standing to do so, they began to strategize their approach and write papers to support it. Blackley first gave the project the codename "Midway," in reference to their intention to attack Sony, a Japanese company, with their eventual product. However, the others in the group didn't think it was Microsofty enough, and wanted something a little less warlike. All the alternative names derived from DirectX, as they saw it ultimately as a DirectX-Box, but still a PC dedicated to games. One amusing alternative was the XXX-Box, which Hase quipped was based on the observation that during the video tape wars between Sony's Betamax and VHS, it was in part Sony's resistance to adult content that led to the VHS victory.

The resulting codename for the project was either X-Box or XBOX, or XBox or xBox or Xbox. It was never clearly stated, in part because at the beginning they never wrote it down for fear of letting rival internal groups learn what they were up to. According to Brown, "The initial secrecy and, later, the period of not wanting to send anything specific in email to prevent the Dolphin/WebTV folks from getting their hands on it, meant we talked with a lot of folks internally and externally purely by phone and just said 'xbox.' It got interpreted however they thought it was spelled."

The 'Bill' Meetings

When it was time to present their ideas to Bill Gates, Brown was able to pull some strings and arrange a meeting for the group, ostensibly to talk about something he had worked on and a hot button for Gates—Unified Graphics Architecture (UGA). The meeting took place on April 30, 1999, and it did start by talking about UGA. But Brown then steered it toward the information he had gathered about PlayStation, showing Gates their sales volume, profitability from games, overall profitability, unit volume, and software attach rate. The data showed that PlayStation had turned out 120 million units, in the range of $60 per unit. "Those are very attractive numbers," says Brown. "Those are 'Bill realm' numbers."

They ended the first meeting by presenting their idea of a controlled environment system that would rival console performance, to be built by third-party hardware manufacturers (OEMs). They described the system in a way that shamelessly hit a lot of Gates' hot buttons, like how slowly PCs boot and how file systems get corrupted over time. By defining their ideal machine in such a way that it would be fast booting and have a clean, uncorrupted operating and file system, they would solve many of the problems that concerned Gates about Windows PCs.

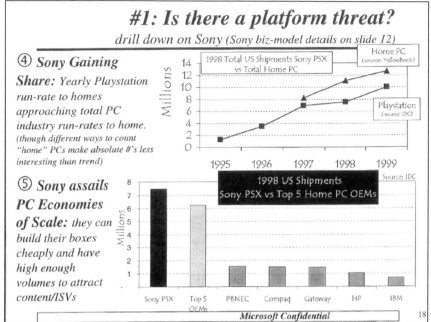

#1: Is there a platform threat?
drill down on Sony (Sony biz-model details on slide 12)

④ **Sony Gaining Share:** *Yearly Playstation run-rate to homes approaching total PC industry run-rates to home.* (though different ways to count "home" PCs make absolute #'s less interesting than trend)

⑤ **Sony assails PC Economies of Scale:** *they can build their boxes cheaply and have high enough volumes to attract content/ISVs*

1998 Total US Shipments Sony PSX vs Total Home PC

Home PC (source: YellowBook)

Playstation (source IDC)

1998 US Shipments Sony PSX vs Top 5 Home PC OEMs

Source: IDC

Microsoft Confidential

18

One of the prime strategies used to convince Bill Gates to support the idea of a Microsoft console was to hammer on the threat from Sony's PlayStation business. Here is one of several slides dealing with the PlayStation threat, taken directly from a PowerPoint deck, which was presented to Gates at a meeting in May of 1999.

range of people, including managers who were technically above the five guys who had just made this proposal to Bill Gates, and they got a ration of grief for it. But they had Gates' attention and had achieved their early goal.

What ensued was a months-long series of meetings, initially with Gates, and later, in July, with Gates and Microsoft president, Steve Ballmer. But at the second meeting, the skunkworks Xbox team encountered an unpleasant surprise. Gates had invited rivals to the party, including VP Craig Mundie, who was representing the WebTV group, the ex-3DO team that Microsoft had recently purchased for over $400 million. There were also representatives of the Windows CE group, who had recently been working on an operating system for the Sega Dreamcast. Both groups claimed to have the experience to take over any project that Microsoft decided to undertake, and Mundie was a very highly-placed executive who outranked them several times over.

In a series of subsequent meetings, the Xbox team continued to hammer at Mundie's groups, provided demos of fast-booting PCs, and fought to convince Gates, and eventually Ballmer, that their vision was the best one for the company. They enlisted the support of Ed Fries; Robbie Bach, who was then the head of the consumer division; Rick Thompson, head of hardware; Rick Rashid of Microsoft Research; and others to help make their case.

Seamus Blackley

In the end, Gates gave the greenlight and the money needed to begin building the Microsoft console system, which he insisted would be powered by Windows.

OK. Maybe

In September 1999, Gates put Microsoft veteran J Allard in charge of the project along with Rick Thompson, who had already been tapped to run the hardware side in a previous meeting in July. Thompson didn't want the responsibility. He already had a full-time job, but the day after the meeting he says, "Steve Ballmer showed up in my office with a baseball bat in his hand, literally, and off I went to go work on the beginnings of the Xbox."

Allard had not been involved in any of the previous meetings. In fact, he had been on a long sabbatical and wasn't all

Kevin Bachus

Nat Brown

After the meeting, Gates fired off an email to a wide

355

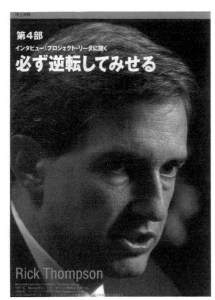

第4部
インタビュー：プロジェクト・リーダに聞く
必ず逆転してみせる

Rick Thompson

Rick Thompson on the cover of a Japanese magazine.

J Allard

that interested in coming back to work. But Gates wanted him because it was Allard who had first introduced the promise of the internet to Bill Gates back in 1995, which prompted a famous memo from Gates—"The Internet Tidal Wave"— and radically changed the focus of the company. Allard had a very special relationship with Gates— so much so that, about a month after being given the project, when it became clear that the Xbox machine would not be able to run a full version of Windows but just a basic kernel with DirectX, Allard was the one who was able to withstand Gates' wrath and get him to accept the inevitable.

Allard had his own people, including his close associate Cam Ferroni, and very few of those who had worked on the Xbox concept up to that point were chosen to join Allard's team. Hase and Bachus stayed with DRG; Berkes went back to his work with DirectX and OpenGL (though not happily); and Blackley, who had initially thought he might lead the group, started the Advanced Technology Group, pulling together a lot of very talented engineers who wrote hundreds of examples of sample code to help developers get up to speed on using the new console.

Meanwhile, the Xbox project was not fully greenlit. Initial efforts focused on planning the hardware, software, and architecture and determining costs. There were fewer meetings, but everyone knew that the project could be cancelled at any time. In fact, there were other meetings going on that could have killed it. Microsoft was looking to purhcase either Nintendo, Sega, or Squaresoft—even going so far as to make offers in the latter two cases. Gates had meetings with the head of Sony to try to convince him to power the PlayStation 2 with Windows, which was unlikely to happen but came too late in any case.

The Moment of Truth

The moment of truth arrived on February 14, 2000. Bill Gates had already been scheduled to speak (and announce Xbox) at GDC in March, but neither he nor Ballmer were completely convinced. This was the do-or-die meeting, known by those who attended it as the "Valentine's Day Massacre." It began just after 4 p.m. and went on for hours while Gates and Ballmer grilled everyone associated with the project. Among those in attendance were Ed Fries, Robbie Bach, J Allard, Craig Mundie, Rick Rashid, Kevin Bachus, Seamus Blackley, Rick Thompson, and a bunch of other Microsfoft senior managers and VPs.

The main points of contention revolved around the finances and business model. As some, like Ballmer and Thompson saw it, they would be selling a $500 device for $300 and losing money on each transaction. In addition, the model had changed from an OEM-built machine to something Microsoft would be manufacturing, along with all the attendant risks. There was no question that on the hardware at least, Microsoft stood to lose billions of dollars, in particular because of the controversial inclusion of a hard drive in the system that would not become cheaper over time, as other components would. Capacity would go up, but price per unit would not.

In the end, however, it was not about price and profit or loss—not directly. It came down to competition. As Ed Fries remembers it, "At some point, Craig Mundie said basically, 'Well? What about the competition?' Meaning Sony, of course. And Bill and Steve looked at each other, and their expressions kind of changed, and Bill says, 'You know, we should do this.' Steve says, 'Yeah, we should do this.' And then they completely changed, you know, 180 degrees from where they were. They turned back to us and said, 'You know, we're going to give you guys everything you need, and we're going to let you go off and be your own part of the company. We'll give you all the resourc-

> "I went to sell Sega to Microsoft, but Mr. Okawa screwed that up… it was a deal that was cut, and he went back again, like twice, to get more money, and Gates finally said no."
>
> -Bernie Stolar, then president of Sega of America

es that you're asking for, and we want you to go off and do this thing and make it be successful.' And that part lasted about five minutes. And then the meeting was over." Yes, there are different stories that people tell, but if Fries' recollection is correct, it was former rival Craig Mundie who saved the day. After that meeting, neither Gates nor Ballmer ever second-guessed the decision, and Xbox went into full development.

Announcement

Gates took the stage at GDC 2000 as planned and announced Xbox, showing demos that were really running on a PC backstage. On stage was a fancy metal X-shaped box designed by Blackley, a prototype that had been used to help sell the concept to potential developers in the previous months. While Blackley assisted Gates on stage, Bachus was backstage managing the actual machines. The event was a huge success, and the race was on!

Rick Thompson, who had led the hardware division for years and helped develop the hardware plan for Xbox, left Microsoft soon afterward, saying that it was simply "against my religion" to support a product that was designed to lose money. His departure was a big loss, but Todd Holmdahl, who had already been leading much of the development, took over and completed the hardware development. Meanwhile, Allard's team completed the software systems and Ed Fries concentrated on getting titles for the console, an effort that included the acquisition of Bungie Studios and the greenlighting of a game that would put Xbox on the map—Halo. (For more about Bungie and Halo, *see page 362*.)

The rapid development of a world-class console system in under two years sounds like a big challenge, and it was. It was not without its hiccups and some thorny moments, but overall the process went amazingly well. According to Holmdahl, "The general architecture was pretty straightforward. We were basically creating a computer that runs the best DirectX-based GPU that you could find at the time and just having it be dedicated to running video games." There were issues with DVD/CD drives that took some time to resolve as well as some confusion with CPUs. The CPU issue got ironed out first, but the problem with the optical drives persisted almost to the last minute. And then came the 9/11 attacks, right at the critical time when they were trying to finalize the consoles. With everything shut down for four days, they had to charter a plane to fly units from the factory in Guadalajara, Mexico, and then work around the

clock to test them. Holmdahl remembers it well: "So we got all the units in—I remember it was a Saturday—and we unloaded them in the parking lot of Millennium D for people on the team to take them home that weekend and test them out. We had an instruction sheet for everybody to use in testing them out. People were sticking in DVDs and playing games, playing with the dash, and trying the controller out all through the weekend. We were using that to gather information in order to make a decision and assess the viability of the product."

Blue Screen Machine?

Xbox was merely an internal codename for the console project. Don Coyner, who was working on market research, recalls that when they asked people what they thought about different companies making a console, such as Apple or Microsoft, the typical response was, "Well, if Microsoft made a video game console it would blue screen all the time, it would take three minutes to boot up, and the best game they would have would be Flight Sim."

The only areas where Microsoft was viewed positively was in their understanding of how to handle online applications and the fact that they had enough money not to bail on it without giving it a chance to succeed. Maybe it was best not to lean heavily on the Microsoft name. The system needed a highly marketable name of its own, but even after generating hundreds of possible names, they weren't yet satisfied.

They decided to hire an expensive naming company to come up with something flashy. According to Kevin Bachus, "They asked us things like, if it was a car,

Bill Gates and Seamus Blackley, with the famous Silver X prototype, announcing Xbox at GDC 2000.

Gates also introduced Xbox at the Consumer Electronics Show in January 2001 and was joined by "The Rock."

what kind of car would it be? Or like, describe it like you would describe a person, and that kind of stuff. So we answered all these questions. They came back with a list of names and they were all terrible. They all actually sounded like car names. The Allterra, the Lanca, and that kind of stuff." After rejecting the first wave of names, the company regrouped and came back all excited, promising a name that would knock their socks off: "Microsoft 11X." That was it. Bachus again: "So I turn to Don Coyner and he goes, 'Yeah. I'll go work on the Xbox trademark.'"

Launch

As the launch date approached, one of the remaining concerns was over the launch title that would drive

sales. They were betting on Halo, but according to Robbie Bach, "Literally, it wasn't until three or four weeks before launch that we knew we had a success."

The actual U.S. launch of Xbox took place in New York at a brand-new Toys"R"Us in Times Square on November 15, 2001. The store was so new that it was still two weeks away from opening, but Microsoft made a deal and turned it into an Xbox launch party. Every billboard in Times Square had Xbox lit up, and Bill Gates was in attendance to give away the first Xbox at midnight.

At the time of its launch, Xbox was technically a match for PlayStation 2, although the two systems had very different architectures, and so it's difficult to compare and categorically say one was better than the other. One area where Xbox did have an advantage was in graphics, where it supported traditional vertex and pixel shaders, and a dedicated transform and lighting unit. The addition of an 8GB hard drive, a first for game consoles, added flexibility and power to the system, and built-in broadband set the stage for some of the system's most powerful game experiences as well as digital downloading. Marketing primarily to hardcore gamers and featuring Halo as their launch title, with a backup cast including Oddworld: Munch's Oddysee; Project Gotham Racing; plus upcoming titles like Splinter Cell, MechAssault, The Elder Scrolls III: Morrowind; and titles from recently acquired Rare, Ltd., such as Banjo-Kazooie and the GoldenEye franchise, Xbox was off to a strong start. A year later, with the successful launch of Xbox Live, they sealed their position as one of the top consoles of the time. However, as predicted, the original Xbox lost billions—by some estimates $8 billion or more—and the franchise didn't begin to earn a profit until the Xbox 360.

A happy Bill Gates at the Xbox launch.

Xbox launch announcement postcard, front and back.

An Early Xbox marketing postcard.

I think we knew that Halo was going to be a big hit by then, and it was going to be good enough to drive the sales of the platform. So by the time we actually hit the launch, it was relatively stress-free in comparison to the time leading up to it.

–Beth Featherstone, senior director, Xbox Global Marketing

Burnout 3: Takedown (*Electronic Arts/Criterion Games*)

More Xbox Games

Conker: Live & Reloaded (*Microsoft /Rare*)

Munch's Oddysee (*Oddworld Inhabitants*)

Crimson Skies (Microsoft/*Zipper Interactive*)

Steel Battalion (*Capcom*)

The Elder Scrolls III:Morrowind (*Bethesda Game Studios*)

Prince of Persia: The Sands of Time (*Ubisoft*)

Fable (*Microsoft/Lionhead*)

I've never seen one like that before...

Ninja Gaiden (*Tecmo*)

Star Wars: Knights of the Old Republic (*BioWare/ LucasArts*)

BUNGiE

To be perfectly clear, Bungie's company name has nothing to do with bungee jumping. All the same, the company has seen its share of gravity-defying moments. In fact, if it takes courage to jump off a bridge with a big rubber band attached to your ankles, it's nothing compared with the risks the developers at Bungie have taken in their pursuit of perfection in gaming.

Alex and Jason respectively. Seropian had created some games previous to meeting Jones, including a Pong clone spelled Gnop! (Pong backwards, in case you didn't notice), and Operation Desert Storm, which he programmed, packaged, and sold as Bungie's first commercial

Bungie's first offices.

Jason Jones communicating his appreciation of the camera.

The Right Chemistry

It all started in 1991 when somehow Alex Seropian, despite being jealous of his "fancy" computer rig, partnered up with Jason Jones after sharing a class in artificial intelligence at the University of Chicago. As is often the case in video game history, one person turned out to be "the business guy," while the other turned out to be "the creative guy." That would be

Alex Seropian in the early Bungie offices.

game. Operation Desert Storm sold 2,500 copies and was followed by Jones' Minotaur: The Labyrinths of Crete for the Macintosh in 1992. Minotaur was notable for its multiplayer focus; its single-player mode was more or less available so that people could discover the secrets of the maze, but it was designed as a multiplayer game. The tagline, "Kill your enemies. Kill your friends' enemies. Kill your friends," appeared in future games, such as Myth: The Fallen Lords and Halo 3.

Bungie in the "South Side"

Bungie's original office was in Chicago, but not in the classy part of town. Their second-floor office, described as a "room and a half," shared the neighborhood with at least one crack house and suffered at least a couple of break-ins. Bungie composer Marty O'Donnell reminisces that it "smelled like a frat house after a really long weekend." Others compared it to something out of Silent Hill.

Pathways

After adding a few more employees to round out the team, in 1993 Bungie released their first profitable game—Pathways into Darkness for the Mac, a Wolfenstein 3D-inspired shooter. Pathways was a critical and financial success, winning several awards. At the time, Bungie was poised to become one of the leaders in the small field of Mac game developers, and their next release was the first of several increasingly popular Mac hits. Originally intended to be a sequel to Pathways, their late 1994

Marathon

release, Marathon, was an evolution in Bungie's continual rise in quality. After months of crunch time—long, grueling hours every day for six months—the team released their first milestone game. Marathon innovated by adding new features to the shooter genre: the ability to use the mouse to look up and down in addition to the standard side-to-side, along with vertical map elements. The game also expanded Bungie's growing commitment to story in games; they even provided virtual computer terminals that allowed players access to more of the backstory and game fiction. Marathon was Bungie's first game

to garner attention from the press outside the small world of Mac gaming, at the same time serving as the Macintosh alternative to PC shooter games like DOOM.

With Bungie's even more successful Marathon sequel, Marathon 2: Durandal, they made the decision, wildly unpopular with their Mac fans, to port the game to the Windows operating system. For the first time, they weren't a Mac-only developer, beginning their gradual but necessary evolution away from Mac exclusivity.

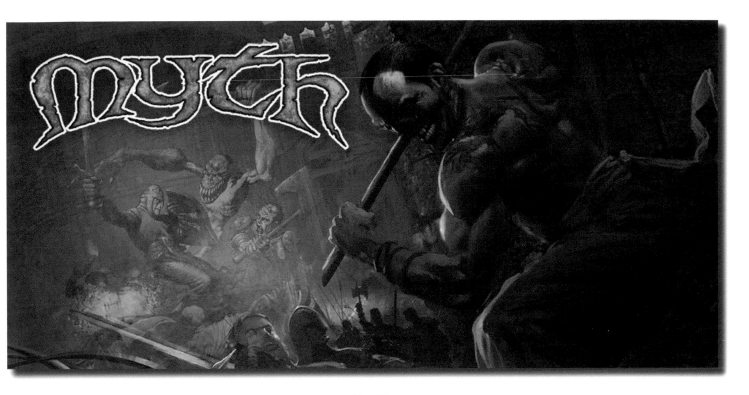

Myth

Not only did Bungie move away from their Macintosh roots, but they also moved away from shooters to create the wildly popular Myth series of strategy games. Myth: The Fallen Lords, which released simultaneously on Mac and Windows 95 machines in 1997, did away with resource grinding in favor of a sophisticated combat engine that allowed for terrain and weather effects, realistic physics, effectiveness of unit formations, friendly fire, and experience/ stat improvements for individual units. Battlefield casualties and damage did not dissolve away as in most games, but remained as a visual, and often grisly, reminder of what had occurred. Myth, like other Bungie games to come, featured both solo and multiplayer modes as well as a deep storyline. The first installment of Myth sold at least a million copies and was followed by Myth II: Soulblighter.

Myth II

Soulblighter sort of lived up to its name by being shipped with a serious installer bug that could nuke the player's system. A massive recall of 500,000 copies ensued. It was, in the words of composer Marty O'Donnell, "A million dollar mistake."

Despite their growth and success, the company was just winging it. As O'Donnell said, in retrospect, "I definitely didn't think Bungie was going to last. It didn't seem like they had a real plan for the future." Jason Jones' assessment: "We had the advantage 20 years ago of being really stupid. I mean, being really young, but that young is stupid." In contrast, Seropian had a more positive way of looking at it. "I think it all starts with the idea that we were our own customer, and that anybody else who was going to play our games, well, we were in their shoes."

Myth II satirical comic
(© Copyright1998 - 2015 Penny Arcade, Inc.)

Oni

Despite the Soulblighter bump in the road, Bungie was doing well enough to open an office in San Jose, CA. Bungie West began work on Oni, a third-person action game that included both shooting and melee combat. Meanwhile, back in Chicago, another project was just beginning.

A lethal uninstaller bug forced Bungie to recall a half a million copies of Myth II. Everyone pitched in to repackage the replacement discs.

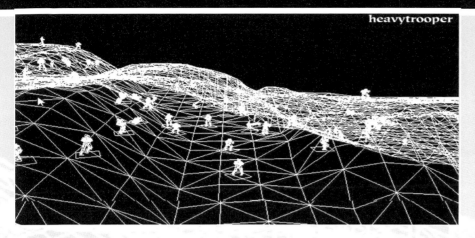
heavytrooper

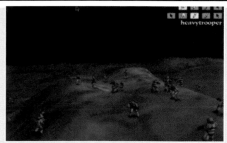
heavytrooper

scoutcar

Left and below: Wireframe and early screenshots for Blam, the early prototype of Halo.

The Next Big No, Really Big Thing

According to Art Director Marcus Lehto, "It started out with three of us making what we thought was going to turn out to be a Myth-like clone with a sci-fi skin on it." It was called Blam, but at first it wasn't really clear what it was going to be. It had tanks and guns and stuff, and a huge map. They knew they had a problem with their goals of combining action gaming with an RTS. As Jones recalls, "We did a lot of thinking about what it meant to be an action game, and could an action game be a real-time strategy game, and the answer was no."

As they experimented with different perspectives, they came to realize that the closer they could take the player into the action, the more involving it became, and ultimately they took the player all the way—inside the hero, in the first-person view. In retrospect, it was a moment of brilliance. It's not that they were the first to create a first-person shooter—far from it—but it is probably one of the decisions that added an all-important refinement to their vision of the game, which they proceeded to execute brilliantly. Where many games start with a very clear design concept, Bungie worked their way in steps toward a solution that was to have a monumental impact on their future, and on the gaming public.

Inside the hero. All the way in.

What's the Score?

Marty O'Donnell remembers the key words he was given for the game's memorable score: "Ancient. Epic. Alien." O'Donnell delivered a powerful piece of music, with pounding kettle drums, moody cellos, and haunting voices, and the day after the score was first delivered, the team was off to Macworld in New York to show the game they had come up with…

They Called It Halo

Halo previewed at Macworld in November 1999. It wowed the audience. It wowed Steve Jobs. Halo looked like a rousing success, but they still had a lot to do. The game was not finished.

Steve Jobs introduces Jason Jones...

...and Jones blows everybody's minds.

A Call from "The Man"

For years, Bungie had considered buyout offers from larger companies, but for various reasons had declined them. But they really needed to do something to complete a project as ambitious as Halo. That's when Ed Fries, head of Microsoft's game division, stepped in. Fries was looking for something with the necessary wow factor to launch with their upcoming Xbox console, and he thought Halo might just be it... if the Bungie team could deliver what their demos promised. So Fries made an offer. It was a huge risk for both companies. Fries and his team were betting on Bungie to produce the blockbuster title he knew he needed for Xbox, and Bungie was looking at creating their first console game—and it had to be not just good, but great! Moreover, it meant leaving the familiarity of Chicago and uprooting everything to move to Seattle. On the other hand, it meant funding, a suite of modern offices on the Microsoft campus, and a chance to become part of history in the making. Jones is reported to have said, "Microsoft is holding the biggest cannon in the world and they're pointing it right at Sony, and we can be the bullet in that cannon."

There's no question that the decision to sell out to Microsoft was unpopular at first, despite the opportunities it represented. Bungie employees valued their independence, and many viewed Microsoft as "the Man" or the "evil empire." And when Fries first showed them the spiffy offices he had arranged for them, they once again rebelled. "I thought they were going to love it," says Fries, "and they hated it." Instead of cubicles and offices, Bungie wanted what they had always had—a big open space. So they tore down the walls and remade the offices in their image.

Ed Fries takes a risk.

Bill Gates visits the Halo crew. The caption at the top reads, "Money Pit Thu Jun 7 16:32:10 2001."

The Halo team were not particularly happy about joining Microsoft or leaving Chicago.

Inside Microsoft's offices, Bungie had the walls torn down. It was a no-cubicle zone.

Jordan Weisman

In the end, it was the game that mattered, and they had plenty of challenges adapting an FPS to a brand new console. As reality set in, the team refocused and ultimately determined their direction, the real scope of the game, and what Halo was really about. They knew they had the chance to be the launch title that defined the Xbox, but they also knew that Fries had other options, such as Malice and Oddworld: Munch's Oddysee. "It wasn't preordained that it was going to be Halo. Halo earned that right by being one of the best titles in development at the time," said Chief Creative Officer Jordan Weisman.

As they had from the beginning, the Halo team relied on their instincts, mad skills, and a passion for perfection. They also worked their asses off to realize their vision as it came more and more clearly into focus.

Controlling the Controller

One of the major challenges facing the Halo team was adapting the first-person shooter genre to the console. They knew they had to nail it. If they failed to move the action from keyboard to controller, Halo would fail. To make the challenge even more difficult, they were working on a brand-new console system. However, they successfully invented a new way to play on consoles, remapping actions and skills to buttons, dual sticks, and triggers. It was different, and it required that players change they way they played on consoles, but that didn't deter many for very long. What Bungie introduced in Halo: Combat Evolved has become the template for

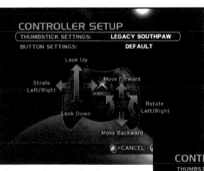

almost all console shooters that followed.

Telling Stories

What every Halo fan knows is that this was a game that soared, not only

in gameplay and technical wizardry, but in story and depth. The introduction of Master Chief; his virtual sidekick, Cortana; and the Convenant took the game far beyond a mere shooting contest and into something bigger, deeper, and, as we experienced it, far more important.

Teamwork

As part of the Microsoft deal, the rights to both Myth and Oni were sold to Take-Two Interactive. Oni was finally released in 2001 to mixed reviews, but after the sale, some of the team moved up from San Jose to help with Halo development. In the end, everybody at Bungie was absorbed into the Halo team, but even so, they faced the real possibility of missing the all-important deadline. One of the features on the chopping block was multiplayer. It wasn't working well enough, and time was running out. Some people were questioning its feasibility, since it required people to lug their consoles and TVs to a central place to play together. But, as COO Pete Parsons says, "Everybody was pushing to keep multiplayer in, but none of us knew just what it would mean."

What multiplayer meant to Halo was immeasurable. Halo was a monster success, thanks to its unique and challenging gameplay, its deep and compelling storyline, its brilliant graphics, its stirring music and sounds, its kick-ass multiplayer, and well... its everything.

People all over the world played together, with, and against each other in multiplayer. With the release of Halo: Combat Evolved in 2001, Bungie became a rock star and helped catapult the Xbox into serious contention with PlayStation.

Pete Parsons

In terms of bungee jumps, developing Halo was definitely one of those experiences of plunging toward the ground and pulling out at the last minute. But it couldn't hold a candle to the death-defying, gut-wrenching story of the development of Halo 2.

That story will have to wait for *High Score 3*…

Meet Cortana

Cortana may not exist in any real sense of the word. She is just a video game character, and not even a real person in the game, but Cortana is cool, and she's an integral part of the Halo experience. But who is Cortana?

Jen Taylor was the original voice actress who brought the character to life. She remembers how she got the part: "I think I auditioned with a British style act, and then I auditioned with just a vaguely Spanish-y, French-y, German-y sound, and then somebody—I think it was Marty—said, 'Just do your own voice. Get in your lower register, and give that to us.'" And Jen Taylor was Cortana.

369

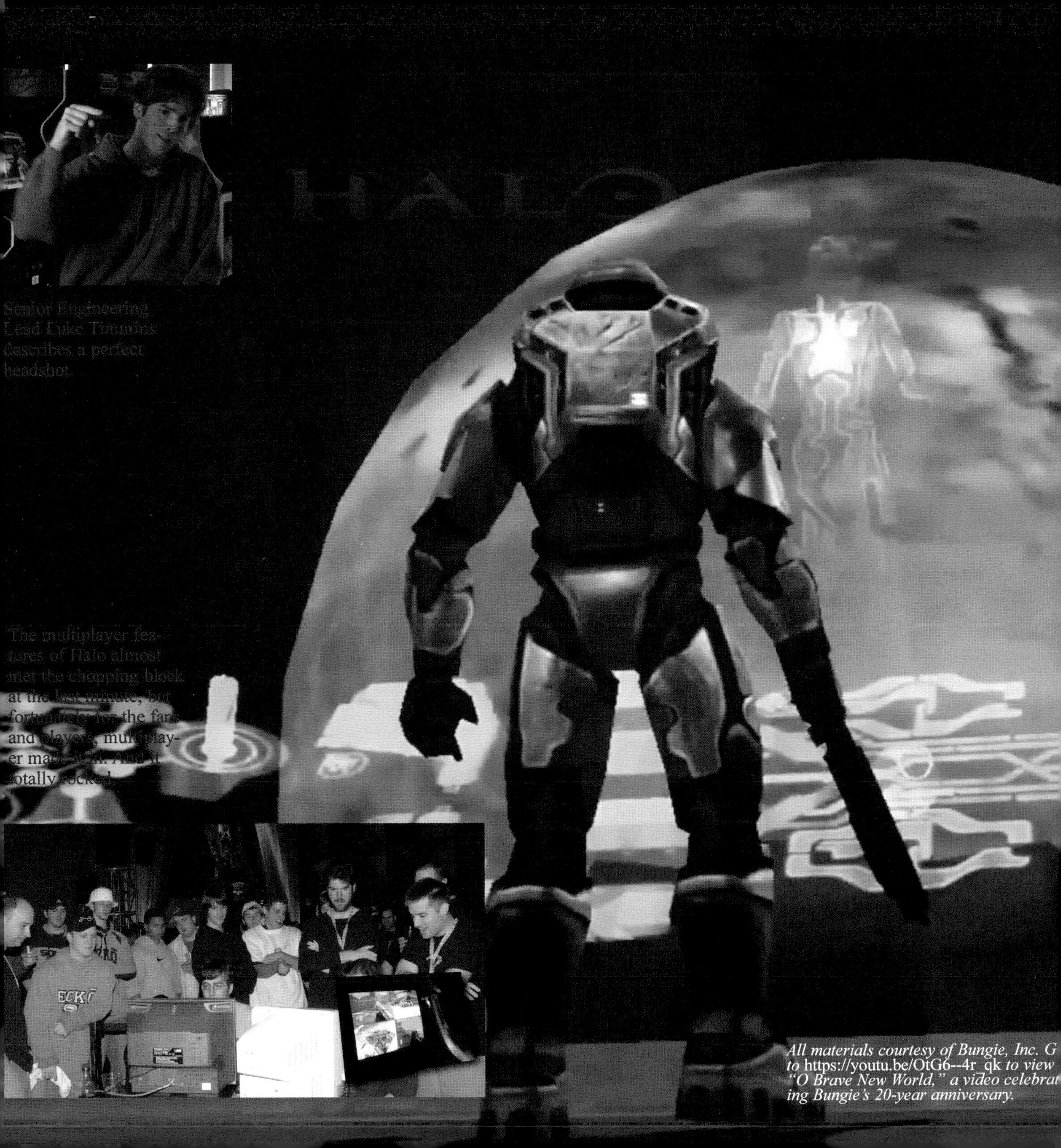

Senior Engineering Lead Luke Timmins describes a perfect headshot.

The multiplayer features of Halo almost met the chopping block at the last minute, but fortunately for the fans and players, multiplayer made it in. And it totally rocked.

All materials courtesy of Bungie, Inc. G to https://youtu.be/OtG6--4r_qk *to view "O Brave New World," a video celebrat ing Bungie's 20-year anniversary.*

ACROSS THE POND

In the original edition of *High Score*, we covered the history of electronic games from a decidedly U.S. perspective. So we thought we'd check with our friends on the other side of the Atlantic to see what the story looked like from there. Of course, we have already mentioned many of the great games that have come from that side of the pond, such as Tomb Raider, Populous, Lemmings, Grand Theft Auto, Donkey Kong Country, Battletoads, Elite, XCOM, Flashback, and Rayman to name only a few. Now we're going to take a closer look.

We started our research expecting the project to be comparatively simple, but we discovered a complex story of individual innovators; companies forming, evolving, disappearing, and reappearing; and products that made history of their own. Particularly in the UK, the cast of characters was just as varied and had just as much impact as in the U.S. Some of them are still in the games industry today. Others have long since gone in different directions. Because it is impossible in the amount of space available to provide a complete picture, this is just a small taste of their rich story.

A Short History of Electronic Games in the UK

Early Adopters in the UK

In Europe, the pioneers of electronic games had their start more on the computer side than the console side. There was no Atari (unless it was an imported machine from the States), so real electronic game development had to wait until the early computer industry emerged. Much like the early computer hackers and pioneers of the U.S., Europe had its own early adopters of digital technology, and inevitably, some of them thought that computers would be perfect for games.

According to Bruce Everiss, an early computer entrepreneur in the UK:

"Before the 1980s if you wanted to buy a computer off the shelf, it would set you back more than £500 (a king's ransom in those days) and would have probably been imported from the States. Therefore, most budding computer owners built their own. After all, if you held an interest in computers, you were probably an electronics nut anyway, used to building radio sets and calculators. Or maybe you'd be an academic or science professional, since the only people lucky enough to use a 'real' computer were those who worked in large universities or research institutes. These early machines may not sound attractive, but it would be foolish to believe that there was no market for them."

Everiss could be thought of, to some degree, as the British equivalent of Paul Terrell, the owner of The Byte Shop in what was to become Silicon Valley (*see page 46*, "Apple: A Modern Fairy Tale"). An accountant by trade, Everiss "begged, borrowed, and stole" to open a shop in Liverpool, which he called Microdigital, in July 1979. The store initially sold Apple, NASCOM, and S100 computers, as well as books and magazines related to computers. It also provided help and repair for kit builders. The company even published a magazine called the Liverpool Software Gazette. According to Eugene Evans (see story on *page 385*), who started

doing odd jobs at Microdigital when he was about 13 and still in school, "It was one of very few computer stores in the UK in 1979, and on Saturdays it was more like a club where a lot of us would hang around, read books, and discuss computers." Unlike his American counterpart, Everiss was outspoken and became something of a personality in England. In 1981, at the age of 22, Everiss received "an offer I couldn't refuse" from a hi-fi chain called Lasky's and helped set up a sort of "store-within-a-store" in the various outlets of Lasky's chain. Within a short time, however, Everiss left, occupying his time with a variety of enterprises ranging from publishing to consulting and ultimately helping run game companies.

Bruce Everiss: Pioneer of the digital revolution in the UK.

One company Everiss consulted with was called Bug-Byte. It was formed by Tony Milner and Tony Baden, both of whom were ex-Microdigital employees and Cambridge graduates with chemistry degrees. They began writing games for the new Sinclair ZX81 and the Commodore VIC-20. Seeing some early success, they hired Dave Lawson, a brilliant self-taught programmer, to help them make games. "Dave had the breakthrough idea of using a more powerful machine to develop games for a less powerful one," says Eugene Evans. "So, using an Apple II with floppy drives and a proper editor, we could write the code, which was in 6502 assembly language, and then just download it over to the VIC-20, which also used the 6502."

Meanwhile, across town, Evans was writing driver software for yet another ex-Microdigital employee who had started the Liverpool Computer Centre and another company called March Communications, which manufactured peripheral boards for Apple II computers. One day, he was delivering a parallel board to Bug-Byte that they would use to connect the Apple and the VIC. "They asked me if I wanted to do a game, and I thought about it and decided it would be fun." Evans programmed a VIC-20 version of the game Alien Panic, which was ported to just about every system. After that, Evans joined Bug-Byte as a game programmer.

The first issue of the *Liverpool Software Gazette*, published November 1979.

Uncle Clive

Clive Sinclair had been making inventions and taking risks in the technology field since the 1960s. By 1980, when he launched the Sinclair ZX80 computer, he had already created a host of products. Some of his failures were dramatic, and in 1976, when his ill-fated Black Watch turned out to be a complete disaster, the only way he stayed in business was with financial infusions from the government. The Black Watch was a futuristic digital watch that used flat panels to display time and date, without the use of any buttons. But it was plagued by problems, not the least of which was that the batteries only lasted ten days, and the chips inside could be fried by static electricity from a wearer's nylon shirt!

Sir Clive Sinclair (also known as Uncle Clive) brought affordable computers to the masses in the UK.

Sinclair has always been an eccentric and restless genius who began his career creating a wide variety of electronic devices, including stereo equipment, calculators, and some digital timepieces. But he is best known today for the computers he helped create. Ironically, his first microcomputer project ended up as an obscure system called New-Brain that was conceived in the late '70s and didn't actually get produced until 1983. His first successful computer was a kit called the MK 14, which sold about 50,000 units to the hobbyist market after its introduction in 1978.

Even as he was entering the newly forming computer business, Sinclair was still developing other products, such as his miniature TV called Microvision, which flopped and ultimately caused the closure of Sinclair Radionics. Sinclair created a new company out of the old Sinclair Instruments Ltd. division and called it Science of Cambridge. It was Science of Cambridge that ultimately released the MK 14 and the ZX80, which appeared in February 1980 at £79.95 in kit form and £99.95 fully assembled. By November of that year, Science of Cambridge became Sinclair Computers Ltd.

Only about 70,000 ZX80s were sold, and it was reputed to be a quirky machine, full of flaws. It was black and white only and lacked sound. "The ZX80 was dreadful, really," recalls Evans, "so bad that when you pressed a button on the keyboard, the screen went black. The processor could only do one thing at a time—handle the keyboard or the screen—not both." However, it was one of the first low-priced computers aimed at home users, not just hobbyists, and nothing else had been seen in its price range other than in kit form. However, in all likelihood, the ZX80 would probably have been long forgotten if it had not been for its successors—the ZX81 and the ZX Spectrum.

The ZX81 would not impress anyone today, and even for its time it was not a breakthrough in technology or capabilities. It had no color or sound, and its touch-sensitive keyboard left much to be desired. What it lacked in impressive technology, however, it more than made up for in price, timing, and good fortune. The ZX81 became a phenomenon, quickly outselling its predecessor in Sinclair's usual mail-order markets. But then the struggling WHSmith newspaper chain, which had stores around the UK, decided to sell the ZX81, and the product took off. By February 1982, sales of the system had risen to 40,000 per month.

With the success of the ZX81, Sinclair teamed up with the watchmaker Timex to create and market the system in the U.S.—the Timex Sinclair 1000—and met with reasonable success. The Timex factory was located in Dundee, Scotland. Timex and Dundee crossed paths again on two other significant gaming creations, but more on that later...

The ZX81 broke the price barrier and set the bar for low-cost computers, sparking a digital revolution in the UK.

Matchless Programmer

Jon Ritman bought his first ZX81 computer at the beginning of 1982 and soon found himself staying up until two in the morning learning all he could about it. Within six months he had completed his first game—Namtir Raiders—which was published by Artic Computing. A born game programmer, Ritman once commented that Namtir Raiders was his first program because "I couldn't think of anything to do with my ZX81 but program a game." Note his name spelled backwards in the title.

In Ritman's own words: "My first attempt at programming a game was really just an attempt to find anything to program, having just learnt how. I had seen an arcade game in a pub (I was camping in the pub's back garden with some mates at the time) and simply tried to copy the rough memory I had of the early levels—I could only do the early levels because I had never been good enough to get any further. When I started this game I had never heard of an assembler, and as a result, I was hand-converting to hex and then entering it with a simple hex editor. Discovering assemblers meant a complete rewrite. Mind you, it was far from easy with the assembler from Bug-Byte only having 256 labels and with the cranky tape-saving system that the ZX81 enjoyed. I think it took about three months to write, but I was working full-time as a TV repairman at the time."

Ritman graduated quickly to the Sinclair Spectrum, and after creating a "truly crap Space Invaders clone" (his words), he created his second commercial game, Cosmic Debris. This was followed by 3D Combat Zone and Bear Bovver, the latter of which caused the words "Ace Programmer" to appear in the

Two of Clive Sinclair's projects—the Black Watch and Microvision—were innovative experiments, but it was the low-cost personal computer in the form of the ZX81 and then the ZX Spectrum that defined Sinclair's success in the '80s.

3D MONSTER MAZE

Few games for the ZX81 were particularly memorable, but J. K. Greye's 3D Monster Maze seems to hold a special place in players' hearts. This first-person maze crawl came out in 1981. It had no sound, blocky and slow black-and-white graphics, and very little in the way of plot or game mechanics.

Compared to maze games such as Wizardry, which came out around the same time, it hardly comes close. But because it was on the ZX81, it stands out as a worthy attempt and is remembered by former British schoolboys to this day.

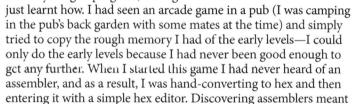

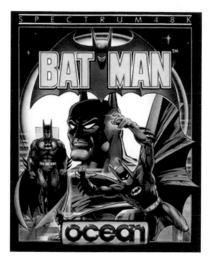

magazines writing about him. All of these titles were published by Artic in 1983.

Ritman teamed up with Chris Clarke, a co-founder of Crystal Computing (which ultimately became the hot game company Design Design), with the idea of creating a top-notch football game. (For the American audience, football = soccer, also known affectionately as "footie.") Having seen International Soccer on the Commodore 64, the pair set about creating a really good game for the Spectrum. They severed connections with Artic to form their own company, resulting in a slight scare when Artic released World Cup Football a week after Ritman and Clarke started their game. But, as Ritman said later, "We weren't too worried once we had seen it."

The resulting game was Match Day, one of the all-time favorite games in the UK. It was published by Ocean Software because, months earlier, Ritman had met some Ocean representatives at a game show and told them he was working on a "superb soccer game. Nine months later they rang and asked if I had written it, and the rest is history." Ritman formed an association with Ocean that lasted for three more game projects.

Riding on the success of Match Day, which was a great two-player game, Ritman had a look at Ultimate's Knight Lore, and, always being interested in gameplay first, he immediately saw the potential of this kind of game. "Just like playing in a Disney cartoon," he told CRASH magazine in a later interview. He decided to see if he could match or better Ultimate's achievement, but he wanted something that would appeal to a wide audience. He wanted a superhero. He got Ocean to obtain a license and then got Bernie Drummond, a friend of his who loved drawing, to do the graphics for the game.

The game took a long time and a lot of effort. "I tend to work in spurts. I don't like to put a problem down until it's solved." Ritman encountered some difficulties with the license. "There was a month delay over the license as well. Batman is not a superhero—he's got no superpowers—he's a detective. The people who own the rights are very careful about what they let people do, and everything had to go to the States first for approval."

With gameplay as his cardinal rule and first priority, Ritman

created a very successful original Batman game. "I'm not an innovator. I take a synthesis of good points. With Batman, take a room for instance: everything you need to solve it is in the room. I try to design a game for everyone, for the games-buying public. I get a lot of satisfaction from writing a game and pleasing people—although the money's nice!"

After Batman, Ritman wanted to revisit Match Day, which remained one of his personal favorite games to play. He added new and advanced features in Match Day II (originally called Three and In). Next came an original and unusual game called Head Over Heels (originally called Foot and Mouth) in which the player basically played the two parts of a split person— Mouth and Foot—with the goal of reuniting the halves. Each body part could solve certain puzzles, but not others, while some puzzles required their combined efforts. Head Over Heels was also very successful.

Ritman seemed to disappear from the game design field after Head Over Heels, despite its success. He spent several years at Rare, Ltd. working on arcade titles, on Game Boy, and on writing the development system for Rare's 16-bit games, including Donkey Kong

Match Day and its sequel were the first big games from Jon Ritman, considered by many to be the best of the early football/soccer games.

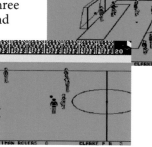

Country for the SNES and Monster Max for the Game Boy. He then formed his own company, called Cranberry Source Ltd., which released QAD: Quintessential Art of Destruction in 1996 and Super Match Soccer for the PC and PlayStation, published by Acclaim in 1998.

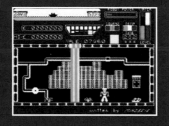
The Acorn Drops

The BBC Microcomputer system from Acorn Computers Ltd. also contributed significantly to the popularity and accessibility of computers in the UK. Acorn was founded by two ex-Sinclair employees, Hermann Hauser and Chris Curry, in 1979. Their first system, the Acorn Atom, was an 8-bit computer with 4K of RAM, sold either as a kit or ready-built. With the success of the Atom, Hauser and Curry began to work on a new system, called the Proton. They intended to include some advanced features such as parallel processing and support for various industry standard peripherals.

While they were working on Proton, an opportunity presented itself. The BBC (British Broadcasting Corporation) was looking for a computer for their computer literacy project, which was inspired in part by a previous BBC documentary, *The Mighty Micro*. The computer selected would be featured on a television show called *The Computer Programme*, which would feature topics such as programming, graphics, AI, sound, and so on. The first system the BBC considered was Sinclair's NewBrain. But it didn't meet their specifications, so they approached both Acorn and another small company, Dragon Data Ltd.

As the story goes, the demonstration of the Proton was scheduled for a Friday, and as of that Monday, Hauser and Curry didn't have a working system. They worked long hours the next few days assembling the machine, but by Wednesday they didn't have it working. At the eleventh hour, they had to put together an operating system; however, the prototype was still not working correctly even at 7:00 a.m. on Friday morning, when a timing issue was discovered and repaired. The meeting, which took place at 10:00 a.m., went well enough for the BBC to approve the Proton—subsequently renamed the BBC Microcomputer—and offer Acorn a contract for 12,000 units.

The BBC Micro (affectionately known as the "Beeb") was featured on a

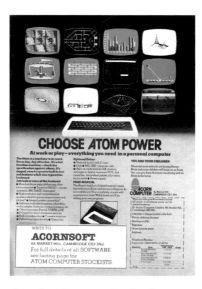

An advertisement for the Acorn Atom that appeared in the January 1982 edition of *Electronics and Computer Monthly*.

The Acorn Atom.

variety of TV shows, starting with *The Computer Programme*, but progressing to several others, such as *The Computer Game Show*, which was reportedly all about keyboards and which used the Beeb for effects. The Beeb was apparently also used to create some of the graphics and special effects in the popular series, *Dr. Who*.

Sales of the BBC Micro continued to grow and, in 1982, the government stepped in and officially backed the computer for use in the school system. Thus, many British kids were first exposed to computers through contact with "the Beeb."

Archimedes

Acorn went on to create more machines and had some successful times, but their major impact on the history of games ended with "the Beeb." In 1989, they did release a powerful RISC-based system called the Archimedes, which featured a small following of gamers. It was not a significant machine in the context of games, but more of a footnote. The interesting

The Acorn Archimedes.

tidbit below came from an anomymous message sent to *Foundation RISK User* magazine, Fred Bloggs being a placeholder name used by programmers:

```
> Just as an aside, there are
    actually quite a
> few Acorn fanatics at Microsoft,
  and it's a
> little known fact that the
  Archimedes version of
> Lemmings was responsible for
  delaying Windows
> 3.1 by about a week because
  a bunch of Windows
> developers refused to get back to
  work until
> they'd completed all the levels!
> 'Fred Bloggs'
> Windows UI Development
```

BBC Micro motherboard.

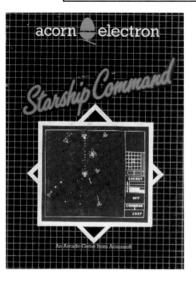

1982: The Full Spectrum

After the BBC Micro and the ZX81, the next really important computer to be developed in the UK was the Sinclair ZX Spectrum. But that's putting it mildly. Certainly from the UK perspective, the Spectrum was important enough to earn Sir Clive Sinclair a fortune, not to mention a knighthood. In collaboration with Timex, the Spectrum was also sold in the U.S. Combined with other international sales, it was by far the most successful computer to come out of the UK. In addition to its legitimate international sales, it was also cloned and copied in many countries in Eastern Europe and Asia.

The Spectrum was designed to compete with popular systems from the States, such as the Commodore 64, and it did a credible job. Gone were the touch-sensitive keys and the monochrome display. The Spectrum's display was in full color, it had a real keyboard, the case was elegantly styled, and best of all, it was inexpensive. Not that the Spectrum lacked problems. One of the main complaints about it was that the keyboard, which—in addition to its bouncy, rubbery keys—was designed so that each key had multiple functions.

Not that the Spectrum lacked problems. One of the main complaints about it was that the keyboard, albeit featuring real rubbery keys, was designed so that each key had multiple functions. The idea was clever—to cram one-key BASIC commands and other functions onto an ordinary keyboard—but in practice many users found it daunting.

There were seven versions of the Spectrum in all, but with the initial launch, there were just two—a 16K version and a 48K version—priced at a reasonable £125 and £175, respectively. The 16K version could be upgraded by another 32K for an additional £60. Peripherals included a disk drive, a serial modem, and a printer. The system was based around a 3.5 MHz Z80A chip, and BASIC was resident in ROM.

The British government and its school system had done a good job of instilling the importance of computers into children's education, and many parents believed that the ZX81, which continued to be produced, and the Spectrum (whose nickname was "Speccy") would join the Beeb as significant learning and working devices. The audience for this low-cost computer that, at last, had color and sound, was vast. And the truth is, what kids did with these machines, whenever possible, was play games.

SWEEVO'S WORLD

"....THE FUNNIEST CARTOON ADVENTURE YOU'LL EVER TAKE PART IN...."

For an intelligent robot, Sweevo is not very bright - he's clumsy, accident-prone and fond of fruit, but not bright. So that when he encounters the Great Dictator, the Horrid Little Girl and the Goose that lays the Golden Erg, his strange faith in apples is shaken to the core......
Confused? You will be, when you enter the outrageous, bizarre and hilarious SWEEVO'S WORLD.

GARGOYLE GAMES LTD
74 KING STREET
DUDLEY
WEST MIDLANDS
DY2 8QB

5 013615 005105

SPECTRUM 48K

SWEEVO'S WORLD

GARGOYLE SPECIAL EDITION

sinclair ZX Spectrum

HUNGRY HORACE

SOFTWARE BY PSION WITH MELBOURNE HOUSE   ROM 16K/48K RAM

Hungry Horace was a popular character who spawned several games.

THE SPLAT CHALLENGE

A totally original game featuring:
ZIPPY
GRASS
RIVERS
PLUMS
SPIKES

7 Levels to Explore.

Progress % Indicator.

High Score Feature.

User Defined Controls.

On Screen Instructions

ALSO WORKS WITH KEMPSTON & A.G.F JOYSTICKS

Splat Evolution by I. Andrew & I. Morgan

SPLAT!

SINCLAIR ZX SPECTRUM

48K

48K SPECTRUM CHALLENGE FROM INCENTIVE SOFTWARE LTD

LOADING SPLAT
Connect the ear socket on the spectrum to the ear socket on your cassette recorder.
Insert the cassette label upwards into your cassette recorder and rewind to the beginning.
Type LOAD"" and then press enter.
Press play on your cassette recorder.
The program will run automatically when loaded. If the program fails to load, rewind the tape and adjust the volume level and try again.

LOUDER SOUND
To amplify the sound effects: connect the mic socket on the Spectrum to mic socket on your cassette recorder. Disconnect ear sockets. Remove cassette and press play on your cassette recorder.

SPLAT © COPYRIGHT 1983
Incentive Software Ltd.
ALL RIGHTS RESERVED WORLDWIDE.
The game and name Splat and all of its Associated Software, Code, Listings, Audio Effects, graphics, illustrations and text are the exclusive property and copyright of Incentive Software Ltd and may not be copied, transferred, reproduced, transmitted, hired, lent, distributed, stored or modified in any form in full or in part without the express written permission of Incentive Software Ltd, 54 London Street, Reading RG1 4SQ, England.

SPLAT!

48K SPECTRUM CHALLENGE FROM INCENTIVE SOFTWARE LTD

Ant Attack: Sandy White in His Own Words...

Sandy White was one of the British game pioneers whose Ant Attack game remains one of the memorable games of the Spectrum era. Ant Attack is certainly one of the first games to introduce an isometric 3D look, although it did come out after Zaxxon*. It was also possibly one of the first to offer a choice of genders for the leading role. And, like many early programmer/developers, Sandy White managed to put his initials into the map.

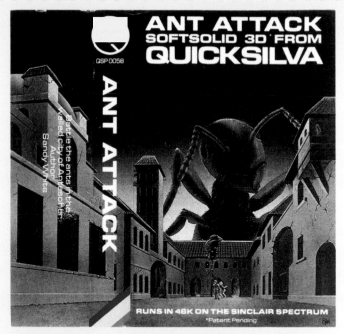

Developers wasted no time developing games for the Spectrum.

"Before writing Ant Attack, I was studying at Edinburgh College of Art, escaping after five years with a degree in sculpture. For much of that time I had been up to my elbows in plaster of Paris, ribbon cable, radio control servos, and Christmas tree bulbs. At the end of '82, I had my own one-man show, which featured three story-telling computer controlled sculptures, each based around the SC/MP chip that was in Sinclair's first computer, the MK 14—that's how I learned to program. It was well received, and even appeared on the telly. Wow! By early '83, like all real artists, I was on the dole. I was 22 when I started writing Ant Attack around March of '83.

Ant Attack sort of evolved. In an attempt to escape from dole-inflicted poverty, I tried to do some work programming an Acorn Atom (6502-based precursor of the BBC computer). It never made me any money, but I did get to borrow the Acorn. It was the first time I'd had a computer with any kind of graphics, as the MK 14 had only a tiny LED calculator display. One idle afternoon I managed to get it to draw a cube, then modified the program so that it drew cubes at random, one on top of the other, lined up by their vertexes. I was amazed to find that it started to draw walls, castles, in fact all sorts of strange and wonderful cityscapes. That was the start of Ant Attack.

Funnily enough, I think I had just seen Superman: The Movie, because the next thing I did was make a little Superman sprite which flew over this weird random landscape, though as history tells, it never occurred to me to make a Superman game. In fact, at this stage it had still not occurred to me to do a game at all! I was still thinking about the sculptural possibilities. Later on, it became apparent that there was a striking similarity between the isometric structures in Ant Attack and etchings by M. C. Escher; so the city was eventually named 'Antescher' in tribute.

I suppose Ant Attack might qualify for being the least designed game in history. Early in '83 I discovered the Sinclair Spectrum—my brother had been given one for Xmas. Suddenly I became aware of games! A few weeks later I had rewritten my Acorn Atom city for the Speccy and was just having fun trying things out. A lot of stuff came out of discussion with my brother and my dad who were really into their Speccy games. I am quite sure someone must have said 'Wouldn't it

379

be cool if you had a little man that could run around in the city.' Basically, I had this engine that drew cubes and did little else, so the first thing I had moving around was a cube. This became a black cube, then a black blob. Then it became a herd of black blobs! What had become interesting to me were the 'flocking' properties that grew out of some simple rules given to the blobs. They could be made to either seek or avoid a cube that you could control with the keyboard. I did at one stage consider doing a sheep

the mnemonics on a sheet of A4, shoving the opcodes in the margin. Trouble was, when you wanted to insert a line somewhere, you had to go back and recalculate all the jump offsets… it was hideously slow. Anyway, once the hex was put together on paper, it was typed into my Softy. The Softy was a ROM emulator with 4 whole K of RAM, which I mapped into the Speccy's memory map via its rear connector. This meant that the whole of Ant Attack had to fit into 4K, leaving aside the data for the city and some BASIC to do

farming game… I bet that would have been a big seller! Anyway, eventually in went a couple of human characters, and because of a bug, one of the blob sprites was drawn as a human and started to follow the other human. Ant Attack was born! The blobs got legs, and it became a kind of hide and seek while avoiding the blobs-with-legs.

People have called it 'technically impressive,' but I don't know about that. Looking back on it, the coding was not particularly fantastic. For instance, I redrew the city every frame instead of simply updating bits that had changed. It is true that it created an impression, though, I'm glad to say. I well remember the press launch; there was a sort of hushed collective gasp—it was the first time anyone had seen isometric 3D! I remember being asked by a writer what exactly I was doing, and struggling to describe it, then recalling the term 'isometric projection' from my memories of school tech drawing classes. The word duly went into gaming vocabulary.

I suppose a big struggle for me was the actual process of coding. I was not using an assembler, as I had never heard of them! This meant that I had to assemble by hand, writing

the scoring screens. Despite all its disadvantages, it did have one enormous compensation. When the Speccy crashed, either because the power supply plug had been wiggled or because of a bug, the code in the Softy was protected and didn't have to be reloaded.

Once I got to the point where I had a semi-playable game, it seemed like a good idea to try and find a publisher. My first thought was to try Sinclair themselves, as Uncle Clive was already my hero from Radionics and MK 14 days, and they were already publishing their own games. I wrote to Clive Sinclair in person, and was a bit disappointed that it was his software manager who replied—still—she sounded positive and asked me to send in a tape. Being very paranoid about the actual code, I sent a video tape of Ant Attack off to Sinclair, only to have it duly returned with a note saying they were unable to view it, as they didn't have a VCR, and suggesting I try some other large software house. I often wonder if they even noticed that they turned down what went on to be a No. 1 bestseller!

Looking around WHSmith's the following day, I picked on Quicksilva as a good alternative, as they were the only publisher at that time who had put out a game with a color sleeve. Everyone else was still at the stage of selling cassettes with black-and-white inserts, many of them simply photocopies, believe it or not. Armed with their number, I duly got onto the phone to Quicksilva. But it was not all plain sailing. I was waffling about this game that had 3D buildings that you could climb on, windows that you could go through, etc., and the reception was, let's say, a little skeptical. I distinctly remember jumping up and down on the floor as I tried to convince the voice on the other end that it was true. It was agreed that I should send down a video tape. Thank goodness QS had a VCR.

The next day they were on the phone. 'We'd like to fly you down to Southampton.' 'Can I bring my girlfriend?' I asked. 'No probs.' So we got on a plane to Gatwick, the first time either of us had flown! We were picked up at the airport by Rod Cousens (who later became Acclaim's CEO) and transported to Quicksilva's Southampton office, cramped into the back of a Ford XR3i. Negotiations began. I thought 50 percent was a reasonable sort of royalty, if a bit generous to Quicksilva, given that they had done none of the work. Yes, perhaps I was a bit naive! I insisted I would go no lower than 25 percent. I think eventually they offered 20 percent and locked us in the Post House hotel until we agreed. We sneaked out early the next morning and flew back to Edinburgh without telling them. The next day I got a call, and they offered 25 percent. Oh yes, we'd been very clever, but not clever enough to specify what it was 25 percent of. Eventually I found I was getting 25 percent of the 'returns,' which means 25 percent of what comes back from the shops—25 percent of 50 percent, or 12.5 percent-ish —a pretty average deal. You live and learn, as they say. Still, it amounted to a fair old amount of dosh, though not by any means the millions that were implied by the press.

In fact, so unworldly was I that I had never even heard of an 'advance,' and more or less had to hitchhike to London for the launch of Ant Attack. Anyway, I digress… The game was not yet finished, and suddenly I was told that for it to be in the shops for Christmas it would have to be completed within a month. At this point a certain amount of planning, and panic, ensued. Whoopee! The scoring screens were written in BASIC for speed, and the code was transcribed by hand from squared paper and into the Spectrum—16K

of hand-compiled data read out as hex numbers and typed in. Meanwhile, cover artwork was being created, blurb written, and the game renamed by QS from Ant Terror—my brilliant name for it (really rolls off the tongue, doesn't it?)—to Ant Attack. I believe they bought the name for a few hundred quid from someone else who had written another Ant Attack. Wonder whatever happened to that?

The cover painting is by talented artist David Rowe, who has since done tons of stuff, like cover artwork for Populous and dungeon interiors for the ITV children's program Knightmare. I asked David how he came up with the Ant Attack cover. 'There would have been a variety of roughs. I liked the Escher references and went for a surrealistic feel to the world and of course a giant ant. I bought a second-hand microscope for £100 (which I still have), captured an ant in a hollowed slide, and drew it from life. I was amazed to discover that they're not black and shiny, but brown, translucent, and hairy. What a mad bastard I was!'

The first time I saw the finished product in a box was at a computer show in London's Barbican, just before the press launch. Everything was very homely by comparison to today's shows. There, standing in a tiny stall with a massive pile of Ant Attack tapes were the founders of Quicksilva. They were selling tapes over the counter like they were hotcakes—it was very exciting! Some bloke called Jeff Minter, from the stall opposite, had apparently been asked what he thought of it, and said it was not bad! At the end of a long day, John Hollis, Time-Gate author and co-founder of QS, asked me where I was staying, and I shrugged, 'Errr… I don't know… I don't exactly have any money.' Certainly, it was true, I was on social security at the time. In a gesture I'll never forget, John opened the stall's till, which had been ringing like a fire bell all day, reached in, and removed its entire contents and thrust them into my hands—a massive, bulging wad of notes.

People ask me if I miss the old days. I suppose there was something quite nice about the fact that you could near enough write a whole game single-handed; but no, I love the sheer pixel power of today's systems too much to want to swap back.

Sandy White's response regarding Ant Attack's 3D environment: "Ant Attack introduced more than the 'look' of isometric; the city map itself was stored in three dimensions down to the last brick. It was effectively a full physical model, rendered in real time using isometric projection, which I think sets it apart from Zaxxon, which will have used a pre-rendered map and is only viewable from one angle... and has strict limits on where you can go within the environment... Yes Zaxxon had the 'look' of isometric, but AA was the full Monty."

381

French version of the CPC 464.

Amstrad

Founded by Alan Michael Sugar, Amstrad (for Alan Michael Sugar TRADing) introduced their CPC 464 home computer in the UK, France, and Germany. Many games were released for Amstrad's CPC (Color Personal Computer) series, although many of them were originally created on other systems such as the BBC Micro or the Sinclair Spectrum.

Dragon Data Ltd.

Dragon Data Ltd. was a spin-off of a toy company (Mettoy) that decided to enter the home computer market in the early '80s. Their first product, the Dragon 32, came out in 1982 and achieved a decent following. The Dragon 32 and its successor, the Dragon 64 (which was little more than a somewhat souped-up 32), were based on the Motorola 6809 chip, which was arguably more powerful than the chips being used in some of the other popular machines, such as the BBC Micro and the Sinclair ZX Spectrum. Strangely, the original design was based almost entirely on the TRS-80, to the point where some accounts suggest that it was nearly a copy, but with some "fixes" to avoid lawsuits.

Despite having a loyal following and presence in some of the posh High Street shops, Dragon Data really didn't match the numbers of the Spectrum, and, despite the loyalty of its users, it wasn't the first choice of game designers. Many games did become available on the Dragon systems, but they were most often created originally on a

different machine. Possible exceptions were Shock Trooper, Speed Racer, Tanglewood, and Airball.

One of the factors that inspired loyalty among Dragon's customers was that the company would send out schematics and machine code listings to any user upon request. They were very supportive of their customer base, which largely consisted of hobbyists and hackers.

By 1984, the company was in trouble and was on the verge of "calling in the receivers" (meaning going bankrupt) when it was bought by a new company, Eurohard SA, which intended on moving production to Spain. The intention was to create computers that supported the new, machine-independent MSX technology, which was adopted in Japan and Holland and was supported by Sony, Sanyo, Hitachi, Toshiba, and Philips, but never really caught on elsewhere.

As early as May 1985, there were signs that Dragon sales were failing to live up to expectations. It is even said that Eurohard took to selling the Dragon systems door-to-door in Spain. At any rate, the story drags on—excuse the pun—for a few more years, but the Dragon systems never achieved any notable success or lived up to the promise of their early days.

Manic Miner/Jet Set Willy

Matthew Smith created Manic Miner, starring Miner Willy, in 1983. It was written for the Sinclair Spectrum and was a platform arcade game that has been compared to Bill Hogue's Miner 2049er, one of the groundbreaking and highly popular games that came out in 1982 in the U.S. This is no coincidence. Miner 2049er was Matthew Smith's favorite game at the time he created Manic Miner. However, the two games are different, and brilliant, each in its own way. Similarly, the two programmers, Smith and Hogue, were mere teenagers when they made these games and each became an overnight sensation when their products were released. (Of course, both games were post-Donkey Kong, which came out in 1981 and pretty much set the standard for this type of platformer.)

The story goes that Matthew Smith actually wrote the game for Bug-Byte, but also sold an almost identical (with slight changes) version to Software Projects, which published that version, as well. It was Software Projects that continued with Smith and published the megahit follow-up game, Jet Set Willy, and its successor, Jet Set Willy II.

Where Miner 2049er was a brilliant example of programming, originally for the Atari 400 system, and contained ten levels (although some later ports contained a difficult to

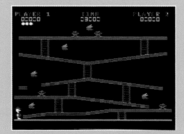

reach 11th level), Manic Miner contained 20 levels and is regarded as a brilliant example of programming for the Spectrum, with continuous music throughout the game and exceptionally smooth graphics.

One famous level, Eugene's Lair, was named for fellow Bug-Byte programmer Eugene Evans. The story goes that Evans told Smith that he didn't think Manic Miner would work (before it was programmed), and so Level 5 was named after him.

Smith continued his success with Jet Set Willy, which was even more popular than Manic Miner. Both games rank among the most memorable Speccy games, although they were also ported to many other systems. Of course, being immensely popular, another sequel was inevitable, but when it came time to do Jet Set Willy II, Matthew Smith, always a highly eccentric and controversial figure, had apparently disappeared, spawning all kinds of rumors—some even surmising that he never existed in the first place. One rumor had him fixing motorbikes in Italy. However, he later reappeared and was quoted in a magazine as saying that there was no mystery at all, that he had spent some time out of the country, that he was back, and that he was still "signing on the dot," which means he was on the dole. JSWII was, overall, disappointing, and pretty much ended the story of Miner Willy and Matthew Smith in the gaming industry.

Jet Set Willy fans have not exactly given up on the game, and today there are JSW editors and various emulated versions. So if you want to play the original game and lots of user-created sequels and versions, it's only a web search away.

The founders of Imagine, Mark Butler and David Lawson.

The Rise and Fall of Imagine Software

As Bug-Byte started to become successful, the phenomenon of the retail computer store also began to become more widespread. It was no longer necessary to sell only by mail order, which had been more or less the norm at that point. Instead of opening an envelope and taking out your £5.50, you might now sell boxes of ten or more to a local shop. Of course, that meant sharing the profits, but the volume was better. To support the new retail outlets, Bug-Byte hired Mark Butler, another Microdigital alumnus, as a sales guy.

Ultimately, Butler and Dave Lawson became friends, and in the wake of disagreements with Bug-Byte management, Butler proposed to Lawson that they go into business for themselves. Lawson would create the games, and Butler could sell them. Lawson agreed and soon left the company to start on the first game, while Butler remained at Bug-Byte until the game was ready. Because Liverpool was a depressed city economically at that time, the two were able to secure a government grant of £25,000 to start the company. Before long, Lawson had completed a simple but fun Space Invaders-like shooter called Arcadia for both the VIC-20 and the newly launched Sinclair Spectrum.

Arcadia, and the newly-formed company, Imagine, were instant successes. They ultimately moved into plush offices and employed almost a hundred programmers, technicians, artists, and musicians. One ex-Microdigital employee who rode the early wave of success was 16-year-old whiz kid programmer Eugene Evans, who at that tender age was reputedly earning £35,000 a year and owned a sports car that he was too young to drive. Evans's comment is, "Don't believe everything you read on the web." However, this was a popular tactic in the ongoing marketing campaign intended to glamorize the electronic games industry. "We had to bring computer games to a wider audience," said Imagine director Bruce Everiss, "and the cult of personality was the tool we used." Interestingly enough, Trip Hawkins used the same strategy, and Bill Budge was his poster boy (*see page 178*).

As Evans tells it, "Bruce was a real mentor to a number of us… he was the one at Bug-Byte who had consulted with us on doing full-page ads with spot color, which was a big thing at the time and was a successful strategy. At Imagine, he got us involved with a PR firm, and it was their idea to promote not just a new game, but the idea of a young guy making computer games and being successful. We never guessed at the response we'd get to that campaign. At the time, there was a lot of unemployment, so people noticed it when I was shown as a teenager making a lot of money and living extravagantly. When I came into work after the ad ran, all our phone lines were ringing. Within a few days, I had been interviewed by journalists from nearly every British newspaper. There were articles and clippings from all over, from Brazil, and from *Reader's Digest*. It was a bit much."

The company promoted a few of its other programmers and overall tried to give a very successful impression. "We would go to the trade shows, and we would all be wearing suits," remembers Evans, "I mean in a place where everyone else was wearing t-shirts and jeans, we looked professional." But all the bravado cost them in the end. The biggest booths, the fanciest offices, the best of everything… after about two or three years, Imagine ran into financial problems. It was partly a sign of the times: game companies were crashing as a backlash to the Atari collapse (*see page 107*), there was a glut of product, although that wasn't the only reason for Imagine's demise.

In Imagine's inimitable way, they were directly responsible for a great deal of the glut. It started in 1982, when there was a shortage of software in the shops. As 1983 rolled around, Imagine realized that it would be a boom year. To gain the most advantage, they booked the entire capacity of Kitdale, the biggest tape duplication firm for the software business, for the time approaching Christmas. The idea was to prevent their competitors from being able to duplicate their product. It was a devious ploy, but one that backfired mightily. Instead of capitalizing

on a boom, Imagine found themselves stuck with hundreds of thousands of tapes that they couldn't sell because of the market crash. Imagine was forced to lower their prices to budget levels in order to sell anything at all. However, the end result was a market flooded with tapes that not only did not sell, but made little to no profit for anyone when they did.

In addition to original titles, Imagine developed conversions of Japanese arcade games.

Megagames

Then there was Dave Lawson's innovative, but ambitious, idea of creating what came to be called "megagames" (variously spelled mega-games or Mega Games). These games came as a response to several factors. The first was the ease with which the game tapes could be copied, simply by hooking one cassette player to another. In addition, Lawson wanted to make bigger games. But how, without a disk drive? His solution was to develop a series of cartridge games with 64K of information. However, none of the systems he wanted to support accepted cartridges, so he had to figure out a way to use the edge connectors that were used for extra memory on the Spectrum and VIC-20 to accept a specially designed cartridge.

"It became a big PR thing," remembers Eugene Evans. "We teased them through ads showing pro-

Imagine began an aggressive marketing campaign for the Megagames before they were completed. This ad features Imagine employees Ian Weatherburn, Mike Glover, John Gibson, and Eugene Evans.

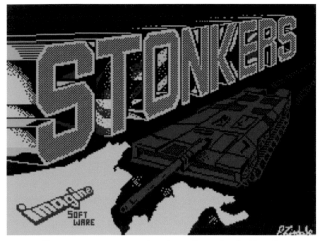

According to accounts at the time, Imagine's Stonkers, well... it "stonk."

grammers, artists doing art, musicians. Everything was 'mega this' and 'mega that.'" But, despite the publicity campaign, the games weren't forthcoming, and some analysts suspected that the high price that they would have to charge (£30) would be out of people's price range, especially as the market was getting more competitive, with budget games selling for as little as £1.99.

At any rate, even as the megagame concept dragged on without results, a deal with a major magazine publisher, which initially promised to be very lucrative, also went sour. The original idea was that Marshall Cavendish would publish a series of game magazines, and Imagine would program games for the Spectrum and the C64 and provide a tape of the games on the cover of each issue. Marshall Cavendish had used a similar strategy with magazines of classical music with cassettes included, or cooking magazines with recipes on index cards. The idea seemed to promise lots of profit for Imagine, and they began to staff up to handle all the games they would need to produce.

In the end, the magazine idea didn't go well. According to articles written at the time, this was largely because Dave Lawson was totally focused on the megagames concept, Mark Butler was off racing motorbikes, and the limited product offered to the magazine publisher was unimpressive.

There were other problems, as well. The two founders, Butler and Lawson, became the central figures in factions within the company, and all was not rosy in the halls and offices of Imagine. In order to handle the expected increase in business from the Marshall Cavendish deal (which would have been worth, in some estimations, £11 million), Imagine had hired many more programmers, artists, and other staff members, now totaling as many as 140 people, which meant 140 paychecks.

The megagames were not progressing well, in spite of colorful ads illustrated by the famous album cover and book artist Roger Dean. (Dean reportedly got £6,000 for the job.) Nothing was going well. An article published in *CRASH* magazine in early 1985 told the story of a BBC television special being shot about Imagine at the time. The emphasis was supposed to be a super-successful software company on the rise, but here is what the film crew found: "So in the middle of shooting a TV programme about a company that was going places fast, Paul Andersen found himself filming one with a huge staff it no longer needed nor could afford, sitting on a vast stock of product it could not sell, with programmers left to their own devices much of the time and producing games that were increasingly unplayable and usually released with bugs still in them (remember Stonkers), run by a management team that was beginning to fall apart at the seams."

"The short version," Eugene Evans added, "is that the company went belly up and splintered into probably a dozen new companies around northern England."

Dave Lawson went off with Imagine's CFO, Ian Hetherington, to form a new company, initially called Finchspeed, which somehow acquired some of Imagine's assets and a few of their key technical personnel while avoiding a massive financial collapse replete with lawsuits, accusations and recriminations, and loads of unhappy people. What was left was purchased by Ocean Ltd.

Some good did come out of Imagine's messy end. Finchspeed, whose initial name was the result of the common practice of "combining a prefix word and a suffix word more or less at random to create the paperwork, then changing the name later," according to Evans, would soon be known by its more recognizable moniker, Psygnosis.

Psygnosis

Hetherington and Lawson started Psygnosis with an investment from Robert Smith, who ran various businesses ranging from a Mercedes dealership to a scrap metal business, and who saw an opportunity to diversify. Smith put Jonathan Ellis in charge of the business side, while Ian Hetherington ran software development.

Along with other assets, Smith had bought out the rights to the megagames, including the announced game, Bandersnatch. While still doing business as Finchspeed, they licensed the property to Sinclair Research and completed a version of the game for the Sinclair QL, calling it Brataccas. After changing their name to Psygnosis, they released the game on Atari ST and Amiga using the same title. This was Psygnosis' first release in 1987.

Psygnosis published quite a few games in the late '80s and, as was common in those days, also published budget games under the name Psyclapse (presumably in memory of the second of the megagames from the Imagine era). Among their first big hits was Shadow of the Beast, a beautifully designed platform game with parallax scrolling, released in 1989. Its success generated two high-powered sequels for Psygnosis. The company also scored on an action game called Ballistix that played like a computerized version of the sport depicted in the movie *Rollerball*.

Without doubt, however, their biggest success came with the 1991 release of the megahit game Lemmings from DMA Design. DMA had previously done a port of Blood Money for Psygnosis, but it was Lemmings and its several sequels that put Psygnosis on the map. (For more on the creation of Lemmings, *see pages 311 and 411.*)

Psygnosis continued into the '90s with a string of games, some of good quality and some forgettable. Notable among Psygnosis' post-Lemmings games was DMA's Walker, which depicted images of "mechanoid" walkers squishing little men, much as someone would squish ants or bugs. The company also sank plenty of cash into the 1994 release, Microcosm, a CD-ROM product reminiscent of Isaac Asimov's *Fantastic Voyage*, except for the fact that you were in the equivalent of a "fighter" flying through the entrails and circulatory system of your patient. In 1998, Psygnosis delivered Sentinel Returns, a remake (with superior graphics and sound) of Geoff Crammond's unique action/puzzle game The Sentinel (*see page 409*).

These post-Lemmings games, however, may never have existed it hadn't been for Tom Randolph, who loved Shadow of the Beast, and Jerry Wolosenko, who ran Psygnosis' North American division and who introduced Randolph to Ian Hetherington. Randolph worked for Fujitsu, which was creating the FM Towns, one of the first computer systems to feature an integrated CD player. Psygnosis was brought on to create games for the

Among Psygnosis' popular games was Shadow of the Beast, developed for Psygnosis by Martin Edmondson and Paul Howarth of Reflections. Reflections also did two sequels as well as Awesome, Ballistix, and their final entry for Psygnosis, Brian the Lion.

machine, using the CD-ROM as a memory device. They also worked with Sega on their early CD machines. When they began talking with Olaf Olafsson, Sony Imagesoft's president, it seemed a natural step to join forces. But Olafsson had more than just collaboration in mind, and in the end, Sony bought Psygnosis. Psygnosis remained a publishing label of Sony for many years, renamed in 2001 as SCE Studio Liverpool, but ultimately was shut down altogether.

Hetherington was highly instrumental in the PlayStation's success. He was well known in the European development community, and was able to attract quite a few developers for the upcoming PSX. Psygnosis also created many of the development tools used in creating games for the original PlayStation.

THE PYSGNOSIS LOGO

Both David Lawson and Robert Smith were fans of Roger Dean's artwork, and so Dean was hired to develop the Psygnosis logos, as well as to create some of the company's game covers. The resultant owl logos became famous throughout the industry, and were arguably the best game company logos of all time.

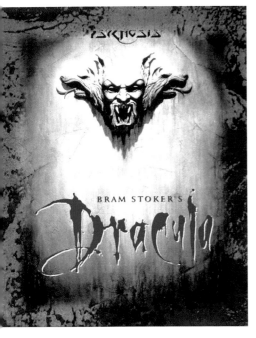

Psygnosis covers were often visually compelling, continuing in the tradition begun by Roger Dean. The image on the left is the cover of the first Psygnosis game, Brataccas, which was originally the megagame Bandersnatch.

Fujitsu's, FM Towns was one of the first computer systems to feature an integrated CD player.

The Halcyon Days
of Jeff Minter

The following interview with the eccentric and brilliant programmer, Jeff Minter (AKA "Yak"), was originally printed in Halcyon Days, *published by James Hague in 1997. The full text is available online at* www.dadgum.com/halcyon.

What led up to the programming of your first commercial game, Andes Attack?
Oh, bloody hell, that goes way back. My first encounter with coding was at sixth form college where they had a Commodore PET, and I taught meself BASIC on that and started writing games for me mates. When I ran out of steam with BASIC I turned to 6502 machine code, hand assembled, by God. The first machine I actually owned was the ZX80, and in fact I did a few pre-Llamasoft games for the ZX80/ZX81 for an outfit called dk'tronics in the UK. However, they treated me spectacularly badly, and so the founding of Llamasoft coincided with my getting my hands on the VIC. Games were just something I did in my spare time before that.

Andes Attack was coded during a period of illness and, to my surprise and delight, sold pretty well when I'd finished it, despite being painfully jerky and buggy now that I look back on it. I think learning to write games as a hobby, just for the benefit of your mates, is a pretty good grounding; your mates don't hesitate to tell you if they think you've made a shitty game! I always knew if I'd done a good 'un because all the chipheads at the college would be staying after hours playing the games and writing their hi-scores on the walls of the computer room--for which I got shit.

How well did "Andes Attack" do commercially?
Not too bad, considering how shitty it actually was. But my God, you should have seen what the competition was like at that time in the UK—some really diabolical stuff that made "Andes Attack" look great by comparison. It was published in the U.S. as "Aggressor" with some minor cosmetic changes, and did okay, but nothing compared to "Gridrunner." It was good enough that it got Llamasoft into the market and got us the hook-up with HES that later proved to be pretty lucrative.

The limitations of the VIC-20 seem severe today. Did they feel constraining at the time?
Well, after using the PET, which had 8K, was monochrome and had no bitmapped graphics or sound, and the ZX80/ZX81, which had 1K, was monochrome, had a membrane keyboard; no sound—Ugh! Bleachh!—the VIC, with a proper keyboard, a sound chip, programmable bitmaps and, above all, color and joystick ports, seemed like the very lap of luxury!

How was your company, Llamasoft, founded?
Basically, I was motivated by seeing "Asteroids" by Bug-Byte on the VIC-20, by S. Munnery. That name is branded on my brain. It was so bad, I mean, unbelievably bad. You only had one spaceship, and the program would poke your ship on the screen, then randomly poke on the asteroids, and fully half the time it would poke a rock right on top of your ship before you even had a chance to move or fire, and it would be "Game Over" before it even started. When you fired, instead of individual bullets that actually moved, you just got this chain of full stops that stuck out of the end of your ship while the VIC made a sound like a vacuum cleaner. Shudder. They were charging seven quid for that pile of wank, and I thought, hell, I could do better than that, so I started work on what would eventually become "Andes Attack." Originally Llamasoft was founded to sell that. After a brief period of misguided partnership with your archetypical dodgy geezer, my mum came into the partnership, we kicked him out, and Llamasoft proper came into being in 1982.

I guess I have to thank S. Munnery for something, even if that game he wrote was execrable!

What were the early years of Llamasoft like, say, 1982-1986?
Absolutely brilliant. It was totally like a dream come true. After a fair-

LLA 21001

Attack Of The Mutant Camels
CBM 64

Planet earth needs you! Hostile aliens have used genetic engineering to mutate camels from normally harmless beasts into 90 foot high, neutronium shielded, laser-spitting death camels!! Can you fly your tiny, manoeuverable fighter over the mountainous landscape to weaken and destroy the camels before they invade the human stronghold! You must withstand withering laser fire and alien UFOs. Game action stretches over 10 screen lengths and features superb scrolling, scanner 1/2 player actions and unbelievable animation! Play this game and you'll never be able to visit a zoo again without getting an itchy trigger finger!

Awesome m/c action!

ATTACK OF THE MUTANT CAMELS JEFF MINTER 1983
The game and name ATTACK OF THE MUTANT CAMELS and all associated software, code, listings, audio effects, graphics, illustrations and text are the exclusive copyright of Llamasoft and may not be copied, transmitted, transferred, reproduced, hired, lent, distributed, stored or modified in any form without the express written permission of LLAMASOFT SOFTWARE, 49 Mount Pleasant, Tadley, England.

Attack Of The Mutant Camels

LLAMASOFT !!

CBM 64

© 1983

Attack Of The Mutant Camels

SCORE PL. 1   HI: LLAMA   SCORE PL. 2
8888888   H : 188   8888888

JETS 4   SECTOR 81   JETS 8

ly slow start, things went ballistic when Gridrunner became a big hit in the U.S., and we made some silly money for a while. Meanwhile, in the UK, we started to get a reputation for games that were weird, but playable. We used to go to five or six big shows in the UK every year, and they were a total blast. I got to meet a lot of great people, sell a lot of games, and drink a lot of beer! I also got to do a lot of stuff I would never have dreamed possible before it all started: go to Peru to be with llamas, get a new car, go skiing every year. It was just great. I was a bloody lucky git to have such a good time!

Was there ever any temptation to sell out?

Not really. I was perfectly happy to do my own thing. We never had any ambitions to become a big software empire.

I'm sure we could have done it if we'd wanted to, but me and my mum liked it the way it was, just me coding, my mum and dad doing the administrative stuff. I'm afraid I was much more interested in having a good time than getting seriously commercial. People have called me a fool for that, but I don't care. I had a great time and don't regret it for a minute.

When did you start to feel that the "golden age" of home computer gaming was drawing to a close?

I guess around 1987 things started getting a bit thin. The biz was becoming more serious, with arcade and movie licenses dominant instead of just a bunch of rogue coders all trying to come up with original stuff. That's what I really liked about the early

scene; there was a very high premium placed on originality in a game. Now you tend to have your genres: driving, bloody endless fighting games, bloody DOOM clones. No disrespect to id, DOOM is a fantastic game, and they created the genre. It's just that now every flipping game, apart from the aforementioned fighting and driving ones, tends to look like DOOM. You wait, I'm going to do something about that one of these days!

You've written quite a few Defender-inspired games. What is it that fascinates you about Defender?

Defender is just a beautiful game design, and the effects, for their time, were astounding. It broke a lot of new ground, introducing the scanner and the smart bomb; it was the first game to provide a coherent play area larger than the screen within which one had complete freedom to maneuver. In playing Defender, one is not just memorizing a pattern, one has to think and respond dynamically to a threat that is constantly changing. You had to take the time to actually learn to fly your ship, but when you'd learned, you could pull off the most beautiful moves. A wonderful game to play, and one that I still play, surrounded though I am with awesome next-gen tech. The game stands the test of time. It's a true classic.

Have you ever met Eugene Jarvis?

Yes, at CES in 1994. He's a lovely bloke, witty and intelligent—very much so—and not at all big-headed, 'specially as he's a god! It was a real case of hero worship for me. Mind you, I have to say I think he made me tone down the difficulty on my Jag implementation of Defender a bit too far. He was the guy we had to satisfy for approval from Williams on Defender 2000. I played Defender on Williams Arcade Classics the other day, and it kicked my ass by comparison to Classic mode on Defender 2000.

Jeff Minter created classic remakes of Eugene Jarvis' great Defender and Dave Theurer's Tempest for the Atari Jaguar, hailed by many as some of the best arcade conversions ever.

What's your philosophy of game design?

Gameplay *Über Alles*. And if you can make it psychedelic too, great! My idea of fun is not so much creating a realistic world with the computer, as creating a surrealistic one. Rather than use the machine to emulate reality, use the machine to go to places that no one ever imagined before. I think that's the real potential of the new generation of ultra-powerful machines, at least as far as my future designs are concerned. I have things in my head that you could create with the power of, say, five PlayStations, that'd have to be made illegal, they'd be so trippy.

How did you hook up with Atari?

I kinda fell in with Atari UK back in the 1980s and, when it was getting impractical to publish our own stuff, did the odd contract for them—Defender 2, Photon Storm. Then I hooked up with Atari U.S. and my old boss, John Skruch—a lovely bloke, you could not ask for a better producer to work for—to work on the Falcon and subsequently on the Jaguar.

I met my first Tramiel shortly after the ST came out. I was at Comdex with Colourspace, my ST lightsynth, and Leonard T. brought his Uncle Jack over to take a look at it! I was pretty awestruck to meet the guys who ran Atari and who founded Commodore, the company that had made the machine I first learned to code on.

Do you prefer reworking classics or creating original games?

I have greatly enjoyed reworking the likes of Defender and Tempest. Those two are probably my fave arcade games, ever. But I would like to do some original stuff now, I think. However, I do count bringing those old games to a new generation of players as one of my proudest achievements. Those designs were so cool.

Minter's secret Easter Egg
level. Not exactly a llama, but...

Do you still program in assembly language, or have you switched to something more fashionable?

Assembly all the way so far. I know the day will come, but for now, there is still a demand for true assembler coders if you know where to look.

What games, from either the 1980s or 1990s, have you been most impressed with?

Star Raiders, Defender, Tempest, Rescue on Fractalus!, F-Zero, and Wipeout on the PlayStation, F-Zero's logical successor. Thrust on the C64. DOOM, Robotron, Tetris—pure elegance! And, of course, the Mario canon on the Nintendos; no denying Shig his greatness.

What do you think, in general, of the games currently on the shelves?

There are only a few must-have games around. There are a lot of technically great games around, but very few have that real spark of gameplay excellence that just makes you drool and need to play all the time. Wipeout on the PlayStation is great. Not only did I love it, but it has managed to addict all my brothers, even those who do not usually play video games—always the sign of a great game if it can do that.

Any chance of a Llamasoft game that doesn't feature yaks or llamas or other furry beasts?

Now what possible reason would I have for giving up my love of beasties?

Some images of Jeff
Minter over the years.

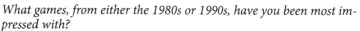

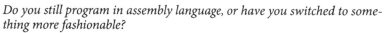

Interview from Halcyon Days *used with permission*

Notable BBC Games and Companies

Although Acorn began as a hardware company and was best known for the BBC Microcomputer, they also ran a software division—Acornsoft—which not only created educational, business, and utility software, but also, according to some, the best of the games available for the Beeb. In the early '80s, from at least 1982 until Superior Software bought their catalog in 1986, they were arguably the preeminent publishers of games for the BBC computers, although there were dozens of competitors. Their biggest hit, worldwide and historically, was without a doubt the classic space trading game, Elite, which was written by two teenage developers—Ian Bell and David Braben.

Elite: Open Space

Elite is one of the original space exploration and trading games, of which there have been many in the years since. It was written for the BBC Micro, which required that the whole program fit in the system's 32K of memory.

Elite was the first of the space exploration games to combine wireframe 3D graphics, free exploration of hundreds of planets, a trade model, combat, and a variety of ships and upgrades in an open style of play. It may also have been one of the first games to use hidden line removal, meaning that it would remove the wireframe lines that were at the back of an object, further enhancing the illusion of 3D. No big deal today, but a big deal back then!

Elite was also a complex and highly immersive game with just the right blend of technology, trade, and combat. According to co-designer Ian Bell in a 1995 interview, "Open games are ones you exist in and play many roles." Certainly, Elite's combination of space combat and trading was the model for games that followed, such as Star Control, Privateer, and many more.

Braben started with the underpowered Acorn Atom while in school. "It took me a long time to learn enough assembler programming to make this go smoothly enough to get a sense of speed, but then I was hooked!" Then he met Ian Bell, who was already working on the BBC Micro game Freefall for Acornsoft. At that time, Braben's game was called Fighter and wasn't complete, but when the two compared notes, and after seeing Star Raiders on the Atari 800, they decided to meet the challenge of making a truly involving and spectacular space game.

We asked Bell and Braben about the influences that led to the development of Elite. Bell cites a general interest in science fiction, plus Traveller (the RPG), *Star Wars*, *2001*, and Douglas Adams' *Hitchhiker's Guide to the Galaxy*. Braben also mentions *2001* and *Star Wars* (and "to a lesser extent," he says, "*Battlestar Galactica*"). In addition, he mentions the fiction of Larry Niven, Isaac Asimov, Jerry Pournelle, Arthur C. Clarke, Robert L. Forward, Orson Scott Card, "and many others."

Elite came out on just about every system imaginable—a true classic!

The story of making Elite, which for its time was a very complex game, was often the story of eking out a few more bytes of memory on a very limited system. The Beeb's 32K of memory was quite a lot at the time, but only about 16K of that was available for the game elements outside of screen handling and "various other elements," according to Braben.

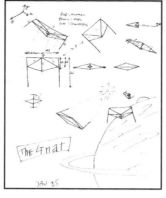

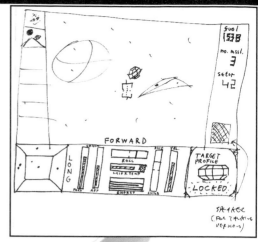

Original Elite design sketches and formulae courtesy of Ian Bell.

The two managed to write their own screen mode and display drivers, gaining another 6K, and continued to take "perverse delight" in saving bytes wherever possible. "This is a little like trying to preserve the meaning of a sentence in English, but to use as few characters as possible in the process. Imagine trying to write the most complicated novel possible in 22,000 characters," states Braben. Like many successful games, Elite was turned down by the first publisher to see it, which Braden remembers well.

"When we first approached publishers with the unfinished (but playable) Elite, the reception was generally frosty. Thorn EMI rejected the game, saying it was a great technical demo but had no score, the 3D was confusing, there was only one life, no goal, took too long to play, and needed the user to provide their own cassette to save their position. They said they might reconsider it if we made it more conventional, with a typical play time of ten minutes.

"In my opinion the features they listed were its strengths, so this was a bit of a blow. We then went to Acornsoft, and the contrast was amazing. This was a company staffed by people who loved games (rather than the 'business' people at Thorn EMI). They absolutely loved Elite, so they became the publishers. They were also hugely supportive, and I am especially grateful to their managing director, David Johnson-Davies."

The pair soon discovered that they had a hit on their hands. Again, according to Braben, "We were contacted by John Taplin, then editor of Channel 4 News, shortly after the game was released. In their studio they used BBC Micros for preparing text. (Haven't times changed!) He came in to find everyone playing this strange game and thought that in itself was newsworthy, so he did a long piece on Ian and me and the game. I was amazed (and delighted) at how positive everyone was about the game—people outside the games business—so this was possibly my first real inkling that we had 'struck it big.'"

Unfortunately, the co-authors of Elite had a falling out during the production of Frontier: Elite II and have not collaborated since. Ian Bell has continued to work on games, including his adaptation of Elite to the NES, and various other interests, such as fluorescent body painting and techno music. David Braben has remained an active designer and developer and has created quite a few games, including Frontier: Elite II. During the five-year development period for Frontier: Elite II, Braben founded Frontier Developments, which has produced several games, including Zarch for the Acorn Archimedes, which was released as Virus on other systems and was later followed by its sequel, V2000. Frontier Developments also released Chris Sawyer's RollerCoaster Tycoon and its sequel, as well as multiple Wallace & Gromit games. They have recently entered the mobile games arena with Darxide for Pocket PC and, at the time of this writing, are about to release Dog's Life, with Elite 4 somewhere around the corner.

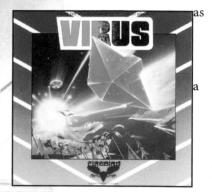

Over Easy? Or Hard-Boiled?

In the U.S., Elite is probably the best known game to come out of the UK in the early days, but if you speak with the Brits about their favorite game of all time, often enough you'll hear them mention an unassuming little platformer called Chuckie Egg. This clucker was hatched by A&F Software, a company whose game history failed to produce any other significant offerings, although they did create a dozen or more games for the Beeb.

But Chuckie Egg was a phenomenon, and a quick web search will turn up several pages of crowing—er, adoration—for this little arcade game, plus emulators and screen-

 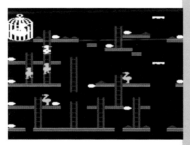

Virtually unknown outside the UK, for some Brits, Chuckie Egg still conjures up some of their fondest early game memories.

shots. The goal of the game was to collect eggs and bird seed while staying clear of marauding ostriches. It had some similarity to Lode Runner, but looked even more crude. You had to run, climb ladders, and negotiate around holes and various elevators while keeping away from the ostriches and other critters that would kill your little guy on contact.

For many former school kids in the UK, Chuckie Egg still nests among their fondest memories.

Nigel Lays a Golden Egg

We asked Nigel Alderton, creator of Chuckie Egg, to tell us a little bit about how the game came into being. Here's what he told us, all these years later:

Q. How did you first come to write Chuckie Egg?
I was totally addicted to arcade games. A newsagent near school had a series of classic machines, one after the other, including Scramble and Donkey Kong. For a while I went there every day on the way to school, on the way home, during lunch hour, during breaks, on the way from lesson-to-lesson if I could get away with it. I'd already written a game for the Speccy called Blaster—a cross between Scramble and Defender that scrolled horizontally, but all the movement was a character at a time. What I really wanted to do was a game where things moved smoothly, pixel by pixel. There were very few games with smooth movement (I even remember reading in a magazine some "expert" stating that pixel movement wasn't possible in the Speccy because of the way the screen was mapped), so I started to develop code for pixel movement and think about ideas for a game.

Q. What was your original inspiration?
Chuckie Egg is a cross between two of my favorite platform arcade games at the time, Donkey Kong and the rather more obscure Space Panic. I just took the bits I liked best from each game and added a few ideas of my own.

Q. What did you imagine the game would be like when you started?
The game was 95 percent designed in my head very early in the coding process and 100 percent designed by halfway through coding, so what you see is pretty much as I had imagined it at the start.

Q. Had you written any games before? If so, what were they?
Just one called Blaster. It was all hand-coded, i.e. I would
- write a routine in assembler
- look up the corresponding machine code for each instruction and write it next to the assembler
- 'POKE' the numbers into memory
- test it

Thinking back I'm amazed that I had the patience.

Q. Why do you think Chuckie Egg was so much fun? What

did you do consciously to make it especially fun? How much was blind luck?

I didn't design by thinking about what other people would like. I just created the sort of game that I would enjoy playing myself. The great thing about writing your own game is obviously that you get to decide exactly what goes in and what doesn't. I was creating my own little world, so without really thinking about what I was doing, I automatically created a world that I would enjoy spending time in. I don't remember taking even one second to consider what other people would think of the game when it was finished. So I suppose it's just luck that other people enjoyed it, too.

Q. With the popularity of Chuckie Egg, did your life change substantially? Did you make a lot of money from it? If not, why not?

Although I didn't realize it at the time, Chuckie Egg did change the course of my life. Because of CE, I walked straight into my first job, no questions asked, which was with Ocean in Manchester. If it wasn't for CE, I don't know what I would have done.

Q. What about Chuckie Egg 2? Did you have anything to do with that?

I'm afraid I don't know much about Chuckie Egg 2. The directors of A&F Software decided to do a follow-up to Chuckie Egg; however, they wanted it done to a very keen deadline, so I kept well clear of the whole thing. To my mind, if you want to create something, you first have to have an idea, then work out how long it's going to take you to bring that idea to fruition. But they were businessmen, so they decided, "We are going to release CE2 in x weeks. Now let's think of a game." Bonkers! They went bust soon after it was released. I don't even think I've ever played it.

Q. Could you imagine a modern 3D version of Chuckie Egg, and has anybody ever approached you about doing one?

There is a Chuckie Egg 3D! Search the net and you'll find it. And there's now a mobile version of the game coming out from Elite.

Superior Software

While at university, Richard Hanson started programming games for the Acorn Atom, some of which were published by a company called Program Power (which later became Micro Power). After earning a degree in computational science, Hanson teamed up with John Dyson and, using total investment of £100 (£50 each), they started Superior Software with four games and began advertising them using small black-and-white ads.

While Dyson ultimately decided to stay at his job as a technician with the BBC, Hanson never left, and continues to run the company at the time of this writing. By 1983 the company began to see major success with sizeable orders for ten of their games, and their first runaway hit was Overdrive, a simple racing game programmed by Peter Johnson.

In the BBC Micro heyday, Superior Software was considered by many to be the quintessential Beeb games producer, and even obtained some publication rights for several of the Acornsoft games in 1986. They re-released Elite, one of the best of Acornsoft's original titles, as well as Revs, Magic Mushrooms, Starship Command, and other Acornsoft games. Over the years, Superior's products were known to be among the best for the Beeb, and at the top of their game they held leading positions in the BBC Micro and Acorn Electron software charts. For instance, in one 1987 chart for the BBC Micro, Superior Software held the top five places plus number seven. Number three on the list was Stryker's Run, programmed by Chris Roberts. (*See page 214 for more on Chris Roberts.*)

Superior's most successful releases include the three Repton games as well as Elite, Ravenskull, Galaforce, Citadel, Thrust, Pipeline, Codename: Droid, Exile, Stryker's Run, Crazee Rider, Karate Combat, Tempest, Revs, The Last Ninja, Predator, Ballistix, SimCity, Quest, Spycat, Superior Soccer, Ricochet, and Perplexity.

> *The computer software business, both then and now, offers a wonderful route for potential rewards for anyone prepared to put in the research and hard work—and it doesn't require a great deal of money to get started.*
> **–Richard Hanson**

including the main character, Repton. An information panel has also been added to the PC version of the game on the right-hand side of the screen. The PC version of Repton 1 features 32 levels and 20 bonus levels for children, which is more than double the number of levels in the BBC Micro version of the game, and the PC version also includes a simple-to-use level editor enabling players to design their own Repton 1 levels."

Years later, under the brand name Superior Interactive, the company embarked on a new phase, beginning with a PC version of Repton 1. Superior has stood the test of time and earned a place in the history of games not only because of its many game releases, but also because it is one of the few companies of that era still in existence today. They have released modernized versions of Repton 1, Repton 2, Repton 3, Ravenskull, Galaforce, Pipeline, and Ricochet. The screenshots below show the original BBC Micro versions of some of the games next to their modern PC counterparts.

Here's what Richard Hanson has to say about the Repton screenshots below: "These two screenshots show the same game position from Level 5 of one Repton 1 scenario. The BBC Micro four-color graphics have been replaced by full-color graphics for all of the game characters,

Richard Hanson

Elite Systems Ltd.

Elite Systems (initially called Richard Wilcox Software) started business in Walsall, England, in August 1984. The occasion for the founding of this company by Steve and Brian Wilcox was to distribute 16-year-old Richard Wilcox's helicopter shooter, Blue Thunder, for the Spectrum and Commodore 64. (Elite Systems is still in business as of 2012. Oh, and, yes, Richard, Steve, and Brian are all related.)

The first published game under the Elite brand was Kokotoni Wilf, which was intended to compete against Jet Set Willy. According to Steve Wilcox, who still runs the company, "It failed, but enjoyed some chart and commercial success nonetheless."

Elite's first hit game was the officially licensed game based on the Airwolf property, making one of the top 5 lists for Christmas 1984. By the middle of 1985, they scored their first number one title by hooking up with the popular British boxing heavyweight Frank Bruno's and releasing Frank Bruno's Boxing. They followed this success with a licensing deal involving three of Capcom's arcade hits, starting with Commando, which once again hit number one. The next year they capitalized on arcade conversions again with Tecmo's Bomb Jack, Capcom's Ghosts 'n Goblins, and Atari's Paperboy—the latter being voted Game of the Year in 1988. With the success of these titles, Elite grew quickly and became one of the significant publishers to come out of the UK.

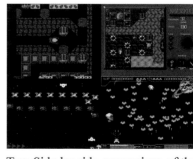

Top: Side-by-side comparison of the BBC and PC versions of Ravenskull. Bottom: Side-by-side comparison of the BBC and PC versions of Galaforce.

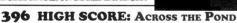

Other high points in the company's history included entering into development and distribution deals with Nintendo in 1990, their co-development of Striker with Rage Software, and their early adoption of the Sony PlayStation in 1995. One of their associate companies, Motivetime, developed the very popular Accolade title, Test Drive: Off-Road.

In all, Elite has produced approximately 75 titles, many of them licensed conversions from arcades, television, and movies. Today, they continue to produce new and retro collections of classic games, including mobile versions of Chuckie Egg, Bomb Jack, Jet Set Willy, Bruce Lee, Ikari Warriors, Buggy Boy, and others.

Lords of Midnight

Mike Singleton is another of those early programmers who started way back in the infancy of home computers. In fact, he developed his first programs on a Sinclair calculator, which was limited to 32 programmable steps. A retired schoolteacher, he began doodling around with the calculator and found himself helping a friend at a betting parlor by programming a routine to handle complex betting in horse races. "There are some very complicated bets. There's one called 'around the clock,' which actually consists of 13 different bets on three horses, and I wrote a little program which would calculate 'around the clock,' and then we decided we would try and do it commercially." After his "around the clock" program, which was ultimately created on a Texas Instruments programmable calculator, Singleton graduated to a Commodore PET, writing more complex betting programs.

For the slow days, Singleton came up with something he called "Computer Race." It was a computerized horse race with actual graphics. "This was specifically designed for betting shop use, say when the racing was off because of bad weather. It was developed to the point where it would do a complete printout of all the operations done during the day, so you had a list of all the races run that day for security purposes, and it was on ROMs, so it couldn't be tampered with."

British betting laws prevented the use of Computer Race, so Singleton created a simplified version of the game for the VIC-20, which later evolved into Shadowfax in 1982. The original graphics were taken from the seminal work of the early Victorian photographer, Eadweard Muybridge, who experimented with time-lapse photography in the 1870s and did a series of photographs of horses for Leland Stanford (founder of Stanford University).

Singleton continued to develop games and began to experiment with the ZX81 when it was released. "Actually, the ZX81 didn't even have 1K's worth of memory. Because of all the bits of bobs inside, there was only about 750 bytes of memory left to play with!" His efforts were to be published by Petsoft, which was doing a deal with Clive Sinclair to develop games. But the deal fell through, and Singleton was left without many options and even less cash. So he called up Clive Sinclair ("he was just Clive then") and was asked to send along his games. After some time, he was invited to Cambridge and shown the ZX81 prototype—actually a ZX81 with a prototype EPROM. Could he create some games for the new system?

What Singleton remembers is that the ZX81 had even less available memory than the ZX80, since it had 32 additional system variables occupying space in its memory banks.

Despite the limited memory, Singleton did come up with something—a collection called Gamespack Number 1, which consisted of six less-than-1K games, all programmed over the two-week Christmas holiday. Gamespack Number 1 sold about 90,000 units and earned the struggling Singleton the massive royalty paycheck of £6,000.

Singleton also created and ran a very successful play-by-mail game called Starlord for several years. In addition, he created a few arcade games, such as Siege, Shadowfax, Snake Pit, and 3-Deep Space, an attempt at doing a 3D game complete with goggles. However, his breakthrough megahit was the first of a planned trilogy called The Lords of Midnight, which is remembered by many to be one of the great games in the history of the Spectrum.

Part of the inspiration for The Lords of Midnight came from seeing The Hobbit by

Shadowfax was Mike Singleton's first big game, based on his work on Computer Race.

Eadweard Muybridge's 19th century time-lapse photography was the basis for Singleton's graphics in Shadowfax.

SOFT 1957 DISC

LUXOR THE MOONPRINCE
He stands on the Downs
of Shadows looking
North to the Tower of
the Moon.

The Lords of Midnight was the first of a planned trilogy of huge adventure games.

Melbourne House. "I was appalled at the speed at which the graphics came up!" He told Terry Pratt, the head of Beyond, that something better could be done. Originally called Lords of Atlantis, Singleton borrowed some ideas he had already come up with for a play-by-mail game "which was more map-based rather than panorama-based…" He referred to the game's original inspiration as "landscaping." To create a world, he drew a large map with felt-tipped pens. "It isn't quite as difficult as it sounds, and really, I bet Tolkien did the same. You start off with a few word endings and tack different syllables on the front until you come up with something that sounds good, so you sit there going 'Ushgarak, Ashgarak, Ighrem' to yourself until you get something that sounds nice or horrible according to what you want."

After the map, Singleton worked on the story before doing any programming. Once he had the basic story, he began to program the game. Lords of Midnight was, for its time, a massive game, with a huge map and complex set of characters. Its sequel, Doomdark's Revenge, was even bigger. But the biggest one of all, the third in the trilogy, was to be titled Eye of the Moon. As far as we can tell, it was never completed under that title, although Singleton continued to program games for years afterward. Following the success of Lords of

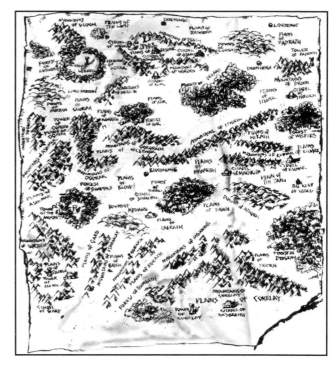

The Lords of Midnight world map.

Midnight and Doomdark's Revenge, Singleton created many additional games over the years, including Ring Cycle, War in Middle Earth, Lords of Chaos, and in 1995, Lords of Midnight 3: The Citadel. About Eye of the Moon, Singleton was quoted in a 1987 issue of *CRASH* magazine as saying, "It'll be finished when it's good and ready."

THE LORDS OF MIDNIGHT
MIKE SINGLETON
GAME OF THE MONTH AUGUST 1984

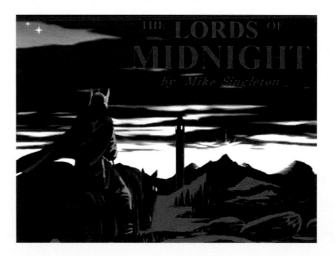

A Down Under Connection

Australia may get little acknowledgment in the history of computer games, but it has been particularly important in three different genres: adventure games, fighting games, and strategy games. Melbourne House (or more precisely Beam Software, a developer distributed by Melbourne) earns the kudos for the first two genres, while Strategic Studies Group (SSG) led the way in the latter. Melbourne House built its initial success on a 1980 book called *30 Programs for the Sinclair ZX80 1K*, but it made its fortune on a product called The Hobbit, a text-based adventure game with occasional still graphics, created by Philip Mitchell in 1982. By the late '80s, the game had sold over a million copies across all platforms. The secret of its success was the popularity of Tolkien and Stuart Richie's excellent Inglish parser.

In addition to the advancement in parser design, The Hobbit featured another intriguing aspect: it was a "real-time" adventure game. If you did nothing, the game kept moving. As Bilbo, you could literally die from doing nothing but watching the screen. The downside of the game (and its successors, Lord of the Rings and Shadows of Mordor) was that it was incredibly buggy. After UK-based Mastertronic (subsequently Virgin Games) acquired Melbourne House, UK developer Synergistic Software took over the Tolkien license under both the Virgin and Melbourne House banner and released a beautiful mix of strategy and adventure for the Amiga

We included this obscure Melbourne House title because... well, why not?

called War in Middle Earth.

In 1985, Melbourne House launched a new genre on the personal computer. Gregg Barnett's The Way of the Exploding Fist (a Sinclair game that loaded via cassette tape), was an early example of the one-on-one martial arts game, which ultimately became one of the most influential genres of game playing when Street Fighter II elevated it to cult status.

The Aussies proved they were masters of the arcade game and not merely sentenced to a lifetime of creating adventure games like the wild parody Denis Through the Drinking Glass and the superhero game Redhawk.

Mastertronic

Part of the relevance of the Melbourne House story is its ultimate acquisition by Mastertronic, a company originally created to produce budget games. The company was founded by three partners, Martin Alper, Frank Herman, and Alan Sharam, none of whom had any particular interest in playing games. They had a vision to create budget games, not to play them.

At first, they had to overcome resistance from the retail trade to the idea of low-cost games with low per-piece profits, but ultimately, they were able to show that they could provide a constant stream of new budget games, meaning a constant stream of sales. The idea worked, and they began to achieve some success. They employed no in-house programming staff, but paid outside developers royalties on a quarterly basis.

Over the years, they released many inexpensive titles, and re-released many of the hits and lesser games from previous years—all at £1.99 per game. Though they may often have lacked for originality or high quality, they made up for it by sheer volume and dirt-cheap pricing.

In 1987, Mastertronic bought Melbourne House and, later in the same year, sold a major share of stock to Richard Branson's The Virgin Group, becoming Virgin Mastertronic. This was also the year they began distributing Sega's Master System consoles and software. By 1991, their business was largely driven by Sega distribution in Europe. They

With graphics and an "educated parser," The Hobbit won a multitude of fans, despite its bugs.

Melbourne House's Redhawk delved into the superhero genre long before Infocomics, and arguably did a better job of it.

Melbourne House's The Way of the Exploding Fist helped establish the martial arts game genre in 1985.

produced games of various sorts and under various names, including M.A.D. (Mastertronic Added Dimension), Tronix, Bulldog Software, Ricochet, and Mastervision. They also opened offices in the U.S. and distributed other titles from the UK to major retailers in the States. They had some successful products as Virgin Mastertronic, and later, Virgin Interactive Entertainment (VIE), ultimately opening offices in Southern California under this header. It was Martin Alper who opened the U.S. office and who also affected game history by encouraging two young developers to go on their own and create the ambitious game they had envisioned (*see page 268*).

The Darlings

Despite their early experience as budget game creators, the Darling brothers showed that they had the skills and vision to create an enduring company capable of ultimately producing Many of the early Mastertronic games were created by two groups—the Darling brothers (David and Richard) and a company called Mr. Chip Software. We have no idea what happened to Mr. Chip, but we have a very good idea where to find the Darling brothers. They got out of their Mastertronic contract as soon as they could and opened their own firm—Codemasters.

more than 60 hit games in the UK. Moreover, they are one of the few companies that began in the UK in the '80s and continues to create games in today's market without a change of name or ownership.

Codemasters was the first UK company to employ compact discs, and they did it in an innovative way, by creating a method that allowed users to hook a standard CD player to their computer to download the game. They have produced games of all genres, including sports, first-person shooters, music creation software, and games from licensed properties. Among their hits are BMX Racer, the Colin McRae Rally series, the Operation Flashpoint series, and many other titles for PC, PlayStation, PlayStation 2, and Xbox. And the best may be

DAVE PERRY IN THE OLD COUNTRY

Dave Perry was born in Ireland, once wanted to be a test pilot, and is one of the great success stories coming out of the UK. He began programming while still in school. He sent some programs to a company called Interface Publications, which published his code in several magazines and books, ultimately creating a book of Perry's programs alone called *Astounding Arcade Games for Your Spectrum+ & Spectrum*. The book sold 13,000 copies.

In 1984, he sent a game called Drakmaze to Mikro-Gen, one of the early game publishers. Later, he joined Mikro-Gen at the request of its managing director, Mike Meek. But joining the company meant he would have to "chuck in" school and live on a salary of £3,200 a year. "Everyone was telling me not to do it." But he packed up his worldly goods and moved to Virginia Water, near Bracknell.

He helped on the highly successful game, Pyjamarama, by Chris Hinsley, writing the Amstrad version, and, when Hinsley became ill on the subway (the "tube"), he ended up fielding questions from the press at the game's launch. Pyjamarama was the second game to feature a typical British working-class bloke named Wally Week, the first being Mikro-Gen's Automania. Demand for more Wally games grew and more games in the series followed, such as Everyone's a Wally and Herbert's Dummy Run,

followed by Perry's first big hit game, Three Weeks in Paradise, where he first began working with Nick Jones, which started a long-time association. Jones had sent in a buggy version of his first game, Galaliens, and it impressed the Mikro-Gen team enough to offer him a job. With Hinsley and Raffaele Cecco, they became the Mikro-Gen development team after that.

Perry's next big project was Stainless Steel, which featured a bird's-eye view of the action. He encountered problems with this approach and vowed, "I'll never do another game from above. I've always done things from the side and always will in the future."

Among his most fondly remembered programs are Supremacy, which was created on the Amiga, and Extreme, which, he says, pushed the Spectrum to the limit. He also did The Terminator for Orion Pictures, after which he was offered a job in the States by Virgin Games.

Dave Perry's story continued in the U.S., where he founded Shiny Entertainment. For more on his story, see page 288.

An early photo of Codemasters, David and Richard Darling.

yet to come: Codemasters is still developing games as of our most recent update in 2016, 30 years after the company's creation.

Hewson

In 1984, Andrew Hewson created Hewson Consultants Ltd., better known simply as Hewson. They initially created games for the Speccy, but ultimately branched out to other systems and even hired programmers from as far away as Germany and Scandinavia. Among their most popular games were Nebulus, which strangely involved guiding a green pig up some rotating towers. Other games that stood out were Stormlord, Cybernoid, and its sequel. When the company became financially challenged in the early '90s, they became 21st Century Entertainment, which created some popular pinball simulations but ultimately went out of business.

U.S. Gold

U.S. Gold was started by Geoff and Anne Brown in Edgbaston, Birmingham, in the early '80s with the idea of taking coin-op games from the States and porting them to popular systems in the UK such as the BBC Micro, Sinclair Spectrum, and Amstrad CPC series. However, they far surpassed their original vision, releasing hundreds of games and several hit titles from 1984 through 1996. In the words of a former employee, their biggest contribution to the industry was "bringing affordable high-quality games to the masses."

Some of their notable releases include Beach Head and Beach Head II, Impossible Mission, Bruce Lee, Gauntlet, Leaderboard, Street Fighter, and Ghouls 'n Ghosts. They ultimately distributed games in the U.S., as well, with some success. In 1996, U.S. Gold merged with their distributor and ultimately became part of Eidos. For more, see Core Design/Eidos on *page 409*.

U.S. Gold were no strangers to controversy. They once released a game called Psycho Pigs UXB, and the billboards showed a picture of a joystick and a picture of a semi-naked woman. The slogan stated, "I know which one I'd rather play with." When they released a game called Chernobyl, which had nothing to do with the meltdown, they were picketed by protesters at their offices in Birmingham.

Geoff Brown went on to create Kaboom Studios, which made news in 2002 with their strip club simulation, Private

Bruce Lee was one of the earliest one-on-one fighting games, although it was basically a platform arcade game. It's difficult to see the resemblance between its 2D graphics and future games like Street Fighter II, but games like Bruce Lee and Karateka were enough to get some of us hooked on fighting games.

Firebird/ Rainbird

In the spring of 1984, British Telecom General Manager Dr. Ederyn Williams decided to create a game company with the name Telecomsoft. According to one source, the original publishing name for the company was going to be "Firefly," but ultimately it became Firebird when it was discovered that Firefly was already

Dancer, and which closed down nearly a year later.

Ocean Software

Ocean Software Ltd. published tons of games—possibly quite literally—from 1987 until 1999 on a variety of platforms. Their output was prolific, but most of it was created by outside development houses. Many of their published titles were ports; others were licenses such as The Addams Family, Batman, Jurassic Park, Robocop, and Terminator 2, although their games were of consistently high quality overall. Although there were some exceptions, Ocean mostly published arcade and action games. If you played arcade or action games during the late '80s and early '90s, chances are you played at least one Ocean offering.

registered.

The company staffed up somewhat, hiring Tony Rainbird from his own company, Micro Gold, and transferring James Leavey to run the marketing and PR. After some marketing analysis, they decided to release two kinds of titles at different price points, known as Firebird Gold and Firebird Silver. One of their marketing points was that they would include screenshots from the games on the game boxes instead of "potentially misleading artwork."

Once the company was set up, they created an ad that called for submissions from hopeful game programmers. They were inundated with replies, and soon were putting out titles on a variety of systems. Their first release was called Snake Bite for the VIC-20. They also released Mickey the Bricky, Bird Strike, Gold Digger, Duck!, Run Baby Run, Exodus, Viking Raiders, Terra Force, and Menace among their first wave of titles. In a second wave, they released Byte Bitten, The Wild Bunch, Acid Drops, Mr. Freeze, Booty, Crazy Caverns, Estra, The Hacker, Headache, Zulu, and GoGo the Ghost. The first Firebird Gold titles were Buggy Blast, Demons of Topaz, and then Gyron.

This was just the beginning. Under its various labels, which later included Rainbird, they released a huge number of original titles, budget titles, and ports. They worked with quite a few different development groups and many of the finest programmers to come out of the UK, including David Braben and Ian Bell, Geoff Crammond, Core Design, and ultimately purchased the design houses Beyond and Odin. They released classics such as Starglider and Starglider 2, Elite, Revs, and Virus.

It wasn't long before the management of British Telecom realized that the game business wasn't a great fit for them as an organization, despite its profitability. In 1988, they attempted to orchestrate a managerial buyout, however terms were not reached, and the company went on the market. At the time prospective buyers were being

shown around the company's upcoming releases included Rick Dangerous, Weird Dreams, Quartz, Oriental Games, Stunt Car Racer, Rainbow Islands, Mr. Heli, P47 Thunderbolt, Action Fighter, and conversions of Carrier Command and Starglider 2. Some of these were sure hits, and some became classics.

MicroProse Ltd., the UK branch of MicroProse (*see page 194*) purchased the company in May 1989 and started new operations, with some of the staff remaining. After taking over the company, MicroProse made some changes, among which was to discontinue the budget Silverbird line. Switching things around, some titles originally intended for Rainbird were moved and published by other divisions within MicroProse, while a couple of games originally intended for the MicroProse label were moved and published as Rainbird titles, including Maelstrom's Midwinter and Pete Cooke's Tower of Babel. Once the last of the titles in development had been released, however, the Firebird label was discontinued altogether, with Rainbird lasting a bit longer, but ultimately succumbing as well.

Magnetic Scrolls

One game that turned heads in the mid-'80s was published by Firebird (Rainbird in the States) but created by a new company called Magnetic Scrolls. The founders of Magnetic Scrolls, Ken Gordon and Anita Sinclair, saw an opportunity to enter the 16-bit computer market with the introduction of the Sinclair QL and the Atari ST. The Pawn was an adventure game set in the mythical land of Kerovnia, and it introduced gamers to some beautiful graphics of a kind not previously seen in electronic games, along with very intelligent and witty writing and puzzle design. The Pawn was released on a variety of systems and was popular in both the UK and the U.S.

The stunning graphics of The Pawn had a similar, although not as striking, effect on players to that of Myst when it came out. Not to overstate the case, but both games were more subtle and traditionally artistic than most of what preceded them, and both took the art of computer graphics to new levels.

Magnetic Scrolls went on to publish several more titles, winning awards and acclaim in all the adventure game circles. Their games covered a wide range of subject matter, and, though they believed strongly in the text adventure format, they weren't afraid to experiment. They were first to provide a cassette tape with audio clues along with the mystery-thriller Corruption, and they introduced a proprietary windowing system in the brilliantly crafted Wonderland.

The Pawn was notable for its great adventure gameplay and for its graphics, which were artistic and considered superior for the time.

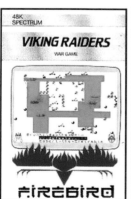

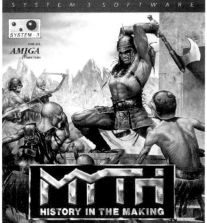

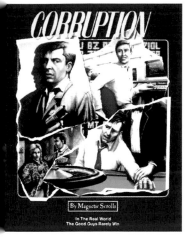

Argonaut Games

Jez San was still a teenager when he founded Argonaut Games in the early '80s. He wrote his first book, *Quantum Theory*, at the age of 18, and his first game was Skyline Attack on the Commodore 64. His second game, the award-winning Starglider, was inspired by the Star Wars arcade game. Starglider was a fast-action first-person game that featured 3D wireframe graphics and even came with a novella written by James Follett, which detailed the game's story. Most versions of the game also contained sampled speech. Published by Rainbird, Starglider put Jez San on the map, and his sequel, Starglider 2, was even better.

But Jez San was not only interested in programming games. He was passionately interested in the technology of games. "We've always pushed the R&D side of the company to achieve new technologies, like 3D rendering and physics."

Some people criticized Argonaut for focusing too much on technology and not enough on gameplay. "Worst of all, this was true," acknowledges San. But that was fixed when Argonaut hired more creative talent and built effective design tools for them to use.

However, a passion for the technology is part of what made Argonaut, and San, one of the most significant game companies and developers of the early '90s. And that's because of their close association with Nintendo.

Argonaut showed Nintendo some of their vector and polygon graphic demos, and the Japanese were impressed by what they had been able to wring out of the machine.

A screenshot from Starfox.

San told them that if they would fund it, Argonaut could design a chip to increase the 3D rendering ability of the SNES ten times. That was an understatement, and the chip they ultimately created, the Super FX, actually increased 3D graphics handling by 40 times.

The results were fantastic for Nintendo, for Argonaut, and for game players as the FX chip found its way into millions of cartridges. Argonaut contributed the first of those—Starfox—in 1993. In fact, the Super FX chip was so successful that the Argonaut team used to joke (privately) that the Super NES was the power supply for the Super FX chip and that the SNES merely displayed the results on the screen.

The success of the Super FX chip prompted a spin-off company called ARC, dedicated to hardware design and development. Among their accomplishments is the Argonaut RISC Core, which was the world's first customizable microprocessor. ARC licenses it to all kinds of hardware product designers.

Argonaut's other hits include Stunt Race FX, Croc and Croc 2, Creature Shock, Alien: Resurrection, and several Harry Potter games. Although Argonaut would eventually shut down, Jez San is still considered to be one of the top experts in interactive design.

Ultimate Play The Game

The story of the Stamper brothers, Chris and Tim, is one that stretches back to the earliest days of computer games in the UK and continues today. First influences? Chris Stamper was hooked as soon as he found out he could control something on a computer, specifically Pong-like games. With a degree in physics and electronics, he built himself an RCA CDP1802 computer and originally set about creating a traffic light control program. In 1980, he quit his job and began repairing and converting arcade games. Around the same time, he purchased a ZX81 computer. By 1982, Chris was convinced that he could create better games than most of what he had seen, so he got two brothers (Tim and Stephen), one girlfriend (Carole), and a college buddy (John), and together they started Ashby Computers & Graphics Ltd. located in Ashby-de-la-Zouch in Leicestershire, England. At first, they created modification kits for arcade games and earned modest cash with those, but they soon began creating original computer games under the company name Ultimate Play The Game.

Living on a shoestring budget in early 1983, the small company was in debt and the partners were getting more and more worried. Their first game, Jetpac, was their only hope. Remarkably, their hope was well-founded. Jetpac sold more than 300,000 units at £5.50 each, earning them more than £1.6 million!

Ultimate proceeded to release three more games in short order—Pssst, which involved spraying garden pests; Tranz Am, a racing game; and Cookie, which took place in a somewhat surreal kitchen. All their games ran smoothly and were written entirely in machine language, as opposed to many other games of the time which were still being written in BASIC. Each of their early games was written to work on the 16K Sinclair Spectrum models. Ultimate games were the first to claim, legitimately, "arcade quality" on the Spectrum.

Ultimate received great press reviews and were definitely at the top of the heap as they headed into 1984 with the release of Lunar Jetman (sequel to Jetpac) and Atic Atac, which was a simple graphic adventure that represented a turning point in their history.

Atic Atac took place in a haunted house and allowed the player to choose between three main characters, each with slightly different abilities. Although simple by today's standards, the game was quite large and ambitious for its time, but more importantly, it set the company in a new direction. Where their earlier games were purely arcade-inspired, after Atic Atac they moved toward more adventure-like gameplay.

The game that followed Atic Atac was called Sabre Wulf, which was followed by Knight Lore, a game played in the isometric 3D perspective that in another time would come to be popularly associated with Diablo and similar games. The Stampers called their isometric technology "Filmation." Simultaneous with the release of Knight Lore, they came out with yet another innovative title: Underwurlde, which was a sequel to Sabre Wulf. (In some ways, Knight Lore was also in the series, as it starred Sabre Wulf's hero, Sabreman.) With each new release, Ultimate outdid itself and reinvented their game mechanics. But they concentrated on the software and eschewed interviews, maintaining an aura of mystery, which intrigued the press and fans alike. Their aura of mystery and inaccessibility became semi-legendary, with stories of journalists pounding on their door to get an interview. But according to Tim Stamper, in a 1988 *CRASH* magazine interview, the years of silence and the publicity effect it had weren't intentional. They simply didn't have time for interviews and appearances. "We worked seven days a week, 5:00 a.m. 'til 1 or 2 in the morning. I don't feel it's any good having engineers who work 9 to 5, because you get a 9 to 5 game…"

Knight Lore itself was an immense success and spawned many imitators. It was considered to be far ahead of its time when released, but the irony is that Knight Lore was actually complete (and Alien 8 half-done) before they released Sabre Wulf. However, they believed that Sabre Wulf sales would have suffered if they had released Knight Lore first, so they held onto it and put out Sabre Wulf. Whether they were correct or not, Sabre Wulf was a huge

Tape box covers for Sabre Wulf and Knight Lore, plus Knight Lore screen on right.

A 1988 company photo of Rare, Ltd. outside their farmhouse studio.

had to strike a deal Tape box cover for Alien 8.

Splash screen for the creatively named Gunfright on right.

hit, and so were Knight Lore, Underwurlde, and Alien 8, each in its own right. Until 1986, Ultimate continued to produce more games—most notably, Nightshade and Gunfight, the last game the Stampers developed for Ultimate. About Gunfight, Chris Stamper said, "Everyone was copying our Knight Lore concept, so we thought we'd do one as well. Get a little bit of the action!"

In 1984 and 1985, Ultimate released a pair of C64 games, their first non-Spectrum games. Staff of Karnath and Entombed were both hit games, but their subsequent C64 releases did not fare well and caused speculation that their magic had dried up.

The Stamper brothers realized that the Spectrum era was about done. To this point, almost all their games had been created on and for the Speccy, with a few ports and a few C64 experiments, but the Stampers were now ready to move on to a new challenge. They set their sites on Japan.

The truth is that they had had a Nintendo game system as early as 1984 and had been considering their entry into the console market for four years before going public with their intentions. They had to make contacts, figure out how to program on the Nintendo machine—without any documentation or help from Nintendo—and they had to strike a deal with Nintendo. The deal they struck turned out to be very lucrative. Instead of being a separate publisher, they licensed their games to Nintendo. So, while most producers of games for the NES were given allocations and limits by Nintendo, the Stampers were able to produce all the games they wanted in their new company, Rare, Ltd. Not only do they create great games, but they have also been shrewd in business and visionary about their future.

Ultimate was sold to U.S. Gold after the Stampers had formed Rare. Yes, the creative minds behind Knight Lore and Sabre Wulf are also the people who brought you R.C. Pro-Am and Battletoads (for the NES), Killer Instinct, GoldenEye, Donkey Kong Country, Banjo-Kazooie, Perfect Dark, Star Fox Adventures, and many other great games in a long and profitable association with Nintendo. (See also page 307.)

Reportedly, some of the old cast of characters have made occasional appearances in Rare's games. Jetpac appears in Donkey Kong 64, and Sabreman (from Sabre Wulf) is reported to appear on the N64 title Banjo-Tooie. We haven't seen them, but perhaps you can find them.

More recently, Rare joined with Microsoft to help bring their exceptional talents to the Xbox. Many of their classic Ultimate Play The Game titles returned in the Rare Replay collection released on the Xbox One in honor of Rare's 30th anniversary. Who knows what other titles from their past may reappear? Meanwhile, Ultimate fans are still hoping for the never-released Mire Mare.

The Quantum Leap

Sir Clive Sinclair figured that if the Spectrum could sell millions, his next machine, the Sinclair QL (for Quantum Leap), would be another record breaker. At a price point of under £400, and featuring a powerful Motorola 68008 processor, two Microdrives, and a lot of other great stuff, it looked on paper to be a clear winner, but then reality set in.

Lack of quality control delayed shipments and produced faulty, inoperable machines, and the QL's launch was a disaster. Worse still, the machine's ROMs had not been completed when it shipped, and a dongle (or special chip board) was necessary to correct the problem.

Meanwhile, the IBM PC was rising in popularity, even as the price of the machines and peripherals dropped. Sinclair's price point advantage was disappearing, and the QL sold miserably—about 100,000 systems. There were games for the QL, of course. There are always games, but the machine never amounted to a major player in the game market.

Subsequent computer introductions, such as the Spectrum+, the Spectrum 128, and the portable Z88 computer released in 1988 all have their place in computer history, but from the games perspective, Uncle Clive's significant contribution ended with the Speccy.

Mirrorsoft

Robert Maxwell (born Jan Ludvik Hoch in Czechoslovakia in 1923) was a controversial, practically mythical figure, who was captured by Nazis in France in 1940 and, after escaping to England, joined the British Army in the liberation of Europe in 1944. He owned many enterprises, beginning with the publishing house Pergamon Press and extending to football teams and other businesses such as the Daily Mirror and Macmillan Publishers. In the '80s, after Sinclair Research Ltd. ran into financial trouble (again), Maxwell purchased the company from Sir Clive, who, once the dust had settled, retained an eight percent share and an important-sounding, but meaningless position. In 1991, facing significant financial difficulties himself, Maxwell died at sea under mysterious circumstances. Many rumors surrounded his death, ranging from suicide to implications that he had been an Israeli spy and was assassinated.

One of Maxwell's business ventures was the software company Mirrorsoft, which was started in 1983 by Jim Mackonochie for Maxwell's Mirror Group Newspapers. Mirrorsoft was formed based on Mackonochie's projection that "by the 1990s most homes would have a terminal, based on a home computer." Mirrorsoft came into being to support that future.

Expecting education to be a more important part of the projection than games, Mirrorsoft placed a lot of their ini-

tial emphasis on early education, starting with one of Mirror Group's comic strip characters, Mr. Men. Early game efforts that had educational content were Phineas Frog and Ancient Quests. Creating software in a wide variety of areas, including adult education and creative uses of the computer, the company did get involved in more mainstream games, as well.

While Mirrorsoft did distribute some Cinemaware titles and the Bitmap Brothers' Speedball in Europe, their own games saw little success outside the UK. Mirrorsoft is usually included in history books like this one because of its involvement in the Tetris story (*see page 204*). Mirrorsoft did release some successful games in the UK, the earliest of which were Caesar the Cat and a good Jet Set Willy clone, Dynamite Dan. Mirrorsoft also owned a major stake in Spectrum HoloByte, which, in turn, was thoroughly investigated after Maxwell's death. The British authorities were firmly convinced that Maxwell and his sons had laundered money through the Spectrum HoloByte operation. (*See also page 202.*)

After Mirrorsoft closed its doors, Mackonochie went on to join Mindscape's SSI division, where he managed the UK development and distribution.

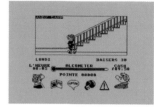

Two of Mirrorsoft's early games: Andy Capp and Caesar the Cat.

A clone of Jet Set Willy, Dynamite Dan sold well for Mirrorsoft.

An amusing story UK-specific story is one about Barbarian: The Ultimate Warrior, released under the Palace Software label in 1987. The cover of the game featured a pair of scantily clad models dressed as "barbarians" in the style common in fantasy fiction. Perhaps this would not have stirred up a hornet's nest, but the woman in the picture was none other than a famous "page 3" girl, the amply endowed Maria Whittaker. Now, most of us in the U.S. and other parts of the world have no idea what a "page 3" girl is. Starting in the '70s, British tabloids got in the habit of publishing a photograph of a nude or topless model, specifically on page 3 of the paper.

The first paper to do so was The Sun, but others followed suit.

Maria Whittaker was a famous, regularly featured page 3 girl, but when she appeared on the game's cover, clad in far more clothes than usual but sporting a skimpy thong bikini, a right to-do ensued. There was much protest and hoopla over the buxom Ms. Whittaker's state of dress on the Barbarian cover, and—this is the ironic part—nothing about the extreme gory violence of the game, which was far more gruesome than just about anything that had been seen previously. Of course, the publicity was highly beneficial to everyone involved, and the voluptuous Ms. Whittaker not only appeared on posters but also on the box art of the sequel, Barbarian II: The Dungeon of Drax.

Note: Psygnosis had previously come out with a Barbarian game, which had no relation to this one at all.

Peter Scott's Signature Style

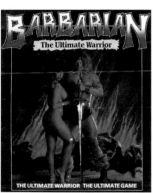

Peter Scott was one of the early computer game programmer/developers who had his own recognizable style, according to his fans. He started programming in school and teamed up with his friend Gary Partis first to create some programs for the school system—networking and a word processor—for which they were paid a one-time fee. But his first games were listings in various magazines for ZX81, Dragon, Oric, Spectrum, and C64 systems. Finally, he bought an Acorn Electron and from there migrated to the Beeb. Many of the magazine games ultimately became, in his words, "proper published games."

Scott wanted to bring the best qualities of games from other systems to the Beeb, and in doing so, he created a style that players recognized as unique. He contracted with a game company called ASL, but some of his games appeared from other publishers, such as Bug-Byte. "For example," he said in an interview, "Hunkidory was one of my first ever games. It was finally published something like two years into my career, by Bug-Byte, a company I didn't even know. And companies sold games to each other. I didn't care so long as I got paid."

While under contract with ASL, Scott saw that the company was selling too few games, so he began sending his games to Superior Software under the pseudonym Dylan. "I had a bank account and checkbook under 'Dylan.'" Among more than 20 games credited to him, Scott created Barbarian for Superior Software in 1987, and the sequel in 1989 (although apparently published under the Palace label).

Scott also did quite a few conversions. He would receive an Atari ST or C64 disk with no instructions and be expected to program a conversion of the game to the BBC Micro. "I'd buy magazines to find cheats. I'd then have to play through the game and convert it from sight. Not easy. And with incredibly tight deadlines. I got the gig because I'd say yes before seeing the game, look at it and go pale, slave over it, and get something ready on time."

By 1991, Scott was ready to move on to something else. He had done two games in 1990—one a version of Predator, based on the license, and the other a version of SimCity. "I wrote Predator in four or five weeks, a fairly crap little shoot-'em-up, finished right before Christmas. It sold by the barrel load. I slaved for six months on SimCity. It sold very few copies. That kinda gets to you, all the effort and pride that went into SimCity, and Arnie's face on the box of Predator wins every time."

The Bitmap Brothers

First of all, they aren't brothers. But The Bitmap Brothers have created a family of truly memorable games. Their first game, Xenon, was published on the Amiga in 1988 and immediately gained attention for its slick look and gameplay. However, it was their second game, Speedball, that became an instant classic. This futuristic sports game combined great gameplay, physics, the slick metallic arena, and a fascinating overhead perspective. All of these elements combined to make Speedball a superior game.

Both Xenon and Speedball did extremely well in the UK and the U.S. The Bitmap Brothers were well established among the top developers after only two games. They are still making games at the time of this writing, including The Chaos Engine, Speedball 2, and World War II: Frontline Command.

Core Design/Eidos

In 1988, with an investment of £16,000, Jeremy Heath-Smith opened the doors of Core Design. Their first product, Rick Dangerous, shot immediately to the top of the UK charts and ultimately won an award as European Game of the Year. That was only the beginning of a long run of hits from this innovative and prolific team. In 1990-91, they released

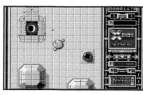

Corporation through Virgin Games, which was one of the earliest first-person shooters, slightly predating id Software's Wolfenstein 3D. Corporation was another hit for Core, along with Chuck Rock, Heimdall, Darkmere, and Thunderhawk.

Tomb Raider screens

In 1994, Core Design became a part of CentreGold, which itself was a merger of game publisher U.S. Gold and the distributor Centresoft. Two years later, in April 1996, CentreGold was acquired by Eidos, a company originally formed in 1990 to research video compression technologies. In 1993, Eidos entered the game publishing business by acquiring Domark, a company established in 1984 in London "to be the biggest publisher of computer games in Europe," according to former Domark chairman Ian Livingstone. Livingstone went on to become Eidos' creative director.

Domark had previously released a string of titles, including Championship Manager and several flight sims. By October of 1996, Tomb Raider was first released on the Sega Saturn, coming out in the next month on the PlayStation and the PC (*see page 302*). Core Design continued to grow as a semi-independent development house

under Eidos, creating a variety of sequels in the Tomb Raider series.

Of course, the overused phrase "the rest is history" certainly applies here. Tomb Raider not only became one of the biggest game series ever released on the computer, but it also spawned two movies and, in some people's opinion, was a big part of the ultimate success of Sony's PlayStation line.

Surprisingly, in 2003, Eidos moved Tomb Raider development to their U.S. subsidiary, Crystal Dynamics, and Core Design founder Jeremy Heath-Smith left the company.

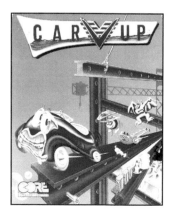

Core Design created many memorable games before Tomb Raider.

Interview with Dave Jones

Dave Jones, the legendary developer, talks about his career and, in particular, his two biggest hits—Lemmings and the Grand Theft Auto series.

Q: When did you first start with computers?

It was when I was in school. Back in 1981, I bought a ZX81 kit and tried to put it together. I was maybe 13 or 14 at the time. I was ambitious.

Q: How did it turn out?

It was a bit of a mess, actually. It didn't run at all. But one of the teachers at school helped me, and we got it working. Then I sort of ran across a book on computers and started reading.

Q: Did this lead immediately to your first game efforts?

Well, it turned out that all the Sinclair computers for the UK were being made there in Dundee where I lived, at Timex, the watch company. And so it was natural for me to go apply for an apprenticeship there after high school. Having actually built one of the kits was unusual. It was great to say I had built one of the machines from scratch. That got me a job as an electronics engineer. It was a good deal. They put you through college, full-time for a year while getting paid. After that you went to the factory, learning various disciplines. They were making the Sinclair Spectrum then—it was around '83. I worked on the ZX81, ZX Spectrum, Sinclair QL (first 16-bit machine), as well as Sinclair peripherals such as the ZX Microdrive, ZX Thermal Printer. It was a good place to get access to computers in the early days. I was at Timex for three or four years.

Q: Did you create any games during that time?

Yes. I wrote one game on the Spectrum with a friend. We called it Moon Shadow. It was my first commercial project, and I found that I liked the programming side even more than the hardware side. So I decided to leave Timex and go back to university to get a four-year software degree.

While I was still at the university, the Amiga 1000 came out in the States. That was around 1986 or '87. Well, I went out and spent my life savings to get one of the machines from the U.S. I was still at the university, but I thought I'd have a go at writing a game on the Amiga. I spent a year working on a game called Menace. It was a shooter on the Amiga. I had a guy in London doing the artwork, and I did all the programming.

I decided to take it to the Personal Computer World Show in London, where I showed it around. That's when I hooked up with Psygnosis. I was just a student and the game was mostly

done. Psygnosis was pretty new then, and said they'd like to publish it. Which they did. It sold around 10,000 copies in the UK—not bad for a university student. Then, in 1989, I did my second game called Blood Money, another Amiga shooter.

About this time, I had a bunch of college friends working on converting games to other formats, like Atari ST, Commodore 64, and the PC. With the success of the games, I saw that there was a lot of opportunity out there. I was torn between completing my degree and going full-time into the games. They said I could take a couple of years off if I wanted and come back to complete my degree, so I got a friend to help me—my first employee—and opened an office. That's when DMA was born.

Q: What does DMA stand for?

Doesn't mean anything. That's what it stands for. Doesn't Mean Anything.

Q: How did you come up with that for a name?

It was really hard to come up with a name; initially, I started to use Acme Software. In the dictionary this is defined as "the pinnacle of perfection," which I thought was great. Everyone else thought of the Road Runner cartoon and did not like it. I got fed up with trying to think of a good name, and decided to use something that: Doesn't Mean Anything.

Q: So what happened next?

Well, we were doing a conversion of Blood Money when we first started, and around lunchtime one day, Mike Dailly, one of our artists, showed us a little animation he had done in DPaint—just a simple little cyclic animation that kept replaying. It showed a little creature walking up a hill, and at the top its head would get lopped off. We thought it was pretty funny, and pretty soon we had Mike create a whole bunch of the little guys, just walking

to the top of the hill and losing their heads. Well, I began to think, "How could we prevent them from losing their heads? How could we save them?" and that was how Lemmings was born. In fact, the name Lemmings was what we first thought of. It's rare that you have the final name of a game from the very beginning, but that was the case with Lemmings.

Q: Let me get this straight. Lemmings was just the third game you ever created?

Yes. We worked on it for about six months and completed ten levels. We thought about the skills we'd want the Lemmings to have, like digging and climbing, but

we wanted to keep it pretty simple, so we chose eight types. In those days, computer programmers often thought in terms of eight, but basically we didn't want people to have to remember too many options.

Anyway, after working on it for six months, we went to visit the Psygnosis offices in Liverpool and dropped a copy off with one of their artists while we went to lunch with some people. When we got back from lunch, Lemmings was on all the computers in the office, and they were all talking about it. "I made it to Level 7." "I finished it." We sort of sprang it on them, and at the end of the day we had a good feeling we were on to something special.

We kept working on it until we had about 100 levels; then we released it. That was in 1991. The day it was released in the UK, Ian [Hetherington—founder of Psygnosis] was calling me every 5,000 presale unit orders he received. This was on the Amiga, and by the day's end, we had sold something like 65,000 units. For the Amiga in the UK, this was very good.

By the time the Lemmings phenomenon was done, I think we had spent more than two additional years, creating Lemmings versions for about 21 different formats. We created Lemmings 2 and ultimately Lemmings 3, but by that time the idea was drying up and I didn't do much work on that version. I mean, it's not so enjoyable to have to do a product because you have to do a product. You want to enjoy what you're working on, and that's hard when it becomes more commercial. Today, Sony owns the copyright, having bought Psygnosis.

Q: So Psygnosis owned the Lemmings copyright, not you?

Yes, it was pretty standard when you were just starting out to give up the copyright to the publisher. It was just the way it was done. So when Sony bought Psygnosis, they got the Lemmings rights with the company.

Q: In the midst of Lemmings' success, you developed a relationship with Nintendo that turned out to be challenging.

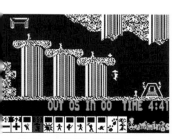

Can you tell us more about that?

Yes. We were contacted by Tony Harman at Nintendo who wanted us to do some games for the Super NES. We came up with a unicycle racing game called Uniracers. It was a fun game—a bit different—with the twist that you had to perform stunts to gain speed.

Q: *I've heard it described as a cross between Sonic the Hedgehog and Tony Hawk's Pro Skater. But you had more difficulties with another Nintendo collaboration.*

You're referring to Body Harvest. Yes, we had some challenges working with the Japanese. Where we had previously created games pretty much without any involvement from the publishers, with Nintendo, they had very specific ideas about how the games should be. Body Harvest was meant to be a free-form, mission-based game, very much a forerunner to Grand Theft Auto, in which you could undertake missions or just spend time killing bugs. But Nintendo at that time was very focused on more role-playing types of games. That was their strategy for the N64. They saw it going one way, and we saw it going another. We tried to add in some of the role-playing elements, but it ended up as a sort of mishmash. Body Harvest could have been as good as GTA, but it was somewhat hampered by our differing visions. In the end, Nintendo didn't publish it, but we were able to release it with Gremlin in the UK, and they got it distributed in the U.S. by Midway.

Our next step was to join up with BMG, who were coming out of the music business, and, possibly because of that, they were more into pop culture and taking risks. They commissioned us to create three games, and the games we came up with were Grand Theft Auto, Silicon Valley for the N64, and Wild Metal Country for the PC.

Q: *Obviously of the three, GTA is the one that most intrigues me.*

GTA started out as a city simulation—a whole living city. Once we had something we could play in, we started putting in things to do. Originally, you could be the police as well as the criminals, and the name of the game was Race and Chase. But everybody wanted to be the criminals. Then one of the marketing guys at BMG came up with the name Grand Theft Auto. It was a great name—short and snappy.

BMG let us do whatever we wanted. They told us to go ahead, and they would handle any backlash. So we spent around 18 months to two years working on it. In actuality, BMG's U.S. division never liked it. It was a top-down perspective, and they didn't believe in it. There was a clash between the UK people and the U.S. people—a friction between them. The original GTA was the kind of game you had to start playing to appreciate. Once you began to play, the top-down perspective didn't matter anymore.

So GTA did really well, but BMG was getting out of the game business, so they sold out to Take-Two. We were working on GTA 2 at the time, which was also top-down perspective. It really took the PlayStation 2 to make it feasible to create the 3D version of the game—GTA III. But GTA III was the same game from a design perspective, and I was ready to leave before it was done. So I left DMA and formed a new company with Tony Harman from Nintendo and the team that did GTA and Wild Metal Country. Ian Hetherington also recently joined us as chairman. We have a great team working on some new-generation online games and technologies.

413

GTA

GTA 2

Q: But you did start out the development of GTA III before you left. Tell me about its success.

GTA III is really the game that took the concept to the mainstream. Before that, it was a gamer's game because you had to see past the graphics. But with the introduction of the 3D perspective, the game became accessible to a much wider audience of players.

Q: What about the criticisms of GTA's violence?

Well, think of it this way. The game underneath GTA is Pac-Man. The pedestrians are the dots, the ghosts are the police, and the weapons are like picking up the Power Pill so you can fight back. I see it as Pac-Man with mature content. Sure, we knew it would be controversial. We made big decisions to keep everything in the game, even if it meant that some of the big chains, such as Wal-Mart, might not carry it. It's hard to do something for all ages. But what we did was take a classic gaming hook and create a game that worked for people.

Q: Even though I have thoughts about the nature of video games and their social value (or lack of it), I think GTA III is a superbly designed game and is rightfully successful. What worries me more is all the copycat mentality in the industry—people who will take the worst concepts of GTA and won't execute with the same skill and care. It can propagate an ugly trend. And I would like to see games with somewhat more redeeming content done with the same skill and care…

At the core, the game is very different from the treatment of the game. People are free to play in any way, but it isn't only about gratuitous violence. And we've done games that are completely different. At the end of the day, it wasn't about trying to glamorize it, but to realize the concept.

Q: So what's next for you? You've created a number of great games and at least two classics. Where do you go now?

As I said before, my new company is devoted to finding new, interesting, and original ways to create games on the Internet, which is currently dominated by first-person games and role-playing. I started Realtime Worlds to try out some things and hopefully come up with something very different. We hope to infuse some fresh air into the world of online games. We've got a concept we're excited about, but it will take some more time to develop the technology.

Q: Finally, tell me some of the games that have most influenced you in your career.

Certainly Populous, particularly for its link-up mode. Playing with someone else is so much more satisfying than sitting alone at the computer playing against the AI. I played Populous once a week with a friend for two solid years. Then there were many early Nintendo games, and particularly Mario 64, which demonstrated how to overcome many problems of 3D games. Counter-Strike for holding people's attention for so many years and for being one of those rare games that can have me jumping out of my chair once or twice. From the old days… Manic Miner, one of the classics in the UK, and the shooters like Salamander and R-Type.

ACROSS THE PACIFIC

Although Japan initially trailed the U.S. in video game development, when they did enter the market, they entered it in a big way. Starting in the mid-'80s, Japanese companies quickly dominated the console arena, a dominance they retained almost unchallenged until Microsoft launched the Xbox. Japanese games also took a lead position on the world stage, with first Donkey Kong, then Mario leading the way. Game franchises such as Mario Bros. and The Legend of Zelda from Nintendo, Sonic the Hedgehog from Sega, Street Fighter and Resident Evil from Capcom, Metal Gear from Konami, and Final Fantasy from Squaresoft—just to name a few—made history and kept on making it.

The influence of Japanese developers on the game industry and game design cannot be overstated. Japanese designers put their stamp on games of all kinds, and continued to surprise and delight players by constantly pushing the envelope and always seeking to improve and innovate in their games. On the console side, they created rivalries that forced innovation and kept the market lively and competitive, and, like Nintendo with the Wii, they proved that they still have surprises and amazing tricks up their sleeves decades after their first innovation.

Across the Pacific: A Japanese Chronology

The three Japanese characters that make up the word "Nintendo" roughly translate to "the place where things are left to heaven"—appropriate for a company that got its start in the gambling halls of Kyoto. Founded in 1889 as a manufacturer of hanafuda, Japanese playing cards with flower designs, Nintendo Co., Ltd. experimented with other product lines and ventures but always found itself most profitable in the world of entertainment.

Hiroshi Yamauchi

As the '60s drew to a close, president Hiroshi Yamauchi, the grandson of the company's founder, created a new department called simply Games. Department head Gunpei Yokoi's gadgets took Japan by storm—Nintendo sold millions of his Ultra toys, including a latticework hand that picked up far-away objects and an indoor pitching machine. By the '70s Nintendo had expanded into the world of electronic toys and games. Although Yokoi's Beam Gun toys that used light-sensor technology from Sharp are the most remembered, other products, like an electronic conga drum called Ele-Conga, were also developed and released during the decade.

Nintendo's first foray into the video game market was through the home, with the Color TV-Game series in 1977. Color TV-Game 6 and 15 were essentially versions of the Magnavox Odyssey systems. That same year, a young designer named Shigeru Miyamoto joined

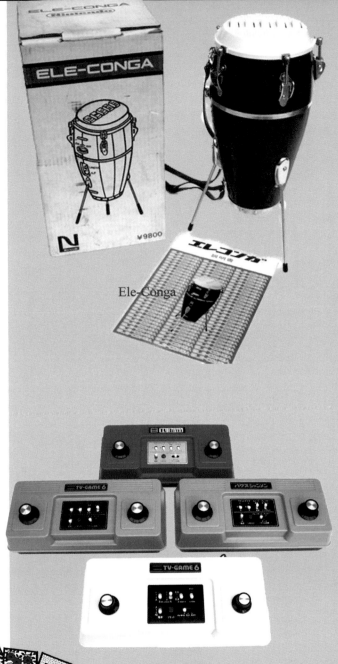

Ele-Conga

Color TV-Game 6 systems.

Original Nintendo hanafuda cards from Nintendo's archives.

Later Nintendo hanafuda cards.

In 1959, Hiroshi Yamauchi negotiated a deal with the Walt Disney Company to produce and distribute several highly successful lines of playing cards with Disney's characters on them.

Block Kuzushi

It was not Nintendo, but a toy company called Epoch that produced the first dedicated home system (TV Tennis) and the first programmable home system (Cassette Vision) in Japan.

the company and designed their next two home game cabinets: a racing game with a life-size steering wheel and a Breakout clone called Block Kuzushi or Block Breaker. The systems sold over one million units altogether, a huge hit compared to the slow sales of other dedicated systems.

This is not to suggest that Nintendo was the only company of note in the early days of the Japanese video game industry, or even that they were the first. That honor, on two fronts, goes to a toy company called Epoch that released Japan's first dedicated game system (TV Tennis) and later Japan's first programmable machine, Cassette Vision.

Soon after, Nintendo expanded into the arcade market, joining their contemporaries in making clones of popular arcade titles. Sheriff was a one-player version of Taito's Western Gun. Space Fever was much like Space Invaders. Radar Scope (see also page 243) was a lot like Galaxian and, for a time, was one of the hottest games in Japan. But when it fizzled in the U.S., Miyamoto was tapped to design a game to take its place across the Pacific. That game was Donkey Kong, and nearly a hundred years after the company's founding, Miyamoto's ape made the Nintendo name known worldwide (see also page 86).

Nintendo continued to produce original arcade games, but their next big success would come on a smaller scale. While Casio and Sharp fought to lower the prices of their digital watches, Nin-

417

Original Super Mario Bros. and Donkey Kong packages for the Famicom, signed by Shigeru Miyamoto.

tendo took advantage of the falling prices of LCDs and integrated circuits to produce handheld games about the size of a cassette tape. The Game & Watch series, from its very first game, Ball, was a giant hit in Japan. Copycat hardware soon flooded the market, but Nintendo's products were recognized above all, especially as the games began to feature their budding licensed properties like Donkey Kong and Mario Bros.

Nintendo stuck with the arcades and the Game & Watch, waiting until 1983 to release the Family Computer, a red-and-white toy-like system that the public quickly dubbed "Famicom" for short. Nintendo shipped more than 440,000 units in their first month, more than double the amount shipped by Sega

when they released their first console, the SG-1000, one day before Nintendo shipped the Famicom.

The Famicom shipped with three launch titles—Donkey Kong, Donkey Kong Jr., and Popeye. Nintendo took a lion's share of the still comparatively small market in 1983, and it wasn't until 1985 that Super Mario Bros.—and the Famicom boom—hit big.

Nintendo sold 3.9 million units in 1986 alone, over ten million sold overall by that time. The Famicom would go on to be a fixture in over 15 million Japanese homes, in many of which it still sits today.

Starting in 1984, other Japanese companies signed up with Nintendo to publish games on the Famicom. Some, like Namco, Konami, Capcom, and Taito, were established, successful arcade game publishers. Others, like Enix and Square, were start-ups formed specifically to publish home video games. Initially, their games could be played on the popular MSX home computers, but soon all of their energy was devoted toward Famicom titles. As a licensor, Nintendo made harsh demands, but the rewards were worth it.

By 1987, the Famicom technology was already four years old and showing its age. This opened the doors for competitors to enter the market with flashier hardware. NEC introduced a machine called the PC Engine that year, and arcade giant Sega, after two failed 8-bit efforts, introduced the 16-bit Mega Drive in 1988. Both machines could display more colorful and detailed graphics than the Famicom, but the game quality was lacking compared to the Famicom titles that were released in those years—

Nintendos's Disk System for the Famicom was successful in Japan, but ultimately Nintendo abandoned the disk format and stuck with cartridges until they introduced the GameCube in 2001.

Sega's Mega Drive was their 16-bit console that, just like NEC's PC Engine, was meant to challenge Nintendo's dominance.

including Enix's megahit Dragon Quest and Nintendo's own Zeruda no Densetsu (The Legend of Zelda). Dragon Quest was a cartridge-based game, but Zeruda no Densetsu was the launch title for Nintendo's Famicom Disk System, an add-on device that played games on compact floppy disk media. It was as successful a console add-on as has ever been, reaching nearly 50% market penetration, but the impermanence of the disk media and the small size of the disks led most publishers, including Nintendo a year later, to stick almost exclusively with cartridges.

To counter Nintendo's software juggernaut, NEC allied with Hudson Soft, the first Nintendo licensee, to create original and appealing PC Engine software like PC Genjin (Bonk's Adventure) and a new version of their Famicom and MSX hit, Bomberman. NEC achieved more success in Japan than Sega did—although strategic anti-Nintendo ad campaigns and the appeal of Mortal Kombat gave Sega the edge in the U.S. These factors weren't effective in Japan, and the Mega Drive finished third in the three-way 16-bit race. The PC Engine might have overtaken the Famicom had Nintendo's Super Famicom, released in 1990, not been so popular.

Unlike the Super Famicom, the Sega Mega Drive was backwards-compatible with the SG-3000 and the SG-1000 systems with the addition of an adapter. While compatibility proved to be a mildly successful feature in America, it didn't matter much to Japanese gamers, very few of whom owned the older Sega systems. Nintendo chose to emphasize the superiority of its new system and planned another amazing release calendar filled with impressive games. Based on the strength of launch titles like Super Mario World, F-Zero, and Pilotwings as well as early titles like Final Fantasy IV from Squaresoft and Final Fight from Capcom, Nintendo shipped 660,000 Super Famicoms in November 1990 and sold all of them on the first day. Later hit titles included Zeruda no Densetsu: Kamigami no

Triforce (The Legend of Zelda: Triforce of the Gods, known as A Link to the Past in America) and Super Mario Kart from Nintendo, Street Fighter II from Capcom, and Final Fantasy V and Dragon Quest V from Squaresoft and Enix, respectively. In 1991, Nintendo shipped an additional three million units.

Even as Nintendo rode its wave of success higher than ever before, the seeds that would topple the king from its throne had already begun to sprout. Still, the earliest days

HUDSON SOFT

Hudson Soft's Famicom and PC Engine titles might not have appealed to the majority of American players, but the company's games were well-known in Japan, starting with Lode Runner, a million-selling hit for the Famicom. A platformer starring their own PR representative, Takahashi Meijin no Bouken Jima (The Great Takahashi's Adventure Island) featured four installments, all of which made it to the U.S., albeit with all references to the real-life Takahashi removed. The U.S. division of the company was run by Bunso Yamada, a Jap-

anese-born executive who made the ignominious choice of "Bunny" for an American nickname before someone suggested that "Bernie" would provoke less laughter. Bernie's division published an extraordinarily difficult game called Starship Hector on the NES, and as the story goes, they pulled one over on Nintendo: to prove to Nintendo that the game was playable, you had to videotape the play from start to finish. To videotape Starship Hector, the programmers allegedly disabled the damage so that hits didn't count.

Bandai entered the disc-based market with their ultimately unsuccessful Playdia system.

Bandai's early toy, the Toyopet Crown, was the first to offer a guarantee.

The U.S. version of Bandai's first game for a Nintendo system was called M.U.S.C.L.E. Tag Team Match.

of CD-ROM technology were not exactly impressive. CD-ROM add-ons to the Mega Drive and PC Engine only served to weaken them in the 16-bit wars by splitting their user bases, and early CD-ROM-only game systems, like Panasonic's 3DO REAL and Bandai's Playdia were market disasters.

And indeed, when the Sega Saturn and Sony PlayStation were released in the waning months of 1994, it seemed as if the system that would topple Nintendo was, if either, Sega's. By the end of that year, the Saturn had sold 500,000 units at ¥44,800 compared to 300,000 PlayStations at ¥39,800. The reason was Virtua Fighter, which was far and away the best Japanese arcade game at the time, and sold on a 1:1 ratio with the system. NEC's entry, the boxy PC-FX, sold 70,000 units its first week but fizzled soon afterward, although it found a niche fan base with numerous anime-inspired exclusive titles.

Bandai

Like many of the successful Japanese game companies, Bandai started long before the digital revolution, making toys. They were incorporated by Naoharu Yamashina with a capital investment of ¥1 million in July 1950, and their first product, the Rhythm Ball, was released in September of the same year.

In 1951, they came out with the B-26 Night Plane, a metallic toy airplane. In the mid-'50s, Bandai's logo used the initials BC, for Bandai Corporation, and they were the first to offer a guarantee on one of their toys, a model car called the Toyopet Crown.

By 1960 they had established overseas sales channels and in 1961, officially changed the name of the company to Bandai. In the '60s, they produced action figures and other toys based on the popular and groundbreaking TV cartoon series, Osamu Tezuka's *Tetsuwan Atom* (*Mighty Atom*, known in the U.S. as *Astro Boy*). Their Naughty Flipper was a gold medal winner in the New York International Innovative Products Exhibition of 1968.

Bandai entered the home video game market in 1985 with a million-selling, cartoonish wrestling game based on the popular Japanese comic *Kinnikuman*. The comic never came to the U.S., but the tiny action figures based on the character did—they were licensed by toy company Mattel and called M.U.S.C.L.E. The game also made its way to the U.S., as M.U.S.C.L.E. Tag Team Match.

Bandai never fully shifted their focus to video games, however. They continued to diversify their business with such widely varied enterprises as film and stage productions, video productions (on contract with the Walt Disney Company), more toys (including *Gundam* and *Ultraman* figures), retail outlets (Shot M78 for *Ultraman* products), and

Bandai's Wonderswan handheld games were popular in Japan, in part due to the inclusion of Square's already popular Final Fantasy games, but the system never made it into distribution in the U.S.

Screenshot above is Final Fantasy for Wonderswan color.

Gunpei Yokoi

even music, with the establishment of the Emotion label.

In 1995, they partnered with Nintendo to release a Super Famicom add-on called Satellaview, which allowed users to download game content from satellite television feeds. In 1996, Bandai hit a worldwide goldmine in the toy market with the Tamagotchi virtual reality pet

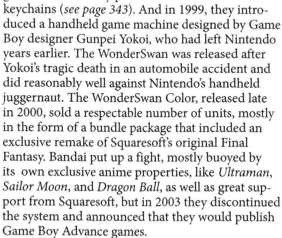

Satellaview

keychains (*see page 343*). And in 1999, they introduced a handheld game machine designed by Game Boy designer Gunpei Yokoi, who had left Nintendo years earlier. The WonderSwan was released after Yokoi's tragic death in an automobile accident and did reasonably well against Nintendo's handheld juggernaut. The WonderSwan Color, released late in 2000, sold a respectable number of units, mostly in the form of a bundle package that included an exclusive remake of Squaresoft's original Final Fantasy. Bandai put up a fight, mostly buoyed by its own exclusive anime properties, like *Ultraman*, *Sailor Moon*, and *Dragon Ball*, as well as great support from Squaresoft, but in 2003 they discontinued the system and announced that they would publish Game Boy Advance games.

Despite moving away from their own hardware, Bandai continued producing noteworthy titles that grew into beloved series, especially in the role-playing realm. .hack (pronounced "dot hack") was a four-game series supported by a tie-in anime, both

of which revolved around a fictional MMO world. After their merger with Namco in 2005 to become Namco Bandai Games, they also gained the prolific Tales series, which grew from Tales of Phantasia's release in 1995 to over a dozen games, with new titles still being developed to date.

A screen from .hack.

Taito

Established in 1953 by a Russian Jew named Michael Kogan, Taito (a Japanese word meaning "far east") initially imported and distributed amusement machines like peanut vending machines. (Taito also

brewed and sold the first Japanese-made vodka.) By the next year, they began leasing jukeboxes; soon they were manufacturing their own.

Taito also began their video game history by importing and distributing American coin-op video games in Japan, but soon

Early Taito game flyers.

began producing their own. Early titles like Davis Cup were more or less Pong clones. In 1974 they introduced Speed Race, which was Japan's first driving video game and the first Japanese game to be exported to the U.S. (by Midway). A reprogrammed U.S. version of Taito's Western Gun, called Gun Fight by Midway, was the first video game to use microprocessors (*see also page 25*).

This technological leap so impressed Taito engineer Tomohiro

Taito's never-released WOWOW satellite television unit.

Nishikado that he decided his next game would use a microprocessor; he called it Space Invaders, and it took Japan—and the world—by storm (*see page 50*).

Taito has never had another success quite like Space Invaders, but its later arcade releases remain true classics in their own right: Qix, Elevator Action, Arkanoid, Darius, Rastan, Double Dragon, Twin Cobra, Operation Wolf, Chase H.Q., and various sequels. In 1992, Taito showed a prototype console system that partnered with the WOWOW satellite television network to download and play arcade-quality CD-ROM games, but the system was never released. Taito released a 25th Anniversary edition of Space Invaders for the PlayStation 2, featuring a dozen different versions of the game, various video extras, and an optional controller in the shape of a miniature Space Invaders arcade cabinet.

Namco

Iwatani and his inspiration.

Iwatani and friend.

Namco was founded in 1955 as Nakamura Manufacturing Ltd. by Masaya Nakamura. His first entrepreneurial project was the installation of mechanical rocking-horse kiddie rides on the roof of a Tokyo department store, and he soon found himself at the helm of a company manufacturing and distributing its own amusement rides and arcade machines.

Namco joined the arcade game business in 1974, when they entered into an agreement with Atari to acquire the company's Japanese arm and distribute its games in Japan. After a falling-out with Atari over Namco's

unauthorized manufacture of Breakout machines, Namco began to create its own games. The company officially changed its name to Namco Ltd. in 1977. In 1978, Namco introduced the shooting game Galaxian (*see also page 54*). It was popular, but the company's future would actually be determined by the next game from Toru Iwatani, a designer whose previous games were all video-pinball simulators like Gee Bee and Cutie Q.

Iwatani's gift for colorful, pop culture designs attracted many women as well as men to his games, but this was only truly realized on a worldwide scale with Pac-Man (*see page 66*). When Nakamura awarded Iwatani a miniscule bonus of $3,500 after Pac-Man had made the company millions, he refused to program any more video games. Iwatani programmed only one more game, called Libble Rabble. As of the early 2000s, he still worked at Namco under the Japanese lifetime employment system, however, and did emerge out of near seclusion in 2003 to promote Pac-Man Vs. for the Nintendo GameCube alongside designer Shigeru Miyamoto, who is perhaps Iwatani's biggest fan.

Namco continued to produce arcade titles, including Pole Position and Xevious. They became a Nintendo licensee in 1985, bringing such titles as Pac-Man and Galaxian into Japanese homes for the first time. They also branched out into new

Nolan Bushnell and other executives from Atari meet with Namco execs at Atari's Japanese headquarters.

ventures, purchasing the Italian Tomato chain of restaurants in 1986. Their 1987 racing game, Final Lap, was the first to offer multiplayer competition.

In 1985, after the American video game market crash, Time Warner sold controlling interest in Atari Games, the arcade arm of Atari, to Namco for $10 million. In 1987, Namco sold its shares back to Time Warner and to Hideyuki Nakajima, the former general manager of Atari Japan under Namco. Nakajima soon went to Nintendo to form licensee Tengen, which published Namco's Famicom games in America, alongside Atari games like Gauntlet (as well as Tetris—*see page 204*).

In 1993, Namco acquired Aladdin's Castle Ltd., making them the largest arcade operator in the U.S. Also in 1993, they opened Wonder Park, an indoor amusement park, and a multifunctional entertainment facility called Wonder City in Yokohama. In 1994, Namco's original arcade business and Aladdin's Castle were consolidated under the name Cybertainment Inc. They continued to expand their arcade presence in later years, establishing arcade parks in Spain, France, Germany, and Israel, as well as the Namco Wonder

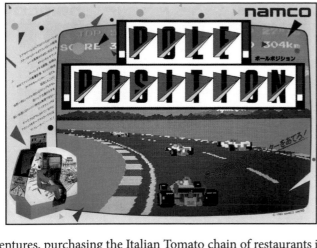

Tower in Kyoto, Japan.

At the same time, the company was introducing landmark next-generation games like Ridge Racer and Tekken, the home versions of which were exclusive to PlayStation. This brought the Namco/Sega rivalry to the home, since Tekken and Ridge Racer were Sony's answers to the Sega titles that were causing the Saturn to beat the PlayStation in Japan.

The rivalry didn't last, however, and Namco and Sega teamed up with Nintendo on the Triforce arcade hardware. Namco's most popular arcade title in Japan by far in those days was Taiko no Tatsujin (Drum Master), a music game that uses a giant traditional taiko drum as a controller. PlayStation 2 versions have sold over a million units combined, while in 2003 a GameCube version called Donkey Konga was released with a bongo drum controller and Nintendo characters.

Data East

Date East was founded in 1976 by Tetsuo Fukuda, and during the '80s they were a major force in the arcade world, with many memorable hits such as Bad Dudes, Karnov, and Fighter's History (which sparked a lawsuit with Capcom over similarities to Street Fighter II). Ironically, Data East's 1984 arcade title, Karate Champ, is arguably the first one-on-one side-view fighting game in arcade history (although Datasoft's Bruce Lee for various computer systems is also in the

Fighter's History sparked a lawsuit with Capcom over similarities to Street Fighter II.

Karate Champ: One of the first side-view arcade fighting games.

Screenshots from Metal Gear Solid 3 (below) and Silent Hill 3 (below right)

running, and a case can be made for Cinematronics' 1979 arcade title, Warrior, depending on how picky you want to be about what defines the genre).

In addition to their many arcade releases, Data East also created many games for the Famicom and NES, beginning with Tag Team Wrestling, Karate Champ, BurgerTime, and Side Pocket, all released in 1986 and 1987. In 1988, they released Karnov, Cobra Command, and Rampage. Sadly, Data East went bankrupt and closed their doors in June 2003.

Konami

Konami was founded on March 21, 1969, by Kagemasa Kozuki, who is still chairman and CEO to this day. Kozuki's original business was jukebox rental and repair. The company became Konami Industry Co., Ltd. in 1973 on a capital investment of ¥1 million and began manufacturing amusement machines.

Konami has a long history of hit games in the arcades and on home systems from MSX to the PlayStation 3. Some of their earliest hits include Akuma-jō Dorakyura (Demon Castle Dracula, now known worldwide as Castlevania), Gradius, Contra, Double Dribble, Teenage Mutant Ninja Turtles, Super C, Rush'n Attack, The Goonies, Track & Field, Silent Scope, and Parodius. More recently, they have taken a lead in the market with the highly acclaimed and innovative Metal Gear Solid, created by Hideo Kojima; two sequels to Silent Scope; the atmospheric Silent Hill series (the last of which was made into a feature movie); as well as their athletic arcade sensation, and precursor to movement games, Dance Dance Revolution. In addition, they have followed up with Guitar Freaks, DrumMania, and Karaoke Revolution, which uses a headset microphone to gauge the player's singing. In all, Konami has released hundreds of unique games of all kinds, putting it among the top game companies in the world.

Konami's Demon Castle Dracula (Castlevania) for the PC Engine.

Mega Man is known as Rockman in Japan.

Capcom

Capcom was founded in 1979 as a manufacturer and distributor of electronic games, and has in the years since reinvented its image at least three times. In the '80s, Capcom was known for addictive and difficult platformers and shooters like Gun.Smoke, Rockman (Mega Man), and Commando. In 1991, Capcom rose to the top of arcades worldwide with Street Fighter II, the game that single-handedly revived the flagging Japanese arcade market and defined the modern fighting game genre. According to Capcom, as of 2003 the Street Fighter series had sold more than 500,000 coin-operated cabinets, over 24 million console versions, and has generated more than a billion dollars in revenue. Street Fighter action figures, plush dolls, lunchboxes, and everything in between were hugely popular on both sides of the Pacific, and its detailed backstory has been the subject of animated and live action features, including the critically panned (but unintentionally campy and hilarious) film starring Jean-Claude Van Damme, Raul Julia, and Ming-Na.

Many of Capcom's early games are well worth remembering, such as their early arcade title 1942, the innovative Bionic Commando, the pure arcade mayhem in Ghosts 'n Goblins, and the first-rate RPG, Breath of Fire. But with Capcom, its biggest hits have been big indeed, and the company has introduced several major franchises in addition to the Street Fighter series.

Released the same year as the original Street Fighter, Mega Man was so popular that Capcom adopted the "Blue Bomber" as its official mascot. A whole series of Mega Man games were produced for Nintendo console systems, and in 1997 Capcom released a fully 3D version called Mega Man Legends.

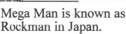

Above right:
Early Capcom:
Poker Ladies.

Mega Man Legends for DS.

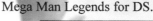

Milla Jovovich in the film
Resident Evil.

In 1996, when Street Fighter mania was in decline, Capcom found a new savior in young designer Shinji Mikami's game Resident Evil, which established the "survival horror" adventure game category with B-movie zombies, bloody corpses, and some genuinely scary moments. As of 2003, the game had sold over 16 million units worldwide, and the franchise continues going strong, with sequels that consistently improve upon the already successful formula. Like their other

KOEI

Yoichi Erikawa founded KOEI Micro-Computer Systems as an outgrowth of his small computer store, and from the first, his products were unique in the marketplace. In 1983, he published Night Life for the Fujitsu FM-7 and later ported it to the FM-11 and other machines. It was probably the first "adult-oriented" computer game in Japan, featuring illustrations of different sexual positions, a rhythm method calculator, and a sex diary. In addition to conversions of Night Life, KOEI released another adult product called Tempting Housewife in the Building. Erikawa soon abandoned the adult games business, despite a continued market demand for the genre.

Using seed money from his adult titles, Erikawa transitioned to his breakthrough game style with a strategy game set in feudal Japan called Nobunaga's Ambition, the prototype for a style of strategy games that mixed economic decision making, human resource management, and diplomatic skill into exciting historical simulations. Before publishing the game he adopted the pseudonym Kou Shibusawa, after the great 19th-century industrialist named Eiichi Shibusawa. He said he admired Shibusawa's entrepreneurial spirit and great vision. Nobunaga's Ambition, set during the historical unification of feudal Japan, became the product that came to define the strategically-oriented nature of early KOEI games like Sangokushi

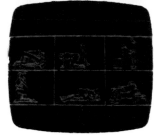

KOEI's first product, Night Life, featured sexual positions, a rhythm method calculator, and a sex diary.

(Romance of the Three Kingdoms, based on Chinese history), Genghis Khan, and Bandit Kings of Ancient China.

In 2001, spurred on by the success of Konami's Bemani series, KOEI expanded into the least likely of markets: music games. They published a game called Gitaroo-Man, created by a tiny Tokyo developer called iNiS. Gitaroo-Man was critically acclaimed, but didn't rack up the sales that KOEI had hoped for.

Erikawa was a visionary in more than just game genres. In the early '80s, the Japanese computer market was a mess. NEC was moving to yet another operating system as it tried to migrate users from PC-8801 to PC-9801, and another OS called MSX (Mitsubishi, Sony, and X for "others") was losing ground rapidly. Erikawa (aka Shibusawa) saw a solution in the midst of the problem. He created an intermediary program called KOEI DOS that would run under any of the systems then popular in Japan. By the late '80s, KOEI was selling Nobunaga's Ambition and Romance of the Three Kingdoms on all platforms. Working from Erikawa's code, an American named Bill Swartz went to

427

Yokohama and managed single-handedly to translate game text, fix a major bug in the code, add some play-balancing, and rewrite the game manuals for both Nobunaga's Ambition and Romance of the Three Kingdoms in a total of four months. Later projects, like Genghis Khan, required teams of people and six months or more to convert.

KOEI gained worldwide recognition when the Famicom version of Nobunaga's Ambition was released in the U.S. in 1990. It was not a mainstream hit, but whenever *Nintendo Power* editors and game counselors were asked to name their favorite games, Nobunaga's Ambition was almost always one of the top two or three choices.

Reinventing themselves yet again, in 1997 KOEI launched the Shin Sangoku Musou (Dynasty Warriors) series, which combines their familiar Chinese historical settings, but this time in fast-paced, arcade-style hack & slash games with a very different brand of strategy. The Dynasty Warriors games have been immensely successful, however, even more than KOEI's original strategy titles.

Activision Japan

One thing about the Japanese market is as true today as it was in the '80s: the Japanese prefer Japanese products to those from the outside. Though games like Wizardry and Ultima had tremendous followings and great sales, both making the conversion from U.S. PC game to Famicom hits, few U.S. companies managed to have any staying power in the early Japanese market. MicroProse, Electronic Arts, Sega, Interplay, Activision, and Acclaim all tried to build Japanese divisions, but only Activision

Japan was able to establish a firm foothold.

Why was Activision Japan successful when others weren't? First, it was established with Japanese staff. Second, it was established with modest expectations. Third, it operated as a Japanese company from the language spoken at company meetings through the company's documents and culture. It did the latter in spite of (or perhaps because of) the obsession of a young American executive who took over the Japanese business after one of Activision CEO Bobby Kotick's famous "company outings." Those "outings" had nothing to do with motivational picnics in the park. They meant that Kotick went through the organizational structure of the company, saying "You're out!" and "You're out!" and "You're out!" When he said "You're out!" to the top executive in Japan, he left Bill Swartz (formerly of KOEI) in command. According to Swartz, Kotick offered these memorable instructions: "Okay. I'll tell dickhead he's off the case. Try not to break anything until I can find someone more competent."

Swartz insisted on running everything in a manner as Japanese as possible. Having worked at KOEI, he knew both the language and the culture. He put what he knew to work in two basic areas: aggressively collecting debts and licensing intellectual properties. Activision Japan's biggest product was Shanghai, a mahjong game that Swartz licensed for digital cameras, dedicated word processors, toys, game consoles, and anything else with a screen and any processing power at all. With 55 different platforms, they sold five million units of the original Shanghai. With arcade machines being such a stable part of the business in Japan, it was logical to license a coin-op version of Shanghai. Hot Bee was the licensee for both a Nintendo Famicom version and the coin-op version.

Both companies made plenty of money on the license, but not until Activision complained to Nintendo that Hot Bee was in default on the agreed advance and Nintendo threatened to halt the manufacture of the cartridges until Hot Bee delivered the funds. Of course, Hot Bee paid while they were over the barrel, but they were angry enough to try to do the coin-op version without Activision's approval. The resulting game was bizarre, featuring cut scenes and backgrounds with weird stuff like nuns in bras and panties hanging their habits on clotheslines.

Eventually, the near-naked nuns version was taken off the market by legal action and replaced by a compromise version. Even then, it didn't take a genius to realize that Hot Bee was shipping far more circuit boards than they had paid royalties on. Activision audited them, and Hot Bee CEO Takahashi said they would pay at the end of the month. No payment came. Next, Activision received a tegata (a distinctly Japanese business practice in which a creditor would receive a post-dated check from the bank, giving the bearer the right to draw money from the bank 30-60 days in the future). Sixty days later, the bank called because the tegata bounced. Immediately, Hot Bee went bankrupt and no more circuit boards were produced.

Activision Japan's biggest success in the U.S., however, was Tenchu. This game, based on the idea of ninja assassins, was originally developed by Acquire for Sony Music Entertainment. An Activision executive named David Grijns discovered the game and insisted that it would do well in the U.S. market. Activision Japan acquired the U.S. rights to the game and made substantial changes. AI and graphics were improved, new and expanded stages were added, and the storyline was lengthened and improved over the Japanese version. The Japanese version of Tenchu sold 100,000 units at full price and another 100,000 units at reduced price, but the Western version of the game sold more than 2 million units overall.

Square Enix

The story of Square Enix is the story of two separate companies, longtime rivals that, one day in 2003, found each other.

Enix

Enix was a small start-up, founded in 1985 with a capital investment of ¥5 million to produce Famicom and MSX games. To find game designers, the company held a game design contest. One of the winners was Yuji Horii. His game, Love Match Tennis, was one of Enix's first personal computer products. Later, Horii decided to make a simpler manga-styled version of computer role-playing games, titling it Dragon Quest (later retitled Dragon Warrior for the U.S. market). With character designs by

Dragon Ball creator Akira Toriyama, the game hit it big thanks to a series of promotional articles in the boy's comic magazine Shonen Jump.

Though Enix expanded to release other titles, Dragon Quest remained its bread and butter, becoming the single most popular game series in Japan and an indelible part of the country's popular culture. Dragon Quest was so popular that the Tokyo government demanded that Enix not release new games on school days after children across the country skipped school en masse to line up for the latest version.

Squaresoft

Square Co., Ltd. (also known as Squaresoft) was first formed in 1983 by Masafumi Miyamoto as the Software Production Department of Den-Yu-Sha Co., Ltd., which was not a game developer but an electric power line company owned by Miyamoto's father. In 1986, the company was incorporated as Square Co., Ltd. Its first games were Hironobu Sakaguchi's The Death Trap and its sequel for the NEC PC-8801. Also among their first efforts were conversions of PC titles like Game Arts' Thexder (a shooting game released by Sierra On-Line in the U.S.) and an original title, King's Knight.

Squaresoft shifted focus to become a player in the console market, specifically for the Famicom Disk System. To accomplish their goals they allied with a few smaller publishers to form the Disk Original Group. DOG turned out to be an unintentionally appropriate acronym, as most of the eleven Disk System titles under the DOG label were awful.

The next move was to team Sakaguchi with the talented 3D programmer, Nasir Gebelli, who was known for his work on the Apple II (*see page 152*). The collaboration paid off. Their

429

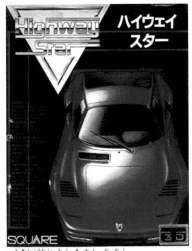

Highway Star, known as Rad Racer in the U.S.

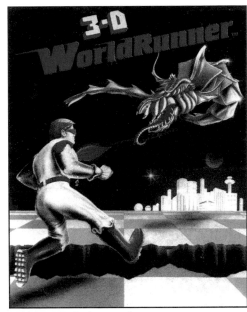

Tobidase Daisakusen, known as 3-D WorldRunner in the U.S.

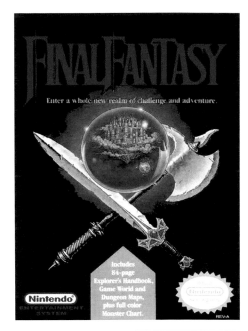

3D games ended up selling the most of all the Square and DOG titles. The cartridge-based Highway Star and Tobidase Daisakusen sold 500,000 copies each. Nintendo released Highway Star in the U.S. as Rad Racer and Acclaim released Tobidase as 3-D WorldRunner, but not even the money from these licenses was enough to keep Square afloat.

Miyamoto was close to shutting down the company's operations entirely when Sakaguchi came to him with the idea for a 2D role-playing game to rival Enix's immensely popular Dragon Quest. According to Sakaguchi, it was called Final Fantasy because it was to be the last game he would create. But it didn't quite work out that way.

Final Fantasy's image stood in direct contrast to Dragon Quest. Where Enix's game was a bright, colorful, cheery adventure, Final Fantasy featured mellow, almost sad music from Nobuo Uematsu and an intricate, deep plot from Sakaguchi. First published in 1987—around the same time as Sega's Phantasy Star, which was quickly released in the U.S.—Final Fantasy didn't make it to the U.S. until Nintendo published it in 1990, three years later. By that time, the larger and more sophisticated Final Fantasy III was already available in Japan.

Square completed an English translation of Final Fantasy II, but Nintendo rejected it, saying that the graphics were too similar to the original, which was entirely correct, considering that the early '90s American consumers expected better graphics with sequels. So the next Final Fantasy to make it across the

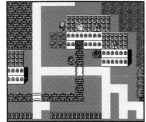

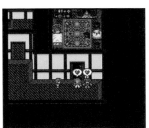

Top to bottom: Final Fantasy, Final Fantasy II, Final Fantasy III, Final Fantasy IV, Final Fantasy V, Final Fantasy VI

Final Fantasy VII

Pacific was Final Fantasy IV, although it was called Final Fantasy II in the U.S. In fact, Squaresoft has released dozens of games only in Japan throughout their history, and the actual FFII, FFIII, FFV, Seiken Densetsu 3 (the follow-up to Secret of Mana, not released in the U.S. but nicknamed Secret of Mana 2), Treasure Hunter G, Rudra no Hihou, Front Mission, and the three-game Romancing SaGa series were not exported. Most of these titles would be exported on later consoles, after their predecessors' popularity created a high enough demand.

With the release of the U.S. Final Fantasy II on the Super Nintendo Entertainment System (SNES), Square's golden age began. Their 16-bit offerings are considered by many to be the best games the company has ever made, including Final Fantasy VI, Chrono Trigger, and *Seiken Densetsu 2* (Legend of the Holy Sword, or Secret of Mana).

Seiken Densetsu 2—Secret of Mana

Kingdom Hearts

Squaresoft also released four black-and-white Game Boy games that were also released in the U.S. under the Final Fantasy name, although none of them were Final Fantasy titles in Japan. The Final Fantasy Legend games were the SaGa series in Japan, and Final Fantasy Adventure was the first Seiken Densetsu—the prequel to Secret of Mana.

In 1994, Squaresoft released Breath of Fire, a great RPG that was actually developed by Capcom for the Super NES. Final Fantasy VI was also released a few months later in the U.S., but was called Final Fantasy III since FFV had not been released stateside. Already huge in Japan, with FFIII, Squaresoft gained more fans and more momentum in the U.S.

The 1994 SNES title Chrono Trigger is possibly the one Square title that rivals Final Fantasy's fan base, and for good reason: it featured the game design talents of Sakaguchi, a storyline by Dragon Quest creator Yuji Horii, and character designs by Dragon Quest and *Dragon Ball* artist Akira Toriyama. It was also the composing debut of Yasunori Mitsuda, who would go on to cult fame as the composer of video game scores like Xenogears and Shadow Hearts.

In 1996, Square created the Nintendo-published title Super Mario RPG. However, incensed that Nintendo was using cartridges for the Nintendo 64 instead of compact disc media, Square cut their ties with Nintendo and began to develop exclusively for PlayStation. A fighting game released later in 1996, Tobal No. 1, contained a demo of the three-CD masterpiece Final Fantasy VII. This epic RPG may have been the single game that skyrocketed the PlayStation to popularity in Japan and, along with Tomb Raider, it helped sell a lot of PlayStation units in the U.S., as well. In fact, bolstered by a TV ad campaign that featured the game's cinematic cut scenes, FFVII was the first Final Fantasy game to sell more copies in the U.S. than in Japan.

Squaresoft continued to produce great games for the PlayStation and its successors, including Bushido Blade, Final Fantasy Tactics, SaGa Frontier, Parasite Eve, Legend of Mana, Vagrant Story, Threads of Fate, Chrono Cross, and, of course, Final Fantasy versions VIII, IX, X, XI… and onward.

From Final Fantasy VII on, Square started raking in the cash with worldwide releases of dozens of PlayStation titles. They put that money to use by establishing Square Pictures in Honolulu and partnering with Columbia Pictures to release a full-length computer-animated feature film, *Final Fantasy: The Spirits Within*, to theaters worldwide in 2001. Even with the voice talents of such notable Hollywood actors as Ming-Na Wen, Donald Sutherland, James Woods, and Steve Buscemi, the Final Fantasy film ended up losing big at the box office. One report suggested that Square lost nearly $70 million on the film, and Square Pictures went out of business that same year. Even so, *The Spirits Within* was one of the most ambitious and stunning works of 3D computer animation that had been produced up until that time and still stands as an artistic tour de force, even if it was not a financial success.

Square took a lickin', but kept on tickin' with new releases of the Final Fantasy series and, in 2002, a new and immensely popular series in collaboration with The Walt Disney Company—Kingdom Hearts. In Kingdom Hearts, the worlds of Disney and Final Fantasy collided, along with top-class voice talent, a fluid battle system, and a great plot that has now been expanded across several sequels, spin-offs, and platforms. Much like Final Fantasy, the Kingdom Hearts series shows no sign of disappearing.

On April 1, 2003, Square merged with Enix to become Square Enix Co., Ltd., putting most of Japan's top RPG series—including Dragon Quest, Final Fantasy, Kingdom Hearts, Star Ocean, and Ogre Battle—under one roof.

Square Enix Co., Ltd. continues to produce great games, extending the Final Fantasy series, expanding into new genres, and creating new original game experiences.

Japanese Video Games

Timeline of Important Dates, guest section by Chris Kohler

1889: Fusajiro Yamauchi founds Nintendo Koppai in Kyoto, to manufacture his handmade hanafuda playing cards.

1907: Nintendo becomes the first Japanese company to manufacture Western-style playing cards.

1933: Company name changed to Yamauchi-Nintendo, a new ferroconcrete building opens next door to the original on Rokujou in Kyoto. Still standing today (with signs in the original pre-World War II backwards lettering.)

1949: Hiroshi Yamauchi becomes third president of Nintendo.

July 1950: Bandai founded in Tokyo.

1951: Yamauchi changes name of company to Nintendo Karuta (playing cards).

1951: Marty Bromley, former manager of game rooms on U.S. military bases, starts importing U.S.-made slot machines and jukeboxes into Japan under the company name Service Games, or Nippon Koraku Bussan. At the same time, another American in Japan, David Rosen, starts a portrait-painting business.

1953: Nintendo manufactures the first plastic-coated playing cards in Japan.

1954: Rosen starts Rosen Enterprises and begins importing American Photomat instant photo booths to Japan. The Japanese name for the machines is Nifun Shashin, or two-minute photo, and they are very popular. They continue to be popular to this day—advanced purikura machines, with on-the-fly image editing, are still all the rage with teenage girls.

1955: Namco founded as Nakamura Amusements.

1956: Rosen expands to import coin-op games to Japan, then is approached by AMF, the American bowling company, to help establish Japan's first civilian bowling alleys. (The only alleys in Japan at the time were on U.S. military bases.) He opens his first alley on top of a movie theater in the high-tech, youth-culture area of Shinjuku in Tokyo; it is an unqualified success. The bowling boom launches in Japan and lasts until the early '70s.

Hiroshi Yamauchi

1959: Nintendo strikes a deal with Disney to use its characters on their cards. Sales shoot up; they sell a record 600,000 packs. Yamauchi lists Nintendo on the Osaka and Kyoto stock exchanges, changes company name to Nintendo Co., Ltd.

1964: Rosen Enterprises and Service Games merge to form Sega Enterprises.

1969: Nintendo creates a Games department, headed by Gunpei Yokoi, who invents the Ultra

Dave Rosen

433

Hand, which becomes a huge hit, selling over a million units. The Ultra series of toys takes off for Nintendo.

1970: Yokoi and new engineer Uemura create the mega-hit Beam Gun series of toys; these would form the foundation of Nintendo's gun games for the Famicom, like Wild Gunman.

1973: Nintendo opens Laser Clay Ranges in Kyoto, converted from old bowling alleys that closed after the fad ended. Games included clay pigeons and Wild Gunman–style cowboy shooting.

1974: Atari closes its ill-fated Japanese operation and partners with Namco to distribute Pong in Japan.

Spring 1975: Shigeru Miyamoto graduates from Kanazawa Municipal College of Arts and Crafts.

12 September 1975: Electronic toys company Epoch releases Terebi Tenisu (TV Tennis), a black-and-white dedicated system that retailed for ¥19,500. This was Japan's first home video game system.

1976: Atari licenses Breakout to Namco but retains exclusive manufacturing rights; yakuza begin pirating Breakout machines. To keep control of the market, Namco produces unlicensed Breakout machines without Atari's approval. Atari sues and wins by the end of the decade.

1977: Nintendo releases their first two video game systems: the low-end Color TV-Game 6 (¥9,800) and the higher-end Color TV-Game 15 (¥15,000). In total, they sell over a million units. Another toy company, Bandai, gets into the act by releasing a dedicated system of their own, TV JACK 1000. They eventually release Japanese versions of American game systems like the Vectrex, Intellivision, and Arcadia.

1977: Nintendo hires Shigeru Miyamoto as a designer.

June 1978: Taito releases Space Invaders, Japan's first megahit video game. A severe shortage of the 100-yen coins required to play the game followed, and the Japanese government had to quadruple production of the coins. Family-run vegetable markets clear out their inventory and fill their store space with nothing but Space Invaders machines.

1978: Namco releases its first original arcade game, a video pinball game designed by Toru Iwatani called Gee Bee.

1979: With Space Invaders a huge hit in the arcades, Epoch releases Terebi Vader, an unlicensed home system that plays only a scaled-down version of Space Invaders. It is a huge hit. The same year, Nintendo releases two more dedicated systems: the ¥12,500 Color TV-Game Racing 112 and the ¥13,500 Color TV-Game Block Kuzushi (Block Breaker). The outer cabinets of these dedicated systems are designed by a new Nintendo employee named Shigeru Miyamoto.

1979: Namco releases Galaxian.

1979: Capcom is founded.

1980: Namco releases Pac-Man in the arcades.

1980: Henk Rogers, an Amsterdam-born graduate of the University of Hawaii living in Yokohama, creates a Japanese version of the top-selling computer game Black Onyx. It is a moderate success and leads Rogers to establish his own software company out of Yokohama, Bullet-Proof Software.

28 April 1980: Nintendo releases Ball, the very first Game & Watch. It costs ¥5,800 and sets off the massive watch game boom. By the end of the year, nearly every major toy and electronics company in Japan has released similar games.

30 July 1981: Epoch releases the low-priced and popular Cassette Vision, Japan's first programmable system. This kicks off the TV-game boom. The system sold for ¥13,500, cassettes for ¥4,000. Eleven titles were available at launch, including Galaxian, Cassette Vader, Baseball, and the cleverly disguised PakPak Monster.

June 1982: Bandai releases the Intellivision.

August 1982: Tomy releases their Pyu-Ta hybrid computer/game system (a game system disguised as a computer, really). The Pyu-Ta is a 16-bit system and costs a whopping ¥59,800.

November 1982: Takara releases its own disguised computer/game system, called the Game Pasocon.

March 1983: Bandai releases the Arcadia.

14 July 1983: Sega releases the SG-1000 for ¥15,000. An optional steering wheel controller plays Safari Race. The system plays mostly Sega games like Congo Bongo. Simultaneously, Sega releases the SC-3000, which is an SG-1000-compatible personal computer, selling for ¥29,800.

15 July 1983: Nintendo releases the Famicom at ¥14,800. Launch titles are Donkey Kong, Donkey Kong Jr., and Popeye.

19 July 1983: Epoch releases the Cassette Vision Jr., a lower-priced, sleeker version of the Cassette Vision.

9 September 1983: Nintendo releases Mario Brothers for the Famicom.

October 1983: Nintendo's longtime cohort Sharp (they worked with Nintendo on the Color TV-Games and, most recently, manufactured the screens for the Game Boy Advance SP) releases a television with a built-in Famicom.

18 February 1984: Nintendo releases the Beam Gun for the Famicom. It is black and shaped like a Wild West–style gun; exactly like the version used for Wild Gunman in the arcades and similar to the Beam Gun cowboy toy sold by Nin-

tendo in the 1970s. Included in the ¥8,500 set is Wild Gunman; soon to follow are Duck Hunt and Hogan's Alley. The Beam Gun was never included with the Famicom like the Zapper was packaged with the NES in America; as such it is a rare collector's item today.

25 April 1984: Namco releases "Video Game Music" on the Alfa Records label, on cassette and LP. It is the first video game soundtrack recording commercially released.

21 June 1984: Nintendo releases Famicom Family BASIC, a cartridge and keyboard set with an optional cassette tape backup drive, allowing users to program their own Famicom games. The set is ¥14,800.

June 1984: Sega releases the SG-1000 II, a redesigned version of their first system with more Famicom-like controllers (the originals were designed more like Atari 7800 controllers).

17 July 1984: Epoch releases the Super Cassette Vision, an all-new system with graphics comparable to the Famicom's.

28 July 1984: Hudson becomes the first third-party Famicom publisher. Their first game, Lode Runner, is released for the Famicom and sells over a million copies. Before this, Hudson had sold a max of 10,000 copies of any game. Their annual profits quadruple. Famicom boom begins.

7 September 1984: Namco becomes a third-party Famicom publisher.

8 November 1984: Xevious is released for the Famicom; keeps the Famicom boom going.

18 July 1985: Enix is founded as a start-up, with capital of ¥5 million, to publish Nintendo games. Their first game is Door Door, created by Yuji Horii, who some sources contend was one of the winners (with fellow future Dragon Quest team member Koichi Nakamura) of a programming contest sponsored by Enix in 1982.

26 July 1985: Nintendo releases the Family Computer Robot. One game, Block (called Stack-Up in the U.S.), is sold separately.

13 August 1985: Nintendo releases the second and last Famicom Robot game, Gyro.

13 September 1985: Friday the 13th, a traditionally unlucky day in America but not in Japan. Nintendo releases Super Mario Bros. for the Famicom. It sells 1,200,000 copies by the end of the month.

October 1985: Sega releases the Sega Mark III, the Japanese version of the Sega Master System.

December 1985: Capcom and Square become Nintendo third parties.

21 February 1986: Nintendo releases the Famicom Disk System, a floppy disk drive add-on for the Famicom. The disks have 1 meg of storage space (twice the size of Super Mario Bros.) and can be re-written at video game stores for as little as ¥500 per game. Major launch title is The Legend of Zelda, which takes up both sides of the disk.

27 March 1986: Enix pins high hopes on its release of Dragon Quest. It is an initial failure, picking up sales only when the boys' manga magazine Shonen Jump agrees to publish a series of articles about the game. *Shonen Jump's* circulation jumps from 4.5 million per week to over 6 million as a result of the DQ tie-ins; a Dragon Quest manga appears in the magazine later.

June 1986: First issue of *Famicom Tsushin* magazine.

3 June 1986: Super Mario Bros. 2 is released for the Famicom Disk System (FDS), directed by Mario Team member Takashi Tezuka. For the first time, Mario and Luigi have different abilities. This game is completely different from the SMB2 that will be released in 1988 in the U.S.

30 July 1986: Konami releases the first 1-meg cartridge game, Ganbare Goemon!, for the Famicom. It is the beginning of a perennially popular series.

August 1986: Sharp releases the Twin Famicom, a combination Famicom/Disk System, for ¥32,000.

6 August 1986: Nintendo releases Metroid for the Disk System, directed by Gunpei Yokoi. Like other Disk System games, it has a three-slot save feature; when it is moved to cart in the U.S. it is changed to a password save method.

Henk Rogers with a system identical to the ones used to create Tetris.

14 April 1987: Henk Rogers' Bullet-Proof Software becomes a Famicom licensee, creating a Go game for the Famicom Disk System (with financial backing from Nintendo). It is later released on cartridge (11 August 1987).

21 October 1987: Nintendo releases the Famicom 3D System (motorized 3D glasses like those released in the U.S. for the Sega Master System) for ¥6,000. They work with 3D Hot Rally for the FDS.

30 October 1987: NEC releases the PC Engine for ¥24,800. Games cost about ¥4,900 each. Only five games appear for the system by year's end, including Kato and Ken, a comedic platform action game starring a popular stand-up comedian duo. Amazingly, this game is released in the U.S. as J.J. & Jeff.

18 December 1987: Final Fantasy released for the Famicom.

29 October 1988: Sega releases the Mega Drive for ¥21,000. It is the first true 16-bit system.

4 December 1988: NEC releases the PC Engine CD-ROM, the first CD-ROM-based video game hardware. It costs an amazing ¥57,800, nearly the same as the original price of the Neo-Geo. Games cost about ¥7,800.

22 December 1988: Henk Rogers' company BPS releases Tetris for the Famicom, under the sketchy license from Andromeda. A rare version has the original license text on the back of the box, reproduced here. Most copies of Tetris have a simple "Licensed to Nintendo" notice. This is Japan's equivalent of Tengen Tetris.

The back of the Japanese version of Tetris for Game Boy. The front can be seen on *page 204*.

21 April 1989: Nintendo releases the Game Boy with the main launch title being Super Mario Land, but no game is bundled with the system.

20 May 1989: Final Fantasy Symphonic Suite, the first live Final Fantasy concert featuring orchestrated music from the Famicom games FFI and FFII composed by Nobuo Uematsu, takes place in Yuport Hall in Tokyo. A recording of the concert is released later that year.

14 July 1989: Nintendo releases Tetris for Game Boy.

1 July 1990: SNK releases the Neo-Geo AES (home) system. It costs ¥58,000.

6 October 1990: Sega Game Gear, one of the first color portable video game system, released for ¥19,800.

20 November 1990: Operation Midnight Shipping. To head off possible theft of Super Famicom shipments by a yakuza ring, Nintendo ships their 16-bit systems to stores in the silence of night. Orders reached 1.5 million, but only 300,000 units shipped that first night, along with launch titles Super Mario World and F-Zero. The price: ¥25,000.

December 1991: Sega releases the Mega-CD add-on for ¥49,800.

20 August 1993: Pioneer releases its LaserActive laserdisc player for ¥89,800. Optional ¥20,000 add-on parts, available that same day, allow the LaserActive to play PC Engine and Mega Drive games.

November 1993: Sony creates Sony Computer Entertainment division.

1 December 1993: Nintendo redesigns and rereleases the Famicom, now with A/V ports, for ¥6,800.

20 March 1994: Matsushita (Panasonic) releases the 3DO REAL in Japan for ¥54,800. In October, an open-priced version (stores can set their own price) and Sanyo's version of the 3DO both hit Japan.

24 June 1994: Hudson releases Takahashi Meijin no Bouken Jima IV, the final Famicom game. (It is released in the U.S. as Hudson's Adventure Island IV.)

August 1994: Bandai releases its own CD-based game system, the Playdia. It is designed to play interactive anime games featuring Bandai properties like Sailor Moon.

22 November 1994: Sega releases the Sega Saturn for ¥44,800. The launch title is Virtua

437

Fighter; many people buy the system on this fact alone. Virtua Fighter is on CD but costs over $100.

3 December 1994: Sony releases the PlayStation. It is cheaper than the Saturn, at ¥39,800, but lacks the killer title of Virtua Fighter; early indications are that the Saturn will succeed. Ironically, Sega releases the Super 32X in Japan on the same day.

23 December 1994: After years of incremental hardware upgrades to the PC Engine, NEC releases its next-generation follow-up, the PC-FX. At ¥49,800 it is not appealing to anyone but hardcore players. It is the size of a PC mini-tower and the same orientation—a very strange system.

23 April 1995: Nintendo releases the Satellaview, an add-on for the Super Famicom that allows players to download games through the popular BS satellite TV service. Certain small games are released only through this service, like Radical Dreamers (the sequel to Chrono Trigger and the inspiration for Chrono Cross) and a Super Famicom version of Wario's Woods. The service runs until June 30, 2000.

21 July 1995: Nintendo releases its ill-fated Virtual Boy for (the reasonably low price of) ¥15,000. It is such a critical and market failure that inventor Gunpei Yokoi quits the company soon after.

12 January 1996: Square moves to Sony to begin producing games for PlayStation. Squaresoft had previously shown a Final Fantasy demo running on SGI workstations (N64 hardware-based).

February 1996: DigiCube starts selling video games in Japanese convenience stores.

March 1996: Feeling pressure from the PlayStation and anticipating the launch of the Nintendo 64, Sega releases a new lower-priced, white-colored Sega Saturn for ¥20,000.

24 May 1996: Square releases its last Super Famicom game, Treasure Hunter G. They will not release another game on a Nintendo system until 2002.

21 June 1996: Nintendo releases the N64 for ¥25,000. Launch titles: Super Mario 64 sells on a one-to-one ratio with the system, Pilotwings 64 sells on a 1:10 ratio, and the third and last launch title, a Shogi (Japanese chess) game from Seta, sells minimal amounts.

23 January 1997: Sega and Bandai announce that they will merge in October. The plans are scrapped on May 27.

31 January 1997: Final Fantasy VII released for the PlayStation.

4 October 1997: Gunpei Yokoi, inventor of the Game & Watch, Game Boy, designer of the Famicom, and creator of Metroid, dies in a car accident. He had left Nintendo before the accident and was designing a portable game system for Bandai.

21 October 1998: After years of minimal hardware upgrades to the Game Boy, Nintendo releases the Game Boy Color. A week later, SNK releases the Neo-Geo Pocket (black-and-white version).

27 November 1998: Sega preemptively begins the next-generation console wars with the early launch of the Dreamcast. The launch lineup, consisting of Godzilla Generations, July, and a disappointingly bad version of Virtua Fighter 3, does not make waves. Each system includes a VMU (Visual Memory Unit) memory card.

4 March 1999: After failed attempts at video game systems since the earliest days, Bandai releases its Won-

RADICAL DREAMERS
— 盗めない宝石 —
©1996 SQUARE

derSwan (black-and-white) portable for ¥4,800. It was designed by the late Gunpei Yokoi; a launch title is the puzzle game GunPey (pronounced the same), designed by his former team members.

19 March 1999: Less than five months after the release of the Neo-Geo Pocket, SNK releases a version with a color screen (NGPC).

1 December 1999: The 64DD (disk drive), promised since before the N64's launch, is finally released in Japan for ¥30,000. It works with a special keyboard and Randnet online software to get the N64 online. Games include the Mario Artist suite, SimCity 64, an expansion pack for F-Zero, and Doshin the Giant, among a few others. A promised add-on pack for The Legend of Zelda: Ocarina of Time is never released.

4 March 2000: Sony releases the PlayStation 2 for ¥39,800, with only a few launch games, and they are underwhelming: Ridge Racer V, Drum-Mania, Eternal Ring, Street Fighter EX3. Perhaps the first system launch with no first-party games. For months, the best-selling PS2 title is the DVD version of *The Matrix*, showing that people only bought the PS2 to use as a DVD player; it is half the price of all other Japanese DVD players at the time.

9 December 2000: Bandai launches the WonderSwan Color, leveraging their partnership with Squaresoft to release a special-edition package that includes the hit launch title Final Fantasy.

31 January 2001: CSK chairman Okawa donates ¥800 million of his personal fortune to keep Sega alive and save the Dreamcast. He dies a month and a half later.

21 March 2001: Nintendo jumps far ahead of the scattershot portable market with the Game Boy Advance at ¥9,800.

14 September 2001: Nintendo launches the GameCube in Japan three days after terrorist attacks kill 3,000 American citizens in New York City and Washington, D.C. The worldwide news buzz is not as big as they had hoped, and neither are sales.

22 February 2002: Microsoft finally launches the Xbox in Japan. Large billboards can be seen in Akihabara and Shibuya, entire subway cars on the Yamanote line are filled with Xbox ads, Bill Gates makes a personal signing appearance at the Ueno Toys"R"Us on launch night, and sales are an absolute disaster. A year and a half later, MS has not broken half a million systems sold in Japan.

1 April 2003: Not an April Fools' joke: Square and Enix merge to form Square Enix, putting Final Fantasy, Dragon Quest, Star Ocean, Kingdom Hearts all under one roof.

27 May 1999: Tokyo District Court rules that video games are not cinematographic works, and therefore the sale of used games is permissible under copyright law. (Enix appeals.)

7 October 1999: Osaka District Court rules that video games are cinematographic works, and therefore the sale of used games is not permissible under copyright law. (The defendant appeals.)

27 March 2001: Tokyo High Court rules that video games are cinematographic works, and therefore the sale of used games is not permissible under copyright law.

29 March 2001: Osaka High Court rules that video games are cinematographic works, and therefore the sale of used games is permissible under copyright law.

Credits

3DO: Box cover artwork and in-game images from the Might and Magic® and Heroes of Might and Magic® product series, and other New World Computing products, are provided courtesy of The 3DO Company. New World Computing is a division of The 3DO Company. All Rights Reserved.

Activision® games and images are the property of Activision, Inc. Photos of the Activision organization, party pictures, Family Tree, Fortune picture, and newspaper ad provided courtesy of Jim Levy. Neither the text nor the materials presented in this book have been reviewed or approved by Activision.

Apple images provided courtesy of Apple Computer, Inc.

Archon™, Archon II: Adept™, Murder on the Zinderneuf' are properties of Free Fall Games. Images from Archon™, Archon Ultra TM, and Murder on the ZinderneufTM provided courtesy of Free Fall Games. Original George Barr Archon Ultra art used with permission.

AT&T: Photographs of transistor developers and the first transistor provided by and property of AT&T Archives. Reprinted with permission of AT&T.

Blizzard Entertainment®: Box cover, cinematic, and in-game images from Diablo®, Diablo II, Diablo® II: Lord of Destruction™, StarCraft®, StarCraft®: Brood War™, Warcraft®, Warcraft® II, and Warcraft® II: Beyond the Dark Portal™ courtesy of Blizzard Entertainment®.

Brian Moriarty photo courtesy of Brian Moriarty.

Broderbund material and photos provided courtesy of the private archives of Doug Carlston. Software © Broderbund Properties LLC, and its licensors. All rights reserved. Some product names are either trademarks or registered trade- marks of Broderbund Properties LLC. All other trademarks or copyrights are the property of their respective owners.

CAPCOM and STREET FIGHTER II are registered trademarks of Capcom Company, Ltd.

Cinemaware: Copyright© 2002 Cinemaware, Inc. Cinemaware, the Cinemaware logo, Heroes Are Forever and Cinematech are trademarks of Cinemaware, Inc. Defender of the Crown, S.D.I., The King of Chicago, Sinbad and the Throne of the Falcon, Rocket Ranger, Lords of the Rising Sun, It Came From the Desert, Antheads: It Came From the Desert II, Wings, and TV Sports are trademarks of Cinemaware, Inc. All Rights Reserved.

Cyan® images of Myst, Riven, Cosmic Osmo, Manhole, Spelunx, and Parable provided courtesy of Cyan Worlds, Inc. Myst is a registered trademark of Cyan, Inc., under license to Ubisoft Entertainment S.A.

Dragon's Lair art property of Bluth Group and Don Bluth, licensed to Dragon's Lair LLC. Used by permission. ©1983 Bluth Group, Ltd. Dirk the Daring and Singe are part of Dragon's Lair 3D action figure series one. The figure line was sculpted by Sculpt This, licensed and produced by AnJon Inc. Eidos games and images are the property of Eidos Interactive Ltd. Tomb Raider/ Laura Croft cover image provided courtesy of Eidos Interactive.The Horde™, The Unholy War™, and Pandemonium"? are properties of Crystal Dynamics, Inc.

Electronic Arts games and images are the property of Electronic Arts. Electronic Arts, EA Sports, Origin, Bullfrog, Maxis, Westwood Studios, and all associated logos are trademarks, registered trademarks or service marks of Electronic Arts Inc. in the U.S. and/or other countries. Neither the text nor the materials presented in this book have been reviewed or approved by Electronic Arts. Photos supplied by Trip Hawkins, Richard Garriot, and Jeff Braun used with permission.

Epic Games: Unreal® images provided courtesy of Epic Games Inc. Unreal is a registered trademark of Epic Games Inc. Used with permission, all rights reserved.

Historical photographs provided by IBM Corporate Archives.Reprinted with permission of IBM.

Historical photographs provided by Intel Corporation. Reprinted with permission of Intel.

Historical photographs provided courtesy of Ralph Baer. Used by permission.

id™ : Images of Commander Keen, Wolfenstein 3D, DOOM, and QUAKE© 1991-2002 Id Software, Inc. All Rights Reserved. Commander Keen™, Wolfenstein 3D®, DOOM®, QUAKE®, the id™ logo, the DOOM™ logo, the QUAKE™ logo, and the id Software ™ name are either registered trademarks of trademarks of Id Software, Inc. in the United States and/or other countries. Images used under license from Id Software, Inc. Special thanks to id Software.

Infocom archive photos provided courtesy of Michael Dornbrook.

Infogrames Entertainment: Asteroids!™, Gunship®, Civilization®, Falcon® 4.0, and Atari® name and logo, and MicroProse® and some Atari® images provided courtesy of Infogrames Interactive, Inc. ©2002 Infogrames Interactive, Inc. Accolade images provided courtesy of Infogrames, Inc. All Rights Reserved. Used with permission.

Intellivision ™ /Blue Sky Rangers images copyright © Intellivision Productions, Inc., www.intellivi-sionlives.com. Used by permission.

lnterplay! games and images are the property of Interplay Entertainment Corp. Earthworm Jim and all related characters © and ™ Interplay Entertainment Corp. Original Earthworm Jim character created by Doug TenNapel. Neither the text nor the materials presented in this book have been reviewed or approved by Interplay.

Konami®: Castlevania Circle of the Moon, Metal Gear, Metal Gear Solid, Time Pilot and Konami® are either trademarks or registered trademarks of KONAMI CORPORATION. ©1989, 2002 KONAMI CORPORATION.

LucasArts Entertainment Company LLC provided the following images: Ballblazer © 1984 LucasArts Entertainment Company LLC. Koronis Rift and Rescue on Fractalus! © 1985 LucasArts Entertainment Company LLC.